W9-ADX-654

Justice

Justice: A Reader

EDITED BY

Michael J. Sandel

OXFORD
UNIVERSITY PRESS
2007

OXFORD

UNIVERSITY PRESS

Oxford University Press, Inc., publishes works that further
Oxford University's objective of excellence
in research, scholarship, and education.

Oxford   New York

Auckland   Cape Town   Dar es Salaam   Hong Kong   Karachi
Kuala Lumpur   Madrid   Melbourne   Mexico City   Nairobi
New Delhi   Shanghai   Taipei   Toronto

With offices in

Argentina   Austria   Brazil   Chile   Czech Republic   France   Greece
Guatemala   Hungary   Italy   Japan   Poland   Portugal   Singapore
South Korea   Switzerland   Thailand   Turkey   Ukraine   Vietnam

Copyright © 2007 by Oxford University Press, Inc.

Published by Oxford University Press, Inc.
198 Madison Avenue, New York, New York 10016

www.oup.com

Oxford is a registered trademark of Oxford University Press

All rights reserved. No part of this publication may be reproduced,
stored in a retrieval system, or transmitted, in any form or by any means,
electronic, mechanical, photocopying, recording, or otherwise,
without the prior permission of Oxford University Press.

Library of Congress Cataloging-in-Publication Data
Justice : a reader / edited by Michael J. Sandel.
p.   cm.
ISBN 978-0-19-533511-8; 978-0-19-533512-5 (pbk.)
1. Justice. 2. Values. 3. Ethics. I. Sandel, Michael J.
JC578.J868 2007
320.01'1—dc22   2007015063

18   19   20

Printed in the United States of America
on acid-free paper

To the Justice teaching fellows

PREFACE

The readings gathered in this volume are the ones I assign in my undergraduate course, "Justice," an introduction to moral and political philosophy that I have taught at Harvard, on and off, for over 25 years. The readings, like the course, include classical and contemporary theories of justice, along with writings about legal and political controversies that raise philosophical questions. The readings are arranged thematically rather than chronologically. The aim of the volume is not to present an overview of the history of political thought, but rather to provide students with a guided journey in moral and political reflection that moves back and forth between philosophical writings and practical issues that illustrate competing conceptions of justice.

While selections include writings by Aristotle, Jeremy Bentham, John Locke, Immanuel Kant, John Stuart Mill, and John Rawls, these works are not presented as artifacts in the history of ideas, but as episodes in arguments in which we are still engaged. The emphasis throughout is on inviting students to engage critically with the philosophers they read—to try to make sense of their arguments and also to assess them. While none of us is fully qualified, as a first- or second-time reader of a great philosopher like Aristotle or Kant, to pass definitive judgment on the adequacy of his arguments, an excess of reverence can spoil the challenge of political philosophy, and dampen the fun. Even the greatest philosophers, after all, were trying to persuade their readers, not to lay down the law. There is much to be gained by engaging with them in a buoyant, probing, confident spirit, unburdened, at least initially, by the weight of their prestige or by too much knowledge of the historical context in which they wrote. This may be another way of saying that political philosophy is best approached in the spirit of an undergraduate—whether or not one is actually an undergraduate by age or enrollment.

Since the aim of the volume is to invite readers to reflect critically on their own moral and political assumptions in the company of philosophers past and present, the readings are ordered in a thematic sequence designed to seem natural, or at least inviting and accessible, to contemporary readers in the Anglo-American world. The volume begins with utilitarianism, an influential current in our moral and political landscape. It then presents some rights-oriented theories that challenge utilitarianism, from libertarianism to the versions of liberal political theory advanced by Locke, Kant, and Rawls. We then turn to Aristotle's virtue-based political theory, followed by readings from the contemporary debate between liberals and their communitarian critics. The volume concludes with selections designed to provoke discussion about morality and law in a pluralist society.

Alert readers may detect in the thematic trajectory, and in the brief introductory remarks to each section, a certain perspective on political philosophy. It is difficult to imagine a way of presenting a subject as rich and contested as justice without making any judgments whatsoever. I have tried nonetheless to strike a balance between letting readers find their own way through these materials, while at the same time offering a set of readings and questions that hang together as a coherent whole. My aim is to propose a journey with a certain shape but without a fixed destination.

There is of course no one best way to introduce students to moral and political philosophy. I can report that the approach reflected in these readings has worked well in my own experience of teaching. I hope that this selection of readings and themes may be useful to others who teach similar courses, and to readers of all ages who are tempted by the challenge of submitting their moral and political convictions to critical examination.

In developing the course from which this volume comes, I have accumulated many debts, not least to the 12,000 undergraduates who have taken the course, and who by their reaction to these materials prompted many revisions and improvements. I owe a special debt to the truly remarkable group of Justice teaching fellows with whom I have been privileged to work. Like the students we taught together, I benefited greatly from their dedication, wisdom, and advice, much of which is reflected in the choice of readings presented here. Since their graduate school days teaching Justice, they have moved on to a dazzling array of pursuits and careers in academia and the professions. With much gratitude, I dedicate this volume to them:

Tamar Abramov, Robert Alcala, Anita Allen, David Anderson, Elizabeth Anderson, David Angel, Scott Angstreich, Fredrick Appel, Vikas Arora, John Arthur, Sandra Badin, Carla Bagnoli, Preeta Bansal, Grant Barnes, John Barrett, Benjamin Barron, Tom Barron, John Bauer, Matthew Baughman, Michael Baur, Karen Bell, Ray Belliotti, Ehud Ben-Or, Ben Berger, McKey Berkman, Alyssa Bernstein, Shalini Bhargava, Christopher Blazejewski, Ryan Billings, Jennifer Bird-Pollan, Carles Boix, Hilary Bok, Pierre Bollinger, Liliana Botcheva, Nicholas Brown, Rachel Brown, Molly Burke, Stephen Butler, David Butt, Leon Calleja, Peter Cannavo, Paolo Carozza, Evan Charney, Dana Chasin, Robert Chesler, Daniel Choi, David Chow, Eric Citron, Stacy Cline, Chloe Cockburn, I. Glenn Cohen, Elizabeth Collery, James Crabtree, John Cranley, Alice Crary, Colin Crawford, Maurizio D'Entreves, Peter De Marneffe, Shanya Dingle, David DiPasquale, Steve Dixon, Sharon Dolovich, Douglas Driemeier, Kurt Dudas, David Duff, Francesco Duina, John Duvivier, Berkley Eddins, Nevan Elam, Bram Elias, Autumn M. Elliott, Ezekiel Emanuel, Karen Engle, Jeff Ernst, Trevor Farrow, John Fellas, Allen Ferrell, Dave Ferrero, Luca Ferrero, Josh Fine, Mike Fischer, April Flakne, Stephanie Flanders, James Fleming, Juliet Floyd, Andreas Follesdal, Richard Forrest, Barbara Fortson, Mary Anne Franks, Paul Franks, Jane Freemiller, Jim Fuerst, Juliet Gainsborough, Scott Gant, Kenneth Garrett, Andrew Geddis, Peter Gerstman, Sally Gibbons, Matthew Gibney, Christopher Gilbert, Eric Giroux, Brian Glasser, Alan Gluck, Elizabeth Grayer, Katie Grzenczyk, Olav Haazen, Mark Hager, Shawn Halbert, Guy Hamlet-Mundlak, Claudia Hammerman, Pamela Harris, Melissa Hart, Katharina Held, Debbie Hellman, Elissa Hendler, Thomas Higley, Christina Ho, Kyle Hoffman, Brad Holyman, Heather Hughes, Von Hughes, Agnieszka Jaworska, Joel Johnson, Neal Johnson, Beth Johnston, Laurie Kahn-Leavitt, Victoria Kamsler, Jonathan Kang, Grace Kao, Anja Karnein, Gregory Keating, Daniel Kelly, Vikas Khanna, Pauline Kim, Karen King, Jeff Klein, Madeline Kochen, Hank Kopel, Amanda Kosonen, Ruben Kraiem, Marc Krickbaum, Douglas Kropp, Anita Krug, William Kuhn, Allison Kuklok, Andrew Kuper, Joel Kurtzberg, He?le`ne Landemore, Stephen Latham, Laurie Kahn Leavitt, Travis Leblanc, Brant Lee, Woo Lee, Christopher Leich, Curtis Leitner, Amod Lele, Patti Lenard, Craig Lerner, David Lessing, Daniel Levin, Katherine Levine, Jeffrey Levy, Jason Linder, Erik Lindseth, Peter Lindsey, Sharon

Lloyd, Diana Lobel, Sara Lord, Daniel Loss, Bruno Macaes, David MacArthur, Ian MacMullen, Jerome Maddox, Danny Maguire, Evan Mandery, Price Marshall, Sally Matless, Peter Mavrick, Kirsten Mayer, Marc Mayerson, Joseph Mazor, Jack McCullough, Jessica McFarland, Zachary McGee, Chris McNeill, Tamara Metz, Aziz Mohammed, Jennifer Montana, Michelle Moody, Josh Moore, Donald Moulds, Russ Muirhead, Daniel Mulhern, Guy Mundlak, Newman Nahas, Larry Nemer, Miriam Nemetz, Robert Neugeboren, Andrew Nevin, Michael Nitsch, Jeremy Ofseyer, Martin O'Neill, Yi-Ping Ong, Eva Orlebeke, Michael Pahl, Raul Pangalangan, Deborah Paul, Bruce Peabody, David Peritz, Andrew Perlman, Lee Perlman, Andrew Peskoe, Arthur Pineau, Joseph Prud'homme, Sylvia Quast, Ofer Raban, Kimberly Ravener, Dan Rearick, Juan Rebolledo, Alison Dundes Renteln, Henry Richardson, Alice Ristroph, Zachariah Robert, Clement Roberts, Mark Roberts, Christopher Robertson, Sarah Robinson, Mark Rollins, Connie Rosati, David Rosenfeld, Jessica Roth, Jed Rubenfeld, Albert Ruesga, Beardsley Ruml, Martin Sandbu, Andrea Sangiovanni, David Schanzer, Bettina Scholz, Kimberly Younce Schooley, Scott Andrew Schroeder, Dov Seidman, Mitsi Sellers, Nathan Shah, James Shannon, Joseph Shea, Josh Shiffrin, Wes Shih, Stephen Siderow, Thomas Simon, Eryn Simmers, Peter Sinclair, Gillian Sinnott, Sarah Song, Jason Springs, Lucas Stanczyk, Jason Steffen, Carol Steiker, Jordan Steiker, David Steiner, Kerry Stirton, John Stopford, Jon Strauss, Scott Styles, Sung-Hee Suh, Andrew Sullivan, Kathleen Sullivan, Talha Syed, Paul Taylor, Hannibal Travis, Dimitri Tymoczko, Brian Ulicny, Geoff Upton, Brandon Van Dyke, John Van Hook, Jane VanLare, Geoffrey Vaughan, Angelo Volandes, Ari Waldman, Alec Walen, Chris Walton, Rory Weiner, Daniel Weinstock, Darren Weirnick, David Welch, Trafford Welden, Leif Wenar, Jeffrey Wieand, Grant Palmer Wiggins, Scott Wilkens, Thad Williamson, Elizabeth Wilson, Peter Winn, Stewart Wood, Michael Woods, Adam Wright, Toby Young, Oksanna Zanft, Michael Zilles, Adam Zoia.

CONTENTS

Justice

Chapter 1

INTRODUCTION: DOING THE RIGHT THING

One way to begin thinking about moral and political philosophy is to ask yourself what you would do if faced with a moral dilemma, or, more precisely, what you hope you would do. For example, most people believe it is wrong to kill an innocent person. But suppose you find yourself in a situation in which killing an innocent person is the only way to prevent many innocent people from dying. Is it the right thing to do? Such questions often confront soldiers and policy-makers during wartime.

Such questions can also arise for judges and juries in criminal trials. *The Queen v. Dudley and Stephens* (1884), a famous English law case, involved four men stranded at sea in a lifeboat. As you read the case, put aside the question of what the law happened to be, and think about the moral question: How do you judge the action of Dudley and Stephens? Was it morally justified or morally wrong?

THE QUEEN V. DUDLEY AND STEPHENS

14 Queen's Bench Division 273
9 December 1884

Criminal Law—Murder—Killing and eating Flesh of Human Being under Pressure of Hunger—"Necessity"—Special Verdict—Certiorari—Offence on High Seas—Jurisdiction of High Court.

A man who, in order to escape death from hunger, kills another for the purpose of eating his flesh, is guilty of murder; although at the time of the act he is in such circumstances that he believes and has reasonable ground for believing that it affords the only chance of preserving his life.

At the trial of an indictment for murder it appeared, upon a special verdict, that the prisoners D. and S., seamen, and the deceased, a boy between seventeen and eighteen, were cast away in a storm on the high seas, and compelled to put into an open boat; that the boat was drifting on the ocean, and was probably more than 1000 miles from land; that on the eighteenth day, when they had been seven days without food and five without water, D. proposed to S. that lots should be cast who should be put to death to save the rest, and that they afterwards thought it would be better to kill the boy that their lives should be saved; that on the twentieth day D., with the assent of S., killed the boy, and both D. and S. fed on his flesh for four days; that at the time of the act there was no sail in sight nor any reasonable prospect of relief; that under these circumstances there appeared to the prisoners every probability that unless they then or very soon fed upon the boy, or one of themselves, they would die of starvation:-

Held, that upon these facts, there was no proof of any such necessity as could justify the prisoners in killing the boy, and that they were guilty of murder.

INDICTMENT for the murder of Richard Parker on the high seas within the jurisdiction of the Admiralty.

At the trial before Huddleston, B., at the Devon and Cornwall Winter Assizes, November 7, 1884, the jury, at the suggestion of the learned judge, found the facts of the case in a special verdict which stated "that on July 5, 1884, the prisoners, Thomas Dudley and Edward Stephens, with one Brooks, all able-bodied English seamen, and the deceased also an English boy, between seventeen and eighteen years of age, the crew of an English yacht, a registered English vessel, were cast away in a storm on the high seas 1600 miles from the Cape of Good Hope, and were compelled to put into an open boat belonging to the said yacht. That in this boat they had no supply of water and no supply of food, except two 11b. tins of turnips, and for three days they had nothing else to subsist upon. That on the fourth day they caught a small turtle, upon which they subsisted for a few days, and this was the only food they had up to the twentieth day when the act now in question was committed. That on the twelfth day the remains of the turtle were entirely consumed, and for the next eight days they had nothing to eat. That they had no fresh water, except such rain as they from time to time caught in their oilskin capes. That the boat was drifting on the ocean, and was probably more than 1000 miles away from land. That on the eighteenth day, when they had been seven days without food and five without water, the prisoners spoke to Brooks as to what should be done if no succour came, and suggested that some one should be sacrificed to save the rest, but Brooks dissented, and the boy, to whom they were understood to refer, was not consulted. That on the 24th of July, the day before the act now in question, the prisoner Dudley proposed to Stephens and Brooks that lots should be cast who should be put to death to save the rest, but Brooks refused to consent, and it was not put to the boy, and in point of fact there was no drawing of lots. That on that day the prisoners spoke of their having families, and suggested it would be better to

kill the boy that their lives should be saved, and Dudley proposed that if there was no vessel in sight by the morrow morning the boy should be killed. That next day, the 25th of July, no vessel appearing, Dudley told Brooks that he had better go and have a sleep, and made signs to Stephens and Brooks that the boy had better be killed. The prisoner Stephens agreed to the act, but Brooks dissented from it. That the boy was then lying at the bottom of the boat quite helpless, and extremely weakened by famine and by drinking sea water, and unable to make any resistance, nor did he ever assent to his being killed. The prisoner Dudley offered a prayer asking forgiveness for them all if either of them should be tempted to commit a rash act, and that their souls might be saved. That Dudley, with the assent of Stephens, went to the boy, and telling him that his time was come, put a knife into his throat and killed him then and there; that the three men fed upon the body and blood of the boy for four days; that on the fourth day after the act had been committed the boat was picked up by a passing vessel, and the prisoners were rescued, still alive, but in the lowest state of prostration. That they were carried to the port of Falmouth, and committed for trial at Exeter. That if the men had not fed upon the body of the boy they would probably not have survived to be so picked up and rescued, but would within the four days have died of famine. That the boy, being in a much weaker condition, was likely to have died before them. That at the time of the act in question there was no sail in sight, nor any reasonable prospect of relief. That under these circumstances there appeared to the prisoners every probability that unless they then fed or very soon fed upon the boy or one of themselves they would die of starvation. That there was no appreciable chance of saving life except by killing some one for the others to eat. That assuming any necessity to kill anybody, there was no greater necessity for killing the boy than any of the other three men." But whether upon the whole matter by the jurors found the killing of Richard Parker by Dudley and Stephens be felony and murder the jurors are ignorant, and pray the advice of the Court thereupon, and if upon the whole matter the Court shall be of opinion that the killing of Richard Parker be felony and murder, then the jurors say that

Dudley and Stephens were each guilty of felony and murder as alleged in the indictment."

The learned judge then adjourned the assizes until the 25th of November at the Royal Courts of Justice. On the application of the Crown they were again adjourned to the 4th of December, and the case ordered to be argued before a Court consisting of five judges.

Dec. 4. . . .

Sir H. James, A. G., for the Crown.

. . . . With regard to the substantial question in the case—whether the prisoners in killing Parker were guilty of murder—the law is that where a private person acting upon his own judgment takes the life of a fellow creature, his act can only be justified on the ground of self-defence—self-defence against the acts of the person whose life is taken. This principle has been extended to include the case of a man killing another to prevent him from committing some great crime upon a third person. But the principle has no application to this case, for the prisoners were not protecting themselves against any act of Parker. If he had had food in his possession and they had taken it from him, they would have been guilty of theft; and if they killed him to obtain this food, they would have been guilty of murder. . . .

A. Collins, Q.C., for the prisoners.

The facts found on the special verdict shew that the prisoners were not guilty of murder, at the time when they killed Parker, but killed him under the pressure of necessity. Necessity will excuse all act which would otherwise be a crime. Stephen, Digest of Criminal Law, art. 32, Necessity. The law as to compulsion by necessity is further explained in Stephen's History of the Criminal Law, vol. ii., p. 108, and an opinion is expressed that in the case often put by casuists, of two drowning men on a plank large enough to support one only, and one thrusting the other off, the survivor could not be subjected to legal punishment. In the American case of The United States v. Holmes n(1), the proposition that a passenger on board a vessel may be thrown overboard to save the others is sanctioned. The law as to inevitable necessity is fully considered in

Russell on Crimes, vol. i. p. 847, and there are passages relating to it in Bracton, vol. ii. p. 277; Hale's Pleas of the Crown, p. 54 and c. 40; East's Pleas of the Crown, p. 221, citing Dalton, c. 98, "Homicide of Necessity," and several cases, amongst others McGrowther's Case n(1); Stratton's Case n(2). Lord Bacon, Bac. Max., Reg. 5, gives the instance of two shipwrecked persons clinging to the same plank and one of them thrusting the other from it, finding that it will not support both, and says that this homicide is excusable through unavoidable necessity and upon the great universal principle of self-preservation, which prompts every man to save his own life in preference to that of another, where one of them must inevitably perish. It is true that Hale's Pleas of the Crown, p. 54, states distinctly that hunger is no excuse for theft, but that is on the ground that there can be no such extreme necessity in this country. In the present case the prisoners were in circumstances where no assistance could be given. The essence of the crime of murder is intention and here the intention of the prisoners was only to preserve their lives. . . .

Dec. 9. The judgment of the Court was delivered by

LORD COLERIDGE, C.J: The two prisoners, Thomas Dudley and Edwin Stephens, were indicted for the murder of Richard Parker on the high seas on the 25th of July in the present year. They were tried before my Brother Huddleston at Exeter on the 6th of November, and, under the direction of my learned Brother, the jury returned a special verdict, the legal effect of which has been argued before us, and on which we are now to pronounce judgment.

The special verdict as, after certain objections by Mr. Collins to which the Attorney General yielded, it is finally settled before us is as follows. [His Lordship read the special verdict as above set out.] From these facts, stated with the cold precision of a special verdict, it appears sufficiently that the prisoners were subject to terrible temptation, to sufferings which might break down the bodily power of the strongest man, and try the conscience of the best. Other details yet more harrowing, facts still more loathsome and appalling, were presented to the jury, and are to be found recorded in my learned Brother's notes. But nevertheless this is clear, that the prisoners put to death a weak and unoffending boy upon the chance of preserving their own lives by feeding upon his flesh and blood after he was killed, and with the certainty of depriving him of any possible chance of survival. The verdict finds in terms that "if the men had not fed upon the body of the boy they would probably not have survived," and that "the boy being in a much weaker condition was likely to have died before them." They might possibly have been picked up next day by a passing ship; they might possibly not have been picked up at all; in either case it is obvious that the killing of the boy would have been an unnecessary and profitless act. It is found by the verdict that the boy was incapable of resistance, and, in fact, made none; and it is not even suggested that his death was due to any violence on his part attempted against, or even so much as feared by, those who killed him. Under these circumstances the jury say that they are ignorant whether those who killed him were guilty of murder, and have referred it to this Court to determine what is the legal consequence which follows from the facts which they have found. . . .

There remains to be considered the real question in the case—whether killing under the circumstances set forth in the verdict be or be not murder. The contention that it could be anything else was, to the minds of us all, both new and strange, and we stopped the Attorney General in his negative argument in order that we might hear what could be said in support of a proposition which appeared to us to be at once dangerous, immoral, and opposed to all legal principle and analogy. All, no doubt, that can be said has been urged before us, and we are now to consider and determine what it amounts to. First it is said that it follows from various definitions of murder in books of authority, which definitions imply, if they do not state, the doctrine, that in order to save your own life you may lawfully take away the life of another, when that other is neither attempting nor threatening yours, nor is guilty of any illegal act whatever towards you or any one else. But if these definitions be looked at they will not be found to sustain this contention. . . .

Now, except for the purpose of testing how far the conservation of a man's own life is in all cases and under all circumstances, an absolute, unqualified, and paramount duty, we exclude from our consideration all the incidents of war. We are dealing with a case of private homicide, not one imposed upon men in the service of their Sovereign and in the defence of their country. Now it is admitted that the deliberate killing of this unoffending and unresisting boy was clearly murder, unless the killing can be justified by some well-recognised excuse admitted by the law. It is further admitted that there was in this case no such excuse, unless the killing was justified by what has been called "necessity." But the temptation to the act which existed here was not what the law has ever called necessity. Nor is this to be regretted. Though law and morality are not the same, and many things may be immoral which are not necessarily illegal, yet the absolute divorce of law from morality would be of fatal consequence; and such divorce would follow if the temptation to murder in this case were to be held by law an absolute defence of it. It is not so. To preserve one's life is generally speaking a duty, but it may be the plainest and the highest duty to sacrifice it. War is full of instances in which it is a man's duty not to live, but to die. The duty, in case of shipwreck, of a captain to his crew, of the crew to the passengers, of soldiers to women and children, as in the noble case of the Birkenhead; these duties impose on men the moral necessity, not of the preservation, but of the sacrifice of their lives for others, from which in no country, least of all, it is to be hoped, in England, will men ever shrink, as indeed, they have not shrunk. It is not correct, therefore, to say that there is any absolute or unqualified necessity to preserve one's life. "Necesse est ut eam, non ut vivam," is a saying of a Roman officer quoted by Lord Bacon himself with high eulogy in the very chapter on necessity to which so much reference has been made. It would be a very easy and cheap display of commonplace learning to quote from Greek and Latin authors, from Horace, from Juvenal, from Cicero, from Euripides, passage after passage, in which the duty of dying for others has been laid down in glowing and emphatic language as resulting from the principles of heathen ethics; it is enough in a Christian country to remind ourselves of the Great Example whom we profess to follow. It is not needful to point out the awful danger of admitting the principle which has been contended for. Who is to be the judge of this sort of necessity? By what measure is the comparative value of lives to be measured? Is it to be strength, or intellect, or what? It is plain that the principle leaves to him who is to profit by it to determine the necessity which will justify him in deliberately taking another's life to save his own. In this case the weakest, the youngest, the most unresisting, was chosen. Was it more necessary to kill him than one of the grown men? The answer must be "No"—

"So spake the Fiend, and with necessity, The tyrant's plea, excused his devilish deeds."

It is not suggested that in this particular case the deeds were "devilish," but it is quite plain that such a principle once admitted might be made the legal cloak for unbridled passion and atrocious crime. There is no safe path for judges to tread but to ascertain the law to the best of their ability and to declare it according to their judgment; and if in any case the law appears to be too severe on individuals, to leave it to the Sovereign to exercise that prerogative of mercy which the Constitution has intrusted to the hands fittest to dispense it.

It must not be supposed that in refusing to admit temptation to be an excuse for crime it is forgotten how terrible the temptation was; how awful the suffering; how hard in such trials to keep the judgment straight and the conduct pure. We are often compelled to set up standards we cannot reach ourselves, and to lay down rules which we could not ourselves satisfy. But a man has no right to declare temptation to be an excuse, though he might himself have yielded to it, nor allow compassion for the criminal to change or weaken in any manner the legal definition of the crime. It is therefore our duty to declare that the prisoners' act in this case was wilful murder, that the facts as stated in the verdict are no legal justification of the homicide; and to say that in our unanimous opinion the prisoners are upon this special verdict guilty of murder.[1]

THE COURT then proceeded to pass sentence of death upon the prisoners.[2]

1. My brother Grove has furnished me with the following suggestion, too late to be embodied in the judgment but well worth preserving: "If the two accused men were justified in killing Parker, then if not rescued in time, two of the three survivors would be justified in killing the third, and of the two who remained the stronger would be justified in killing the weaker, so that three men might be justifiably killed to give the fourth a chance of surviving."—C.
2. This sentence was afterwards commuted by the Crown to six months' imprisonment.

Chapter 2

Utilitarianism

One way of thinking about the right thing to do, perhaps the most natural and familiar way, is to ask what will produce the greatest happiness for the greatest number of people. This way of thinking about morality finds its clearest statement in the philosophy of Jeremy Bentham (1748–1832). In his *Introduction to the Principles of Morals and Legislation* (1789), Bentham argues that the principle of utility should be the basis of morality and law. By utility, he means whatever promotes pleasure or prevents pain.

Bentham's utilitarianism is open to a number of objections. One is that maximizing utility, or collective happiness, may come at the expense of violating individual rights. Suppose, for example, that a large majority despises a minority religion, and wants it banned. Would the happiness of the majority justify banning the religion of the few? John Stuart Mill (1806–1873) sought to rescue utilitarianism from the objections to which Bentham's version seemed vulnerable. In his essay *Utilitarianism* (1861), Mill argues that respect for justice and individual rights as "the most sacred and binding part of all morality" is compatible with the idea that justice rests ultimately on utilitarian considerations. Here then is a question to consider as you read Mill: Can the utility principle support the idea that certain individual rights should be upheld even if doing so makes the majority very unhappy? If not, which should give way—respect for individual rights, or the utility principle itself?

Principles of Morals and Legislation

Jeremy Bentham

Chapter I. Of the Principle of Utility

I. Nature has placed mankind under the governance of two sovereign masters, *pain* and *pleasure*. It is for them alone to point out what we ought to do, as well as to determine what we shall do. On the one hand the standard of right and wrong, on the other the chain of causes and effects, are fastened to their throne. They govern us in all we do, in all we say, in all we think: every effort we can make to throw off our subjection, will serve but to demonstrate and confirm it. In words a man may pretend to abjure their empire: but in reality he will remain subject to it all the while. The *principle of utility*[1] recognises this subjection, and assumes it for the foundation of

1. Note by the Author, July 1822.
   To this denomination has of late been added, or substituted, the *greatest happiness* or *greatest felicily* principle:

that system, the object of which is to rear the fabric of felicity by the hands of reason and of law. Systems which attempt to question it, deal in sounds instead of sense, in caprice instead of reason, in darkness instead of light.

But enough of metaphor and declamation: it is not by such means that moral science is to be improved.

II. The principle of utility is the foundation of the present work: it will be proper therefore at the outset to give an explicit and determinate account of what is meant by it. By the principle[2] of utility is meant that principle which approves or disapproves of every action whatsoever, according to the tendency which it appears to have to augment or diminish the happiness of the party whose interest is in question: or, what is the same thing in other words, to promote or to oppose that happiness. I say of every action whatsoever; and therefore not only of every action of a private individual, but of every measure of government.

III. By utility is meant that property in any object, whereby it tends to produce benefit, advantage, pleasure, good, or happiness, (all this in the present case comes to the same thing) or (what comes again to the same thing) to prevent the happening of mischief, pain, evil, or unhappiness to the party whose interest is considered: if that party be the community in general, then the

happiness of the community: if a particular individual, then the happiness of that individual.

IV. The interest of the community is one of the most general expressions that can occur in the phraseology of morals: no wonder that the meaning of it is often lost. When it has a meaning, it is this. The community is a fictitious *body*, composed of the individual persons who are considered as constituting as it were its *members*. The interest of the community then is, what?— the sum of the interests of the several members who compose it.

V. It is in vain to talk of the interest of the community, without understanding what is the interest of the individual[3]. A thing is said to promote the interest, or to be *for* the interest, of an individual, when it tends to add to the sum total of his pleasures: or, what comes to the same thing, to diminish the sum total of his pains.

VI. An action then may be said to be conformable to the principle of utility, or, for shortness sake, to utility, (meaning with respect to the community at large) when the tendency it has to augment the happiness of the community is greater than any it has to diminish it.

VII. A measure of government (which is but a particular kind of action, performed by a particular person or persons) may be said to be conformable to or dictated by the principle of utility, when in like manner the tendency which it has to augment the happiness of the community is greater than any which it has to diminish it.

VIII. When an action, or in particular a measure of government, is supposed by a man to be conformable to the principle of utility, it may be

---

this for shortness, instead of saying at length that *principle* which states the greatest happiness of all those whose interest is in question, as being the right and proper, and only right and proper and universally desirable, end of human action: of human action in every situation, and in particular in that of a functionary or set of functionaries exercising the powers of Government. The word *utility* does not so clearly point to the ideas of *pleasure* and *pain* as the words *happiness* and *felicity* do: nor does it lead us to the consideration of the *number*, of the interests affected; to the *number*, as being the circumstance, which contributes, in the largest proportion, to the formation of the standard here in question: the *standard of right and wrong*, by which alone the propriety of human conduct, in every situation, can with propriety be tried. This want of a sufficiently manifest connexion between the ideas of *happiness* and *pleasure* on the one hand, and the idea of *utility* on the other, I have every now and then found operating, and with but too much efficiency, as a bar to the acceptance, that might otherwise have been given, to this principle.

2. The word principle is derived from the Latin principium: which seems to be compounded of the two words

primus, first, or chief, and *cipium*, a termination which seems to be derived from *capio*, to take, as in *mancipium*, *municipium*; to which are analogous, *auceps*, *forceps*, and others. It is a term of very vague and very extensive signification: it is applied to any thing which is conceived to serve as a foundation or beginning to any series of operations: in some cases, of physical operations; but of mental operations in the present case.

The principle here in question may be taken for an act of the mind; a sentiment; a sentiment of approbation; a sentiment which, when applied to an action, approves of its utility, as that quality of it by which the measure of approbation or disapprobation bestowed upon it ought to be governed.

3. Interest is one of those words, which not having any superior *genus*, cannot in the ordinary way be defined.

convenient, for the purposes of discourse, to imagine a kind of law or dictate, called a law or dictate of utility: and to speak of the action in question, as being conformable to such law or dictate.

IX. A man may be said to be a partizan of the principle of utility, when the approbation or disapprobation he annexes to any action, or to any measure, is determined by and proportioned to the tendency which he conceives it to have to augment or to diminish the happiness of the community: or in other words, to its conformity or unconformity to the laws or dictates of utility.

X. Of an action that is conformable to the principle of utility one may always say either that it is one that ought to be done, or at least that it is not one that ought not to be done. One may say also, that it is right it should be done; at least that it is not wrong it should be done: that it is a right action; at least that it is not a wrong action. When thus interpreted, the words *ought*, and *right* and *wrong*, and others of that stamp, have a meaning: when otherwise, they have none.

XI. Has the rectitude of this principle been ever formally contested? It should seem that it had, by those who have not known what they have been meaning. Is it susceptible of any direct proof? it should seem not: for that which is used to prove every thing else, cannot itself be proved: a chain of proofs must have their commencement somewhere. To give such proof is as impossible as it is needless.

XII. Not that there is or ever has been that human creature breathing, however stupid or perverse, who has not on many, perhaps on most occasions of his life, deferred to it. By the natural constitution of the human frame, on most occasions of their lives men in general embrace this principle, without thinking of it: if not for the ordering of their own actions, yet for the trying of their own actions, as well as of those of other men. There have been, at the same time, not many, perhaps, even of the most intelligent, who have been disposed to embrace it purely and without reserve. There are even few who have not taken some occasion or other to quarrel with it, either on account of their not understanding always how to apply it, or on account of some prejudice or other which they were afraid to examine into, or could not bear to part with. For such is the stuff that man is made of: in principle and in practice, in a right

track and in a wrong one, the rarest of all human qualities is consistency.

XIII. When a man attempts to combat the principle of utility, it is with reasons drawn, without his being aware of it, from that very principle itself[4]. His arguments, if they prove any thing, prove not that the principle is *wrong*, but that, according to the applications he supposes to be made of it, it is *misapplied*. Is it possible for a man to move the earth? Yes; but he must first find out another earth to stand upon.

XIV. To disprove the propriety of it by arguments is impossible; but, from the causes that have been mentioned, or from some confused or partial view of it, a man may happen to be disposed not to relish it. Where this is the case, if he thinks the settling of his opinions on such a subject worth the trouble, let him take the following steps, and at length, perhaps, he may come to reconcile himself to it.

---

4. 'The principle of utility, (I have heard it said) is a dangerous principle: it is dangerous on certain occasions to consult it.' This is as much as to say, what? that it is not consonant to utility, to consult utility: in short, that it is *not* consulting it, to consult it.

Addition by the Author, July 1822.

Not long after the publication of the Fragment on Government, anno 1776, in which, in the character of an all-comprehensive and all-commanding principle, the principle of *utility* was brought to view, one person by whom observation to the above effect was made was *Alexander Wedderburn*, at that time Attorney or Solicitor General, after wards successively Chief Justice of the Common Pleas, and Chancellor of England, under the successive titles of Lord Lough borough and Earl of Rosslyn. It was made—not indeed in my hearing, but in the hearing of a person by whom it was almost immediately communicated to me. So far from being self-contradictory, it was a shrewd and perfectly true one. By that distinguished functionary, the state of the Government was thoroughly understood: by the obscure individual, at that time not so much as supposed to be so: his disquisitions had not been as yet applied, with any thing like a comprehensive view, to the field of Constitutional Law, nor therefore to those features of the English Government, by which the greatest happiness of the ruling *one* with or without that of a favoured few, are now so plainly seen to be the only ends to which the course of it has at any time been directed. The *principle of utility* was an appellative, at that time employed—employed by me, as it had been by others, to designate that which, in a more perspicuous and instructive manner, may, as above, be designated by the name of the *greatest happiness principle*. 'This principle

1. Let him settle with himself, whether he would wish to discard this principle altogether; if so, let him consider what it is that all his reasonings (in matters of politics especially) can amount to?

2. If he would, let him settle with himself, whether he would judge and act without any principle, or whether there is any other he would judge and act by?

3. If there be, let him examine and satisfy himself whether the principle he thinks he has found is really any separate intelligible principle; or whether it be not a mere principle in words, a kind of phrase, which at bottom expresses neither more nor less than the mere averment of his own unfounded sentiments; that is, what in another person he might be apt to call caprice?

4. If he is inclined to think that his own approbation or disapprobation, annexed to the idea of an act, without any regard to its consequences, is a sufficient foundation for him to judge and act upon, let him ask himself whether his sentiment is to be a standard of right and wrong, with respect to every other man, or whether every man's sentiment has the same privilege of being a standard to itself?

(said Wedderburn) is a dangerous one.' Saying so, he said that which, to a certain extent, is strictly true; a principle, which lays down, as the only *right* and justifiable end of Government, the greatest happiness of the greatest number—how can it be denied to be a dangerous one? dangerous it unquestionably is, to every government which has for its *actual* end or object, the greatest happiness of a certain *one*, with or without the addition of some comparatively small number of others, whom it is matter of pleasure or accommodation to him to admit, each of them, to a share in the concern, on the footing of so many junior partners. *Dangerous* it therefore really was, to the interest—the sinister interest—of all those functionaries, himself included, whose interest it was, to maximize delay, vexation, and expense, in judicial and other modes of procedure, for the sake of the prolit, extractible out of the expense. In a Government which had for its end in view the greatest happiness of the greatest number, Alexander Wedderburn might have been Attorney General and then Chancellor: but he would not have been Attorney General with £15,000 a year, nor Chancellor, with a peerage with a veto upon all justice, with £25,000 a year, and with 500 sinecures at his disposal, under the name of Ecclesiastical Benefices, besides *et cæteras*.

5. In the first case, let him ask himself whether his principle is not despotical, and hostile to all the rest of human race?

6. In the second case, whether it is not anarchial, and whether at this rate there are not as many different standards of right and wrong as there are men? and whether even to the same man, the same thing, which is right to-day, may not (without the least change in its nature) be wrong to-morrow? and whether the same thing is not right and wrong in the same place at the same time? and in either case, whether all argument is not at an end? and whether, when two men have said, 'I like this,' and 'I don't like it,' they can (upon such a principle) have any thing more to say?

7. If he should have said to himself, No: for that the sentiment which he proposes as a standard must be grounded on reflection, let him say on what particulars the reflection is to turn? if on particulars having relation to the utility of the act, then let him say whether this is not deserting his own principle, and borrowing assistance from that very one in opposition to which he sets it up: or if not on those particulars, on what other particulars?

8. If he should be for compounding the matter, and adopting his own principle in part, and the principle of utility in part, let him say how far he will adopt it?

9. When he has settled with himself where he will stop, then let him ask himself how he justifies to himself the adopting it so far? and why he will not adopt it any farther?

10. Admitting any other principle than the principle of utility to be a right principle, a principle that it is right for a man to pursue; admitting (what is not true) that the word *right* can have a meaning without reference to utility, let him say whether there is any such thing as a *motive* that a man can have to pursue the dictates of it: if there is, let him say what that motive is, and how it is to be distinguished from those which enforce the dictates of utility: if not, then lastly let him say what it is this other principle can be good for?

Chapter IV, Value of a Lot of Pleasure or Pain, How to Be Measured

I. Pleasures then, and the avoidance of pains, are the *ends* that the legislator has in view; it behoves him therefore to understand their *value*. Pleasures and pains are the instruments he has to work with: it behoves him therefore to understand their force, which is again, in other words, their value.

II. To a person considered by *himself*, the value of a pleasure or pain considered *by itself*, will be greater or less, according to the four following *circumstances*[1]:

1. Its *intensity*.
2. Its *duration*.
3. Its *certainty* or *uncertainty*.
4. Its *propinquity* or *remoteness*.

III. These are the circumstances which are to be considered in estimating a pleasure or a pain considered each of them by itself. But when the value of any pleasure or pain is considered for the purpose of estimating the tendency of any *act* by which it is produced, there are two other circumstances to be taken into the account; these are,

5. Its *fecundity*, or the chance it has of being followed by sensations of the *same* kind: that is, pleasures, if it be a pleasure: pains, if it be a pain.
6. Its *purity*, or the chance it has of not being followed by sensations of the *opposite* kind: that is, pains, if it be a pleasure: pleasures, if it be a pain.

These two last, however, are in strictness scarcely to be deemed properties of the pleasure or the pain itself; they are not, therefore, in strictness to be taken into the account of the value of that pleasure or that pain. They are in strictness to be deemed properties only of the act, or other event, by which such pleasure or pain has been produced; and accordingly are only to be taken into the account of the tendency of such act or such event.

IV. To a *number* of persons, with reference to each of whom to the value of a pleasure or a pain is considered, it will be greater or less, according to seven circumstances: to wit, the six preceding ones; viz.

1. Its *intensity*.
2. Its *duration*.
3. Its *certainty* or *uncertainty*.
4. Its *propinquity* or *remoteness*.
5. Its *fecundity*.
6. Its *purity*.

And one other; to wit:

7. Its *extent*; that is, the number of persons to whom it *extends*; or (in other words) who are affected by it.

V. To take an exact account then of the general tendency of any act, by which the interests of a community are affected, proceed as follows. Begin with any one person of those whose interests seem most immediately to be affected by it: and take an account,

1. Of the value of each distinguishable *pleasure* which appears to be produced by it in the *first* instance.
2. Of the value of each *pain* which appears to be produced by it in the *first* instance.
3. Of the value of each pleasure which appears to be produced by it *after* the first. This constitutes the *fecundity* of the first *pleasure* and the *impurity* of the first *pain*.
4. Of the value of each *pain* which appears to be produced by it after the first. This constitutes the *fecundity* of the first *pain*, and the *impurity* of the first pleasure.
5. Sum up all the values of all the *pleasures* on the one side, and those of all the pains on the other. The balance, if it be on the side of pleasure, will give the *good* tendency of the act upon the whole, with respect to the interests of that *individual* person; if on the side of pain, the *bad* tendency of it upon the whole.
6. Take an account of the *number* of persons whose interests appear to be concerned; and

---

1. These circumstances have since been denominated *elements* or *dimensions* of *value* in a pleasure or a pain.

   Not long after the publication of the first edition, the following memoriter verses were framed, in the view of lodging more effectually, in the memory, these points, on which the whole fabric of morals and legislation may be seen to rest.

   Intense, long, certain, speedy, fruitful, pure—
   Such marks in *pleasures* and in *pains* endure.
   Such pleasures seek if *private* be thy end:
   If it be *public*, wide let them *extend*
   Such *pains* avoid, whichever be thy view:
   If pains *must* come, let them *extend* to few.

repeat the above process with respect to each. *Sum up* the numbers expressive of the degrees of *good* tendency, which the act has, with respect to each individual, in regard to whom the tendency of it is *good* upon the whole: do this again with respect to each individual, in regard to whom the tendency of it is *good* upon the whole: do this again with respect to each individual, in regard to whom the tendency of it is *bad* upon the whole. Take the *balance* which if on the side of *pleasure*, will give the general *good tendency* of the act, with respect to the total number or community of individuals concerned; if on the side of pain, the general *evil tendency*, with respect to the same community.

VI. It is not to be expected that this process should be strictly pursued previously to every moral judgment, or to every legislative or judicial operation. It may, however, be always kept in view: and as near as the process actually pursued on these occasions approaches to it, so near will such process approach to the character of an exact one.

VII. The same process is alike applicable to pleasure and pain, in whatever shape they appear: and by whatever denomination they are distinguished: to pleasure, whether it be called *good* (which is properly the cause or instrument of pleasure) or *profit* (which is distant pleasure, or the cause or instrument of, distant pleasure,) or *convenience*, or *advantage, benefit, emolument, happiness,* and so forth: to pain, whether it be called *evil,*

(which corresponds to *good*) or *mischief*, or *inconvenience*. or *disadvantage*, or *loss*, or *unhappiness*, and so forth.

VIII. Nor is this a novel and unwarranted, any more than it is a useless theory. In all this there is nothing but what the practice of mankind, wheresoever they have a clear view of their own interest, is perfectly conformable to. An article of property, an estate in land, for instance, is valuable, on what account? On account of the pleasures of all kinds which it enables a man to produce, and what comes to the same thing the pains of all kinds which it enables him to avert. But the value of such an article of property is universally understood to rise or fall according to the length or shortness of the time which a man has in it: the certainty or uncertainty of its coming into possession: and the nearness or remoteness of the time at which, if at all, it is to come into possession. As to the *intensity* of the pleasures which a man may derive from it, this is never thought of, because it depends upon the use which each particular person may come to make of it; which cannot be estimated till the particular pleasures he may come to derive from it, or the particular pains he may come to exclude by means of it, are brought to view. For the same reason, neither does he think of the *fecundity* or *purity* of those pleasures.

Thus much for pleasure and pain, happiness and unhappiness, in *general*. We come now to consider the several particular kinds of pain and pleasure.

Utilitarianism

John Stuart Mill

Chapter I. General Remarks

There are few circumstances among those which make up the present condition of human knowledge, more unlike what might have been expected, or more significant of the backward state in which speculation on the most important subjects still lingers, than the little progress which has been made in the decision of the controversy respecting the criterion of right and wrong. From the dawn of philosophy, the question concerning the *summum*

bonum, or, what is the same thing, concerning the foundation of morality, has been accounted the main problem in speculative thought, has occupied the most gifted intellects, and divided them into sects and schools, carrying on a vigorous warfare against one another. And after more than two thousand years the same discussions continue, philosophers are still ranged under the same contending banners, and neither thinkers nor mankind at large seem nearer to being unanimous on the subject, than when the youth Socrates listened to the old Protagoras, and asserted (if Plato's dialogue be grounded on a real conversation) the theory of utilitarianism against the popular morality of the so-called sophist.

It is true that similar confusion and uncertainty, and in some cases similar discordance, exist respecting the first principles of all the sciences, not excepting that which is deemed the most certain of them—mathematics; without much impairing, generally indeed without impairing at all, the trustworthiness of the conclusions of those sciences. An apparent anomaly, the explanation of which is, that the detailed doctrines of a science are not usually deduced from, nor depend for their evidence upon, what are called its first principles. Were it not so, there would be no science more precarious, or whose conclusions were more insufficiently made out, than algebra; which derives none of its certainty from what are commonly taught to learners as its elements, since these, as laid down by some of its most eminent teachers, are as full of fictions as English law, and of mysteries as theology. The truths which are ultimately accepted as the first principles of a science, are really the last results of metaphysical analysis, practiced on the elementary notions with which the science is conversant; and their relation to the science is not that of foundations to an edifice, but of roots to a tree, which may perform their office equally well though they be never dug down to and exposed to light. But though in science the particular truths precede the general theory, the contrary might be expected to be the case with a practical art, such as morals or legislation. All action is for the sake of some end, and rules of action, it seems natural to suppose, must take their whole character and colour from the end to which they are subservient. When we engage in a pursuit, a clear and precise conception of what we are pursuing would seem to be the first thing we need, instead of the last we are to look forward to. A test of right and wrong must be the means, one would think, of ascertaining what is right or wrong, and not a consequence of having already ascertained it.

The difficulty is not avoided by having recourse to the popular theory of a natural faculty, a sense or instinct, informing us of right and wrong. For—besides that the existence of such a moral instinct is itself one of the matters in dispute—those believers in it who have any pretensions to philosophy, have been obliged to abandon the idea that it discerns what is right or wrong in the particular case in hand,

as our other senses discern the sight or sound actually present. Our moral faculty, according to all those of its interpreters who are entitled to the name of thinkers, supplies us only with the general principles of moral judgments; it is a branch of our reason, not of our sensitive faculty; and must be looked to for the abstract doctrines of morality, not for perception of it in the concrete. The intuitive, no less than what may be termed the inductive, school of ethics, insists on the necessity of general laws. They both agree that the morality of an individual action is not a question of direct perception, but of the application of a law to an individual case. They recognize also, to a great extent, the same moral laws; but differ as to their evidence, and the source from which they derive their authority. According to the one opinion, the principles of morals are evident *a priori*, requiring nothing to command assent, except that the meaning of the terms be understood. According to the other doctrine, right and wrong, as well as truth and falsehood, are questions of observation and experience. But both hold equally that morality must be deduced from principles; and the intuitive school affirm as strongly as the inductive, that there is a science of morals. Yet they seldom attempt to make out a list of the *a priori* principles which are to serve as the premises of the science; still more rarely do they make any effort to reduce those various principles to one first principle, or common ground of obligation. They either assume the ordinary precepts of morals as of *a priori* authority, or they lay down as the common groundwork of those maxims, some generality much less obviously authoritative than the maxims themselves, and which has never succeeded in gaining popular acceptance. Yet to support their pretensions there ought either to be some one fundamental principle or law, at the root of all morality, or if there be several, there should be a determinate order of precedence among them; and the one principle, or the rule for deciding between the various principles when they conflict, ought to be self-evident.

To inquire how far the bad effects of this deficiency have been mitigated in practice, or to what extent the moral beliefs of mankind have been vitiated or made uncertain by the absence of any distinct recognition of an ultimate standard, would imply a complete survey and criticism, of past and present ethical doctrine. It would, however, be easy to show that whatever steadiness or consistency these moral beliefs have, attained, has been mainly due to the tacit influence of a standard not recognized. Although the nonexistence of an acknowledged first principle has made ethics not so much a guide as a consecration of men's actual sentiments, still, as men's sentiments, both of favour and of aversion, are greatly influenced by what they suppose to be the effects of things upon their happiness, the principle of utility, or as Bentham latterly called it, the greatest happiness principle, has had a large share in forming the moral doctrines even of those who most scornfully reject its authority. Nor is there any school of thought which refuses to admit that the influence of actions on happiness is a most material and even predominant consideration in many of the details of morals, however unwilling to acknowledge it as the fundamental principle of morality, and the source of moral obligation. I might go much further, and say that to all those *a priori* moralists who deem it necessary to argue at all, utilitarian arguments are indispensable. It is not my present purpose to criticize these thinkers; but I cannot help referring, for illustration, to a systematic treatise by one of the most illustrious of them, the *Metaphysics of Ethics*, by Kant. This remarkable man, whose system of thought will long remain one of the landmarks in the history of philosophical speculation, does, in the treatise in question, lay down a universal first principle as the origin and ground of moral obligation; it is this: "So act, that the rule on which thou actest would admit of being adopted as a law by all rational beings." But when he begins to deduce from this precept any of the actual duties of morality, he fails, almost grotesquely, to show that there would be any contradiction, any logical (not to say physical) impossibility, in the adoption by all rational beings of the most outrageously immoral rules of conduct. All he shows is that the *consequences* of their universal adoption would be such as no one would choose to incur.

On the present occasion, I shall, without further discussion of the other theories, attempt to contribute something towards the understanding and appreciation of the Utilitarian or Happiness theory, and towards such proof as it is susceptible of. It is evident that this cannot be proof in the ordinary and popular meaning of the term. Questions of ultimate ends are not amenable to direct proof. Whatever can be proved to be good, must be so by being shown to be a means to something admitted to be good without proof. The medical art is proved to be good by its conducing to health; but how is it

possible to prove that health is good? The art of music is good, for the reason, among others, that it produces pleasure; but what proof is it possible to give that pleasure is good? If, then, it is asserted that there is a comprehensive formula, including all things which are in themselves good, and that whatever else is good, is not so as an end, but as a mean, the formula may be accepted or rejected, but is not a subject of what is commonly understood by proof. We are not, however, to infer that its acceptance or rejection must depend on blind impulse, or arbitrary choice. There is a larger meaning of the word proof, in which this question is as amenable to it as any other of the disputed questions of philosophy. The subject is within the cognizance of the rational faculty; and neither does that faculty deal with it solely in the way of intuition. Considerations may be presented capable of determining the intellect either to give or withhold its assent to the doctrine; and this is equivalent to proof.

We shall examine presently of what nature are these considerations; in what manner they apply to the case, and what rational grounds, therefore, can be given for accepting or rejecting the utilitarian formula. But it is a preliminary condition of rational acceptance or rejection, that the formula should be correctly understood. I believe that the very imperfect notion ordinarily formed of its meaning, is the chief obstacle which impedes its reception; and that could it be cleared, even from only the grosser misconceptions, the question would be greatly simplified, and a large proportion of its difficulties removed. Before, therefore, I attempt to enter into the philosophical grounds which can be given for assenting to the utilitarian standard, I shall offer some illustrations of the doctrine itself; with the view of showing more clearly what it is, distinguishing it from what it is not, and disposing of such of the practical objections to it as either originate in, or are closely connected with, mistaken interpretations of its meaning. Having thus prepared the ground, I shall afterwards endeavor to throw such light as I can upon the question, considered as one of philosophical theory.

Chapter II. What Utilitarianism Is

A passing remark is all that needs be given to the ignorant blunder of supposing that those who stand up for utility as the test of right and wrong, use the term in that restricted and merely colloquial sense in which utility is opposed to pleasure. An apology is due to the philosophical opponents of utilitarianism, for even the momentary appearance of confounding them with any one capable of so absurd a misconception; which is the more extraordinary, inasmuch as the contrary accusation, of referring everything to pleasure, and that too in its grossest form, is another of the common charges against utilitarianism: and, as has been pointedly remarked by an able writer, the same sort of persons, and often the very same persons, denounce the theory 'as impracticably dry when the word utility precedes the word pleasure, and as too practicably voluptuous when the word pleasure precedes the word utility'. Those who know anything about the matter are aware that every writer, from Epicurus to Bentham, who maintained the theory of utility, meant by it, not something to be contradistinguished from pleasure, but pleasure itself, together with exemption from pain; and instead of opposing the useful to the agreeable or the ornamental, have always declared that the useful means these, among other things. Yet the common herd, including the herd of writers, not only in newspapers and periodicals, but in books of weight and pretension, are perpetually falling into this shallow mistake. Having caught up the word utilitarian, while knowing nothing whatever about it but its sound, they habitually express by it the rejection, or the neglect, of pleasure in some of its forms; of beauty, of ornament, or of amusement. Nor is the term thus ignorantly misapplied solely in disparagement, but occasionally in compliment; as though it implied superiority to frivolity and the mere pleasures of the moment. And this perverted use is the only one in which the word is popularly known, and the one from which the new generation are acquiring their sole notion of its meaning. Those who introduced the word[1], but who had for many years discontin-

---

1. The author of this essay has reason for believing himself to be the first person who brought the word utilitarian into use. He did not invent it, but adopted it from a passing expression in Mr. Galt's *Annals of the Parish*. After using it as a designation for several years, he and others abandoned it from a growing dislike to anything resembling a badge or watchword of sectarian distinction. But as a name for one single opinion, not a set of opinions— to denote the recognition of utility as a standard, not any particular way of applying it—the term supplies a want in the language, and offers, in many cases, a convenient mode of avoiding tiresome circumlocution.

ued it as a distinctive appellation, may well feel themselves called upon to resume it, if by doing so they can hope to contribute anything towards rescuing it from this utter degradation.

The creed which accepts as the foundation of morals, Utility, or the Greatest Happiness Principle, holds that actions are right in proportion as they tend to promote happiness, wrong as they tend to produce the reverse of happiness. By happiness is intended pleasure, and the absence of pain; by unhappiness, pain, and the privation of pleasure. To give a clear view of the moral standard set up by the theory, much more requires to be said; in particular, what things it includes in the ideas of pain and pleasure; and to what extent this is left an open question. But these supplementary explanations do not affect the theory of life on which this theory of morality is grounded—namely, that pleasure, and freedom from pain, are the only things desirable as ends; and that all desirable things (which are as numerous in the utilitarian as in any other scheme) are desirable either for the pleasure inherent in themselves, or as means to the promotion of pleasure and the prevention of pain.

Now, such a theory of life excites in many minds, and among them in some of the most estimable in feeling and purpose, inveterate dislike. To suppose that life has (as they express it) no higher end than pleasure—no better and nobler object of desire and pursuit—they designate as utterly mean and groveling; as a doctrine worthy only of swine, to whom the followers of Epicurus were, at a very early period, contemptuously likened; and modern holders of the doctrine are occasionally made the subject of equally polite comparisons by its German, French, and English assailants.

When thus attacked, the Epicureans have always answered, that it is not they, but their accusers, who represent human nature in a degrading light; since the accusation supposes human beings to be capable of no pleasures except those of which swine are capable. If this supposition were true, the charge could not be gainsaid, but would then be no longer an imputation; for if the sources of pleasure were precisely the same to human beings and to swine, the rule of life which is good enough for the one would be good enough for the other. The comparison of the Epicurean life to that of beasts is felt as degrading, precisely because a beast's pleasures do not satisfy a human being's conceptions of happiness. Human beings have faculties more elevated than the animal appetites, and when once made conscious of them, do not regard anything as happiness which does not include their gratification. I do not, indeed, consider the Epicureans to have been by any means faultless in drawing out their scheme of consequences from the utilitarian principle. To do this in any sufficient manner, many Stoic, as well as Christian elements require to be included. But there is no known Epicurean theory of life which does not assign to the pleasures of the intellect, of the feelings and imagination, and of the moral sentiments, a much higher value as pleasures than to those of mere sensation. It must be admitted, however, that utilitarian writers in general have placed the superiority of mental over bodily pleasures chiefly in the greater permanency, safety, uncostliness, etc., of the former—that is, in their circumstantial advantages rather than in their intrinsic nature. And on all these points utilitarians have fully proved their case; but they might have taken the other, and, as it may be called, higher ground, with entire consistency. It is quite compatible with the principle of utility to recognize the fact, that some *kinds* of pleasure are more desirable and more valuable than others. It would be absurd that while, in estimating all other things, quality is considered as well as quantity, the estimation of pleasures should be supposed to depend on quantity alone.

If I am asked, what I mean by difference of quality in pleasures, or what makes one pleasure more valuable than another, merely as a pleasure, except its being greater in amount, there is but one possible answer. Of two pleasures, if there be one to which all or almost all who have experience of both give a decided preference, irrespective of any feeling of moral obligation to prefer it, that is the more desirable pleasure. If one of the two is, by those who are competently acquainted with both, placed so far above the other that they prefer it, even though knowing it to be attended with a greater amount of discontent, and would not resign it for any quantity of the other pleasure which their nature is capable of, we are justified in ascribing to the preferred enjoyment a superiority in quality, so far outweighing quantity as to render it, in comparison, of small account.

Now it is an unquestionable fact that those who are equally acquainted with, and equally capable of appreciating and enjoying, both, do give a most marked preference to the manner of existence which employs their higher faculties. Few human creatures would consent to be changed into any of the lower animals, for a promise of the fullest allowance of a beast's pleasures; no intelligent human being would consent to be a fool, no instructed person would be an ignoramus, no person of feeling and conscience would be selfish and base, even though they should be persuaded that the fool, the dunce, or the rascal is better satisfied with his lot than they are with theirs. They would not resign what they possess more than he for the most complete satisfaction of all the desires which they have in common with him. If they ever fancy they would, it is only in cases of unhappiness so extreme, that to escape from it they would exchange their lot for almost any other, however undesirable in their own eyes. A being of higher faculties requires more to make him happy, is capable probably of more acute suffering, and certainly accessible to it at more points, than one of an inferior type; but in spite of these liabilities, he can never really wish to sink into what he feels to be a lower grade of existence. We may give what explanation we please of this unwillingness; we may attribute it to pride, a name which is given indiscriminately to some of the most and to some of the least estimable feelings of which mankind are capable; we may refer it to the love of liberty and personal independence, an appeal to which was with the Stoics one of the most effective means for the inculcation of it; to the love of power, or to the love of excitement, both of which do really enter into and contribute to it: but its most appropriate appellation is a sense of dignity, which all human beings possess in one form or other, and in some, though by no means in exact, proportion to their higher faculties, and which is so essential a part of the happiness of those in whom it is strong, that nothing which conflicts with it could be, otherwise than momentarily, an object of desire to them. Whoever supposes that this preference takes place at a sacrifice of happiness—that the superior being, in anything like equal circumstances, is not happier than the inferior—confounds the two very different ideas, of happiness, and content. It is indisputable that the being whose capacities of enjoyment are low, has the greatest chance of having them fully satisfied; and a highly endowed being will always feel that any happiness which he can look for, as the world is constituted, is imperfect. But he can learn to bear its imperfections, if they are at all bearable; and they will not make him envy the being who is indeed unconscious of the imperfections, but only because he feels not at all the good which those imperfections qualify. It is better to be a human being dissatisfied than a pig satisfied; better to be Socrates dissatisfied than a fool satisfied. And if the fool, or the pig, are of a different opinion, it is because they only know their own side of the question. The other party to the comparison knows both sides.

It may be objected, that many who are capable of the higher pleasures, occasionally, under the influence of temptation, postpone them to the lower. But this is quite compatible with a full appreciation of the intrinsic superiority of the higher. Men often, from infirmity of character, make their election for the nearer good, though they know it to be the less valuable; and this no less when the choice is between two bodily pleasures, than when it is between bodily and mental. They pursue sensual indulgences to the injury of health, though perfectly aware that health is the greater good. It may be further objected, that many who begin with youthful enthusiasm for everything noble, as they advance in years sink into indolence and selfishness. But I do not believe that those who undergo this very common change, voluntarily choose the lower description of pleasures in preference to the higher. I believe that before they devote themselves exclusively to the one, they have already become incapable of the other. Capacity for the nobler feelings is in most natures a very tender plant, easily killed, not only by hostile influences, but by mere want of sustenance; and in the majority of young persons it speedily dies away if the occupations to which their position in life has devoted them, and the society into which it has thrown them, are not favourable to keeping that higher capacity in exercise. Men lose their high aspirations as they lose their intellectual tastes, because they have not time or opportunity for indulging them; and they addict themselves to inferior pleasures, not because they deliberately prefer them, but because they are either the only ones to which they have access, or the only ones which

they are any longer capable of enjoying. It may be questioned whether any one who has remained equally susceptible to both classes of pleasures, ever knowingly and calmly preferred the lower; though many, in all ages, have broken down in an ineffectual attempt to combine both.

From this verdict of the only competent judges, I apprehend there can be no appeal. On a question which is the best worth having of two pleasures, or which of two modes of existence is the most grateful to the feelings, apart from its moral attributes and from its consequences, the judgment of those who are qualified by knowledge of both, or, if they differ, that of the majority among them, must be admitted as final. And there needs be the less hesitation to accept this judgment respecting the quality of pleasures, since there is no other tribunal to be referred to even on the question of quantity. What means are there of determining which is the acutest of two pains, or the intensest of two pleasurable sensations, except the general suffrage of those who are familiar with both? Neither pains nor pleasures are homogeneous, and pain is always heterogeneous with pleasure. What is there to decide whether a particular pleasure is worth purchasing at the cost of a particular pain, except the feelings and judgment of the experienced? When, therefore, those feelings and judgment declare the pleasures derived from the higher faculties to be preferable *in kind*, apart from the question of intensity, to those of which the animal nature, disjoined from the higher faculties, is susceptible, they are entitled on this subject to the same regard.

I have dwelt on this point, as being a necessary part of a perfectly just conception of Utility or Happiness, considered as the directive rule of human conduct. But it is by no means an indispensable condition to the acceptance of the utilitarian standard; for that standard is not the agent's own greatest happiness, but the greatest amount of happiness altogether; and if it may possibly be doubted whether a noble character is always the happier for its nobleness, there can be no doubt that it makes other people happier, and that the world in general is immensely a gainer by it. Utilitarianism, therefore, could only attain its end by the general cultivation of nobleness of character, even if each individual were only benefited by the nobleness of others, and his own, so far as happiness is concerned, were a sheer deduction from the benefit. But the bare enunciation of such an absurdity as this last, renders refutation superfluous.

According to the Greatest Happiness Principle, as above explained, the ultimate end, with reference to and for the sake of which all other things are desirable (whether we are considering our own good or that of other people), is an existence exempt as far as possible from pain, and as rich as possible in enjoyments, both in point of quantity and quality; the test of quality, and the rule for measuring it against quantity, being the preference felt by those who in their opportunities of experience, to which must be added their habits of self-consciousness and self-observation, are best furnished with the means of comparison. This, being, according to the utilitarian opinion, the end of human action, is necessarily also the standard of morality; which may accordingly be defined, the rules and precepts for human conduct, by the observance of which an existence such as has been described might be, to the greatest extent possible, secured to all mankind; and not to them only, but, so far as the nature of things admits, to the whole sentient creation.

Against this doctrine, however, arises another class of objectors, who say that happiness, in any form, cannot be the rational purpose of human life and action; because, in the first place, it is unattainable: and they contemptuously ask, what right hast thou to be happy? a question which Mr. Carlyle clenches by the addition, What right, a short time ago, hadst thou even *to be*? Next, they say, that men can do *without* happiness; that all noble human beings have felt this, and could not have become noble but by learning the lesson of *Entsagen*, or renunciation; which lesson, thoroughly learnt and submitted to, they affirm to be the beginning and necessary condition of all virtue.

The first of these objections would go to the root of the matter were it well founded; for if no happiness is to be had at all by human beings, the attainment of it cannot be the end of morality, or of any rational conduct. Though, even in that case, something might still be said for the utilitarian theory; since utility includes not solely the pursuit of happiness, but the prevention or mitigation of unhappiness; and if the former aim be chimerical, there will be all the greater scope and more imperative need for the latter, so long at least as mankind think fit to live, and do not take refuge in the simultaneous act of suicide recommended under certain conditions by Novalis. When, however, it is thus positively asserted to be impossible that human life should be happy, the assertion, if not something like a verbal quibble, is at least an exaggeration. If by happiness be meant a continuity of highly pleasurable excitement, it is evident enough that this is impossible. A state of exalted pleasure lasts only moments, or in some cases, and with some intermissions, hours or days, and is the occasional brilliant flash of enjoyment, not its permanent and steady flame. Of this the philosophers who have taught that happiness is the end of life were as fully aware as those who taunt them. The happiness which they meant was not a life of rapture; but moments of such, in an existence made up of few and transitory pains, many and various pleasures, with a decided predominance of the active over the passive, and having as the foundation of the whole, not to expect more from life than it is capable of bestowing. A life thus composed, to those who have been fortunate enough to obtain it, has always appeared worthy of the name of happiness. And such an existence is even now the lot of many, during some considerable portion of their lives. The present wretched education, and wretched social arrangements, are the only real hindrance to its being attainable by almost all.

The objectors perhaps may doubt whether human beings, if taught to consider happiness as the end of life, would be satisfied with such a moderate share of it. But great numbers of mankind have been satisfied with much less. The main constituents of a satisfied life appear to be two, either of which by itself is often found sufficient for the purpose: tranquillity, and excitement. With much tranquillity, many find that they can be content with very little pleasure: with much excitement, many can reconcile themselves to a considerable quantity of pain. There is assuredly no inherent impossibility in enabling even the mass of mankind to unite both; since the two are so far from being incompatible that they are in natural alliance, the prolongation of either being a preparation for, and exciting a wish for, the other.

It is only those in whom indolence amounts to a vice, that do not desire excitement after an interval of repose: it is only those in whom the need of excitement is a disease, that feel the tranquillity which follows excitement dull and insipid, instead of pleasurable in direct proportion to the excitement which preceded it. When people who are tolerably fortunate in their outward lot do not find in life sufficient enjoyment to make it valuable to them, the cause generally is, caring for nobody but themselves. To those who have neither public nor private affections, the excitements of life are much curtailed, and in any case dwindle in value as the time approaches when all selfish interests must be terminated by death: while those who leave after them objects of personal affection, and especially those who have also cultivated a fellow-feeling with the collective interests of mankind, retain as lively an interest in life on the eve of death as in the vigour of youth and health. Next to selfishness, the principal cause which makes life unsatisfactory is want of mental cultivation. A cultivated mind—I do not mean that of a philosopher, but any mind to which the fountains of knowledge have been opened, and which has been taught, in any tolerable degree, to exercise its faculties—finds sources of inexhaustible interest in all that surrounds it; in the objects of nature, the achievements of art, the imaginations of poetry, the incidents of history, the ways of mankind, past and present, and their prospects in the future. It is possible, indeed, to become indifferent to all this, and that too without having exhausted a thousandth part of it; but only when one has had from the beginning no moral or human interest in these things, and has sought in them only the gratification of curiosity.

Now there is absolutely no reason in the nature of things why an amount of mental culture sufficient to give an intelligent interest in these objects of contemplation, should not be the inheritance of every one born in a civilized country. As little is there an inherent necessity that any human being should be a selfish egotist, devoid of every feeling or care but those which centre in his own miserable individuality. Something far superior to this is sufficiently common even now, to give ample earnest of what the human species may be made. Genuine private affections and a sincere interest in the public good, are possible, though in unequal degrees, to every rightly brought up human being. In a world in which there is so much to interest, so much to enjoy, and so much also to correct and improve, every one who has this moderate amount of moral and intellectual requisites is capable of an existence which may be called enviable; and unless such a person, through bad laws, or subjection to the will of others, is denied the liberty to use the sources of happiness within his reach, he will not fail to find this enviable existence, if he escape the positive evils of life, the great sources of physical and mental suffering—such as indigence, disease, and the unkindness, worthlessness, or premature loss of objects of affection. The main stress of the problem lies, therefore, in the contest with these calamities, from which it is a rare good fortune entirely to escape; which, as things now are, cannot be obviated, and often cannot be in any material degree mitigated. Yet no one whose opinion deserves a moment's consideration can doubt that most of the great positive evils of the world are in themselves removable, and will, if human affairs continue to improve, be in the end reduced within narrow limits. Poverty, in any sense implying suffering, may be completely extinguished by the wisdom of society, combined with the good sense and providence of individuals. Even that most intractable of enemies, disease, may be indefinitely reduced in dimensions by good physical and moral education, and proper control of noxious influences; while the progress of science holds out a promise for the future of still more direct conquests over this detestable foe. And every advance in that direction relieves us from some, not only of the chances which cut short our own lives, but, what concerns us still more, which deprive us of those in whom our happiness is wrapt up. As for vicissitudes of fortune, and other disappointments connected with worldly circumstances, these are principally the effect either of gross imprudence, of ill-regulated desires, or of bad or imperfect social institutions. All the grand sources, in short, of human suffering are in a great degree, many of them almost entirely, conquerable by human care and effort; and though their removal is grievously slow—though a long succession of generations will perish in the breach before the conquest is completed, and this world becomes all that, if will and knowledge were not wanting, it might easily be made—yet every mind sufficiently intelligent and generous to bear a part, however small and unconspicuous, in the endeavour, will draw a noble enjoyment from the contest itself, which he would not for any bribe in the form of selfish indulgence consent to be without.

And this leads to the true estimation of what is said by the objectors concerning the possibility, and the obligation, of learning to do without happiness. Unquestionably it is possible to do without happiness; it is done involuntarily by nineteen-twentieths of mankind, even in those parts of our present world which are least deep in barbarism; and it often has to be done voluntarily by the hero or the martyr, for the sake of something which he prizes more than his individual happiness. But this something, what is it, unless the happiness of others or some of the requisites of happiness? It is noble to be capable of resigning entirely one's own portion of happiness, or chances of it: but, after all, this self-sacrifice must be for some end; it is not its own end; and if we are told that its end is not happiness, but virtue, which is better than happiness, I ask, would the sacrifice be made if the hero or martyr did not believe that it would earn for others immunity from similar sacrifices? Would it be made if he thought that his renunciation of happiness for himself would produce no fruit for any of his fellow creatures, but to make their lot like his, and place them also in the condition of persons who have renounced happiness? All honour to those who can abnegate for themselves the personal enjoyment of life, when by such renunciation they contribute worthily to increase the amount of happiness in the world; but he who does it, or professes to do it, for any other purpose, is no more deserving of admiration than the ascetic mounted on his pillar. He may be an inspiring proof of what men *can* do, but assuredly not an example of what they *should*.

Though it is only in a very imperfect state of the world's arrangements that any one can best serve the happiness of others by the absolute sacrifice of his own, yet so long as the world is in that imperfect state, I fully acknowledge that the readiness to make such a sacrifice is the highest virtue which can be found in man. I will add, that in this condition the world, paradoxical as the assertion may be, the conscious ability to do without happiness gives the best prospect of realizing, such happiness as is attainable. For nothing except that consciousness can raise a person above the chances of life, by making him feel that, let fate and fortune do their worst, they have not power to subdue him: which, once felt, frees him from excess of anxiety concerning the evils of life, and enables him, like many a Stoic in the worst times of the Roman Empire, to cultivate in tranquillity the sources of satisfaction accessible to him, without concerning himself about the uncertainty of their duration, any more than about their inevitable end.

Meanwhile, let utilitarians never cease to claim the morality of self devotion as a possession which belongs by as good a right to them, as either to the Stoic or to the Transcendentalist. The utilitarian morality does recognize in human beings the power of sacrificing their own greatest good for the good of others. It only refuses to admit that the sacrifice is itself a good. A sacrifice which does not increase, or tend to increase, the sum total of happiness, it considers as wasted. The only self-renunciation which it applauds, is devotion to the happiness, or to some of the means of happiness, of others; either of mankind collectively, or of individuals within the limits imposed by the collective interests of mankind.

I must again repeat, what the assailants of utilitarianism seldom have the justice to acknowledge, that the happiness which forms the utilitarian standard of what is right in conduct, is not the agent's own happiness, but that of all concerned. As between his own happiness and that of others, utilitarianism requires him to be as strictly impartial as a disinterested and benevolent spectator. In the golden rule of Jesus of Nazareth, we read the complete spirit of the ethics of utility. To do as you would be done by, and to love your neighbour as yourself, constitute the ideal perfection of utilitarian morality. As the means of making the nearest approach to this ideal, utility would enjoin, first, that laws and social arrangements should place the happiness, or (as speaking practically it may be called) the interest, of every individual, as nearly as possible in harmony with the interest of the whole; and secondly, that education and opinion, which have so vast a power over human character, should so use that power as to establish in the mind of every individual an indissoluble association between his own happiness and the good of the whole; especially between his own happiness and the practice of such modes of conduct, negative and positive, as regard for the universal happiness prescribes; so that not only he may be unable to conceive the possibility of happiness to himself, consistently with conduct opposed to the general good, but also that a direct impulse to promote the general good may be in every individual one of the habitual motives of action, and the sentiments connected therewith may fill a large and prominent place in every human being's sentient existence. If the, impugners of the utilitarian morality represented it to their own minds in this its, true character, I know not what recommendation possessed by any other morality they could possibly affirm to be wanting to it; what more beautiful or more exalted developments of human nature any other ethical system can be supposed to foster, or what springs of action, not accessible to the utilitarian, such systems rely on for giving effect to their mandates.

The objectors to utilitarianism cannot always be charged with representing it in a discreditable light. On the contrary, those among them who entertain anything like a just idea of its disinterested character, sometimes find fault with its standard as being too high for humanity. They say it is exacting too much to require that people shall always act from the inducement of promoting the general interests of society. But this is to mistake the very meaning of a standard of morals, and confound the rule of action with the motive of it. It is the business of ethics to tell us what are our duties, or by what test we may know them; but no system of ethics requires that the sole motive of all we do shall be a feeling of duty; on the contrary, ninety-nine hundredths of all our actions are done from other motives, and rightly so done, if the rule of duty does not condemn them. It is the more unjust to utilitarianism that this particular misapprehension should be made a ground of objection to it, inasmuch as utilitarian moralists have gone beyond almost all others in affirming that the motive has nothing to do with the morality of the action, though much with the worth of

the agent. He who saves a fellow creature from drowning does what is morally right, whether his motive be duty, or the hope of being paid for his trouble[2]; he who betrays the friend that trusts him, is guilty of a crime, even if his object be to serve another friend to whom he is under greater obligations. But to speak only of actions done from the motive of duty, and in direct obedience to principle: it is a misapprehension of the utilitarian mode of thought, to conceive it as implying that people should fix their minds upon so wide a generality as the world, or society at large. The great majority of good actions are intended not for the benefit of the world, but for that of individuals, of which the good of the world is

---

2. An opponent, whose intellectual and moral fairness is a pleasure to acknowledge (the Rev. J. Llewellyn Davies), has objected to this passage, saying, 'Surely the rightness or wrongness of saving, a man from drowning does depend very much upon the motive with which it is done. Suppose that a tyrant, when his enemy jumped into the sea to escape from him, saved him from drowning simply in order that he might inflict upon him more exquisite tortures, would it tend to clearness to speak of that rescue as a "morally right action"? Or suppose again, according to one of the stock illustrations of ethical inquiries, that a man betrayed a trust received from a friend, because the discharge of it would fatally injure that friend himself or some one belonging to him, would utilitarianism compel one to call the betrayal "a crime" as much as if it had been done from the meanest motive?'

I submit, that he who saves another from drowning in order to kill him by torture afterwards, does not differ only in motive from him who does the same thing from duty or benevolence; the act itself is different. The rescue of the man is, in the case supposed, only the necessary first step of an act far more atrocious than leaving him to drown would have been. Had Mr Davies said, "The rightness or wrongness of saving a man from drowning does depend very much—not upon the motive, but 'upon the *intention*', no utilitarian would have differed from him. Mr Davies, by an oversight too common not to be quite venial, has in this case confounded the very different ideas of Motive and Intention. There is no point which utilitarian thinkers (and Bentham preeminently) have taken more pains to illustrate than this. The morality of the action depends entirely upon the intention—that is, upon what the agent *wills to do*. But the motive, that is, the feeling which makes him will so to do, when it makes no difference in the act, makes none in the morality: though it makes a great difference in our moral estimation of the agent, especially if it indicates a good or a bad habitual *disposition*—a bent of character from which useful, or from which hurtful actions are likely to arise.

made up; and the thoughts of the most virtuous man need not on these occasions travel beyond the particular persons concerned, except so far as is necessary to assure himself that in benefiting them he is not violating the rights, that is, the legitimate and authorized expectations, of any one else. The multiplication of happiness is, according to the utilitarian ethics, the object of virtue: the occasions on which any person (except one in a thousand) has it in his power to do this on an extended scale, in other words to be a public benefactor, are but exceptional; and on these occasions alone is he called on to consider public utility; in every other case, private utility, the interest or happiness of some few persons, is all he has to attend to. Those alone the influence of whose actions extends to society in general, need concern themselves habitually about large an object. In the case of abstinences indeed-of things which people forbear to do from moral considerations, though the consequences in the particular case might be beneficial—it would be unworthy of an intelligent agent not to be consciously aware that the action is of a class which, if practiced generally, would be generally injurious, and that this is the ground of the obligation to abstain from it. The amount of regard for the public interest implied in this recognition, is no greater than is demanded by every system of morals, for they all enjoin to abstain from whatever is manifestly pernicious to society.

The same considerations dispose of another reproach against the doctrine of utility, founded on a still grosser misconception of the purpose of a standard of morality, and of the very meaning of the words right and wrong. It is often affirmed that utilitarianism renders men cold and unsympathising; that it chills their moral feelings towards individuals; that it makes them regard only the dry and hard consideration of the consequences of actions, not taking into their moral estimate the qualities from which those actions emanate. If the assertion means that they do not allow their judgment respecting the rightness or wrongness of an action to be influenced by their opinion of the qualities of the person who does it, this is a complaint not against utilitarianism, but against having any standard of morality at all; for certainly no known ethical standard decides an action to be

good or bad because it is done by a good or a bad man, still less because done by an amiable, a brave, or a benevolent man, or the contrary. These considerations are relevant, not to the estimation of actions, but of persons; and there is nothing in the utilitarian theory inconsistent with the fact that there are other things which interest us in persons besides the rightness and wrongness of their actions. The Stoics, indeed, with the paradoxical misuse of language which was part of their system, and by which they strove to raise themselves above all concern about anything but virtue, were fond of saying that he who has that has everything; that he, and only he, is rich, is beautiful, is a king. But no claim of this description is made for the virtuous man by the utilitarian doctrine. Utilitarians are quite aware that there are other desirable possessions and qualities besides virtue, and are perfectly willing to allow to all of them their full worth. They are also aware that a right action does not necessarily indicate a virtuous character, and that actions which are blamable, often proceed from qualities entitled to praise. When this is apparent in any particular case, it modifies their estimation, not certainly of the act, but of the agent. I grant that they are, notwithstanding, of opinion, that in the long run the best proof of a good character is good actions; and resolutely refuse to consider any mental disposition as good, of which the predominant tendency is to produce bad conduct. This makes them unpopular with many people; but it is an unpopularity which they must share with every one who regards the distinction between right and wrong in a serious light; and the reproach is not one which a conscientious utilitarian need be anxious to repel.

If no more be meant by the objection than that many utilitarians look on the morality of actions, as measured by the utilitarian standard, with too exclusive a regard, and do not lay sufficient stress upon the other beauties of character which go towards making a human being lovable or admirable, this may be admitted. Utilitarians who have cultivated their moral feelings, but not their sympathies nor their artistic perceptions, do fall into this mistake; and so do all other moralists under the same conditions. What can be said in excuse for other moralists is equally available for them, namely, that, if there is to be any error, it is better that it should be on that side. As a matter of fact, we may affirm that among utilitarians as among adherents of other systems, there is every imaginable degree of rigidity and of laxity in the application of their standard: some are even puritanically rigorous, while others are as indulgent as can possibly be desired by sinner or by sentimentalist. But on the whole, a doctrine which brings prominently forward the interest that mankind have in the repression and prevention of conduct which violates the moral law, is likely to be inferior to no other in turning the sanctions of opinion again such violations. It is true, the question, What does violate the moral law? is one on which those who recognize different standards of morality are likely now and then to differ. But difference of opinion on moral questions was not first introduced into the world by utilitarianism, while that doctrine does supply, if not always an easy, at all events a tangible and intelligible mode of deciding such differences.

It may not be superfluous to notice a few more of the common misapprehensions of utilitarian ethics, even those which are so obvious and gross that it might appear impossible for any person of candour and intelligence to fall into them; since persons, even of considerable mental endowments, often give themselves so little trouble to understand the bearings of any opinion against which they entertain a prejudice, and men are in general so little conscious of this voluntary ignorance as a defect, that the vulgarest misunderstandings of ethical doctrines are continually met with in the deliberate writings of persons of the greatest pretensions both to high principle and to philosophy. We not uncommonly hear the doctrine of utility inveighed against as a *godless* doctrine. If it be necessary to say anything at all against so mere an assumption, we may say that the question depends upon what idea we have formed of the moral character of the Deity. If it be a true belief that God desires, above all things, the happiness of his creatures, and that this was his purpose in their creation, utility is not only not a godless doctrine, but more profoundly religious than any other. If it be meant that utilitarianism does not recognize the revealed will of God as the supreme law of morals, I answer, that a utilitarian who believes in the perfect goodness and wisdom of God, necessarily believes that whatever God

has thought fit to reveal on the subject of morals, must fulfill the requirements of utility in a supreme degree. But others besides utilitarians have been of opinion that the Christian revelation was intended, and is fitted, to inform the hearts and minds of mankind with a spirit which should enable them to find for themselves what is right, and incline them to do it when found, rather than to tell them, except in a very general way, what it is; and that we need a doctrine of ethics, carefully followed out, to *interpret* to us the will God. Whether this opinion is correct or not, it is superfluous here to discuss; since whatever aid religion, either natural or revealed, can afford to ethical investigation, is as open to the utilitarian moralist as to any other. He can use it as the testimony of God to the usefulness or hurtfulness of any given course of action, by as good a right as others can use it for the indication of a transcendental law, having no connection with usefulness or with happiness.

Again, Utility is often summarily stigmatized as an immoral doctrine by giving it the name of Expediency, and taking advantage of the popular use of that term to contrast it with Principle. But the Expedient, in the sense in which it is opposed to the Right, generally means that which is expedient for the particular interest of the agent himself; as when a minister sacrifices the interests of his country to keep himself in place. When it means anything better than this, it means that which is expedient for some immediate object, some temporary purpose, but which violates a rule whose observance is expedient in a much higher degree. The Expedient, in this sense, instead of being the same thing with the useful, is a branch of the hurtful. Thus, it would often be expedient, for the purpose of getting over some momentary embarrassment, or attaining some object immediately useful to ourselves or others, to tell a lie. But inasmuch as the cultivation in ourselves of a sensitive feeling on the subject of veracity, is one of the most useful, and the enfeeblement of that feeling one of the most hurtful, things to which our conduct can be instrumental; and inasmuch as any, even unintentional, deviation from truth, does that much towards weakening the trustworthiness of human assertion, which is not only the principal support of all present social well-being, but the insufficiency of which does more than any one thing that can be named to keep back civilization, virtue, everything on which human happiness on the largest scale depends; we feel that the violation, for a present advantage, of a rule of such transcendent expediency, is not expedient, and that he who, for the sake of a convenience to himself or to some other individual, does what depends on him to deprive mankind of the good, and inflict upon them the evil, involved in the greater or less reliance which they can place in each other's word, acts the part of one of their worst enemies. Yet that even this rule, sacred as it is, admits of possible exceptions, is acknowledged by all moralists; the chief of which is when the withholding of some fact (as of information from a malefactor, or of bad news from a person dangerously ill) would save an individual (especially an individual other than oneself) from great and unmerited evil, and when the withholding can only be effected by denial. But in order that the exception may not extend itself beyond the need, and may have the least possible effect in weakening reliance on veracity, it ought to be recognized, and, if possible, its limits defined; and if the principle of utility is good for anything, it must be good for weighing these conflicting utilities against one another, and marking out the region within which one or the other preponderates.

Again, defenders of utility often find themselves called upon to reply to such objections as this—that there is not time, previous to action, for calculating and weighing the effects of any line of conduct on the general happiness. This is exactly as if any one were to say that it is impossible to guide our conduct by Christianity, because there is not time, on every occasion on which anything has to be done, to read through the Old and New Testaments. The answer to the objection is, that there has been ample time, namely, the whole past duration of the human species. During all that time, mankind have been learning by experience the tendencies of actions; on which experience all the prudence, as well as all the morality of life, are dependent. People talk as if the commencement of this course of experience had hitherto been put off, and as if, at the moment when some man feels tempted to meddle with the property or life of another, he had to begin considering for the first time whether murder and theft are injurious

to human happiness. Even then I do not think that he would find the question very puzzling; but, at all events, the matter is now done to his hand. It is truly a whimsical supposition that, if mankind were agreed in considering utility to be the test of morality, they would remain without any agreement as to what is useful, and would take no measures for having their notions on the subject taught to the young, and enforced by law and opinion. There is no difficulty in proving any ethical standard whatever to work ill, if we suppose universal idiocy to be conjoined with it; but on any hypothesis short of that, mankind must by this time have acquired positive beliefs as to the effects of some actions on their happiness; and the beliefs which have thus come down are the rules of morality for the multitude, and for the philosopher until he has succeeded in finding better. That philosophers might easily do this, even now, on many subjects; that the received code of ethics is by no means of divine right; and that mankind have still much to learn as to the effects of actions on the general happiness, I admit, or rather, earnestly maintain. The corollaries from the principle of utility, like the precepts of every practical art, admit of indefinite improvement, and, in a progressive state of the human mind, their improvement is perpetually going on. But to consider the rules of morality as improveable, is one thing; to pass over the intermediate generalizations entirely, and endeavour to test each individual action directly by the first principle, is another. It is a strange notion that the acknowledgment of a first principle is inconsistent with the admission of secondary ones. To inform a traveler respecting the place of his ultimate destination, is not to forbid the use of landmarks and direction-posts on the way. The proposition that happiness is the end and aim of morality, does not mean that no road ought to be laid down to that goal, or that persons going thither should not be advised to take one direction rather than another. Men really ought to leave off talking a kind of nonsense on this subject, which they would neither talk nor listen to on other matters of practical concernment. Nobody argues that the art of navigation is not founded on astronomy, because sailors cannot wait to calculate the Nautical Almanac. Being rational creatures, they go to sea with it ready calculated; and all rational creatures go out upon the sea of life with their minds made up on the common questions of right and wrong, as well as on many of the far more difficult questions of wise and foolish. And this, as long as foresight is a human quality, it is to be presumed they will continue to do. Whatever we adopt as the fundamental principle of morality, we require subordinate principles to apply it by; the impossibility of doing without them, being common to all systems, can afford no argument against any one in particular; but gravely to argue as if no such secondary principles could be had, and as if mankind had remained till now, and always must remain, without drawing any general conclusions from the experience of human life, is as high a pitch, I think, as absurdity has ever reached in philosophical controversy.

The remainder of the stock arguments against utilitarianism mostly consist in laying to its charge the common infirmities of human nature, and the general difficulties which embarrass conscientious persons in shaping their course through life. We are told that a utilitarian will be apt to make his own particular case an exception to moral rules, and, when under temptation, will see a utility in the breach of a rule, greater than he will see in its observance. But is utility the only creed which is able to furnish us with excuses for evil doing, and means of cheating our own conscience? They are afforded in abundance by all doctrines which recognize as a fact in morals the existence of conflicting considerations; which all doctrines do, that have been believed by sane persons. It is not the fault of any creed, but of the complicated nature of human affairs, that rules of conduct cannot be so framed as to require no exceptions, and that hardly any kind of action can safely be laid down as either always obligatory or always condemnable. There is no ethical creed which does not temper the rigidity of its laws, by giving a certain latitude, under the moral responsibility of the agent, for accommodation to peculiarities of circumstances; and under every creed, at the opening thus made, self-deception and dishonest casuistry get in. There exists no moral system under which there do not arise unequivocal cases of conflicting obligation. These are the real difficulties, the knotty points both in the theory of ethics, and in the conscientious guidance of personal conduct. They are overcome practically, with greater or with less success, according to the intellect and virtue of the individual; but it can hardly be pretended that any one will be the less qualified for dealing with them, from possessing an ultimate standard to which conflicting rights and duties can be referred. If utility is the ultimate source of moral obligations, utility may be invoked to decide between them when their demands are incompatible. Though the application of the standard may be difficult, it is better than none at all: while in other systems, the moral laws all claiming independent authority, there is no common umpire entitled to interfere between them; their claims to precedence one over another rest on little better than sophistry, and unless determined, as they generally are, by the unacknowledged influence of considerations of utility, afford a free scope for the action of personal desires and partialities. We must remember that only in these cases of conflict between secondary principles is it requisite that first principles should be appealed to. There is no case of moral obligation in which some secondary principle is not involved; and if only one, there can seldom be any real doubt which one it is, in the mind of any person by whom the principle itself is recognized.

Chapter III. Of the Ultimate Sanction of the Principle of Utility

The Question is often asked, and properly so, in regard to any supposed moral standard—What is its sanction? what are the motives to obey it? or more specifically, what is the source of its obligation? whence does it derive its binding force? It is a necessary part of moral philosophy to provide the answer to this question; which, though frequently assuming the shape of an objection to the utilitarian morality, as if it had some special applicability to that above others, really arises in regard to all standards. It arises, in fact, whenever a person is called on to *adopt* a standard, or refer morality to any basis on which he has not been accustomed to rest it. For the customary morality, that which education and opinion have consecrated, is the only one which presents itself to the mind with the feeling of being *in itself* obligatory; and when a person is asked to believe that this morality *derives* its obligation from some general principle round which custom has not thrown the same halo, the assertion is to him a paradox; the supposed corollaries seem to have a more binding force than the original theorem; the superstructure seems to stand better without, than with, what is represented as its foundation. He says to himself, I feel that I am bound not to rob or murder, betray or deceive; but why am I bound to promote the general happiness? If my own happiness lies in something else, why may I not give that the preference?

If the view adopted by the utilitarian philosophy of the nature of the moral sense be correct, this difficulty will always present itself, until the influences which form moral character have taken the same hold of the principle which they have taken of some of the consequences-until, by the improvement of education, the feeling of unity with our fellow-creatures shall be (what it cannot be denied that Christ intended it to be) as deeply rooted in our character, and to our own consciousness as completely a part of our nature, as the horror of crime is in an ordinarily well brought up young person. In the meantime, however, the difficulty has no peculiar application to the doctrine of utility, but is inherent in every attempt to analyze morality and reduce it to principles; which, unless the principle is already in men's minds invested with as much sacredness as any of its applications, always seems to divest them of a part of their sanctity.

The principle of utility either has, or there is no reason why it might not have, all the sanctions which belong to any other system of morals. Those sanctions are either external or internal. Of the external sanctions it is not necessary to speak at any length. They are, the hope of favour and the fear of displeasure, from our fellow creatures or from the Ruler of the Universe, along with whatever we may have of sympathy or affection for them, or of love and awe of Him, inclining us to do his will independently of selfish consequences. There is evidently no reason why all these motives for observance should not attach themselves to the utilitarian morality, as completely and as powerfully as to any other. Indeed, those of them which refer to our fellow creatures are sure to do so, in proportion to the amount of general intelligence; for whether there be any other ground of moral obligation than the general happiness or not, men do desire happiness; and however imperfect may be their own practice, they desire and commend all conduct in others towards themselves, by which they think their happiness is promoted. With regard to the religious motive, if men believe, as most profess to do, in the goodness of God, those who think that conduciveness to the general happiness is the essence, or even only the criterion of good, must necessarily believe that it is also that which God approves. The whole force therefore of external reward and punishment, whether physical or moral, and whether proceeding from God or from our fellow men, together with all that the capacities of human nature admit of disinterested devotion to either, become available to enforce the utilitarian morality, in proportion as that morality is recognized; and the more powerfully, the more the appliances of education and general cultivation are bent to the purpose.

So far as to external sanctions. The internal sanction of duty, whatever our standard of duty may be, is one and the same—a feeling in our own mind; a pain, more or less intense, attendant on violation of duty, which in properly cultivated moral natures rises, in the more serious cases, into shrinking from it as an impossibility. This feeling, when disinterested, and connecting itself with the pure idea of duty, and not with some particular form of it, or with any of the merely accessory circumstances, is the essence of Conscience; though in that complex phenomenon as it actually exists, the simple fact is in general all encrusted over with collateral associations, derived from sympathy, from love, and still more from fear; from all the forms of religious feeling; from the recollections of childhood and of all our past life; from self-esteem, desire of the esteem of others, and occasionally even self-abasement. This extreme complication is, I apprehend, the origin of the sort of mystical character which, by a tendency of the human mind of which there are many other examples, is apt to be attributed to the idea of moral obligation, and which leads people to believe that the idea cannot possibly attach itself to any other objects than those which, by a supposed mysterious law, are found in our present experience to excite it. Its binding force, however, consists in the existence of a mass of feeling which must be broken through in order to do what violates our standard of right, and which, if we do nevertheless violate that standard, will probably have to be encountered afterwards in the form of remorse. Whatever theory we have of the nature or origin of conscience, this is what essentially constitutes it.

The ultimate sanction, therefore, of all morality (external motives apart) being a subjective feeling in our own minds, I see nothing embarrassing to those whose standard is utility, in the question, what is the sanction of that particular standard? We may answer, the same as of all other moral standards—the conscientious feelings of mankind. Undoubtedly this sanction has no binding efficacy on those who do not possess the feelings it appeals to; but neither will these persons be more obedient to any other moral principle than to the utilitarian one. On them morality of any kind has no hold but through the external sanctions. Meanwhile the feelings exist, a fact in human nature, the reality of which, and the great power with which they are capable of acting on those in whom they have been duly cultivated, are proved by experience. No reason has ever been shown why they may not be cultivated to as great intensity in connection with the utilitarian, as with any other rule of morals.

There is, I am aware, a disposition to believe that a person who sees in moral obligation a transcendental fact, an objective reality belonging to the province of "Things in themselves," is likely to be more obedient to it than one who believes it to be entirely subjective, having its seat in human consciousness only. But whatever a person's opinion may be on this point of Ontology, the force he is really urged by is his own subjective feeling, and is exactly measured by its strength. No one's belief that duty is an objective reality is stronger than the belief that God is so; yet the belief in God, apart from the expectation of actual reward and punishment, only operates on conduct through, and in proportion to, the subjective religious feeling. The sanction, so far as it is disinterested, is always in the mind itself; and the notion therefore of the transcendental moralists must be, that this sanction will not exist *in* the mind unless it is believed to have its root out of the mind; and that if a person is able to say to himself, This which is restraining me, and which is called my conscience, is only a feeling in my own mind, he

may possibly draw the conclusion that when the feeling ceases the obligation ceases, and that if he find the feeling inconvenient, he may disregard it, and endeavour to get rid of it. But is this danger confined to the utilitarian morality? Does the belief that moral obligation has its seat outside the mind make the feeling of it too strong to be got rid of? The fact is so far otherwise, that all moralists admit and lament the ease with which, in the generality of minds, conscience can be silenced or stifled. The question, Need I obey my conscience? is quite as often put to themselves by persons who never heard of the principle of utility, as by its adherents. Those whose conscientious feelings are so weak as to allow of their asking this question, if they answer it affirmatively, will not do so because they believe in the transcendental theory, but because of the external sanctions.

It is not necessary, for the present purpose, to decide whether the feeling of duty is innate or implanted. Assuming it to be innate, it is an open question to what objects it naturally attaches itself; for the philosophic supporters of that theory are now agreed that the intuitive perception is of principles of morality and not of the details. If there be anything innate in the matter, I see no reason why the feeling which is innate should not be that of regard to the pleasures and pains of others. If there is any principle of morals which is intuitively obligatory, I should say it must be that. If so, the intuitive ethics would coincide with the utilitarian, and there would be no further quarrel between them. Even as it is, the intuitive moralists, though they believe that there are other intuitive moral obligations, do already believe this to one; for they unanimously hold that a large *portion* of morality turns upon the consideration due to the interests of our fellow-creatures. Therefore, if the belief in the transcendental origin of moral obligation gives any additional efficacy to the internal sanction, it appears to me that the utilitarian principle has already the benefit of it.

On the other hand, if, as is my own belief, the moral feelings are not innate, but acquired, they are not for that reason the less natural. It is natural to man to speak, to reason, to build cities, to cultivate the ground, though these are acquired faculties. The moral feelings are not indeed a part of our nature, in the sense of being in any perceptible degree present in all of us; but this, unhappily, is a fact admitted by those who believe the most strenuously in their transcendental origin. Like the other acquired capacities above referred to, the moral faculty, if not a part of our nature, is a natural outgrowth from it; capable, like them, in a certain small degree, of springing up spontaneously; and susceptible of being brought by cultivation to a high degree of development. Unhappily it is also susceptible, by a sufficient use of the external sanctions and of the force of early impressions, of being cultivated in almost any direction: so that there is hardly anything so absurd or so mischievous that it may not, by means of these influences, be made to act on the human mind with all the authority of conscience. To doubt that the same potency might be given by the same means to the principle of utility, even if it had no foundation in human nature, would be flying in the face of all experience.

But moral associations which are wholly of artificial creation, when intellectual culture goes on, yield by degrees to the dissolving force of analysis: and if the feeling of duty, when associated with utility, would appear equally arbitrary; if there were no leading department of our nature, no powerful class of sentiments, with which that association would harmonize, which would make us feel it congenial, and incline us not only to foster it in others (for which we have abundant interested motives), but also to cherish it in ourselves—if there were not, in short, a natural basis of sentiment for utilitarian morality, it might well happen that this association also, even after it had been implanted by education, might be analyzed away.

But there *is* this basis of powerful natural sentiment; and this it is which, when once the general happiness is recognized as the ethical standard, will constitute the strength of the utilitarian morality. This firm foundation is that of the social feelings of mankind—the desire to be in unity with our fellow creatures, which is already a powerful principle in human nature, and happily one of those which tend to become stronger, even without express inculcation, from the influences of advancing civilization. The social state is at once so natural, so necessary, and so habitual to man, that, except in some unusual circumstances or by an effort of voluntary abstraction, he never conceives himself otherwise than as a member of a body; and this association is riveted more and more, as mankind are further removed from the state of savage independence. Any condition, therefore, which is essential to a state of society, becomes more and more an inseparable part of every person's conception of the state of things which he is born into, and which is the destiny of a human being.

Now, society between human beings, except in the relation of master and slave, is manifestly impossible on any other footing than that the interests of all are to be consulted. Society between equals can only exist on the understanding that the interests of all are to be regarded equally. And since in all states of civilization, every person, except an absolute monarch, has equals, every one is obliged to live on these terms with somebody; and in every age some advance is made towards a state in which it will be impossible to live permanently on other terms with anybody. In this way people grow up unable to conceive as possible to them a state of total disregard of other people's interests. They are under a necessity of conceiving themselves as at least abstaining from all the grosser injuries, and (if only for their own protection) living in a state of constant protest against them. They are also familiar with the fact of co-operating with others and proposing to themselves a collective, not an individual interest as the aim (at least for the time being) of their actions. So long as they are co-operating, their ends are identified with those of others; there is at least a temporary feeling that the interests of others are their own interests. Not only does all strengthening of social ties, and all healthy growth of society, give to each individual a stronger personal interest in practically consulting the welfare of others; it also leads him to identify his *feelings* more and more with their good, or at least with an even greater degree of practical consideration for it. He comes, as though instinctively, to be conscious of himself as a being who *of course* pays regard to others. The good of others becomes to him a thing naturally and necessarily to be attended to, like any of the physical conditions of our existence. Now, whatever amount of this feeling a person has, he is urged by the strongest motives both of interest and of sympathy to demonstrate it, and to the utmost of his power encourage it in others; and even if he has none of it himself, he is as greatly interested as any one else that others should have it. Consequently the smallest germs of the feeling are laid hold of and nourished by the contagion of sympathy and the influences of education; and a complete web of corroborative association is woven round it, by the powerful agency of the external sanctions.

This mode of conceiving ourselves and human life, as civilization goes on, is felt to be more and more natural. Every step in political improvement renders it more so, by removing the sources of opposition of interest, and leveling those inequalities of legal privilege between individuals or classes, owing to which there are large portions of mankind whose happiness it is still practicable to disregard. In an improving state of the human mind, the influences are constantly on the increase, which tend to generate in each individual a feeling of unity with all the rest; which, if perfect, would make him never think of, or desire, any beneficial condition for himself, in the benefits of which they are not included. If we now suppose this feeling of unity to be taught as a religion, and the whole force of education, of institutions, and of opinion, directed, as it once was in the case of religion, to make every person grow up from infancy surrounded on all sides both by the profession and the practice of it, I think that no one, who can realize this conception, will feel any misgiving about the sufficiency of the ultimate sanction for the Happiness morality. To any ethical student who finds the realization difficult, I recommend, as a means of facilitating it, the second of M. Comte's two principle works, the *Traite de Politique Positive*. I entertain the strongest objections to the system of politics and morals set forth in that treatise; but I think it has superabundantly shown the possibility of giving to the service of humanity, even without the aid of belief in a Providence, both the psychological power and the social efficacy of a religion; making it take hold of human life, and colour all thought, feeling, and action, in a manner of which the greatest ascendancy ever exercised by any religion may be but a type and foretaste; and of which the danger is, not that it should be insufficient but that it should be so excessive as to interfere unduly with human freedom and individuality.

Neither is it necessary to the feeling which constitutes the binding force of the utilitarian morality on those who recognize it, to wait for those social influences which would make its obligation felt by mankind at large. In the comparatively early state of human advancement in which we now live, a person cannot indeed feel that entireness of sympathy with all others, which would make any real discordance in the general direction of their conduct in life impossible; but already a person in whom the social feeling is at all developed, cannot bring himself to think of the rest of his fellow creatures as struggling rivals with him for the means of happiness, whom he must desire to see defeated in their object in order that he may succeed in his. The deeply rooted conception which every individual even now has of himself as a social being, tends to make him feel it one of his natural wants that there should be harmony between his feelings and aims and those of his fellow creatures. If differences of opinion and of mental culture make it impossible for him to share many of their actual feelings—perhaps make him denounce and defy those feelings—he still needs to be conscious that his real aim and theirs do not conflict; that he is not opposing himself to what they really wish for, namely their own good, but is, on the contrary, promoting it. This feeling in most individuals is much inferior in strength to their selfish feelings, and is often wanting altogether. But to those who have it, it possesses all the characters of a natural feeling. It does not present itself to their minds as a superstition of education, or a law despotically imposed by the power of society, but as an attribute which it would not be well for them to be without. This conviction is the ultimate sanction of the greatest happiness morality. This it is which makes any mind, of well-developed feelings, work with, and not against, the outward motives to care for others, afforded by what I have called the external sanctions; and when those sanctions are wanting, or act in an opposite direction, constitutes in itself a powerful internal binding force, in proportion to the sensitiveness and thoughtfulness of the character; since few but those whose mind is a moral blank, could bear to lay out their course of life on the plan of paying no regard to others except so far as their own private interest compels.

Chapter IV. Of What Sort of Proof the Principle of Utility Is Susceptible

It has already been remarked, that questions of ultimate ends do not admit of proof, in the ordinary acceptation of the term. To be incapable of proof by reasoning is common to all first principles, to the first premises of our knowledge, as well as to those of our conduct. But the former, being matters of fact, may be the subject of a direct appeal to the faculties which judge of fact—namely, our senses, and our internal consciousness. Can an appeal be made to the same faculties on questions of practical ends? Or by what other faculty is cognizance taken of them?

Questions about ends are, in other words, questions what things are desirable. The utilitarian doctrine is, that happiness is desirable, and the only thing desirable, as an end; all other things being only desirable as means to that end. What ought to be required of this doctrine, what conditions is it requisite that the doctrine should fulfill—to make good its claim to be believed?

The only proof capable of being given that an object is visible, is that people actually see it. The only proof that a sound is audible, is that people hear it; and so of the other sources of our experience. In like manner, I apprehend, the sole evidence it is possible to produce that anything is desirable, is that people do actually desire it. If the end which the utilitarian doctrine proposes to itself were not, in theory and in practice, acknowledged to be an end, nothing could ever convince any person that it was so. No reason can be given why the general happiness is desirable, except that each person, so far as he believes it to be attainable, desires his own happiness. This, however, being a fact, we have not only all the proof which the case admits of, but all which it is possible to require, that happiness is a good, that each person's happiness is a good to that person, and the general happiness, therefore, a good to the aggregate of all persons. Happiness has made out its title as *one* of the ends of conduct, and consequently one of the criteria of morality.

But it has not, by this alone, proved itself to be the sole criterion. To do that, it would seem, by the same rule, necessary to show, not only that people desire happiness, but that they never desire anything else. Now it is palpable that they do desire things which, in common language, are decidedly distinguished from happiness. They desire, for example, virtue, and the absence of vice, no less really than pleasure and the absence of pain. The desire of virtue is not as universal, but

it is as authentic a fact, as the desire of happiness. And hence the opponents of the utilitarian standard deem that they have a right to infer that there are other ends of human action besides happiness, and that happiness is not the standard of approbation and disapprobation.

But does the utilitarian doctrine deny that people desire virtue, or maintain that virtue is not a thing to be desired? The very reverse. It maintains not only that virtue is to be desired, but that it is to be desired disinterestedly, for itself. Whatever may be the opinion of utilitarian moralists as to the original conditions by which virtue is made virtue, however they may believe (as they do) that actions and dispositions are only virtuous because they promote another end than virtue, yet this being granted, and it having been decided, from considerations of this description, what *is* virtuous, they not only place virtue at the very head of the things which are good as means to the ultimate end, but they also recognize as a psychological fact the possibility of its being, to the individual, a good in itself, without looking to any end beyond it; and hold, that the mind is not in a right state, not in a state conformable to Utility, not in the state most conducive to the general happiness, unless it does love virtue in this manner—as a thing desirable in itself, even although, in the individual instance, it should not produce those other desirable consequences which it tends to produce, and on account of which it is held to be virtue. This opinion is not, in the smallest degree, a departure from the Happiness principle. The ingredients of happiness are very various, and each of them is desirable in itself, and not merely when considered as swelling an aggregate. The principle of utility does not mean that any given pleasure, as music, for instance, or any given exemption from pain, as for example health, is to be looked upon as means to a collective something termed happiness, and to be desired on that account. They are desired and desirable in and for themselves; besides being means, they are a part of the end. Virtue, according to the utilitarian doctrine, is not naturally and originally part of the end, but it is capable of becoming so; and in those who love it disinterestedly it has become so, and is desired and cherished, not as a means to happiness, but as a part of their happiness.

To illustrate this farther, we may remember that virtue is not the only thing, originally a means, and which if it were not a means to anything else, would be and remain indifferent, but which by association with what it is a means to, comes to be desired for itself, and that too with the utmost intensity. What, for example, shall we say of the love of money? There is nothing originally more desirable about money than about any heap of glittering pebbles. Its worth is solely that of the things which it will buy; the desires for other things than itself, which it is a means of gratifying. Yet the love of money is not only one of the strongest moving forces of human life, but money is, in many cases, desired in and for itself; the desire to possess it is often stronger than the desire to use it, and goes on increasing when all the desires which point to ends beyond it, to be compassed by it, are falling off. It may, then, be said truly, that money is desired not for the sake of an end, but as part of the end. From being a means to happiness, it has come to be itself a principal ingredient of the individual's conception of happiness. The same may be said of the majority of the great objects of human life: power, for example, or fame; except that to each of these there is a certain amount of immediate pleasure annexed, which has at least the semblance of being naturally inherent in them—a thing which cannot be said of money. Still, however, the strongest natural attraction, both of power and of fame, is the immense aid they give to the attainment of our other wishes; and it is the strong association thus generated between them and all our objects of desire, which gives to the direct desire of them the intensity it often assumes, so as in some characters to surpass in strength all other desires. In these cases the means have become a part of the end, and a more important part of it than any of the things which they are means to. What was once desired as an instrument for the attainment of happiness, has come to be desired for its own sake. In being desired for its own sake it is, however, desired as *part* of happiness. The person is made, or thinks he would be made, happy by its mere possession; and is made unhappy by failure to obtain it. The desire of it is not a different thing from the desire of happiness, any more than the love of music, or the desire of health. They are included in happiness. They are

some of the elements of which the desire of happiness is made up. Happiness is not an abstract idea, but a concrete whole; and these are some of its parts. And the utilitarian standard sanctions and approves their being so. Life would be a poor thing, very ill provided with sources of happiness, if there were not this provision of nature, by which things originally indifferent, but conducive to, or otherwise associated with, the satisfaction of our primitive desires, become in themselves sources of pleasure more valuable than the primitive pleasures, both in permanency, in the space of human existence that they are capable of covering, and even in intensity.

Virtue, according to the utilitarian conception, is a good of this description. There was no original desire of it, or motive to it, save its conduciveness to pleasure, and especially to protection from pain. But through the association thus formed, it may be felt a good in itself, and desired as such with as great intensity as any other good; and with this difference between it and the love of money, of power, or of fame—that all of these may, and often do, render the individual noxious to the other members of the society to which he belongs, whereas there is nothing which makes him so much a blessing to them as the cultivation of the disinterested love of virtue. And consequently, the utilitarian standard, while it tolerates and approves those other acquired desires, up to the point beyond which they would be more injurious to the general happiness than promotive of it, enjoins and requires the cultivation of the love of virtue up to the greatest strength possible, as being above all things important to the general happiness.

It results from the preceding considerations, that there is in reality nothing desired except happiness. Whatever is desired otherwise than as a means to some end beyond itself, and ultimately to happiness, is desired as itself a part of happiness, and is not desired for itself until it has become so. Those who desire virtue for its own sake, desire it either because the consciousness of it is a pleasure, or because the consciousness of being without it is a pain, or for both reasons united; as in truth the pleasure and pain seldom exist separately, but almost always together—the same person feeling pleasure in the degree of virtue attained, and pain in not having attained more. If one of these gave him no pleasure, and the other no pain, he would not love or desire virtue, or would desire it only for the other benefits which it might produce to himself or to persons whom he cared for.

We have now, then, an answer to the question, of what sort of proof the principle of utility is susceptible. If the opinion which I have now stated is psychologically true—if human nature is so constituted as to desire nothing which is not either a part of happiness or a means of happiness, we can have no other proof, and we require no other, that these are the only things desirable. If so, happiness is the sole end of human action, and the promotion of it the test by which to judge of all human conduct; from whence it necessarily follows that it must be the criterion of morality, since a part is included in the whole.

And now to decide whether this is really so; whether mankind do desire nothing for itself but that which is a pleasure to them, or of which the absence is a pain; we have evidently arrived at a question of fact and experience, dependent, like all similar questions, upon evidence. It can only be determined by practiced self-consciousness and self-observation, assisted by observation of others. I believe that these sources of evidence, impartially consulted, will declare that desiring a thing and finding it pleasant, aversion to it and thinking of it as painful, are phenomena entirely inseparable, or rather two parts of the same phenomenon—in strictness of language, two different modes of naming the same psychological fact; that to think of an object as desirable (unless for the sake of its consequences), and to think of it as pleasant, are one and the same thing; and that to desire anything, except in proportion as the idea of it is pleasant, is a physical and metaphysical impossibility.

So obvious does this appear to me, that I expect it will hardly be disputed; and the objection made will be, not that desire can possibly be directed to anything ultimately except pleasure and exemption from pain, but that the will is a different thing from desire; that a person of confirmed virtue, or any other person whose purposes are fixed, carries out his purposes without any thought of the pleasure he has in contemplating them, or expects to derive from their fulfillment; and persists in acting on them, even though these pleasures are much diminished, by changes in his character or decay of his passive sensibilities, or

are outweighed by the pains which the pursuit of the purposes may bring upon him. All this I fully admit, and have stated it elsewhere, as positively and emphatically as any one. Will, the active phenomenon, is a different thing from desire, the state of passive sensibility, and though originally an offshoot from it, may in time take root and detach itself from the parent stock; so much so, that in the case of an habitual purpose, instead of willing the thing because we desire it, we often desire it only because we will it. This, however, is but an instance of that familiar fact, the power of habit, and is nowise confined to the case of virtuous actions. Many indifferent things, which men originally did from a motive of some sort, they continue to do from habit. Sometimes this is done unconsciously, the consciousness coming only after the action; at other times with conscious volition, but volition which has become habitual, and is put in operation by the force of habit, in opposition perhaps to the deliberate preference, as often happens with those who have contracted habits of vicious or hurtful indulgence.

Third and last comes the case in which the habitual act of will in the individual instance is not in contradiction to the general intention prevailing at other times, but in fulfillment of it, as in the case of the person of confirmed virtue, and of all who pursue deliberately and consistently any determinate end. The distinction between will and desire thus understood is an authentic and highly important psychological fact; but the fact consists solely in this—that will, like all other parts of our constitution, is amenable to habit, and that we may will from habit what we no longer desire for itself or desire only because we will it. It is not the less true that will, in the beginning, is entirely produced by desire; including in that term the repelling influence of pain as well as the attractive one of pleasure. Let us take into consideration, no longer the person who has a confirmed will to do right, but him in whom that virtuous will is still feeble, conquerable by temptation, and not to be fully relied on; by what means can it be strengthened? How can the will to be virtuous, where it does not exist in sufficient force, be implanted or awakened? Only by making the person *desire* virtue—by making him think of it in a pleasurable light, or of its absence in a painful one. It is by associating the doing right with pleasure, or the doing wrong with pain, or by eliciting and impressing and bringing home to the person's experience the pleasure naturally involved in the one or the pain in the other, that it is possible to call forth that will to be virtuous, which, when confirmed, acts without any thought of either pleasure or pain. Will is the child of desire, and passes out of the dominion of its parent only to come under that of habit. That which is the result of habit affords no presumption of being intrinsically good; and there would be no reason for wishing that the purpose of virtue should become independent of pleasure and pain, were it not that the influence of the pleasurable and painful associations which prompt to virtue is not sufficiently to be depended on for unerring constancy of action until it has acquired the support of habit. Both in feeling and in conduct, habit is the only thing which imparts certainty; and it is because of the importance to others of being able to rely absolutely on one's feelings and conduct, and to oneself of being able to rely on one's own, that the will to do right ought to be cultivated into this habitual independence. In other words, this state of the will is a means to good, not intrinsically a good; and does not contradict the doctrine that nothing is a good to human beings but in so far as it is either itself pleasurable, or a means of attaining pleasure or averting pain.

But if this doctrine be true, the principle of utility is proved. Whether it is so or not, must now be left to the consideration of the thoughtful reader.

Chapter V. On the Connection between Justice and Utility

In all ages of speculation, one of the strongest obstacles to the reception of the doctrine that Utility or Happiness is the criterion of right and wrong, has been drawn from the idea of justice. The powerful sentiment, and apparently clear perception, which that word recalls with a rapidity and certainty resembling an instinct, have seemed to the majority of thinkers to point to an inherent quality in things; to show that the just must have an existence in Nature as something absolute, generically distinct from every variety of the expedient, and, in idea, opposed to it, though (as is commonly acknowledged) never, in the long run, disjoined from it in fact.

In the case of this, as of our other moral sentiments, there is no necessary connection between the question of its origin, and that of its binding force. That a feeling is bestowed on us by Nature, does not necessarily legitimate all its promptings. The feeling of justice might be a peculiar instinct, and might yet require, like our other instincts, to be controlled and enlightened by a higher reason. If we have intellectual instincts, leading us to judge in a particular way, as well as animal instincts that prompt us to act in a particular way, there is no necessity that the former should be more infallible in their sphere than the latter in theirs; it may as well happen that wrong judgments are occasionally suggested by those, as wrong actions by these. But though it is one thing to believe that we have natural feelings of justice, and another to acknowledge them as an ultimate criterion of conduct, these two opinions are very closely connected in point of fact. Mankind are always predisposed to believe that any subjective feeling, not otherwise accounted for, is a revelation of some objective reality. Our present object is to determine whether the reality, to which the feeling of justice corresponds, is one which needs any such special revelation; whether the justice or injustice of an action is a thing intrinsically peculiar, and distinct from all its other qualities, or only a combination of certain of those qualities, presented under a peculiar aspect. For the purpose of this inquiry it is practically important to consider whether the feeling itself, of justice and injustice, is *sui generis* like our sensations of color and taste, or a derivative feeling, formed by a combination of others. And this it is the more essential to examine, as people are in general willing enough to allow, that objectively the dictates of justice coincide with a part of the field of general expediency; but inasmuch as the subjective mental feeling of justice is different from that which commonly attaches to simple expediency, and, except in the extreme cases of the latter, is far more imperative in its demands, people find it difficult to see, in justice, only a particular kind or branch of general utility, and think that its superior binding force requires a totally different origin.

To throw light upon this question, it is necessary to attempt to ascertain what is the distinguishing character of justice, or of injustice; what is the quality, or whether there is any quality, attributed in common to all modes of conduct designated as unjust (for justice, like many other moral attributes, is best defined by its opposite), and distinguishing them from such modes of conduct as are disapproved, but without having that particular epithet of disapprobation applied to them. If in everything which men are accustomed to characterize as just or unjust, some one common attribute or collection of attributes is always present, we may judge whether this particular attribute or combination of attributes would be capable of gathering round it a sentiment of that peculiar character and intensity by virtue of the general laws of our emotional constitution, or whether the sentiment is inexplicable, and requires to be regarded as a special provision of Nature. If we find the former to be the case, we shall, in resolving this question, have resolved also the main problem; if the latter, we shall have to seek for some other mode of investigating it.

To find the common attributes of a variety of objects, it is necessary to begin by surveying the objects themselves in the concrete. Let us therefore advert successively to the various modes of action, and arrangements of human affairs, which are classed, by universal or widely spread opinion, as Just or as Unjust. The things well known to excite the sentiments associated with those names are of a very multifarious character. I shall pass them rapidly in review, without studying any particular arrangement.

In the first place, it is mostly considered unjust to deprive any one of his personal liberty, his property, or any other thing which belongs to him by law. Here, therefore, is one instance of the application of the terms just and unjust in a perfectly definite sense, namely, that it is just to respect, unjust to violate, the *legal rights* of any one. But this judgment admits of several exceptions, arising from the other forms in which the notions of justice and injustice present themselves. For example, the person who suffers the deprivation may (as the phrase is) have *forfeited* the rights which he is so deprived of—a case to which we shall return presently. But also—

Secondly; the legal rights of which he is deprived, may be rights which *ought* not to have belonged to him; in other words, the law which confers on him these rights, may be a bad law. When it is so, or when (which is the same thing for our purpose) it is supposed to be so, opinions will differ as to the justice or injustice of infringing it. Some maintain that no law, however bad, ought to be disobeyed by an individual citizen; that his opposition to it, if shown at all, should only be shown in endeavoring to get it altered by competent authority. This opinion (which condemns many of the most illustrious benefactors of mankind, and would often protect pernicious institutions against the only weapons which, in the state of things existing at the time, have any chance of succeeding against them) is defended, by those who hold it, on grounds of expediency; principally on that of the importance, to the common interest of mankind, of maintaining inviolate the sentiment of submission to law. Other persons, again, hold the directly contrary opinion, that any law, judged to be bad, may blamelessly be disobeyed, even though it be not judged to be unjust, but only inexpedient; while others would confine the license of disobedience to the case of unjust laws; but again, some say, that all laws which are inexpedient are unjust; since every law imposes some restriction on the natural liberty of mankind, which restriction is an injustice, unless legitimated by tending to their good. Among these diversities of opinion, it seems to be universally admitted that there may be unjust laws, and that law, consequently, is not the ultimate criterion of justice, but may give to one person a benefit, or impose on another an evil, which justice condemns. When, however, a law is thought to be unjust, it seems always to be regarded as being so in the same way in which a breach of law is unjust, namely, by infringing somebody's right; which, as it cannot in this case be a legal right, receives a different appellation, and is called a moral right. We may say, therefore, that a second case of injustice consists in taking or withholding from any person that to which he has a *moral right*.

Thirdly, it is universally considered just that each person should obtain that (whether good or evil) which he *deserves*, and unjust that he should obtain a good, or be made to undergo an evil, which he does not deserve. This is, perhaps, the clearest and most emphatic form in which the idea of justice is conceived by the general mind.

As it involves the notion of desert, the question arises, what constitutes desert? Speaking in a general way, a person is understood to deserve good if he does right, evil if he does wrong; and in a more particular sense, to deserve good from those to whom he does or has done good, and evil from those to whom he does or has done evil. The precept of returning good for evil has never been regarded as a case of the fulfillment of justice, but as one in which the claims of justice are waived, in obedience to other considerations.

Fourthly, it is confessedly unjust to *break faith* with any one: to violate an engagement, either express or implied, or disappoint expectations raised by our conduct, at least if we have raised those expectations knowingly and voluntarily. Like the other obligations of justice already spoken of, this one is not regarded as absolute, but as capable of being overruled by a stronger obligation of justice on the other side; or by such conduct on the part of the person concerned as is deemed to absolve us from our obligation to him, and to constitute a *forfeiture* of the benefit which he has been led to expect.

Fifthly, it is, by universal admission, inconsistent with justice to be *partial*—to show favour or preference to one person over another, in matters to which favour and preference do not properly apply. Impartiality, however, does not seem to be regarded as a duty in itself, but rather as instrumental to some other duty; for it is admitted that favour and preference are not always censurable, and indeed the cases in which they are condemned are rather the exception than the rule. A person would be more likely to be blamed than applauded for giving his family or friends no superiority in good offices over strangers, when he could do so without violating any other duty; and no one thinks it unjust to seek one person in preference to another as a friend, connection, or companion. Impartiality where rights are concerned is of course obligatory, but this is involved in the more general obligation of giving to every one his right. A tribunal, for example, must be impartial, because it is bound to award, without regard to any other consideration, a disputed object to the one of two parties who has the right to it. There are other cases in which impartiality means, being solely influenced by desert; as with those who, in the capacity of judges, preceptors, or parents, administer reward and punishment as such. There are cases, again, in which it means, being solely influenced by consideration for the public interest; as in making a selection among candidates for a government employment. Impartiality, in short, as an obligation of justice, may be said to mean, being exclusively influenced by the considerations which it is supposed ought to influence the particular case in hand; and resisting the solicitation of any motives which prompt to conduct different from what those considerations would dictate.

Nearly allied to the idea of impartiality is that of *equality*, which often enters as a component part both into the conception of justice and into the practice of it, and, in the eyes of many persons, constitutes its essence. But in this, still more than in any other case, the notion of justice varies in different persons, and always conforms in its variations to their notion of utility. Each person maintains that equality is the dictate of justice, except where he thinks that expediency requires inequality. The justice of giving equal protection to the rights of all, is maintained by those who support the most outrageous inequality in the rights themselves. Even in slave countries it is theoretically admitted that the rights of the slave, such as they are, ought to be as sacred as those of the master; and that a tribunal which fails to enforce them with equal strictness is wanting in justice; while, at the same time, institutions which leave to the slave scarcely any rights to enforce, are not deemed unjust, because they are not deemed inexpedient. Those who think that utility requires distinctions of rank do not consider it unjust that riches and social privileges should be unequally dispensed; but those who think this inequality inexpedient, think it unjust also. Whoever thinks that government is necessary sees no injustice in as much inequality as is constituted by giving to the magistrate powers not granted to other people. Even among those who hold leveling doctrines, there are as many questions of justice as there are differences of opinion about expediency. Some Communists consider it unjust that the produce of the labour of the community should be shared on any other principle than that of exact equality; others think it just that those should receive most whose wants are greatest; while others hold that those who work harder, or who produce more, or whose services are more valuable to the community, may justly claim a larger quota in the division of the produce. And the sense of natural justice may be plausibly appealed to in behalf of every one of these opinions.

Among so many diverse applications of the term "justice," which yet is not regarded as ambiguous, it is a matter of some difficulty to seize the mental link which holds them together, and on which the moral sentiment adhering to the term essentially depends. Perhaps, in this embarrassment, some help may be derived from the history of the word, as indicated by its etymology.

In most, if not in all, languages, the etymology of the word which corresponds to "just," points distinctly to an origin connected with the ordinances of law. *Justum* is a form of *jussum*, that which has been ordered. *Dikaion* comes directly from *dike*, a suit at law. *Recht*, from which came *right* and *righteous*, is synonymous with law. The courts of justice, the administration of justice, are the courts and the administration of law. *La justice*, in French, is the established term for judicature. I am not committing the fallacy imputed with some show of truth to Horne Tooke, of assuming that a word must still continue to mean what it originally meant. Etymology is slight evidence of what the idea now signified is, but the very best evidence of how it sprang up. There can, I think, be no doubt that the *idee mere*, the primitive element, in the formation of the notion of justice, was conformity to law. It constituted the entire idea among the Hebrews, up to the birth of Christianity; as might be expected in the case of a people whose laws attempted to embrace all subjects on which precepts were required, and who believed those laws to be a direct emanation from the Supreme Being. But other nations, and in particular the Greeks and Romans, who knew that their laws had been made originally, and still continued to be made, by men, were not afraid to admit that those men might make bad laws; might do, by law, the same things, and from the same motives, which if done by individuals without the sanction of law, would be called unjust. And hence the sentiment of injustice came to be attached, not to all violations of law, but only to violations of such laws as *ought* to exist, including such as

ought to exist, but do not, and to laws themselves, if supposed to be contrary to what ought to be law. In this manner the idea of law and of its injunctions was still predominant in the notion of justice, even when the laws actually in force ceased to be accepted as the standard of it.

It is true that mankind consider the idea of justice and its obligations as applicable to many things which neither are, nor is it desired that they should be, regulated by law. Nobody desires that laws should interfere with the whole detail of private life; yet every one allows that in all daily conduct a person may and does show himself to be either just or unjust. But even here, the idea of the breach of what ought to be law, still lingers in a modified shape. It would always give us pleasure, and chime in with our feelings of fitness, that acts which we deem unjust should be punished, though we do not always think it expedient that this should be done by the tribunals. We forego that gratification on account of incidental inconveniences. We should be glad to see just conduct enforced and injustice repressed, even in the minutest details, if we were not, with reason, afraid of trusting the magistrate with so unlimited an amount of power over individuals. When we think that a person is bound in justice to do a thing, it is an ordinary form of language to say, that he ought to be compelled to do it. We should be gratified to see the obligation enforced by anybody who had the power. If we see that its enforcement by law would be inexpedient, we lament the impossibility, we consider the impunity given to injustice as an evil, and strive to make amends for it by bringing a strong expression of our own and the public disapprobation to bear upon the offender. Thus the idea of legal constraint is still the generating idea of the notion of justice, though undergoing several transformations before that notion, as it exists in an advanced state of society, becomes complete.

The above is, I think, a true account, as far as it goes, of the origin and progressive growth of the idea of justice. But we must observe, that it contains, as yet, nothing to distinguish that obligation from moral obligation in general. For the truth is, that the idea of penal sanction, which is the essence of law, enters not only into the conception of injustice, but into that of any kind of wrong. We do not call anything wrong, unless we mean to imply that a person ought to be punished in some way or other for doing it—if not by law, by the opinion of his fellow-creatures; if not by opinion, by the reproaches of his own conscience. This seems the real turning point of the distinction between morality and simple expediency. It is a part of the notion of Duty in every one of its forms, that a person may rightfully be compelled to fulfill it. Duty is a thing which may be *exacted* from a person, as one exacts a debt. Unless we think that it may be exacted from him, we do not call it his duty. Reasons of prudence, or the interest of other people, may militate against actually exacting it; but the person himself, it is clearly understood, would not be entitled to complain. There are other things, on the contrary, which we wish that people should do; which we like or admire them for doing, perhaps dislike or despise them for not doing, but yet admit that they are not bound to do; it is not a case of moral obligation; we do not blame them, that is, we do not think that they are proper objects of punishment. How we come by these ideas of deserving and not deserving punishment, will appear, perhaps, in the sequel; but I think there is no doubt that this distinction lies at the bottom of the notions of right and wrong; that we call any conduct wrong, or employ, instead, some other term of dislike or disparagement, according as we think that the person ought, or ought not, to be punished for it[3]; and we say, it would be right, to do so and so, or merely that it would be desirable or laudable, according as we would wish to see the person whom it concerns, compelled, or only persuaded and exhorted, to act in that manner.

This, therefore, being the characteristic difference which marks off, not justice, but morality in general, from the remaining provinces of expediency and worthiness; the character is still to be sought which distinguishes justice from other branches of morality. Now it is known that ethical writers divide moral duties into two classes, denoted by the ill-chosen expressions, duties of perfect and of imperfect obligation; the latter

being those in which, though the act is obligatory, the particular occasions of performing it are left to our choice, as in the case of charity or beneficence, which we are indeed bound to practice, but not towards any definite person, nor at any prescribed time. In the more precise language of philosophic jurists, duties of perfect obligation are those duties in virtue of which a correlative *right* resides in some person or persons; duties of imperfect obligation are those moral obligations which do not give birth to any right. I think it will be found that this distinction exactly coincides with that which exists between justice and the other obligations of morality. In our survey of the various popular acceptations of justice, the term appeared generally to involve the idea of a personal right—a claim on the part of one or more individuals, like that which the law gives when it confers a proprietary or other legal right. Whether the injustice consists in depriving a person of a possession, or in breaking faith with him, or in treating him worse than he deserves, or worse than other people who have no greater claims—in each case the supposition implies two things—a wrong done, and some assignable person who is wronged. Injustice may also be done by treating a person better than others; but the wrong in this case is to his competitors, who are also assignable persons. It seems to me that this feature in the case—a right in some person, correlative to the moral obligation—constitutes the specific difference between justice, and generosity or beneficence. Justice implies something which it is not only right to do, and wrong not to do, but which some individual person can claim from us as his moral right. No one has a moral right to our generosity or beneficence, because we are not morally bound to practice those virtues towards any given individual. And it will be found with respect to this, as to every correct definition, that the instances which seem to conflict with it are those which most confirm it. For if a moralist attempts, as some have done, to make out that mankind generally, though not any given individual, have a right to all the good we can do them, he at once, by that thesis, includes generosity and beneficence within the category of justice. He is obliged to say, that our utmost exertions are *due* to our fellow creatures, thus assimilating them to a debt; or that nothing

---

3. See this point enforced and illustrated by Professor Bain, in an admirable chapter (entitled "The Ethical Emotions, or the Moral Sense"), of the second of the two treatises composing his elaborate and profound work on the Mind.

less can be a sufficient *return* for what society does for us, thus classing the case as one of gratitude; both of which are acknowledged cases of justice. Wherever there is right, the case is one of justice, and not of the virtue of beneficence; and whoever does not place the distinction between justice and morality in general, where we have now placed it, will be found to make no distinction between them at all, but to merge all morality in justice.

Having thus endeavoured to determine the distinctive elements which enter into the composition of the idea of justice, we are ready to enter on the inquiry, whether the feeling, which accompanies the idea, is attached to it by a special dispensation of nature, or whether it could have grown up, by any known laws, out of the idea itself; and in particular, whether it can have originated in considerations of general expediency.

I conceive that the sentiment itself does not arise from anything which would commonly, or correctly, be termed an idea of expediency; but that though the sentiment does not, whatever is moral in it does.

We have seen that the two essential ingredients in the sentiment of justice are, the desire to punish a person who has done harm, and the knowledge or belief that there is some definite individual or individuals to whom harm has been done.

Now it appears to me, that the desire to punish a person who has done harm to some individual is a spontaneous outgrowth from two sentiments, both in the highest degree natural, and which either are or resemble instincts; the impulse of self-defense, and the feeling of sympathy.

It is natural to resent, and to repel or retaliate, any harm done or attempted against ourselves, or against those with whom we sympathize. The origin of this sentiment it is not necessary here to discuss. Whether it be an instinct or a result of intelligence, it is, we know, common to all animal nature; for every animal tries to hurt those who have hurt, or who it thinks are about to hurt, itself or its young. Human beings, on this point, only differ from other animals in two particulars. First, in being capable of sympathizing, not solely with their offspring, or, like some of the more noble animals, with some superior animal who is kind to them, but with all human, and even with all sentient, beings; secondly, in having a more devel-

oped intelligence, which gives a wider range to the whole of their sentiments, whether self-regarding or sympathetic. By virtue of his superior intelligence, even apart from his superior range of sympathy, a human being is capable of apprehending a community of interest between himself and the human society of which he forms a part, such that any conduct which threatens the security of the society generally, is threatening to his own, and calls forth his instinct (if instinct it be) of self-defense. The same superiority of intelligence joined to the power of sympathizing with human beings generally, enables him to attach himself to the collective idea of his tribe, his country, or mankind, in such a manner that any act hurtful to them, raises his instinct of sympathy, and urges him to resistance.

The sentiment of justice, in that one of its elements which consists of the desire to punish, is thus, I conceive, the natural feeling of retaliation or vengeance, rendered by intellect and sympathy applicable to those injuries, that is, to those hurts, which wound us through, or in common with, society at large. This sentiment, in itself, has nothing moral in it; what is moral is, the exclusive subordination of it to the social sympathies, so as to wait on and obey their call. For the natural feeling would make us resent indiscriminately whatever any one does that is disagreeable to us; but when moralized by the social feeling, it only acts in the directions conformable to the general good: just persons resenting a hurt to society, though not otherwise a hurt to themselves, and not resenting a hurt to themselves, however painful, unless it be of the kind which society has a common interest with them in the repression of.

It is no objection against this doctrine to say, that when we feel our sentiment of justice outraged, we are not thinking of society at large, or of any collective interest, but only of the individual case. It is common enough certainly, though the reverse of commendable, to feel resentment merely because we have suffered pain; but a person whose resentment is really a moral feeling, that is, who considers whether an act is blamable before he allows himself to resent it—such a person, though he may not say expressly to himself that he is standing up for the interest of society, certainly does feel that he is asserting a rule which is for the benefit of others as well as for his own.

If he is not feeling this, if he is regarding the act solely as it affects him individually, he is not consciously just; he is not concerning himself about the justice of his actions. This is admitted even by anti-utilitarian moralists. When Kant (as before remarked) propounds as the fundamental principle of morals, "So act, that thy rule of conduct might be adopted as a law by all rational beings," he virtually acknowledges that the interest of mankind collectively, or at least of mankind indiscriminately, must be in the mind of the agent when conscientiously deciding on the morality of the act. Otherwise he uses words without a meaning; for, that a rule even of utter selfishness could not *possibly* be adopted by all rational beings—that there is any insuperable obstacle in the nature of things to its adoption—cannot be even plausibly maintained. To give any meaning to Kant's principle, the sense put upon it must be, that we ought to shape our conduct by a rule which all rational beings might adopt *with benefit to their collective interest.*

To recapitulate: the idea of justice supposes two things— a rule of conduct, and a sentiment which sanctions the rule. The first must be supposed common to all mankind, and intended for their good. The other (the sentiment) is a desire that punishment may be suffered by those who infringe the rule. There is involved, in addition, the conception of some definite person who suffers by the infringement, whose rights (to use the expression appropriated to the case) are violated by it. And the sentiment of justice appears to me to be, the animal desire to repel or retaliate a hurt or damage to oneself, or to those with whom one sympathizes, widened so as to include all persons, by the human capacity of enlarged sympathy, and the human conception of intelligent self-interest. From the latter elements, the feeling derives its morality; from the former, its peculiar impressiveness, and energy of self-assertion.

I have, throughout, treated the idea of a *right* residing in the injured person, and violated by the injury, not as a separate element in the composition of the idea and sentiment, but as one of the forms in which the other two elements clothe themselves. These elements are, a hurt to some assignable person or persons on the one hand, and a demand for punishment on the other. An examination of our own minds, I think, will show, that

these two things include all that we mean when we speak of violation of a right. When we call anything a person's right, we mean that he has a valid claim on society to protect him in the possession of it, either by the force of law, or by that of education and opinion. If he has what we consider a sufficient claim, on whatever account, to have something guaranteed to him by society, we say that he has a right to it. If we desire to prove that anything does not belong to him by right, we think this done as soon as it is admitted that society ought not to take measures for securing it to him, but should leave him to chance, or to his own exertions. Thus, a person is said to have a right to what he can earn in fair professional competition, because society ought not to allow any other person to hinder him from endeavoring to earn in that manner as much as he can. But he has not a right to three hundred a-year, though he may happen to be earning it; because society is not called on to provide that he shall earn that sum. On the contrary, if he owns ten thousand pounds three per cent stock, he *has* a right to three hundred a-year because society has come under an obligation to provide him with an income of that amount.

To have a right, then, is, I conceive, to have something which society ought to defend me in the possession of. If the objector goes on to ask, why it ought, I can give him no other reason than general utility. If that expression does not seem to convey a sufficient feeling of the strength of the obligation, nor to account for the peculiar energy of the feeling, it is because there goes to the composition of the sentiment, not a rational only, but also an animal element—the thirst for retaliation; and this thirst derives its intensity, as well as its moral justification, from the extraordinarily important and impressive kind of utility which is concerned. The interest involved is that of security, to every one's feelings the most vital of all interests. All other earthly benefits are needed by one person, not needed by another; and many of them can, if necessary, be cheerfully foregone, or replaced by something else; but security no human being can possibly do without on it we depend for all our immunity from evil, and for the whole value of all and every good, beyond the passing moment; since nothing but the gratification of the instant could be of any worth to us, if we could be deprived of anything the next instant by whoever was momentarily stronger than ourselves. Now this most indispensable of all necessaries, after physical nutriment, cannot be had, unless the machinery for providing it is kept unintermittedly in active play. Our notion, therefore, of the claim we have on our fellow-creatures to join in making safe for us the very groundwork of our existence, gathers feelings around it so much more intense than those concerned in any of the more common cases of utility, that the difference in degree (as is often the case in psychology) becomes a real difference in kind. The claim assumes that character of absoluteness, that apparent infinity, and incommensurability with all other considerations, which constitute the distinction between the feeling of right and wrong and that of ordinary expediency and inexpediency. The feelings concerned are so powerful, and we count so positively on finding a responsive feeling in others (all being alike interested), that *ought* and *should* grow into *must*, and recognized indispensability becomes a moral necessity, analogous to physical, and often not inferior to it in binding force exhorted.

If the preceding analysis, or something resembling it, be not the correct account of the notion of justice—if justice be totally independent of utility, and be a standard *per se*, which the mind can recognize by simple introspection of itself—it is hard to understand why that internal oracle is so ambiguous, and why so many things appear either just or unjust, according to the light in which they are regarded.

We are continually informed that Utility is an uncertain standard, which every different person interprets differently, and that there is no safety but in the immutable, ineffaceable, and unmistakable dictates of justice, which carry their evidence in themselves, and are independent of the fluctuations of opinion. One would suppose from this that on questions of justice there could be no controversy; that if we take that for our rule, its application to any given case could leave us in as little doubt as a mathematical demonstration. So far is this from being the fact, that there is as much difference of opinion, and as much discussion, about what is just, as about what is useful to society. Not only have different nations and individuals different notions of justice, but in the mind of

one and the same individual, justice is not some one rule, principle, or maxim, but many, which do not always coincide in their dictates, and in choosing between which, he is guided either by some extraneous standard, or by his own personal predilections.

For instance, there are some who say that it is unjust to punish any one for the sake of example to others; that punishment is just, only when intended for the good of the sufferer himself. Others maintain the extreme reverse, contending that to punish persons who have attained years of discretion, for their own benefit, is despotism and injustice, since if the matter at issue is solely their own good, no one has a right to control their own judgment of it; but that they may justly be punished to prevent evil to others, this being the exercise of the legitimate right of self-defense. Mr. Owen, again, affirms that it is unjust to punish at all; for the criminal did not make his own character; his education, and the circumstances which surrounded him, have made him a criminal, and for these he is not responsible. All these opinions are extremely plausible; and so long as the question is argued as one of justice simply, without going down to the principles which lie under justice and are the source of its authority, I am unable to see how any of these reasoners can be refuted. For in truth every one of the three builds upon rules of justice confessedly true. The first appeals to the acknowledged injustice of singling out an individual, and making a sacrifice, without his consent, for other people's benefit. The second relies on the acknowledged justice of self-defense, and the admitted injustice of forcing one person to conform to another's notions of what constitutes his good. The Owenite invokes the admitted principle, that it is unjust to punish any one for what he cannot help. Each is triumphant so long as he is not compelled to take into consideration any other maxims of justice than the one he has selected; but as soon as their several maxims are brought face to face, each disputant seems to have exactly as much to say for himself as the others. No one of them can carry out his own notion of justice without trampling upon another equally binding. These are difficulties; they have always been felt to be such; and many devices have been invented to turn rather than to overcome them. As a refuge from the last of the three, men imagined what they called the freedom of the will—fancying that they could not justify punishing a man whose will is in a thoroughly hateful state, unless it be supposed to have come into that state through no influence of anterior circumstances. To escape from the other difficulties, a favorite contrivance has been the fiction of a contract, whereby at some unknown period all the members of society engaged to obey the laws, and consented to be punished for any disobedience to them, thereby giving to their legislators the right, which it is assumed they would not otherwise have had, of punishing them, either for their own good or for that of society. This happy thought was considered to get rid of the whole difficulty, and to legitimate the infliction of punishment, in virtue of another received maxim of justice, *volenti non fit injuria*— that is not unjust which is done with the consent of the person who is supposed to be hurt by it. I need hardly remark, that even if the consent were not a mere fiction, this maxim is not superior in authority to the others which it is brought in to supersede. It is, on the contrary, an instructive specimen of the loose and irregular manner in which supposed principles of justice grow up. This particular one evidently came into use as a help to the coarse exigencies of courts of law, which are sometimes obliged to be content with very uncertain presumptions, on account of the greater evils which would often arise from any attempt on their part to cut finer. But even courts of law are not able to adhere consistently to the maxim, for they allow voluntary engagements to be set aside on the ground of fraud, and sometimes on that of mere mistake or misinformation.

Again, when the legitimacy of inflicting punishment is admitted, how many conflicting conceptions of justice come to light in discussing the proper apportionment of punishments to offenses. No rule on the subject recommends itself so strongly to the primitive and spontaneous sentiment of justice, as the *lex talionis*, an eye for an eye and a tooth for a tooth. Though this principle of the Jewish and of the Mohammedan law has been generally abandoned in Europe as a practical maxim, there is, I suspect, in most minds, a secret hankering after it; and when retribution accidentally falls on an offender in that precise shape, the general feeling of satisfaction evinced bears witness how natural is the sentiment to which this repayment in kind is acceptable. With many, the test of justice in penal infliction is that the punishment should be proportioned to the offense; meaning that it should be exactly measured by the moral guilt of the culprit (whatever be their standard for measuring moral guilt): the consideration, what amount of punishment is necessary to deter from the offense, having nothing to do with the question of justice, in their estimation; while there are others to whom that consideration is all in all; who maintain that it is not just, at least for man, to inflict on a fellow creature, whatever may be his offenses., any amount of suffering beyond the least that will suffice to prevent him from repeating, and others from imitating, his misconduct.

To take another example from a subject already once referred to. In a co-operative industrial association, is it just or not that talent or skill should give a title to superior remuneration? On the negative side of the question it is argued, that whoever does the best he can, deserves equally well, and ought not in justice to be put in a position of inferiority for no fault of his own; that superior abilities have already advantages more than enough, in the admiration they excite, the personal influence they command, and the internal sources of satisfaction attending them, without adding to these a superior share of the world's goods; and that society is bound in justice rather to make compensation to the less favored, for this unmerited inequality of advantages, than to aggravate it. On the contrary side it is contended, that society receives more from the more efficient laborer; that his services being more useful, society owes him a larger return for them; that a greater share of the joint result is actually his work, and not to allow his claim to it is a kind of robbery; that if he is only to receive as much as others, he can only be justly required to produce as much, and to give a smaller amount of time and exertion, proportioned to his superior efficiency. Who shall decide between these appeals to conflicting principles of Justice? Justice has in this case two sides to it, which it is impossible to bring into harmony, and the two disputants have chosen opposite sides; the one looks to what it is just that the individual should receive, the other to what it is just that the community should give. Each, from his own point of view, is unanswerable; and any choice between them, on grounds of justice, must be perfectly arbitrary. Social utility alone can decide the preference.

How many, again, and how irreconcilable, are the standards of justice to which reference is made in discussing the repartition of taxation. One opinion is, that payment to the State should be in numerical proportion to pecuniary means. Others think that justice dictates what they term graduated taxation—taking a higher percentage from those who have more to spare. In point of natural justice a strong case might be made for disregarding means altogether, and taking the same absolute sum (whenever it could be got) from everyone; as the subscribers to a mess, or to a club, all pay the same sum for the same privileges, whether they can all equally afford it or not. Since the protection (it might be said) of law and government is afforded to, and is equally required by all, there is no injustice in making all buy it at the same price. It is reckoned justice, not injustice, that a dealer should charge to all customers the same price for the same article, not a price varying according to their means of payment. This doctrine, as applied to taxation, finds no advocates, because it conflicts so strongly with man's feelings of humanity and of social expediency; but the principle of justice which it invokes is as true and as binding as those which can be appealed to against it. Accordingly it exerts a tacit influence on the line of defense employed for other modes of assessing taxation. People feel obliged to argue that the State does more for the rich than for the poor, as a justification for its taking more from them: though this is in reality not true, for the rich would be far better able to protect themselves, in the absence of law or government, than the poor, and indeed would probably be successful in converting the poor into their slaves. Others, again, so far defer to the same conception of justice, as to maintain that all should pay an equal capitation tax for the protection of their persons (these being of equal value to all), and an unequal tax for the protection of their property, which is unequal. To this others reply, that the all of one man is as valuable to him as the all of another. From these confusions there is no other mode of extrication than the utilitarian.

Is, then the difference between the just and the expedient a merely imaginary distinction? Have mankind been under a delusion in thinking that justice is a more sacred thing than policy, and that the latter ought only to be listened to after the former has been satisfied? By no means. The exposition we have given of the nature and origin of the sentiment, recognizes a real distinction; and no one of those who profess the most sublime contempt for the consequences of actions as an element in their morality, attaches more importance to the distinction than I do. While I dispute the pretensions of any theory which sets up an imaginary standard of justice not grounded on utility, I account the justice which is grounded on utility to be the chief part, and incomparably the most sacred and binding part, of all morality. Justice is a name for certain classes of moral rules, which concern the essentials of human well-being more nearly, and are therefore of more absolute obligation, than any other rules for the guidance of life; and the notion which we have found to be of the essence of the idea of justice—that of a right residing in an individual—implies and testifies to this more binding obligation.

The moral rules which forbid mankind to hurt one another (in which we must never forget to include wrongful interference with each other's freedom) are more vital to human well-being than any maxims, however important, which only point out the best mode of managing some department of human affairs. They have also the peculiarity, that they are the main element in determining the whole of the social feelings of mankind. It is their observance which alone preserves peace among human beings; if obedience to them were not the rule, and disobedience the exception, every one would see in every one else an enemy, against whom he must be perpetually guarding himself. What is hardly less important, these are the precepts which mankind have the strongest and the most direct inducements for impressing upon one another. By merely giving to each other prudential instruction or exhortation, they may gain, or think they gain, nothing: in inculcating on each other the duty of positive beneficence they have an unmistakable interest, but far less in degree; a person may possibly not need the benefits of others; but he always needs that they should not do him hurt. Thus the moralities which protect every individual from being harmed by others, either directly or by being hindered in his freedom of pursuing his own good, are at once those which he himself has most at heart, and those which he has the strongest interest in publishing and enforcing by word and deed. It is by a person's observance of these that his fitness to exist as one of the fellowship of human beings is tested and decided; for on that depends his being a nuisance or not to those with whom he is in contact. Now it is these moralities primarily which compose the obligations of justice. The most marked cases of injustice, and those which give the tone to the feeling of repugnance which characterizes the sentiment, are acts of wrongful aggression, or wrongful exercise of power over someone; the next are those which consist in wrongfully withholding from him something which is his due—in both cases, inflicting on him a positive hurt, either in the form of direct suffering, or of the privation of some good which he had reasonable ground, either of a physical or of a social kind, for counting upon.

The same powerful motives which command the observance of these primary moralities, enjoin the punishment of those who violate them; and as the impulses of self-defense, of defense of others, and of vengeance, are all called forth against such persons, retribution, or evil for evil, becomes closely connected with the sentiment of justice, and is universally included in the idea. Good for good is also one of the dictates of justice; and this, though its social utility is evident, and though it carries with it a natural human feeling, has not at first sight that obvious connection with hurt or injury, which, existing in the most elementary cases of just and unjust, is the source of the characteristic intensity of the sentiment. But the connection, though less obvious, is not less real. He who accepts benefits, and denies a return of them when needed, inflicts a real hurt, by disappointing one of the most natural and reasonable of expectations, and one which he must at least tacitly have encouraged, otherwise the benefits would seldom have been conferred. The important rank, among human evils and wrongs, of the disappointment of expectation, is shown in the fact that it constitutes the principal criminality of two such highly immoral acts as a breach of friendship and a breach of promise. Few hurts which human beings can sustain are greater, and none wound more, than when that on which they habitually and with full assurance relied, fails them in the hour of need; and few wrongs are greater than this mere withholding of good; none excite more resentment, either in the person suffering, or in a sympathizing spectator. The principle, therefore, of giving to each what they deserve, that is, good for good as well as

evil for evil, is not only included within the idea of justice as we have defined it, but is a proper object of that intensity of sentiment, which places the just, in human estimation, above the simply expedient.

Most of the maxims of justice current in the world, and commonly appealed to in its transactions, are simply instrumental to carrying into effect the principles of justice which we have now spoken of. That a person is only responsible for what he has done voluntarily, or could voluntarily have avoided, that it is unjust to condemn any person unheard; that the punishment ought to be proportioned to the offense, and the like, are maxims intended to prevent the just principle of evil for evil from being perverted to the infliction of evil without that justification. The greater part of these common maxims have come into use from the practice of courts of justice, which have been naturally led to a more complete recognition and elaboration than was likely to suggest itself to others, of the rules necessary to enable them to fulfill their double function—of inflicting punishment when due, and of awarding to each person his right.

That first of judicial virtues, impartiality, is an obligation of justice, partly for the reason last mentioned; as being a necessary condition of the fulfillment of the other obligations of justice. But this is not the only source of the exalted rank, among human obligations, of those maxims of equality and impartiality, which, both in popular estimation and in that of the most enlightened are included among the precepts of justice. In one point of view, they may be considered as corollaries from the principles already laid down. If it is a duty to do to each according to his deserts, returning good for good as well as repressing evil by evil, it necessarily follows that we should treat all equally well (when no higher duty forbids) who have deserved equally well of *us*, and that society should treat all equally well who have deserved equally well of *it*, that is, who have deserved equally well absolutely. This is the highest abstract standard of social and distributive justice; towards which all institutions, and the efforts of all virtuous citizens, should be made in the utmost possible degree to converge. But this great moral duty rests upon a still deeper foundation, being a direct emanation from the first principle of morals, and not a mere logical corollary from secondary or derivative doctrines. It is involved in the very meaning of Utility, or the Greatest Happiness

Principle. That principle is a mere form of words without rational signification, unless one person's happiness, supposed equal in degree (with the proper allowance made for kind), is counted for exactly as much as another's. Those conditions being supplied, Bentham's dictum, "everybody to count for one, nobody for more than one", might be written under the principle of utility as an explanatory commentary[4]. The equal claim of everybody to happiness in the estimation of the moralist and the

4. This implication, in the first principle of the utilitarian scheme, of perfect impartiality between persons, is regarded by Mr. Herbert Spencer (in his *Social Statics*) as a disproof of the pretensions of utility to be a sufficient guide to right; since (he says) the principle of utility presupposes the anterior principle, that everybody has an equal right to happiness. It may be more correctly described as supposing that equal amounts of happiness are equally desirable, whether felt by the same or by different persons. This, however, is not a *pre*supposition; not a premise needful to support the principle of utility, but the very principle itself; for what is the principle of utility, if it be not that "happiness" and "desirable" are synonymous terms? If there is any anterior principle implied, it can be no other than this, that the truths of arithmetic are applicable to the valuation of happiness, as of all other measurable quantities.

(Mr. Herbert Spencer, in a private communication on the subject of the preceding Note, objects to being considered an opponent of utilitarianism, and states that he regards happiness as the ultimate end of morality; but deems that end only partially attainable by empirical generalizations from the observed results of conduct, and completely attainable only by deducing, from the laws of life and the conditions of existence, what kinds of action necessarily tend to produce happiness, and what kinds to produce unhappiness. What the exception of the word "necessarily," I have no dissent to express from this doctrine; and (omitting that word) I am not aware that any modern advocate of utilitarianism is of a different opinion. Bentham, certainly, to whom in the *Social Statics* Mr. Spencer particularly referred, is, least of all writers, chargeable with unwillingness to deduce the effect of actions on happiness from the laws of human nature and the universal conditions of human life. The common charge against him is of relying too exclusively upon such deductions, and declining altogether to be bound by the generalizations from specific experience which Mr. Spencer thinks that utilitarians generally confine themselves to. My own opinion (and, as I collect, Mr. Spencer's) is, that in ethics, as in all other branches of scientific study, the consilience of the results of both these processes, each corroborating and verifying the other, is requisite to give to any general proposition the kind degree of evidence which constitutes scientific proof.)

legislator, involves an equal claim to all the means of happiness, except in so far as the inevitable conditions of human life, and the general interest, in which that of every individual is included, set limits to the maxim; and those limits ought to be strictly construed. As every other maxim of justice, so this is by no means applied or held applicable universally; on the contrary, as I have already remarked, it bends to every person's ideas of social expediency. But in whatever case it is deemed applicable at all, it is held to be the dictate of justice. All persons are deemed to have a *right* to equality of treatment, except when some recognized social expediency requires the reverse. And hence all social inequalities which have ceased to be considered expedient, assume the character not of simple inexpediency, but of injustice, and appear so tyrannical, that people are apt to wonder how they ever could have. Been tolerated—forgetful that they themselves perhaps tolerate other inequalities under an equally mistaken notion of expediency, the correction of which would make that which they approve seem quite as monstrous as what they have at last learnt to condemn. The entire history of social improvement has been a series of transitions, by which one custom or institution after another, from being a supposed primary necessity of social existence, has passed into the rank of a universally stigmatized injustice and tyranny. So it has been with the distinctions of slaves and freemen, nobles and serfs, patricians and plebeians; and so it will be, and in part already is, with the aristocracies of color, race, and sex.

It appears from what has been said, that justice is a name for certain moral requirements, which, regarded collectively, stand higher in the scale of social utility, and are therefore of more paramount obligation, than any others; though particular cases may occur in which some other social duty is so important, as to overrule any one of the general maxims of justice. Thus, to save a life, it may not only be allowable, but a duty, to steal, or take by force, the necessary food or medicine, or to kidnap, and compel to officiate, the only qualified medical practitioner. In such cases, as we do not call anything justice which is not a virtue, we usually say, not that justice must give way to some other moral principle, but that what is just in ordinary cases is, by reason of that other principle, not just in the particular case. By this useful accommodation of language, the character of indefeasibility attributed to justice is kept up, and we are saved from the necessity of maintaining that there can be laudable injustice.

The considerations which have now been adduced resolve, I conceive, the only real difficulty in the utilitarian theory of morals. It has always been evident that all cases of justice are also cases of expediency; the difference is in the peculiar sentiment which attaches to the former, as contradistinguished from the latter. If this characteristic sentiment has been sufficiently accounted for; if there is no necessity to assume for it any peculiarity of origin; if it is simply the natural feeling of resentment, moralized by being made coextensive with the demands of social good; and if this feel-ing not only does but ought to exist in all the classes of cases to which the idea of justice corresponds—that idea no longer presents itself as a stumbling block to the utilitarian ethics. Justice remains the appropriate name for certain social utilities which are vastly more important, and therefore more absolute and imperative, than any others are as a class (though not more so than others may be in particular cases); and which, therefore, ought to be, as well as naturally are, guarded by a sentiment not only different in degree, but also in kind; distinguished from the milder feeling which attaches to the mere idea of promoting human pleasure or convenience, at once by the more definite nature of its commands, and by the sterner character of its sanctions.

Chapter 3

LIBERTARIANISM

If you conclude, even provisionally, that utilitarianism does not provide an adequate basis for individual rights, you might wonder what other, stronger justification for rights is available. Libertarians offer one answer to this question. Libertarians are best known as advocates of free markets and critics of government regulation. Underlying their laissez-faire stance is the idea that each of us has a fundamental right to liberty—a right to do whatever we want with the things we own, provided we do not violate other people's rights to do the same.

If the libertarian theory of rights is correct, then only a minimal state—one that enforces contracts, protects private property, and keeps the peace—is morally justified. Laws that try to protect people from harming themselves (such as motorcycle helmet laws) or that require some people to help others (by redistributing wealth from the rich to the poor, for example) violate the right to liberty. At the heart of the libertarian philosophy is the idea that we own ourselves and the fruits of our labor. As the proprietors of our own person, each of us has the right to decide what to do with our bodies and our labor, with the money we earn and the goods we possess.

Here is a challenge to bear in mind while reading the libertarians: If you accept the idea that we own ourselves, must you also accept the conclusion that all paternalist and redistributive laws are unjust? If, on the other hand, you believe that government should tax the rich to help the poor, how do you answer the libertarian argument that such laws are a form of coerced charity that makes every person the property (perhaps even the slave) of the majority?

FREE TO CHOOSE

Milton & Rose Friedman

Created Equal

"Equality," "liberty"—what precisely do these words from the Declaration of Independence mean? Can the ideals they express be realized in practice? Are equality and liberty consistent one with the other, or are they in conflict?

Since well before the Declaration of Independence, these questions have played a central role in the history of the United States. The attempt to answer them has shaped the intellectual climate of opinion, led to bloody war, and produced major changes in economic and political institutions. This attempt continues to dominate our political debate. It will shape our future as it has our past.

In the early decades of the Republic, equality meant equality before God; liberty meant the liberty to shape one's own life. The obvious conflict between the Declaration of Independence and the institution of slavery occupied the center of the stage. That conflict was finally resolved by the Civil War. The debate then moved to a different level. Equality came more and more to be interpreted as "equality of opportunity" in the sense that no one should be prevented by arbitrary obstacles from using his capacities to pursue his own objectives. That is still its dominant meaning to most citizens of the United States.

Neither equality before God nor equality of opportunity presented any conflict with liberty to shape one's own life. Quite the opposite. Equality and liberty were two faces of the same basic value—that every individual should be regarded as an end in himself.

A very different meaning of equality has emerged in the United States in recent decades—equality of outcome. Everyone should have the same level of living or of income, should finish the race at the same time. Equality of outcome is in clear conflict with liberty. The attempt to promote it has been a major source of bigger and bigger government, and of government-imposed restrictions on our liberty.

Equality Before God

When Thomas Jefferson, at the age of thirty-three, wrote "all men are created equal," he and his contemporaries did not take these words literally. They did not regard "men"—or as we would say today, "persons"—as equal in physical characteristics, emotional reactions, mechanical and intellectual abilities. Thomas Jefferson himself was a most remarkable person. At the age of twenty-six he designed his beautiful house at Monticello (Italian for "little mountain"), supervised its construction, and, indeed, is said to have done some of the work himself. In the course of his life, he was an inventor, a scholar, an author, a statesman, governor of the State of Virginia, President of the United States, Minister to France, founder of the University of Virginia—hardly an average man.

The clue to what Thomas Jefferson and his contemporaries meant by equal is in the next phrase of the Declaration—"endowed by their Creator with certain unalienable rights; that among these are Life, Liberty, and the pursuit of Happiness." Men were equal before God. Each person is precious in and of himself. He has unalienable rights, rights that no one else is entitled to invade. He is entitled to serve his own purposes and not to be treated simply as an instrument to promote someone else's purposes. "Liberty" is part of the definition of equality, not in conflict with it.

Equality before God—personal equality—is important precisely because people are not identical. Their different values, their different tastes, their different capacities will lead them to want to lead very different lives. Personal equality requires respect for their right to do so, not the imposition on them of someone else's values or judgment. Jefferson had no doubt that some men were superior to others, that there was an elite. But that did not give them the right to rule others.

If an elite did not have the right to impose its will on others, neither did any other group, even a majority. Every person was to be his own ruler—provided that he did not interfere with the similar right of others. Government was established to protect that right—from fellow citizens and from external threat—not to give a majority unbridled rule. Jefferson had three achievements he wanted to be remembered for inscribed on his tombstone: the Virginia statute for religious freedom (a precursor of the U.S. Bill of Rights designed to protect minorities against domination by majorities), authorship of the Declaration of Independence, and the founding of the University of Virginia. The goal of the framers of the Constitution of the United States, drafted by Jefferson's contemporaries, was a national government strong enough to defend the country and promote the general welfare but at the same time sufficiently limited in power to protect the individual citizen, and the separate state governments, from domination by the national government. Democratic, in the sense of widespread participation in government, yes; in the political sense of majority rule, clearly no.

Similarly, Alexis de Tocqueville, the famous French political philosopher and sociologist, in his classic *Democracy in America*, written after a lengthy visit in the 1830s, saw equality, not majority rule, as the outstanding characteristic of America. "In America," he wrote, the aristocratic element has always been feeble from its birth; and if at the present day it is not actually destroyed, it is at any rate so completely disabled, that we can scarcely assign to it any degree of influence on the course of affairs. The democratic principle, on the contrary, has gained so much strength by time, by events, and by legislation, as to have become not only predominant but all-powerful. There is no family or corporate authority....

America, then, exhibits in her social state a most extraordinary phenomenon. Men are there seen on a greater equality in point of fortune and intellect, or, in other words, more equal in their strength, than in any other country of the world, or in any age of which history has preserved the remembrance.

Tocqueville admired much of what he observed, but he was by no means an uncritical admirer, fearing that democracy carried too far might undermine civic virtue. As he put it, "There is . . . a manly and lawful passion for equality which incites men to wish all to be powerful and honored. This passion tends to elevate the humble to the rank of the great; but there exists also in the human heart a depraved taste for equality, which impels the weak to attempt to lower the powerful to their own level, and reduces men to prefer equality in slavery to inequality with freedom."

It is striking testimony to the changing meaning of words that in recent decades the Democratic party of the United States has been the chief instrument for strengthening that government power which Jefferson and many of his contemporaries viewed as the greatest threat to democracy. And it has striven to increase government power in the name of a concept of "equality" that is almost the opposite of the concept of equality Jefferson identified with liberty and Tocqueville with democracy.

Of course the practice of the founding fathers did not always correspond to their preaching. The most obvious conflict was slavery. Thomas Jefferson himself owned slaves until the day he died—July 4, 1826. He agonized repeatedly about slavery, suggested in his notes and correspondence plans for eliminating slavery, but never publicly proposed any such plans or campaigned against the institution.

Yet the Declaration he drafted had either to be blatantly violated by the nation he did so much to create and form, or slavery had to be abolished. Little wonder that the early decades of the Republic saw a rising tide of controversy about the institution of slavery. That controversy ended in a civil war that, in the words of Abraham Lincoln's Gettysburg Address, tested whether a "nation, conceived in liberty and dedicated to the proposition that all men are created equal . . . can long endure." The nation endured, but only at a tremendous cost in lives, property, and social cohesion.

Equality of Opportunity

Once the Civil War abolished slavery and the concept of personal equality—equality before God and the law—came closer to realization, emphasis shifted, in intellectual discussion and in government and private policy, to a different concept—equality of opportunity.

Literal equality of opportunity—in the sense of "identity"—is impossible. One child is born blind, another with sight. One child has parents deeply concerned about his welfare who provide a background of culture and understanding; another has dissolute, improvident parents. One child is born in the United States, another in India, or China, or Russia. They clearly do not have identical opportunities open to them at birth, and there is no way that their opportunities can be made identical.

Like personal equality, equality of opportunity is not to be interpreted literally. Its real meaning is perhaps best expressed by the French expression dating from the French Revolution: *Une carrière ouverte aux les talents*—a career open to the talents. No arbitrary obstacles should prevent people from achieving those positions for which their talents fit them and which their values lead them to seek. Not birth, nationality, color, religion, sex, nor any other irrelevant characteristic should determine the opportunities that are open to a person—only his abilities.

On this interpretation, equality of opportunity simply spells out in more detail the meaning of personal equality, of equality before the law. And like personal equality, it has meaning and importance precisely because people are different in their genetic and cultural characteristics, and hence both want to and can pursue different careers.

Equality of opportunity, like personal equality, is not inconsistent with liberty; on the contrary, it is an essential component of liberty. If some people are denied access to particular positions in life for which they are qualified simply because of their ethnic background, color, or religion, that is an interference with their right to "Life, Liberty, and the pursuit of Happiness." It denies equality of opportunity and, by the same token, sacrifices the freedom of some for the advantage of others.

Like every ideal, equality of opportunity is incapable of being fully realized. The most serious departure was undoubtedly with respect to the blacks, particularly in the South but in the North as well. Yet there was also tremendous progress for blacks and for other groups. The very concept of a "melting pot" reflected the goal of equality of opportunity. So also did the expansion of "free" education at elementary, secondary, and higher levels—though, as we shall see in the next chapter, this development has not been an unmixed blessing.

The priority given to equality of opportunity in the hierarchy of values generally accepted by the public after the Civil War is manifested particularly in economic policy. The catchwords were free enterprise, competition, laissez-faire. Everyone was to be free to go into any business, follow any occupation, buy any property, subject only to the agreement of the other parties to the transaction. Each was to have the opportunity to reap the benefits if he succeeded, to suffer the costs if he failed. There were to be no arbitrary obstacles. Performance, not birth, religion, or nationality, was the touchstone.

One corollary was the development of what many who regarded themselves as the cultural elite sneered at as vulgar materialism—an emphasis on the almighty dollar, on wealth as both the symbol and the seal of success. As Tocqueville pointed out, this emphasis reflected the unwillingness of the community to accept the traditional criteria in feudal and aristocratic societies, namely birth and parentage. Performance was the obvious alternative, and the accumulation of wealth was the most readily available measure of performance.

Another corollary, of course, was an enormous release of human energy that made America an increasingly productive and dynamic society in which social mobility was an everyday reality. Still another, perhaps surprisingly, was an explosion in charitable activity. This explosion was made possible by the rapid growth in wealth. It took the form it did—of nonprofit hospitals, privately endowed colleges and universities, a plethora of charitable organizations directed to helping the poor—because of the dominant values of the society, including, especially, promotion of equality of opportunity.

Of course, in the economic sphere as elsewhere, practice did not always conform to the ideal. Government *was* kept to a minor role; no major obstacles to enterprise were erected, and by the end of the nineteenth century, positive government measures, especially the Sherman Anti-Trust Law, were adopted to eliminate private barriers to competition. But extralegal arrangements continued to interfere with the freedom of individuals to enter various businesses or professions, and social practices unquestionably gave special advantages to persons born in the "right" families, of the "right" color, and practicing the "right" religion. However, the rapid rise in the economic and social position of various less privileged groups demonstrates that these obstacles were by no means insurmountable.

In respect of government measures, one major deviation from free markets was in foreign trade, where Alexander Hamilton's *Report on Manufactures* had enshrined tariff protection for domestic industries as part of the American way. Tariff protection was inconsistent with thoroughgoing equality of opportunity and, indeed, with the free immigration of persons, which was the rule until World War I, except only for Orientals. Yet it could be rationalized both by the needs of national defense and on the very different ground that equality stops at the water's edge—an illogical rationalization that is adopted also by most of today's proponents of a very different concept of equality.

Equality of Outcome

That different concept, equality of outcome, has been gaining ground in this century. It first affected government policy in Great Britain and on the European continent. Over the past half-century it has increasingly affected government policy in the United States as well. In some intellectual circles the desirability of equality of outcome has become an article of religious faith: everyone should finish the race at the same time. As the Dodo said in *Alice in Wonderland,* "*Everybody* has won, and *all* must have prizes."

For this concept, as for the other two, "equal" is not to be interpreted literally as "identical." No one really maintains that everyone, regardless of age or sex or other physical qualities, should have identical rations of each separate item of food, clothing, and so on. The goal is rather "fairness," a much vaguer notion—indeed, one that it is difficult, if not impossible, to define precisely. "Fair shares for all" is the modern slogan that has replaced Karl Marx's, "To each according to his needs, from each according to his ability."

This concept of equality differs radically from the other two. Government measures that promote personal equality or equality of opportunity enhance liberty; government measures to achieve "fair shares for all" reduce liberty. If what people get is to be determined by "fairness," who is to decide what is "fair"? As a chorus of voices asked the Dodo, "But who is to give the prizes?" "Fairness" is not an objectively determined concept once it departs from identity. "Fairness," like "needs," is in the eye of the beholder. If all are to have "fair shares," someone or some group of people must decide what shares are fair—and they must be able to impose their decisions on others, taking from those who have more than their "fair" share and giving to those who have less. Are those who make and impose such decisions equal to those for whom they decide? Are we not in George Orwell's *Animal Farm,* where "all animals are equal, but some animals are more equal than others"?

In addition, if what people get is determined by "fairness" and not by what they produce, where are the "prizes" to come from? What incentive is there to work and produce? How is it to be decided who is to be the doctor, who the lawyer, who the garbage collector, who the street sweeper? What assures that people will accept the roles assigned to them and perform those roles in accordance with their abilities? Clearly, only force or the threat of force will do.

The key point is not merely that practice will depart from the ideal. Of course it will, as it does

with respect to the other two concepts of equality as well. The point is rather that there is a fundamental conflict between the *ideal* of "fair shares" or of its precursor, "to each according to his needs," and the *ideal* of personal liberty. This conflict has plagued every attempt to make equality of outcome the overriding principle of social organization. The end result has invariably been a state of terror: Russia, China, and, more recently, Cambodia offer clear and convincing evidence. And even terror has not equalized outcomes. In every case, wide inequality persists by any criterion; inequality between the rulers and the ruled, not only in power, but also in material standards of life.

The far less extreme measures taken in Western countries in the name of equality of outcome have shared the same fate to a lesser extent. They, too, have restricted individual liberty. They, too, have failed to achieve their objective. It has proved impossible to define "fair shares" in a way that is generally acceptable, or to satisfy the members of the community that they are being treated "fairly." On the contrary, dissatisfaction has mounted with every additional attempt to implement equality of outcome.

Much of the moral fervor behind the drive for equality of outcome comes from the widespread belief that it is not fair that some children should have a great advantage over others simply because they happen to have wealthy parents. Of course it is not fair. However, unfairness can take many forms. It can take the form of the inheritance of property—bonds and stocks, houses, factories; it can also take the form of the inheritance of talent—musical ability, strength, mathematical genius. The inheritance of property can be interfered with more readily than the inheritance of talent. But from an ethical point of view, is there any difference between the two? Yet many people resent the inheritance of property but not the inheritance of talent.

Look at the same issue from the point of view of the parent. If you want to assure your child a higher income in life, you can do so in various ways. You can buy him (or her) an education that will equip him to pursue an occupation yielding a high income; or you can set him up in a business that will yield a higher income than he could earn as a salaried employee; or you can leave him property, the income from which will enable him to live better. Is there any ethical difference among these three ways of using your property? Or again, if the state leaves you any money to spend over and above taxes, should the state permit you to spend it on riotous living but not to leave it to your children?

The ethical issues involved are subtle and complex. They are not to be resolved by such simplistic formulas as "fair shares for all." Indeed, if we took that seriously, youngsters with less musical skill should be given the greatest amount of musical training in order to compensate for their inherited disadvantage, and those with greater musical aptitude should be prevented from having access to good musical training; and similarly with all other categories of inherited personal qualities. That might be "fair" to the youngsters lacking in talent, but would it be "fair" to the talented, let alone to those who had to work to pay for training the youngsters lacking talent, or to the persons deprived of the benefits that might have come from the cultivation of the talents of the gifted?

Life is not fair. It is tempting to believe that government can rectify what nature has spawned. But it is also important to recognize how much we benefit from the very unfairness we deplore.

There's nothing fair about Marlene Dietrich's having been born with beautiful legs that we all want to look at; or about Muhammad Ali's having been born with the skill that made him a great fighter. But on the other side, millions of people who have enjoyed looking at Marlene Dietrich's legs or watching one of Muhammad Ali's fights have benefited from nature's unfairness in producing a Marlene Dietrich and a Muhammad Ali. What kind of a world would it be if everyone were a duplicate of everyone else?

It is certainly not fair that Muhammad Ali should be able to earn millions of dollars in one night. But wouldn't it have been even more unfair to the people who enjoyed watching him if, in the pursuit of some abstract ideal of equality, Muhammad Ali had not been permitted to earn more for one night's fight—or for each day spent in preparing for a fight—than the lowest man on the totem pole could get for a day's unskilled work on the docks? It might have been possible to do that, but the result would have been to deny people the opportunity to watch Muhammad Ali.

We doubt very much that he would have been willing to undergo the arduous regimen of training that preceded his fights, or to subject himself to the kind of fights he has had, if he were limited to the pay of an unskilled dockworker.

Still another facet of this complex issue of fairness can be illustrated by considering a game of chance, for example, an evening at baccarat. The people who choose to play may start the evening with equal piles of chips, but as the play progresses, those piles will become unequal. By the end of the evening, some will be big winners, others big losers. In the name of the ideal of equality, should the winners be required to repay the losers? That would take all the fun out of the game. Not even the losers would like that. They might like it for the one evening, but would they come back again to play if they knew that whatever happened, they'd end up exactly where they started?

This example has a great deal more to do with the real world than one might at first suppose. Every day each of us makes decisions that involve taking a chance. Occasionally it's a big chance—as when we decide what occupation to pursue, whom to marry, whether to buy a house or make a major investment. More often it's a small chance, as when we decide what movie to go to, whether to cross the street against the traffic, whether to buy one security rather than another. Each time the question is, who is to decide what chances we take? That in turn depends on who bears the consequences of the decision. If we bear the consequences, we can make the decision. But if someone else bears the consequences, should we or will we be permitted to make the decision? If you play baccarat as an agent for someone else with his money, will he, or should he, permit you unlimited scope for decision making? Is he not almost certain to set some limit to your discretion? Will he not lay down some rules for you to observe? To take a very different example, if the government (i.e., your fellow taxpayers) assumes the costs of flood damage to your house, can you be permitted to decide freely whether to build your house on a floodplain? It is no accident that increasing government intervention into personal decisions has gone hand in hand with the drive for "fair shares for all."

The system under which people make their own choices—and bear most of the consequences of their decisions—is the system that has prevailed for most of our history. It is the system that gave the Henry Fords, the Thomas Alva Edisons, the George Eastmans, the John D. Rockefellers, the James Cash Penneys the incentive to transform our society over the past two centuries. It is the system that gave other people an incentive to furnish venture capital to finance the risky enterprises that these ambitious inventors and captains of industry undertook. Of course, there were many losers along the way—probably more losers than winners. We don't remember their names. But for the most part they went in with their eyes open. They knew they were taking chances. And win or lose, society as a whole benefited from their willingness to take a chance.

The fortunes that this system produced came overwhelmingly from developing new products or services, or new ways of producing products or services, or of distributing them widely. The resulting addition to the wealth of the community as a whole, to the well-being of the masses of the people, amounted to many times the wealth accumulated by the innovators. Henry Ford acquired a great fortune. The country acquired a cheap and reliable means of transportation and the techniques of mass production. Moreover, in many cases the private fortunes were largely devoted in the end to the benefit of society. The Rockefeller, Ford, and Carnegie foundations are only the most prominent of the numerous private benefactions which are so outstanding a consequence of the operation of a system that corresponded to "equality of opportunity" and "liberty" as these terms were understood until recently.

One limited sample may give the flavor of the outpouring of philanthropic activity in the nineteenth and early twentieth century. In a book devoted to "cultural philanthropy in Chicago from the 1880's to 1917," Helen Horowitz writes:

At the turn of the century, Chicago was a city of contradictory impulses: it was both a commercial center dealing in the basic commodities of an industrial society and a community caught in the winds of cultural uplift. As one commentator put it, the city was "a strange combination of pork and Plato."

A major manifestation of Chicago's drive toward culture was the establishment of the city's great cultural institutions in the 1880's and early 1890's (the Art Institute, the Newberry Library,

the Chicago Symphony Orchestra, the University of Chicago, the Field Museum, the Crerar Library). . . .

These institutions were a new phenomenon in the city. Whatever the initial impetus behind their founding, they were largely organized, sustained, and controlled by a group of businessmen. . . . Yet while privately supported and managed, the institutions were designed for the whole city. Their trustees had turned to cultural philanthropy not so much to satisfy personal aesthetic or scholarly yearnings as to accomplish social goals. Disturbed by social forces they could not control and filled with idealistic notions of culture, these businessmen saw in the museum, the library, the symphony orchestra, and the university a way to purify their city and to generate a civic renaissance.

Philanthropy was by no means restricted to cultural institutions. There was, as Horowitz writes in another connection, "a kind of explosion of activity on many different levels." And Chicago was not an isolated case. Rather, as Horowitz puts it, "Chicago seemed to epitomize America." The same period saw the establishment of Hull House in Chicago under Jane Addams, the first of many settlement houses established throughout the nation to spread culture and education among the poor and to assist them in their daily problems. Many hospitals, orphanages, and other charitable agencies were set up in the same period.

There is no inconsistency between a free market system and the pursuit of broad social and cultural goals, or between a free market system and compassion for the less fortunate, whether that compassion takes the form, as it did in the nineteenth century, of private charitable activity, or, as it has done increasingly in the twentieth, of assistance through government—provided that in both cases it is an expression of a desire to help others. There is all the difference in the world, however, between two kinds of assistance through government that seem superficially similar: first, 90 percent of us agreeing to impose taxes on ourselves in order to help the bottom 10 percent, and second, 80 percent voting to impose taxes on the top 10 percent to help the bottom 10 percent— William Graham Sumner's famous example of B and C deciding what D shall do for A. The first may be wise or unwise, an effective or an ineffective way to help the disadvantaged—but it is consistent with belief in both equality of opportunity and liberty. The second seeks equality of outcome and is entirely antithetical to liberty.

Who Favors Equality of Outcome?

There is little support for the goal of equality of outcome despite the extent to which it has become almost an article of religious faith among intellectuals and despite its prominence in the speeches of politicians and the preambles of legislation. The talk is belied alike by the behavior of government, of the intellectuals who most ardently espouse egalitarian sentiments, and of the public at large.

For government, one obvious example is the policy toward lotteries and gambling. New York State—and particularly New York City—is widely and correctly regarded as a stronghold of egalitarian sentiment. Yet the New York State government conducts lotteries and provides facilities for off-track betting on races. It advertises extensively to induce its citizens to buy lottery tickets and bet on the races—at terms that yield a very large profit to the government. At the same time it tries to suppress the "numbers" game, which, as it happens, offers better odds than the government lottery (especially when account is taken of the greater ease of avoiding tax on winnings). Great Britain, a stronghold, if not the birthplace, of egalitarian sentiment, permits private gambling clubs and betting on races and other sporting events. Indeed, wagering is a national pastime and a major source of government income.

For intellectuals, the clearest evidence is their failure to practice what so many of them preach. Equality of outcome can be promoted on a do-it-yourself basis. First, decide exactly what you mean by equality. Do you want to achieve equality within the United States? In a selected group of countries as a whole? In the world as a whole? Is equality to be judged in terms of income per person? Per family? Per year? Per decade? Per lifetime? Income in the form of money alone? Or including such nonmonetary items as the rental value of an owned home; food grown for one's own use; services rendered by members of the family not employed for money, notably the housewife? How are physical and mental handicaps or advantages to be allowed for?

However you decide these issues, you can, if you are an egalitarian, estimate what money income would correspond to your concept of equality. If your actual income is higher than that, you can keep that amount and distribute the rest to people who are below that level. If your criterion were to encompass the world—as most egalitarian rhetoric suggests it should—something less than, say, $200 a year (in 1979 dollars) per person would be an amount that would correspond to the conception of equality that seems implicit in most egalitarian rhetoric. That is about the average income per person worldwide.

What Irving Kristol has called the "new class"—government bureaucrats, academics whose research is supported by government funds or who are employed in government financed "think-tanks," staffs of the many so-called "general interest" or "public policy" groups, journalists and others in the communications industry—are among the most ardent preachers of the doctrine of equality. Yet they remind us very much of the old, if unfair, saw about the Quakers: "They came to the New World to do good, and ended up doing well." The members of the new class are in general among the highest paid persons in the community. And for many among them, preaching equality and promoting or administering the resulting legislation has proved an effective means of achieving such high incomes. All of us find it easy to identify our own welfare with the welfare of the community.

Of course, an egalitarian may protest that he is but a drop in the ocean, that he would be willing to redistribute the excess of his income over his concept of an equal income if everyone else were compelled to do the same. On one level this contention that compulsion would change matters is wrong—even if everyone else did the same, his specific contribution to the income of others would still be a drop in the ocean. His individual contribution would be just as large if he were the only contributor as if he were one of many. Indeed, it would be more valuable because he could target his contribution to go to the very worst off among those he regards as appropriate recipients. On another level compulsion would change matters drastically: the kind of society that would emerge if such acts of redistribution were voluntary is altogether different—and, by our standards, infinitely preferable—to the kind that would emerge if redistribution were compulsory.

Persons who believe that a society of enforced equality is preferable can also practice what they preach. They can join one of the many communes in this country and elsewhere, or establish new ones. And, of course, it is entirely consistent with a belief in personal equality or equality of opportunity and liberty that any group of individuals who wish to live in that way should be free to do so. Our thesis that support for equality of outcome is word-deep receives strong support from the small number of persons who have wished to join such communes and from the fragility of the communes that have been established.

Egalitarians in the United States may object that the fewness of communes and their fragility reflect the opprobrium that a predominantly "capitalist" society visits on such communes and the resulting discrimination to which they are subjected. That may be true for the United States but as Robert Nozick has pointed out, there is one country where that is not true, where, on the contrary, egalitarian communes are highly regarded and prized. That country is Israel. The kibbutz played a major role in early Jewish settlement in Palestine and continues to play an important role in the state of Israel. A disproportionate fraction of the leaders of the Israeli state were drawn from the kibbutzim. Far from being a source of disapproval, membership in a kibbutz confers social status and commands approbation. Everyone is free to join or leave a kibbutz, and kibbutzim have been viable social organizations. Yet at no time, and certainly not today, have more than about 5 percent of the Jewish population of Israel chosen to be members of a kibbutz. That percentage can be regarded as an upper estimate of the fraction of people who would voluntarily choose a system enforcing equality of outcome in preference to a system characterized by inequality, diversity, and opportunity.

Public attitudes about graduated income taxes are more mixed. Recent referenda on the introduction of graduated state income taxes in some states that do not have them, and on an increase in the extent of graduation in other states, have generally been defeated. On the other hand, the federal income tax is highly graduated, at least on paper, though it also contains a large number of provisions ("loopholes") that greatly reduce the extent of graduation in practice. On this showing, there is at least public tolerance of a moderate amount of redistributive taxation.

However, we venture to suggest that the popularity of Reno, Las Vegas, and now Atlantic City is no less faithful an indication of the preferences of the public than the federal income tax, the editorials in the *New York Times* and the *Washington Post*, and the pages of the *New York Review of Books*.

Consequences of Egalitarian Policies

In shaping our own policy, we can learn from the experience of Western countries with which we share a common intellectual and cultural background, and from which we derive many of our values. Perhaps the most instructive example is Great Britain, which led the way in the nineteenth century toward implementing equality of opportunity and in the twentieth toward implementing equality of outcome.

Since the end of World War II, British domestic policy has been dominated by the search for greater equality of outcome. Measure after measure has been adopted designed to take from the rich and give to the poor. Taxes were raised on income until they reached a top rate of 98 percent on property income and 83 percent on "earned" income, and were supplemented by ever heavier taxes on inheritances. State-provided medical, housing, and other welfare services were greatly expanded, along with payments to the unemployed and the aged. Unfortunately, the results have been very different from those that were intended by the people who were quite properly offended by the class structure that dominated Britain for centuries. There has been a vast redistribution of wealth, but the end result is not an equitable distribution.

Instead, new classes of privileged have been created to replace or supplement the old: the bureaucrats, secure in their jobs, protected against inflation both when they work and when they retire; the trade unions that profess to represent the most downtrodden workers but in fact consist of the highest paid laborers in the land—the aristocrats of the labor movement; and the new millionaires—people who have been cleverest at

finding ways around the laws, the rules, the regulations that have poured from Parliament and the
bureaucracy, who have found ways to avoid paying taxes on their income and to get their wealth
overseas beyond the grasp of the tax collectors.
A vast reshuffling of income and wealth, yes;
greater equity, hardly.

The drive for equality in Britain failed, not
because the wrong measures were adopted—
though some no doubt were; not because they
were badly administered—though some no
doubt were; not because the wrong people
administered them—though no doubt some did.
The drive for equality failed for a much more
fundamental reason. It went against one of the
most basic instincts of all human beings. In the
words of Adam Smith, "The uniform, constant,
and uninterrupted effort of every man to better
his condition"—and, one may add, the condition
of his children and his children's children. Smith,
of course, meant by "condition" not merely
material well-being, though certainly that was
one component. He had a much broader concept
in mind, one that included all of the values
by which men judge their success—in particular
the kind of social values that gave rise to the outpouring of philanthropic activities in the
nineteenth century.

When the law interferes with people's pursuit of
their own values, they will try to find a way around.
They will evade the law, they will break the law, or
they will leave the country. Few of us believe in a
moral code that justifies forcing people to give up
much of what they produce to finance payments to
persons they do not know for purposes they may
not approve of. When the law contradicts what most
people regard as moral and proper, they will break
the law—whether the law is enacted in the name of
a noble ideal such as equality or in the naked interest of one group at the expense of another. Only fear
of punishment, not a sense of justice and morality,
will lead people to obey the law.

When people start to break one set of laws, the
lack of respect for the law inevitably spreads to all
laws, even those that everyone regards as moral
and proper—laws against violence, theft, and vandalism. Hard as it may be to believe, the growth of
crude criminality in Britain in recent decades
may well be one consequence of the drive for
equality.

In addition, that drive for equality has driven
out of Britain some of its ablest, best-trained, most
vigorous citizens, much to the benefit of the
United States and other countries that have given
them a greater opportunity to use their talents for
their own benefit. Finally, who can doubt the effect
that the drive for equality has had on efficiency and
productivity? Surely, that is one of the main reasons
why economic growth in Britain has fallen so far
behind its continental neighbors, the United States,
Japan, and other nations over the past few decades.

We in the United States have not gone as far
as Britain in promoting the goal of equality
of outcome. Yet many of the same consequences
are already evident—from a failure of egalitarian
measures to achieve their objectives, to a reshuffling of wealth that by no standards can be regarded as equitable, to a rise in criminality, to a
depressing effect on productivity and efficiency.

Capitalism and Equality

Everywhere in the world there are gross
inequities of income and wealth. They offend
most of us. Few can fail to be moved by the contrast between the luxury enjoyed by some and the
grinding poverty suffered by others.

In the past century a myth has grown up that
free market capitalism—equality of opportunity
as we have interpreted that term—increases such
inequalities, that it is a system under which the
rich exploit the poor.

Nothing could be further from the truth.
Wherever the free market has been permitted to
operate, wherever anything approaching equality
of opportunity has existed, the ordinary man has
been able to attain levels of living never dreamed
of before. Nowhere is the gap between rich and
poor wider, nowhere are the rich richer and the
poor poorer, than in those societies that do not
permit the free market to operate. That is true of
feudal societies like medieval Europe, India before
independence, and much of modern South
America, where inherited status determines
position. It is equally true of centrally planned
societies, like Russia or China or India since
independence, where access to government
determines position. It is true even where central
planning was introduced, as in all three of these
countries, in the name of equality.

Russia is a country of two nations: a small privileged upper class of bureaucrats, Communist party officials, technicians; and a great mass of people living little better than their great-grandparents did. The upper class has access to special shops, schools, and luxuries of all kind; the masses are condemned to enjoy little more than the basic necessities. We remember asking a tourist guide in Moscow the cost of a large automobile that we saw and being told, "Oh, those aren't for sale; they're only for the Politburo." Several recent books by American journalists document in great detail the contrast between the privileged life of the upper classes and the poverty of the masses. Even on a simpler level, it is noteworthy that the average wage of a foreman is a larger multiple of the average wage of an ordinary worker in a Russian factory than in a factory in the United States—and no doubt he deserves it. After all, an American foreman only has to worry about being fired; a Russian foreman also has to worry about being shot.

China, too, is a nation with wide differences in income—between the politically powerful and the rest; between city and countryside; between some workers in the cities and other workers. A perceptive student of China writes that "the inequality between rich and poor regions in China was more acute in 1957 than in any of the larger nations of the world except perhaps Brazil." He quotes another scholar as saying, "These examples suggest that the Chinese industrial wage structure is not significantly more egalitarian than that of other countries." And he concludes his examination of equality in China, "How evenly distributed would China's income be today? Certainly, it would not be as even as Taiwan's or South Korea's. . . . On the other hand, income distribution in China is obviously more even than in Brazil or South America. . . . We must conclude that China is far from being a society of complete equality. In fact, income differences in China may be quite a bit greater than in a number of countries commonly associated with `fascist' elites and exploited masses."

Industrial progress, mechanical improvement, all of the great wonders of the modern era have meant relatively little to the wealthy. The rich in Ancient Greece would have benefited hardly at all from modern plumbing: running servants replaced running water. Television and radio—the patricians of Rome could enjoy the leading musicians and actors in their home, could have the leading artists as domestic retainers. Ready-to-wear clothing, supermarkets—all these and many other modern developments would have added little to their life. They would have welcomed the improvements in transportation and in medicine, but for the rest, the great achievements of Western capitalism have redounded primarily to the benefit of the ordinary person. These achievements have made available to the masses conveniences and amenities that were previously the exclusive prerogative of the rich and powerful.

In 1848 John Stuart Mill wrote: "Hitherto it is questionable if all the mechanical inventions yet made have lightened the day's toil of any human being. They have enabled a greater population to live the same life of drudgery and imprisonment, and an increased number of manufacturers and others to make fortunes. They have increased the comforts of the middle classes. But they have not yet begun to effect those great changes in human destiny, which it is in their nature and in their futurity to accomplish."

No one could say that today. You can travel from one end of the industrialized world to the other and almost the only people you will find engaging in backbreaking toil are people who are doing it for sport. To find people whose day's toil has not been lightened by mechanical invention, you must go to the noncapitalist world: to Russia, China, India or Bangladesh, parts of Yugoslavia; or to the more backward capitalist countries—in Africa, the Mideast, South America; and until recently, Spain or Italy.

Conclusion

A society that puts equality—in the sense of equality of outcome—ahead of freedom will end up with neither equality nor freedom. The use of force to achieve equality will destroy freedom, and the force, introduced for good purposes, will end up in the hands of people who use it to promote their own interests.

On the other hand, a society that puts freedom first will, as a happy by-product, end up with both greater freedom and greater equality. Though a by-product of freedom, greater equality is not an accident. A free society releases the energies and abilities of people to pursue their own objectives. It prevents some people from arbitrarily suppressing others. It does not prevent some people from achieving positions of privilege, but so long as freedom is maintained, it prevents those positions of privilege from becoming institutionalized; they are subject to continued attack by other able, ambitious people. Freedom means diversity but also mobility. It preserves the opportunity for today's disadvantaged to become tomorrow's privileged and, in the process, enables almost everyone, from top to bottom, to enjoy a fuller and richer life.

ANARCHY, STATE, AND UTOPIA

Robert Nozick

Distributive Justice

The minimal state is the most extensive state that can be justified. Any state more extensive violates people's rights. Yet many persons have put forth reasons purporting to justify a more extensive state. It is impossible within the compass of this book to examine all the reasons that have been put forth. Therefore, I shall focus upon those generally acknowledged to be most weighty and influential, to see precisely wherein they fail. In this chapter we consider the claim that a more extensive state is justified, because necessary (or the best instrument) to achieve distributive justice; in the next chapter we shall take up diverse other claims.

The term "distributive justice" is not a neutral one. Hearing the term "distribution," most people presume that some thing or mechanism uses some principle or criterion to give out a supply of things. Into this process of distributing shares some error may have crept. So it is an open question, at least, whether *redistribution* should take place; whether we should do again what has already been done once, though poorly. However, we are not in the position of children who have been given portions of pie by someone who now makes last minute adjustments to rectify careless cutting. There is no *central* distribution, no person or group entitled to control all the resources, jointly deciding how they are to be doled out. What each person gets, he gets from others who give to him in exchange for something, or as a gift. In a free society, diverse persons control different resources, and new holdings arise out of the voluntary exchanges and actions of persons. There is no more a distributing or distribution of shares than there is a distributing of mates in a society in which persons choose whom they shall marry. The total result is the product of many individual decisions which the different individuals involved are entitled to make. Some uses of the term "distribution," it is true, do not imply a previous distributing appropriately judged by some criterion (for example, "probability distribution"); nevertheless, despite the title of this chapter, it would be best to use a terminology that clearly is neutral. We shall speak of people's holdings; a principle of justice in holdings describes (part of) what justice tells us (requires) about holdings. I shall state first what I take to be the correct view about justice in holdings, and then turn to the discussion of alternate views.

Section I. The Entitlement Theory

The subject of justice in holdings consists of three major topics. The first is the *original acquisition of holdings*, the appropriation of unheld things. This includes the issues of how unheld things may come to be held, the process, or processes, by which unheld things may come to be held, the things that may come to be held by these processes, the extent of what comes to be held by a particular process, and so on. We shall refer to the complicated truth about this topic, which we shall not formulate here, as the principle of justice in acquisition. The second topic concerns the *transfer of holdings* from one person to another. By what processes may a person transfer holdings to another? How may a person acquire a holding from another who holds it? Under this topic come general descriptions of voluntary exchange, and gift and (on the other hand) fraud, as well as reference to particular conventional details fixed upon in a given society. The complicated truth about this subject (with placeholders for conventional details) we shall call the principle of justice in transfer. (And we shall suppose it also includes principles governing how a person may divest himself of a holding, passing it into an unheld state.)

If the world were wholly just, the following inductive definition would exhaustively cover the subject of justice in holdings.

1. A person who acquires a holding in accordance with the principle of justice in acquisition is entitled to that holding.
2. A person who acquires a holding in accordance with the principle of justice in transfer, from someone else entitled to the holding, is entitled to the holding.
3. No one is entitled to a holding except by (repeated) applications of 1 and 2.

The complete principle of distributive justice would say simply that a distribution is just if everyone is entitled to the holdings they possess under the distribution.

A distribution is just if it arises from another just distribution by legitimate means. The legitimate means of moving from one distribution to another are specified by the principle of justice in transfer. The legitimate first "moves" are specified by the principle of justice in acquisition.[1] Whatever arises from a just situation by just steps is itself just. The means of change specified by the principle of justice in transfer preserve justice. As correct rules of inference are truth-preserving, and any conclusion deduced via repeated application of such rules from only true premises is itself true, so the means of transition from one situation to another specified by the principle of justice in transfer are justice-preserving, and any situation actually arising from repeated transitions in accor-

dance with the principle from a just situation is itself just. The parallel between justice-preserving transformations and truth-preserving transformations illuminates where it fails as well as where it holds. That a conclusion could have been deduced by truth-preserving means from premises that are true suffices to show its truth. That from a just situation a situation *could* have arisen via justice-preserving means does *not* suffice to show its justice. The fact that a thief's victims voluntarily *could* have presented him with gifts does not entitle the thief to his ill-gotten gains. Justice in holdings is historical; it depends upon what actually has happened. We shall return to this point later.

Not all actual situations are generated in accordance with the two principles of justice in holdings: the principle of justice in acquisition and the principle of justice in transfer. Some people steal from others, or defraud them, or enslave them, seizing their product and preventing them from living as they choose, or forcibly exclude others from competing in exchanges. None of these are permissible modes of transition from one situation to another. And some persons acquire holdings by means not sanctioned by the principle of justice in acquisition. The existence of past injustice (previous violations of the first two principles of justice in holdings) raises the third major topic under justice in holdings: the rectification of injustice in holdings. If past injustice has shaped present holdings in various ways, some identifiable and some not, what now, if anything, ought to be done to rectify these injustices? What obligations do the performers of injustice have toward those whose position is worse than it would have been had the injustice not been done? Or, than it would have been had compensation been paid promptly? How, if at all, do things change if the beneficiaries and those made worse off are not the direct parties in the act of injustice, but, for example, their descendants? Is an injustice done to someone whose holding was itself based upon an unrectified injustice? How far back must one go in wiping clean the historical slate of injustices? What may victims of injustice permissibly do in order to rectify the injustices being done to them, including the many injustices done by persons acting through their government? I do not know of a thorough or theoretically sophisticated treatment of such

---

1. Applications of the principle of justice in acquisition may also occur as part of the move from one distribution to another. You may find an unheld thing now and appropriate it. Acquisitions also are to be understood as included when, to simplify, I speak only of transitions by transfers.

issues. Idealizing greatly, let us suppose theoretical investigation will produce a principle of rectification. This principle uses historical information about previous situations and injustices done in them (as defined by the first two principles of justice and rights against interference), and information about the actual course of events that flowed from these injustices, until the present, and it yields a description (or descriptions) of holdings in the society. The principle of rectification presumably will make use of its best estimate of subjunctive information about what would have occurred (or a probability distribution over what might have occurred, using the expected value) if the injustice had not taken place. If the actual description of holdings turns out not to be one of the descriptions yielded by the principle, then one of the descriptions yielded must be realized.[2]

The general outlines of the theory of justice in holdings are that the holdings of a person are just if he is entitled to them by the principles of justice in acquisition and transfer, or by the principle of rectification of injustice (as specified by the first two principles). If each person's holdings are just, then the total set (distribution) of holdings is just. To turn these general outlines into a specific theory we would have to specify the details of each of the three principles of justice in holdings: the principle of acquisition of holdings, the principle of transfer of holdings, and the principle of rectification of violations of the first two principles. I shall not attempt that task here. (Locke's principle of justice in acquisition is discussed below.)

Historical Principles and End-Result Principles

The general outlines of the entitlement theory illuminate the nature and defects of other conceptions of distributive justice. The entitle-

ment theory of justice in distribution is *historical;* whether a distribution is just depends upon how it came about. In contrast, *current time-slice principles* of justice hold that the justice of a distribution is determined by how things are distributed (who has what) as judged by some *structural* principle(s) of just distribution. A utilitarian who judges between any two distributions by seeing which has the greater sum of utility and, if the sums tie, applies some fixed equality criterion to choose the more equal distribution, would hold a current time-slice principle of justice. As would someone who had a fixed schedule of trade-offs between the sum of happiness and equality. According to a current time-slice principle, all that needs to be looked at, in judging the justice of a distribution, is who ends up with what; in comparing any two distributions one need look only at the matrix presenting the distributions. No further information need be fed into a principle of justice. It is a consequence of such principles of justice that any two structurally identical distributions are equally just. (Two distributions are structurally identical if they present the same profile, but perhaps have different persons occupying the particular slots. My having ten and your having five, and my having five and your having ten are structurally identical distributions.) Welfare economics is the theory of current time-slice principles of justice. The subject is conceived as operating on matrices representing only current information about distribution. This, as well as some of the usual conditions (for example, the choice of distribution is invariant under relabeling of columns), guarantees that welfare economics will be a current time-slice theory, with all of its inadequacies.

Most persons do not accept current time-slice principles as constituting the whole story about distributive shares. They think it relevant in assessing the justice of a situation to consider not only the distribution it embodies, but also how that distribution came about. If some persons are in prison for murder or war crimes, we do not say that to assess the justice of the distribution in the society we must look only at what this person has, and that person has, and that person has, . . . at the current time. We think it relevant to ask whether someone did something so that he

2. If the principle of rectification of violations of the first two principles yields more than one description of holdings, then some choice must be made as to which of these is to be realized. Perhaps the sort of considerations about distributive justice and equality that I argue against play a legitimate role in *this* subsidiary choice. Similarly, there may be room for such considerations in deciding which otherwise arbitrary features a statute will embody, when such features are unavoidable because other considerations do not specify a precise line; yet a line must be drawn.

deserved to be punished, deserved to have a lower share. Most will agree to the relevance of further information with regard to punishments and penalties. Consider also desired things. One traditional socialist view is that workers are entitled to the product and full fruits of their labor; they have earned it; a distribution is unjust if it does not give the workers what they are entitled to. Such entitlements are based upon some past history. No socialist holding this view would find it comforting to be told that because the actual distribution *A* happens to coincide structurally with the one he desires *D*, *A* therefore is no less just than *D*: it differs only in that the "parasitic" owners of capital receive under *A* what the workers are entitled to under *D*, and the workers receive under *A* what the owners are entitled to under *D*, namely very little. This socialist rightly, in my view, holds onto the notions of earning, producing, entitlement, desert, and so forth, and he rejects current time-slice principles that look only to the structure of the resulting set of holdings. (The set of holdings resulting from what? Isn't it implausible that how holdings are produced and come to exist has no effect at all on who should hold what?) His mistake lies in his view of what entitlements arise out of what sorts of productive processes.

We construe the position we discuss too narrowly by speaking of *current* time-slice principles. Nothing is changed if structural principles operate upon a time sequence of current time-slice profiles and, for example, give someone more now to counterbalance the less he has had earlier. A utilitarian or an egalitarian or any mixture of the two over time will inherit the difficulties of his more myopic comrades. He is not helped by the fact that *some* of the information others consider relevant in assessing a distribution is reflected, unrecoverably, in past matrices. Henceforth, we shall refer to such unhistorical principles of distributive justice, including the current time-slice principles, as *end-result principles* or *end-state principles*.

In contrast to end-result principles of justice, *historical principles* of justice hold that past circumstances or actions of people can create differential entitlements or differential deserts to things. An injustice can be worked by moving from one distribution to another structurally identical one, for the second, in profile the same, may violate people's entitlements or deserts; it may not fit the actual history.

Patterning

The entitlement principles of justice in holdings that we have sketched are historical principles of justice. To better understand their precise character, we shall distinguish them from another subclass of the historical principles. Consider, as an example, the principle of distribution according to moral merit. This principle requires that total distributive shares vary directly with moral merit; no person should have a greater share than anyone whose moral merit is greater. (If moral merit could be not merely ordered but measured on an interval or ratio scale, stronger principles could be formulated.) Or consider the principle that results by substituting "usefulness to society" for "moral meric" in the previous principle. Or instead of "distribute according to moral merit," or "distribute according to usefulness to society," we might consider "distribute according to the weighted sum of moral merit, usefulness to society, and need," with the weights of the different dimensions equal. Let us call a principle of distribution *patterned* if it specifies that a distribution is to vary along with some natural dimension, weighted sum of natural dimensions, or lexicographic ordering of natural dimensions. And let us say a distribution is patterned if it accords with some patterned principle. (I speak of natural dimensions, admittedly without a general criterion for them, because for any set of holdings some artificial dimensions can be gimmicked up to vary along with the distribution of the set.) The principle of distribution in accordance with moral merit is a patterned historical principle, which specifies a patterned distribution. "Distribute according to I.Q." is a patterned principle that looks to information not contained in distributional matrices. It is not historical, however, in that it does not look to any past actions creating differential entitlements to evaluate a distribution; it requires only distributional matrices whose columns are labeled by I.Q. scores. The distribution in a society, however, may be composed of such simple patterned distributions, without itself being simply patterned. Different sectors may operate different patterns, or some combination of patterns may operate in different proportions across a society. A distribution composed in this manner, from a small number of patterned distributions, we also shall term "patterned." And we extend the use of "pattern" to include the overall designs put forth by combinations of end-state principles.

Almost every suggested principle of distributive justice is patterned: to each according to his moral merit, or needs, or marginal product, or how hard he tries, or the weighted sum of the foregoing, and so on. The principle of entitlement we have sketched is *not* patterned.[3] There is no one natural dimension or weighted sum or combination of a small number of natural dimensions that yields the distributions generated in accordance with the principle of entitlement. The set of holdings that results when some persons receive their marginal products, others win at gambling, others receive a share of their mate's income, others receive gifts from foundations, others receive interest on loans, other receive gifts from admirers, others receive returns on investment, others make for themselves much of what they have, others find things, and so on, will not be patterned. Heavy strands of patterns will run through it; significant portions of the variance in holdings will be accounted for by pattern-variables. If most people most of the time choose to transfer some of their entitlements to others only in exchange for something from them, then a large part of what many people hold will vary with what they held that others wanted. More details are

provided by the theory of marginal productivity. But gifts to relatives, charitable donations, bequests to children, and the like, are not best conceived, in the first instance, in this manner. Ignoring the strands of pattern, let us suppose for the moment that a distribution actually arrived at by the operation of the principle of entitlement is random with respect to any pattern. Though the resulting set of holdings will be unpatterned, it will not be incomprehensible, for it can be seen as arising from the operation of a small number of principles. These principles specify how an initial distribution may arise (the principle of acquisition of holdings) and how distributions may be transformed into others (the principle of transfer of holdings). The process whereby the set of holdings is generated will be intelligible, though the set of holdings itself that results from this process will be unpatterned.

The writings of F. A. Hayek focus less than is usually done upon what patterning distributive justice requires. Hayek argues that we cannot know enough about each person's situation to distribute to each according to his moral merit (but would justice demand we do so if we did have this knowledge?); and he goes on to say, "our objection is against all attempts to impress upon society a deliberately chosen pattern of distribution, whether it be an order of equality or of inequality." However, Hayek concludes that in a free society there will be distribution in accordance with value rather than moral merit; that is, in accordance with the perceived value of a person's actions and services to others. Despite his rejection of a patterned conception of distributive justice, Hayek himself suggests a pattern he thinks justifiable: distribution in accordance with the perceived benefits given to others, leaving room for the complaint that a free society does not realize exactly this pattern. Stating this patterned strand of a free capitalist society more precisely, we get "To each according to how much he benefits others who have the resources for benefiting those who benefit them." This will seem arbitrary unless some acceptable initial set of holdings is specified, or unless it is held that the operation of the system over time washes out any significant effects from the initial set of holdings. As an example of the latter, if almost anyone would have bought a car from Henry Ford, the supposition that it was an arbitrary matter who held the money then (and so bought) would not place

3. One might try to squeeze a patterned conception of distributive justice into the framework of the entitlement conception, by formulating a gimmicky obligatory "principle of transfer" that would lead to the pattern. For example, the principle that if one has more than the mean income one must transfer everything one holds above the mean to persons below the mean so as to bring them up to (but not over) the mean. We can formulate a criterion for a "principle of transfer" to rule out such obligatory transfers, or we can say that no correct principle of transfer, no principle of transfer in a free society will be like this. The former is probably the better course, though the latter also is true.

Alternatively, one might think to make the entitlement conception instantiate a pattern, by using matrix entries that express the relative strength of a person's entitlements as measured by some real-valued function. But even if the limitation to natural dimensions failed to exclude this function, the resulting edifice would *not* capture our system of entitlements to *particular* things.

Henry Ford's earnings under a cloud. In any event, *his* coming to hold it is not arbitrary. Distribution according to benefits to others *is* a major patterned strand in a free capitalist society, as Hayek correctly points our, but it is only a strand and does not constitute the whole pattern of a system of entitlements (namely, inheritance, gifts for arbitrary reasons, charity, and so on) or a standard that one should insist a society fit. Will people tolerate for long a system yielding distributions that they believe are unpatterned? No doubt people will not long accept a distribution they believe is *unjust*. People want their society to be and to look just. But must the look of justice reside in a resulting pattern rather than in the underlying generating principles? We are in no position to conclude that the inhabitants of a society embodying an entitlement conception of justice in holdings will find it unacceptable. Still, it must be granted that were people's reasons for transferring some of their holdings to others always irrational or arbitrary, we would find this disturbing. (Suppose people always determined what holdings they would transfer, and to whom, by using a random device.) We feel more comfortable upholding the justice of an entitlement system if most of the transfers under it are done for reasons. This does not mean necessarily that all deserve what holdings they receive. It means only that there is a purpose or point to someone's transferring a holding to one person rather than to another; that usually we can see what the transferrer thinks he's gaining, what cause he thinks he's serving, what goals he thinks he's helping to achieve, and so forth. Since in a capitalist society people often transfer holdings to others in accordance with how much they perceive these others benefiting them, the fabric constituted by the individual transactions and transfers is largely reasonable and intelligible.[4] (Gifts to loved ones, bequests to children, charity to the needy also are nonarbitrary components of the fabric.) In stressing the large strand of distribution in accordance with benefit to others, Hayek shows the point of

many transfers, and so shows that the system of transfer of entitlements is not just spinning its gears aimlessly. The system of entitlements is defensible when constituted by the individual aims of individual transactions. No overarching aim is needed, no distributional pattern is required.

To think that the task of a theory of distributive justice is to fill in the blank in "to each according to his ———" is to be predisposed to search for a pattern; and the separate treatment of "from each according to his ———" treats production and distribution as two separate and independent issues. On an entitlement view these are *not* two separate questions. Whoever makes something, having bought or contracted for all other held resources used in the process (transferring some of his holdings for these cooperating factors), is entitled to it. The situation is *not* one of something's getting made, and there being an open question of who is to get it. Things come into the world already attached to people having entitlements over them. From the point of view of the historical entitlement conception of justice in holdings, those who start afresh to complete "to each according to his ———" treat objects as if they appeared from nowhere, out of nothing. A complete theory of justice might cover this limit case as well; perhaps here is a use for the usual conceptions of distributive justice.

So entrenched are maxims of the usual form that perhaps we should present the entitlement conception as a competitor. Ignoring acquisition and rectification, we might say:

> From each according to what he chooses to do, to each according to what he makes for himself (perhaps with the contracted aid of others) and what others choose to do for him and choose to give him of what they've been given previously (under this maxim) and haven't yet expended or transferred.

This, the discerning reader will have noticed, has its defects as a slogan. So as a summary and great

4. We certainly benefit because great economic incentives operate to get others to spend much time and energy to figure out how to serve us by providing things we will want to pay for. It is not mere paradox mongering to wonder whether capitalism should be criticized for most rewarding and hence encouraging, not individualists like Thoreau who go about their own lives, but

people who are occupied with serving others and winning them as customers. But to defend capitalism one need not think businessmen are the finest human types. (I do not mean to join here the general maligning of businessmen, either.) Those who think the finest should acquire the most can try to convince their fellows to transfer resources in accordance with *that* principle.

simplification (and not as a maxim with any independent meaning) we have:

From each as they choose, to each as they are chosen.

How Liberty Upsets Patterns

It is not clear how those holding alternative conceptions of distributive justice can reject the entitlement conception of justice in holdings. For suppose a distribution favored by one of these nonentitlement conceptions is realized. Let us suppose it is your favorite one and let us call this distribution D_1; perhaps everyone has an equal share, perhaps shares vary in accordance with some dimension you treasure. Now suppose that Wilt Chamberlain is greatly in demand by basketball teams, being a great gate attraction. (Also suppose contracts run only for a year, with players being free agents.) He signs the following sort of contract with a team: In each home game, twenty-five cents from the price of each ticket of admission goes to him. (We ignore the question of whether he is "gouging" the owners, letting them look out for themselves.) The season starts, and people cheerfully attend his team's games; they buy their tickets, each time dropping a separate twenty-five cents of their admission price into a special box with Chamberlain's name on it. They are excited about seeing him play; it is worth the total admission price to them. Let us suppose that in one season one million persons attend his home games, and Wilt Chamberlain winds up with $250,000, a much larger sum than the average income and larger even than anyone else has. Is he entitled to this income? Is this new distribution D_2, unjust? If so, why? There is *no* question about whether each of the people was entitled to the control over the resources they held in D_1; because that was the distribution (your favorite) that (for the purposes of argument) we assumed was acceptable. Each of these persons *chose* to give twenty-five cents of their money to Chamberlain. They could have spent it on going to the movies, or on candy bars, or on copies of *Dissent* magazine, or of *Montly Review*. But they all, at least one million of them, converged on giving it to Wilt Chamberlain in exchange for watching him play basketball. If D_1 was a just distribution, and people voluntarily moved from it to D_2, transferring parts of their shares they were given under D_1 (what was it for if not to do something with?), isn't D_2 also just? If the people were entitled to dispose of the resources to which they were entitled (under D_1), didn't this include their being entitled to give it to, or exchange it with, Wilt Chamberlain? Can anyone else complain on grounds of justice? Each other person already has his legitimate share under D_1. Under D_1, there is nothing that anyone has that anyone else has a claim of justice against. After someone transfers something to Wilt Chamberlain, third parties *still* have their legitimate shares; *their* shares are not changed. By what process could such a transfer among two persons give rise to a legitimate claim of distributive justice on a portion of what was transferred, by a third party who had no claim of justice on any holding of the others *before* the transfer?[5] To cut off objections irrelevant here, we might imagine the exchanges occurring in a socialist society, after hours. After playing whatever basketball he does in his daily work, or doing whatever other daily work he does, Wilt Chamberlain decides to put in *overtime* to earn additional money. (First his work quota is set; he works time over that.) Or imagine it is a skilled juggler people like to see, who puts on shows after hours.

Why might someone work overtime in a society in which it is assumed their needs are satisfied? Perhaps because they care about things

5. Might not a transfer have instrumental effects on a third party, changing his feasible options? (But what if the two parties to the transfer independently had used their holdings in this fashion?) I discuss this question below, but note here that this question concedes the point for distributions of ultimate intrinsic noninstrumental goods (pure utility experiences, so to speak) that are transferrable. It also might be objected that the transfer might make a third party more envious because it worsens his position relative to someone else. I find it incomprehensible how this can be thought to involve a claim of justice. On envy, see Chapter 8.

Here and elsewhere in this chapter, a theory which incorporates elements of pure procedural justice might find what I say acceptable, *if* kept in its proper place; that is, if background institutions exist to ensure the satisfaction of certain conditions on distributive shares. But if these institutions are not themselves the sum or invisible-hand result of people's voluntary (nonaggressive) actions, the constraints they impose require justification. At no point does *our* argument assume any background institutions more extensive than those of the minimal night-watchman state, a state limited to protecting persons against murder, assault, theft, fraud, and so forth.

other than needs. I like to write in books that I read, and to have easy access to books for browsing at odd hours. It would be very pleasant and convenient to have the resources of Widener Library in my back yard. No society, I assume, will provide such resources close to each person who would like them as part of his regular allotment (under D_1). Thus, persons either must do without some extra things that they want, or be allowed to do something extra to get some of these things. On what basis could the inequalities that would eventuate be forbidden? Notice also that small factories would spring up in a socialist society, unless forbidden. I melt down some of my personal possessions (under D_1) and build a machine out of the material. I offer you, and others, a philosophy lecture once a week in exchange for your cranking the handle on my machine, whose products I exchange for yet other things, and so on. (The raw materials used by the machine are given to me by others who possess them under D_1, in exchange for hearing lectures.) Each person might participate to gain things over and above their allotment under D_1. Some persons even might want to leave their job in socialist industry and work full time in this private sector. I shall say something more about these issues in the next chapter. Here I wish merely to note how private property even in means of production would occur in a socialist society that did not forbid people to use as they wished some of the resources they are given under the socialist distribution D_1. The socialist society would have to forbid capitalist acts between consenting adults.

The general point illustrated by the Wilt Chamberlain example and the example of the entrepreneur in a socialist society is that no end-state principle or distributional patterned principle of justice can be continuously realized without continuous interference with people's lives. Any favored pattern would be transformed into one unfavored by the principle, by people choosing to act in various ways; for example, by people exchanging goods and services with other people, or giving things to other people, things the transferrers are entitled to under the favored distributional pattern. To maintain a pattern one must either continually interfere to stop people from transferring resources as they wish to, or continually (or periodically) interfere to take from

some persons resources that others for some reason chose to transfer to them. (But if some time limit is to be set on how long people may keep resources others voluntarily transfer to them, why let them keep these resources for *any* period of time? Why not have immediate confiscation?) It might be objected that all persons voluntarily will choose to refrain from actions which would upset the pattern. This presupposes unrealistically (1) that all will most want to maintain the pattern (are those who don't, to be "reeducated" or forced to undergo "self-criticism"?), (2) that each can gather enough information about his own actions and the ongoing activities of others to discover which of his actions will upset the pattern, and (3) that diverse and far-flung persons can coordinate their actions to dovetail into the pattern. Compare the manner in which the market is neutral among persons' desires, as it reflects and transmits widely scattered information via prices, and coordinates persons' activities.

It puts things perhaps a bit too strongly to say that every patterned (or end-state) principle is liable to be thwarted by the voluntary actions of the individual parties transferring some of their shares they receive under the principle. For perhaps some *very* weak patterns are not so thwarted. Any distributional pattern with any egalitarian component is overturnable by the voluntary actions of individual persons over time; as is every patterned condition with sufficient content so as actually to have been proposed as presenting the central core of distributive justice. Still, given the possibility that some weak conditions or patterns may not be unstable in this way, it would be better to formulate an explicit description of the kind of interesting and contentful patterns under discussion, and to prove a theorem about their instability. Since the weaker the patterning, the more likely it is that the entitlement system itself satisfies it, a plausible conjecture is that any patterning either is unstable or is satisfied by the entitlement system.

Redistribution and Property Rights

Apparently, patterned principles allow people to choose to expend upon themselves, but not upon others, those resources they are entitled to (or rather, receive) under some favored distributional pattern D_1. For if each of several persons chooses to expend some of his D_1 resources upon one other person, then that other person will receive more than his D_1 share, disturbing the favored distributional pattern. Maintaining a distributional pattern is individualism with a vengeance! Patterned distributional principles do not give people what entitlement principles do, only better distributed. For they do not give the right to choose what to do with what one has; they do not give the right to choose to pursue an end involving (intrinsically, or as a means) the enhancement of another's position. To such views, families are disturbing; for within a family occur transfers that upset the favored distributional pattern. Either families themselves become units to which distribution takes place, the column occupiers (on what rationale?), or loving behavior is forbidden. We should note in passing the ambivalent position of radicals toward the family. Its loving relationships are seen as a model to be emulated and extended across the whole society, at the same time that it is denounced as a suffocating institution to be broken and condemned as a focus of parochial concerns that interfere with achieving radical goals. Need we say that it is not appropriate to enforce across the wider society the relationships of love and care appropriate within a family, relationships which are voluntarily undertaken?[6] Incidentally, love is an interesting instance of another relationship that is historical, in that (like justice) it depends upon what actually occurred. An adult may come to love another because of the other's characteristics; but it is the other person, and not the characteristics, that is loved. The love is not transferrable to someone else with the same characteristics, even to one who "scores" higher for these characteristics. And the

love endures through changes of the characteristics that gave rise to it. One loves the particular person one actually encountered. Why love is historical, attaching to persons in this way and not to characteristics, is an interesting and puzzling question.

Proponents of patterned principles of distributive justice focus upon criteria for determining who is to receive holdings; they consider the reasons for which someone should have something, and also the total picture of holdings. Whether or not it is better to give than to receive, proponents of patterned principles ignore giving altogether. In considering the distribution of goods, income, and so forth, their theories are theories of recipient justice; they completely ignore any right a person might have to give something to someone. Even in exchanges where each party is simultaneously giver and recipient, patterned principles of justice focus only upon the recipient role and its supposed rights. Thus discussions tend to focus on whether people (should) have a right to inherit, rather than on whether people (should) have a right to bequeath or on whether persons who have a right to hold also have a right to choose that others hold in their place. I lack a good explanation of why the usual theories of distributive justice are so recipient oriented; ignoring givers and transferrers and their rights is of a piece with ignoring producers and their entitlements. But why is it *all* ignored?

Patterned principles of distributive justice necessitate *re*distributive activities. The likelihood is small that any actual freely-arrived-at set of holdings fits a given pattern; and the likelihood is nil that it will continue to fit the pattern as people exchange and give. From the point of view of an entitlement theory, redistribution is a serious matter indeed, involving, as it does, the violation of people's rights. (An exception is those takings that fall under the principle of the rectification of injustices.) From other points of view, also, it is serious.

Taxation of earnings from labor is on a par with forced labor.[7] Some persons find this claim obviously true: taking the earnings of n hours labor is like taking n hours from the person; it is like forcing the person to work n hours for

---

6. One indication of the stringency of Rawls' difference principle, which we attend to in the second part of this chapter, is its inappropriateness as a governing principle even within a family of individuals who love one another. Should a family devote its resources to maximizing the position of its least well off and least talented child, holding back the other children or using resources for their education and development only if they will follow a policy through their lifetimes of maximizing the position of their least fortunate sibling? Surely not. How then can this even be considered as the appropriate policy for enforcement in the wider society? (I discuss below what I think would be Rawls' reply: that some principles apply at the macro level which do not apply to microsituations.)

7. I am unsure as to whether the arguments I present below show that such taxation merely *is* forced labor; so that "is on a par with" means "is one kind of," Of alternatively, whether the arguments emphasize the great

another's purpose. Others find the claim absurd. But even these, *if* they object to forced labor, would oppose forcing unemployed hippies to work for the benefit of the needy.[8] And they would also object to forcing each person to work five extra hours each week for the benefit of the needy. But a system that takes five hours' wages in taxes does not seem to them like one that forces someone to work five hours, since it offers the person forced a wider range of choice in activities than does taxation in kind with the particular labor specified. (But we can imagine a gradation of systems of forced labor, from one that specifies a particular activity, to one that gives a choice among two activities, to . . .; and so on up.) Furthermore, people envisage a system with something like a proportional tax on everything above the amount necessary for basic needs. Some think this does not force someone to work extra hours, since there is no fixed number of extra hours he is forced to work, and since he can avoid the tax entirely by earning only enough to cover his basic needs. This is a very uncharacteristic view of forcing for those who *also* think people are forced to do something *whenever* the alternatives they face are considerably worse. However, *neither* view is correct. The fact that others intentionally intervene, in violation of a side constraint against aggression, to threaten force to limit the alternatives, in this case to paying taxes or (presumably the worse alternative) bare subsistence, makes the taxation system one of forced labor and distinguishes it from other cases of limited choices which are not forcings.

The man who chooses to work longer to gain an income more than sufficient for his basic needs prefers some extra goods or services to the leisure and activities he could perform during the possible nonworking hours; whereas the man who chooses not to work the extra time prefers the

leisure activities to the extra goods or services he could acquire by working more. Given this, if it would be illegitimate for a tax system to seize some of a man's leisure (forced labor) for the purpose of serving the needy, how can it be legitimate for a tax system to seize some of a man's goods for that purpose? Why should we treat the man whose happiness requires certain material goods or services differently from the man whose preferences and desires make such goods unnecessary for his happiness? Why should the man who prefers seeing a movie (and who has to earn money for a ticket) be open to the required call to aid the needy, while the person who prefers looking at a sunset (and hence need earn no extra money) is not? Indeed, isn't it surprising that redistributionists choose to ignore the man whose pleasures are so easily attainable without extra labor, while adding yet another burden to the poor unfortunate who must work for his pleasures? If anything, one would have expected the reverse. Why is the person with the nonmaterial or nonconsumption desire allowed to proceed unimpeded to his most favored feasible alternative, whereas the man whose pleasures or desires involve material things and who must work for extra money (thereby serving whomever considers his activities valuable enough to pay him) is constrained in what he can realize? Perhaps there is no difference in principle. And perhaps some think the answer concerns merely administrative convenience. (These questions and issues will not disturb those who think that forced labor to serve the needy or to realize some favored end-state pattern is acceptable.) In a fuller discussion we would have (and want) to extend our argument to include interest, entrepreneurial profits, and so on. Those who doubt that this extension can be carried through, and who draw the line here at taxation of income from labor, will have to state rather complicated patterned *historical* principles of distributive justice, since end-state principles would not distinguish *sources* of income in any way. It is enough for now to get away from end-state principles and to make clear how various patterned principles are dependent upon particular views about the sources or the illegitimacy or the lesser legitimacy of profits, interest, and so on; which particular views may well be mistaken.

What sort of right over others does a legally institutionalized end-state pattern give one? The

similarities between such taxation and forced labor, to show it is plausible and illuminating to view such taxation in the light of forced labor. This latter approach would remind one of how John Wisdom conceives of the claims of metaphysicians.

8. Nothing hangs on the fact that here and elsewhere I speak loosely of *needs*, since I go on, each time, to reject the criterion of justice which includes it. If, however, something did depend upon the notion, one would want to examine it more carefully. For a skeptical view, see Kenneth Minogue. *The Liberal Mind*, (New York: Random House, 1963), pp. 103–112.

central core of the notion of a property right in X, relative to which other parts of the notion are to be explained, is the right to determine what shall be done with X; the right to choose which of the constrained set of options concerning X shall be realized or attempted. The constraints are set by other principles or laws operating in the society; in our theory, by the Lockean rights people possess (under the minimal state). My property rights in my knife allow me to leave it where I will, but not in your chest. I may choose which of the acceptable options involving the knife is to be realized. This notion of property helps us to understand why earlier theorists spoke of people as having property in themselves and their labor. They viewed each person as having a right to decide what would become of himself and what he would do, and as having a right to reap the benefits of what he did.

This right of selecting the alternative to be realized from the constrained set of alternatives may be held by an *individual* or by a *group* with some procedure for reaching a joint decision; or the right may be passed back and forth, so that one year I decide what's to become of X, and the next year you do (with the alternative of destruction, perhaps, being excluded). Or, during the same time period, some types of decisions about X may be made by me, and others by you. And so on. We lack an adequate, fruitful, analytical apparatus for classifying the *types* of constraints on the set of options among which choices are to be made, and the *types* of ways decision powers can be held, divided, and amalgamated. A *theory* of property would, among other things, contain such a classification of constraints and decision modes, and from a small number of principles would follow a host of interesting statements about the *consequences* and effects of certain combinations of constraints and modes of decision.

When end-result principles of distributive justice are built into the legal structure of a society, they (as do most patterned principles) give each citizen an enforceable claim to some portion of the total social product; that is, to some portion of the sum total of the individually and jointly made products. This total product is produced by individuals laboring, using means of production others have saved to bring into existence, by people organizing production or creating means to produce new things or things in a new way. It is on this batch of individual activities that patterned distributional principles give each individual an enforceable claim. Each person has a claim to the activities and the products of other persons, independently of whether the other persons enter into particular relationships that give rise to these claims, and independently of whether they voluntarily take these claims upon themselves, in charity or in exchange for something.

Whether it is done through taxation on wages or on wages over a certain amount, or through seizure of profits, or through there being a big *social pot* so that it's not clear what's coming from where and what's going where, patterned principles of distributive justice involve appropriating the actions of other persons. Seizing the results of someone's labor is equivalent to seizing hours from him and directing him to carry on various activities. If people force you to do certain work, or unrewarded work, for a certain period of time, they decide what you are to do and what purposes your work is to serve apart from your decisions. This process whereby they take this decision from you makes them a *part-owner* of you; it gives them a property right in you. Just as having such partial control and power of decision, by right, over an animal or inanimate object would be to have a property right in it.

End-state and most patterned principles of distributive justice institute (partial) ownership by others of people and their actions and labor. These principles involve a shift from the classical liberals; notion of self-ownership to a notion of (partial) property rights in *other* people.

Considerations such as these confront end-state and other patterned conceptions of justice with the question of whether the actions necessary to achieve the selected pattern don't themselves violate moral side constraints. Any view holding that there are moral side constraints on actions, that not all moral considerations can be built into end states that are to be achieved (see Chapter 3, pp. 28–30), must face the possibility that some of its goals are not achievable by any morally permissible available means. An entitlement theorist will face such conflicts in a society that deviates from the principles of justice for the generation of holdings, if and only if the only actions available to realize the principles themselves violate some moral constraints. Since deviation from the first two principles of justice (in acquisition and transfer) will involve other persons' direct and aggressive intervention to violate rights, and since moral constraints will not exclude defensive or retributive action in such cases, the entitlement theorist's problem rarely will be pressing. And whatever difficulties he has in applying the principle of rectification to persons who did not themselves violate the first two principles are difficulties in balancing the conflicting considerations so as correctly to formulate the complex principle of rectification itself; he will not violate moral side constraints by applying the principle. Proponents of patterned conceptions of justice, however, often will face head-on clashes (and poignant ones if they cherish each party to the clash) between moral side constraints on how individuals may be treated and their patterned conception of justice that presents an end state or other pattern that *must* be realized.

May a person emigrate from a nation that has institutionalized some end-state or patterned distributional principle? For some principles (for example, Hayek's) emigration presents no theoretical problem. But for others it is a tricky matter. Consider a nation having a compulsory scheme of minimal social provision to aid the neediest (or one organized so as to maximize the position of the worst-off group); no one may opt out of participating in it. (None may say, "Don't compel me to contribute to others and don't provide for me via this compulsory mechanism if I am in need.") Everyone above a certain level is forced to contribute to aid the needy. But if emigration from the country were allowed, anyone could choose to move to another country that did not have compulsory social provision but otherwise was (as much as possible) identical. In such a case, the person's *only* motive for leaving would be to avoid participating in the compulsory scheme of social provision. And if he does leave, the needy in his initial country will receive no (compelled) help from him. What rationale yields the result that the person be permitted to emigrate, yet forbidden to stay and opt out of the compulsory scheme of social provision? If providing for the needy is of overriding importance, this does militate against allowing internal opting out; but it also speaks against allowing external emigra-

tion. (Would it also support, to some extent, the kidnapping of persons living in a place without compulsory social provision, who could be forced to make a contribution to the needy in your community?) Perhaps the crucial component of the position that allows emigration solely to avoid certain arrangements, while not allowing anyone internally to opt out of them, is a concern for fraternal feelings within the country. "We don't want anyone here who doesn't contribute, who doesn't care enough about the others to contribute." That concern, in this case, would have to be tied to the view that forced aiding tends to produce fraternal feelings between the aided and the aider (or perhaps merely to the view that the knowledge that someone or other voluntarily is not aiding produces unfraternal feelings).

Locke's Theory of Acquisition

Before we turn to consider other theories of justice in detail, we must introduce an additional bit of complexity into the structure of the entitlement theory. This is best approached by considering Locke's attempt to specify a principle of justice in acquisition. Locke views property rights in an unowned object as originating through someone's mixing his labor with it. This gives rise to many questions. What are the boundaries of what labor is mixed with? If a private astronaut clears a place on Mars, has he mixed his labor with (so that he comes to own) the whole planet, the whole uninhabited universe, or just a particular plot? Which plot does an act bring under ownership? The minimal (possibly disconnected) area such that an act decreases entropy in that area, and not elsewhere? Can virgin land (for the purposes of ecological investigation by high-flying airplane) come under ownership by a Lockean process? Building a fence around a territory presumably would make one the owner of only the fence (and the land immediately underneath it).

Why does mixing one's labor with something make one the owner of it? Perhaps because one owns one's labor, and so one comes to own a previously unowned thing that becomes permeated with what one owns. Ownership seeps over into the rest. But why isn't mixing what I own with what I don't own a way of losing what I own rather than a way of gaining what I don't? If I own a can of tomato juice and spill it in the sea so that its molecules (made radioactive, so I can check this) mingle evenly throughout the sea, do I thereby come to own the sea, or have I foolishly dissipated my tomato juice? Perhaps the idea, instead, is that laboring on something improves it and makes it more valuable; and anyone is entitled to own a thing whose value he has created. (Reinforcing this, perhaps, is the view that laboring is unpleasant. If some people made things effortlessly, as the cartoon characters in *The Yellow Submarine* trail flowers in their wake, would they have lesser claim to their own products whose making didn't *cost* them anything?) Ignore the fact that laboring on something may make it less valuable (spraying pink enamel paint on a piece of driftwood that you have found). Why should one's entitlement extend to the whole object rather than just to the *added value* one's labor has produced? (Such reference to value might also serve to delimit the extent of ownership; for example, substitute "increases the value of" for "decreases entropy in" in the above entropy criterion.) No workable or coherent value-added property scheme has yet been devised, and any such scheme presumably would fall to objections (similar to those) that fell the theory of Henry George.

It will be implausible to view improving an object as giving full ownership to it, if the stock of unowned objects that might be improved is limited. For an object's coming under one person's ownership changes the situation of all others. Whereas previously they were at liberty (in Hohfeld's sense) to use the object, they now no longer are. This change in the situation of others (by removing their liberty to act on a previously unowned object) need not worsen their situation. If I appropriate a grain of sand from Coney Island, no one else may now do as they will with *that* grain of sand. But there are plenty of other grains of sand left for them to do the same with. Or if not grains of sand, then other things. Alternatively, the things I do with the grain of sand I appropriate might improve the position of others, counterbalancing their loss of the liberty to use that grain. The crucial point is whether appropriation of an unowned object worsens the situation of others.

Locke's proviso that there be "enough and as good left in common for others" (sect. 27) is meant to ensure that the situation of others is not worsened. (If this proviso is met is there any motivation for his further condition of nonwaste?) It is often said that this proviso once held but now no longer does. But there appears to be an argument for the conclusion that if the proviso no longer holds, then it cannot ever have held so as to yield permanent and inheritable property rights. Consider the first person Z for whom there is not enough and as good left to appropriate. The last person Y to appropriate left Z without his previous liberty to act on an object, and so worsened Z's situation. So Y's appropriation is not allowed under Locke's proviso. Therefore the next to last person X to appropriate left Y in a worse position, for X's act ended permissible appropriation. Therefore X's appropriation wasn't permissible. But then the appropriator two from last, W, ended permissible appropriation and so, since it worsened X's position, W's appropriation wasn't permissible. And so on back to the first person A to appropriate a permanent property right.

This argument, however, proceeds too quickly. Someone may be made worse off by another's appropriation in two ways: first, by losing the opportunity to improve his situation by a particular appropriation or any one; and second, by no longer being able to use freely (without appropriation) what he previously could. A *stringent* requirement that another not be made worse off by an appropriation would exclude the first way if nothing else counterbalances the diminution in opportunity, as well as the second. A *weaker* requirement would exclude the second way, though not the first. With the weaker requirement, we cannot zip back so quickly from Z to A, as in the above argument; for though person Z can no longer *appropriate*, there may remain some for him to *use* as before. In this case Y's appropriation would not violate the weaker Lockean condition. (With less remaining that people are at liberty to use, users might face more inconvenience, crowding, and so on; in that way the situation of others might be worsened, unless appropriation stopped far short of such a point.) It is arguable that no one legitimately can complain if the weaker provision is satisfied. However, since this is less clear than in the case of the more stringent proviso, Locke may have intended this stringent proviso by "enough and as good" remaining, and perhaps he meant the nonwaste condition to delay the end point from which the argument zips back.

Is the situation of persons who are unable to appropriate (there being no more accessible and useful unowned objects) worsened by a system allowing appropriation and permanent property? Here enter the various familiar social considerations favoring private property: it increases the social product by putting means of production in the hands of those who can use them most efficiently (profitably); experimentation is encouraged, because with separate persons controlling resources, there is no one person or small group whom someone with a new idea must convince to try it out; private property enables people to decide on the pattern and types of risks they wish to bear, leading to specialized types of risk bearing; private property protects future persons by leading some to hold back resources from current consumption for future markets; it provides alternate sources of employment for unpopular persons who don't have to convince any one person or small group to hire them, and so on. These considerations enter a Lockean theory to support the claim that appropriation of private property satisfies the intent behind the "enough and as good left over" proviso, *not* as a utilitarian justification of property. They enter to rebut the claim that because the proviso is violated no natural right to private property can arise by a Lockean process. The difficulty in working such an argument to show that the proviso is satisfied is in fixing the appropriate base line for comparison. Lockean appropriation makes people no worse off than they would be *how*? This question of

fixing the baseline needs more detailed investigation than we are able to give it here. It would be desirable to have an estimate of the general economic importance of original appropriation in order to see how much leeway there is for differing theories of appropriation and of the location of the baseline. Perhaps this importance can be measured by the percentage of all income that is based upon untransformed raw materials and given resources (rather than upon human actions), mainly rental income representing the unimproved value of land, and the price of raw material *in situ*, and by the percentage of current wealth which represents such income in the past.[9]

We should note that it is not only persons favoring *private* property who need a theory of how property rights legitimately originate. Those believing in collective property, for example those believing that a group of persons living in an area jointly own the territory, or its mineral resources, also must provide a theory of how such property rights arise; they must show why the persons living there have rights to determine what is done with the land and resources there that persons living elsewhere don't have (with regard to the same land and resources).

9. I have not seen a precise estimate. David Friedman, *The Machinery of Freedom* (N.Y.: Harper & Row, 1973), pp. xiv, xv, discusses this issue and suggests 5 percent of U.S. national income as an upper limit for the first two factors mentioned. However he does not attempt to estimate the percentage of current wealth which is based upon such income in the past. (The vague notion of "based upon" merely indicates a topic needing investigation.)

The Constitution of Liberty

Friedrich A. Hayek

Equality, Value, and Merit

I have no respect for the passion for equality, which seems to me merely idealizing envy.

Oliver Wendell Holmes, Jr.

1. The great aim of the struggle for liberty has been equality before the law. This equality under the rules which the state enforces may be supplemented by a similar equality of the rules that men voluntarily obey in their relations with one another. This extension of the principle of equality to the rules of moral and social conduct is the chief expression of what is commonly called the democratic spirit—and probably that aspect of it that does most to make inoffensive the inequalities that liberty necessarily produces.

Equality of the general rules of law and conduct, however, is the only kind of equality conducive to liberty and the only equality which we can secure without destroying liberty. Not only has liberty nothing to do with any other sort of equality, but it is even bound to produce inequality in many respects. This is the necessary result and part of the justification of individual liberty : if the result of individual liberty did not demonstrate that some manners of living are more successful than others, much of the case for it would vanish.

It is neither because it assumes that people are in fact equal nor because it attempts to make them equal that the argument for liberty demands that government treat them equally. This argument not only recognizes that individuals are very different but in a great measure rests on that assumption. It insists that these individual differences provide no justification for government to treat them differently. And it objects to the differences in treatment by the state that would be necessary if persons who are in fact very different were to be assured equal positions in life.

Modern advocates of a more far-reaching material equality usually deny that their demands are based on any assumption of the factual equality of all men. It is nevertheless still widely believed that this is the main justification for such demands. Nothing, however, is more damaging to the demand for equal treatment than to base it on so obviously untrue an assumption as that of the factual equality of all men. To rest the case for equal treatment of national or racial minorities on the assertion that they do not differ from other men is implicitly to admit that factual inequality would justify unequal treatment; and the proof that some differences do, in fact, exist would not be long in forthcoming. It is of the essence of the demand for equality before the law that people should be treated alike in spite of the fact that they are different.

2. The boundless variety of human nature— the wide range of differences in individual capacities and potentialities—is one of the most distinctive facts about the human species. Its evolution has made it probably the most variable among all kinds of creatures. It has been well said that

"biology, with variability as its cornerstone, confers on every human individual a unique set of attributes which give him a dignity he could not otherwise possess. Every newborn baby is an unknown quantity so far as potentialities are concerned because there are many thousands of unknown interrelated genes and gene-patterns which contribute to his make-up. As a result of nature and nurture the newborn infant may become one of the greatest of men or women ever to have lived. In every case he or she has the making of a distinctive individual. . . . If the differences are not very important, then freedom is not very important and the idea of individual worth is not very important." The writer justly adds that the widely held uniformity theory of human nature, "which on the surface appears to accord with democracy . . . would in time undermine the very basic ideals of freedom and individual worth and render life as we know it meaningless."

It has been the fashion in modern times to minimize the importance of congenital differences between men and to ascribe all the important differences to the influence of environment. However important the latter may be, we must not overlook the fact that individuals are very different from the outset. The importance of individual differences would hardly be less if all people were brought up in very similar environments. As a statement of fact, it just is not true that "all men are born equal." We may continue to use this hallowed phrase to express the ideal that legally and morally all men ought to be treated alike. But if we want to understand what this ideal of equality can or should mean, the first requirement is that we free ourselves from the belief in factual equality.

From the fact that people are very different it follows that, if we treat them equally, the result must be inequality in their actual position, and that the only way to place them in an equal position would be to treat them differently. Equality before the law and material equality are therefore not only different but are in conflict with each other; and we can achieve either the one or the other, but not both at the same time. The equality before the law which freedom requires leads to material inequality. Our argument will be that, though where the state must use coercion for other reasons, it should treat all people alike, the desire of making people more alike in their condition cannot be accepted in a free society as a justification for further and discriminatory coercion.

We do not object to equality as such. It merely happens to be the case that a demand for equality is the professed motive of most of those who desire to impose upon society a preconceived pattern of distribution. Our objection is against all attempts to impress upon society a deliberately chosen pattern of distribution, whether it be an order of equality or of inequality. We shall indeed see that many of those who demand an extension of equality do not really demand equality but a distribution that conforms more closely to human conceptions of individual merit and that their desires are as irreconcilable with freedom as the more strictly egalitarian demands.

If one objects to the use of coercion in order to bring about a more even or a more just distribution, this does not mean that one does not regard these as desirable. But if we wish to preserve a free society, it is essential that we recognize that the desirability of a particular object is not sufficient justification for the use of coercion. One may well feel attracted to a community in which there are no extreme contrasts between rich and poor and may welcome the fact that the general increase in wealth seems gradually to reduce those differences. I fully share these feelings and certainly regard the degree of social equality that the United States has achieved as wholly admirable.

There also seems no reason why these widely felt preferences should not guide policy in some respects. Wherever there is a legitimate need for government action and we have to choose between different methods of satisfying such a need, those that incidentally also reduce inequality may well be preferable. If, for example, in the law of intestate succession one kind of provision will be more conducive to equality than another, this may be a strong argument in its favor. It is a different matter, however, if it is demanded that, in order to produce substantive equality, we should abandon the basic postulate of a free society, namely, the limitation of all coercion by equal law. Against this we shall hold that economic inequality is not one of the evils which justify our resorting to discriminatory coercion or privilege as a remedy.

3. Our contention rests on two basic propositions which probably need only be stated to win fairly general assent. The first of them is an expression of the belief in a certain similarity of all human beings: it is the proposition that no man or group of men possesses the capacity to determine conclusively the potentialities of other human beings and that we should certainly never trust anyone invariably to exercise such a capacity. However great the differences between men may be, we have no ground for believing that they will ever be so great as to enable one man's mind in a particular instance to comprehend fully all that another responsible man's mind is capable of.

The second basic proposition is that the acquisition by any member of the community of additional capacities to do things which may be valuable must always be regarded as a gain for that community. It is true that particular people may be worse off because of the superior ability of some new competitor in their field; but any such additional ability in the community is likely to benefit the majority. This implies that the desirability of increasing the abilities and opportunities of any individual does not depend on whether the same can also be done for the others—provided, of course, that others are not thereby deprived of the opportunity of acquiring the same or other abilities which might have been accessible to them had they not been secured by that individual.

Egalitarians generally regard differently those differences in individual capacities which are inborn and those which are due to the influences of environment, or those which are the result of "nature" and those which are the result of "nurture." Neither, be it said at once, has anything to do with moral merit. Though either may greatly affect the value which an individual has for his fellows, no more credit belongs to him for having been born with desirable qualities than for having grown up under favorable circumstances. The distinction between the two is important only because the former advantages are due to circumstances clearly beyond human control, while the latter are due to factors which we might be able to alter. The important question is whether there is a case for so changing our institutions as to eliminate as much as possible those advantages due to environment. Are we to agree that "all inequalities that rest on birth and inherited property ought to be abolished and none remain unless it is an effect of superior talent and industry"?

The fact that certain advantages rest on human arrangements does not necessarily mean that we could provide the same advantages for all or that, if they are given to some, somebody else is thereby deprived of them. The most important factors to be considered in this connection are the family, inheritance, and education, and it is against the inequality which they produce that criticism is mainly directed. They are, however, not the only important factors of environment. Geographic conditions such as climate and landscape, not to speak of local and sectional differences in cultural and moral traditions, are scarcely less important. We can, however, consider here only the three factors whose effects are most commonly impugned.

So far as the family is concerned, there exists a curious contrast between the esteem most people profess for the institution and their dislike of the fact that being born into a particular family should confer on a person special advantages. It seems to be widely believed that, while useful qualities which a person acquires because of his native gifts under conditions which are the same for all are socially beneficial, the same qualities become somehow undesirable if they are the result of environmental advantages not available to others. Yet it is difficult to see why the same useful quality which is welcomed when it is the result of a person's natural endowment should be less valuable when it is the product of such circumstances as intelligent parents or a good home.

The value which most people attach to the institution of the family rests on the belief that, as a rule, parents can do more to prepare their children for a satisfactory life than anyone else. This means not only that the benefits which particular people derive from their family environment will be different but also that these benefits may operate cumulatively through several generations. What reason can there be for believing that a desirable quality in a person is less valuable to society if it has been the result of family background than if it has not? There is, indeed, good reason to think that there are some socially valuable qualities which will be rarely acquired in a single generation but which will generally be formed only by the continuous efforts of two or three. This means simply that there are parts of the cultural heritage of a society that are more effectively transmitted through the family. Granted this, it would be unreasonable to deny that a society is likely to get a better elite if ascent is not limited to one generation, if individuals are not deliberately made to start from the same level, and if children are not deprived of the chance to benefit from the better education and material environment which their parents may be able to provide. To admit this is merely to recognize that belonging to a particular family is part of the individual personality, that society is made up as much of families as of individuals, and that the transmission of the heritage of civilization within the family is as important a tool in man's striving toward better things as is the heredity of beneficial physical attributes.

4. Many people who agree that the family is desirable as an instrument for the transmission of morals, tastes, and knowledge still question the desirability of the transmission of material property. Yet there can be little doubt that, in order that the former may be possible, some continuity of standards, of the external forms of life, is essential, and that this will be achieved only if it is possible to transmit not only immaterial but also material advantages. There is, of course, neither greater merit nor any greater injustice involved in some people being born to wealthy parents than there is in others being born to kind or intelligent parents. The fact is that it is no less of an advantage to the community if at least some children can start with the advantages which at any given time only wealthy homes can offer than if some children inherit great intelligence or are taught better morals at home.

We are not concerned here with the chief argument for private inheritance, namely, that it seems essential as a means to preserve the dispersal in the control of capital and as an inducement for its accumulation. Rather, our concern here is whether the fact that it confers unmerited benefits on some is a valid argument against the institution. It is unquestionably one of the institutional causes of inequality. In the present context we need not inquire whether liberty demands unlimited freedom of bequest. Our problem here is merely whether people ought to be free to pass on to children or others such material possessions as will cause substantial inequality.

Once we agree that it is desirable to harness the natural instincts of parents to equip the new generation as well as they can, there seems no sensible ground for limiting this to non-material benefits. The family's function of passing on standards and traditions is closely tied up with the possibility of transmitting material goods. And it is difficult to see how it would serve the true interest of society to limit the gain in material conditions to one generation.

There is also another consideration which, though it may appear somewhat cynical, strongly suggests that if we wish to make the best use of the natural partiality of parents for their children, we ought not to preclude the transmission of property. It seems certain that among the many ways in which those who have gained power and influence might provide for their children, the bequest of a fortune is socially by far the cheapest. Without this outlet, these men would look for other ways of providing for their children, such as placing them in positions which might bring them the income and the prestige that a fortune would have done; and this would cause a waste of resources and an injustice much greater than is caused by the inheritance of property. Such is the case with all societies in which inheritance of property does not exist, including the Communist. Those who dislike the inequalities caused by inheritance should therefore recognize that, men being what they are, it is the least of evils, even from their point of view.

5. Though inheritance used to be the most widely criticized source of inequality, it is today probably no longer so. Egalitarian agitation now tends to concentrate on the unequal advantages due to differences in education. There is a growing tendency to express the desire to secure equality of conditions in the claim that the best education we have learned to provide for some should be made gratuitously available for all and that, if this is not possible, one should not be allowed to get a better education than the rest merely because one's parents are able to pay for it, but only those and all those who can pass a uniform test of ability should be admitted to the benefits of the limited resources of higher education.

The problem of educational policy raises too many issues to allow of their being discussed incidentally under the general heading of equality. We shall have to devote a separate chapter to them at the end of this book. For the present we shall only point out that enforced equality in this field can hardly avoid preventing some from getting the education they otherwise might. Whatever we might do, there is no way of preventing those advantages which only some can have, and which it is desirable that some should have, from going to people who neither individually merit them nor will make as good a use of them as some other person might have done. Such a problem cannot be satisfactorily solved by the exclusive and coercive powers of the state.

It is instructive at this point to glance briefly at the change that the ideal of equality has undergone in this field in modern times. A hundred years ago, at the height of the classical liberal movement, the demand was generally expressed by the phrase *la carrière ouverte aux talents*. It was a demand that all man-made obstacles to the rise of some should be removed, that all privileges of individuals should be abolished, and that what the state contributed to the chance of improving one's conditions should be the same for all. That so long as people were different and grew up in different families this could not assure an equal start was fairly generally accepted. It was understood that the duty of government was not to ensure that everybody had the same prospect of reaching a given position but merely to make available to all on equal terms those facilities which in their nature depended on government action. That the results were bound to be different, not only because the individuals were different, but also because only a small part of the relevant circumstances depended on government action, was taken for granted.

This conception that all should be allowed to try has been largely replaced by the altogether different conception that all must be assured an equal start and the same prospects. This means little less than that the government, instead of providing the same circumstances for all, should aim at controlling all conditions relevant to a particular individual's prospects and so adjust them to his capacities as to assure him of the same prospects as everybody else. Such deliberate adaptation of opportunities to individual aims and capacities would, of course, be the opposite of freedom. Nor could it be justified as a means of making the best use of all available knowledge except on the assumption that government knows best how individual capacities can be used.

When we inquire into the justification of these demands, we find that they rest on the discontent that the success of some people often produces in those that are less successful, or, to put it bluntly, on envy. The modern tendency to gratify this passion and to disguise it in the respectable garment of social justice is developing into a serious threat to freedom. Recently an attempt was made to base these demands on the argument that it ought to be the aim of politics to remove all sources of discontent. This would, of course, necessarily mean that it is the responsibility of government to see that nobody is healthier or possesses a happier temperament, a better-suited spouse or more prospering children, than anybody else. If really all unfulfilled desires have a claim on the community, individual responsibility is at an end. However human, envy is certainly not one of the sources of discontent that a free society can eliminate. It is probably one of the essential conditions for the preservation of such a society that we do not countenance envy, not sanction its demands by camouflaging it as social justice, but treat it, in the words of John Stuart Mill, as "the most anti-social and evil of all passions."

6. While most of the strictly egalitarian demands are based on nothing better than envy, we must recognize that much that on the surface appears as a demand for greater equality is in fact a demand for a juster distribution of the good things of this world and springs therefore from much more creditable motives. Most people will object not to the bare fact of inequality but to the fact that the differences in reward do not correspond to any recognizable differences in the merits of those who receive them. The answer commonly given to this is that a free society on the whole achieves this kind of justice. This, however, is an indefensible contention if by justice is meant proportionality of reward to moral merit. Any attempt to found the case for freedom on this argument is very damaging to it, since it concedes that material rewards ought to be made to correspond to recognizable merit and then opposes the conclusion that most people will draw from this by an assertion which is untrue.

The proper answer is that in a free system it is neither desirable nor practicable that material rewards should be made generally to correspond to what men recognize as merit and that it is an essential characteristic of a free society that an individual's position should not necessarily depend on the views that his fellows hold about the merit he has acquired.

This contention may appear at first so strange and even shocking that I will ask the reader to suspend judgment until I have further explained the distinction between value and merit. The difficulty in making the point clear is due to the fact that the term "merit," which is the only one available to describe what I mean, is also used in a wider and vaguer sense. It will be used here exclusively to describe the attributes of conduct that make it deserving of praise, that is, the moral character of the action and not the value of the achievement.

As we have seen throughout our discussion, the value that the performance or capacity of a person has to his fellows has no necessary connection with its ascertainable merit in this sense. The inborn as well as the acquired gifts of a person clearly have a value to his fellows which does not depend on any credit due to him for possessing them. There is little a man can do to alter the fact that his special talents are very common or exceedingly rare. A good mind or a fine voice, a beautiful face or a skilful hand, and a ready wit or an attractive personality are in a large measure as independent of a person's efforts as the opportunities or the experiences he has had. In all these instances the value which a person's capacities or services have for us and for which he is recompensed has little relation to anything that we can call moral merit or deserts. Our problem is whether it is desirable that people should enjoy advantages in proportion to the benefits which their fellows derive from their activities or whether the distribution of these advantages should be based on other men's views of their merits.

Reward according to merit must in practice mean reward according to assessable merit, merit that other people can recognize and agree upon and not merit merely in the sight of some higher power. Assessable merit in this sense presupposes that we can ascertain that a man has done what some accepted rule of conduct demanded of him and that this has cost him some pain and effort. Whether this has been the case cannot be judged by the result: merit is not a matter of the objective outcome but of subjective effort. The attempt to achieve a valuable result may be highly meritorious but a complete failure, and full success may be entirely the result of accident and thus without merit. If we know that a man has done his best, we will often wish to see him rewarded irrespective of the result; and if we know that a most valuable achievement is almost entirely due to luck or favorable circumstances, we will give little credit to the author.

We may wish that we were able to draw this distinction in every instance. In fact, we can do so only rarely with any degree of assurance. It is possible only where we possess all the knowledge which was at the disposal of the acting person, including a knowledge of his skill and confidence, his state of mind and his feelings, his capacity for attention, his energy and persistence, etc. The possibility of a true judgment of merit thus depends on the presence of precisely those conditions whose general absence is the main argument for liberty. It is because we want people to use knowledge which we do not possess that we let them decide for themselves. But insofar as we want them to be free to use capacities and knowledge of facts which we do not have, we are not in a position to judge the merit of their achievements. To decide on merit presupposes that we can judge whether people have made such use of their opportunities as they ought to have made and how much effort of will or self-denial this has cost them; it presupposes also that we can distinguish between that part of their achievement which is due to circumstances within their control and that part which is not.

7. The incompatibility of reward according to merit with freedom to choose one's pursuit is most evident in those areas where the uncertainty of the outcome is particularly great and our individual estimates of the chances of various kinds of effort very different. In those speculative efforts which we call "research" or "exploration," or in economic activities which we commonly describe as "speculation," we cannot expect to attract those best qualified for them unless we give the successful ones all the credit or gain, though many others may have striven as meritoriously. For the same reason that nobody can know beforehand who will be the successful ones, nobody can say who has earned greater merit. It would clearly not serve our purpose if we let all who have honestly striven share in the prize. Moreover, to do so would make it necessary that somebody have the right to decide who is to be allowed to strive for it. If in their pursuit of uncertain goals people are to use their own knowledge and capacities, they must be guided, not by what other people think they ought to do, but by the value others attach to the result at which they aim.

What is so obviously true about those undertakings which we commonly regard as risky is scarcely less true of any chosen object we decide to pursue. Any such decision is beset with uncertainty, and if the choice is to be as wise as it is humanly possible to make it, the alternative results anticipated must be labeled according to their value. If the remuneration did not correspond to the value that the product of a man's efforts has for his fellows, he would have no basis for deciding whether the pursuit of a given object is worth the effort and risk. He would necessarily have to be told what to do, and some other person's estimate of what was the best use of his capacities would have to determine both his duties and his remuneration.

The fact is, of course, that we do not wish people to earn a maximum of merit but to achieve a maximum of usefulness at a minimum of pain and sacrifice and therefore a minimum of merit. Not only would it be impossible for us to reward all merit justly, but it would not even be desirable that people should aim chiefly at earning a maximum of merit. Any attempt to induce them to do this would necessarily result in people being rewarded differently for the same service. And it is only the value of the result that we can judge with any degree of confidence, not the different degrees of effort and care that it has cost different people to achieve it.

The prizes that a free society offers for the result serve to tell those who strive for them how much effort they are worth. However, the same prizes will go to all those who produce the same result, regardless of effort. What is true here of the remuneration for the same services rendered by different people is even more true of the relative remuneration for different services requiring different gifts and capacities: they will have little relation to merit. The market will generally offer for services of any kind the value they will have for those who benefit from them; but it will rarely be known whether it was necessary to offer so much in order to obtain these services, and often, no doubt, the community could have had them for much less. The pianist who was reported not long ago to have said that he would perform even if he had to pay for the privilege probably described the position of many who earn large incomes from activities which are also their chief pleasure.

8. Though most people regard as very natural the claim that nobody should be rewarded more than he deserves for his pain and effort, it is nevertheless based on a colossal presumption. It presumes that we are able to judge in every individual instance how well people use the different opportunities and talents given to them and how meritorious their achievements are in the light of all the circumstances which have made them possible. It presumes that some human beings are in a position to determine conclusively what a person is worth and are entitled to determine what he may achieve. It presumes, then, what the argument for liberty specifically rejects: that we can and do know all that guides a person's action.

A society in which the position of the individuals was made to correspond to human ideas of moral merit would therefore be the exact opposite of a free society. It would be a society in which people were rewarded for duty performed instead of for success, in which every move of every individual was guided by what other people thought he ought to do, and in which the individual was thus relieved of the responsibility and the risk of decision. But if nobody's knowledge is sufficient to guide all human action, there is also no human being who is competent to reward all efforts according to merit.

In our individual conduct we generally act on the assumption that it is the value of a person's performance and not his merit that determines our obligation to him. Whatever may be true in more intimate relations, in the ordinary business of life we do not feel that, because a man has rendered us a service at a great sacrifice, our debt to

him is determined by this, so long as we could have had the same service provided with ease by somebody else. In our dealings with other men we feel that we are doing justice if we recompense value rendered with equal value, without inquiring what it might have cost the particular individual to supply us with these services. What determines our responsibility is the advantage we derive from what others offer us, not their merit in providing it. We also expect in our dealings with others to be remunerated not according to our subjective merit but according to what our services are worth to them. Indeed, so long as we think in terms of our relations to particular people, we are generally quite aware that the mark of the free man is to be dependent for his livelihood not on other people's views of his merit but solely on what he has to offer them. It is only when we think of our position or our income as determined by "society" as a whole that we demand reward according to merit.

Though moral value or merit is a species of value, not all value is moral value, and most of our judgments of value are not moral judgments. That this must be so in a free society is a point of cardinal importance; and the failure to distinguish between value and merit has been the source of serious confusion. We do not necessarily admire all activities whose product we value; and in most instances where we value what we get, we are in no position to assess the merit of those who have provided it for us. If a man's ability in a given field is more valuable after thirty years' work than it was earlier, this is independent of whether these thirty years were most profitable and enjoyable or whether they were a time of unceasing sacrifice and worry. If the pursuit of a hobby produces a special skill or an accidental invention turns out to be extremely useful to others, the fact that there is little merit in it does not make it any less valuable than if the result had been produced by painful effort.

This difference between value and merit is not peculiar to any one type of society—it would exist anywhere. We might, of course, attempt to make rewards correspond to merit instead of value, but we are not likely to succeed in this. In attempting it, we would destroy the incentives which enable people to decide for themselves what they should do. Moreover, it is more than doubtful whether even a fairly successful attempt to make rewards correspond to merit would produce a more attractive or even a tolerable social order. A society in which it was generally presumed that a high income was proof of merit and a low income of the lack of it, in which it was universally believed that position and remuneration corresponded to merit, in which there was no other road to success than the approval of one's conduct by the majority of one's fellows, would probably be much more unbearable to the unsuccessful ones than one in which it was frankly recognized that there was no necessary connection between merit and success.

It would probably contribute more to human happiness if, instead of trying to make remuneration correspond to merit, we made clearer how uncertain is the connection between value and merit. We are probably all much too ready to ascribe personal merit where there is, in fact, only superior value. The possession by an individual or a group of a superior civilization or education certainly represents an important value and constitutes an asset for the community to which they belong; but it usually constitutes little merit. Popularity and esteem do not depend more on merit than does financial success. It is, in fact, largely because we are so used to assuming an often non-existent merit wherever we find value that we balk when, in particular instances, the discrepancy is too large to be ignored.

There is every reason why we ought to endeavor to honor special merit where it has gone without adequate reward. But the problem of rewarding action of outstanding merit which we wish to be widely known as an example is different from that of the incentives on which the ordinary functioning of society rests. A free society produces institutions in which, for those who prefer it, a man's advancement depends on the judgment of some superior or of the majority of his fellows. Indeed, as organizations grow larger and more complex, the task of ascertaining the individual's contribution will become more difficult; and it will become increasingly necessary that, for many, merit in the eyes of the managers rather than the ascertainable value of the contribution should determine the rewards. So long as this does not produce a situation in which a single comprehensive scale of merit is imposed

upon the whole society, so long as a multiplicity of organizations compete with one another in offering different prospects, this is not merely compatible with freedom but extends the range of choice open to the individual.

9. Justice, like liberty and coercion, is a concept which, for the sake of clarity, ought to be confined to the deliberate treatment of men by other men. It is an aspect of the intentional determination of those conditions of people's lives that are subject to such control. Insofar as we want the efforts of individuals to be guided by their own views about prospects and chances, the results of the individual's efforts are necessarily unpredictable, and the question as to whether the resulting distribution of incomes is just has no meaning. Justice does require that those conditions of people's lives that are determined by government be provided equally for all. But equality of those conditions must lead to inequality of results. Neither the equal provision of particular public facilities nor the equal treatment of different partners in our voluntary dealings with one another will secure reward that is proportional to merit. Reward for merit is reward for obeying the wishes of others in what we do, not compensation for the benefits we have conferred upon them by doing what we thought best.

It is, in fact, one of the objections against attempts by government to fix income scales that the state must attempt to be just in all it does. Once the principle of reward according to merit is accepted as the just foundation for the distribution of incomes, justice would require that all who desire it should be rewarded according to that principle. Soon it would also be demanded that the same principle be applied to all and that incomes not in proportion to recognizable merit not be tolerated. Even an attempt merely to distinguish between those incomes or gains which are "earned" and those which are not will set up a principle which the state will have to try to apply but cannot in fact apply generally. And every such attempt at deliberate control of some remunerations is bound to create further demands for new controls. The principle of distributive justice, once introduced, would not be fulfilled until the whole of society was organized in accordance with it. This would produce a kind of society which in all essential respects would be the opposite of a free society—a society in which authority decided what the individual was to do and how he was to do it.

10. In conclusion we must briefly look at another argument on which the demands for a more equal distribution are frequently based, though it is rarely explicitly stated. This is the contention that membership in a particular community or nation entitles the individual to a particular material standard that is determined by the general wealth of the group to which he belongs. This demand is in curious conflict with the desire to base distribution on personal merit. There is clearly no merit in being born into a particular community, and no argument of justice can be based on the accident of a particular individual's being born in one place rather than another. A relatively wealthy community in fact regularly confers advantages on its poorest members unknown to those born in poor communities. In a wealthy community the only justification its members can have for insisting on further advantages is that there is much private wealth that the government can confiscate and redistribute and that men who constantly see such wealth being enjoyed by others will have a stronger desire for it than those who know of it only abstractly, if at all.

There is no obvious reason why the joint efforts of the members of any group to ensure the maintenance of law and order and to organize the provision of certain services should give the members a claim to a particular share in the wealth of this group. Such claims would be especially difficult to defend where those who advanced them were unwilling to concede the same rights to those who did not belong to the same nation or community. The recognition of such claims on a national scale would in fact only create a new kind of collective (but not less exclusive) property right in the resources of the nation that could not be justified on the same grounds as individual property. Few people would be prepared to recognize the justice of these demands on a world scale. And the bare fact that within a given nation the majority had the actual power to enforce such demands, while in the

world as a whole it did not yet have it, would hardly make them more just.

There are good reasons why we should endeavor to use whatever political organization we have at our disposal to make provision for the weak or infirm or for the victims of unforeseeable disaster. It may well be true that the most effective method of providing against certain risks common to all citizens of a state is to give every citizen protection against those risks. The level on which such provisions against common risks can be made will necessarily depend on the general wealth of the community.

It is an entirely different matter, however, to suggest that those who are poor, merely in the sense that there are those in the same community who are richer, are entitled to a share in the wealth of the latter or that being born into a group that has reached a particular level of civilization and comfort confers a title to a share in all its benefits. The fact that all citizens have an interest in the common provision of some services is no justification for anyone's claiming as a right a share in all the benefits. It may set a standard for what some ought to be willing to give, but not for what anyone can demand.

National groups will become more and more exclusive as the acceptance of this view that we have been contending against spreads. Rather than admit people to the advantages that living in their country offers, a nation will prefer to keep them out altogether; for, once admitted, they will soon claim as a right a particular share in its wealth. The conception that citizenship or even residence in a country confers a claim to a particular standard of living is becoming a serious source of international friction. And since the only justification for applying the principle within a given country is that its government has the power to enforce it, we must not be surprised if we find the same principle being applied by force on an international scale. Once the right of the majority to the benefits that minorities enjoy is recognized on a national scale, there is no reason why this should stop at the boundaries of the existing states.

Chapter 4

LOCKE: PROPERTY RIGHTS

One of the difficult things about reading the political theory of John Locke (1632–1704) is that it seems so familiar, especially to those who have grown up in the American system of government. His Second Treatise of Government (1690) argues that legitimate government is a limited government based on consent, in which the majority rules but may not violate people's fundamental rights. At first glance, Locke's theory of government may seem too obvious to be interesting. But its surface familiarity conceals some intriguing questions. For example: Just how limited are the powers of government, according to Locke? A legitimate government may not violate our natural right to life, liberty, and property. But Locke allows that government can legitimately take our property through taxation and require citizens to sacrifice their lives in war. If government may do these things, what would count as a law that violated our rights?

Some libertarians claim Locke as an ally. They point to his account of how private property can arise in "the state of nature," before government arrives on the scene. Central to Locke's account is the idea that "every man has a property in his own person. This nobody has any right to but himself." When I mix my labor with some unowned thing—by picking apples in the wild or cultivating unowned land—that thing becomes mine, my private property.

This much seems to accord with the libertarian notion of self-ownership. But Locke qualifies this notion in an important way. He rejects the idea that we have the right to dispose of our life and liberty as we please. To the contrary, no one, Locke insists, has the right to alienate his natural rights by selling himself into slavery, or placing his life or his property under the arbitrary power of someone else. For Locke, the right to life, liberty, and property is an unalienable right; it is not ours to give away, even by our own consent. Do these limits on what we may do with our life, liberty, and property suggest a tension between Locke's conception of rights and that of the libertarians? If so, which do you find more persuasive?

SECOND TREATISE OF GOVERNMENT

John Locke

An Essay Concerning the True Original, Extent and End of Civil Government

Chapter I

IT having been shewn in the foregoing discourse:

1. That Adam had not, either by natural right of fatherhood or by positive donation from God, any such authority over his children, or dominion over the world, as is pretended.

2. That if he had, his heirs yet had no right to it.

3. That if his heirs, there being no law of nature nor positive law of God that determines which is the right heir in all cases that may arise, the right of succession, and consequently of bearing rule, could not have been certainly determined.

4. That if even that had been determined, yet the knowledge of which is the eldest line of Adam's posterity, being so long since utterly lost, that in the races of mankind and families of the world there remains not to one above another the least pretence to be the eldest house, and to have the right of inheritance.

All these premises having, as I think, been clearly made out, it is impossible that the rulers now on earth should make any benefit, or derive any the least shadow of authority from that which is held to be the foundation of all power, Adam's private dominion and paternal jurisdiction; so that he that will not give just occasion to think that all government in the world is the product only of force and violence, and that men live together by no other rules but that of beasts, where the strongest carries it, and so lay a foundation for perpetual disorder and mischief, tumult, sedition, and rebellion (things that the followers of that hypothesis so loudly cry out against), must of necessity find out another rise of government, another original of political power, and another way of designing and knowing the persons that have it, than what Sir Robert Filmer hath taught us.

2. To this purpose, I think it may not be amiss to set down what I take to be political power; that the power of a magistrate over a subject may be distinguished from that of a father over his children, a master over his servant, a husband over his wife, and a lord over his slave. All which distinct powers happening sometimes together in the same man, if he be considered under these different relations, it may help us to distinguish these powers one from another, and shew the difference betwixt a ruler of a commonwealth, a father of a family, and a captain of a galley.

3. Political power, then, I take to be a right of making laws with penalties of death, and consequently all less penalties, for the regulating and preserving of property, and of employing the force of the community in the execution of such laws, and in the defence of the commonwealth from foreign injury; and all this only for the public good.

Chapter II. Of the State of Nature

4. To understand political power aright, and derive it from its original, we must consider what state all men are naturally in, and that is a state of perfect freedom to order their actions and dispose of their possessions and persons as they think fit, within the bounds of the law of nature, without asking leave, or depending upon the will of any other man.

A state also of equality, wherein all the power and jurisdiction is reciprocal, no one having more than another; there being nothing more evident than that creatures of the same species and rank, promiscuously born to all the same advantages of nature, and the use of the same faculties, should also be equal one amongst another without subordination or subjection, unless the Lord and Master of them all should by any manifest declaration of his will set one above another, and confer on him, by an evident and clear appointment, an undoubted right to dominion and sovereignty.

5. This equality of men by nature the judicious Hooker looks upon as so evident in itself and beyond all question, that he makes it the foundation of that obligation to mutual love amongst men on which he builds the duties they owe one another, and from whence he derives the great maxims of justice and charity. His words are:

"The like natural inducement hath brought men to know that it is no less their duty to love others than themselves; for seeing those things which are equal must needs all have one measure, if I cannot but wish to receive good, even as much at every man's hands as any man can wish unto his own soul, how should I look to have any part of my desire herein satisfied, unless myself be careful to satisfy the like desire, which is undoubtedly in other men, being of one and the same nature? To have anything offered them repugnant to this desire, must needs in all respects grieve them as much as me, so that, if I do harm, I must look to suffer, there being no reason that others should shew greater measures of love to me than they have by me shewed unto them. My desire, therefore, to be loved of my equals in nature as much as possible may be, imposeth upon me a natural duty of bearing to themward fully the like affection; from which relation of equality between ourselves and them that are as ourselves, what several rules and canons natural reason hath drawn for direction of life no man is ignorant." Eccl. Pol., lib. i.

6. But though this be a state of liberty, yet it is not a state of licence; though man in that state have an uncontrollable liberty to dispose of his person or possessions, yet he has not liberty to destroy himself, or so much as any creature in his possession, but where some nobler use than its bare preservation calls for it. The state of nature has a law of nature to govern it, which obliges every one; and reason, which is that law, teaches all mankind who will but consult it, that, being all equal and independent, no one ought to harm another in his life, health, liberty, or possessions. For men being all the workmanship of one omnipotent and infinitely wise Maker—all the servants of one sovereign Master, sent into the world by his order, and about his business—they are his property, whose workmanship they are, made to last during his, not one another's pleasure; and being furnished with like faculties, sharing all in one community of nature, there cannot be supposed any such subordination among us, that may authorize us to destroy one another, as if we were made for one another's uses, as the inferior ranks of creatures are for ours. Every one, as he is bound to preserve himself, and not to quit his station wilfully, so, by the like reason, when his own preservation comes not in competition, ought he, as much as he can, to pre-

serve the rest of mankind, and may not, unless it be to do justice on an offender, take away or impair the life, or what tends to the preservation of the life, the liberty, health, limb, or goods of another.

7. And that all men may be restrained from invading others' rights, and from doing hurt to one another, and the law of nature be observed, which willeth the peace and preservation of all mankind, the execution of the law of nature is in that state put into every man's hand, whereby every one has a right to punish the transgressors of that law to such a degree as may hinder its violation. For the law of nature would, as all other laws that concern men in this world, be in vain if there were nobody that, in the state of nature, had a power to execute that law, and thereby preserve the innocent and restrain offenders. And if any one in the state of nature may punish another for any evil he has done, every one may do so. For in that state of perfect equality, where naturally there is no superiority or jurisdiction of one over another, what any may do in prosecution of that law, every one must needs have a right to do.

8. And thus in the state of nature one man comes by a power over another; but yet no absolute or arbitrary power, to use a criminal, when he has got him in his hands, according to the passionate heats or boundless extravagancy of his own will; but only to retribute to him so far as calm reason and conscience dictate what is proportionate to his transgression, which is so much as may serve for reparation and restraint. For these two are the only reasons why one man may lawfully do harm to another, which is that we call punishment. In transgressing the law of nature, the offender declares himself to live by another rule than that of reason and common equity, which is that measure God has set to the actions of men, for their mutual security; and so he becomes dangerous to mankind, the tie which is to secure them from injury and violence being slighted and broken by him. Which, being a trespass against the whole species, and the peace and safety of it, provided for by the law of nature, every man upon this score, by the right he hath to preserve mankind in general, may restrain, or, where it is necessary, destroy things noxious to them, and so may bring such evil on any one who hath transgressed that law, as may make him

repent the doing of it, and thereby deter him, and by his example others, from doing the like mischief. And in this case, and upon this ground, every man hath a right to punish the offender, and be executioner of the law of nature.

9. I doubt not but this will seem a very strange doctrine to some men: but before they condemn it, I desire them to resolve me by what right any prince or state can put to death or punish an alien, for any crime he commits in their country. 'Tis certain their laws, by virtue of any sanction they receive from the promulgated will of the legislative, reach not a stranger: they speak not to him, nor, if they did, is he bound to hearken to them. The legislative authority, by which they are in force over the subjects of that commonwealth, hath no power over him. Those who have the supreme power of making laws in England, France, or Holland, are to an Indian but like the rest of the world—men without authority. And, therefore, if by the law of nature every man hath not a power to punish offences against it, as he soberly judges the case to require, I see not how the magistrates of any community can punish an alien of another country; since in reference to him they can have no more power than what every man naturally may have over another.

10. Besides the crime which consists in violating the law, and varying from the right rule of reason, whereby a man so far becomes degenerate, and declares himself to quit the principles of human nature, and to be a noxious creature, there is commonly injury done to some person or other, and some other man receives damage by his transgression: in which case he who hath received any damage has, besides the right of punishment common to him with other men, a particular right to seek reparation from him that has done it. And any other person, who finds it just, may also join with him that is injured, and assist him in recovering from the offender so much as may make satisfaction for the harm he has suffered.

11. From these two distinct rights—the one of punishing the crime, for restraint and preventing the like offence, which right of punishing is in everybody; the other of taking reparation, which belongs only to the injured party—comes it to pass that the magistrate, who by being magistrate hath the common right of punishing put into his

hands, can often, where the public good demands not the execution of the law, remit the punishment of criminal offences by his own authority, but yet cannot remit the satisfaction due to any private man for the damage he has received. That, he who has suffered the damage has a right to demand in his own name, and he alone can remit. The damnified person has this power of appropriating to himself the goods or service of the offender, by right of self-preservation, as every man has a power to punish the crime, to prevent its being committed again, by the right he has of preserving all mankind, and doing all reasonable things he can in order to that end. And thus it is that every man in the state of nature has a power to kill a murderer, both to deter others from doing the like injury, which no reparation can compensate, by the example of the punishment that attends it from everybody, and also to secure men from the attempts of a criminal who, having renounced reason, the common rule and measure God hath given to mankind, hath, by the unjust violence and slaughter he hath committed upon one, declared war against all mankind, and therefore may be destroyed as a lion or a tiger, one of those wild savage beasts with whom men can have no society nor security. And upon this is grounded that great law of nature, "Whoso sheddeth man's blood, by man shall his blood be shed." And Cain was so fully convinced that every one had a right to destroy such a criminal, that after the murder of his brother he cries out, "Every one that findeth me shall slay me;" so plain was it writ in the hearts of all mankind.

12. By the same reason may a man in the state of nature punish the lesser breaches of that law. It will perhaps be demanded, With death? I answer, Each transgression may be punished to that degree, and with so much severity, as will suffice to make it an ill bargain to the offender, give him cause to repent, and terrify others from doing the like. Every offence that can be committed in the state of nature, may, in the state of nature, be also punished equally, and as far forth as it may, in a commonwealth. For though it would be beside my present purpose to enter here into the particulars of the law of nature, or its measures of punishment, yet it is certain there is such a law, and that, too, as intelligible and plain to a rational creature and a studier of that law as the positive

laws of commonwealths; nay, possibly plainer, as much as reason is easier to be understood than the fancies and intricate contrivances of men, following contrary and hidden interests put into words; for so truly are a great part of the municipal laws of countries, which are only so far right as they are founded on the law of nature, by which they are to be regulated and interpreted.

13. To this strange doctrine—*viz.*, That in the state of nature every one has the executive power of the law of nature—I doubt not but it will be objected that it is unreasonable for men to be judges in their own cases, that self-love will make men partial to themselves and their friends: and on the other side, that ill-nature, passion, and revenge will carry them too far in punishing others; and hence nothing but confusion and disorder will follow; and that therefore God hath certainly appointed government to restrain the partiality and violence of men. I easily grant that civil government is the proper remedy for the inconveniences of the state of nature, which must certainly be great where men may be judges in their own case, since 'tis easy to be imagined that he who was so unjust as to do his brother an injury, will scarce be so just as to condemn himself for it. But I shall desire those who make this objection, to remember that absolute monarchs are but men; and if government is to be the remedy of those evils which necessarily follow from men's being judges in their own cases, and the state of nature is therefore not to be endured, I desire to know what kind of government that is, and how much better it is than the state of nature, where one man commanding a multitude has the liberty to be judge in his own case, and may do to all his subjects whatever he pleases, without the least liberty to any one to question or control those who execute his pleasure; and in whatsoever he doth, whether led by reason, mistake, or passion, must be submitted to? Much better it is in the state of nature, wherein men are not bound to submit to the unjust will of another: and if he that judges, judges amiss in his own or any other case, he is answerable for it to the rest of mankind.

14. 'Tis often asked as a mighty objection, Where are, or ever were there, any men in such a state of nature? To which it may suffice as an answer at present: That since all princes and rulers of independent governments all through the world are in a state of nature, 'tis plain the world never was, nor ever will be, without numbers of men in that state. I have named all governors of independent communities, whether they are or are not in league with others. For 'tis not every compact that puts an end to the state of nature between men, but only this one of agreeing together mutually to enter into one community, and make one body politic; other promises and compacts men may make one with another, and yet still be in the state of nature. The promises and bargains for truck, etc., between the two men in the desert island, mentioned by Garcilasso de la Vega in his history of Peru; or between a Swiss and an Indian, in the woods of America, are binding to them, though they are perfectly in a state of nature in reference to one another. For truth and keeping of faith belong to men as men, and not as members of society.

15. To those that say there were never any men in the state of nature, I will not only oppose the authority of the judicious Hooker, Eccl. Pol., lib. i, sect. 10, where he says, "The laws which have been hitherto mentioned," *i.e.*, the laws of nature, "do bind men absolutely, even as they are men, although they have never any settled fellowship, and never any solemn agreement amongst themselves what to do or not to do; but forasmuch as we are not by ourselves sufficient to furnish ourselves with competent store of things needful for such a life as our nature doth desire—a life fit for the dignity of man—therefore to supply those defects and imperfections which are in us, as living single and solely by ourselves, we are naturally induced to seek communion and fellowship with others; this was the cause of men's uniting themselves at first in politic societies," but I moreover affirm that all men are naturally in that state, and remain so, till by their own consents they make themselves members of some politic society; and I doubt not, in the sequel of this discourse, to make it very clear.

Chapter III. Of the State of War

16. THE state of war is a state of enmity and destruction; and therefore declaring by word or action, not a passionate and hasty, but a sedate, settled design upon another man's life, puts him in a state of war with him against whom he has declared such an intention, and so has exposed his life to the other's power to be taken away by him,

or any one that joins with him in his defence and espouses his quarrel; it being reasonable and just I should have a right to destroy that which threatens me with destruction. For by the fundamental law of nature, man being to be preserved as much as possible, when all cannot be preserved, the safety of the innocent is to be preferred; and one may destroy a man who makes war upon him, or has discovered an enmity to his being, for the same reason that he may kill a wolf or a lion; because such men are not under the ties of the common law of reason, have no other rule but that of force and violence, and so may be treated as beasts of prey, those dangerous and noxious creatures that will be sure to destroy him whenever he falls into their power.

17. And hence it is that he who attempts to get another man into his absolute power does thereby put himself into a state of war with him; it being to be understood as a declaration of a design upon his life. For I have reason to conclude that he who would get me into his power without my consent, would use me as he pleased when he had got me there, and destroy me too, when he had a fancy to it; for nobody can desire to have me in his absolute power, unless it be to compel me by force to that which is against the right of my freedom, *i.e.*, make me a slave. To be free from such force is the only security of my preservation; and reason bids me look on him as an enemy to my preservation who would take away that freedom which is the fence to it; so that he who makes an attempt to enslave me, thereby puts himself into a state of war with me. He that in the state of nature would take away the freedom that belongs to any one in that state, must necessarily be supposed to have a design to take away everything else, that freedom being the foundation of all the rest; as he that in the state of society would take away the freedom belonging to those of that society or commonwealth, must be supposed to design to take away from them everything else, and so be looked on as in a state of war.

18. This makes it lawful for a man to kill a thief who has not in the least hurt him, nor declared any design upon his life, any farther than by the use of force so to get him in his power as to take away his money or what he pleases from him; because using force, where he has no right, to get me into his power, let his pretence be what

it will, I have no reason to suppose that he who would take away my liberty would not, when he had me in his power, take away everything else. And therefore it is lawful for me to treat him as one who has put himself into a state of war with me, *i.e.*, kill him if I can; for to that hazard does he justly expose himself, whoever introduces a state of war and is aggressor in it.

19. And here we have the plain difference between the state of nature and the state of war, which however some men have confounded, are as far distant as a state of peace, good will, mutual assistance, and preservation, and a state of enmity, malice, violence, and mutual destruction, are one from another. Men living together according to reason, without a common superior on earth with authority to judge between them, are properly in the state of nature. But force, or a declared design of force, upon the person of another, where there is no common superior on earth to appeal to for relief, is the state of war; and 'tis the want of such an appeal gives a man the right of war even against an aggressor, though he be in society and a fellow-subject. Thus a thief, whom I cannot harm, but by appeal to the law, for having stolen all that I am worth, I may kill, when he sets on to rob me but of my horse or coat; because the law, which was made for my preservation, where it cannot interpose to secure my life from present force, which if lost is capable of no reparation, permits me my own defence, and the right of war, a liberty to kill the aggressor, because the aggressor allows not time to appeal to our common judge, nor the decision of the law, for remedy in a case where the mischief may be irreparable. Want of a common judge with authority puts all men in a state of nature; force without right upon a man's person makes a state of war, both where is, and is not, a common judge.

20. But when the actual force is over, the state of war ceases between those that are in society, and are equally on both sides subjected to the fair determination of the law; because then there lies open the remedy of appeal for the past injury, and to prevent future harm. But where no such appeal is, as in the state of nature, for want of positive laws and judges with authority to appeal to, the state of war once begun continues, with a right to the innocent party to destroy the other whenever he can, until the aggressor offers peace, and

desires reconciliation on such terms as may repair any wrongs he has already done, and secure the innocent for the future. Nay, where an appeal to the law and constituted judges lies open, but the remedy is denied by a manifest perverting of justice and a barefaced wresting of the laws, to protect or indemnify the violence or injuries of some men or party of men, there it is hard to imagine anything but a state of war. For wherever violence is used and injury done, though by hands appointed to administer justice, it is still violence and injury, however coloured with the name, pretences, or forms of law; the end whereof being to protect and redress the innocent, by an unbiassed application of it to all who are under it; wherever that is not *bona fide* done, war is made upon the sufferers, who having no appeal on earth to right them, they are left to the only remedy in such cases, an appeal to heaven.

21. To avoid this state of war (wherein there is no appeal but to heaven, and wherein every the least difference is apt to end, where there is no authority to decide between the contenders) is one great reason of men's putting themselves into society and quitting the state of nature. For where there is an authority, a power on earth, from which relief can be had by appeal, there the continuance of the state of war is excluded, and the controversy is decided by that power. Had there been any such court, any superior jurisdiction on earth, to determine the right between Jephtha and the Ammonites, they had never come to a state of war; but we see he was forced to appeal to heaven. "The Lord, the Judge," says he, "be judge this day between the children of Israel and the children of Ammon" (Judges xi. 27), and then prosecuting and relying on his appeal, he leads out his army to battle. And, therefore, in such controversies, where the question is put, Who shall be judge? it cannot be meant, Who shall decide the controversy? Every one knows what Jephtha here tells us, that "the Lord the Judge" shall judge. Where there is no judge on earth, the appeal lies to God in heaven. That question, then, cannot mean, Who shall judge whether another hath put himself in a state of war with me, and whether I may, as Jephtha did, appeal to heaven in it? Of that I myself can only be judge in my own conscience, as I will answer it at the great day, to the supreme Judge of all men.

Chapter IV. Of Slavery

22. THE natural liberty of man is to be free from any superior power on earth, and not to be under the will or legislative authority of man, but to have only the law of nature for his rule. The liberty of man in society is to be under no other legislative power but that established by consent in the commonwealth; nor under the dominion of any will or restraint of any law, but what that legislative shall enact according to the trust put in it. Freedom then is not what Sir Robert Filmer tells us, O. A.55, "a liberty for every one to do what he lists, to live as he pleases, and not to be tied by any laws." But freedom of men under government is to have a standing rule to live by, common to every one of that society, and made by the legislative power erected in it; a liberty to follow my own will in all things, where the rule prescribes not; and not to be subject to the inconstant, uncertain, unknown, arbitrary will of another man; as freedom of nature is to be under no other restraint but the law of nature.

23. This freedom from absolute, arbitrary power is so necessary to, and closely joined with, a man's preservation, that he cannot part with it but by what forfeits his preservation and life together. For a man not having the power of his own life cannot by compact, or his own consent, enslave himself to any one, nor put himself under the absolute, arbitrary power of another to take away his life when he pleases. Nobody can give more power than he has himself; and he that cannot take away his own life, cannot give another power over it. Indeed, having by his fault forfeited his own life by some act that deserves death, he to whom he has forfeited it may (when he has him in his power) delay to take it, and make use of him to his own service; and he does him no injury by it. For whenever he finds the hardship of his slavery outweigh the value of his life, 'tis in his power by resisting the will of his master to draw on himself the death he desires.

24. This is the perfect condition of slavery, which is nothing else but the state of war continued between a lawful conqueror and a captive. For if once compact enter between them, and make an agreement for a limited power on the one side, and obedience on the other, the state of war and slavery ceases as long as the compact

endures. For, as has been said, no man can by agreement pass over to another that which he hath not in himself, a power over his own life.

I confess we find among the Jews as well as other nations that men did sell themselves; but 'tis plain this was only to drudgery, not to slavery. For it is evident the person sold was not under an absolute, arbitrary, despotical power. For the master could not have power to kill him, at any time, whom at a certain time he was obliged to let go free out of his service; and the master of such a servant was so far from having an arbitrary power over his life, that he could not at pleasure so much as maim him, but the loss of an eye or tooth set him free. (Exod. xxi.)

Chapter V. Of Property

25. WHETHER we consider natural reason, which tells us that men being once born have a right to their preservation, and consequently to meat and drink and such other things as nature affords for their subsistence; or revelation, which gives us an account of those grants God made of the world to Adam, and to Noah and his sons, 'tis very clear that God, as King David says, Psalm cxv. 16, "has given the earth to the children of men," given it to mankind in common. But this being supposed, it seems to some a very great difficulty how any one should ever come to have a property in anything. I will not content myself to answer that if it be difficult to make out property upon a supposition that God gave the world to Adam and his posterity in common, it is impossible that any man but one universal monarch should have any property upon a supposition that God gave the world to Adam and his heirs in succession, exclusive of all the rest of his posterity. But I shall endeavour to shew how men might come to have a property in several parts of that which God gave to mankind in common, and that without any express compact of all the commoners.

26. God, who hath given the world to men in common, hath also given them reason to make use of it to the best advantage of life and convenience. The earth and all that is therein is given to men for the support and comfort of their being. And though all the fruits it naturally produces, and beasts it feeds, belong to mankind in common, as they are produced by the spontaneous hand of nature; and nobody has originally a private dominion exclusive of the rest of mankind in any of them as they are thus in their natural state; yet being given for the use of men, there must of necessity be a means to appropriate them some way or other before they can be of any use or at all beneficial to any particular man. The fruit or venison which nourishes the wild Indian, who knows no enclosure, and is still a tenant in common, must be his, and so his, *i.e.*, a part of him, that another can no longer have any right to it, before it can do any good for the support of his life.

27. Though the earth and all inferior creatures be common to all men, yet every man has a property in his own person; this nobody has any right to but himself. The labour of his body and the work of his hands we may say are properly his. Whatsoever, then, he removes out of the state that nature hath provided and left it in, he hath mixed his labour with, and joined to it something that is his own, and thereby makes it his property. It being by him removed from the common state nature placed it in, it hath by this labour something annexed to it that excludes the common right of other men. For this labour being the unquestionable property of the labourer, no man but he can have a right to what that is once joined to, at least where there is enough and as good left in common for others.

28. He that is nourished by the acorns he picked up under an oak, or the apples he gathered from the trees in the wood, has certainly appropriated them to himself. Nobody can deny but the nourishment is his. I ask, then, When did they begin to be his? when he digested? or when he ate? or when he boiled? or when he brought them home? or when he picked them up? And 'tis plain, if the first gathering made them not his, nothing else could. That labour put a distinction between them and common; that added something to them more than nature, the common mother of all, had done, and so they became his private right. And will any one say he had no right to those acorns or apples he thus appropriated, because he had not the consent of all mankind to make them his? Was it a robbery thus to assume to himself what belonged to all in common? If such a consent as that was necessary, man had starved, notwithstanding the plenty God

had given him. We see in commons which remain so by compact that 'tis the taking any part of what is common and removing it out of the state nature leaves it in, which begins the property; without which the common is of no use. And the taking of this or that part does not depend on the express consent of all the commoners. Thus the grass my horse has bit, the turfs my servant has cut, and the ore I have dug in any place where I have a right to them in common with others, become my property without the assignation or consent of anybody. The labour that was mine removing them out of that common state they were in, hath fixed my property in them.

29. By making an explicit consent of every commoner necessary to any one's appropriating to himself any part of what is given in common, children or servants could not cut the meat which their father or master had provided for them in common without assigning to every one his peculiar part. Though the water running in the fountain be every one's, yet who can doubt but that in the pitcher is his only who drew it out? His labour hath taken it out of the hands of nature, where it was common, and belonged equally to all her children, and hath thereby appropriated it to himself.

30. Thus this law of reason makes the deer that Indian's who hath killed it; 'tis allowed to be his goods who hath bestowed his labour upon it, though before it was the common right of every one. And amongst those who are counted the civilized part of mankind, who have made and multiplied positive laws to determine property, this original law of nature, for the beginning of property in what was before common, still takes place; and by virtue thereof, what fish any one catches in the ocean, that great and still remaining common of mankind, or what ambergris any one takes up here, is, by the labour that removes it out of that common state nature left it in, made his property who takes that pains about it. And even amongst us, the hare that any one is hunting is thought his who pursues her during the chase. For being a beast that is still looked upon as common, and no man's private possession, whoever has employed so much labour about any of that kind as to find and pursue her has thereby removed her from the state of nature wherein she was common, and hath begun a property.

31. It will perhaps be objected to this, that if gathering the acorns, or other fruits of the earth, etc., makes a right to them, then any one may engross as much as he will. To which I answer, Not so. The same law of nature, that does by this means give us property, does also bound that property too. "God has given us all things richly" (1 Tim. vi. 12), is the voice of reason confirmed by inspiration. But how far has he given it us? To enjoy. As much as any one can make use of to any advantage of life before it spoils, so much he may by his labour fix a property in; whatever is beyond this is more than his share, and belongs to others. Nothing was made by God for man to spoil or destroy. And thus considering the plenty of natural provisions there was a long time in the world, and the few spenders, and to how small a part of that provision the industry of one man could extend itself, and engross it to the prejudice of others—especially keeping within the bounds, set by reason, of what might serve for his use—there could be then little room for quarrels or contentions about property so established.

World made by God

32. But the chief matter of property being now not the fruits of the earth, and the beasts that subsist on it, but the earth itself, as that which takes in and carries with it all the rest, I think it is plain that property in that, too, is acquired as the former. As much land as a man tills, plants, improves, cultivates, and can use the product of, so much is his property. He by his labour does as it were enclose it from the common. Nor will it invalidate his right to say, everybody else has an equal title to it; and therefore he cannot appropriate, he cannot enclose, without the consent of all his fellow-commoners, all mankind. God, when he gave the world in common to all mankind, commanded man also to labour, and the penury of his condition required it of him. God and his reason commanded him to subdue the earth, *i.e.*, improve it for the benefit of life, and therein lay out something upon it that was his own, his labour. He that, in obedience to this command of God, subdued, tilled, and sowed any part of it, thereby annexed to it something that was his property, which another had no title to, nor could without injury take from him.

33. Nor was this appropriation of any parcel of land, by improving it, any prejudice to any

other man, since there was still enough and as good left; and more than the yet unprovided could use. So that in effect there was never the less left for others because of his enclosure for himself. For he that leaves as much as another can make use of, does as good as take nothing at all. Nobody could think himself injured by the drinking of another man, though he took a good draught, who had a whole river of the same water left him to quench his thirst; and the case of land and water, where there is enough of both, is perfectly the same.

34. God gave the world to men in common; but since he gave it them for their benefit, and the greatest conveniencies of life they were capable to draw from it, it cannot be supposed he meant it should always remain common and uncultivated. He gave it to the use of the industrious and rational (and labour was to be his title to it), not to the fancy or covetousness of the quarrelsome and contentious. He that had as good left for his improvement as was already taken up, needed not complain, ought not to meddle with what was already improved by another's labour; if he did, 'tis plain he desired the benefit of another's pains, which he had no right to, and not the ground which God had given him in common with others to labour on, and whereof there was as good left as that already possessed, and more than he knew what to do with, or his industry could reach to.

35. 'Tis true, in land that is common in England, or any other country where there is plenty of people under government, who have money and commerce, no one can enclose or appropriate any part without the consent of all his fellow-commoners: because this is left common by compact, *i.e.*, by the law of the land, which is not to be violated. And though it be common in respect of some men, it is not so to all mankind; but is the joint property of this country, or this parish. Besides, the remainder, after such enclosure, would not be as good to the rest of the commoners as the whole was, when they could all make use of the whole; whereas in the beginning and first peopling of the great common of the world it was quite otherwise. The law man was under was rather for appropriating. God commanded, and his wants forced him, to labour. That was his property, which could not be taken from

him wherever he had fixed it. And hence subduing or cultivating the earth, and having dominion, we see are joined together. The one gave title to the other. So that God, by commanding to subdue, gave authority so far to appropriate. And the condition of human life, which requires labour and materials to work on, necessarily introduces private possessions.

36. The measure of property nature has well set by the extent of men's labour and the conveniencies of life. No man's labour could subdue or appropriate all; nor could his enjoyment consume more than a small part; so that it was impossible for any man, this way, to intrench upon the right of another, or acquire to himself a property to the prejudice of his neighbour, who would still have room for as good and as large a possession (after the other had taken out his) as before it was appropriated. This measure did confine every man's possession to a very moderate proportion, and such as he might appropriate to himself without injury to anybody, in the first ages of the world, when men were more in danger to be lost by wandering from their company in the then vast wilderness of the earth than to be straitened for want of room to plant in. And the same measure may be allowed still without prejudice to anybody, as full as the world seems. For supposing a man or family in the state they were at first peopling of the world by the children of Adam or Noah; let him plant in some inland vacant places of America, we shall find that the possessions he could make himself, upon the measures we have given, would not be very large, nor, even to this day, prejudice the rest of mankind, or give them reason to complain or think themselves injured by this man's encroachment, though the race of men have now spread themselves to all the corners of the world, and do infinitely exceed the small number that was at the beginning. Nay, the extent of ground is of so little value without labour, that I have heard it affirmed that in Spain itself a man may be permitted to plough, sow, and reap, without being disturbed, upon land he has no other title to but only his making use of it. But, on the contrary, the inhabitants think themselves beholden to him who by his industry on neglected and consequently waste land has increased the stock of corn which they wanted. But be this as it will, which I lay no stress on, this

· Locke couldn't have known about global warming, pop. growth

I dare boldly affirm—that the same rule of propriety, *viz.*, that every man should have as much as he could make use of, would hold still in the world without straitening anybody, since there is land enough in the world to suffice double the inhabitants, had not the invention of money, and the tacit agreement of men to put a value on it, introduced (by consent) larger possessions and a right to them; which how it has done I shall by and by shew more at large.

37. This is certain, that in the beginning, before the desire of having more than man needed had altered the intrinsic value of things, which depends only on their usefulness to the life of man; or had agreed that a little piece of yellow metal which would keep without wasting or decay should be worth a great piece of flesh or a whole heap of corn, though men had a right to appropriate by their labour, each one to himself, as much of the things of nature as he could use, yet this could not be much, nor to the prejudice of others, where the same plenty was still left to those who would use the same industry. To which let me add, that he who appropriates land to himself by his labour does not lessen but increase the common stock of mankind. For the provisions serving to the support of human life produced by one acre of enclosed and cultivated land are (to speak much within compass) ten times more than those which are yielded by an acre of land of an equal richness lying waste in common. And therefore he that encloses land, and has a greater plenty of the conveniencies of life from ten acres than he could have from an hundred left to nature, may truly be said to give ninety acres to mankind: for his labour now supplies him with provisions out of ten acres, which were but the product of an hundred lying in common. I have here rated the improved land very low, in making its product but as ten to one, when it is much nearer an hundred to one. For I ask, whether in the wild woods and uncultivated waste of America, left to nature without any improvement, tillage, or husbandry, a thousand acres yield the needy and wretched inhabitants as many conveniencies of life as ten acres of equally fertile land do in Devonshire, where they are well cultivated?

Before the appropriation of land, he who gathered as much of the wild fruit, killed, caught, or tamed as many of the beasts as he could; he that

so employed his pains about any of the spontaneous products of nature as any way to alter them from the state which nature put them in, by placing any of his labour on them, did thereby acquire a propriety in them. But if they perished in his possession without their due use: if the fruits rotted, or the venison putrefied before he could spend it, he offended against the common law of nature, and was liable to be punished; he invaded his neighbour's share, for he had no right farther than his use called for any of them and they might serve to afford him conveniencies of life.

38. The same measures governed the possession of land too. Whatsoever he tilled and reaped, laid up, and made use of before it spoiled, that was his peculiar right; whatsoever he enclosed and could feed and make use of, the cattle and product was also his. But if either the grass of his enclosure rotted on the ground, or the fruit of his planting perished without gathering and laying up, this part of the earth, notwithstanding his enclosure, was still to be looked on as waste, and might be the possession of any other. Thus, at the beginning, Cain might take as much ground as he could till and make it his own land, and yet leave enough for Abel's sheep to feed on; a few acres would serve for both their possessions. But as families increased, and industry enlarged their stocks, their possessions enlarged with the need of them; but yet it was commonly without any fixed property in the ground they made use of, till they incorporated, settled themselves together, and built cities; and then, by consent, they came in time to set out the bounds of their distinct territories, and agree on limits between them and their neighbours, and, by laws within themselves, settled the properties of those of the same society. For we see that in that part of the world which was first inhabited, and therefore like to be the best peopled, even as low down as Abraham's time they wandered with their flocks and their herds, which were their substance, freely up and down; and this Abraham did in a country where he was a stranger: whence it is plain that at least a great part of the land lay in common; that the inhabitants valued it not, nor claimed property in any more than they made use of. But when there was not room enough in the same place for their herds to feed together, they by consent, as Abraham and Lot did (Gen. xiii. 5), separated and

enlarged their pasture where it best liked them. And for the same reason Esau went from his father and his brother, and planted in Mount Seir (Gen. xxxvi. 6).

39. And thus, without supposing any private dominion and property in Adam over all the world, exclusive of all other men, which can no way be proved, nor any one's property be made out from it; but supposing the world given as it was to the children of men in common, we see how labour could make men distinct titles to several parcels of it for their private uses, wherein there could be no doubt of right, no room for quarrel.

40. Nor is it so strange, as perhaps before consideration it may appear, that the property of labour should be able to overbalance the community of land. For 'tis labour indeed that puts the difference of value on everything; and let any one consider what the difference is between an acre of land planted with tobacco or sugar, sown with wheat or barley, and an acre of the same land lying in common without any husbandry upon it, and he will find that the improvement of labour makes the far greater part of the value. I think it will be but a very modest computation to say that of the products of the earth useful to the life of man nine-tenths are the effects of labour; nay, if we will rightly estimate things as they come to our use, and cast up the several expenses about them—what in them is purely owing to nature, and what to labour—we shall find that in most of them ninety-nine hundredths are wholly to be put on the account of labour.

41. There cannot be a clearer demonstration of anything than several nations of the Americans are of this, who are rich in land and poor in all the comforts of life; whom nature having furnished as liberally as any other people with the materials of plenty—i.e., a fruitful soil, apt to produce in abundance what might serve for food, raiment, and delight—yet, for want of improving it by labour, have not one-hundredth part of the conveniencies we enjoy. And a king of a large and fruitful territory there, feeds, lodges, and is clad worse than a day-labourer in England.

42. To make this a little clearer, let us but trace some of the ordinary provisions of life through their several progresses before they come to our use, and see how much they receive of their value

from human industry. Bread, wine, and cloth are things of daily use and great plenty; yet, notwithstanding, acorns, water, and leaves or skins must be our bread, drink, and clothing, did not labour furnish us with these more useful commodities. For whatever bread is more worth than acorns, wine than water, and cloth or silk than leaves, skins, or moss, that is wholly owing to labour and industry; the one of these being the food and raiment which unassisted nature furnishes us with; the other, provisions which our industry and pains prepare for us; which how much they exceed the other in value when any one hath computed, he will then see how much labour makes the far greatest part of the value of things we enjoy in this world. And the ground which produces the materials is scarce to be reckoned in as any, or at most but a very small, part of it; so little that even amongst us land that is left wholly to nature, that hath no improvement of pasturage, tillage, or planting, is called, as indeed it is, waste, and we shall find the benefit of it amount to little more than nothing.

This shows how much numbers of men are to be preferred to largeness of dominions; and that the increase of lands and the right employing of them is the great art of government: and that prince, who shall be so wise and godlike as by established laws of liberty to secure protection and encouragement to the honest industry of mankind, against the oppression of power and narrowness of party, will quickly be too hard for his neighbours: but this by the by.

To return to the argument in hand.

43. An acre of land that bears here twenty bushels of wheat, and another in America which, with the same husbandry, would do the like, are without doubt of the same natural intrinsic value; but yet the benefit mankind receives from the one in a year is worth £5, and from the other possibly not worth a penny, if all the profit an Indian received from it were to be valued and sold here; at least, I may truly say, not one-thousandth. 'Tis labour, then, which puts the greatest part of value upon land, without which it would scarcely be worth anything; 'tis to that we owe the greatest part of all its useful products, for all that the straw, bran, bread of that acre of wheat is more worth than the product of an acre of as good land which lies waste, is all the effect of labour. For 'tis not

barely the ploughman's pains, the reaper's and thresher's toil, and the baker's sweat, is to be counted into the bread we eat; the labour of those who broke the oxen, who digged and wrought the iron and stones, who felled and framed the timber employed about the plough, mill, oven, or any other utensils, which are a vast number, requisite to this corn, from its being seed to be sown to its being made bread, must all be charged on the account of labour, and received as an effect of that. Nature and the earth furnished only the almost worthless materials as in themselves. 'Twould be a strange catalogue of things that industry provided and made use of, about every loaf of bread before it came to our use, if we could trace them—iron, wood, leather, bark, timber, stone, bricks, coals, lime, cloth, dyeing drugs, pitch, tar, masts, ropes, and all the materials made use of in the ship that brought any of the commodities made use of by any of the workmen to any part of the work, all which 'twould be almost impossible, at least too long, to reckon up.

44. From all which it is evident that, though the things of nature are given in common, yet man, by being master of himself and proprietor of his own person and the actions or labour of it, had still in himself the great foundations of property; and that which made up the great part of what he applied to the support or comfort of his being, when invention and arts had improved the conveniencies of life, was perfectly his own, and did not belong in common to others.

45. Thus labour, in the beginning, gave a right of property, wherever any one was pleased to employ it upon what was common, which remained a long while the far greater part, and is yet more than mankind makes use of. Men at first, for the most part, contented themselves with what unassisted nature offered to their necessities; and though afterwards, in some parts of the world (where the increase of people and stock, with the use of money, had made land scarce, and so of some value), the several communities settled the bounds of their distinct territories, and, by laws within themselves, regulated the properties of the private men of their society, and so, by compact and agreement, settled the property which labour and industry began—and the leagues that have been made between several states and kingdoms, either expressly or tacitly disowning all claim and right to the land in the other's possession, have, by common consent, given up their pretences to their natural common right, which originally they had to those countries; and so have, by positive agreement, settled a property amongst themselves in distinct parts and parcels of the earth—yet there are still great tracts of ground to be found which (the inhabitants thereof not having joined with the rest of mankind in the consent of the use of their common money) lie waste, and are more than the people who dwell on it do or can make use of, and so still lie in common; though this can scarce happen amongst that part of mankind that have consented to the use of money.

46. The greatest part of things really useful to the life of man, and such as the necessity of subsisting made the first commoners of the world look after, as it doth the Americans now, are generally things of short duration, such as, if they are not consumed by use, will decay and perish of themselves: gold, silver, and diamonds are things that fancy or agreement have put the value on more than real use and the necessary support of life. Now, of those good things which nature hath provided in common, every one had a right (as hath been said) to as much as he could use, and property in all he could effect with his labour; all that his industry could extend to, to alter from the state nature had put it in, was his. He that gathered a hundred bushels of acorns or apples had thereby a property in them; they were his goods as soon as gathered. He was only to look that he used them before they spoiled, else he took more than his share, and robbed others; and, indeed, it was a foolish thing, as well as dishonest, to hoard up more than he could make use of. If he gave away a part to anybody else, so that it perished not uselessly in his possession, these he also made use of; and if he also bartered away plums that would have rotted in a week, for nuts that would last good for his eating a whole year, he did no injury; he wasted not the common stock, destroyed no part of the portion of goods that belonged to others, so long as nothing perished uselessly in his hands. Again, if he would give his nuts for a piece of metal, pleased with its colour; or exchange his sheep for shells, or wool for a sparkling pebble or a diamond, and keep those by him all his life, he invaded not the right of others; he might heap up

as much of these durable things as he pleased, the exceeding of the bounds of his just property not lying in the largeness of his possession, but the perishing of anything uselessly in it.

47. And thus came in the use of money—some lasting thing that men might keep without spoiling, and that, by mutual consent, men would take in exchange for the truly useful but perishable supports of life.

48. And as different degrees of industry were apt to give men possessions in different proportions, so this invention of money gave them the opportunity to continue and enlarge them; for supposing an island, separate from all possible commerce with the rest of the world, wherein there were but an hundred families—but there were sheep, horses, and cows, with other useful animals, wholesome fruits, and land enough for corn for a hundred thousand times as many, but nothing in the island, either because of its commonness or perishableness, fit to supply the place of money—what reason could any one have there to enlarge his possessions beyond the use of his family and a plentiful supply to its consumption, either in what their own industry produced, or they could barter for like perishable useful commodities with others? Where there is not something both lasting and scarce, and so valuable to be hoarded up, there men will not be apt to enlarge their possessions of land, were it never so rich, never so free for them to take; for I ask, what would a man value ten thousand or an hundred thousand acres of excellent land, ready cultivated, and well stocked too with cattle, in the middle of the inland parts of America, where he had no hopes of commerce with other parts of the world, to draw money to him by the sale of the product? It would not be worth the enclosing, and we should see him give up again to the wild common of nature whatever was more than would supply the conveniencies of life to be had there for him and his family.

49. Thus in the beginning all the world was America, and more so than that is now, for no such thing as money was anywhere known. Find out something that hath the use and value of money amongst his neighbours, you shall see the same man will begin presently to enlarge his possessions.

50. But since gold and silver, being little useful to the life of man in proportion to food, rai-ment, and carriage, has its value only from the consent of men, whereof labour yet makes, in great part, the measure, it is plain that men have agreed to a disproportionate and unequal possession of the earth; they having, by a tacit and voluntary consent, found out a way how a man may fairly possess more land than he himself can use the product of, by receiving in exchange for the overplus, gold and silver, which may be hoarded up without injury to any one; these metals not spoiling or decaying in the hands of the possessor. This partage of things in an inequality of private possessions men have made practicable, out of the bounds of society, and without compact, only by putting a value on gold and silver, and tacitly agreeing in the use of money. For in governments the laws regulate the right of property, and the possession of land is determined by positive constitutions.

51. And thus, I think, it is very easy to conceive without any difficulty how labour could at first begin a title of property in the common things of nature, and how the spending it upon our uses bounded it; so that there could then be no reason of quarrelling about title, nor any doubt about the largeness of possession it gave. Right and conveniency went together; for as a man had a right to all he could employ his labour upon, so he had no temptation to labour for more than he could make use of. This left no room for controversy about the title, nor for encroachment on the right of others; what portion a man carved to himself was easily seen, and it was useless, as well as dishonest, to carve himself too much, or take more than he needed....

Chapter VII. Of Political or Civil Society

77. GOD having made man such a creature, that in his own judgment it was not good for him to be alone, put him under strong obligations of necessity, convenience, and inclination to drive him into society, as well as fitted him with understanding and language to continue and enjoy it. The first society was between man and wife, which gave beginning to that between parents and children; to which, in time, that between master and servant came to be added; and though all these might, and commonly did meet together, and make up but one family, wherein the master or

mistress of it had some sort of rule proper to a family; each of these, or all together, came short of political society, as we shall see, if we consider the different ends, ties, and bounds of each of these.

78. Conjugal society is made by a voluntary compact between man and woman, and though it consists chiefly in such a communion and right in one another's bodies as is necessary to its chief end, procreation, yet it draws with it mutual support and assistance, and a communion of interests too, as necessary not only to unite their care and affection, but also necessary to their common offspring, who have a right to be nourished and maintained by them till they are able to provide for themselves.

79. For the end of conjunction between male and female being not barely procreation, but the continuation of the species, this conjunction betwixt male and female ought to last, even after procreation, so long as is necessary to the nourishment and support of the young ones, who are to be sustained by those that got them till they are able to shift and provide for themselves. This rule, which the infinite wise Maker hath set to the works of his hands, we find the inferior creatures steadily obey. In those viviparous animals which feed on grass, the conjunction between male and female lasts no longer than the very act of copulation, because the teat of the dam being sufficient to nourish the young till it be able to feed on grass, the male only begets, but concerns not himself for the female or young, to whose sustenance he can contribute nothing. But in beasts of prey the conjunction lasts longer, because the dam not being able well to subsist herself and nourish her numerous offspring by her own prey alone, a more laborious as well as more dangerous way of living than by feeding on grass, the assistance of the male is necessary to the maintenance of their common family, which cannot subsist till they are able to prey for themselves but by the joint care of male and female. The same is to be observed in all birds (except some domestic ones where plenty of food excuses the cock from feeding and taking care of the young brood), whose young needing food in the nest, the cock and hen continue mates till the young are able to use their wing and provide for themselves.

80. And herein I think lies the chief, if not the only, reason why the male and female in mankind are tied to a longer conjunction than other creatures, *viz.*, because the female is capable of conceiving, and *de facto* is commonly with child again, and brings forth, too, a new birth, long before the former is out of a dependency for support on his parents' help, and able to shift for himself, and has all the assistance is due to him from his parents; whereby the father, who is bound to take care for those he hath begot, is under an obligation to continue in conjugal society with the same woman longer than other creatures, whose young being able to subsist of themselves before the time of procreation returns again, the conjugal bond dissolves of itself, and they are at liberty till Hymen at his usual anniversary season summons them again to choose new mates. Wherein one cannot but admire the wisdom of the great Creator, who having given to man foresight, and an ability to lay up for the future as well as to supply the present necessity, hath made it necessary that society of man and wife should be more lasting than of male and female amongst other creatures, that so their industry might be encouraged, and their interest better united to make provision and lay up goods for their common issue, which uncertain mixture or easy and frequent solutions of conjugal society would mightily disturb.

81. But though these are ties upon mankind which make the conjugal bonds more firm and lasting in man than the other species of animals, yet it would give one reason to inquire why this compact, where procreation and education are secured, and inheritance taken care for, may not be made determinable, either by consent, or at a certain time, or upon certain conditions, as well as any other voluntary compacts, there being no necessity in the nature of the thing, nor to the ends of it, that it should always be for life—I mean to such as are under no restraint of any positive law which ordains all such contracts to be perpetual.

82. But the husband and wife, though they have but one common concern, yet having different understandings, will unavoidably sometimes have different wills too; it therefore being necessary that the last determination—*i.e.*, the rule—should be placed somewhere, it naturally falls to the man's share, as the abler and the stronger. But this, reaching but to the things of their common interest and property, leaves the wife in the full and free possession of what by contract is her

peculiar right, and at least gives the husband no more power over her life than she has over his. The power of the husband being so far from that of an absolute monarch, that the wife has in many cases a liberty to separate from him, where natural right or their contract allows it, whether that contract be made by themselves in a state of nature, or by the customs or laws of the country they live in; and the children upon such separation fall to the father's or mother's lot, as such contract does determine.

83. For all the ends of marriage being to be obtained under politic government, as well as in the state of nature, the civil magistrate doth not abridge the right or power of either naturally necessary to those ends—*viz.*, procreation and mutual support and assistance whilst they are together—but only decides any controversy that may arise between man and wife about them. If it were otherwise, and that absolute sovereignty and power of life and death naturally belonged to the husband, and were necessary to the society between man and wife, there could be no matrimony in any of those countries where the husband is allowed no such absolute authority. But the ends of matrimony requiring no such power in the husband, the condition of conjugal society put it not in him, it being not at all necessary to that state. Conjugal society could subsist and attain its ends without it; nay, community of goods, and the power over them, mutual assistance and maintenance, and other things belonging to conjugal society, might be varied and regulated by that contract which unites man and wife in that society, as far as may consist with procreation and the bringing up of children till they could shift for themselves; nothing being necessary to any society that is not necessary to the ends for which it is made.

84. The society betwixt parents and children, and the distinct rights and powers belonging respectively to them, I have treated of so largely in the foregoing chapter that I shall not here need to say anything of it; and I think it is plain that it is far different from a politic society.

85. Master and servant are names as old as history, but given to those of far different condition; for a freeman makes himself a servant to another by selling him for a certain time the service he undertakes to do in exchange for wages he is to receive; and though this commonly puts him into the family of his master, and under the ordinary discipline thereof, yet it gives the master but a temporary power over him, and no greater than what is contained in the contract between them. But there is another sort of servants, which by a peculiar name we call slaves, who, being captives taken in a just war, are by the right of nature subjected to the absolute dominion and arbitrary power of their masters. These men having, as I say, forfeited their lives, and with them their liberties, and lost their estates—and being, in the state of slavery, not capable of any property—cannot in that state be considered as any part of civil society, the chief end whereof is the preservation of property.

86. Let us therefore consider a master of a family, with all these subordinate relations of wife, children, servants, and slaves, united under the domestic rule of a family, which, what resemblance soever it may have in its order, offices, and number too, with a little commonwealth, yet is very far from it both in its constitution, power, and end; or, if it must be thought a monarchy, and the paterfamilias the absolute monarch in it, absolute monarchy will have but a very shattered and short power, when 'tis plain, by what has been said before, that the master of the family has a very distinct and differently limited power, both as to time and extent, over those several persons that are in it; for, excepting the slave (and the family is as much a family, and his power as paterfamilias as great, whether there be any slaves in his family or no), he has no legislative power of life and death over any of them, and none, too, but what a mistress of a family may have as well as he. And he certainly can have no absolute power over the whole family, who has but a very limited one over every individual in it. But how a family or any other society of men differ from that, which is properly political society, we shall best see by considering wherein political society itself consists.

87. Man being born, as has been proved, with a title to perfect freedom, and an uncontrolled enjoyment of all the rights and privileges of the law of nature equally with any other man or number of men in the world, hath by nature a power not only to preserve his property—that is, his life, liberty, and estate—against the injuries and attempts of other men, but to judge of and punish the breaches of that law in others as he is per-

suaded the offence deserves, even with death itself, in crimes where the heinousness of the fact in his opinion requires it. But because no political society can be nor subsist without having in itself the power to preserve the property, and, in order thereunto, punish the offences of all those of that society; there, and there only, is political society, where every one of the members hath quitted this natural power, resigned it up into the hands of the community in all cases that exclude him not from appealing for protection to the law established by it. And thus all private judgment of every particular member being excluded, the community comes to be umpire, by settled, standing rules, indifferent, and the same to all parties; and by men having authority from the community for the execution of those rules, decides all the differences that may happen between any members of that society concerning any matter of right, and punishes those offences which any member hath committed against the society, with such penalties as the law has established; whereby it is easy to discern who are and who are not in political society together. Those who are united into one body, and have a common established law and judicature to appeal to, with authority to decide controversies between them and punish offenders, are in civil society one with another; but those who have no such common appeal— I mean on earth—are still in the state of nature, each being, where there is no other, judge for himself and executioner, which is, as I have before shewn it, the perfect state of nature.

88. And thus the commonwealth comes by a power to set down what punishment shall belong to the several transgressions which they think worthy of it, committed amongst the members of that society (which is the power of making laws) as well as it has the power to punish any injury done unto any of its members by any one that is not of it (which is the power of war and peace); and all this for the preservation of the property of all the members of that society as far as is possible. But though every man who has entered into civil society, and is become a member of any commonwealth, has thereby quitted his power to punish offences against the law of nature in prosecution of his own private judgment, yet with the judgment of offences, which he has given up to the legislative in all cases where he can appeal to the magistrate, he has given a right to the commonwealth to employ his force for the execution of the judgments of the commonwealth whenever he shall be called to it; which, indeed, are his own judgments, they being made by himself or his representative. And herein we have the original of the legislative and executive power of civil society, which is to judge by standing laws how far offences are to be punished when committed within the commonwealth, and also to determine, by occasional judgments founded on the present circumstances of the fact, how far injuries from without are to be vindicated; and in both these to employ all the force of all the members when there shall be need.

89. Wherever, therefore, any number of men are so united into one society, as to quit every one his executive power of the law of nature, and to resign it to the public, there, and there only, is a political, or civil society. And this is done wherever any number of men, in the state of nature, enter into society to make one people, one body politic, under one supreme government, or else when any one joins himself to, and incorporates with, any government already made. For hereby he authorizes the society, or, which is all one, the legislative thereof, to make laws for him, as the public good of the society shall require, to the execution whereof his own assistance (as to his own decrees) is due. And this puts men out of a state of nature into that of a commonwealth, by setting up a judge on earth with authority to determine all the controversies and redress the injuries that may happen to any member of the commonwealth; which judge is the legislative, or magistrates appointed by it. And wherever there are any number of men, however associated, that have no such decisive power to appeal to, there they are still in the state of nature.

90. Hence it is evident that absolute monarchy, which by some men is counted the only government in the world, is indeed inconsistent with civil society, and so can be no form of civil government at all. For the end of civil society being to avoid and remedy those inconveniencies of the state of nature which necessarily follow from every man's being judge in his own case, by setting up a known authority to which every one of that society may appeal upon any injury received or controversy that may arise, and which every

one of the society ought to obey[1]; wherever any persons are, who have not such an authority to appeal to and decide any difference between them, there those persons are still in the state of nature. And so is every absolute prince, in respect of those who are under his dominion.

91. For he being supposed to have all, both legislative and executive, power in himself alone, there is no judge to be found; no appeal lies open to any one who may fairly and indifferently and with authority decide, and from whose decision relief and address may be expected of any injury or inconvenience that may be suffered from the prince or by his order; so that such a man, however entitled—Czar, or Grand Seignior, or how you please—is as much in the state of nature, with all under his dominion, as he is with the rest of mankind. For wherever any two men are, who have no standing rule and common judge to appeal to on earth for the determination of controversies of right betwixt them, there they are still in the state of nature,[2] and under all the inconveniencies of it, with only this woeful difference to the subject, or rather slave, of an absolute prince: that, whereas in the ordinary state of nature he has a liberty to judge of his right, and according to the best of his power to maintain it; now, whenever his property is invaded by the will and order of his monarch, he has not only no appeal, as those in society ought to have, but, as if he were degraded from the common state of rational creatures, is denied a liberty to judge of or to defend his right; and so is exposed to all the misery and inconveniencies that a man can fear from one who, being in the unrestrained state of nature, is yet corrupted with flattery, and armed with power.

92. For he that thinks absolute power purifies men's blood, and corrects the baseness of human nature, need read but the history of this or any other age, to be convinced of the contrary. He that would have been insolent and injurious in the woods of America, would not probably be much better in a throne; where, perhaps, learning and religion shall be found out to justify all that he shall do to his subjects, and the sword presently silence all those that dare question it. For what the protection of absolute monarchy is, what kind of fathers of their countries it makes princes to be, and to what a degree of happiness and security it carries civil society, where this sort of government is grown to perfection, he that will look into the late relation of Ceylon may easily see.

93. In absolute monarchies, indeed, as well as other governments of the world, the subjects have an appeal to the law and judges, to decide any controversies and restrain any violence that may happen betwixt the subjects themselves, one amongst another. This every one thinks necessary, and believes he deserves to be thought a declared enemy to society and mankind who should go about to take it away. But whether this be from a true love of mankind and society, and such a charity as we owe all one to another, there is reason to doubt. For this is no more than what every man who loves his own power, profit, or greatness may, and naturally must do, keep those animals from hurting or destroying one another who labour and drudge only for his pleasure and advantage; and so are taken care of, not out of any love the master has for them, but love of himself, and the profit they bring him. For if it be asked, what security, what fence is there, in such a state, against

1. "The public power of all society is above every soul contained in the same society, and the principal use of that power is to give laws unto all that are under it, which laws in such cases we must obey, unless there be reason shewed which may necessarily enforce that the law of reason or of God doth enjoin the contrary."—Hooker (*Eccl. Pol.*, lib. i, sect. 16).
2. To take away all such mutual grievances, injuries, and wrongs, *i.e.*, such as attend men in the state of nature, there was no way but only by growing into composition and agreement amongst themselves by ordaining some kind of government public, and by yielding themselves subject thereunto, that unto whom they granted authority to rule and govern, by them the peace, tranquillity, and happy estate of the rest might be procured. Men always knew that where force and injury was offered, they might be defenders of themselves. They knew that, however men may seek their own commodity, yet if this were done with injury unto others, it was not to be suffered, but by all men and all good means to be withstood. Finally, they knew that no man might, in reason, take upon him to determine his own right, and according to his own determination proceed in maintenance thereof, in as much as every man is towards himself, and them whom he greatly affects, partial; and therefore, that strifes and troubles would be endless, except they gave their common consent, all to be ordered by some whom they should agree upon, without which consent there would be no reason that one man should take upon him to be lord or judge over another."—Hooker (*ibid.*, sect. 10).

the violence and oppression of this absolute ruler, the very question can scarce be borne. They are ready to tell you that it deserves death only to ask after safety. Betwixt subject and subject, they will grant, there must be measures, laws and judges, for their mutual peace and security; but as for the ruler, he ought to be absolute, and is above all such circumstances; because he has power to do more hurt and wrong, 'tis right when he does it. To ask how you may be guarded from harm or injury on that side where the strongest hand is to do it, is presently the voice of faction and rebellion. As if when men quitting the state of nature entered into society, they agreed that all of them but one should be under the restraint of laws, but that he should still retain all the liberty of the state of nature, increased with power, and made licentious by impunity. This is to think that men are so foolish that they take care to avoid what mischiefs may be done them by polecats or foxes, but are content, nay, think it safety, to be devoured by lions.

94. But, whatever flatterers may talk to amuse people's understandings, it hinders not men from feeling; and when they perceive that any man, in what station soever, is out of the bounds of the civil society which they are of, and that they have no appeal on earth against any harm they may receive from him, they are apt to think themselves in the state of nature in respect of him whom they find to be so; and to take care, as soon as they can, to have that safety and security in civil society for which it was first instituted, and for which only they entered into it. And, therefore, though perhaps at first (as shall be shewn more at large hereafter in the following part of this discourse), some one good and excellent man, having got a pre-eminency amongst the rest, had this deference paid to his goodness and virtue, as to a kind of natural authority, that the chief rule, with arbitration of their differences, by a tacit consent devolved into his hands, without any other caution but the assurance they had of his uprightness and wisdom; yet when time, giving authority and (as some men would persuade us) sacredness of customs which the negligent and unforeseeing innocence of the first ages began, had brought in successors of another stamp, the people finding their properties not secure under the government, as then it was (whereas government has no

other end but the preservation of property),[3] could never be safe nor at rest, nor think themselves in civil society, till the legislature was placed in collective bodies of men, call them senate, parliament, or what you please. By which means every single person became subject, equally with other the meanest men, to those laws, which he himself, as part of the legislative, had established; nor could any one by his own authority avoid the force of the law when once made, nor by any pretence of superiority plead exemption, thereby to license his own, or the miscarriages of any of his dependents. No man in civil society can be exempted from the laws of it.[4] For if any man may do what he thinks fit, and there be no appeal on earth for redress or security against any harm he shall do, I ask whether he be not perfectly still in the state of nature, and so can be no part or member of that civil society; unless any one will say the state of nature and civil society are one and the same thing, which I have never yet found any one so great a patron of anarchy as to affirm.

Chapter VIII. Of the Beginning of Political Societies

95. MEN being, as has been said, by nature all free, equal, and independent, no one can be put out of this estate, and subjected to the political power of another, without his own consent. The only way whereby any one divests himself of his natural liberty and puts on the bonds of civil society is by agreeing with other men to join and unite into a community for their comfortable, safe, and peaceable living one amongst another, in

3. "At the first, when some certain kind of regiment was once appointed, it may be that nothing was then farther thought upon for the manner of governing, but all permitted unto their wisdom and discretion which were to rule till, by experience, they found this for all parts very inconvenient, so as the thing which they had devised for a remedy did indeed but increase the sore which it should have cured. They saw that to live by one man's will became the cause of all men's misery. This constrained them to come unto laws wherein all men might see their duty beforehand, and know the penalties of transgressing them."—Hooker (*Eccl. Pol.*, lib. i, sect. 10).
4. "Civil law, being the act of the whole body politic, doth therefore overrule each several part of the same body."—Hooker (*ibid.*).

a secure enjoyment of their properties, and a greater security against any that are not of it. This any number of men may do, because it injures not the freedom of the rest; they are left as they were in the liberty of the state of nature. When any number of men have so consented to make one community or government, they are thereby presently incorporated, and make one body politic, wherein the majority have a right to act and conclude the rest.

96. For when any number of men have, by the consent of every individual, made a community, they have thereby made that community one body, with a power to act as one body, which is only by the will and determination of the majority. For that which acts any community being only the consent of the individuals of it, and it being necessary to that which is one body to move one way, it is necessary the body should move that way whither the greater force carries it, which is the consent of the majority; or else it is impossible it should act or continue one body, one community, which the consent of every individual that united into it agreed that it should; and so every one is bound by that consent to be concluded by the majority. And therefore we see that in assemblies empowered to act by positive laws, where no number is set by that positive law which empowers them, the act of the majority passes for the act of the whole, and of course determines, as having by the law of nature and reason the power of the whole.

97. And thus every man, by consenting with others to make one body politic under one government, puts himself under an obligation to every one of that society, to submit to the determination of the majority, and to be concluded by it; or else this original compact, whereby he with others incorporates into one society, would signify nothing, and be no compact, if he be left free and under no other ties than he was in before in the state of nature. For what appearance would there be of any compact? What new engagement if he were no farther tied by any decrees of the society, than he himself thought fit, and did actually consent to? This would be still as great a liberty as he himself had before his compact, or any one else in the state of nature hath, who may submit himself and consent to any acts of it if he thinks fit.

98. For if the consent of the majority shall not in reason be received as the act of the whole, and conclude every individual, nothing but the consent of every individual can make anything to be the act of the whole, but such a consent is next to impossible ever to be had, if we consider the infirmities of health and avocations of business, which in a number, though much less than that of a commonwealth, will necessarily keep many away from the public assembly. To which if we add the variety of opinions, and contrariety of interests, which unavoidably happen in all collections of men, the coming into society upon such terms would be only like Cato's coming into the theatre, only to go out again. Such a constitution as this would make the mighty Leviathan of a shorter duration than the feeblest creatures, and not let it outlast the day it was born in; which cannot be supposed, till we can think that rational creatures should desire and constitute societies only to be dissolved. For where the majority cannot conclude the rest, there they cannot act as one body, and consequently will be immediately dissolved again.

99. Whosoever therefore out of a state of nature unite into a community must be understood to give up all the power necessary to the ends for which they unite into society, to the majority of the community, unless they expressly agreed in any number greater than the majority. And this is done by barely agreeing to unite into one political society, which is all the compact that is, or needs be, between the individuals that enter into or make up a commonwealth. And thus that which begins and actually constitutes any political society is nothing but the consent of any number of freemen capable of a majority to unite and incorporate into such a society. And this is that, and that only, which did or could give beginning to any lawful government in the world.

100. To this I find two objections made.

First: That there are no instances to be found in story of a company of men, independent and equal one amongst another, that met together, and in this way began and set up a government.

Secondly: 'Tis impossible of right that men should do so, because all men being born under government, they are to submit to that, and are not at liberty to begin a new one.

101. To the first there is this to answer: That it is not at all to be wondered that history gives us

but a very little account of men that lived together in the state of nature. The inconveniencies of that condition, and the love and want of society, no sooner brought any number of them together, but they presently united and incorporated if they designed to continue together. And if we may not suppose men ever to have been in the state of nature, because we hear not much of them in such a state, we may as well suppose the armies of Salmanasser or Xerxes were never children, because we hear little of them till they were men, and embodied in armies. Government is everywhere antecedent to records, and letters seldom come in amongst a people, till a long continuation of civil society has, by other more necessary arts, provided for their safety, ease, and plenty. And then they begin to look after the history of their founders, and search into their original, when they have outlived the memory of it. For 'tis with commonwealths as with particular persons, they are commonly ignorant of their own birth and infancies. And if they know anything of their original, they are beholden for it to the accidental records that others have kept of it. And those that we have of the beginning of any polities in the world, excepting that of the Jews, where God himself immediately interposed, and which favours not at all paternal dominion, are all either plain instances of such a beginning as I have mentioned, or at least have manifest footsteps of it.

102. He must shew a strange inclination to deny evident matter of fact when it agrees not with his hypothesis, who will not allow that the beginning of Rome and Venice were by the uniting together of several men free and independent one of another, amongst whom there was no natural superiority or subjection. And if Josephus Acosta's word may be taken, he tells us that in many parts of America there was no government at all. "There are great and apparent conjectures," says he, "that these men," speaking of those of Peru, "for a long time had neither kings nor commonwealths, but lived in troops, as they do this day in Florida, the Cheriquanas, those of Brazil, and many other nations, which have no certain kings, but as occasion is offered in peace or war, they choose their captains as they please" (l. i, c. 25). If it be said that every man there was born subject to his father, or the head of his family, that the sub-

jection due from a child to a father took not away his freedom of uniting into what political society he thought fit, has been already proved. But be that as it will, these men, 'tis evident, were actually free; and whatever superiority some politicians now would place in any of them, they themselves claimed it not; but by consent were all equal, till by the same consent they set rulers over themselves. So that their politic societies all began from a voluntary union, and the mutual agreement of men freely acting in the choice of their governors and forms of government.

103. And I hope those who went away from Sparta with Palantus, mentioned by Justin, l. iii, c. 4, will be allowed to have been freemen, independent one of another, and to have set up a government over themselves, by their own consent. Thus I have given several examples out of history of people free and in the state of nature that, being met together, incorporated and began a commonwealth. And if the want of such instances be an argument to prove that government were not nor could not be so begun, I suppose the contenders for paternal empire were better let it alone than urge it against natural liberty. For if they can give so many instances, out of history, of governments begun upon paternal right, I think (though at best an argument from what has been, to what should of right be, has no great force) one might, without any great danger, yield them the cause. But if I might advise them in the case, they would do well not to search too much into the original of governments as they have begun *de facto*, lest they should find at the foundation of most of them something very little favourable to the design they promote and such a power as they contend for.

104. But to conclude, reason being plain on our side that men are naturally free, and the examples of history shewing that the governments of the world, that were begun in peace, had their beginning laid on that foundation, and were made by the consent of the people, there can be little room for doubt, either where the right is, or what has been the opinion or practice of mankind, about the first erecting of governments.

105. I will not deny, that if we look back as far as history will direct us, towards the original of commonwealths, we shall generally find them under the government and administration of one

man. And I am also apt to believe that where a family was numerous enough to subsist by itself, and continued entire together, without mixing with others, as it often happens where there is much land and few people, the government commonly began in the father. For the father having, by the law of nature, the same power with every man else to punish as he thought fit any offences against that law, might thereby punish his transgressing children, even when they were men, and out of their pupilage; and they were very likely to submit to his punishment, and all join with him against the offender, in their turns, giving him thereby power to execute his sentence against any transgression, and so in effect make him the lawmaker and governor over all that remained in conjunction with his family. He was fittest to be trusted; paternal affection secured their property and interest under his care; and the custom of obeying him in their childhood made it easier to submit to him rather than to any other. If therefore they must have one to rule them, as government is hardly to be avoided amongst men that live together, who so likely to be the man as he that was their common father; unless negligence, cruelty, or any other defect of mind or body, made him unfit for it? But when either the father died, and left his next heir, for want of age, wisdom, courage, or any other qualities, less fit for rule; or where several families met and consented to continue together, there 'tis not to be doubted but they used their natural freedom to set up him whom they judged the ablest and most likely to rule well over them. Conformable hereunto we find the people of America, who (living out of the reach of the conquering swords and spreading domination of the two great empires of Peru and Mexico) enjoyed their own natural freedom, though, *cæteris paribus*, they commonly prefer the heir of their deceased king; yet if they find him any way weak or uncapable, they pass him by and set up the stoutest and bravest man for their ruler.

106. Thus, though looking back as far as records give us any account of peopling the world, and the history of nations, we commonly find the government to be in one hand; yet it destroys not that which I affirm, *viz.*, that the beginning of politic society depends upon the consent of the individuals to join into and make one society; who, when they are thus incorporated, might set up what form of government they thought fit. But this having given occasion to men to mistake, and think that by nature government was monarchical, and belonged to the father, it may not be amiss here to consider why people in the beginning generally pitched upon this form, which, though perhaps the father's preeminence might in the first institution of some commonwealths give a rise to, and place in the beginning, the power in one hand; yet it is plain that the reason that continued the form of government in a single person was not any regard or respect to paternal authority, since all petty monarchies, that is, almost all monarchies, near their original, have been commonly—at least upon occasion—elective.

107. First then, in the beginning of things, the father's government of the childhood of those sprung from him having accustomed them to the rule of one man, and taught them that where it was exercised with care and skill, with affection and love to those under it, it was sufficient to procure and preserve to men all the political happiness they sought for in society. It was no wonder that they should pitch upon and naturally run into that form of government, which from their infancy they had been all accustomed to, and which, by experience, they had found both easy and safe. To which if we add, that monarchy being simple and most obvious to men whom neither experience had instructed in forms of government, nor the ambition or insolence of empire had taught to beware of the encroachments of prerogative, or the inconveniencies of absolute power, which monarchy in succession was apt to lay claim to, and bring upon them; it was not at all strange that they should not much trouble themselves to think of methods of restraining any exorbitances of those to whom they had given the authority over them, and of balancing the power of government, by placing several parts of it in different hands. They had neither felt the oppression of tyrannical dominion, nor did the fashion of the age, nor their possessions or way of living (which afforded little matter for covetousness or ambition), give them any reason to apprehend or provide against it; and therefore 'tis no wonder they put themselves into such a frame of government as was not only, as I said, most obvious and simple, but also best suited to their pres-

ent state and condition, which stood more in need of defence against foreign invasions and injuries than of multiplicity of laws. The equality of a simple poor way of living, confining their desires within the bounds of each man's small property, made few controversies, and so no need of many laws to decide them, or variety of officers to superintend the process or look after the execution of justice, where there were but few trespasses and few offenders. Since, then, those who liked one another so well as to join into society, cannot but be supposed to have some acquaintance and friendship together, and some trust one in another, they could not but have greater apprehensions of others than of one another; and therefore their first care and thought cannot but be supposed to be how to secure themselves against foreign force. 'Twas natural for them to put themselves under a frame of government which might best serve to that end, and choose the wisest and bravest man to conduct them in their wars, and lead them out against their enemies, and in this chiefly be their ruler.

108. Thus we see that the kings of the Indians in America—which is still a pattern of the first ages in Asia and Europe whilst the inhabitants were too few for the country, and want of people and money gave men no temptation to enlarge their possessions of land, or contest for wider extent of ground—are little more than generals of their armies; and though they command absolutely in war, yet at home and in time of peace they exercise very little dominion, and have but a very moderate sovereignty, the resolutions of peace and war being ordinarily either in the people or in a council. Though the war itself, which admits not of plurality of governors, naturally devolves the command into the king's sole authority.

109. And thus in Israel itself, the chief business of their judges and first kings seems to have been to be captains of war, and leaders of their armies; which (besides what is signified by going out and in before the people, which was, to march forth to war, and home again in the heads of their forces) appears plainly in the story of Jephtha. The Ammonites making war upon Israel, the Gileadites in fear send to Jephtha, a bastard of their family whom they had cast off, and article with him, if he will assist them against the Ammonites, to make him their ruler; which they do in these words: "And the people made him head and captain over them" (Judges xi. 11), which was, as it seems, all one as to be judge. "And he judged Israel" (Judges xii. 7), that is, was their captain-general, six years. So when Jotham upbraids the Shechemites with the obligation they had to Gideon, who had been their judge and ruler he tells them "He fought for you, and adventured his life for, and delivered you out of the hands of Midian" (Judges ix. 17). Nothing mentioned of him but what he did as a general; and indeed that is all is found in his history, or in any of the rest of the judges. And Abimelech particularly is called king, though at most he was but their general. And when, being weary of the ill-conduct of Samuel's sons, the children of Israel desired a king "like all the nations, to judge them and to go out before them, and to fight their battles" (1 Sam. viii. 20), God, granting their desire, says to Samuel: "I will send thee a man, and thou shalt anoint him to be captain over my people Israel, that he may save my people out of the hands of the Philistines" (ix. 16). As if the only business of a king had been to lead out their armies, and fight in their defence; and accordingly at his inauguration pouring a vial of oil upon him, declares to Saul that "the Lord had anointed him to be captain over his inheritance" (x. 1). And, therefore, those who, after Saul's being solemnly chosen and saluted king by the tribes at Mizpah, were unwilling to have him their king, make no other objection but this: "How shall this man save us?" (verse 27) as if they should have said, "This man is unfit to be our king, not having skill and conduct enough in war to be able to defend us." And when God resolved to transfer the government to David, it is in these words: "But now thy kingdom shall not continue. The Lord hath sought him a man after his own heart, and the Lord hath commanded him to be captain over his people" (xiii. 4). As if the whole kingly authority were nothing else but to be their general; and, therefore, the tribes who had stuck to Saul's family, and opposed David's reign, when they came to Hebron with terms of submission to him, they tell him, amongst other arguments, they had to submit to him as to their king, that he was, in effect, their king in Saul's time, and therefore, they had no reason but to receive him as their king now. "Also," say they, "in time past, when

Saul was king over us, thou wast he that leddest out and broughtest in Israel, and the Lord said unto thee, 'Thou shalt feed my people Israel, and thou shalt be a captain over Israel.'"

110. Thus, whether a family by degrees grew up into a commonwealth, and the fatherly authority being continued on to the elder son, every one in his turn growing up under it, tacitly submitted to it; and the easiness and equality of it not offending any one, every one acquiesced, till time seemed to have confirmed it, and settled a right of succession by prescription; or whether several families, or the descendants of several families, whom chance, neighbourhood, or business brought together, uniting into society, the need of a general, whose conduct might defend them against their enemies in war, and the great confidence the innocency and sincerity of that poor but virtuous age (such as are almost all those which begin governments that ever come to last in the world) gave men one of another, made the first beginners of commonwealths generally put the rule into one man's hand, without any other express limitation or restraint, but what the nature of the thing and the end of government required. Whichever of those it was that at first put the rule into the hands of a single person certain it is nobody was entrusted with it but for the public good and safety, and to those ends, in the infancies of commonwealths, those who had it commonly used it. And unless they had done so, young societies could not have subsisted. Without such nursing fathers, tender and careful of the public weal, all governments would have sunk under the weakness and infirmities of their infancy, and the prince and people had soon perished together.

111. But though the golden age (before vain ambition, and *amor sceleratus habendi*, evil concupiscence, had corrupted men's minds into a mistake of true power and honour) had more virtue, and consequently better governors, as well as less vicious subjects; and there was then no stretching prerogative, on the one side, to oppress the people, nor consequently, on the other, any dispute about privilege, to lessen or restrain the power of the magistrate, and so no contest betwixt rulers and people about governors or government.[5] Yet,

when ambition and luxury in future ages would retain and increase the power, without doing the business for which it was given, and, aided by flattery, taught princes to have distinct and separate interests from their people, men found it necessary to examine more carefully the original and rights of government, and to find out ways to restrain the exorbitances and prevent the abuses of that power which, they having entrusted in another's hands only for their own good, they found was made use of to hurt them.

112. Thus we may see how probable it is that people that were naturally free, and by their own consent either submitted to the government of their father, or united together out of different families to make a government, should generally put the rule into one man's hands, and choose to be under the conduct of a single person, without so much as by express conditions limiting or regulating his power, which they thought safe enough in his honesty and prudence, though they never dreamt of monarchy being *jure divino*, which we never heard of among mankind till it was revealed to us by the divinity of this last age; nor ever allowed paternal power to have a right to dominion, or to be the foundation of all government. And thus much may suffice to show that, as far as we have any light from history, we have reason to conclude that all peaceful beginnings of government have been laid in the consent of the people. I say peaceful, because I shall have occasion in another place to speak of conquest, which some esteem a way of beginning of governments.

The other objection I find urged against the beginning of politics in the way I have mentioned is this, *viz.*:

113. That all men being born under government, some or other, it is impossible any of them should ever be free and at liberty to unite together and begin a new one, or ever be able to erect a lawful government.

---

5. "At first, when some certain kind of regiment was once approved, it may be nothing was then farther thought upon for the manner of governing, but all permitted unto their wisdom and discretion, which were to rule, till by experience they found this for all parts very inconvenient, so as the thing which they had devised for a remedy did indeed but increase the sore which it should have cured. They saw that to live by one man's will became the cause of all men's misery. This constrained them to come unto laws wherein all men might see their duty beforehand and know the penalties of transgressing them."—Hooker (*Eccl. Pol.*, lib. i, sect. 10).

If this argument be good, I ask, how came so many lawful monarchies into the world? For if anybody, upon this supposition, can show me any one man, in any age of the world, free to begin a lawful monarchy, I will be bound to show him ten other free men at liberty at the same time to unite and begin a new government under a regal, or any other form; it being demonstration that if any one, born under the dominion of another, may be so free as to have a right to command others in a new and distinct empire, every one that is born under the dominion of another may be so free too, and may become a ruler or subject of a distinct separate government. And so by this their own principle either all men, however born, are free, or else there is but one lawful prince, one lawful government in the world. And then they have nothing to do but barely to shew us which that is; which, when they have done, I doubt not but all mankind will easily agree to pay obedience to him.

114. Though it be a sufficient answer to their objection to shew that it involves them in the same difficulties that it doth those they use it against, yet I shall endeavour to discover the weakness of this argument a little farther.

"All men," say they, "are born under government, and therefore they cannot be at liberty to begin a new one. Every one is born a subject to his father, or his prince, and is therefore under the perpetual tie of subjection and allegiance." 'Tis plain mankind never owned nor considered any such natural subjection that they were born in, to one or to the other that tied them without their own consents, to a subjection to them and their heirs.

115. For there are no examples so frequent in history, both sacred and profane, as those of men withdrawing themselves and their obedience from the jurisdiction they were born under, and the family or community they were bred up in, and setting up new governments in other places; from whence sprang all that number of petty commonwealths in the beginning of ages, and which always multiplied, as long as there was room enough, till the stronger or more fortunate swallowed the weaker; and those great ones again breaking to pieces, dissolved into lesser dominions. All which are so many testimonies against paternal sovereignty, and plainly prove that it was not the natural right of the father descending to his heirs that made governments in the beginning, since it was impossible upon that ground there should have been so many little kingdoms; all must have been but only one universal monarchy, if men had not been at liberty to separate themselves from their families and the government, be it what it will, that was set up in it, and go and make distinct commonwealths and other governments as they thought fit.

116. This has been the practice of the world from its first beginning to this day; nor is it now any more hindrance to the freedom of mankind that they are born under constituted and ancient polities that have established laws and set forms of government, than if they were born in the woods amongst the unconfined inhabitants that run loose in them. For those who would persuade us that by being born under any government we are naturally subjects to it, and have no more any title or pretence to the freedom of the state of nature, have no other reason (bating that of paternal power, which we have already answered) to produce for it, but only because our fathers or progenitors passed away their natural liberty, and thereby bound up themselves and their posterity to a perpetual subjection to the government which they themselves submitted to. 'Tis true that whatever engagements or promises any one has made for himself, he is under the obligation of them, but cannot by any compact whatsoever bind his children or posterity. For his son when a man being altogether as free as his father, any act of the father can no more give away the liberty of the son than it can of anybody else. He may indeed annex such conditions to the land he enjoyed as a subject of any commonwealth as may oblige his son to be of that community, if he will enjoy those possessions which were his father's, because that estate being his father's property he may dispose or settle it as he pleases.

117. And this has generally given the occasion to mistake in this matter, because commonwealths not permitting any part of their dominions to be dismembered, nor to be enjoyed by any but those of their community, the son cannot ordinarily enjoy the possessions of his father but under the same terms his father did, by becoming a member of the society; whereby he puts himself presently under the government he finds there established, as much as any other subject of that commonwealth. And thus the consent of freemen, born under

government, which only makes them members of it, being given separately in their turns, as each comes to be of age, and not in a multitude together, people take no notice of it, and thinking it not done at all, or not necessary, conclude they are naturally subjects as they are men.

118. But 'tis plain governments themselves understand it otherwise; they claim no power over the son, because of that they had over the father; nor look on children as being their subjects by their father's being so. If a subject of England have a child by an English woman in France, whose subject is he? Not the King of England's, for he must have leave to be admitted to the privileges of it; nor the King of France's, for how then has his father a liberty to bring him away and breed him as he pleases? And whoever was judged as a traitor or deserter, if he left or warred against a country, for being barely born in it of parents that were aliens there? 'Tis plain then by the practice of governments themselves, as well as by the law of right reason, that a child is born a subject of no country or government. He is under his father's tuition and authority till he comes to age of discretion, and then he is a freeman, at liberty what government he will put himself under, what body politic he will unite himself to. For if an Englishman's son, born in France, be at liberty, and may do so, 'tis evident there is no tie upon him by his father's being a subject of this kingdom; nor is he bound up by any compact of his ancestors. And why then hath not his son by the same reason, the same liberty, though he be born anywhere else? Since the power that a father hath naturally over his children is the same wherever they be born, and the ties of natural obligations are not bounded by the positive limits of kingdoms and commonwealths.

119. Every man being, as has been shewn, naturally free, and nothing being able to put him into subjection to any earthly power but only his own consent, it is to be considered what shall be understood to be a sufficient declaration of a man's consent to make him subject to the laws of any government. There is a common distinction of an express and a tacit consent, which will concern our present case. Nobody doubts but an express consent of any man entering into any society makes him a perfect member of that society, a subject of that government. The difficulty is,

what ought to be looked upon as a tacit consent, and how far it binds, *i.e.*, how far any one shall be looked on to have consented, and thereby submitted to any government, where he has made no expressions of it at all. And to this I say that every man that hath any possessions, or enjoyment of any part of the dominions of any government, doth thereby give his tacit consent, and is as far forth obliged to obedience to the laws of that government during such enjoyment as any one under it; whether this his possession be of land to him and his heirs for ever, or a lodging only for a week; or whether it be barely travelling freely on the highway; and in effect it reaches as far as the very being of any one within the territories of that government.

120. To understand this the better, it is fit to consider that every man when he at first incorporates himself into any commonwealth, he, by his uniting himself thereunto, annexes also, and submits to the community, those possessions which he has or shall acquire that do not already belong to any other government; for it would be a direct contradiction for any one to enter into society with others for the securing and regulating of property, and yet to suppose his land, whose property is to be regulated by the laws of the society, should be exempt from the jurisdiction of that government to which he himself, the proprietor of the land, is a subject. By the same act, therefore, whereby any one unites his person, which was before free, to any commonwealth, by the same he unites his possessions, which were before free, to it also; and they become, both of them, person and possession, subject to the government and dominion of that common-wealth as long as it hath a being. Whoever therefore from thence-forth by inheritance, purchases, permission, or otherwise, enjoys any part of the land so annexed to, and under the government of that commonwealth, must take it with the condition it is under, that is, of submitting to the government of the commonwealth under whose jurisdiction it is, as far forth as any subject of it.

121. But since the government has a direct jurisdiction only over the land, and reaches the possessor of it (before he has actually incorporated himself in the society), only as he dwells upon, and enjoys that: the obligation any one is under, by virtue of such enjoyment, to submit to the gov-

ernment, begins and ends with the enjoyment; so that whenever the owner, who has given nothing but such a tacit consent to the government, will by donation, sale, or otherwise, quit the said possession, he is at liberty to go and incorporate himself into any other commonwealth, or to agree with others to begin a new one, *in vacuis locis*, in any part of the world they can find free and unpossessed. Whereas he that has once by actual agreement and any express declaration given his consent to be of any commonwealth is perpetually and indispensably obliged to be and remain unalterably a subject to it, and can never be again in the liberty of the state of nature; unless, by any calamity, the government he was under comes to be dissolved, or else by some public acts cuts him off from being any longer a member of it.

122. But submitting to the laws of any country, living quietly and enjoying privileges and protection under them, makes not a man a member of that society. This is only a local protection and homage due to and from all those who, not being in the state of war, come within the territories belonging to any government, to all parts whereof the force of its law extends. But this no more makes a man a member of that society, a perpetual subject of that commonwealth, than it would make a man a subject to another in whose family he found it convenient to abide for some time; though whilst he continued in it he were obliged to comply with the laws, and submit to the government he found there. And thus we see, that foreigners by living all their lives under another government, and enjoying the privileges and protection of it, though they are bound even in conscience to submit to its administration as far forth as any denizen, yet do not thereby come to be subjects or members of that commonwealth. Nothing can make any man so, but his actually entering into it by positive engagement, and express promise and compact. This is that which I think concerning the beginning of political societies, and that consent which makes any one a member of any commonwealth.

Chapter IX. Of the Ends of Political Society and Government

123. If man in the state of nature be so free, as has been said; if he be absolute lord of his own person and possessions, equal to the greatest, and subject to nobody, why will he part with his freedom? Why will he give up this empire, and subject himself to the dominion and control of any other power? To which 'tis obvious to answer, that though in the state of nature he hath such a right, yet the enjoyment of it is very uncertain, and constantly exposed to the invasion of others. For all being kings as much as he, every man his equal, and the greater part no strict observers of equity and justice, the enjoyment of the property he has in this state is very unsafe, very unsecure. This makes him willing to quit a condition, which, however free, is full of fears and continual dangers; and 'tis not without reason that he seeks out and is willing to join in society with others, who are already united, or have a mind to unite, for the mutual preservation of their lives, liberties, and estates, which I call by the general name, property.

124. The great and chief end, therefore, of men's uniting into commonwealths, and putting themselves under government, is the preservation of their property; to which in the state of nature there are many things wanting.

First, There wants an established, settled, known law, received and allowed by common consent to be the standard of right and wrong, and the common measure to decide all controversies between them. For though the law of nature be plain and intelligible to all rational creatures; yet men, being biased by their interest, as well as ignorant for want of study of it, are not apt to allow of it as a law binding to them in the application of it to their particular cases.

125. Secondly, In the state of nature there wants a known and indifferent judge, with authority to determine all differences according to the established law. For every one in that state, being both judge and executioner of the law of nature, men being partial to themselves, passion and revenge is very apt to carry them too far, and with too much heat in their own cases, as well as negligence and unconcernedness, to make them too remiss in other men's.

126. Thirdly, In the state of nature there often wants power to back and support the sentence when right, and to give it due execution. They who by any injustice offended will seldom fail, where they are able, by force to make good their injustice; such resistance many times makes the

punishment dangerous, and frequently destructive to those who attempt it.

127. Thus mankind, notwithstanding all the privileges of the state of nature, being but in an ill condition while they remain in it, are quickly driven into society. Hence it comes to pass that we seldom find any number of men live any time together in this state. The inconveniencies that they are therein exposed to by the irregular and uncertain exercise of the power every man has of punishing the transgressions of others, make them take sanctuary under the established laws of government, and therein seek the preservation of their property. 'Tis this makes them so willingly give up every one his single power of punishing, to be exercised by such alone, as shall be appointed to it amongst them; and by such rules as the community, or those authorized by them to that purpose, shall agree on. And in this we have the original right and rise of both the legislative and executive power, as well as of the governments and societies themselves.

128. For in the state of nature, to omit the liberty he has of innocent delights, a man has two powers.

The first is to do whatsoever he thinks fit for the preservation of himself and others within the permission of the law of nature, by which law, common to them all, he and all the rest of mankind are of one community, make up one society, distinct from all other creatures. And were it not for the corruption and viciousness of degenerate men there would be no need of any other, no necessity that men should separate from this great and natural community, and by positive agreements combine into smaller and divided associations.

The other power a man has in the state of nature is the power to punish the crimes committed against that law. Both these he gives up when he joins in a private, if I may so call it, or particular political society, and incorporates into any commonwealth separate from the rest of mankind.

129. The first power, *viz.*, of doing whatsoever he thought fit for the preservation of himself and the rest of mankind, he gives up to be regulated by laws made by the society, so far forth as the preservation of himself and the rest of that society shall require; which laws of the society in many things confine the liberty he had by the law of nature.

130. Secondly, The power of punishing he wholly gives up, and engages his natural force (which he might before employ in the execution of the law of nature, by his own single authority as he thought fit), to assist the executive power of the society, as the law thereof shall require. For being now in a new state, wherein he is to enjoy many conveniencies, from the labour, assistance, and society of others in the same community, as well as protection from its whole strength; he has to part also with as much of his natural liberty, in providing for himself, as the good, prosperity, and safety of the society shall require; which is not only necessary but just, since the other members of the society do the like.

131. But though men when they enter into society give up the equality, liberty, and executive power they had in the state of nature into the hands of the society, to be so far disposed of by the legislative as the good of the society shall require; yet it being only with an intention in every one the better to preserve himself, his liberty, and property (for no rational creature can be supposed to change his condition with an intention to be worse), the power of the society, or legislative constituted by them, can never be supposed to extend farther than the common good, but is obliged to secure every one's property by providing against those three defects abovementioned that made the state of nature so unsafe and uneasy. And so whoever has the legislative or supreme power of any commonwealth is bound to govern by established standing laws, promulgated and known to the people, and not by extemporary decrees; by indifferent and upright judges, who are to decide controversies by those laws; and to employ the force of the community at home only in the execution of such laws, or abroad to prevent or redress foreign injuries, and secure the community from inroads and invasion. And all this to be directed to no other end but the peace, safety, and public good of the people.

Chapter X. Of the Forms of a Commonwealth

132. THE majority having, as has been shewed, upon men's first uniting into society, the whole power of the community naturally in them, may employ all that power in making laws for the community from time to time, and executing those laws by officers of their own appointing; and then the form of the government

is a perfect democracy; or else may put the power of making laws into the hands of a few select men, and their heirs or successors, and then it is an oligarchy; or else into the hands of one man, and then it is a monarchy; if to him and his heirs, it is an hereditary monarchy; if to him only for life, but upon his death the power only of nominating a successor to return to them, an elective monarchy. And so accordingly of these the community may make compounded and mixed forms of government, as they think good. And if the legislative power be at first given by the majority to one or more persons only for their lives, or any limited time, and then the supreme power to revert to them again; when it is so reverted, the community may dispose of it again anew into what hands they please, and so constitute a new form of government. For the form of government depending upon the placing the supreme power, which is the legislative, it being impossible to conceive that an inferior power should prescribe to a superior, or any but the supreme make laws, according as the power of making laws is placed, such is the form of the commonwealth.

133. By commonwealth, I must be understood all along to mean, not a democracy, or any form of government, but any independent community, which the Latins signified by the word *civitas*, to which the word which best answers in our language is commonwealth, and most properly expresses such a society of men, which community or city in English does not; for there may be subordinate communities in a government, and city amongst us has quite a different notion from commonwealth. And therefore to avoid ambiguity I crave leave to use the word commonwealth in that sense, in which I find it used by King James the First, and I take it to be its genuine signification; which if anybody dislike, I consent with him to change it for a better.

Chapter XI. Of the Extent of the Legislative Power

134. The great end of men's entering into society being the enjoyment of their properties in peace and safety, and the great instrument and means of that being the laws established in that society: the first and fundamental positive law of all commonwealths is the establishing of the legislative power; as the first and fundamental natural law, which is to govern even the legislative itself, is the preservation of the society, and (as far as will consist with the public good) of every person in it. This legislative is not only the supreme power of the commonwealth, but sacred and unalterable in the hands where the community have once placed it; nor can any edict of anybody else, in what form soever conceived, or by what power soever backed, have the force and obligation of a law, which has not its sanction from that legislative which the public has chosen and appointed. For without this the law could not have that, which is absolutely necessary to its being a law, the consent of the society, over whom nobody can have a power to make laws,[6] but by their own consent, and by authority received from them; and therefore all the obedience, which by the most solemn ties any one can be obliged to pay, ultimately terminates in this supreme power, and is directed by those laws which it enacts; nor can any oaths to any foreign power whatsoever, or any domestic subordinate power, discharge any member of the society from his obedience to the legislative, acting pursuant to their trust; nor oblige him to any obedience contrary to the laws so enacted, or farther than they do allow; it being ridiculous to imagine one can be tied ultimately to obey any power in the society which is not the supreme.

135. Though the legislative, whether placed in one or more, whether it be always in being, or only by intervals, though it be the supreme power in every commonwealth, yet,

---

6. "The lawful power of making laws to command whole politic societies of men, belonging so properly unto the same entire societies, that for any prince or potentare, of what kind soever upon earth, to exercise the same of himself, and not by express commission immediately and personally received from God, or else by authority derived at the first from their consent, upon whose persons they impose laws, it is no better than mere tyranny. Laws they are not, therefore, which public approbation hath not made so."—Hooker (*Eccl. Pol.*, lib. i, sect. 10). "Of this point, therefore, we are to note, that sith men naturally have no full and perfect power to command whole politic multitudes of men, therefore utterly without our consent we could in such sort be at no man's commandment living. And to be commanded we do consent, when that society, whereof we be a part, hath at any time before consented, without revoking the same after by the like universal agreement.

"Laws therefore human, of what kind soever, are available by consent."—Hooker (*ibid.*).

First, It is not nor can possibly be absolutely arbitrary over the lives and fortunes of the people. For it being but the joint power of every member of the society given up to that person, or assembly, which is legislator; it can be no more than those persons had in a state of nature before they entered into society, and gave it up to the community. For nobody can transfer to another more power than he has in himself; and nobody has an absolute arbitrary power over himself, or over any other, to destroy his own life, or take away the life or property of another. A man, as has been proved, cannot subject himself to the arbitrary power of another; and having in the state of nature no arbitrary power over the life, liberty, or possession of another, but only so much as the law of nature gave him for the preservation of himself, and the rest of mankind; this is all he doth, or can give up to the commonwealth, and by it to the legislative power, so that the legislative can have no more than this. Their power, in the utmost bounds of it, is limited to the public good of the society.[7] It is a power that hath no other end but preservation, and therefore can never have a right to destroy, enslave, or designedly to impoverish the subjects. The obligations of the law of nature cease not in society, but only in many cases are drawn closer, and have by human laws known penalties annexed to them to enforce their observation. Thus the law of nature stands as an eternal rule to all men, legislators as well as others. The rules that they make for other men's actions must, as well as their own and other men's actions, be conformable to the law of nature, *i.e.*, to the will of God, of which that is a declaration, and the fundamental law of nature being the preservation of mankind, no human sanction can be good or valid against it.

136. Secondly, The legislative, or supreme authority, cannot assume to itself a power to rule by extemporary arbitrary decrees, but is bound to dispense justice and decide the rights of the subject by promulgated standing laws,[8] and known authorized judges. For the law of nature being unwritten, and so nowhere to be found but in the minds of men, they who through passion or interest shall miscite or misapply it, cannot so easily be convinced of their mistake where there is no established judge. And so it serves not, as it ought, to determine the rights, and fence the properties of those that live under it, especially where every one is judge, interpreter, and executioner of it too, and that in his own case; and he that has right on his side, having ordinarily but his own single strength, hath not force enough to defend himself from injuries, or punish delinquents. To avoid these inconveniencies, which disorder men's properties in the state of nature, men unite into societies, that they may have the united strength of the whole society to secure and defend their properties, and may have standing rules to bound it, by which every one may know what is his. To this end it is that men give up all their natural power to the society which they enter into, and the community put the legislative power into such hands as they think fit, with this trust, that they shall be governed by declared laws, or else their peace, quiet, and property will still be at the same uncertainty as it was in the state of nature.

137. Absolute arbitrary power, or governing without settled standing laws, can neither of them consist with the ends of society and government, which men would not quit the freedom of the state of nature for, and tie themselves up under, were it not to preserve their lives, liberties, and

---

7. Two foundations there are which bear up public societies; the one a natural inclination whereby all men desire sociable life and fellowship; the other an order, expressly or secretly agreed upon, touching the manner of their union in living together. The latter is that which we call the law of a commonweal, the very soul of a politic body, the parts whereof are by law animated, held together, and set on work in such actions as the common good requireth. Laws politic, ordained for external order and regiment amongst men, are never framed as they should be, unless presuming the will of man to be inwardly obstinate, rebellious, and averse from all obedience to the sacred laws of his nature; in a word, unless presuming man to be in regard of his depraved mind little better than a wild beast, they do accordingly provide notwithstanding, so to frame his outward actions, that they be no hindrance unto the common good, for which societies are instituted. Unless they do this they are not perfect."—Hooker (*Eccl. Pol.*, lib. i, sect. 10).

8. "Human laws are measures in respect of men whose actions they must direct, howbeit such measures they are as have also their higher rules to be measured by, which rules are two—the law of God and the law of nature; so that laws human must be made according to the general laws of nature, and without contradiction to any positive law of Scripture, otherwise they are ill made."—Hooker (*Eccl. Pol.*, lib. iii, sect. 9).

"To constrain men to anything inconvenient doth seem unreasonable."—(*ibid.*, lib. i, sect. 10).

fortunes; and by stated rules of right and property to secure their peace and quiet. It cannot be supposed that they should intend, had they a power so to do, to give to any one, or more, an absolute arbitrary power over their persons and estates, and put a force into the magistrate's hand to execute his unlimited will arbitrarily upon them. This were to put themselves into a worse condition than the state of nature, wherein they had a liberty to defend their right against the injuries of others, and were upon equal terms of force to maintain it, whether invaded by a single man or many in combination. Whereas, by supposing they have given up themselves to the absolute arbitrary power and will of a legislator, they have disarmed themselves, and armed him, to make prey of them when he pleases. He being in a much worse condition who is exposed to the arbitrary power of one man who has the command of 100,000, than he that is exposed to the arbitrary power of 100,000 single men; nobody being secure that his will, who hath such a command, is better than that of other men, though his force be 100,000 times stronger. And, therefore, whatever form the commonwealth is under, the ruling power ought to govern by declared and received laws, and not by extemporary dictates and undetermined resolutions. For then mankind will be in a far worse condition than in the state of nature, if they shall have armed one, or a few men, with the joint power of a multitude to force them to obey at pleasure the exorbitant and unlimited decrees of their sudden thoughts, or unrestrained, and, till that moment, unknown wills, without having any measures set down which may guide and justify their actions. For all the power the government has, being only for the good of the society, as it ought not to be arbitrary and at pleasure, so it ought to be exercised by established and promulgated laws; that both the people may know their duty and be safe and secure within the limits of the law; and the rulers too kept within their due bounds, and not be tempted by the power they have in their hands to employ it to such purposes, and by such measures as they would not have known, and own not willingly.

138. Thirdly, The supreme power cannot take from any man any part of his property without his own consent. For the preservation of property being the end of government, and that for which men enter into society, it necessarily supposes and requires that the people should have property, without which they must be supposed to lose that, by entering into society, which was the end for which they entered into it; too gross an absurdity for any man to own. Men, therefore, in society having property, they have such a right to the goods which by the law of the community are theirs, that nobody hath a right to take their substance or any part of it from them, without their own consent; without this they have no property at all. For I have truly no property in that which another can by right take from me when he pleases, against my consent. Hence it is a mistake to think that the supreme or legislative power of any commonwealth can do what it will, and dispose of the estates of the subjects arbitrarily, or take any part of them at pleasure. This is not much to be feared in governments where the legislative consists, wholly or in part, in assemblies which are variable, whose members, upon the dissolution of the assembly, are subjects under the common laws of their country, equally with the rest. But in governments where the legislative is in one lasting assembly, always in being, or in one man, as in absolute monarchies, there is danger still, that they will think themselves to have a distinct interest from the rest of the community, and so will be apt to increase their own riches and power by taking what they think fit from the people. For a man's property is not at all secure, though there be good and equitable laws to set the bounds of it between him and his fellow subjects, if he who commands those subjects have power to take from any private man what part he pleases of his property, and use and dispose of it as he thinks good.

139. But government, into whatsoever hands it is put, being, as I have before shewn, entrusted with this condition, and for this end, that men might have and secure their properties, the prince, or senate, however it may have power to make laws for the regulating of property between the subjects one amongst another, yet can never have a power to take to themselves the whole or any part of the subjects' property without their own consent. For this would be in effect to leave them no property at all. And to let us see that even absolute power, where it is necessary, is not arbitrary by being absolute, but is still limited by

that reason, and confined to those ends, which required it in some cases to be absolute, we need look no farther than the common practice of martial discipline. For the preservation of the army, and in it of the whole commonwealth, requires an absolute obedience to the command of every superior officer, and it is justly death to disobey or dispute the most dangerous or unreasonable of them; but yet we see that neither the sergeant, that could command a soldier to march up to the mouth of a cannon, or stand in a breach, where he is almost sure to perish, can command that soldier to give him one penny of his money; nor the general, that can condemn him to death for deserting his post, or for not obeying the most desperate orders, can yet, with all his absolute power of life and death, dispose of one farthing of that soldier's estate, or seize one jot of his goods; whom yet he can command anything, and hang for the least disobedience. Because such a blind obedience is necessary to that end for which the commander has his power, *viz.*, the preservation of the rest; but the disposing of his goods has nothing to do with it.

140. 'Tis true governments cannot be supported without great charge, and 'tis fit every one who enjoys his share of the protection should pay out of his estate his proportion for the maintenance of it. But still it must be with his own consent, *i.e.*, the consent of the majority, giving it either by themselves or their representatives chosen by them. For if any one shall claim a power to lay and levy taxes on the people, by his own authority, and without such consent of the people, he thereby invades the fundamental law of property, and subverts the end of government. For what property have I in that which another may by right take when he pleases to himself?

141. Fourthly, The legislative cannot transfer the power of making laws to any other hands; for it being but a delegated power from the people, they who have it cannot pass it over to others. The people alone can appoint the form of the commonwealth, which is by constituting the legislative, and appointing in whose hands that shall be. And when the people have said, We will submit to rules, and be governed by laws made by such men, and in such forms, nobody else can say other men shall make laws for them; nor can the people be bound by any laws but such as are

enacted by those whom they have chosen and authorized to make laws for them.

142. These are the bounds which the trust that is put in them by the society, and the law of God and nature, have set to the legislative power of every commonwealth, in all forms of government.

First, They are to govern by promulgated established laws, not to be varied in particular cases, but to have one rule for rich and poor, for the favourite at court and the countryman at plough.

Secondly, These laws also ought to be designed for no other end ultimately but the good of the people.

Thirdly, They must not raise taxes on the property of the people without the consent of the people, given by themselves or their deputies. And this properly concerns only such governments where the legislative is always in being, or at least where the people have not reserved any part of the legislative to deputies, to be from time to time chosen by themselves.

Fourthly, The legislative neither must nor can transfer the power of making laws to anybody else, or place it anywhere but where the people have....

Chapter XVIII. Of Tyranny

199. As usurpation is the exercise of power which another hath a right to, so tyranny is the exercise of power beyond right, which nobody can have a right to. And this is making use of the power any one has in his hands, not for the good of those who are under it, but for his own private separate advantage. When the governor, however entitled, makes not the law but his will the rule, and his commands and actions are not directed to the preservation of the properties of his people, but the satisfaction of his own ambition, revenge, covetousness, or any other irregular passion.

200. If one can doubt this to be truth or reason, because it comes from the obscure hand of a subject, I hope the authority of a king will make it pass with him. King James the First in his speech to the parliament, 1603, tells them thus: "I will ever prefer the weal of the public and of the whole commonwealth, in making of good laws and constitutions, to any particular and private ends of mine; thinking ever the wealth and weal of the commonwealth to be my greatest weal and worldly felicity; a point wherein a lawful

king doth directly differ from a tyrant. For I do acknowledge that the special and greatest point of difference, that is between a rightful king and a usurping tyrant, is this: that whereas the proud and ambitious tyrant doth think his kingdom and people are only ordained for satisfaction of his desires and unreasonable appetites; the righteous and just king doth by the contrary acknowledge himself to be ordained for the procuring of the wealth and property of his people." And again, in his speech to the parliament, 1609, he hath these words: "The king binds himself by a double oath, to the observation of the fundamental laws of his kingdom; tacitly, as by being a king, and so bound to protect as well the people, as the laws of his kingdom, and expressly by his oath at his coronation; so as every just king, in a settled kingdom, is bound to observe that paction made to his people by his laws, in framing his government agreeable thereunto, according to that paction which God made with Noah after the deluge. Hereafter, seedtime and harvest, and cold and heat, and summer and winter, and day and night, shall not cease while the earth remaineth. And therefore a king governing in a settled kingdom leaves to be a king and degenerates into a tyrant, as soon as he leaves off to rule according to his laws." And a little after, "Therefore all kings that are not tyrants, or perjured, will be glad to bound themselves within the limits of their laws. And they that persuade them the contrary are vipers and pests, both against them and the commonwealth." Thus that learned king, who well understood the notions of things, makes the difference betwixt a king and a tyrant to consist only in this, that one makes the laws the bounds of his power, and the good of the public the end of his government; the other makes all give way to his own will and appetite.

201. 'Tis a mistake to think this fault is proper only to monarchies; other forms of government are liable to it as well as that. For wherever the power, that is put in any hands for the government of the people and the preservation of their properties, is applied to other ends, and made use of to impoverish, harass, or subdue them to the arbitary and irregular commands of those that have it, there it presently becomes tyranny, whether those that thus use it are one or many. Thus we read of the thirty tyrants at Athens, as well as one at Syracuse; and the intolerable dominion of the Decemviri at Rome was nothing better.

202. Wherever law ends tyranny begins, if the law be transgressed to another's harm. And whosoever in authority exceeds the power given him by the law, and makes use of the force he has under his command to compass that upon the subject which the law allows not, ceases in that to be a magistrate; and, acting without authority, may be opposed as any other man who by force invades the right of another. This is acknowledged in subordinate magistrates. He that hath authority to seize my person in the street, may be opposed as a thief and a robber if he endeavours to break into my house to execute a writ, notwithstanding that I know he has such a warrant and such a legal authority as will empower him to arrest me abroad. And why this should not hold in the highest, as well as in the most inferior magistrate, I would gladly be informed. Is it reasonable that the eldest brother, because he has the greatest part of his father's estate, should thereby have a right to take away any of his younger brothers' portions? Or that a rich man, who possessed a whole country, should from thence have a right to seize, when he pleased, the cottage and garden of his poor neighbour? The being rightfully possessed of great power and riches, exceedingly beyond the greatest part of the sons of Adam, is so far from being an excuse, much less a reason, for rapine and oppression, which the endamaging another without authority is, that it is a great aggravation of it. For the exceeding the bounds of authority is no more a right in a great than in a petty officer, no more justifiable in a king than a constable; but is so much the worse in him, in that he has more trust put in him, has already a much greater share than the rest of his brethren, and is supposed, from the advantages of his education, employment, and counsellors, to be more knowing in the measures of right and wrong.

203. May the commands then of a prince be opposed? May he be resisted as often as any one shall find himself aggrieved, and but imagine he has not right done him? This will unhinge and overturn all polities, and, instead of government and order, leave nothing but anarchy and confusion.

204. To this I answer, that force is to be opposed to nothing but to unjust and unlawful

116 Chapter IV Locke: Property Rights

force; whoever makes any opposition in any other case draws on himself a just condemnation both from God and man, and so no such danger or confusion will follow, as is often suggested. For,

205. First, As, in some countries, the person of the prince by the law is sacred, and so, whatever he commands or does, his person is still free from all question or violence, not liable to force, or any judicial censure or condemnation. But yet opposition may be made to the illegal acts of any inferior officer, or other commissioned by him, unless he will, by actually putting himself into a state of war with his people, dissolve the government, and leave them to that defence which belongs to every one in the state of nature. For of such things who can tell what the end will be? And a neighbour kingdom has shewn the world an odd example. In all other cases the sacredness of the person exempts him from all inconveniencies, whereby he is secure, whilst the government stands, from all violence and harm whatsoever; than which there cannot be a wiser constitution. For the harm he can do in his own person not being likely to happen often, nor to extend itself far; nor being able by his single strength to subvert the laws, nor oppress the body of the people, should any prince have so much weakness and ill nature as to be willing to do it, the inconveniency of some particular mischiefs that may happen sometimes, when a heady prince comes to the throne, are well recompensed by the peace of the public and security of the government in the person of the chief magistrate thus set out of the reach of danger; it being safer for the body that some few private men should be sometimes in danger to suffer than that the head of the republic should be easily and upon slight occasions exposed.

206. Secondly, But this privilege, belonging only to the king's person, hinders not but they may be questioned, opposed, and resisted who use unjust force, though they pretend a commission from him which the law authorizes not. As is plain in the case of him that has the king's writ to arrest a man, which is a full commission from the king; and yet he that has it cannot break open a man's house to do it, nor execute this command of the king upon certain days, nor in certain places, though this commission have no such exception in it; but they are the limitations of the law, which

if any one transgress, the king's commission excuses him not. For the king's authority being given him only by the law, he cannot empower any one to act against the law, or justify him by his commission in so doing. The commission or command of any magistrate where he has no authority being as void and insignificant as that of any private man; the difference between the one and the other being that the magistrate has some authority so far and to such ends, and the private man has none at all. For 'tis not the commission, but the authority, that gives the right of acting, and against the laws there can be no authority. But, not-withstanding such resistance, the king's person and authority are still both secured, and so no danger to governor or government.

207. Thirdly, Supposing a government wherein the person of the chief magistrate is not thus sacred, yet this doctrine of the lawfulness of resisting all unlawful exercises of his power will not upon every slight occasion endanger him or embroil the government. For where the injured party may be relieved, and his damages repaired by appeal to the law, there can be no pretence for force, which is only to be used where a man is intercepted from appealing to the law. For nothing is to be accounted hostile force, but where it leaves not the remedy of such an appeal. And 'tis such force alone that puts him that uses it into a state of war, and makes it lawful to resist him. A man with a sword in his hand demands my purse in the highway, when perhaps I have not 12d. in my pocket; this man I may lawfully kill. To another I deliver £100 to hold only whilst I alight, which he refuses to restore me when I am got up again, but draws his sword to defend the possession of it by force if I endeavour to retake it. The mischief this man does me is a hundred, or possibly a thousand times more than the other perhaps intended me (whom I killed before he really did me any), and yet I might lawfully kill the one, and cannot so much as hurt the other lawfully. The reason whereof is plain, because the one using force, which threatened my life, I could not have time to appeal to the law to secure it, and when 'twas gone it was too late to appeal. The law could not restore life to my dead carcase. The loss was irreparable, which to prevent the law of nature gave me a right to destroy him who had put himself into a state of war with me, and threatened my destruction. But

in the other case, my life not being in danger, I may have the benefit of appealing to the law, and have reparation for my £100 that way.

208. Fourthly, But if the unlawful acts done by the magistrate be maintained (by the power he has got), and the remedy which is due by law be by the same power obstructed, yet the right of resisting, even in such manifest acts of tyranny, will not suddenly or on slight occasions disturb the government. For if it reach no farther than some private men's cases, though they have a right to defend themselves and recover by force what by unlawful force is taken from them; yet the right to do so will not easily engage them in a contest wherein they are sure to perish; it being as impossible for one or a few oppressed men to disturb the government, where the body of the people do not think themselves concerned in it, as for a raving madman or heady malcontent to overturn a well-settled state, the people being as little apt to follow the one as the other.

209. But if either these illegal acts have extended to the majority of the people; or if the mischief and oppression has lighted only on some few, but in such cases as the precedent and consequences seem to threaten all, and they are persuaded in their consciences, that their laws, and with them their estates, liberties, and lives are in danger, and perhaps their religion too; how they will be hindered from resisting illegal force used against them I cannot tell. This is an inconvenience, I confess, that attends all governments whatsoever, when the governors have brought it to this pass, to be generally suspected of their people; the most dangerous state they can possibly put themselves in, wherein they are the less to be pitied, because it is so easy to be avoided; it being as impossible for a governor, if he really means the good of his people, and the preservation of them and their laws together, not to make them see and feel it, as it is for the father of a family not to let his children see he loves and takes care of them.

210. But if all the world shall observe pretences of one kind and actions of another; arts used to elude the law, and the trust of prerogative (which is an arbitrary power in some things left in the prince's hand to do good, not harm to the people) employed contrary to the end for which it was given: if the people shall find the ministers and subordinate magistrates chosen suitable to

such ends, and favoured or laid by proportionably as they promote or oppose them: if they see several experiments made of arbitrary power, and that religion under-hand favoured (though publicly proclaimed again) which is readiest to introduce it, and the operators in it supported as much as may be; and when that cannot be done, yet approved still, and liked the better: if a long train of actions shew the councils all tending that way; how can a man any more hinder himself from being persuaded in his own mind which way things are going, or from casting about how to save himself, than he could from believing the captain of the ship he was in was carrying him and the rest of the company of Algiers, when he found him always steering that course, though cross winds, leaks in his ship, and want of men and provisions did often force him to turn his course another way for some time, which he steadily returned to again as soon as the wind, weather, and other circumstances would let him?

Chapter XIX. Of the Dissolution of Government

211. HE that will with any clearness speak of the dissolution of government ought, in the first place, to distinguish between the dissolution of the society and the dissolution of the government. That which makes the community, and brings men out of the loose state of nature into one politic society, is the agreement which every one has with the rest to incorporate and act as one body, and so be one distinct commonwealth. The usual, and almost only way whereby this union is dissolved, is the inroad of foreign force making a conquest upon them. For in that case (not being able to maintain and support themselves as one entire and independent body) the union belonging to that body which consisted therein must necessarily cease, and so every one return to the state he was in before, with a liberty to shift for himself and provide for his own safety as he thinks fit in some other society. Whenever the society is dissolved, it is certain the government of that society cannot remain. Thus conquerors' swords often cut up governments by the roots, and mangle societies to pieces, separating the subdued or scattered multitude from the protection of and dependence on that society which ought to have preserved them from violence. The

world is too well instructed in, and too forward to allow of, this way of dissolving of governments, to need any more to be said of it; and there wants not much argument to prove that where the society is dissolved, the government cannot remain—that being as impossible as for the frame of a house to subsist when the materials of it are scattered and displaced by a whirlrwind, or jumbled into a confused heap by an earthquake.

212. Besides this overturning from without, governments are dissolved from within.

First, When the legislative is altered. Civil society being a state of peace amongst those who are of it, from whom the state of war is excluded by the umpirage which they have provided in their legislative, for the ending all differences that may arise amongst any of them, 'tis in their legislative that the members of a commonwealth are united and combined together in one coherent living body. This is the soul that gives form, life, and unity to the commonwealth. From hence the several members have their mutual influence, sympathy, and connexion. And, therefore, when the legislative is broken or dissolved, dissolution and death follow. For the essence and union of the society consisting in having one will, the legislative, when once established by the majority, has the declaring and, as it were, keeping of that will. The constitution of the legislative is the first and fundamental act of the society, whereby provision is made for the continuation of their union, under the direction of persons and bonds of laws made by persons authorized thereunto by the consent and appointment of the people, without which no one man or number of men amongst them can have authority of making laws that shall be binding to the rest. When any one or more shall take upon them to make laws, whom the people have not appointed so to do, they make laws without authority, which the people are not therefore bound to obey; by which means they come again to be out of subjection, and may constitute to themselves a new legislative, as they think best, being in full liberty to resist the force of those who without authority would impose anything upon them. Every one is at the disposure of his own will, when those, who had by the delegation of the society the declaring of the public will, are excluded from it, and others usurp the place who have no such authority or delegation.

213. This being usually brought about by such in the commonwealth who misuse the power they have, it is hard to consider it aright, and know at whose door to lay it, without knowing the form of government in which it happens. Let us suppose, then, the legislative placed in the concurrence of three distinct persons.

1. A single hereditary person having the constant supreme executive power, and with it the power of convoking and dissolving the other two within certain periods of time.
2. An assembly of hereditary nobility.
3. An assembly of representatives chosen *pro tempore* by the people. Such a form of government supposed, it is evident,

214. First, That when such a single person or prince sets up his own arbitrary will in place of the laws which are the will of the society, declared by the legislative, then the legislative is changed. For that being in effect the legislative, whose rules and laws are put in execution and required to be obeyed; when other laws are set up, and other rules pretended and enforced, than what the legislative constituted by the society have enacted, 'tis plain that the legislative is changed. Whoever introduces new laws, not being thereunto authorized by the fundamental appointment of the society, or subverts the old, disowns and overturns the power by which they were made, and so sets up a new legislative.

215. Secondly, When the prince hinders the legislative from assembling in its due time, or from acting freely, pursuant to those ends for which it was constituted, the legislative is altered. For 'tis not a certain number of men, no, nor their meeting, unless they have also freedom of debating and leisure of perfecting what is for the good of the society, wherein the legislative consists. When these are taken away or altered so as to deprive the society of the due exercise of their power, the legislative is truly altered. For it is not names that constitute governments, but the use and exercise of those powers that were intended to accompany them; so that he who takes away the freedom, or hinders the acting of the legislative in its due seasons, in effect takes away the legislative, and puts an end to the government.

216. Thirdly, When, by the arbitrary power of the prince, the electors or ways of elections are

altered, without the consent and contrary to the common interest of the people, there also the legislative is altered. For if others than those whom the society hath authorized thereunto do choose, or in another way than what the society hath prescribed, those chosen are not the legislative appointed by the people.

217. Fourthly, The delivery also of the people into the subjection of a foreign power, either by the prince, or by the legislative, is certainly a change of the legislative, and so a dissolution of the government. For the end why people entered into society being to be preserved one entire, free, independent society, to be governed by its own laws, this is lost whenever they are given up into the power of another.

218. Why in such a constitution as this the dissolution of the government in these cases is to be imputed to the prince, is evident; because he, having the force, treasure, and offices of the state to employ, and often persuading himself, or being flattered by others, that as supreme magistrate he is incapable of control, he alone is in a condition to make great advances towards such changes, under pretence of lawful authority, and has it in his hands to terrify or suppress opposers, as factious, seditious, and enemies to the government. Whereas no other part of the legislative or people is capable by themselves to attempt any alteration of the legislative, without open and visible rebellion, apt enough to be taken notice of, which, when it prevails, produces effects very little different from foreign conquest. Besides, the prince in such a form of government, having the power of dissolving the other parts of the legislative, and thereby rendering them private persons, they can never, in opposition to him, or without his concurrence, alter the legislative by a law, his consent being necessary to give any of their decrees that sanction. But yet so far as the other parts of the legislative any way contribute to any attempt upon the government, and do either promote, or not, what lies in them, hinder such designs, they are guilty, and partake in this, which is certainly the greatest crime men can be guilty of one towards another.

219. There is one way more whereby such a government may be dissolved, and that is, when he who has the supreme executive power neglects and abandons that charge, so that the laws already made can no longer be put in execution. This is demonstratively to reduce all to anarchy, and so effectually to dissolve the government. For laws not being made for themselves, but to be by their execution the bonds of the society, to keep every part of the body politic in its due place and function; when that totally ceases, the government visibly ceases, and the people become a confused multitude without order or connexion. Where there is no longer the administration of justice, for the securing of men's rights, nor any remaining power within the community to direct the force, or provide for the necessities of the public, there certainly is no government left. Where the laws cannot be executed, it is all one as if there were no laws; and a government without laws is, I suppose, a mystery in politics, inconceivable to human capacity, and inconsistent with human society.

220. In these and the like cases, when the government is dissolved, the people are at liberty to provide for themselves by erecting a new legislative, differing from the other, by the change of persons, or form, or both, as they shall find it most for their safety and good. For the society can never, by the fault of another, lose the native and original right it has to preserve itself, which can only be done by a settled legislative, and a fair and impartial execution of the laws made by it. But the state of mankind is not so miserable that they are not capable of using this remedy, till it be too late to look for any. To tell people they may provide for themselves by erecting a new legislative, when by oppression, artifice, or being delivered over to a foreign power, their old one is gone, is only to tell them they may expect relief when it is too late, and the evil is past cure. This is in effect no more than to bid them first be slaves, and then to take care of their liberty; and when their chains are on tell them they may act like freemen. This, if barely so, is rather mockery than relief; and men can never be secure from tyranny if there be no means to escape it till they are perfectly under it. And therefore it is that they have not only a right to get out of it, but to prevent it.

221. There is therefore, secondly, another way whereby governments are dissolved, and that is when the legislative or the prince, either of them, act contrary to their trust.

First, The legislative acts against the trust reposed in them when they endeavour to invade the property of the subject, and to make themselves or any part of the community masters or arbitrary disposers of the lives, liberties, or fortunes of the people.

222. The reason why men enter into society is the preservation of their property; and the end why they choose and authorize a legislative is that there may be laws made, and rules set, as guards and fences to the properties of all the members of the society, to limit the power and moderate the dominion of every part and member of the society. For since it can never be supposed to be the will of the society that the legislative should have a power to destroy that which every one designs to secure by entering into society, and for which the people submitted themselves to legislators of their own making; whenever the legislators endeavour to take away and destroy the property of the people, or to reduce them to slavery under arbitrary power, they put themselves into a state of war with the people, who are thereupon absolved from any farther obedience, and are left to the common refuge which God hath provided for all men against force and violence. Whensoever, therefore, the legislative shall transgress this fundamental rule of society, and either by ambition, fear, folly, or corruption, endeavour to grasp themselves or put into the hands of any other an absolute power over the lives, liberties, and estates of the people, by this breach of trust they forfeit the power the people had put into their hands for quite contrary ends, and it devolves to the people; who have a right to resume their original liberty, and by the establishment of the new legislative (such as they shall think fit) provide for their own safety and security, which is the end for which they are in society. What I have said here concerning the legislative in general, holds true also concerning the supreme executor, who having a double trust put in him, both to have a part in the legislative and the supreme execution of the law, acts against both when he goes about to set up his own arbitrary will as the law of the society. He acts also contrary to his trust when he either employs the force, treasure, and offices of the society, to corrupt the representatives, and gain them to his purposes; or openly pre-engages the electors, and prescribes to their choice such whom he has by solicitations, threats, promises, or otherwise, won

to his designs, and employs them to bring in such, who have promised beforehand what to vote and what to enact. Thus to regulate candidates and electors, and new-model the ways of election, what is it but to cut up the government by the roots, and poison the very fountain of public security? For the people having reserved to themselves the choice of their representatives as the fence to their properties, could do it for no other end but that they might always be freely chosen, and, so chosen, freely act and advise as the necessity of the commonwealth and the public good should upon examination and mature debate be judged to require. This, those who give their votes before they hear the debate, and have weighed the reasons on all sides, are not capable of doing. To prepare such an assembly as this, and endeavour to set up the declared abettors of his own will for the true representatives of the people and the lawmakers of the society, is certainly as great a breach of trust, and as perfect a declaration of a design to subvert the government, as is possible to be met with. To which if one shall add rewards and punishments visibly employed to the same end, and all the arts of perverted law made use of to take off and destroy all that stand in the way of such a design, and will not comply and consent to betray the liberties of their country, 'twill be past doubt what is doing. What power they ought to have in the society, who thus employ it contrary to the trust that went along with it in its first institution, is easy to determine; and one cannot but see that he who has once attempted any such thing as this cannot any longer be trusted.

223. To this perhaps it will be said, that the people being ignorant and always discontented, to lay the foundation of government in the unsteady opinion and uncertain humour of the people is to expose it to certain ruin; and no government will be able long to subsist if the people may set up a new legislative whenever they take offence at the old one. To this I answer: Quite the contrary. People are not so easily got out of their old forms as some are apt to suggest. They are hardly to be prevailed with to amend the acknowledged faults in the frame they have been accustomed to. And if there be any original defects, or adventitious ones introduced by time or corruption, 'tis not an easy thing to get them changed, even when all the world sees there is an opportunity for it. This

slowness and aversion in the people to quit their old constitutions has, in the many revolutions which have been seen in this kingdom, in this and former ages, still kept us to, or after some interval of fruitless attempts still brought us back again to, our old legislative of King, Lords, and Commons. And whatever provocations have made the crown be taken from some of our princes' heads, they never carried the people so far as to place it in another line.

224. But 'twill be said, this hypothesis lays a ferment for frequent rebellion. To which I answer:

First, No more than any other hypothesis. For when the people are made miserable, and find themselves exposed to the ill-usage of arbitary power, cry up their governors as much as you will for sons of Jupiter, let them be sacred and divine, descended, or authorized from heaven, give them out for whom or what you please, the same will happen. The people generally ill-treated, and contrary to right, will be ready upon any occasion to ease themselves of a burden that sits heavy upon them. They will wish and seek for the opportunity, which in the change, weakness, and accidents of human affairs, seldom delays long to offer itself. He must have lived but a little while in the world who has not seen examples of this in his time, and he must have read very little who cannot produce examples of it in all sorts of governments in the world.

225. Secondly, I answer, such revolutions happen not upon every little mismanagement in public affairs. Great mistakes in the ruling part, many wrong and inconvenient laws, and all the slips of human frailty, will be borne by the people without mutiny or murmur. But if a long train of abuses, prevarications, and artifices, all tending the same way, make the design visible to the people— and they cannot but feel what they lie under, and see whither they are going—'tis not to be wondered that they should then rouse themselves and endeavour to put the rule into such hands which may secure to them the ends for which government was at first erected; and without which ancient names and specious forms are so far from being better that they are much worse than the state of nature or pure anarchy; the inconveniencies being all as great and as near, but the remedy farther off and more difficult.

226. Thirdly, I answer, that this doctrine of a power in the people of providing for their safety anew by a new legislative, when their legislators have acted contrary to their trust by invading their property, is the best fence against rebellion, and the probablest means to hinder it. For rebellion being an opposition, not to persons, but authority, which is founded only in the constitutions and laws of the government; those, whoever they be, who by force break through, and by force justify their violation of them, are truly and properly rebels. For when men, by entering into society and civil government, have excluded force, and introduced laws for the preservation of property, peace, and unity amongst themselves, those who set up force again in opposition to the laws do *rebellare*—that is, bring back again the state of war—and are properly rebels; which they who are in power (by the pretence they have to authority, the temptation of force they have in their hands, and the flattery of those about them) being likeliest to do, the properest way to prevent the evil is to shew them the danger and injustice of it, who are under the greatest temptation to run into it.

227. In both the fore-mentioned cases, when either the legislative is changed or the legislators act contrary to the end for which they were constituted, those who are guilty are guilty of rebellion. For if any one by force takes away the established legislative of any society, and the laws by them made pursuant to their trust, he thereby takes away the umpirage which every one had consented to for a peaceable decision of all their controversies, and a bar to the state of war amongst them. They who remove, or change the legislative, take away this decisive power, which nobody can have but by the appointment and consent of the people; and so destroying the authority which the people did, and nobody else can set up, and introducing a power which the people hath not authorized, they actually introduce a state of war, which is that of force without authority. And thus by removing the legislative established by the society (in whose decisions the people acquiesced and united, as to that of their own will), they untie the knot and expose the people anew to the state of war. And if those who by force take away the legislative are rebels, the legislators themselves, as has been shewn, can be

no less esteemed so, when they who were set up for the protection and preservation of the people, their liberties and properties, shall by force invade and endeavour to take them away; and so they, putting themselves into a state of war with those who made them the protectors and guardians of their peace, are properly and with the greatest aggravation *rebellantes*, rebels.

228. But if they who say it lays a foundation for rebellion mean that it may occasion civil wars or intestine broils, to tell the people they are absolved from obedience when illegal attempts are made upon their liberties or properties, and may oppose the unlawful violence of those who were their magistrates, when they invade their properties contrary to the trust put in them; and that therefore this doctrine is not to be allowed, being so destructive to the peace of the world: they may as well say upon the same ground that honest men may not oppose robbers or pirates because this may occasion disorder or bloodshed. If any mischief come in such cases, it is not to be charged upon him who defends his own right, but on him that invades his neighbour's. If the innocent honest man must quietly quit all he has, for peace sake, to him who will lay violent hands upon it, I desire it may be considered what a kind of peace there will be in the world, which consists only in violence and rapine, and which is to be maintained only for the benefit of robbers and oppressors. Who would not think it an admirable peace betwixt the mighty and the mean, when the lamb without resistance yielded his throat to be torn by the imperious wolf? Polyphemus's den gives us a perfect pattern of such a peace and such a government, wherein Ulysses and his companions had nothing to do but quietly to suffer themselves to be devoured. And no doubt Ulysses, who was a prudent man, preached up passive obedience, and exhorted them to a quiet submission by representing to them of what concernment peace was to mankind, and by shewing the inconveniencies might happen if they should offer to resist Polyphemus, who had now the power over them.

229. The end of government is the good of mankind; and which is best for mankind, that the people should be always exposed to the boundless will of tyranny, or that the rulers should be sometimes liable to be opposed when they grow exor-

bitant in the use of their power, and employ it for the destruction and not the preservation of the properties of their people?

230. Nor let any one say that mischief can arise from hence, as often as it shall please a busy head or turbulent spirit to desire the alteration of the government. 'Tis true such men may stir whenever they please, but it will be only to their own just ruin and perdition. For till the mischief be grown general, and the ill-designs of the rulers become visible, or their attempts sensible to the greater part, the people who are more disposed to suffer than right themselves by resistance are not apt to stir. The examples of particular injustice, or oppression of here and there an unfortunate man, move them not. But if they universally have a persuasion grounded upon manifest evidence that designs are carrying on against their liberties, and the general course and tendency of things cannot but give them strong suspicions of the evil intention of their governors, who is to be blamed for it? Who can help it if they who might avoid it bring themselves into this suspicion? Are the people to be blamed, if they have the sense of rational creatures, and can think of things no otherwise than as they find and feel them? And is it not rather their fault, who put things into such a posture, that they would not have them thought to be as they are? I grant that the pride, ambition, and turbulency of private men have sometimes caused great disorders in commonwealths, and factions have been fatal to states and kingdoms. But whether the mischief hath oftener begun in the people's wantonness, and a desire to cast off the lawful authority of their rulers, or in the rulers' insolence, and endeavours to get and exercise an arbitrary power over their people; whether oppression or disobedience gave the first rise to the disorder, I leave it to impartial history to determine. This I am sure, whoever, either ruler or subject, by force goes about to invade the rights of either prince or people, and lays the foundation for overturning the constitution and frame of any just government, is highly guilty of the greatest crime I think a man is capable of, being to answer for all those mischiefs of blood, rapine, and desolation, which the breaking to pieces of governments brings on a country. And he who does it is justly to be esteemed the common enemy and pest of mankind, and is to be treated accordingly.

231. That subjects or foreigners, attempting by force on the properties of any people, may be resisted with force, is agreed on all hands. But that magistrates, doing the same thing, may be resisted, hath of late been denied. As if those who had the greatest privileges and advantages by the law, had thereby power to break those laws by which alone they were set in a better place than their brethren. Whereas their offence is thereby the greater, both as being ungrateful for the greater share they have by the law, and breaking also that trust which is put into their hands by their brethren.

232. Whosoever uses force without right, as every one does in society who does it without law, puts himself into a state of war with those against whom he so uses it; and in that state all former ties are cancelled, all other rights cease, and every one has a right to defend himself and to resist the aggressor. This is so evident that Barclay himself, that great assertor of the power and sacredness of kings, is forced to confess, that it is lawful for the people in some cases to resist their king; and that too in a chapter wherein he pretends to shew that the divine law shuts up the people from all manner of rebellion. Whereby it is evident, even by his own doctrine, that, since they may in some cases resist, all resisting of princes is not rebellion. His words are these:

233. But if any one should ask: Must the people, then, always lay themselves open to the cruelty and rage of tyranny? Must they see their cities pillaged and laid in ashes, their wives and children exposed to the tyrant's lust and fury, and themselves and families reduced by their king to ruin, and all the miseries of want and oppression, and yet sit still? Must men alone be debarred the common privilege of opposing force with force, which nature allows so freely to all other creatures for their preservation from injury? I answer: Self-defence is a part of the law of nature; nor can it be denied the community, even against the king himself. But to revenge themselves upon him must by no means be allowed them, it being not agreeable to that law. Wherefore, if the king shall shew an hatred, not only to some particular persons, but sets himself against the body of the commonwealth, whereof he is the head, and shall, with intolerable ill-usage, cruelly tyrannize over the whole or a considerable part of the people, in this case the people have a

right to resist and defend themselves from injury. But it must be with this caution, that they only defend themselves, but do not attack their prince. They may repair the damages received, but must not, for any provocation, exceed the bounds of due reverence and respect. They may repulse the present attempt, but must not revenge past violences. For it is natural for us to defend life and limb; but that an inferior should punish a superior, is against nature. The mischief which is designed them, the people may prevent before it be done; but when it is done, they must not revenge it on the king, though author of the villainy. This, therefore, is the privilege of the people in general, above what any private person hath: that particular men are allowed by our adversaries themselves (Buchanan only excepted), to have no other remedy but patience; but the body of the people may, with respect, resist intolerable tyranny; for when it is but moderate, they ought to endure it.

234. Thus far that great advocate of monarchical power allows of resistance.

235. 'Tis true he has annexed two limitations to it to no purpose.

First, He says, it must be with reverence.

Secondly, It must be without retribution or punishment; and the reason he gives is, because an inferior cannot punish a superior.

First, How to resist force without striking again, or how to strike with reverence, will need some skill to make intelligible. He that shall oppose an assault only with a shield to receive the blows, or in any more respectful posture, without a sword in his hand, to abate the confidence and force of the assailant, will quickly be at an end of his resistance, and will find such a defence serve only to draw on himself the worse usage. This is as ridiculous a way of resisting as Juvenal thought it of fighting: *ubi tu pulsas, ego vapulo tantum.* And the success of the combat will be unavoidably the same he there describes it:—

Libertas pauperis hæc est:
Pulsatus rogat, et pugnis concisus adorat,
Ut liceat paucis cum dentibus inde reverti.

This will always be the event of such an imaginary resistance, where men may not strike again. He, therefore, who may resist, must be allowed to strike. And then let our author or anybody else join a knock on the head, or a cut on the face, with as much reverence and respect as he thinks fit. He that can reconcile blows and reverence may, for aught I know, deserve for his pains a civil, respectful cudgelling, wherever he can meet with it.

Secondly, As to his second, An inferior cannot punish a superior; that is true, generally speaking, whilst he is his superior. But to resist force with force, being the state of war that levels the parties, cancels all former relation of reverence, respect, and superiority; and then the odds that remains is, that he who opposes the unjust aggressor has this superiority over him—that he has a right, when he prevails, to punish the offender, both for the breach of the peace, and all the evils that followed upon it. Barclay, therefore, in another place, more coherently to himself, denies it to be lawful to resist a king in any case. But he there assigns two cases whereby a king may un-king himself. His words are:

237. What, then, can there no case happen wherein the people may of right and by their own authority help themselves take arms, and set upon their king imperiously domineering over them? None at all whilst he remains a king: "Honour the king," and "He that resists the power resists the ordinance of God," are divine oracles that will never permit it. The people, therefore, can never come by a power over him, unless he does something that makes him cease to be a king; for then he divests himself of his crown and dignity, and returns to the state of a private man, and the people become free and superior, the power which they had in the interregnum, before they crowned him king, devolving to them again. But there are but few miscarriages which bring the matter to this state. After considering it well on all sides, I can find but two. Two cases there are, I say, whereby a king *ipso facto* becomes no king, and loses all power and regal authority over his people, which are also taken notice of by Winzerus.

The first is, if he endeavour to overturn the government—that is, if he have a purpose and design to ruin the kingdom and commonwealth, as it is recorded of Nero that he resolved to cut off the senate and people of Rome, lay the city waste with fire and sword, and then remove to some other place. And of Caligula, that he openly declared that he would be no longer a head to the people or senate, and that he had it in his thoughts to cut off the worthiest men of both ranks, and then retire to Alexandria; and he wished that the people had but one neck that he might despatch them all at a blow. Such designs as these, when any king harbours in his thoughts and seriously promotes, he immediately gives up all care and thought of the commonwealth, and consequently forfeits the power of governing his subjects, as a master does the dominion over his slaves whom he hath abandoned.

238. The other case is, when a king makes himself dependent of another, and subjects his kingdom, which his ancestors left him, and the people put free into his hands, to the dominion of another; for, however perhaps it may not be his intention to prejudice the people, yet because he has hereby lost the principal part of regal dignity, *viz.*, to be, next and immediately under God, supreme in his kingdom, and also because he betrayed or forced his people, whose liberty he ought to have carefully preserved, into the power and dominion of a foreign nation. By this, as it were, alienation of his kingdom, he himself loses the power he had in it before, without transferring any the least right to those on whom he would have bestowed it; and so by this act sets the people free, and leaves them at their own disposal. One example of this is to be found in the Scotch annals.

239. In these cases Barclay, the great champion of absolute monarchy, is forced to allow that a king may be resisted and ceases to be a king. That is, in short, not to multiply cases, in whatsoever he has no authority, there he is no king and may be resisted; for wheresoever the authority ceases, the king ceases too, and becomes like other men who have no authority. And these two cases he instances in, differ little from those above-mentioned, to be destructive to governments, only that he has omitted the principle from which his doctrine flows; and that is the breach of trust in not preserving the form of government agreed on, and in not intending the end of government itself, which is the public good and preservation of property. When a king has dethroned himself and put himself in a state of war with his people, what shall hinder them from prosecuting him who is no king, as they would any other man who has put himself into a state of war with them?

Barclay, and those of his opinion, would do well to tell us. This farther I desire may be taken notice of out of Barclay, that he says, the mischief that is designed them, the people may prevent before it be done: whereby he allows resistance when tyranny is but in design. Such designs as these (says he) when any king harbours in his thoughts and seriously promotes, he immediately gives up all care and thought of the commonwealth; so that, according to him, the neglect of the public good is to be taken as an evidence of such design, or at least for a sufficient cause of resistance. And the reason of all he gives in these words, Because he betrayed or forced his people whose liberty he ought carefully to have preserved. What he adds, into the power and dominion of a foreign nation, signifies nothing, the fault and forfeiture lying in the loss of their liberty which he ought to have preserved, and not in any distinction of the persons to whose dominion they were subjected. The people's right is equally invaded and their liberty lost whether they are made slaves to any of their own or a foreign nation; and in this lies the injury, and against this only have they the right of defence. And there are instances to be found in all countries which shew that 'tis not the change of nations in the persons of their governors, but the change of government that gives the offence. Bilson, a bishop of our church, and a great stickler for the power and prerogative of princes, does, if I mistake not, in his treatise of *Christian Subjection*, acknowledge that princes may forfeit their power and their title to the obedience of their subjects; and if there needed authority in a case where reason is so plain, I could send my reader to Bracton, Fortescue, and the author of *The Mirror*, and others, writers that cannot be suspected to be ignorant of our government or enemies to it. But I thought Hooker alone might be enough to satisfy those men who, relying on him for their ecclesiastical polity, are by a strange fate carried to deny those principles upon which he builds it. Whether they are herein made the tools of cunninger workmen, to pull down their own fabric, they were best look. This I am sure, their civil policy is so new, so dangerous, and so destructive to both rulers and people that, as former ages never could bear the broaching of it, so, it may be hoped, those to come, redeemed from the impositions of those Egyptian under-

taskmasters, will abhor the memory of such servile flatterers, who, whilst it seemed to serve their turn, resolved all government into absolute tyranny, and would have all men born to what their mean souls fitted them for, slavery.

240. Here, 'tis like, the common question will be made: Who shall be judge whether the prince or legislative act contrary to their trust? This, perhaps, ill-affected and factious men may spread amongst the people, when the prince only makes use of his due prerogative. To this I reply: The people shall be judge; for who shall be judge whether his trustee or deputy acts well, and according to the trust reposed in him, but he who deputes him, and must, by having deputed him, have still a power to discard him when he fails in his trust? If this be reasonable in particular cases of private men, why should it be otherwise in that of the greatest moment, where the welfare of millions is concerned, and also where the evil, if not prevented, is greater, and the redress very difficult, dear, and dangerous?

241. But farther, this question, who shall be judge, cannot mean that there is no judge at all; for where there is no judicature on earth to decide controversies amongst men, God in heaven is judge. He alone, 'tis true, is judge of the right; but every man is judge for himself, as in all other cases, so in this, whether another hath put himself into a state of war with him, and whether he should appeal to the Supreme Judge, as Jephtha did.

242. If a controversy arise betwixt a prince and some of the people, in a matter where the law is silent or doubtful, and the thing be of great consequence, I should think the proper umpire in such a case should be the body of the people; for in cases where the prince hath a trust reposed in him, and is dispensed from the common ordinary rules of the law; there, if any men find themselves aggrieved, and think the prince acts contrary to or beyond that trust, who so proper to judge as the body of the people (who at first lodged that trust in him) how far they meant it should extend? But if the prince, or whoever they be in the administration, decline that way of determination, the appeal then lies nowhere but to heaven; force between either persons who have no known superior on earth, or which permits no appeal to a judge on earth, being properly a state of war, wherein the appeal lies only to heaven;

and in that state the injured party must judge for himself when he will think fit to make use of that appeal and put himself upon it.

243. To conclude, the power that every individual gave the society, when he entered into it, can never revert to the individuals again as long as the society lasts, but will always remain in the community; because without this there can be no community, no commonwealth, which is contrary to the original agreement; so also when the society hath placed the legislative in any assembly of men, to continue in them and their successors, with direction and authority for providing such successors, the legislative can never revert to the people whilst that government lasts; because having provided a legislative with power to continue for ever, they have given up their political power to the legislative and cannot resume it. But if they have set limits to the duration of their legislative, and made this supreme power in any person or assembly only temporary; or else, when by the miscarriages of those in authority it is forfeited; upon the forfeiture, or at the determination of the time set, it reverts to the society, and the people have a right to act as supreme, and continue the legislative in themselves; or erect a new form, or under the old form place it in new hands, as they think good.

Chapter 5

MARKETS AND MORALS: SURROGATE MOTHERHOOD, MILITARY SERVICE

One way of testing utilitarian and libertarian theories is to consider arguments for and against the use of markets in some controversial settings. Are there some goods that should be not be bought and sold? If so, why are markets objectionable means of allocating these goods? Consider military service. What do you think of the Civil War system, which allowed conscripts to hire a substitute to take their place? Or, to take another market controversy, what about surrogacy contracts, in which a couple pays a woman to become pregnant with their child, and to turn it over at birth? Do your views about markets in these cases challenge or support utilitarian and libertarian assumptions?

TRAGIC CHOICES

Guido Calabresi and Philip Bobbit

Prior to 1776, the American colonies passed literally hundreds of statutes and ordinances providing for the raising of militias; typically these empowered authorities to recruit and pay men under arms rather than draft them into service. One commentator has observed that, during that period, the colonies "required all able-bodied men between the ages of 16 and 50 to compose the militia. . . . A fine was generally imposed upon those unable to attend [drill]." These were the colonial soldiers who fought the Indians and the French.

With the dawning of the Revolution the Continental Congress recommended, but was not empowered to direct, that the states furnish troops to the Continental Army.

In 1780 the Congress asked for 41,760 men from the states but received only 21,015. When combined with the various militias then in uni-

form, this represented a total force of only about half the number which had been serving in 1776. Not only the increasing difficulty of raising forces, but the short duration of their service when they could be inducted, doubtless prompted George Washington to propose, upon being elected President, that a national force be raised and maintained by the compulsory draft of men between eighteen and twenty-five years of age. The new Congress rejected this scheme.

The wars with Britain in 1812 and Mexico in 1845 were fought with state militias and volunteers. Not until the Civil War did the United States face a struggle which moved its Congress to institute a form of compulsory conscription.

When hostilities began, the Northern armies totaled slightly more than 15,000 men. President Abraham Lincoln's call for 75,000 volunteers to serve for ninety days was met by more than 90,000 men. When it became clear that a more protracted struggle was to take place, Congress authorized the President to accept a million volunteers for three years; this was followed, a year later in 1862, by a similar authorization for 300,000 men. The tepid response to this last call made clear that the initial enlistments represented about the full, hard core of enthusiastic sentiment. Although the forthcoming recruitment eventually produced more than 400,000 volunteers, a panicky Congress passed, searcely two weeks after its 1862 call, the Militia Act of 1862 which empowered the President to direct the states to levy drafts upon the state militias, thereby to fulfill quotas for the national army.

The Militia Act was the first draft act in the United States; reaction to it was said to have been "immediate and unfavorable." It was argued that the draft was insulting to citizens who would otherwise have volunteered; that it was timed seriously to impede that year's harvest; that it was unnecessary. But the most violent objection centered on the bill's provision that enabled a drafted citizen to hire a substitute in his place. The effect of this provision was to stop all voluntary enlistment. This in turn increased the demand for draftees and thus the cost of hiring a substitute; a lucrative arbitrage in service conducted by brokers arose and desertion increased.

In part to respond to the criticism which accompanied this ill-conceived measure, Congress passed a superseding statute in 1863. The new act granted to the War Department the power to induct draftees directly into the federal force, and set a flat fee of $300 for exemption from induction. This latter provision was thought to remedy the trade in substitutes (the price for which had risen to $1,500 in some places) and thereby to provide a pool of eligible men as well as a sum of money which could be used for bounties to encourage enlistment and re-enlistment. In this way it was hoped that any gap in induction and deployment could be closed.

As might have been expected, the open pricing of service by the Congress—even though it brought exemption within the range of relatively less well-off people, it was still close to a year's wages for the average workingman—evoked furious and sustained outrage. In Ohio, draft resisters

were fired on by federal infantry; in Indiana and Illinois, the officers conducting the draft were murdered and their records destroyed. A single draft riot, in July 1863 in New York City, took the lives of more than 1,000. A year later, President Lincoln issued a new call for volunteers, and signed into law a statute eliminating the $300 avoidance option. At war's end, local enlistment efforts produced the vast majority of soldiers in the Northern ranks.

The first draft was something less than a success. Of the 292,441 names drawn, only 9,881 were held to service: 164,395 men were exempted for physical or other reasons; 26,002 furnished substitutes; 52,288 registrants paid the $300 commutation fee.

In 1866, the difficulties with Civil War conscription were the subject of a study commissioned to review draft procedures. Every one of its major suggestions was adopted more than fifty years later when forced conscription was next employed. The author recommended, in part, "that the military be relieved, as far as possible, of any local administration in any future draft; that a personal registration at some designated spot be held rather than a house-to-house canvass; and that there be no bounties or purchases of substitutes."

American military manpower needs in the Cuban, Philippine, and border conflicts did not require a resumption of the draft, in part because of the enthusiasm with which public opinion greeted these conflicts and the mode of warfare then prevailing. The staggering British and French losses during 1914–16 apparently disabused the American administration of any thought that similar conscription measures would suffice in the European theater. In February 1917, the day following the United States rupture of diplomatic relations with Germany, President Woodrow Wilson directed his Secretary of War to prepare a program which would institute a draft as the exclusive means of recruiting and maintaining a national army. The Act passed by Congress in May of that year embodied this concept; the national army was to be composed entirely of draftees. Regulars and a National Guard were to be volunteers where possible but authority was granted to use forced conscription to bring even those forces to designated levels; bounties and substitutes were forbidden. Liability to the draft covered all male citizens, though conscription was authorized only for those twenty-one to thirty-one years old. Ministers and divinity students, some public officials, those men with dependents, and those serving in certain occupations were exempted; conscientious objectors were exempted from combat service.

In the three months from the Act's passage to the first lottery which determined the order of induction, 10 million men registered. In two more months, another 14 million were enrolled. Of these, 2,810,296 were drafted before the end of the war in 1918. The administrator in charge of this logistical triumph seems to have been convinced that "scrupulous fairness" was the essential factor to success and commentators concede that "hardly a charge of unfairness or discrimination" was made at the time. Be that as it may, by August 1918, 16,000 men were being held in New York City for failure to register or appear when drafted. During this period a move to adopt a permanent system of universal military training failed to pass the Senate. At the end of the war, the draft lapsed and the United States returned to a voluntary system.

Many persons today recall the sickening rapidity with which France fell in 1939 and Europe was again the locus of international conflict. But it is hard even for them to remember the impassioned debates occasioned by the proposal, in the summer of 1940, of the Selective Training and Service Act. The United States was not at war and the advisability of our entry into war was itself sharply disputed. It was the conviction of many that a peacetime draft was a measure designed by the Roosevelt administration to take the country into war. When it passed, service was limited to one year. The Act authorized a national draft using a lottery method much the same as that used in 1917. Service was limited to one year; no more than 900,000 men were to be inducted; and their service was limited to actions in the Western Hemisphere. Again, bounties and substitutes were prohibited.

The Act was unpopular, and thus, when in August 1941 Congress voted on an extension of service, passage came by one vote in the House. By this slender margin, the Act was renewed for eighteen months; four months later Pearl Harbor was attacked.

With the declarations of war against Japan, Germany, and Italy, Congress removed the territorial restrictions on service and extended its duration to the life of the conflict. By mid-1942 various modifications were introduced: All males between eighteen and sixty-five were required to be registered; the lottery was discarded and registrants were called by order of date of birth; voluntary enlistments were severely restricted, apparently so that first-order determinations with respect to the production of war materiel, which underlay the system of exemptions or channeling, could be more easily fulfilled. By August 1945, more than 9.5 million men had been inducted.

The 1940 Act, in its subsequent incarnations, continued until March 31, 1947. But less than a year after that President Harry Truman requested draft legislation; the subsequent statute, the Selective Service Act of 1948, remained the basic method for conscription until its repeal at the close of American ground action in Vietnam. For most of those years, call-ups were small and "the chief problem in the administration of the draft [was] to manage a deferment system that could successfully reduce the overabundant supply of potential draftees."

During the Korean and Vietnam conflicts, vigorous controversy focused on the winnowing methods by which second-order allocations were made by the 1948 Act. Under that Act, all eighteen-year-old males were required to register for induction with a local draft board. Liability for induction continued until age twenty-six, or age thirty-five if initial liability had been deferred. The local board classified the registrant according to various categories which reflected his order, vis-à-vis other registrants, as to priority of induction. Information by which these categories were actuated was provided by the registrants. First-order determinations by the Department of Defense were prorated among the states and then, by state administration, among the local boards. Among that category deemed eligible for service, the local boards exercised broad discretion within guidelines which preferred, that is, drafted first, older registrants and delinquents and drafted last young nonvolunteers. (Volunteers counted toward meeting the local quota, thus heightening even further geographical disparities.) All sorts of appeals were available to the registrant dissatisfied with his classification; and a new classification was, of course, required by each relevant change in the registrant's status.

A good lawyer became extremely useful to the reluctant soldier. A complicated system of deferments operated among the categories whereby some registrants were moved to the bottom of the call-up list. This was the case, at various periods during the many revisions to the regulations promulgated bureaucratically under the statute, for those physically or mentally unfit for combat service, college students, graduate students, fathers with a dependent child, farmers employed in the production of "substantial" quantities of agricultural commodities, Peace Corps and VISTA volunteers, medical students, those conscientious objectors willing to perform non-combat service. The deferment applied over two dimensions, that is, for the life of the condition by virtue of which it was created, and across that period, not designated a "national emergency" by the President, as provided by the statute, when manpower needs could be satisfied by the call-up of nondeferred registrants. Often the application for deferment, if successful (though not, paradoxically, its grant absent a request by the registrant), acted to extend the limit of liability, although, with the exception of physicians, the relatively short duration of high manpower needs and, recently, the preference for younger men, mooted this provision. Deferments are, nevertheless, to be distinguished from exemptions, for instance, those granted to ministers and divinity students, conscientious objectors to any participation, aliens, veterans and the orphans of veterans, which removed such categories from the liability pool together.

This system—of broad liability and broad, though vague, deferments—operated with various modifications during the period when draft calls went from 108,000 in 1964 to 299,000 in 1968. Even the latter figure fails to convey the omnipresent nature of the draft in these years; to it one must add the further statistic that more than half the voluntary enlistments during this period occurred as a result of individual efforts to avoid compulsory conscription. (At various times bounties, choice of branch and duration of service were offered as inducements to volunteer.) The controversy surrounding the draft during these years is too fresh in our memories to require repetition. On campuses in every part of the country there prevailed a reckless irritability among students that was at once the product of anxiety at the prospect of being called and guilt in the knowledge that one's contemporaries without academic refuge were being sent to war.

In November 1969 the Nixon administration signed into law a proposal which permitted it to reduce the period of liability from seven years (eighteen to twenty-six) to one year, the latter being the calendar year following a registrant's nineteenth birthday. Also, draft selection was to be determined by lot, preference being paired with birth dates drawn at random, and not, as previously, by age. Deferment for graduate students (except medical and dental students) had somewhat before been curtailed by regulation; those then in graduate schools were allowed a set time in which to finish. In April of the following year, an Executive Order provided that occupational and paternity deferments be phased out. Then, in September 1971, the Draft Extension and Military Pay Bill was enacted, eliminating undergraduate student deferments for those thereafter entering college and establishing a uniform national call to insure that registrants throughout the country with the same lottery number would be equally liable to induction, despite the fact that some local boards had larger pools of nondeferred from which to draw. At about the same time demands for military forces began to diminish significantly, thus reducing the likelihood of an unlucky draw.

All of the underlying statutes providing for compulsory conscription were in form extensions of the 1948 Act. By 1973 only about 50,000 registrants were being drafted and in July of that year the statute was allowed to lapse. An all-volunteer combat force, with a small draft for physicians and added reliance on civilians for some support tasks, replaced the mixed military of draftees and coerced, and noncoerced, volunteers. "The key element," the Secretary of Defense wrote at the time, in the change-over, "was a substantial and costly increase in pay and allowances for personnel in the lower enlisted grades." Thus are we brought full circle to the system of bounties and substitutes, though one considerably more concealed than that which operated during the Civil War.

From the preceding discussion it should be apparent that a mixture of approaches has been used in allocating wartime service or, what is the same, exemption from that service and its deathly risks. Mixtures over time no less than mixtures at any given time have varied in part in reaction to approaches previously used.

BATTLE CRY OF FREEDOM: THE CIVIL WAR ERA

James M. McPherson

[...] A prime issue in both elections was the draft, enacted by Congress on March 3, 1863. Democrats added conscription to emancipation and military arrests in their catalogue of Republican sins. The Enrollment Act of 1863 was designed mainly as a device to stimulate volunteering by the threat of a draft. As such it worked, but with such inefficiency, corruption, and perceived injustice that it became one of the most divisive issues of the war and served as a model of how *not* to conduct a draft in future wars.

By the beginning of 1863 recruitment in the North arrived at the same impasse it had reached in the South a year earlier. The men likely to enlist for patriotic reasons or adventure or peer-group pressure were already in the army. War weariness and the grim realities of army life discouraged further volunteering. The booming war economy had shrunk the number of unemployed men to the vanishing point. The still tentative enlistment of black soldiers could scarcely begin to replace losses from disease and combat and desertion during the previous six months. Like the Confederacy in early 1862, the Union army in 1863 faced a serious manpower loss through expiration of enlistments: 38 two-year regiments raised in 1861, and 92 nine-month militia regiments organized in 1862 were due to go home during the spring and summer of 1863. This prompted Congress to act.

In its nationalizing tendencies the resulting law was similar to the recently passed Banking Act. State governors had taken the lead in the organization of volunteer regiments in 1861–62. The draft was a national process. Congress authorized a Provost Marshals Bureau in the War Department to enforce conscription. This Bureau sent to each congressional district a number of provost marshals whose first task was to enroll every male citizen and immigrant who had filed for citizenship aged twenty to forty-five.[1] This became the basis for each district's quota in the four calls for new troops that Lincoln issued after passage of the conscription act in March 1863. In the first draft (July 1863), provost marshals called up 20 percent of the enrollees, chosen by lot in each district. In the three drafts of 1864, the War Department assigned each district a quota determined by its pro rata share of the number of soldiers called for by the president, after adjustment for men who had already enlisted from the district. Each district had fifty days to fill its quota with volunteers. Those that failed to do so then held a lottery draft to obtain a sufficient number of men to meet the quota.

If a man's name was drawn in this lottery, one of several things would happen to him next—the least likely of which was induction into the army. Of the men chosen in the four drafts, more than one-fifth (161,000 of 776,000) "failed to report"—fleeing instead to the West, to Canada, or to the woods. Of those who did report to the provost marshal's office, one-eighth were sent home because of already filled quotas. Three-fifths of the remaining 522,000 were exempted for physical or mental disability or because they convinced the inducting officer that they were the sole means of support for a widow, an orphan sibling, a motherless child, or an indigent parent. Unlike the Confederate Congress, Union lawmakers allowed no occupational exemptions. But a draftee who passed the physical exam and could not claim any dependent relatives still had two options: he could hire a substitute, which exempted him from this and any future draft; or he could pay a commutation fee of $300, which exempted him from this draft but not necessarily the next one.[2] Of the 207,000 men who were drafted, 87,000 paid the commutation fee and 74,000 furnished substitutes, leaving only 46,000 who went personally into the army. The pool of substitutes was furnished by eighteen- and nineteen-year olds and by immigrants who had

---

1. Men eligible for the draft were divided into two classes. Class 1 included all single men and married men aged 20 to 35. Class 2 included married men over 35. Men from class 2 would not be drafted until class 1 had been exhausted. In practice, that meant virtually never.

2. Criticisms of commutation led to its repeal in 1864—except for conscientious objectors—so that with this minor exception the commutation option did not apply to the last two drafts of July and December 1864.

not filed for citizenship, who were not liable to conscription.[3]

There were numerous opportunities for fraud, error, and injustice in this cumbersome and confusing process. The enrollment of men eligible for the draft was only as good as the officials who carried it out—and some of them were venal or incompetent. Enrollers probably missed even more of the floating population than census takers missed. On the other hand, some officials padded their rolls with fictitious names in order to draw their pay without doing the hard work of canvassing door to door. Timid enrollers feared to venture into Butternut counties of the Midwest, coal-mining districts of Pennsylvania, tough neighborhoods in New York, and other areas hostile to the draft and to the war. Many men "skedaddled" to avoid enrollment. Consequently some districts were under-enrolled while others had padded lists, with resulting inequities in quotas. Governors and congressmen brought pressure for adjustment of quotas, and some districts had to be re-enrolled. Governor Seymour of New York (a Democrat) accused the administration of padding the enrollment in Democratic districts to increase their quotas. Although discrepancies between Democratic and Republican districts did sometimes occur, the usual reason was not a Republican plot but rather a smaller previous enlistment from Democratic districts, leaving a larger quota to be conscripted.

Numerous openings for fraud also existed after enrollment was completed and men whose names had been drawn were called for examination. Surgeons could be bribed, false affidavits claiming dependent support could be filed, and other kinds of under-the-table influence could be exerted. Some potential draftees feigned insanity or dis-

ease. Others practiced self-mutilation. Some naturalized citizens claimed to be aliens.

In the South, the privilege of hiring a substitute had produced the bitter slogan of "rich man's war and poor man's fight." In the North, commutation was even more unpopular than substitution. "Three Hundred Dollars or Your Life" blazoned the headlines in Democratic newspapers. A parody of a popular recruiting song made the rounds: "We Are Coming, Father Abraham, Three Hundred Dollars More."[4] The price of commutation amounted to almost a year's wages for an unskilled laborer. "*The rich are exempt!*" proclaimed an Iowa editor. "Did you ever know aristocratic legislation to so directly point out the poor man as inferior to the rich?" On the face of it, the privileges of commutation and substitution did seem to make the conscription act, in the words of a modern historian, "one of the worst pieces of class legislation ever passed by the United States Congress."[5]

But a closer examination challenges this conclusion. Substitution was hallowed by tradition, having existed in European countries (even in France during the *levée en masse*), in American states during the Revolution, in the militia, and in the Confederacy. The Republican architects of the draft law inserted commutation as a means of putting a cap on the price of substitutes. In the South the cost of a substitute had already soared above $1,000. The commutation alternative in the North would prevent the price of a substitute going much higher than $300. Republicans saw this as a way of bringing exemption within reach of the working class instead of discriminating against them.

Of course a draft without either substitution or commutation would have been more equitable. But substitution was so deeply rooted in precedent as to be viewed as a right. Civil War experience changed this perception, and after twenty months of such experience the Confederacy repealed substitution in December 1863. But the North retained it through all four of its draft calls (also a period of about twenty months). Commutation

3. This and the following paragraphs are based on several studies, especially Fred A. Shannon, *The Organization and Administration of the Union Army, 1861–1865*, 2 vols. (Cleveland, 1928), I, 195–323, II, 11–260; Eugene C. Murdock, *Patriotism Limited 1862–1865: The Civil War Draft and the Bounty System* (Kent, Ohio, 1967); Murdock, *One Million Men: The Civil War Draft in the North* (Madison, 1971); and Peter Levine, "Draft Evasion in the North during the Civil War, 1863–1865," *JAH*, 67 (1981), 816–34. Nearly all draftees were under 30 years of age, for older men generally were able to claim exemption for cause or to pay for commutation or a substitute.

4. Basil L. Lee, *Discontent in New York City 1861–1865* (Washington, 1943), 90; Foote, *Civil War*, II, 151.
5. Robert E. Sterling, "Civil War Draft Resistance in the Middle West," Ph.D. dissertation, Northern Illinois University, 1974, pp. 167, 150.

remained an alternative in the first two Union drafts (summer 1863 and spring 1864). In these drafts it worked as Republicans said it would. Studies of conscription in New York and Ohio have found virtually no correlation between wealth and commutation. Districts in New York with low per capita wealth had about the same percentage of men who paid commutation (or hired substitutes) as those with higher wealth. In four Ohio districts—two rural and two urban—the proportion of unskilled laborers who commuted was 18 percent, compared with 22 percent for skilled laborers, 21 percent for merchants, bankers, manufacturers, doctors, lawyers, and clerks, and 47 percent for farmers and farm laborers. Since skilled and unskilled laborers had the highest percentage of "failure to report" when their names were drawn, it appears that at least in Ohio the laborers and farmers were *more* likely than men in white-collar jobs to avoid the draft. In this respect it does not seem to have been especially a poor man's fight.[6]

Yet the outcry against "blood money" prompted Congress to repeal commutation in July 1864, despite warnings by some Republicans that this would drive the price of substitutes beyond the reach of the poor. The warning proved to be only partly true. The proportion of laborers and farmers who bought their way out of the last two drafts declined by half after the abolition of commutation. But the percentage of exemptions purchased by white-collar and professional classes also declined by almost half. And in the four drafts taken together the poor seem to have suffered little comparative disadvantage. In New York City districts with the highest concentration of Irish immigrants, 98 percent of the men not otherwise exempted paid commutation or hired substitutes. The following table provides a detailed occupational breakdown of men whose names were drawn in four sample Ohio districts:[7]

How could laborers come up with the price of commutation or a substitute? Few of them did, out of their own pockets. But numerous cities and counties appropriated funds raised by property taxes to pay the $300 for those who could not afford it. Tammany Hall ward committees collected money to hire substitutes for draftees, and political machines elsewhere followed suit. Several factories and businesses and railroads bought exemptions for drafted workers with funds contributed by employers and by a 10 percent levy on wages. Draft insurance societies sprang up everywhere to offer a $300 policy for premiums of a few dollars a month. In this manner more than three-quarters of all draftees who reported to the provost marshal's office and were not exempted for cause were able to buy their way out of serving.

What kind of conscription was this, in which only 7 percent of the men whose names were drawn actually served? The answer: it was not conscription at all, but a clumsy carrot and stick device to stimulate volunteering. The stick was the threat of being drafted and the carrot was a bounty for volunteering. In the end this method worked, for while only 46,000 drafted men served and another 74,000 provided substitutes, some 800,000 men enlisted or re-enlisted voluntarily during the two years after passage of the conscription act. While the social and economic cost of this process was high, Americans seemed willing to pay the price because compulsory service was contrary to the country's values and traditions. Alexis de Tocqueville's words a generation earlier were still relevant in 1863: "In America conscription is unknown and men are induced to enlist by bounties. The notions and habits of the people . . . are so opposed to compulsory recruitment that I do not think it can ever be sanctioned by their laws."[8]

Yet in the end, bounty-stimulated volunteering came to seem an even greater evil than the draft. Implicit bounties began in the first days of the war, when soldiers' aid societies raised money to help support the families of men who gave up their jobs to go off to war. States, counties, and municipalities also appropriated funds for this purpose. These patriotic subsidies aroused no

6. James W. Geary, "Civil War Conscription in the North: A Historiographical Review, *CWH* (1986), 208–28; Eugene C. Murdock, "Was It a 'Poor Man's Fight'?" *CWH*, 10 (1964), 241–45; Murdock, *Patriotism Limited*, 211–15; Hugh C. Earnhart, "Commutation: Democratic or Undemocratic?" *CWH*, 12 (1966), 132–42; Levine, "Draft Evasion," *loc. cit.*, 820–29.

7. Calculated from the raw data presented in Earnhart, "Commutation," *loc. cit.*, 138–42.

8. Quoted in Adrian Cook, *The Armies of the Streets: The New York City Draft Riots of 1863* (Lexington, Ky., 1974), 48.

Occupation	Failed to Report	Exempted for Cause	Commuted or Hired Substitute	Held to Service
Unskilled Laborer	24.9%	45.1%	24.2%	5.8%
Skilled Laborer	25.7%	43.8%	21.9%	8.6%
Farmer & Farm Laborer	16.1%	34.1%	30.9%	18.9%
Merchant, Manufacturer, Banker, Broker	22.6%	46.3%	29.1%	2.0%
Clerk	26.2%	47.7%	24.3%	1.8%
Professional	16.3%	48.5%	28.9%	6.3%

controversy. In the summer of 1862, however, several northern localities found it necessary to pay explicit bounties in order to fill quotas under Lincoln's two calls for troops. A year later the shock of the first draft enrollment and lottery, which provoked bitter resistance in many areas, caused communities to resolve to fill future quotas by any means possible to avoid a draft. Lincoln's three calls for troops in 1864 produced a bidding war to buy volunteers. Private associations raised money for bounties. Cities and counties competed for recruits. The federal government got into the act in October 1863 with a $300 bounty (financed by the $300 commutation fee) for volunteers and re-enlistees.

The half-billion dollars paid in bounties by the North represented something of a transfer of wealth from rich to poor—an ironic counterpoint to the theme of rich man's war/poor man's fight. By 1864 a canny recruit could pyramid local, regional, and national bounties into grants of $1,000 or more. Some men could not resist the temptation to take this money, desert, assume a different name, travel to another town, and repeat the process. Several of these "bounty jumpers" got away with the practice several times. "Bounty brokers" went into business to seek the best deals for their clients—with a cut of the bounty as payment. They competed with "substitute brokers" for a share of this lucrative trade in cannon fodder. Relatively few of the bounty men or substitutes actually became cannon fodder, however, for many deserted before they ever got into action and others allowed themselves to be captured at the first contact with the enemy. Thus while the conscription-substitute-bounty system produced three-quarters of a million new men,[9]

they did little to help win the war. This task fell mainly on the pre-bounty veterans of 1861 and 1862—who with exaggerated contempt viewed many of the bounty men and substitutes of 1864 as "off-scourings of northern slums . . . dregs of every nation . . . branded felons . . . thieves, burglars, and vagabonds."[10]

One notorious facet of the bounty and substitute business was the crimping of immigrants. Immigration had declined sharply during the first half of the war, but picked up again in 1863 because of wartime labor shortages. Some of these immigrants came with the intention of joining the army to cash in on bounties or substitute fees. Others were virtually kidnapped into the service by unscrupulous "runners." The substantial number of immigrants in the Union army gave rise to longstanding southern myth that "the majority of Yankee soldiers were foreign hirelings."[11] But in fact quite the opposite was true. Immigrants were proportionally under-represented in the Union's armed services. Of some two million white soldiers and sailors, half a million had been born abroad. While immigrants therefore constituted 25 percent of the servicemen, 30 percent of the males of military age in the Union states were foreign-born. Despite the fighting reputation of the Irish Brigade, the Irish were the most under-represented group in proportion to population, followed by German Catholics. Other immigrant groups enlisted in rough proportion to their share of the population.[12]

9. More than 150,000 re-enlisting veterans also received bounties.

10. Wiley, *Billy Yank*, 343–44; Bruce Catton, *A Stillness at Appomattox* (Garden City, N.Y., 1957), 25–29.
11. Wiley, *Billy Yank*, 428n. 51, quoting an unnamed southern historian who made this assertion in 1951.
12. Data on the number of foreign-born soldiers in the Union army are contained in Benjamin A. Gould, *Investigations in Military and Anthropological Statistics of American Soldiers* (New York, 1869); in Ella Lonn,

The under-representation of Catholic immigrants can be explained in part by the Democratic allegiance of these groups and their opposition to Republican war aims, especially emancipation. Some of them had not yet filed for citizenship—or claimed not to have done so—and were therefore exempt from the draft. Although this group furnished a large number of substitutes and bounty men during the final year of war—thereby achieving an inglorious visibility—they also furnished a large number of deserters and bounty jumpers. Together with Butternuts from the Ohio River valley, they likewise provided many of those who "skedaddled" to escape the draft.[13] This ethnocultural pattern reinforced economic class, for Butternuts and Catholic immigrants were concentrated in the lower end of the wealth and income scale. Perhaps this confirms the theme of a "rich man's war"—for many of these people wanted no part of the war—but it modifies the "poor man's fight" notion. This modification is borne out by the following table comparing previous occupations of white Union soldiers with the occupational distribution of males in the states from which they came.[14]

From this table it might appear that the white-collar class was the most under-represented group in the army. But this appearance is deceptive, for the median age of soldiers at enlistment was 23.5 years while the occupational data from the census were for all adult males. Two-fifths of the soldiers were twenty-one or younger. Studies of nineteenth-century occupational mobility have shown that 10 percent or more of young men who started out as laborers subsequently moved up the occupational ladder.[15] If one could control for the age of soldiers, it seems likely that the only category significantly under-represented would be unskilled workers.

Even if the dichotomy rich man's war/poor man's fight lacked objective reality, it remained a powerful symbol to be manipulated by Democrats who made conscription a partisan and class issue. While 100 percent of the congressional Republicans supported the draft bill, 88 percent of the Democrats voted against it.[16] Scarcely any other issue except emancipation evoked such clearcut partisan division. Indeed, Democrats linked these two issues in their condemnation of the draft as an unconstitutional means to achieve the unconstitutional end of freeing the slaves. A democratic convention in the Midwest pledged that "we will not render support to the present Administration in its wicked Abolition crusade [and] we will *resist* to the *death* all attempts to draft any of our citizens into the army." Democratic newspapers hammered at the theme that the draft would force white working men to fight for the freedom of blacks who would come north and

Foreigners in the Union Army and Navy (Baton Rouge, 1951), esp. 581–82; in Wiley, *Billy Yank*, 306–15; in William F. Fox, *Regimental Losses in the American Civil War 1861–1865* (Albany, 1889), 62–63; and in Edward Channing, *The War for Southern Independence* (Vol. 6 of his *History of the United States*, New York, 1925), 426n. An excellent analysis of this matter in the state with the highest proportion of foreign-born men, Wisconsin, finds that while more than half of the males of military age had been born abroad, only 40 percent of the Wisconsin soldiers were foreign-born. Richard N. Current, *The History of Wisconsin: The Civil War Era 1848–1873* (Madison, 1976), 306, 335.

13. Levine, "Draft Evasion," *loc. cit.*, 820–34; Sterling, "Midwest Draft Resistance," 251–62.

14. The data for occupations of all males in 1860 are drawn from the occupational tables in the 1860 printed census. The samples of the previous occupations of Union soldiers are from: 1) a U.S. Sanitary Commission survey of the occupations of 666,530 Union soldiers from all Union states except Maryland and Delaware; 2) Bell Wiley's sample of 13,392 white Union soldiers in 114 companies from all the free states plus Missouri. (California, Oregon, and the territories are not included in these data.) The Sanitary Commission and Wiley samples were drawn from company muster rolls and are representative of the proportion of soldiers from the various states. The Sanitary Commission data were reported in Gould, *Investigations in Military and Anthropological*

Statistics, and the Wiley data were kindly supplied to the author by Wiley before his death. I am indebted to his generosity and to the painstaking labor of Patricia McPherson, who compiled the occupational data from the 1860 census.

15. Stephan Thernstrom, *The Other Bostonians: Poverty and Progress in the American Metropolis* (Cambridge, Mass., 1973), esp. table on p. 234. This table summarizes the results of studies of occupational mobility in several cities. These studies show that an average of 15 to 20 percent of the young blue-collar workers eventually moved into white-collar jobs, while 5 to 10 percent of the young white-collar workers eventually dropped to blue-collar positions. These studies do not measure the occupational mobility of farm boys, who may have experienced a higher rate of movement into white-collar jobs.

16. CG, 37 Cong., 3 Sess., pp. 1293, 1389.

Occupational Categories	Union Soldiers (U.S. Sanitary Commission Sample)	Union Soldiers (Bell Wiley Sample)	All Males (From 1860 Census)
Farmers and farm laborers	47.5%	47.8%	42.9%
Skilled laborers	25.1	25.2	24.9
Unskilled laborers	15.9	15.1	16.7
White-collar and commercial	5.1	7.8	10.0
Professional	3.2	2.9	3.5
Miscellaneous and unknown	3.2	1.2	2.0

take away their jobs. The editor of New York's leading Catholic weekly told a mass meeting that "when the President called upon them to go and carry on a war for the nigger, he would be d—d if he believed they would go." In a Fourth of July 1863 speech to Democrats in the city, Governor Seymour warned Republicans who pleaded military necessity for emancipation and conscription: "Remember this—that the bloody and treasonable doctrine of public necessity can be proclaimed by a mob as well as by a government."[17]

Such rhetoric inflamed smoldering tensions. Draft dodgers and mobs killed several enrollment officers during the spring and summer. Anti-Negro violence erupted in a number of cities. Nowhere was the tinder more flammable than in New York City, with its large Irish population and powerful Democratic machine. Crowded into noisome tenements in a city with the worst disease mortality and highest crime rate in the Western world, working in low-skill jobs for marginal wages, fearful of competition from black workers, hostile toward the Protestant middle and upper classes who often disdained or exploited them, the Irish were ripe for revolt against this war waged by Yankee Protestants for black freedom. Wage increases had lagged 20 percent or more behind price increases since 1861. Numerous strikes had left a bitter legacy, none more than a longshoremen's walkout in June 1863 when black stevedores under police protection took the place of striking Irishmen.

Into this setting came draft officers to begin the drawing of names on Saturday, July 11. Most of the militia and federal troops normally sta-

tioned in the city were absent in Pennsylvania pursuing Lee's army after the battle of Gettysburg. The first day's drawing went quietly enough, but on Sunday hundreds of angry men congregated in bars and vowed to attack the draft offices next morning. They made good their threat, setting off four days of escalating mob violence that terrorized the city and left at least 105 people dead. It was the worst riot in American history.[18]

Many of the men (and women) in the mobs indulged in indiscriminate looting and destruction. But as in most riots, the mobs singled out certain targets that were related to the underlying causes of the outbreak. Draft offices and other federal property went up in flames early in the rioting. No black person was safe. Rioters beat several, lynched a half-dozen, smashed the homes and property of scores, and burned the Colored Orphan Asylum to the ground. Mobs also fell upon several business establishments that employed blacks. Rioters tried to attack the offices of Republican newspapers and managed to burn out the ground floor of the *Tribune* while howling for Horace Greeley's blood. Several editors warded off the mob by arming their employees with rifles; Henry Raymond of the *Times* borrowed three recently invented Gatling guns from the army to defend his building. Rioters sacked the homes of several prominent Republicans and

17. Convention quoted in Gray, *Hidden Civil War*, 123; Editor James McMaster of *Freeman's Journal* quoted in Lee, *Discontent in New York City*, 239; Seymour quoted in Cook, *Armies of the Streets*, 53.

18. Exaggerated contemporary estimates of more than a thousand persons killed found their way into popular histories of the riot. But the careful research of Adrian Cook has established that only 105 people were definitely killed, and another dozen or so deaths may have been linked to the rioting. Eleven of those killed were black victims of the mob, eight were soldiers, and two were policemen; the rest were rioters. Cook, *Armies of the Streets*, 193–94, 310n.

abolitionists. With shouts of "Down with the rich" and "There goes a $300 man" they attacked well-dressed men who were incautious enough to show themselves on the streets. These hints of class warfare were amplified by assaults on the property of reputed anti-labor employers and the destruction of street-sweeping machines and grain-loading elevators that had automated the jobs of some of the unskilled workers who made up the bulk of the rioters. Several Protestant churches and missions were burned by the mobs whose membership was at least two-thirds Irish.[19]

Untrained in riot control, New York's police fought the mobs courageously but with only partial

19. *Ibid.*, passim, esp. 117, 195–96.

success on July 13 and 14. Army officers desperately scraped together a few hundred troops to help. The War Department rushed several regiments from Pennsylvania to New York, where on July 15 and 16 they poured volleys into the ranks of rioters with the same deadly effect they had produced against rebels at Gettysburg two weeks earlier. By July 17 an uneasy peace returned to the shattered city. Determined to carry out the draft in New York lest successful resistance there spawn imitation elsewhere, the government built up troop strength in Manhattan to 20,000 men who enforced calm during the resumption of drafting on August 19. By then the city council had appropriated funds to pay the commutation fees of drafted men—including, no doubt, some of the rioters.

All Go Down Together

James Traub

When Richard Nixon abolished the draft in 1973, I was one of the beneficiaries. I had just become eligible, and in the normal course of things I would have been assigned a lottery number. Of course, it's unlikely that I would have donned a uniform even if I had come up No. 1; there was always a way out if you had access to the right lawyers and doctors. At the time, I knew literally no one who served—no one. Thanks to college deferment, during the Vietnam War, college students served at only half the rate of high-school graduates, and the higher up you went in the socioeconomic scale, the likelier it was that you would keep out of harm's way.

But what if conscription were equitable and were used to fill a military that was widely respected rather than scorned? This was the case, after all, in the period between the Korean and Vietnam Wars, when military service was widely accepted as the price of citizenship. Why wouldn't that be true today? Why wouldn't it be just the kind of sacrifice young Americans would agree to make at a time of heightened patriotism? The idea has been in the air since earlier this year, when Representative Charles Rangel of New York introduced a bill to restore conscription. Since

Rangel got a grand total of 11 co-sponsors, it is safe to say that conscription is an idea whose time has not come, but it's still one worth thinking seriously about.

The most obvious objection to a restoration of the draft is that the all-volunteer force, as it is known, is one of the most successful institutions in the country. The A.V.F. is both the world's most powerful fighting force and a shining example of harmonious race relations and affirmative action. When asked about the draft, Secretary of Defense Donald H. Rumsfeld has essentially said, Why fix what isn't broken? There are several answers to this question. First of all, the war on terrorism is already straining the military and imposing terrible burdens on reservists. Second, we may soon be redefining such civilian tasks as border patrol and airport security as military ones, thus requiring a much larger uniformed force. Charles Moskos, a professor of sociology at Northwestern and an expert on military affairs, has proposed a three-tier draft involving a military, a homeland defense and a civilian component, the last essentially a form of "national service." So a draft would satisfy manpower needs that an all-volunteer force might not. It would also almost certainly be cheaper.

But the ultimate justification for conscription must be moral. Both Rangel and Moskos argue that the A.V.F. recruits working-class young men and women with bleak job prospects and pays them to put their lives on the line. "These people should not have to die merely because they were born to a class of people that lacked the advantages of other people," as Rangel says. There is also an important issue of political philosophy. Conscription assumes a relationship between citizen and state that makes most conservatives, and many liberals, uncomfortable. Libertarian conservatives like Milton Friedman object vehemently to any form of compulsion on the part of the state that's not absolutely unavoidable. Liberals have traditionally feared the use to which the state puts its soldiers. In 1970, at the height of the Vietnam War, the political philosopher Michael Walzer wrote that since many citizens are bound to find almost any use of military power unjust, conscription may be justified only when the state's very existence is threatened. We owe the state no more than that.

But is that so? In the age of terrorism, doesn't the imperative of self-defense go well beyond acts of direct territorial threat? What's more, is the draft really a form of tyranny? We live in a culture in which everyone has rights and no one has obligations; the social contract has never been so

wan. Perhaps now that our collective safety is jeopardized, the time has come to rethink that contract. Moskos says that in the Princeton class of 1956, from which he graduated, 450 of 750 men served in the military. Last year, Moskos says, 3 of Princeton's approximately 1,000 graduates served. That can't be a good thing for the country.

Of course, the country was at peace in 1956. A young man or woman drafted today might very well face combat—and might even have to serve in a war, like Iraq, that he or she considered wrongheaded—the Walzer problem. Perhaps draftees could be permitted to elect other forms of national service. But a truly democratic draft might also, as Rangel suggests, alter the strategic calculus: if the children of journalists, legislators and policy experts were called to military service, we might do a more thorough, and a more honest, job of deciding exactly what it is that's worth fighting for.

I have a 12-year-old son. The idea that in six or seven years Alex might be drafted is a little bit comical, but mostly appalling. My wife thinks I'm crazy even to suggest the idea. Nevertheless, it's true that we live in a genuinely threatening world; that is, alas, the very reason that military service, or at least some kind of service, should be mandatory, rather than a matter of individual conscience or marketplace choice.

In the Matter of Baby "M"

Superior Court of New Jersey
March 31, 1987

Opinion by Judge Sorkow

This court is confronted with circumstances in which on February 6, 1985, the parties to this litigation, with great joy and expectation, entered into a surrogate arrangement. It was an arrangement where both—the prospective family and the surrogate mother—wanted the child; albeit, for different purposes. . . . The couple sought to bring into existence a child by conscious pre-arrangement

which, as far as biologically possible, would be genetically their own. The surrogate consciously chose to bear a child for another couple with the understanding that she would not contest but would consent to their adoption of it. . . .

Concerns have been expressed about the efficacy of surrogate arrangements. They are: 1) that the child will not be protected; 2) the potential for exploitation of the surrogate mother; 3) the alleged denigration of human dignity by recognizing any agreement in which a child is produced for money; 4) surrogacy is invalid because it is contrary to adoption statutes and other child benefit laws such as statutes establishing standards for termination of parental rights; 5) it will undermine traditional notions of family; and 6) surrogacy allows an elite economic group to use a poorer group of people to achieve their purposes. . . .

The second argument against surrogacy is that the surrogate mother will be exploited. To the contrary. It is the private adoption that has that great potential for, if not actual, exploitation of the mother. In the private adoption, the woman is already pregnant. The biological father may be unknown or at best uninterested in his obligations. The woman may want to keep the child but cannot do so for financial reasons. There is the risk of illegal consideration being paid to the mother. In surrogacy, none of these "downside" elements appear. The arrangement is made when the desire and intention to have a family exist on the couple's part. The surrogate has an opportunity to consult, take advice and consider her act and is not forced into the relationship. She is not yet pregnant.

The third argument is that to produce or deal with a child for money denigrates human dignity. With that premise, this court urgently agrees. The 13th Amendment to the United States Constitution is still valid law. The law of adoption in New Jersey does prohibit the exchange of any consideration for obtaining a child. The fact is, however, that the money to be paid to the surrogate is not being paid for the surrender of the child to the father. And that is just the point—at birth, mother and father have equal rights to the child absent any other agreement. The biological father pays the surrogate for her willingness to be impregnated and carry his child to term. At birth, the father does not purchase the child. It is his own biological genetically related child. He cannot purchase what is already his. . . .

The sixth and final argument suggests that an elite upper economic group of people will use the lower economic group of woman to "make their babies." This argument is insensitive and offensive to the intense drive to procreate naturally and when that is impossible, to use what lawful means are possible to gain a child. This intense desire to propagate the species is fundamental. It is within the soul of all men and women regardless of economic status. . . .

The court was . . . told by the parties that they all understood their obligations under the contract. Specifically, it was understood by all that Mr. Stern's sperm would be used to artificially inseminate Mrs. Whitehead. Upon conception, Mrs. Whitehead would carry the child and when she gave birth, she would then surrender the infant to the biological father and his wife. Mrs. Whitehead would also voluntarily renounce her parental rights to permit Mrs. Stern to adopt the infant. Mrs. Stern, it must be noted, is not a party to the contract. This was to avoid any possible inference that there is a violation of *N.J.S.A.* 9:3–54 (which prohibits giving a consideration to obtain an adoptable child). Mr. Whitehead signed a certification pursuant to *N.J.S.A.* 9:17–44 establishing his non-paternity. Mr. Stern agreed to pay Mrs. Whitehead $10,000 for conceiving and bearing his child.

Fundamentally, when there were no time constraints, when Mrs. Whitehead was not pregnant, when each party had the opportunity to obtain advice (legal, medical and/or psychological), the parties expressed their respective offers and acceptances to each other and reduced their understanding to a writing. If the mutual promises were not sufficient to establish a valid consideration, then certainly there was consideration when there was conception. The male gave his sperm; the female gave her egg in their pre-planned effort to create a child—thus, a contract.

For the past year, there has been a child in being. She is alive and well. She is tangible proof of that which the Whiteheads and Mr. Stern in concert agreed to do. The child was conceived with a mutual understanding by the parties of her future life. Except now, Mrs. Whitehead has failed to perform one of her last promises, which was to surrender the child and renounce parental rights. She has otherwise performed the personal service that she had undertaken—conception and carrying the child to term. The terms of the contract have been executed but for the surrender.

It is argued that Mrs. Whitehead should have a time period after delivery to determine if she wants to surrender the child. Such a rule has been developed in Kentucky by the use of Kentucky's private placement adoption statute. Use of laws not intended for their intended purpose creates forced and confusing results. There should be no use of the New Jersey adoption statutes to accommodate or deny surrogacy contracts. Indeed, again it is held that there is no law governing surrogacy contracts in New Jersey and the laws of adoption do not apply to surrogacy contracts. The sole legal concepts that control are *parens patriae* and best interests of the child. To wait for birth, to plan, pray and dream of the joy it will bring and then be told that the child will not come home, that a new set of rules applies and to ask a court to approve such a result deeply offends the conscience of this court. A person who has promised is entitled to rely on the concommitant promise of the other promisor. This court holds therefore that in New Jersey, although the surrogacy contract is signed, the surrogate may nevertheless renounce and terminate the contract until the time of conception. She may be subject then for such monetary damages as may be proven. Specific performance to compel the promised conception, gestation, and birth shall not be available to the male promisor. However, once conception has occurred the parties rights are fixed, the terms of the contract are firm and performance will be anticipated with the joy that only a newborn can bring.

Having defined a new rule of law, this court hastens to add an exception. After conception, only the surrogate shall have the right, to the exclusion of the sperm donor, to decide whether to abort the fetus. Her decision to abort must comply with the guidelines set forth in *Roe v. Wade*, 410 *U.S.* 113 (1973).

Roe, supra, establishes and recognizes the unique and singular quality of woman. That only woman has the constitutionally protected right to determine the manner in which her body and person shall be used. The surrogate parenting agreement fails to recognize this fact; hence, the clause it contains prohibiting abortion except as allowed by the male promisor is void and unenforceable.

It is argued that the contract in this case is one of adhesion. . . . By definition, a contract of adhesion is one in which one party has no alternative but to accept or reject the other party's terms and there are no options by which the party may obtain the product or service. Here, neither party has a superior bargaining position. Each had what the other wanted. A price for the service each was to

perform was struck and a bargain reached. One did not force the other. Neither had expertise that left the other at a disadvantage. Neither had disproportionate bargaining power. Although the contract was a form, there is no proof that it was absolute and could not be altered. Defendant offered no proof to this end. Mrs. Whitehead, acknowledged that minor changes were bargained for. There is no evidence of an absence of good faith or fair dealing. This is not a contract of adhesion.

Defendants argue unconscionability. They claim the terms are manifestly unfair or oppressive. These terms were known to Mrs. Whitehead from her earlier surrogate contracting experience. She read the second contract, albeit briefly, prior to signing it. She was aware of her compensation. She had been pregnant before and had to be aware of the risks of pregnancy. Her obligation included physical examination for her own welfare as well as the welfare of the fetus. Mrs. Whitehead says that Mr. Stern undertook no risks. To compare the risk of pregnancy in a woman to the donation of sperm by the man would be unconscionable. This, however, is the bargain Mrs. Whitehead sought and obtained. Mr. Stern did take a risk, however, whether the child would be normal or abnormal, whether accepted or rejected he would have a lifetime obligation and responsibility to the child as its natural and biological father.

To the issue of unconscionability, defendants fail to show proof of overreaching or disproportionate bargaining that result in an unfair contract. Mrs. Whitehead was anxious to contract. At the New Brunswick meeting, she pressed for a definitive statement by the Sterns. She knew just what she was bargaining for. This court finds that she has changed her mind, reneged on her promise and now seeks to avoid her obligations. Unconscionability claims arise, more often than not, in consumer contracts for products or services. The seller is in the dominant position and the buyer must comply or there is no deal. Not so here—either party could have walked away from the other. Either party would then have continued on ICNY's roster of available surrogates and childless families seeking a surrogate. They chose not to do so. The bargain here was one for totally personal service. It was a very scarce service Mrs. Whitehead was providing. Indeed, it might even be said she had the dominant bargaining position for without her Mr. Stern had no other immediate source available. Each party sought each other to fulfill their needs.

It is argued by *amicus* that the $10,000 to be paid Mrs. Whitehead is so low as to be unconscionable. In counterpoint, it is stated that not all services can be compensated by money. Millions of men and women work for each other in their marital relationship. There may even be mutual inequality in the value of the work performed but the benefits obtained from the relationship serve to reject the concept of equating societal acts to a monetary balancing. Perhaps the risk was great for the money to be paid but the risk was what Mrs. Whitehead chose to assume and at the agreed upon fee. And it is assumed she received other intangible benefits and satisfaction from doing what she did. Her original application set forth her highly altruistic purpose. Notwithstanding *amicus'* position, all in this world cannot be equated to money. . . .

For the foregoing reasons, this court concludes and holds that the surrogate-parenting agreement is a valid and enforceable contract pursuant to the laws of New Jersey. The rights of the parties to contract are constitutionally protected under the 14th Amendment of the United States Constitution. This court further finds that Mrs. Whitehead has breached her contract in two ways: 1) by failing to surrender to Mr. Stern the child born to her and Mr. Stern and 2) by failing to renounce her parental rights to that child. . . .

At this point the court would enter its order for specific performance, but an additional inquiry is necessary. Since we here deal with a human life of only one year, since we treat with, as the guardian *ad litem* has said "the most precious and unique thing on this earth, a small vulnerable and lovable child," inquiry must be made to determine if the result of such an order for specific performance would be in the child's best interest. This court holds that whether there will be specific performance of this surrogacy contract depends on whether doing so is in the child's best interest. . . . It is for all these reasons and because of all of the facts found by this court as the trier of fact that we find by clear and convincing evidence, indeed by a measure of evidence reaching beyond reasonable doubt, that Melissa's best interests will be served by being placed in her father's sole custody.

Now having found that the best interests of the child will be enhanced and served in paternal custody, that there is no evidence of fraud, overreaching or violation of any other principle of equity by Mr. Stern, this court having evaluated the equities finds them weighted in favor of Mr. Stern. Enforcing the contract will leave Mr. and Mrs. Whitehead in the same position that they were in when the contract was made. To not enforce the contract will give them the child and deprive Mr. Stern of his promised benefits. This court therefore will specifically enforce the surrogate-parenting agreement to compel delivery of the child to the father and to terminate the mother's parental rights.

In the Matter of Baby M

Supreme Court of New Jersey
February 3, 1988

The opinion of the Court was delivered by Wilentz, C.J.

OPINION: In this matter the Court is asked to determine the validity of a contract that purports to provide a new way of bringing children into a family. For a fee of $10,000, a woman agrees to be artificially inseminated with the semen of another woman's husband; she is to conceive a child, carry it to term, and after its birth surrender it to the natural father and his wife. The intent of the contract is that the child's natural mother will thereafter be forever separated from her child. The wife is to adopt the child, and she and the natural father are to be regarded as its parents for all purposes. The contract providing for this is called a "surrogacy contract," the natural mother inappropriately called the "surrogate mother."

We invalidate the surrogacy contract because it conflicts with the law and public policy of this State. While we recognize the depth of the yearning of infertile couples to have their own children, we find the payment of money to a "surrogate" mother illegal, perhaps criminal, and potentially degrading to women. Although in this case we grant custody to the natural father, the evidence having clearly proved such custody to be in the best interests of the infant, we void both the termination of the surrogate mother's parental rights and the adoption of the child by the wife/stepparent. We thus restore the "surrogate" as the mother of the child. We remand the issue of the natural mother's visitation rights to the trial court, since that issue was not reached below and the record before us is not sufficient to permit us to decide it *de novo.*

We find no offense to our present laws where a woman voluntarily and without payment agrees to act as a "surrogate" mother, provided that she is not subject to a binding agreement to surrender her child. Moreover, our holding today does not preclude the Legislature from altering the current statutory scheme, within constitutional limits, so as to permit surrogacy contracts. Under current law, however, the surrogacy agreement before us is illegal and invalid. . . .

Under the contract, the natural mother is irrevocably committed before she knows the strength of her bond with her child. She never makes a totally voluntary, informed decision, for quite clearly any decision prior to the baby's birth is, in the most important sense, uninformed, and any decision after that, compelled by a pre-existing contractual commitment, the threat of a lawsuit, and the inducement of a $10,000 payment, is less than totally voluntary. Her interests are of little concern to those who controlled this transaction.

Although the interest of the natural father and adoptive mother is certainly the predominant interest, realistically the *only* interest served, even they are left with less than what public policy requires. They know little about the natural mother, her genetic makeup, and her psychological and medical history. Moreover, not even a superficial attempt is made to determine their awareness of their responsibilities as parents.

Worst of all, however, is the contract's total disregard of the best interests of the child. There is not the slightest suggestion that any inquiry will be made at any time to determine the fitness of the Sterns as custodial parents, of Mrs. Stern as an adoptive parent, their superiority to Mrs. Whitehead, or the effect on the child of not living with her natural mother.

This is the sale of a child, or, at the very least, the sale of a mother's right to her child, the only mitigating factor being that one of the purchasers is the father. Almost every evil that prompted the prohibition on the payment of money in connection with adoptions exists here.

The differences between an adoption and a surrogacy contract should be noted, since it is asserted that the use of money in connection with surrogacy does not pose the risks found where money buys an adoption.

First, and perhaps most important, all parties concede that it is unlikely that surrogacy will survive without money. Despite the alleged selfless motivation of surrogate mothers, if there is no payment, there will be no surrogates, or very few. That conclusion contrasts with adoption; for obvious reasons, there remains a steady supply, albeit insufficient, despite the prohibitions against payment. The adoption itself, relieving the natural mother of the financial burden of supporting an infant, is in some sense the equivalent of payment.

Second, the use of money in adoptions does not *produce* the problem—conception occurs, and usually the birth itself, before illicit funds are offered. With surrogacy, the "problem," if one views it as such, consisting of the purchase of a woman's procreative capacity, at the risk of her life, is caused by and originates with the offer of money.

Third, with the law prohibiting the use of money in connection with adoptions, the built-in financial pressure of the unwanted pregnancy and the consequent support obligation do not lead the mother to the highest paying, ill-suited, adoptive parents. She is just as well-off surrendering the child to an approved agency. In surrogacy, the highest bidders will presumably become the adoptive parents regardless of suitability, so long as payment of money is permitted.

Fourth, the mother's consent to surrender her child in adoptions is revocable, even after surrender of the child, unless it be to an approved agency, where by regulation there are protections against an ill-advised surrender. In surrogacy, consent occurs so early that no amount of advice would satisfy the potential mother's need, yet the consent is irrevocable.

The main difference, that the unwanted pregnancy is unintended while the situation of the surrogate mother is voluntary and intended, is really not significant. Initially, it produces stronger reactions of sympathy for the mother whose pregnancy was unwanted than for the surrogate mother, who "went into this with her eyes wide open." On reflection, however, it appears that the essential evil is the same, taking advantage of a woman's circumstances (the unwanted pregnancy or the need for money) in order to take away her child, the difference being one of degree.

In the scheme contemplated by the surrogacy contract in this case, a middle man, propelled by profit, promotes the sale. Whatever idealism may have motivated any of the participants, the profit motive predominates, permeates, and ultimately governs the transaction. The demand for children is great and the supply small. The availability of contraception, abortion, and the greater willingness of single mothers to bring up their children has led to a shortage of babies offered for adoption. The situation is ripe for the entry of the middleman who will bring some equilibrium into the market by increasing the supply through the use of money.

Intimated, but disputed, is the assertion that surrogacy will be used for the benefit of the rich at the expense of the poor. In response it is noted that the Sterns are not rich and the Whiteheads not poor. Nevertheless, it is clear to us that it is unlikely that surrogate mothers will be as proportionately numerous among those women in the top twenty percent income bracket as among those in the bottom twenty percent. Put differently, we doubt that infertile couples in the low-income bracket will find upper income surrogates.

In any event, even in this case one should not pretend that disparate wealth does not play a part simply because the contrast is not the dramatic "rich versus poor." At the time of trial, the Whiteheads' net assets were probably negative—Mrs. Whitehead's own sister was foreclosing on a second mortgage. Their income derived from Mr. Whitehead's labors. Mrs. Whitehead is a homemaker, having previously held part-time jobs. The Sterns are both professionals, she a medical doctor, he a biochemist. Their combined income when both were working was about $89,500 a year and their assets sufficient to pay for the surrogacy contract arrangements.

The point is made that Mrs. Whitehead *agreed* to the surrogacy arrangement, supposedly fully understanding the consequences. Putting aside the issue of how compelling her need for money may have been, and how significant her understanding of the consequences, we suggest that her consent is irrelevant. There are, in a civilized society, some things that money cannot buy. In America, we decided long ago that merely because conduct purchased by money was "voluntary" did not mean that it was good or beyond regulation and prohibition. *West Coast Hotel Co. v. Parrish*, 300 *U.S.* 379 (1937). Employers can no longer buy labor at the lowest price they can bargain for, even though that labor is "voluntary," 29 *U.S.C.* § 206 (1982), or buy women's labor for less money than paid to men for the same job, 29 *U.S.C.* § 206(d), or purchase the agreement of children to perform oppressive labor, 29 *U.S.C.* § 212, or purchase the agreement of workers to subject themselves to unsafe or unhealthful working conditions, 29 *U.S.C.* §§ 651 to 678. (Occupational Safety and Health Act of 1970). There are, in short, values that society deems more important than granting to wealth whatever it can buy, be it labor, love, or life. Whether this principle recommends prohibition of surrogacy, which presumably sometimes results in great satisfaction to all of the parties, is not for us to say. We note here only that, under existing law, the fact that Mrs. Whitehead "agreed" to the arrangement is not dispositive.

The long-term effects of surrogacy contracts are not known, but feared—the impact on the child who learns her life was bought, that she is the offspring of someone who gave birth to her only to obtain money; the impact on the natural mother as the full weight of her isolation is felt along with the full reality of the sale of her body and her child; the impact on the natural father and adoptive mother once they realize the consequences of their conduct. Literature in related areas suggests these are substantial considerations, although, given the newness of surrogacy, there is little information.

The surrogacy contract is based on, principles that are directly contrary to the objectives of our laws. It guarantees the separation of a child from its mother; it looks to adoption regardless of suitability; it totally ignores the child; it takes the child from the mother regardless of her wishes and her maternal fitness; and it does all of this, it accomplishes all of its goals, through the use of money.

Beyond that is the potential degradation of some women that may result from this arrangement. In many cases, of course, surrogacy may bring satisfaction, not only to the infertile couple, but to the surrogate mother herself. The fact, however, that many women may not perceive surrogacy negatively but rather see it as an opportunity does not diminish its potential for devastation to other women.

In sum, the harmful consequences of this surrogacy arrangement appear to us all too palpable. In New Jersey the surrogate mother's agreement to sell her child is void. Its irrevocability infects the entire contract, as does the money that purports to buy it.

Is Women's Labor a Commodity?

Elizabeth S. Anderson

In the past few years the practice of commercial surrogate motherhood has gained notoriety as a method for acquiring children. A commercial surrogate mother is anyone who is paid money to bear a child for other people and terminate her parental rights, so that the others may raise the child as exclusively their own. The growth of commercial surrogacy has raised with new urgency a class of concerns regarding the proper scope of the market. Some critics have objected to commercial surrogacy on the ground that it improperly treats children and women's reproductive capacities as commodities.[1] The prospect of reducing children to consumer durables and women to baby factories surely inspires revulsion. But are there good reasons behind the revulsion? And is this an accurate description of what commercial surrogacy implies? This article offers a theory about what things are properly regarded as commodities which supports the claim that commercial surrogacy constitutes an unconscionable commodification of children and of women's reproductive capacities.

What Is a Commodity?

The modern market can be characterized in terms of the legal and social norms by which it governs the production, exchange, and enjoyment of commodities. To say that something is properly regarded as a commodity is to claim that the norms of the market are appropriate for regulating its production, exchange, and enjoyment. To the extent that moral principles or ethical ideals preclude the application of market norms to a good, we may say that the good is not a (proper) commodity.

Why should we object to the application of a market norm to the production or distribution of a good? One reason may be that to produce or distribute the good in accordance with the norm is to *fail to value it in an appropriate way*. Consider, for example, a standard Kantian argument against slavery, or the commodification of persons. Slaves are treated in accordance with the market norm that owners may use commodities to satisfy their own interests without regard for the interests of the commodities themselves. To treat a person without regard for her interests is to fail to respect her. But slaves are persons who may not be merely used in this fashion, since as rational beings

The author thanks David Anderson, Steven Darwall, Ezekiel Emanuel, Daniel Hausman, Don Herzog, Robert Nozick, Richard Pildes, John Rawls, Michael Sandel, Thomas Scanlon, and Howard Wial for helpful comments and criticisms.

1. See, for example, Gena Corea, *The Mother Machine* (New York: Harper and Row, 1985), pp. 216, 219: Angela Holder. "Surrogate Motherhood: Babies for Fun and Profit," *Case and Comment* 90 (1985): 3–11; and Margaret Jane Radin, "Market Inalienability," *Harvard Law Review* 100 (June 1987): 1849–1937.

they possess a dignity which commands respect. In Kantian theory, the problem with slavery is that it treats beings worthy of *respect* as if they were worthy merely of *use*. "Respect" and "use" in this context denote what we may call different *modes of valuation*. We value things and persons in other ways than by respecting and using them. For example, love, admiration, honor, and appreciation constitute distinct modes of valuation. To value a thing or person in a distinctive way involves treating it in accordance with a particular set of norms. For example, courtesy expresses a mode of valuation we may call "civil respect," which differs from Kantian respect in that it calls for obedience to the rules of etiquette rather than to the categorical imperative.

Any ideal of human life includes a conception of how different things and persons should be valued. Let us reserve the term "use" to refer to the mode of valuation proper to commodities, which follows the market norm of treating things solely in accordance with the owner's nonmoral preferences. Then the Kantian argument against commodifying persons can be generalized to apply to many other cases. It can be argued that many objects which are worthy of a higher mode of valuation than use are not properly regarded as mere commodities.[2] Some current arguments against the colorization of classic black-and-white films take this form. Such films have been colorized by their owners in an attempt to enhance their market value by attracting audiences unused to black-and-white cinematography. But some opponents of the practice object that such treatment of the film classics fails to appreciate their aesthetic and historical value. True appreciation of these films would preclude this kind of crass commercial exploitation, which debases their aesthetic qualities in the name of profits. Here the argument rests on the claim that the goods in question are worthy of appreciation, not merely of use.

The ideals which specify how one should value certain things are supported by a conception of human flourishing. Our lives are enriched and elevated by cultivating and exercising the capacity to appreciate art. To fail to do so reflects poorly on ourselves. To fail to value things appropriately is to embody in one's life an inferior conception of human flourishing.[3]

These considerations support a general account of the sorts of things which are appropriately regarded as commodities. Commodities are those things which are properly treated in accordance with the norms of the modern market. We can question the application of market norms to the production, distribution, and enjoyment of a good by appealing to ethical ideals which support arguments that the good should be valued in some other way than use. Arguments of the latter sort claim that to allow certain market norms to govern our treatment of a thing expresses a mode of valuation not worthy of it. If the thing is to be valued appropriately, its production, exchange, and enjoyment must be removed from market norms and embedded in a different set of social relationships.

The Case of Commercial Surrogacy

Let us now consider the practice of commercial surrogate motherhood in the light of this theory of commodities. Surrogate motherhood as a commercial enterprise is based upon contracts

2. The notion of valuing something more highly than another can be understood as follows. Some preferences are neither obligatory nor admirable. To value a thing as a mere use-object is to treat it solely in accordance with such nonethical preferences. To value a thing or person more highly than as a mere use-object is to recognize it as having some special intrinsic worth, in virtue of which we form preferences about how to treat the thing which we regard as obligatory or admirable. The person who truly appreciates art does not conceive of art merely as a thing which she can use as she pleases, but as something which commands appreciation. It would be contemptible to willfully destroy the aesthetic qualities of a work of art simply to satisfy some of one's nonethical preferences, and it is a mark of a cultivated and hence admirable person that she has preferences for appreciating art. This account of higher and lower modes of valuation is indebted to Charles Taylor's account of higher and lower values. See Charles Taylor, "The Diversity of Goods," in *Utilitarianism and Beyond*, ed. Amartya Sen and Bernard Williams (Cambridge: Cambridge University Press, 1982). pp. 129–44.

3. This kind of argument shows why treating something as a commodity may be deplorable. Of course, more has to be said to justify prohibiting the commodification of a thing. I shall argue below that the considerations against the commodification of children and of women's labor are strong enough to justify prohibiting the practice of commercial surrogacy.

involving three parties: the intended father, the broker, and the surrogate mother. The intended father agrees to pay a lawyer to find a suitable surrogate mother and make the requisite medical and legal arrangements for the conception and birth of the child, and for the transfer of legal custody to himself.[4] The surrogate mother agrees to become impregnated with the intended father's sperm, to carry the resulting child to term, and to relinquish her parental rights to it, transferring custody to the father in return for a fee and medical expenses. Both she and her husband (if she has one) agree not to form a parent-child bond with her child and to do everything necessary to effect the transfer of the child to the intended father. At current market prices, the lawyer arranging the contract can expect to gross $15,000 from the contract, while the surrogate mother can expect a $10,000 fee.[5]

The practice of commercial surrogacy has been defended on four main grounds. First, given the shortage of children available for adoption and the difficulty of qualifying as adoptive parents, it may represent the only hope for some people to be able to raise a family. Commercial surrogacy should be accepted as an effective means for realizing this highly significant good. Second, two fundamental human rights support commercial surrogacy: the right to procreate and freedom of contract. Fully informed autonomous adults should have the right to make whatever arrangements they wish for the use of their bodies and the reproduction of children, so long as the children themselves are not harmed. Third, the labor of the surrogate mother is said to be a labor of love. Her altruistic acts should be permitted and encouraged.[6]

4. State laws against selling babies prevent the intended father's wife (if he has one) from being a party to the contract.
5. See Katie Marie Brophy, "A Surrogate Mother Contract to Bear a Child," *Journal of Family Law* 20 (1981–82): 263–91, and Noel Keane, "The Surrogate Parenting Contract," *Adelphia Law Journal* 2 (1983): 45–53, for examples and explanations of surrogate parenting contracts.
6. Mary Warnock, *A Question of Life* (Oxford: Blackwell, 1985), p. 45. This book reprints the Warnock Report on Human Fertilization and Embryology, which was commissioned by the British government for the purpose of recommending legislation concerning surrogacy and other issues. Although the Warnock Report mentions the promotion of altruism as one defense of surrogacy, it strongly condemns the practice overall.

Finally, it is argued that commercial surrogacy is no different in its ethical implications from many already accepted practices which separate genetic, gestational, and social parenting, such as artificial insemination by donor, adoption, wet-nursing, and day care. Consistency demands that society accept this new practice as well.[7]

In opposition to these claims, I shall argue that commercial surrogacy does raise new ethical issues, since it represents an invasion of the market into a new sphere of conduct, that of specifically women's labor—that is, the labor of carrying children to term in pregnancy. When women's labor is treated as a commodity, the women who perform it are degraded. Furthermore, commercial surrogacy degrades children by reducing their status to that of commodities. Let us consider each of the goods of concern in surrogate motherhood—the child, and women's reproductive labor—to see how the commercialization of parenthood affects people's regard for them.

Children as Commodities

The most fundamental calling of parents to their children is to love them. Children are to be loved and cherished by their parents, not to be used or manipulated by them for merely personal advantage. Parental love can be understood as a passionate, unconditional commitment to nurture one's child, providing it with the care, affection, and guidance it needs to develop its capacities to maturity. This understanding of the way parents should value their children informs our interpretation of parental rights over their children. Parents' rights over their children are trusts, which they must always exercise for the sake of the child. This is not to deny that parents have their own aspirations in raising children. But the child's interests beyond subsistence are not definable independently of the flourishing of the family, which is the object of specifically parental aspirations. The proper exercise of parental rights includes those acts which promote their shared life as a family,

7. John Robertson, "Surrogate Mothers: Not So Novel after All," *Hastings Center Report*, October 1983, pp. 28–34; John Harris, *The Value of Life* (Boston: Routledge and Kegan Paul, 1985).

which realize the shared interests of the parents and the child.

The norms of parental love carry implications for the ways other people should treat the relationship between parents and their children. If children are to be loved by their parents, then others should not attempt to compromise the integrity of parental love or work to suppress the emotions supporting the bond between parents and their children. If the rights to children should be understood as trusts, then if those rights are lost or relinquished, the duty of those in charge of transferring custody to others is to consult the best interests of the child.

Commercial surrogacy substitutes market norms for some of the norms of parental love. Most importantly, it requires us to understand parental rights no longer as trusts but as things more like property rights—that is, rights of use and disposal over the things owned. For in this practice the natural mother deliberately conceives a child with the intention of giving it up for material advantage. Her renunciation of parental responsibilities is not done for the child's sake, nor for the sake of fulfilling an interest she shares with the child, but typically for her own sake (and possibly, if "altruism" is a motive, for the intended parents' sakes). She and the couple who pay her to give up her parental rights over her child thus treat her rights as a kind of property right. They thereby treat the child itself as a kind of commodity, which may be properly bought and sold.

Commercial surrogacy insinuates the norms of commerce into the parental relationship in other ways. Whereas parental love is not supposed to be conditioned upon the child having particular characteristics, consumer demand is properly responsive to the characteristics of commodities. So the surrogate industry provides opportunities to adoptive couples to specify the height, I.Q., race, and other attributes of the surrogate mother, in the expectation that these traits will be passed on to the child.[8] Since no industry assigns agents to look after the "interests" of its commodities, no one represents the child's interests in the surrogate industry. The surrogate agency promotes the

adoptive parents' interests and not the child's interests where matters of custody are concerned. Finally, as the agent of the adoptive parents, the broker has the task of policing the surrogate (natural) mother's relationship to her child, using persuasion, money, and the threat of a lawsuit to weaken and destroy whatever parental love she may develop for her child.[9]

All of these substitutions of market norms for parental norms represent ways of treating children as commodities which are degrading to them. Degradation occurs when something is treated in accordance with a lower mode of valuation than is proper to it. We value things not just "more" or "less," but in qualitatively higher and lower ways. To love or respect someone is to value her in a higher way than one would if one merely used her. Children are properly loved by their parents and respected by others. Since children are valued as mere use-objects by the mother and the surrogate agency when they are sold to others, and by the adoptive parents when they seek to conform the child's genetic makeup to their own wishes, commercial surrogacy degrades children insofar as it treats them as commodities.[10]

One might argue that since the child is most likely to enter a loving home, no harm comes to it from permitting the natural mother to treat it as property. So the purchase and sale of infants is unobjectionable, at least from the point of view of children's interests.[11] But the sale of an infant has an expressive significance which this argument

8. See "No Other Hope for Having a Child," *Time*, 19 January 1987, pp. 50–51. Radin argues that women's traits are also commodified in this practice. See "Market Inalienability," pp. 1932–35.

9. Here I discuss the surrogate industry as it actually exists today. I will consider possible modifications of commercial surrogacy in the final section below.

10. Robert Nozick has objected that my claims about parental love appear to be culture-bound. Do not parents in the Third World, who rely on children to provide for the family subsistence, regard their children as economic goods? In promoting the livelihood of their families, however, such children need not be treated in accordance with market norms—that is, as commodities. In particular, such children usually remain a part of their families, and hence can still be loved by their parents. But insofar as children are treated according to the norms of modern capitalist markets, this treatment is deplorable wherever it takes place.

11. See Elizabeth Landes and Richard Posner, "The Economics of the Baby Shortage," *Journal of Legal Studies* 7 (1978): 323–48, and Richard Posner, "The Regulation of the Market in Adoptions," *Boston University Law Review* 67 (1987): 59–72.

fails to recognize. By engaging in the transfer of children by sale, all of the parties to the surrogate contract express a set of attitudes toward children which undermine the norms of parental love. They all agree in treating the ties between a natural mother and her children as properly loosened by a monetary incentive. Would it be any wonder if a child born of a surrogacy agreement feared resale by parents who have such an attitude? And a child who knew how anxious her parents were that she have the "right" genetic makeup might fear that her parent's love was contingent upon her expression of these characteristics.[12]

The unsold children of surrogate mothers are also harmed by commercial surrogacy. The children of some surrogate mothers have reported their fears that they may be sold like their half-brother or half-sister, and express a sense of loss at being deprived of a sibling.[13] Furthermore, the widespread acceptance of commercial surrogacy would psychologically threaten all children. For it would change the way children are valued by people (parents and surrogate brokers)—from being loved by their parents and respected by others, to being sometimes used as objects of commercial profit-making.[14]

Proponents of commercial surrogacy have denied that the surrogate industry engages in the sale of children. For it is impossible to sell to someone what is already his own, and the child is already the father's own natural offspring. The payment to the surrogate mother is not for her child, but for her services in carrying it to term.[15] The claim that the parties to the surrogate contract treat children as commodities, however, is based on the way they treat the *mother's* rights over her child. It is irrelevant that the natural father also has some rights over the child; what he pays for is exclusive rights to it. He would not pay her for the "service" of carrying the child to term if she refused to relinquish her parental rights to it. That the mother regards only her labor and not her child as requiring compensation is also irrelevant. No one would argue that the baker does not treat his bread as property just because he sees the income from its sale as compensation for his labor and expenses and not for the bread itself, which he doesn't care to keep.[16]

Defenders of commercial surrogacy have also claimed that it does not differ substantially from other already accepted parental practices. In the institutions of adoption and artificial insemination by donor (AID), it is claimed, we already grant parents the right to dispose of their children.[17] But these practices differ in significant respects from commercial surrogacy. The purpose

12. Of course, where children are concerned, it is irrelevant whether these fears are reasonable. One of the greatest fears of children is separation from their parents. Adopted children are already known to suffer from separation anxiety more acutely than children who remain with their natural mothers, for they feel that their original mothers did not love them. In adoption, the fact that the child would be even worse off if the mother did not give it up justifies her severing of ties and can help to rationalize this event to the child. But in the case of commercial surrogacy, the severing of ties is done not for the child's sake, but for the parents' sakes. In the adoption case there are explanations for the mother's action which may quell the child's doubts about being loved which are unavailable in the case of surrogacy.

13. Kay Longcope, "Surrogacy: Two Professionals on Each Side of Issue Give Their Arguments for Prohibition and Regulation." *Boston Globe*, 23 March 1987, pp. 18–19; and Iver Peterson, "Baby M Case: Surrogate Mothers Vent Feelings." *New York Times*, 2 March 1987, pp. B1, B4.

14. Herbert Krimmel, "The Case against Surrogate Parenting," *Hastings Center Report*, October 1983, pp. 35–37.

15. Judge Sorkow made this argument in ruling on the famous case of Baby M. See *In Re Baby M*, 217 N.J. Super. 313. Reprinted in *Family Law Reporter* 13 (1987): 2001–30. Chief Justice Wilentz of the New Jersey Supreme Court overruled Sorkow's judgment. See *In the Matter of Baby M*, 109 N.J. 396, 537 A.2d 1227 (1988).

16. Sallyann Payton has observed that the law does not permit the sale of parental rights, only their relinquishment or forced termination by the state and these acts are subject to court review for the sake of the child's best interests. But this legal technicality does not change the moral implications of the analogy with baby-selling. The mother is still paid to do what she can to relinquish her parental rights and to transfer custody of the child to the father. Whether or not the courts occasionally prevent this from happening, the actions of the parties express a commercial orientation to children which is degrading and harmful to them. The New Jersey Supreme Court ruled that surrogacy contracts are void precisely because they assign custody without regard to the child's best interests. See *In the Matter of Baby M*, p. 1246.

17. Robertson, "Surrogate Mothers: Not So Novel after All," p. 32; Harris, *The Value of Life*, pp. 144–45.

of adoption is to provide a means for placing children in families when their parents cannot or will not discharge their parental responsibilities. It is not a sphere for the existence of a supposed parental right to dispose of one's children for profit. Even AID does not sanction the sale of fully formed human beings. The semen donor sells only a product of his body, not his child, and does not initiate the act of conception.

Two developments might seem to undermine the claim that commercial surrogacy constitutes a degrading commerce in children. The first is technological: the prospect of transplanting a human embryo into the womb of a genetically unrelated woman. If commercial surrogacy used women only as gestational mothers and not as genetic mothers, and if it was thought that only genetic and not gestational parents could properly claim that a child was "theirs," then the child born of a surrogate mother would not be hers to sell in the first place. The second is a legal development: the establishment of the proposed "consent-intent" definition of parenthood.[18] This would declare the legal parents of a child to be whoever consented to a procedure which leads to its birth, with the intent of assuming parental responsibilities for it. This rule would define away the problem of commerce in children by depriving the surrogate mother of any legal claim to her child at all, even if it was hers both genetically and gestationally.[19]

There are good reasons, however, not to undermine the place of genetic and gestational ties in these ways. Consider first the place of genetic ties. By upholding a system of involuntary (genetic) ties of obligation among people, even when the adults among them prefer to divide their rights and obligations in other ways, we help

18. See Philip Parker, "Surrogate Motherhood: The Interaction of Litigation, Legislation and Psychiatry," *International Journal of Law and Psychiatry* 5 (1982): 341–54.
19. The consent-intent rule would not, however, change the fact that commercial surrogacy replaces parental norms with market norms. For the rule itself embodies the market norm which acknowledges only voluntary, contractual relations among people as having moral force. Whereas familial love invites children into a network of unwilled relationships broader than those they have with their parents, the willed contract creates an exclusive relationship between the parents and the child only.

to secure children's interests in having an assured place in the world, which is more firm than the wills of their parents. Unlike the consent-intent rule, the principle of respecting genetic ties does not make the obligation to care for those whom one has created (intentionally or not) contingent upon an arbitrary desire to do so. It thus provides children with a set of preexisting social sanctions which give them a more secure place in the world. The genetic principle also places children in a far wider network of associations and obligations than the consent-intent rule sanctions. It supports the roles of grandparents and other relatives in the nurturing of children, and provides children with a possible focus of stability and an additional source of claims to care if their parents cannot sustain a well-functioning household.

In the next section I will defend the claims of gestational ties to children. To deny these claims, as commercial surrogacy does, is to deny the significance of reproductive labor to the mother who undergoes it and thereby to dehumanize and degrade the mother herself. Commercial surrogacy would be a corrupt practice even if it did not involve commerce in children.

Women's Labor as a Commodity

Commercial surrogacy attempts to transform what is specifically women's labor—the work of bringing forth children into the world—into a commodity. It does so by replacing the parental norms which usually govern the practice of gestating children with the economic norms which govern ordinary production processes. The application of commercial norms to women's labor reduces the surrogate mothers from persons worthy of respect and consideration to objects of mere use.

Respect and consideration are two distinct modes of valuation whose norms are violated by the practices of the surrogate industry. To respect a person is to treat her in accordance with principles she rationally accepts—principles consistent with the protection of her autonomy and her rational interests. To treat a person with consideration is to respond with sensitivity to her and to her emotional relations with others, refraining from manipulating or denigrating these for one's own purposes. Given the understanding of respect as a dispassionate, impersonal regard for people's interests, a different ethical concept—consideration—is needed to capture the engaged and sensitive regard we should have for people's emotional relationships. The failure of consideration on the part of the other parties to the surrogacy contract explains the judgment that the contract is not simply disrespectful of the surrogate mother, but callous as well.[20]

The application of economic norms to the sphere of women's labor violates women's claims to respect and consideration in three ways. First, by requiring the surrogate mother to repress whatever parental love she feels for the child, these norms convert women's labor into a form of alienated labor. Second, by manipulating and denying legitimacy to the surrogate mother's evolving perspective on her own pregnancy, the norms of the market degrade her. Third, by taking advantage of the surrogate mother's noncommercial motivations without offering anything but what the norms of commerce demand in return, these norms leave her open to exploitation. The fact that these problems arise in the attempt to commercialize the labor of bearing children shows that women's labor is not properly regarded as a commodity.

The key to understanding these problems is the normal role of the emotions in noncommercialized pregnancies. Pregnancy is not simply a biological process but also a social practice. Many social expectations and considerations surround women's gestational labor, marking it off as an occasion for the parents to prepare themselves to welcome a new life into their family. For example, obstetricians use ultrasound not simply for diagnostic purposes but also to encourage maternal bonding with the fetus.[21] We can all recognize that it is good, although by no means inevitable, for loving bonds to be established between the mother and her child during this period.

In contrast with these practices, the surrogate industry follows the putting-out system of manufacturing. It provides some of the raw materials of production (the father's sperm) to the surrogate mother, who then engages in production of the child. Although her labor is subject to periodic

supervision by her doctors and by the surrogate agency, the agency does not have physical control over the product of her labor as firms using the factory system do. Hence, as in all putting-out systems, the surrogate industry faces the problem of extracting the final product from the mother. This problem is exacerbated by the fact that the social norms surrounding pregnancy are designed to encourage parental love for the child. The surrogate industry addresses this problem by requiring the mother to engage in a form of emotional labor.[22] In the surrogate contract, she agrees not to form or to attempt to form a parent-child relationship with her offspring.[23] Her labor is alienated, because she must divert it from the end which the social practices of pregnancy rightly promote—an emotional bond with her child. The surrogate contract thus replaces a norm of parenthood, that during pregnancy one create a loving attachment to one's child, with a norm of commercial production, that the producer shall not form any special emotional ties to her product.

The demand to deliberately alienate oneself from one's love for one's own child is a demand which can reasonably and decently be made of no one. Unless we were to remake pregnancy into a form of drudgery which is only performed for a wage, there is every reason to expect that many women who do sign a surrogate contract will, despite this fact, form a loving attachment to the child they bear. For this is what the social practices surrounding pregnancy encourage. Treating women's labor as just another kind of commercial production process violates the precious emotional ties which the mother may rightly and properly establish with her "product," the child, and thereby violates her claims to consideration.[24]

---

20. I thank Steven Darwall and David Anderson for clarifying my thoughts on this point.
21. I am indebted to Dr. Ezekiel Emanuel for this point.
22. One engages in emotional labor when one is paid to express or repress certain emotions. On the concept of emotional labor and its consequences for workers, see Arlie Hochschild, *The Managed Heart* (Berkeley and Los Angeles: University of California Press, 1983).
23. Noel Keane and Dennis Breo, *The Surrogate Mother* (New York: Everest House, 1981), p. 291; Brophy, "A Surrogate Mother Contract," p. 267. The surrogate's husband is also required to agree to this clause of the contract.
24. One might ask why this argument does not extend to all cases in which one might form an emotional attachment to an object one has contracted to sell. If I sign a contract with you to sell my car to you, can

Commercial surrogacy is also a degrading practice. The surrogate mother, like all persons, has an independent evaluative perspective on her activities and relationships. The realization of her dignity demands that the other parties to the contract acknowledge rather than evade the claims which her independent perspective makes upon them. But the surrogate industry has an interest in suppressing, manipulating, and trivializing her perspective, for there is an ever-present danger that she will see her involvement in her pregnancy from the perspective of a parent rather than from the perspective of a contract laborer.

How does this suppression and trivialization take place? The commercial promoters of surrogacy commonly describe the surrogate mothers as inanimate objects: mere "hatcheries," "plumbing," or "rented property"—things without emotions which could make claims on others.[25] They also refuse to acknowledge any responsibility for the consequences of the mother's emotional labor. Should she suffer psychologically from being forced to give up her child, the father is not liable to pay for therapy after her pregnancy, although he is liable for all other medical expenses following her pregnancy.[26]

The treatment and interpretation of surrogate mothers' grief raises the deepest problems of degradation. Most surrogate mothers experience grief upon giving up their children—in 10 percent of cases, seriously enough to require therapy.[27] Their grief is not compensated by the $10,000 fee they receive. Grief is not an intelligible response to a successful deal, but rather reflects the subject's

judgment that she has suffered a grave and personal loss. Since not all cases of grief resolve themselves into cases of regret, it may be that some surrogate mothers do not regard their grief, in retrospect, as reflecting an authentic judgment on their part. But in the circumstances of emotional manipulation which pervade the surrogate industry, it is difficult to determine which interpretation of her grief more truly reflects the perspective of the surrogate mother. By insinuating a trivializing interpretation of her emotional responses to the prospect of losing her child, the surrogate agency may be able to manipulate her into accepting her fate without too much fuss, and may even succeed in substituting its interpretation of her emotions for her own. Since she has already signed a contract to perform emotional labor—to express or repress emotions which are dictated by the interests of the surrogate industry—this might not be a difficult task.[28] A considerate treatment of the mothers' grief, on the other hand, would take the evaluative basis of their grief seriously.

Some defenders of commercial surrogacy demand that the provision for terminating the surrogate mother's parental rights in her child be legally enforceable, so that peace of mind for the adoptive parents can be secured.[29] But the surrogate industry makes no corresponding provision for securing the peace of mind of the surrogate. She is expected to assume the risk of a transformation of her ethical and emotional perspective on herself and her child with the same impersonal detachment with which a futures trader assumes the risk of a fluctuation in the price of pork bellies. By applying the market norms of enforcing contracts to the surrogate mother's case, commercial surrogacy treats a moral transformation as if it were merely an economic change.[30]

I back out if I decide I am too emotionally attached to it? My argument is based upon the distinctive characteristics of parental love—a mode of valuation which should not be confused with less profound modes of valuation which generate sentimental attachments to things. The degree to which other modes of valuation generate claims to consideration which tell against market norms remains an open question.

25. Corea, *The Mother Machine*, p. 222.

26. Keane and Breo, *The Surrogate Mother*, p. 292.

27. Kay Longcope, "Standing Up for Mary Beth," *Boston Globe*, 5 March 1987, p. 83; Daniel Goleman, "Motivations of Surrogate Mothers," *New York Times*, 20 January 1987, p. C1; Robertson, "Surrogate Mothers: Not So Novel after All," pp. 30, 34 n. 8. Neither the surrogate mothers themselves nor psychiatrists have been able to predict which women will experience such grief.

28. See Hochschild. *The Managed Heart*, for an important empirical study of the dynamics of commercialized emotional labor.

29. Keane and Breo, *The Surrogate Mother*, pp. 236–37.

30. For one account of how a surrogate mother who came to regret her decision viewed her own moral transformation, see Elizabeth Kane: *Birth Mother: The Story of America's First Legal Surrogate Mother* (San Diego: Harcourt Brace Jovanovich, 1988). I argue below that the implications of commodifying women's labor are not significantly changed even if the contract is unenforceable.

The manipulation of the surrogate mother's emotions which is inherent in the surrogate parenting contract also leaves women open to grave forms of exploitation. A kind of exploitation occurs when one party to a transaction is oriented toward the exchange of "gift" values, while the other party operates in accordance with the norms of the market exchange of commodities. Gift values, which include love, gratitude, and appreciation of others, cannot be bought or obtained through piecemeal calculations of individual advantage. Their exchange requires a repudiation of a self-interested attitude, a willingness to give gifts to others without demanding some specific equivalent good in return each time one gives. The surrogate mother often operates according to the norms of gift relationships. The surrogate agency, on the other hand, follows market norms. Its job is to get the best deal for its clients and itself, while leaving the surrogate mother to look after her own interests as best as she can. This situation puts the surrogate agencies in a position to manipulate the surrogate mothers' emotions to gain favorable terms for themselves. For example, agencies screen prospective surrogate mothers for submissiveness, and emphasize to them the importance of the motives of generosity and love. When applicants question some of the terms of the contract, the broker sometimes intimidates them by questioning their character and morality: If they were really generous and loving they would not be so solicitous about their own interests.[31]

Some evidence supports the claim that most surrogate mothers are motivated by emotional needs and vulnerabilities which lead them to view their labor as a form of gift and not a purely commercial exchange. Only 1 percent of applicants to surrogate agencies would become surrogate mothers for money alone; the others have emotional as well as financial reasons for applying. One psychiatrist believes that most, if not all, of the 35 percent of applicants who had had a previous abortion or given up a child for adoption wanted to become surrogate mothers in order to resolve their guilty feelings or deal with their unresolved loss by going through a process of losing a child again.[32] Women who feel that giving up another child is an effective way to punish themselves for past abortions, or a form of therapy for their emotional problems, are not likely to resist manipulation by surrogate brokers.

Many surrogate mothers see pregnancy as a way to feel "adequate," "appreciated," or "special." In other words, these women feel inadequate, unappreciated, or unadmired when they are not pregnant.[33] Lacking the power to achieve some worthwhile status in their own right, they must subordinate themselves to others' definitions of their proper place (as baby factories) in order to get from them the appreciation they need to attain a sense of self-worth. But the sense of self-worth one can attain under such circumstances is precarious and ultimately self-defeating. For example, those who seek gratitude on the part of the adoptive parents and some opportunity to share the joys of seeing their children grow discover all too often that the adoptive parents want nothing to do with them.[34] For while the surrogate mother sees in the arrangement some basis for establishing the personal ties she needs to sustain her emotionally, the adoptive couple sees it as an impersonal commercial contract, one of whose main advantages to them is that all ties between them and the surrogate are ended once the terms of the contract are fulfilled.[35] To them, her presence is a threat to marital unity and a competing object for the child's affections.

These considerations should lead us to question the model of altruism which is held up to women by the surrogacy industry. It is a strange

31. Susan Ince, "Inside the Surrogate Industry," in *Test-Tube Women*, ed. Rita Arditti, Ranate Duelli Klein, and Shelley Minden (Boston: Pandora Press, 1984), p. 110.

32. Philip Parker, "Motivation of Surrogate Mothers: Initial Findings," *American Journal of Psychiatry* 140 (1983): 117–18.

33. The surrogate broker Noel Keane is remarkably open about reporting the desperate emotional insecurities which shape the lives of so many surrogate mothers, while displaying little sensitivity to the implications of his taking advantage of these motivations to make his business a financial success. See especially Keane and Breo, *The Surrogate Mother*, pp. 247ff.

34. See, for example, the story of the surrogate mother Nancy Barrass in Anne Fleming, "Our Fascination with Baby M." *New York Times Magazine*, 29 March 1987, p. 38.

35. For evidence of these disparate perspectives, see Peterson, "Baby M Case: Surrogate Mothers Vent Feelings," p. B4.

form of altruism which demands such radical self-effacement, alienation from those whom one benefits, and the subordination of one's body, health, and emotional life to the independently defined interests of others.[36] Why should this model of "altruism" be held up to *women*? True altruism does not involve such subordination, but rather the autonomous and self-confident exercise of skill, talent, and judgment. (Consider the dedicated doctor.) The kind of altruism we see admired in surrogate mothers involves a lack of self-confidence, a feeling that one can be truly worthy only through self-effacement. This model of altruism, far from affirming the freedom and dignity of women, seems all too conveniently designed to keep their sense of self-worth hostage to the interests of a more privileged class.[37]

The primary distortions which arise from treating women's labor as a commodity—the surrogate mother's alienation from loved ones, her degradation, and her exploitation—stem from a common source. This is the failure to acknowledge and treat appropriately the surrogate mother's emotional engagement with her labor. Her labor is alienated, because she must suppress her emotional ties with her own child, and may be manipulated into reinterpreting these ties in a trivializing way. She is degraded, because her independent ethical perspective is denied, or demoted to the status of a cash sum. She is exploited, because her emotional needs and vulnerabilities are not treated as characteristics which call for consideration, but as factors which may be manipulated to encourage her to make a grave

self-sacrifice to the broker's and adoptive couple's advantage. These considerations provide strong grounds for sustaining the claims of women's labor to its "product," the child. The attempt to redefine parenthood so as to strip women of parental claims to the children they bear does violence to their emotional engagement with the project of bringing children into the world.

Commercial Surrogacy, Freedom, and the Law

In the light of these ethical objections to commercial surrogacy, what position should the law take on the practice? At the very least, surrogate contracts should not be enforceable. Surrogate mothers should not be forced to relinquish their children if they have formed emotional bonds with them. Any other treatment of women's ties to the children they bear is degrading.

But I think these arguments support the stronger conclusion that commercial surrogate contracts should be illegal, and that surrogate agencies who arrange such contracts should be subject to criminal penalties.[38] Commercial surrogacy constitutes a degrading and harmful traffic in children, violates the dignity of women, and subjects both children and women to a serious risk of exploitation. But are these problems inherent in the practice of commercial surrogacy? Defenders of the practice have suggested three reforms intended to eliminate these problems: (1) give the surrogate mother the option of keeping her child after birth; (2) impose stringent regulations on private surrogate agencies; (3) replace private surrogate agencies with a state-run monopoly on surrogate arrangements. Let us consider each of these options in turn.

Some defenders of commercial surrogacy suggest that the problem of respecting the surrogate mother's potential attachment to her child can be solved by granting the surrogate mother the option

36. The surrogate mother is required to obey all doctor's orders made in the interests of the child's health. (See Brophy, "A Surrogate Mother Contract"; Keane, "The Surrogate Parenting Contract"; and Ince, "Inside the Surrogate Industry.") These orders could include forcing her to give up her job, travel plans, and recreational activities. The doctor could confine her to bed, and order her to submit to surgery and take drugs. One can hardly exercise an autonomous choice over one's health if one could be held in breach of contract and liable for $35,000 damages for making a decision contrary to the wishes of one's doctor.

37. See Corea, *The Mother Machine*, pp. 227–33, and Christine Overall, *Ethics and Human Reproduction* (Boston: Allen and Unwin, 1987), pp. 122–28. Both emphasize the social conditions which undermine the claim that women choose to be surrogate mothers under conditions of autonomy.

38. Both of these conclusions follow the Warnock commission's recommendations. See Warnock, *A Question of Life*, pp. 43–44, 46–47. Since the surrogate mother is a victim of commercial surrogacy arrangements, she should not be prosecuted for entering into them. And my arguments are directed only against surrogacy as a commercial enterprise.

to reserve her parental rights after birth.[39] But such an option would not significantly change the conditions of the surrogate mother's labor. Indeed, such a provision would pressure the agency to demean the mother's self-regard more than ever. Since it could not rely on the law to enforce the adoptive parents' wishes regardless of the surrogate's feelings, it would have to make sure that she assumed the perspective which it and its clients have of her: as "rented plumbing."

Could such dangers be avoided by careful regulation of the surrogate industry? Some have suggested that exploitation of women could be avoided by such measures as properly screening surrogates, setting low fixed fees (to avoid tempting women in financial duress), and requiring independent counsel for the surrogate mother.[40] But no one knows how to predict who will suffer grave psychological damage from surrogacy, and the main forms of duress encountered in the industry are emotional rather than financial. Furthermore, there is little hope that regulation would check the exploitation of surrogate mothers. The most significant encounters between the mothers and the surrogate agencies take place behind closed doors. It is impossible to regulate the multifarious ways in which brokers can subtly manipulate the emotions of the vulnerable to their own advantage. Advocates of commercial surrogacy claim that their failure rate is extremely low, since only five out of the first five hundred cases were legally contested by surrogate mothers. But we do not know how many surrogate mothers were browbeaten into relinquishing their children, feel violated by their treatment, or would feel violated had their perspectives not been manipulated by the other parties to the contract. The dangers of exploiting women through commercial surrogacy are too great to ignore, and too deep to effectively regulate.

Could a state-run monopoly on surrogate arrangements eliminate the risk of degrading and exploiting surrogate mothers?[41] A nonprofit state

agency would arguably have no incentive to exploit surrogates, and it would screen the adoptive parents for the sake of the best interests of the child. Nevertheless, as long as the surrogate mother is paid money to bear a child and terminate her parental rights, the commercial norms leading to her degradation still apply. For these norms are constitutive of our understanding of what the surrogate contract is for. Once such an arrangement becomes socially legitimized, these norms will govern the understandings of participants in the practice and of society at large, or at least compete powerfully with the rival parental norms. And what judgment do these norms make of a mother who, out of love for her child, decides that she cannot relinquish it? They blame her for commercial irresponsibility and flighty emotions. Her transformation of moral and emotional perspective, which she experiences as real but painful growth, looks like a capricious and selfish exercise of will from the standpoint of the market, which does not distinguish the deep commitments of love from arbitrary matters of taste.[42]

The fundamental problem with commercial surrogacy is that commercial norms are inherently manipulative when they are applied to the sphere of parental love. Manipulation occurs whenever norms are deployed to psychologically coerce others into a position where they cannot defend their own interests or articulate their own perspective without being charged with irresponsibility or immorality for doing so. A surrogate contract is inherently manipulative, since the very form of the contract invokes commercial norms which, whether upheld by the law or by social custom only, imply that the mother should feel guilty and irresponsible for loving her own child.

But hasn't the surrogate mother decided in advance that she is not interested in viewing her relationship to her child in this way? Regardless of her initial state of mind, once she enters the contract, she is not free to develop an autonomous perspective on her relationship with her child. She is contractually bound to manipulate her emotions

39. Barbara Cohen, "Surrogate Mothers: Whose Baby Is It?" *American Journal of Law and Medicine* 10 (1984): 282; Peter Singer and Deane Wells, *Making Babies* (New York: Scribner, 1985), pp. 106–7, 111.
40. Harris, *The Value of Life*, pp. 143–44, 156.
41. Singer and Wells support this recommendation in *Making Babies*, pp. 110–11. See also the dissenting

opinion of the Warnock commission, *A Question of Life*, pp. 87–89.
42. See Fleming, "Our Fascination with Baby M," for a sensitive discussion of Americans' conflicting attitudes toward surrogate mothers who find they cannot give up their children.

to agree with the interests of the adoptive parents. Few things reach deeper into the self than a parent's evolving relationship with her own child. To lay claim to the course of this relationship in virtue of a cash payment constitutes a severe violation of the mother's personhood and a denial of the mother's autonomy.

Two final objections stand in the way of criminalizing commercial surrogacy. Prohibiting the practice might be thought to infringe two rights: the right of procreation, and the right to freedom of contract. Judge Harvey Sorkow, in upholding the legality and enforceability of commercial surrogate parenting contracts, based much of his argument on an interpretation of the freedom to procreate. He argued that the protection of the right to procreate requires the protection of noncoital means of procreation, including commercial surrogacy. The interests upheld by the creation of the family are the same, regardless of the means used to bring the family into existence.[43]

Sorkow asserts a blanket right to procreate, without carefully examining the specific human interests protected by such a right. The interest protected by the right to procreate is that of being able to create and sustain a family life with some integrity. But the enforcement of surrogate contracts against the will of the mother destroys one family just as surely as it creates another. And the same interest which generates the right to procreate also generates an obligation to uphold the integrity of family life which constrains the exercise of this right.[44] To recognize the legality of commercial surrogate contracts would undermine the integrity of families by giving public sanction to a practice which expresses contempt for the moral and emotional ties which bind a mother to her children, legitimates the view that these ties are merely the product of arbitrary will, properly loosened by the offering of a monetary incentive, and fails to respect the claims of genetic and gestational ties to children which provide children with a more secure place in the world than commerce can supply.

The freedom of contract provides weaker grounds for supporting commercial surrogacy. This freedom is already constrained, notably in preventing the purchase and sale of human beings. Yet one might object that prohibiting surrogate contracts could undermine the status of women by implying that they do not have the competence to enter into and rationally discharge the obligations of commercial contracts. Insofar as the justification for prohibiting commercial surrogacy depends upon giving special regard to women's emotional ties to their children, it might be thought to suggest that women as a group are too emotional to subject themselves to the dispassionate discipline of the market. Then prohibiting surrogate contracts would be seen as an offensive, paternalistic interference with the autonomy of the surrogate mothers.

We have seen, however, that the content of the surrogate contract itself compromises the autonomy of surrogate mothers. It uses the norms of commerce in a manipulative way and commands the surrogate mothers to conform their emotions to the interests of the other parties to the contract. The surrogate industry fails to acknowledge the surrogate mothers as possessing an independent perspective worthy of consideration. And it takes advantage of motivations—such as self-effacing "altruism"—which women have formed under social conditions inconsistent with genuine autonomy. Hence the surrogate industry itself, far from expanding the realm of autonomy for women, actually undermines the external and internal conditions required for fully autonomous choice by women.

If commercial surrogate contracts were prohibited, this would be no cause for infertile couples to lose hope for raising a family. The option of adoption is still available, and every attempt should be made to open up opportunities for adoption to couples who do not meet standard requirements—for example, because of age. While there is a shortage of healthy white infants available for adoption, there is no shortage of children of other races, mixed-race children, and older and handicapped children who desperately need to be adopted. Leaders of the surrogate industry have

43. *In Re Baby M*, p. 2022. See also Robertson, "Surrogate Mothers: Not So Novel after All," p. 32.
44. The Catholic Church makes this principle the fundamental basis for its own criticism of surrogate motherhood. See Congregation for the Doctrine of the Faith, "Instruction on Respect for Human Life In Its Origin and on the Dignity of Procreation: Replies to Certain Questions of the Day," reproduced in *New York Times*, 11 March 1987, pp. A14–A17.

proclaimed that commercial surrogacy may replace adoption as the method of choice for infertile couples who wish to raise families. But we should be wary of the racist and eugenic motivations which make some people rally to the surrogate industry at the expense of children who already exist and need homes.

The case of commercial surrogacy raises deep questions about the proper scope of the market in modern industrial societies. I have argued that there are principled grounds for rejecting the substitution of market norms for parental norms to govern the ways women bring children into the world. Such substitutions express ways of valuing mothers and children which reflect an inferior conception of human flourishing. When market norms are applied to the ways we allocate and understand parental rights and responsibilities, children are reduced from subjects of love to objects of use. When market norms are applied to the ways we treat and understand women's reproductive labor, women are reduced from subjects of respect and consideration to objects of use. If we are to retain the capacity to value children and women in ways consistent with a rich conception of human flourishing, we must resist the encroachment of the market upon the sphere of reproductive labor. Women's labor is *not* a commodity.

Chapter 6

KANT: FREEDOM AS AUTONOMY

The *Groundwork for the Metaphysics of Morals* (1785) by Immanuel Kant (1724–1804) is one of the most important works of moral philosophy ever written. But it is not an easy read. One way to approach it is with certain questions in mind: Why, according to Kant, is utilitarianism wrong? Why, for that matter, is it a mistake to base morality on any interest, desire, or empirically given end, including the aim of maximizing happiness? And if no interest or empirically given end can serve as the basis for morality, what other basis could there be?

Kant's answer is that reason is the basis of the moral law. But this answer raises a further question. Different people reason differently. Does this mean that morality is one thing for me and another for you? Kant does not think so. But if reason is the source of morality, how can there be a single, universal moral law, rather than a plurality of such laws? If you can figure out the answer this question, you will be well on your way to making sense of Kant's moral theory.

These questions about the source of the moral law suggest that Kant has a specially demanding conception of morality. According to this conception, morality cannot consist in a hypothetic imperative: "If you want this, then do that." Instead, morality must take the form of a categorical imperative. I must do the right thing because it is right, not because it will promote my interests or satisfy my desires. If morality must take the form of a categorical imperative, what does it command? How does it tell us to act? Kant offers several formulations of the categorical imperative. In assessing them, it will help to consider the practical illustrations that Kant offers.

Kant also has a specially demanding conception of freedom. We commonly think that freedom consists in the ability to pursue our desires unimpeded. But Kant rejects this idea. How can we think of ourselves as free, he asks, if all we are doing is pursuing desires given by nature or circumstance, desires that we have not chosen? Kant seems to have a point. What conception of freedom would not be vulnerable to this challenge? See if you can make sense of Kant's answer to this question. If you can, you will begin to see the connection between Kant's conception of morality and his conception of freedom.

Groundwork for the Metaphysics of Morals

Immanuel Kant

Translated by Arnulf Zweig

Preface

I. [Ethics as a Branch of Philosophy]

Ancient Greek philosophy was divided into three sciences: *physics*, *ethics*, and *logic*. This division fits the nature of the subject perfectly and needs no improvement except perhaps to add the principle on which that division rests. By doing this we may be able to guarantee its completeness as well as to determine its necessary subdivisions correctly.

All rational knowledge is either *material* and considers some object or other or *formal*, concerned just with the form of the understanding and the form of reason itself, and with the universal rules of thinking as such, whatever its objects might be. Formal philosophy is called *logic*. Material philosophy, which is concerned with specific objects and their laws, consists of two parts; for those laws are either laws of *nature* or laws of *freedom*. The science of the first is called *physics*, that of the second *ethics*. The former science is also called natural philosophy, the latter moral philosophy.[1]

2. [Two Parts of Ethics: Empirical and Rational]

Logic can have no empirical part, that is, it can have no part in which the universal and necessary laws of thinking are based on facts taken from experience. Otherwise it would not be logic—that is, it would not be an authoritative set of rules for the understanding or for reason, rules that are valid, and must be shown to be valid, for all thinking. On the other hand, both natural philosophy and moral philosophy can have an empirical part. The reason is that natural philosophy has to formulate nature's

---

Editors' note: footnotes marked with small arabic numerals are the translator's; Kant's own footnotes are marked with an asterisk (*).

1. *Naturlehre* and *Sittenlehre*, literally 'Doctrine of Nature' and 'Doctrine of Morals', where 'doctrine' [*Lehre*] means a body of principles.

---

laws in so far as nature is an object of experience, while moral philosophy has to define the laws of the human will, to the extent that the will is affected by nature. Laws of nature are laws according to which everything happens; laws of freedom are laws according to which everything ought to happen, although these laws also weigh the conditions under which what ought to happen very often does not happen.

We can call any philosophy that is based on experience *empirical*. We can call it *pure* philosophy if it sets forth its teachings entirely on the basis of a priori principles. When pure philosophy is merely formal, it is called *logic*; but if it is limited to specific objects of the understanding, pure philosophy is then called *metaphysics*.

In this way there arises the idea of a two-fold metaphysics—*a metaphysics of nature* and *a metaphysics of morals*. Thus physics will have an empirical part, but also a rational part; and similarly ethics, although here the empirical part might be given the special title *practical anthropology*, the term *moral philosophy* being properly used to refer just to the rational part.

3. [Why the Rational Part is Needed and Should Come First]

All professions, handicrafts, and arts have made progress by the division of labour. That is to say, one person can accomplish something most perfectly and easily if he confines himself to a particular job that differs significantly from other jobs in the treatment it requires. Where various tasks are not thus distinguished and divided, where everyone is a jack-of- all-trades, industry remains at a primitive level. It might be worth considering whether pure philosophy, in all its divisions, does not require its own specialist. Perhaps the learned profession as a whole would be better off if a warning were issued—a warning to those who call themselves 'independent thinkers' but who belittle as 'hair-splitters' those who work on the purely rational part of philosophy: For these people are used to marketing a mixture of the empirical and the rational (in various proportions unknown even to themselves, as they pander to the public's taste), but they should be warned against engaging at one and the same time in rational and empirical disciplines, two so different enterprises, involving such different techniques. For each job perhaps requires a special talent and the attempt to combine both in one person produces mere bunglers. Here, however, I ask only whether the nature of science does not require that the empirical part should always be scrupulously separated from the rational one, and that (empirical) physics proper should be prefaced by a metaphysic of nature, while practical anthropology should be prefaced by a metaphysic of morals. Each of these prior sciences must be scrupulously cleansed of everything empirical if we are to know how much pure reason can accomplish in each case and from what sources it can by itself create its own teaching a priori. I leave it an open question whether the latter business is to be conducted by all moralists (whose name is legion) or only by those who feel a calling for the subject.

Since my aim here is directed strictly to moral philosophy, I confine the proposed question to this single point. Is it not a matter of utmost importance to forge for once a pure moral philosophy, completely cleansed of everything that may be only empirical and that really belongs to anthropology? That there must be such a philosophy is already evident if one looks at the common idea of duty and of moral laws. For everyone must admit that a law has to carry with it absolute necessity if it is to be morally valid—valid, that is, as a basis of obligation; and everyone must grant that the commandment, 'Thou shalt not lie' could not hold merely for human beings, as if other rational beings had no obligation to abide by it. So it is with all other genuine moral laws. Consequently, the ground of obligation must here be sought, not in the nature of human beings or in facts about the way the world is, but solely a priori in concepts of pure reason. Every other precept, based on principles of mere experience—even a precept that might in a certain sense be considered universal—can indeed be called a practical rule, but never a moral law, so far as it rests even slightly (perhaps only in its motive) on empirical grounds.

Thus moral laws and their principles are essentially different from all the rest of practical knowledge, in which there is some empirical element. Furthermore, the whole of moral philosophy is based entirely on the part of it that is non-empirical, i.e., pure. When applied to man, it does not borrow in the slightest from our knowledge of human beings (i.e., from anthropology). Rather, it prescribes to man, as a rational being, laws a priori. These laws certainly require in addition a power of judgement sharpened by experience, partly in order to distinguish the cases to which they apply, partly to obtain for these laws access to the human will and impetus to their practice. For man, affected by so many inclinations, is indeed capable of grasping the idea of a pure practical reason, but it is not so easy for him to render this idea concretely effective in his conduct of life.

A metaphysic of morals is thus indispensably necessary not merely because one wants to investigate and understand the source of practical principles which are present a priori in our reason, but because morality itself remains subjected to all sorts of corruption as long as this guiding thread, this ultimate norm for correct moral judgement, is lacking. For if any action is to be morally good, it is not enough that it should *conform* to the moral law—it must also be done *for the sake of that law*. Where this is not the case, the conformity is just very coincidental and precarious, since the non-moral ground will now and then produce actions that accord with the law, but it will often produce actions that transgress it. But the moral law in its purity and authenticity (and in the field of action it is precisely this that matters most) can be found nowhere else than in a pure philosophy. Pure philosophy (metaphysics) must therefore come first, and without it there can be no moral philosophy at all. A philosophy that mixes these pure principles with empirical ones does not even deserve to be called philosophy (since philosophy is distinguished from common rational knowledge precisely because it treats in separate sciences what the latter apprehends only in a disordered way). Still less does it deserve to be called moral philosophy, since by this confusion of a priori and empirical principles it spoils the purity of morality itself and works against its own purpose.

4. [Focus on A Priori Principles of Willing Distinguishes Kant's Project from Wolff's]

It would be a mistake to think that what is here demanded has already been done by the celebrated Wolff in the preparatory study to his moral philosophy—that is, in what he entitles 'Universal Practical Philosophy'—and consequently to think that we do not need to break entirely new ground. Precisely because Wolff's work was supposed to be a universal practical philosophy, it did not take into consideration a special kind of will—a will motivated completely by a priori principles apart from any empirical motives, a pure will, as we might call it. Rather, Wolff's concern was with willing in general, together with all the actions and conditions that belong to volition in this general sense. Because of this it differs from a metaphysic of morals in the same way that general logic differs from transcendental philosophy. General logic sets forth the activities and rules of thinking *in general*, while transcendental philosophy speaks of the special activities and rules of *pure* thinking—that is, of thinking whereby objects are cognized completely a priori. For the metaphysics of morals has to examine the idea and the principles of a possible *pure* will, and not the acts and conditions of human volition generally, which are drawn largely from psychology. The fact that this 'universal practical philosophy' does talk (though quite unjustifiably) of moral laws and duty is no objection to what I am claiming. For the authors of that science remain true to their idea of it in this respect as well: they do not distinguish motives which, as such, are prescribed completely a priori by reason alone and are genuinely moral, from empirical motives which the understanding promotes to general concepts merely by comparison of experiences. On the contrary, without taking into account the difference in their origin they consider motives only as regards to their relative strength or weakness (looking upon all of them as of the same kind) and construct on this basis their concept of *obligation*. This concept is anything but moral; but a concept of that sort is all we can expect from a philosophy which ignores the question of *origin* and fails to decide whether all possible practical concepts are a priori or only a posteriori.

5. [*The Groundwork* Contrasted with a Critique of Practical Reason and a Metaphysics of Morals]

As a prelude to a metaphysics of morals, which I intend to publish someday, I present this *Groundwork*. Strictly speaking, there is no other foundation for a metaphysics of morals than the critique of *pure practical reason*, just as there is no other foundation for metaphysics than the critique of pure speculative reason, which I have already published. But, in the first place, the former critique is not as indispensable as the latter, since even the most ordinary human intelligence can easily be brought to a high degree of correctness and completeness in moral matters, while reason's theoretical but pure employment is, by contrast, totally dialectical. Secondly, I hold that a critique of practical reason, if it is to be complete, must demonstrate the unity of practical and theoretical reason under a single comprehensive principle, since ultimately there can only be one reason which has to be differentiated solely in its application. However, I found that I could not as yet achieve this completeness without bringing up considerations of quite another sort and confusing the reader. This is why I have used the title *Groundwork for the Metaphysics of Morals* rather than *Critique of Pure Practical Reason*.

But, in the third place, since a metaphysics of morals, in spite of its frightening title, is capable of a high degree of popularity and appeal to ordinary minds, I think it useful to publish this preliminary work on its foundation separately, so as to avoid having to insert the subtleties unavoidable here into the later, more easily understood work.

6. [The Aims, Method, and Parts of the *Groundwork*]

The present groundwork, however, aims only to seek out and establish *the supreme principle of morality*. This aim constitutes a complete project all by itself and must be kept separate from every other moral investigation. It is true that my claims about this central question, a question so important and yet until now so inadequately debated, would be greatly clarified by seeing the application of that supreme principle to the whole system, and they would be strongly confirmed by the adequacy the principle would manifest throughout. All the same, I had to forgo this advantage, which in any case would be more flattering to myself than helpful to others. For the convenience of a principle in use and its apparent adequacy do not constitute a secure proof of its correctness. They rather awaken a certain bias against examining and weighing it rigorously and independently of its consequences.

The method I have adopted in this book is, I believe, one which will work best if we proceed analytically from common knowledge to the formulation of its supreme principle and then back again synthetically from an examination of this principle and its origins to the common knowledge in which we find its application. Hence the division turns out to be as follows:

1. Chapter One: Passage from the common rational knowledge of morality to the philosophical.
2. Chapter Two. Transition from popular moral philosophy to a metaphysic of morals.
3. Chapter Three. Final step from a metaphysic of morals to a critique of pure practical reason.

Chapter One. Passage from the Common Rational Knowledge of Morality to the Philosophical

7. [The Unqualified Value of a Good Will]

It is impossible to imagine anything at all in the world, or even beyond it, that can be called good without qualification—except a *good will*. Intelligence, wit, judgement, and the other mental talents, whatever we may call them, or courage, decisiveness, and perseverance, are, as qualities of *temperament*, certainly good and desirable in many respects; but they can also be extremely bad and harmful when the will which makes use of these *gifts of nature* and whose specific quality we refer to as *character*, is not good. It is exactly the same with *gifts of fortune*. Power, wealth, honour, even health and that total well-being and contentment with one's condition which we call 'happiness',[2]

can make a person bold but consequently often reckless as well, unless a good will is present to correct their influence on the mind, thus adjusting the whole principle of one's action to render it conformable to universal ends[3]. It goes without saying that the sight of a creature enjoying uninterrupted prosperity, but never feeling the slightest pull of a pure and good will, cannot excite approval in a rational and impartial spectator. Consequently, a good will seems to constitute the indispensable condition even of our worthiness to be happy.

Some qualities, even though they are helpful to this good will and can make its task very much easier, nevertheless have no intrinsic unconditional worth. Rather, they presuppose a good will which puts limits on the esteem in which they are rightly held and forbids us to regard them as absolutely good. Moderation in emotions and passions, self-control, and sober reflection are not only good in many respects: they may even seem to constitute part of the inner worth of a person. Yet they are far from being properly described as good without qualification (however unconditionally they were prized by the ancients). For without the principles of a good will those qualities may become exceedingly bad; the passionless composure of a villain makes him not merely more dangerous but also directly more detestable in our eyes than we would have taken him to be without it.

A good will is not good because of its effects or accomplishments, and not because of its adequacy to achieve any proposed end: it is good only by virtue of its willing—that is, it is good in itself. Considered in itself it is to be treasured as incomparably higher than anything it could ever bring about merely in order to satisfy some inclination or, if you like, the sum total of all inclinations.

---

2. *Glückseligkeit.* 'Happiness', the usual translation, does not entirely capture Kant's meaning, as various passages show. At G 4: 399 *Glückseligkeit* is described as the satisfaction of all inclinations as a sum, and at G 4: 418, it is said to require 'an absolute whole, a maximum, of well-

being in my present and in every future state', clearly not something implied by modern usage of 'happiness'. *Glückseligkeit* is archaic, and actually meant something like 'blessedness' or 'felicity', a German equivalent of the Latin *beatitudo*. Happiness, in German, at least nowadays, is *Glück, Glücklichkeit, Freude, Zufriedenheit*. However, 'felicity' is a rare word, 'blessedness' carries religious overtones often inappropriate to Kant's discussion, and 'happiness' fits naturally Kant's attack on 'the principle of one's own happiness'. Where appropriate, 'perfect happiness' is used in this translation.

3. *allgemein zweckmässig*

Even if it were to happen that, because of some particularly unfortunate fate or the miserly bequest of a stepmotherly nature, this will were completely powerless to carry out its aims; if with even its utmost effort it still accomplished nothing, so that only good will itself remained (not, of course, as a mere wish, but as the summoning of every means in our power), even then it would still, like a jewel, glisten in its own right, as something that has its full worth in itself. Its utility or ineffectuality can neither add to nor subtract from this worth. Utility would be merely, as it were, its setting, enabling us to handle it better in our ordinary dealings or to attract to it the attention of those who are not yet experts, but not why we recommend it to experts and determine its worth.

8. [Good Will, Not Happiness, Is the Natural End of Reason]

Yet there is something so strange in this idea of the absolute worth of a mere will, all utility being left out of account, that, in spite of all the agreement this idea receives even from common reason, the suspicion must arise that perhaps its hidden basis is merely some high-flown fantasy, and that we may have misunderstood the purpose of nature in appointing reason as ruler of our will. Let us therefore examine this idea from this perspective.

In the natural constitution of an organized being—that is, a being properly equipped for life—we take it as a principle that no instrument for any purpose will be found in that being unless it is also the most appropriate and best adapted for that purpose. Now if nature's real purpose for a being possessed of reason and a will were its *preservation*, its *welfare*, or in a word its *happiness*, then nature would have hit on a very bad arrangement if it assigned the creature's reason the job of carrying out this purpose. For all the actions this creature has to perform with this end in view, and the whole rule of its conduct, would have been disclosed to it far more precisely by instinct; and the end in question could have been attained far more surely by instinct than it ever could be by reason. If, in that case, reason had been given to this favoured creature additionally, its service would have been only to contemplate the fortunate constitution of the creature's nature,

to admire it, enjoy it, and be grateful to its beneficent Cause. But reason would not have been given in order that this creature would subject its faculty of desire to such feeble and defective guidance or to meddle incompetently with nature's purpose. In a word, nature would have prevented reason from striking out into a practical use and from presuming, with its feeble insights, to think out for itself a plan for happiness and for the means of attaining it. Nature would herself have taken over not only the choice of ends but also that of means, and would with wise foresight have entrusted both to instinct alone.

And in fact we do find that the more one devotes one's cultivated reason to the enjoyment of life and happiness, the further away does one get from true contentment. This is why a certain degree of *misology*, i.e., hatred of reason, arises in many people, including those who have been most tempted by this use of reason, if only they are candid enough to admit it. For, according to their calculation of all the benefits they draw—I will not say from the invention of all the arts of common luxury, but even from the sciences (which in the final analysis seem to them to be only a luxury of the understanding)—they find that instead of gaining in happiness they have in fact only brought more trouble on their heads. They therefore come to envy, rather than despise, more ordinary people, who are closer to being guided by mere natural instinct and who do not let their reason have much influence on conduct. To this extent we must admit that the judgement of those who seek to moderate—and even to reduce below zero—the boasting glorification of benefits that reason is supposed to provide in the way of happiness and contentment with life, is by no means morose or ungrateful for the kindness of the world's ruler. That judgement rather is based on the idea that our existence has another and much worthier purpose, for which, and not for happiness, our reason is properly intended, an end which, therefore, is the supreme condition to which our private ends must for the most part be subordinated.

For since reason is not sufficiently competent to guide the will safely with regard to its objects and the satisfaction of all our needs (which it in part even multiplies)—a goal to which an implanted natural instinct would have led us much more certainly—and since reason is nevertheless given to us a practical faculty—that is, as one which is supposed to influence the *will*; since, finally, reason was absolutely necessary for this purpose, as nature has everywhere distributed her abilities so as to fit the functions they are to perform; reason's true vocation must therefore be to produce a *will* which is *good in itself*, not just *good as a means* to some further end. Such a will must not be the sole and complete good, but it must be the highest good and the condition of all the rest, even of all our longing for happiness. In that case it is entirely compatible with the wisdom of nature that the cultivation of reason, which is required for the former unconditional purpose, may in many ways, at least in this life, restrict the attainment of the second, conditional purpose—happiness—and indeed that it can even reduce it to less than nothing. Nor does nature here violate its own purpose, for reason, which recognizes as its highest practical vocation the establishment of a good will, is capable only of its own peculiar kind of satisfaction—satisfaction from fulfilling a purpose which reason alone determines, even if this fulfilment damages the ends of inclination.

9. [The Concept of Duty Includes the Concept of a Good Will]

We must thus develop the concept of a will estimable in itself and good apart from any further aim. This concept is already present in the natural, healthy mind, which requires not so much instruction as merely clarification. It is this concept that always holds the highest place in estimating the total worth of our actions and it constitutes the condition of all the rest. Let us then take up the concept of *duty*, which includes that of a good will, the latter however being here under certain subjective limitations and obstacles. These, so far from hiding a good will or disguising it, rather bring it out by contrast and make it shine forth more brightly.

10. [A Good Will Is Manifested When We Act out of Duty Rather than Inclination; Only Such Acts Have Moral Worth]

I will here omit all actions already recognized as opposed to duty, even if they may be useful from this or that perspective; for about these it makes no sense even to ask the question whether they might have been done *out of duty* since they are directly opposed to it. I will also set aside actions that in fact accord with duty, yet for one has no *direct inclination*, but which one performs because impelled to do so by some other inclination. For in such a case it is easy to decide whether the action [which accords with duty] was done *out of duty* or for some self-interested goal. This distinction is far more difficult to perceive when the action accords with duty but the agent has in addition a *direct* inclination to do it. For example, it is certainly in accord with duty that a shopkeeper should not overcharge an inexperienced customer; and, where there is much business, a prudent merchant refrains from doing this and maintains a fixed general price for everybody, so that a child can buy from him just as well as anyone else. People thus get *honest* treatment. But this is not nearly enough to justify our believing that the shopkeeper acted in this way out of duty or from principles of honesty; his interests required him to act as he did. We cannot assume him to have in addition a direct inclination towards his customers, leading him, as it were out of love, to give no one preferential treatment over another person in the matter of price. Thus the action was done neither out of duty nor from immediate inclination, but solely out of self-interest.

On the other hand, it is a duty to preserve one's life, and every one also has a direct inclination to do it. But for that reason the often-fearful care that most people take for their lives has no intrinsic worth, and the maxim of their action has no moral merit. They do protect their lives *in conformity with duty*, but not *out of duty*. If, by contrast, disappointments and hopeless misery have entirely taken away someone's taste for life; if that wretched person, strong in soul and more angered at fate than fainthearted or cast down, longs for death and still preserves life without loving it—not out of inclination or fear but out of duty—then indeed that person's maxim has moral worth.

It is a duty to help others where one can, and besides this many souls are so compassionately disposed that, without any further motive of vanity or self-interest, they find an inner pleasure in spreading joy around them, taking delight in the contentment of others, so far as they have brought it about. Yet I maintain that, however dutiful and kind an action of this sort may be, it still has no genuinely moral worth. It is on a level with other inclinations—for example, the inclination to pursue honour, which if fortunate enough to aim at something generally useful and consistent with duty, something consequently honourable, deserves praise and encouragement but not esteem. For its maxim lacks the moral merit of such actions done not out of inclination but out of *duty*. Suppose then that the mind of this humanitarian were overclouded by sorrows of his own which extinguished all compassion for the fate of others, but that he still had the power to assist others in distress; suppose though that their adversity no longer stirred him, because he is pre-occupied with his own; and now imagine that, though no longer moved by any inclination, he nevertheless tears himself out of this deadly apa-thy and does the action without any inclination, solely out of duty. Then for the first time his action has its genuine moral worth. Furthermore, if nature had put little sympathy into this or that person's heart; if he, though an honest man, were cold in temperament and indifferent to the suf-ferings of others—perhaps because he has the special gifts of patience and fortitude in his own sufferings and he assumes or even demands the same of others; if such a man (who would in truth not be the worst product of nature) were not exactly fashioned by nature to be a humani-tarian, would he not still find in himself a source from which he might give himself a worth far higher than that of a good-natured temperament? Assuredly he would. It is precisely in this that the worth of character begins to show—a moral worth, and incomparably the highest—namely, that he does good, not out of inclination, but out of duty.

To secure one's own happiness[4] is a duty (at least indirectly); for discontent with one's condi-tion when pressed by many cares and amidst unsatisfied needs might easily become a *great temptation to transgress one's duties*. But even apart from duty, all human beings already have by their own nature the strongest and deepest inclination towards happiness, because it is precisely in this idea that all the inclinations come together. The

prescription for happiness is, however, often so constituted that it greatly interferes with some inclinations, and yet we cannot form a precise conception of the satisfaction of all inclinations as a sum, the conception to which we give the name "happiness". Hence it is not surprising that a single inclination, well defined as to what it promises and as to the time at which it can be sat-isfied, may outweigh a fluctuating idea; so, for example, a man who suffers from gout, may choose to enjoy whatever he likes and put up with what he must—because according to his cal-culations he has at least not sacrificed the enjoy-ment of the present moment to some possibly groundless expectations of happiness allegedly attached to health. But even in this case, if the universal inclination to happiness has failed to determine his will, and if good health, at least for him, did not enter into his calculations, what would remain, as in other cases, is a law—the law that he ought to promote his happiness, not out of inclina-tion, but out of duty. And only from this law would his conduct begin to have real moral worth.

It is doubtless in this sense that we should understand too the passages from Scripture in which we are commanded to love our neighbour and even our enemy. For love as inclination can-not be commanded; but kindness done out of duty—although no inclination impels us, and even although natural and unconquerable aver-sion stands in our way—is *practical love*, not *patho-logical love*. It resides in the will and not in the partiality of feeling, in principles of action and not in melting compassion; and it is this practical love alone that can be commanded.

11. [What Makes Acts out of Duty Morally Worthy Is Not Their Actual or Intended Results, but the Underlying Principle on Which They Are Based]

The second proposition is this: The moral worth of an action done out of duty has its moral worth, not *in the objective* to be reached by that action, but in the maxim in accordance with which the action is decided upon; it depends, therefore, not on actualizing the object of the action, but solely on the *principle of volition* in accordance with which the action was done, with-out any regard for objects of the faculty of desire.

4. *Glückseligkeit*

It is clear from our previous discussion that the objectives we may have in acting, and also our actions' effects considered as ends and as what motivates our volition, can give to actions no unconditional or moral worth. Where then can this worth be found if not in the willing of the action's hoped for effect? It can be found nowhere but *in the principle of the will*, irrespective of the ends that can be brought about by such action. For the will stands, so to speak, at the crossroads between its a priori principle, which is formal, and its a posteriori motivation,[5] which is material; and since it must be determined by something, it will have to be determined by the formal principle of volition, since every material principle is ruled out when an action is done out of duty.

12. [Duty and Respect for Law]

The third proposition, which follows from the two preceding, I would express in this way: *Duty is the necessity of an act done out of respect for the law.* While I can certainly have an *inclination* for an object that results from my proposed action, I can never *respect it*, precisely because it is nothing but an effect of a will and not its activity. Similarly I cannot respect any inclination whatsoever, whether it be my own inclination or that of another. At most I can approve of that towards which I feel an inclination, and occasionally I can like the object of somebody else's inclination myself—that is, see it as conducive to my own advantage. But the only thing that could be an object of respect (and thus a commandment) for me is something that is conjoined with my will purely as a ground and never as a consequence, something that does not serve my inclination but overpowers it or at least excludes it entirely from my decision-making—consequently, nothing but the law itself. Now if an action done out of duty is supposed to exclude totally the influence of inclination, and, along with inclination, every object of volition, then nothing remains that could determine the will except objectively *the law* and subjectively *pure respect* for this practical law. What is left therefore is the maxim,[*] to obey

this sort of law even when doing so is prejudicial to all my inclinations.

13. [Identification of the Principle of a Good Will: The Formula of Universal Law]

Thus the moral worth of an action depends neither on the result expected from that action nor on any principle of action that has to borrow its motive from this expected result. For all these results (such as one's own pleasurable condition or even the promotion of the happiness of others) could have been brought about by other causes as well. It would not require the will of a rational being to produce them, but it is only in such a will that the highest and unconditional good can be found. That pre-eminent good which we call "moral" consists therefore in nothing but *the idea of the law* in itself, which certainly *is present only in a rational being*—so far as that idea, and not an expected result, is the determining ground of the will. And this pre-eminent good is already present in the person who acts in accordance with this idea; we need not await the result of the action in order to find it.[*]

jectively as a practical principle for all rational beings if reason had full control over the faculty of desire) is a practical *law*.
[*] It might be objected that instead of clearly resolving the question by means of a concept of reason I have tried to take refuge in an obscure feeling, under the cover of the word '*respect*' [*Achtung*]. However, though respect is a feeling, it is not a feeling that we are caused to *receive* by some (external) influence; rather, it is a feeling that is *self-generated* by a rational concept, and it is therefore different in kind from feelings of the first sort, all of which can be reduced to inclination or fear. What I recognize directly as a law for myself, I recognize with respect, which means nothing more than the consciousness of my will's *submission* to the law, without the mediation of any other influences on my mind. The direct determination of the will by the law, and the awareness of that determination, is called '*respect*', so we should see respect as the *effect* of the law on a person rather than as what *produces* the law. Actually, respect is the thought of something of such worth that it breaches my self-love. It is neither an object of inclination nor an object of fear, though it is somewhat analogous to both. The sole *object* of respect is the [moral] *law*—that law which we impose *on ourselves* and yet recognize as necessary in itself. As a law, we must submit to it without any consulting of self-love; as self-imposed it is nevertheless a consequence of our will. Considered in the first way, it is analogous to

5. *Triebfeder*
[*] A *maxim* is the subjective principle of volition: an objective principle (that is, one which would also serve sub-

But what kind of law can it be, the idea of which must determine the will, even without considering the expected result, if that will is to be called good absolutely and without qualification? Since I have robbed the will of every inducement that might arise for it from its obeying any particular law, the only thing remaining that could serve the will as a principle is the universal conformity of actions to law as such. That is, I ought never to act in such a way *that I could not also will that my maxim should become a universal law*. Here it is the mere conformity to law as such (without presupposing any law prescribing particular actions) that serves the will as its principle, and must so serve it if duty is not to be a totally empty delusion and a chimerical concept. Common human reason, when engaged in making practical judgements, also agrees with this completely and has that principle constantly in view.

14. [Example: The Wrongness of a Lying Promise]

Suppose, for example, the question is this: May I, when in distress, make a promise with the intention not to keep it? Here I easily distinguish the different meanings this question can have, whether it is prudent to make a false promise, or whether it is in accord with duty. The first no doubt can often be the case. Of course I see that [even for prudence] it is not enough just to extricate myself from my present predicament by means of this deception; I need to consider whether this lie might give rise to even greater troubles than those from which I am escaping, since, for all my supposed *cunning*, it is not so easy to foresee all the consequences, e.g., the loss of trust may cost me more than all the misfortune I am now trying to avoid. I must consider therefore whether it might be *more* prudent for me to act on a general maxim and make it a habit to issue a promise only when I intend to keep it. But

fear; considered in the second way, analogous to inclination. All respect for a person is actually only respect for the law (of righteousness, etc.,) that that person exemplifies. Because we regard the development of our talents as a duty, we see a talented person also as a sort of *example of a law* (to strive to resemble that person), and this is what constitutes our respect. Any moral so-called *interest* consists solely in *respect* for the law.

it is soon clear to me that such a maxim is always based solely on fear of consequences. To tell the truth out of duty is something entirely different from telling the truth out of fear of troublesome consequences; for in the first case the concept of the action itself already contains a law for me, while in the second case I must first look around to see how I am likely to be affected by the action. For deviating from the principle of duty is quite certainly bad; but deserting my prudential maxim can often be greatly to my advantage, though it is admittedly safer to stick to it. If, on the other hand, I want to find out most quickly but unerringly the answer to a different question—whether a deceitful promise accords with duty—I must ask myself 'Would I really be content if my maxim (the maxim of getting out of a difficulty by making a false promise) were to hold as a universal law (one valid both for myself and for others)'? And could I really say to myself, 'Let everyone be allowed to make a false promise if they find themselves in difficulties from which there is otherwise no escape'? I immediately see that I can indeed will the lie, but I cannot will a universal law to lie. For with such a law, there would actually be no promising at all, since it would be futile for me to allege my intentions with regard to some future actions to others who would not believe me, or who, if they did so overhastily, would pay me back in the same coin. Consequently my maxim, as soon as it became a universal law, would necessarily subvert itself.

Thus I need no far-reaching acuteness to know what I have to do in order that my volition can be morally good. Inexperienced in the ways of the world and incapable of anticipating all its actual events, I ask myself only, 'Can you will that your maxim become a universal law?' If not, that maxim must be repudiated, and not because of any impending disadvantage to you or even to others, but because it cannot fit as a principle into a possible universal legislation, and reason forces me to offer my immediate respect to such legislation. As yet I have no *insight* into the grounds of that respect (something the philosopher may investigate), but I do at least understand this much: it is the appreciation of something whose worth far exceeds all the worth of anything favoured by inclination. I understand too that the necessity that I act out of *pure* respect for the practical law is what constitutes duty. To duty every other motive must give way, because it is the condition of a will good *in itself*, whose worth transcends all else.

15. [The General Competence of Ordinary Human Reason and Judgement]

Considering the moral knowledge of common human reason we have thus arrived at its principle, a principle it admittedly does not think about abstractly in such a universal formulation; but which it really does always have in view and employs as the standard in its judging. It would be easy to show here how common human reason, with this compass in hand, knows very well how to distinguish what is good or evil, consistent or inconsistent with duty, in all cases that present themselves. Without attempting to teach it anything new, one merely has to make reason attend, as Socrates did, to its own principle. Therefore neither science nor philosophy is needed in order for us to know what one has to do to be honest and good, and even to be wise and virtuous. This is something that we could have suspected from the start: that knowledge of what it is incumbent upon everyone to do, and so also to know, would be attainable by everyone, even the most ordinary human being. Here we cannot help but be impressed when we notice the great advantage that the power of practical judgement has over theoretical judgement, in the minds of ordinary people. In theoretical judgements, if common reason dares to go beyond the laws of experience and the perceptions of the senses, it falls into sheer inconceivabilities and self-contradictions, or at least into a chaos of uncertainty, obscurity, and vacillation. On the practical side, however, the power of judgement first begins to look its best when the ordinary mind excludes all sensuous motives from its practical laws. The ordinary mind then becomes even subtle—perhaps vexing itself with its conscience or with other claims regarding what is to be called "right", or trying to determine honestly for its own instruction the worth of various actions. But what is most important, the common understanding has, in the latter case, as good a chance of hitting the mark as any philosopher has. Indeed its chances are almost better than a philosopher's, since the latter's

judgement has no principle different from that of ordinary intelligence, and a philosopher's judgement may easily be confused by a mass of strange and irrelevant considerations and caused to turn from the right path. Would it not be wise therefore to accept the judgement of common reason in moral matters, or to bring in philosophy at most to make the system of morals more complete and comprehensible and to present its rules in formulations more convenient to use (especially in disputation)—but not to lead the common human understanding away from its happy simplicity in matters of action and set it on a new path of inquiry and instruction?

16. [Why Moral Philosophy Is Needed]

A wonderful thing about innocence—but also something very bad—is that it cannot defend itself very well and is easily led astray. For this reason even wisdom—which otherwise is more a matter of acting than knowing—also needs science, not in order to learn from it, but in order to gain access and durability for what it prescribes. Human beings feel within themselves a powerful counterweight opposed to all the commandments of duty, which reason portrays as so worthy of esteem: the counterweight of needs and inclinations, whose total satisfaction people sum up under the name 'happiness'. But reason, without promising anything to inclination, dictates its prescriptions relentlessly, thus treating with neglect and contempt those blustering and seemingly legitimate claims (which refuse to be suppressed by any commandment). From this there arises a *natural dialectic*—that is, a tendency to quibble with these strict laws of duty, to cast doubt on their validity or at least on their purity and strictness, and, if possible, to make them conform better to our wishes and inclinations. This means corrupting their very foundations and destroying their dignity—a result that even common practical reason cannot ultimately endorse.

In this way *common human reason* is driven, not by any cognitive need (which never touches it so long as it is content to be mere sound reason), but on practical grounds, driven to leave its own sphere and take a step into the field of *practical philosophy*. There it seeks instruction and precise direction as to the source of its own principle and about the correct function of this principle in contrast with maxims based on need and inclination. It ventures into philosophy so as to escape from the perplexity caused by conflicting claims and so as to avoid the risk of losing all genuine moral principles through the obscurity into which it easily falls. Thus, just as happens in its theoretical use, a *dialectic* arises unnoticed when practical common reason is cultivated, and it is forced to seek help in philosophy. As with the theoretical use of reason, the conflict will be resolved only by a thorough critical examination of our reason.

Chapter Two. Transition from Popular Moral Philosophy to a Metaphysics of Morals

17. [The Need for A Priori Method in Ethics]

Although we have drawn our previous concept of duty from the common use of our practical reason, this by no means implies that we have treated it as a concept derived from experience. On the contrary, if we pay attention to our experience of what human beings do and fail to do, we encounter frequent and, I must admit, justified complaints that one cannot in fact point to any sure examples of the disposition to act out of pure duty. Thus we hear the charge that, although many things may be done that are in accord with what duty commands, it still remains doubtful whether those actions are really done out of duty, and doubtful therefore whether they have moral worth. That is why there have always been philosophers who absolutely denied the reality of this disposition in human conduct and ascribed everything we do to more or less refined self-love. But those philosophers have not denied the correctness of the concept of morality. Rather, they have spoken with sincere regret of the frailty and corruption of human nature, noble enough to take as its rule an Idea so worthy of respect, but at the same time too weak to follow it, so that reason, which should serve as the law-giver to human nature, is used only to serve the interests of our inclinations, either singly or, at most, to maximize their compatibility. It is in fact

absolutely impossible to identify by experience, with complete certainty, a single case in which the maxim of an action—an action that accords with duty—was based exclusively on moral reasons[6] and the thought of one's duty. There are cases when the most searching self-examination comes up with nothing but duty as the moral reason that could have been strong enough to move us to this or that good action or to some great sacrifice. But we cannot conclude from this with certainty that the real determining cause of our will was not some secret impulse of self-love, disguising itself as that Idea of duty. So we like to flatter ourselves with the false claim to a nobler motive[7] but in fact we can never, even with the most rigorous self-examination, completely uncover our hidden motivations.[8] For when moral worth is the issue, what counts is not the actions which one sees, but their inner principles, which one does not see.

Furthermore, there is no better way to serve the interests of those who mock all morality as a mere phantom of the brain, an illusion with which, out of vanity, the human imagination puffs itself up, than to concede that concepts of duty must be drawn solely from experience (as people find it only too easy to believe about all other concepts). For by conceding this we prepare an assured victory for those scoffers. Out of charity I am willing to grant that most of our actions are in accord with duty; but if we look more closely at the devising and striving that lies behind them, then everywhere we run into the dear self which is always there; and it is this and not the strict command of duty (which would often require self-denial) that underlies our intentions. One need not be an enemy of virtue but only a dispassionate observer who does not immediately confuse even the liveliest wish for goodness with its reality, to become doubtful at certain moments whether any genuine virtue can really be found in the world. (Such doubts occur particularly as one grows older and experience renders one's power of judgement and observation shrewder and more discerning.) And at that point only one thing can protect us against a complete

6. *moralischen Gründen*
7. *Bewegungsgrunde*
8. *Triebfeder*

abandonment of our Ideas of duty, or can preserve in us a well-founded respect for its law: the clear conviction that even if there never were any actions springing from such pure sources, the question at issue here is not whether this or that actually occurs. The question is rather whether reason, by itself and independently of all appearances, commands what ought to be done, actions of which the world has perhaps never until now provided an example—actions whose feasibility might well be doubted by those who rest everything on experience—which are nevertheless commanded inexorably by reason. For example, the duty to be totally sincere in one's friendships can be demanded of everyone even if up to now there may never have existed a totally sincere friend. For this duty, as duty in general, lies prior to all experience in the Idea of a power of reason which determines the will by a priori grounds.

Unless we wish to deny to the concept of morality all truth and all application to a possible object, we must grant that its law is so broad in meaning that it must be valid not merely for human beings, but for all rational beings as such, and valid not merely under contingent conditions and subject to exceptions, but with absolute necessity. It is therefore clear that no experience could warrant even the possibility of such absolutely certain and necessary laws.[9] For by what right can we make something that is perhaps valid only under the contingent human conditions into an object of unlimited respect and view it as universally prescribed for every rational creature? And how could laws for determining our will be taken as laws for determining the will of rational beings in general—and only on that account laws for determining our will—if these laws were merely empirical and did not have their source completely a priori in pure, but practical, reason?

18. [Moral Principles Not Derivable from Examples]

Nor could one give morality worse advice than by trying to derive it from examples. For every example of morality presented to me must itself first be assessed with moral principles to see whether it deserves to be used as an original example, i.e., as a model. By no means can it have the authority to give us the concept of morality. Even the Holy One of the Gospels must first be compared with our ideal of moral perfection before we can acknowledge Him to be such. Even He says of Himself: 'Why do you call Me (whom you see) good? There is none good (the archetype of the good) but the one God alone (whom you do not see).' But where do we get the concept of God as the highest good? Only from the *Idea* of moral perfection which reason designs a priori and connects inseparably with the concept of a free will. Imitation has no place in moral matters, and examples serve us only for encouragement—that is, they set beyond doubt the feasibility of doing what the law commands and they make perceptible what the law prescribing conduct expresses in more general terms; but examples can never justify our guiding ourselves by examples and setting aside their true origin which resides in reason.

19. [The Inadequacy of Popular Practical Philosophy]

If, then, there is no genuine supreme principle of morality that is not grounded on pure reason alone, independently of all experience, I think it should be unnecessary even to ask whether it is desirable to exhibit these concepts in general (abstractly)—these concepts which, together with their corresponding principles, hold a priori, in so far as knowledge which establishes this is to be distinguished from common knowledge and described as philosophical. But nowadays it may well be necessary to raise this question. For if we took a vote on which is to be preferred, pure rational knowledge detached from everything empirical—that is to say, a metaphysic of morals—or popular practical philosophy, we can easily guess on which side the majority would stand.

It is certainly most commendable to descend to the level of folk concepts[10] once the ascent to the principles of pure reason has been satisfactorily completed. This ascent could be described as first *grounding* moral philosophy on metaphysics and subsequently, when moral philosophy has

9. *apodiktische Gesetze*

10. *Volksbegriffe*

been established, winning *acceptance* for it by giving it a popular character. But it is utterly absurd to aim at popularity in our first investigation, on which the whole correctness of our principles depends. Not only can such a procedure never lay claim to the extremely rare merit of *truly philosophical popularity*, since it takes no skill to be generally understandable once one renounces all thorough probing: what that popularizing produces is a disgusting mishmash of second-hand observations and half-reasoned principles. Empty-headed people regale themselves with this, because it is something useful in everyday chitchat. More insightful people, on the other hand, are confused by it and avert their eyes, dissatisfied but not knowing how to help themselves. They turn away, but philosophers who see through this deception get little hearing if they urge those moralists to postpone this so-called popularizing for a while until the achievement of some definite insight earns them the right to be popular.

We need only look at essays on morality written in this fashionable style. What we run into is a marvellous medley—now the talk is of the particular vocation of human nature (but along with this also the Idea of a rational nature as such), now they talk of perfection, now of happiness, here moral feeling and there the fear of God; a little of this and a little of that. But it never occurs to anyone to ask whether the principles of morality are to be sought at all in our knowledge of human nature (which we can get only from experience); nor does it occur to them that if this is not so—if these principles are to be found completely a priori and free from empirical elements in concepts of pure reason and absolutely nowhere else, even to the slightest extent—they had better pursue the latter investigation altogether separately, as pure practical philosophy, or (if one may use a word so much vilified) as a metaphysics* of morals. They do not see that this investigation must be completed entirely

by itself and that the public, which demands popularity, should be put off until the outcome of this undertaking is at hand.

Nevertheless, such a completely isolated metaphysics of morals, mixed with no anthropology, no theology, no physics or hyperphysics, still less with occult qualities (which one might call 'hypophysical'), is not only an indispensable underlying support for all theoretical and precisely defined knowledge of duties; it is also something to be desired and of the utmost importance for the actual fulfilment of moral precepts. For the pure thought of duty and of the moral law generally, unmixed with any additional empirical inducements, has an influence on the human heart much more powerful than all other motivations[11],** that may arise from the field of experience, so much so that reason, conscious of its own dignity, despises these and is able gradually to become their master. The thought of duty and the moral law has this influence through reason alone (and reason first learns from this that by itself it is able to be practical [as well as theoretical]). A mixed moral theory, on the other hand, compounded of motives[12] derived from feeling or inclination and also of rational concepts, must

---

11. *Triebfeder*

** I have a letter from the late, distinguished Professor Sulzer, in which he asks me why moral teachings are so ineffective, even though they contain much that is convincing to reason. My answer was delayed because I wanted it to be complete. Yet it is just this: the teachers themselves fail to make their concepts clear, and they over-do their job by looking for all sorts of inducements to moral goodness, spoiling their medicine altogether by their very attempt to make it really powerful. For the most ordinary observation shows that when a righteous act is represented as being done with a steadfast mind in complete disregard of any advantage in this world or another, and even under the greatest temptations of need or enticement, it far surpasses and eclipses any similar act that was affected even in the slightest by an extraneous incentive; it uplifts the soul and arouses the wish that we too could act in this way. Even children of moderate age feel this impression, and one should never present duties to them in any other way. [Editor's note: Johann Georg Sulzer (1720–79) was a prominent aesthetician and so-called 'popular philosopher', important in Berlin intellectual circles. The only extant letter from Sulzer to Kant does not in fact raise the particular question Kant here ascribes to him.]

12. *Triebfedern.*

---

* We can, if we wish, distinguish pure moral philosophy (metaphysics) from applied (applied, that is, to human nature—just as pure mathematics is distinguished from applied mathematics and pure logic from applied logic). Using this terminology immediately reminds us that moral principles are not grounded on the peculiarities of human nature, but must be established a priori by themselves, though it must be possible to derive practical rules for human beings from them as well, just as it is for every kind of rational being.

make the mind vacillate between [different] sources of motivation[13] that cannot be brought under any single principle and that can guide us only by sheer accident to the good, and often to the evil.

20. [Conclusions about Method in Basic Moral Philosophy]

From what has been said, it is clear that all moral concepts have their seat and origin in reason completely a priori, and this is just as true of the most ordinary human intellect as of the most highly theoretical. Moral principles cannot be abstracted from any empirical, and therefore merely contingent, cognition. Their worthiness to serve as supreme practical principles lies precisely in this purity of their origin. Everything empirical added to them subtracts just that much from their genuine influence and from the unqualified worth of the corresponding actions. It is of the utmost necessity—and not only from a cognitive point of view, where our concern is exclusively with theory,[14] but it is also of the utmost importance for action, that we derive these concepts and laws from pure reason, enunciating them pure and unmixed, and indeed determine the scope of this whole practical but pure sphere of rational cognition—that is, of this whole faculty of pure practical reason. But in doing this, we must not make its principles depend on the particular nature of human reason—as speculative philosophy allows and even at times requires. Since moral laws must hold for every rational being as such, our principles must instead be derived from the universal concept of a rational being as such. In this way the whole of ethics, which does require anthropology for its *application* to human beings, should at first be expounded independently of this and fully, as pure philosophy, that is, as metaphysics (which is quite possible to do in a totally separate branch of knowledge such as this). We are well aware that without possessing such a metaphysics it is not only futile to try to determine precisely, for purposes of speculative judgement, the moral element of duty in all actions which accord with duty; it is impossible to establish morality on genuine principles even for merely ordinary practical purposes and particularly for moral instruction, if we lack such a metaphysics. Only in this way can we produce pure moral dispositions and engraft them onto the minds of human beings for the sake of the world's highest good.

In this study we must not go merely from common moral judgement (which is here worthy of great respect) to philosophical judgement, as has already been done, but advance by natural steps from a popular philosophy which goes no further than it can grope by means of examples, to metaphysics (which is not restricted by anything empirical, and—since it must survey the totality of this kind of rational knowledge—extends itself even to Ideas, where examples themselves forsake us). We must pursue and portray in detail the faculty of practical reason, from its general ordinances right up to the point where the concept of duty arises from it.

21. [Practical Reason, Imperfect Wills, and the Idea of Imperatives]

Everything in nature works in accordance with laws. Only a rational being has the power to act in accordance with the idea of laws—that is, in accordance with principles—and thus has a will. Since reason is required if we are to derive actions from laws, the will is nothing else than practical reason. If reason were inevitably to determine the will, then, in a being of this kind, actions which are recognized as objectively necessary would also be subjectively necessary—that is to say, the will would be a power to choose only that which reason independently of inclination recognizes to be practically necessary, that is, sees to be good. But if reason by itself alone is not sufficient to determine the will; if the will is exposed also to subjective conditions (certain incentives) which do not always harmonize with the objective ones; if, in a word, (as in actually the case with human beings) the will is not of itself completely in accord with reason; then actions which are recognized to be objectively necessary are subjectively contingent, and the determining of such a will in accordance with objective laws is constraint,[15] that is, the relation between objective

13. *Bewegursachen*
14. *Spekulation*

15. Or, alternatively, *necessitation, obligation: Nötigung*

laws and an incompletely good will can be represented as the determining of a rational being's will by principles that are indeed principles of reason, but principles to which this will by its own nature is not necessarily obedient.

The idea of an objective principle, in so far as it constrains a will, is called a commandment[16] (of reason), and the formulation of this commandment is a called an Imperative.

22. [Types of Imperative]

All imperatives are expressed by a 'must'.[17] Thereby they mark a constraint, that is to say, the relation of an objective law of reason to a will that in its subjective constitution is not necessarily determined by this law. Imperatives say that something would be good to do or to leave undone; but they say this to a will that does not always do something simply because it has been informed that it is a good thing to do. Practical good however is something that determines the will by means of what reason presents to it, and therefore not by means of subjective causes but objectively—that is, by reasons[18] that are valid for every rational being as such. The practical good is distinguished from the pleasant, which influences the will solely through the medium of sensation as a result of purely subjective causes, effective only for the senses of this person or that, not as a principle of reason valid for everyone.*

A perfectly good will would thus be just as much subject to objective laws (laws of the Good), but it could not for that reason be thought to be constrained[19] to act lawfully, since by its own subjective constitution, it can be moved only by the concept of the Good. Hence no imperatives hold for the divine will or, more generally, for a holy will. The "must"[20] is here out of place, because the "willing"[21] is already of itself necessarily in agreement with the law. For this reason imperatives are only formulas for expressing the relation of objective laws of willing in general to the subjective imperfection of the will of this or that rational being—for example, the human will.

All imperatives command either hypothetically or categorically. Hypothetical imperatives declare a possible action to be practically necessary as a means to the attainment of something else that one wants (or that one may want). A categorical imperative would be one that represented an action as itself objectively necessary, without regard to any further end.

Since every practical law presents a possible action as good and therefore as necessary for a subject whose actions are determined by reason, all imperatives are therefore formulae for determining an action which is necessary according to the principle of a will in some way good. If the action would be good only as a means to something else, the imperative is hypothetical; if the action is thought of as good in itself and therefore as necessary for a will which of itself conforms to reason as its principle, then the imperative is categorical.

An imperative therefore states which of my possible actions would be good. The imperative formulates a practical rule for a will that does not perform an action immediately just because that action is good, partly because the subject does not always know that a good action is good, partly

---

16. *Gebot*
17. *Sollen*, an 'ought'
18. *Gründe*
* The dependence of the faculty of desire on sensations is called an inclination, and thus an inclination always indicates a *need*. The dependence of a contingently determinable will on principles of reason is called an *interest*. Hence an interest is found only where there is a dependent will which of itself is not always in accord with reason; to God's will we cannot ascribe any interest. But even the human will can *take an interest* in something without therefore *acting out of interest*. The first expression signifies *practical* interest in the action; the second signifies *pathological* interest in the object of the action. [Ed. note: pathological = a feeling one is *caused* or *made* to have by something outside one's own will.] The first indicates only dependence of the will on principles of reason in themselves; the second its dependence on principles of reason at the service of inclination—that is to say, where reason merely sup-

plies a practical rule for meeting the needs of inclination. In the first case what interests me is the action; in the second case what interests me is the object of the action (so far as this object is pleasant to me). We have seen in Chapter One that in an action done out of duty one must consider not the interest in the object, but the interest in the action itself and its rational principle (namely, the law).

19. *genötigt*, constrained, necessitated or obligated
20. *Sollen*
21. *Wollen*, the willing or desire

because, even if he did know this, his maxims might still be contrary to the objective principles of practical reason.

A hypothetical imperative thus says only that an action is good for some purpose or other, either possible or actual. In the first case it is a problematic practical principle; in the second case an assertoric practical principle. A categorical imperative, which declares an action to be objectively necessary of itself without reference to any purpose—that is, even without any further end—ranks as an apodictic practical principle.

What is possible only through the powers of some rational being can also be thought of as a possible purpose of some will. Consequently, if we think of principles of action as stating what is necessary in order to achieve some possible purpose, there are in fact infinitely many principles of action. All sciences have a practical part consisting of projects, which suppose that some end is possible for us, and imperatives, which tell us how that end is to be reached. These imperatives can in general be called imperatives of *skill*. Here there is no question at all as to whether the end is reasonable and good, but only about what one would have to do to attain it. The prescriptions required by a doctor in order to cure a patient and those that a poisoner needs in order to bring about certain death are of equal value so far as each will accomplish its purpose perfectly. Since young people do not know what ends may occur to them in the course of life, parents try to make their children learn *many kinds* of things. They try carefully to teach *skill* in the use of means to *various* desired ends, not knowing with certainty which possible end may in the future become an actual goal adopted by their pupil. Their anxiety in this matter is so great that they commonly neglect to form and correct their children's judgements about the worth of things that they might possibly adopt as ends.

There is, however, *one* end that we may presuppose as actual in all rational beings (so far as they are dependent beings to whom imperatives apply); and thus there is one aim which they not only *might* have, but which we can assume with certainty that they all *do* have by a necessity of nature and that aim is *perfect happiness*.[22] The

hypothetical imperative which affirms the practical necessity of an action as a means to the promotion of perfect happiness is an assertoric imperative. We must not characterize it as necessary merely for some uncertain, merely possible purpose, but as necessary for a purpose that we can presuppose a priori and with certainty to be present in everyone because it belongs to the essence of human beings. Now we can call skill in the choice of the means to one's own greatest well-being "prudence"* in the narrowest sense of the word. So the imperative concerning the choice of means to one's own happiness—that is, the precept of prudence—still remains hypothetical; the action is commanded not absolutely but only as a means to a further end.

Finally, there is one imperative which commands a certain line of conduct directly, without assuming or being conditional on any further goal to be reached by that conduct. This imperative is categorical. It is concerned not with the material of the action and its anticipated result, but with its form and with the principle from which the action itself results. And what is essentially good in the action consists in the [agent's] disposition,[23] whatever the result may be. This imperative may be called the imperative of morality.

Volition in accordance with these three kinds of principles is also sharply distinguished by the dissimilarity in how they constrain the will. To make this dissimilarity obvious, I think we would name them most appropriately if we called them rules of skill, counsels of prudence, or commandments (laws) of morality, respectively. For only law carries with it the concept of necessity, an unconditional and objective and therefore universally valid necessity; and commandments are laws that must be obeyed, even against inclination. Counsels do indeed involve necessity, but a necessity valid

---

22. *Glückseligkeit*. On the various meanings of this word, see footnote 2 in Ch. One. In this translation, 'perfect happiness' is the usual rendering.

* The word 'prudence' (*Klugheit*) is used in two senses; in one sense it can be called 'worldly wisdom' (*Weltklugheit*); in a second sense, 'personal wisdom' (*Privatklugheit*). The first is a person's skill in influencing others in order to use them for his own ends. The second is the ability to combine all of these ends to his own lasting advantage. The latter is properly that to which the value of the former can itself be traced; and if a person is prudent in the first sense, but not in the second, we might better say that he is clever and astute, but on the whole imprudent.

23. *Gesinnung*

only under a subjective and contingent condition—namely, depending on whether this or that human being counts this or that as essential to his happiness. As against this, a categorical imperative is limited by no condition and can actually be called a commandment in the strict sense, being absolutely, although practically, necessary. We could also call imperatives of the first kind technical (concerned with art), imperatives of the second kind pragmatic* (concerned with well-being), and imperatives of the third kind moral (concerned with free conduct as such—that is, with morals).

23. [How Are Hypothetical Imperatives Possible?]

The question now arises 'How are all these imperatives possible?' This question does not ask how an action commanded by the imperative can be performed, but merely how we can understand the constraining of the will, which imperatives express in setting us a task. How an imperative of skill is possible requires no special discussion. Whoever wills the end also wills (so far as reason has decisive influence on his actions) the means which are indispensably necessary and in his power. This proposition is analytic as far as willing[24] is concerned. For when I will an object as an effect of my action I already conceive of my causality as an acting cause—that is, the use of means is included in the concept of the end; and the imperative merely extracts the concept of actions necessary to this end from the concept of willing an end. (Of course synthetic propositions are required in determining the means to a pro-

posed end, but these propositions are concerned, not with the ground, the act of will, but with how to actualize the object.) Mathematics teaches, and certainly by synthetic propositions alone, that in order to bisect a line according to a reliable principle I must make two intersecting arcs from each of its extremities. But if I know that the aforesaid effect can be produced only by such an action, then the proposition 'If I fully will the effect, I must also will the action required to produce it' is analytic. For it is one and the same thing to think of something as an effect that is in a certain way possible through me and to think of myself as acting in this same way.

If it were only that easy to provide a definite concept of perfect happiness the imperatives of prudence would coincide entirely with those of skill and would be equally analytic. For then it could be said in this case as in the former case, 'Whoever wills the end, also (necessarily, according to reason) wills the sole means which are in his power.' Unfortunately, however, the concept of perfect happiness is such a vague concept that although everyone wants it, they can never say definitely and self-consistently what it really is that they wish and will. The reason for this is that all the elements that belong to the concept of happiness are empirical—that is, they must be borrowed from experience; but the Idea of perfect happiness requires an absolute whole, a maximum, of well-being in my present and in every future state. Now it is impossible for even the most insightful and most capable but finite being to form here a definite concept of what he really wants. Is it riches that he wants? How much anxiety, envy, and intrigue might he not bring on his own head in this way! Is it knowledge and insight? This might just give him an eye even sharper in seeing evils at present hidden from him and yet unavoidable, making those evils all the more frightful, or it might add a load of still further needs to the desires which already give him trouble enough. Is it long life? Who will guarantee that it would not be a life of long misery? Is it at least health? How often has not physical infirmity kept someone from excesses into which perfect health would have let him fall!—and so on. In short, he has no principle by which he is able to decide with complete certainty what would make him truly happy, since for this he

---

* It seems to me that the proper meaning of the word 'pragmatic' can be defined most accurately in this way. For *sanctions* that do not properly speaking spring from the law of states as necessary statutes, but arise from *provision* for the general welfare are called pragmatic. We say that a *history* is written pragmatically when it teaches *prudence*—that is, when it instructs the world how to provide for its interests better than, or at least as well as, the world of other times has done.

24. *Das Wollen.* The words 'Wollen' and 'will' here could perhaps be translated as 'wanting' and 'wants', though the German words carry a somewhat stronger feeling than what we might call 'casual wanting'. In some uses of 'Ich will' there is a suggestion of commitment to the object one 'wills' but in many ordinary uses 'Ich will' just means 'I want'. In the present context, however, 'willing' seems preferable.

would require omniscience. Thus we cannot act on definite principles in order to be happy, but only on empirical counsels, for example, of diet, frugality, politeness, reserve, and so on—things which experience shows contribute most to well-being on the average. Hence the imperatives of prudence, strictly speaking, do not command at all—that is, they cannot exhibit actions objectively as practically necessary. They should be taken as pieces of advice (*consilia*), rather than as commandments (*praecepta*), of reason. The problem of determining certainly and universally what action will promote the perfect happiness of a rational being is completely insoluble; and consequently in regard to this there is no imperative possible which in the strictest sense could command us to do what will make us happy, since perfect happiness is an ideal, not of reason, but of imagination—an ideal resting merely on empirical grounds, of which it is vain to expect that they should determine an action by which we could attain the totality of a series of consequences which is in fact infinite. Nevertheless, if we were to assume that the means to happiness could be discovered with certainty, this imperative of prudence would be an analytic practical proposition; for it differs from the imperative of skill only in this—that in the latter the end is merely possible, while in the former the end is given. In spite of this difference, since both command solely the means to something assumed to be willed as an end, the imperative that commands him who wills the end to will the means is in both cases analytic. Thus, the possibility of an imperative of prudence also poses no difficulty.

24. [How Is a Categorical Imperative Possible?]

By contrast, 'How is the imperative of morality possible?' is beyond all doubt the one question in need of solution. For the moral imperative is in no way hypothetical, and consequently the objective necessity, which it affirms, cannot be supported by any presupposition, as was the case with hypothetical imperatives. But we must never forget that it is impossible to settle by any example, i.e., empirically, whether there is any imperative of this kind at all; we should rather worry that all imperatives that seem to be categorical may yet be hypothetical in

some hidden way. For example, when it is said, 'You must abstain from making deceitful promises,' one assumes that the necessity for this abstention is not mere advice so as to avoid some further evil—as though the meaning of what was said was, You ought not to make a deceitful promise lest, when it comes to light, you destroy your credit. On the contrary, an action of this kind would have to be considered as bad in itself, and the imperative of the prohibition would be therefore categorical. Even so, no example can show with certainty that the will would be determined here solely by the law without any further motivation,[25] although it may appear to be so; for it is always possible that fear of disgrace, perhaps also hidden dread of other risks, may unconsciously influence the will. Who can prove by experience the non-existence of a cause? For experience shows only that we do not perceive it. In such a case, however, the so-called moral imperative, which as such appears to be categorical and unconditional, would in fact be only a pragmatic prescription calling attention to our own advantage and merely instructing us to take this into account.

We shall thus have to investigate entirely a priori the possibility of a categorical imperative, since here we do not enjoy the advantage of having its reality given in experience so that the discussion of its possibility would be needed merely to explain, and not to establish it. However, we can see the following at least provisionally: that the categorical imperative alone purports to be a practical law, while all the rest may be called principles of the will but not laws; for an action that is necessary merely to achieve some arbitrary purpose can be considered as in itself contingent, and we can always escape from the prescription if we abandon the purpose; whereas an unconditional commandment does not leave it open to the will to do the opposite at its discretion and therefore alone carries with it that necessity which we demand from a law.

In the second place, with this categorical imperative or law of morality the reason for our difficulty (in comprehending its possibility) is a very serious one. We have here a synthetic a priori practical proposition;* and since in theoretical

25. *Triebfeder*
* I connect the deed with the will a priori and thus necessarily, without supposing as a condition that there is any inclination for this deed (although I make this

knowledge there is so much difficulty in comprehending the possibility of propositions of this kind, we may well assume that the difficulty will be no less in the practical sphere.

25. [The Universal Law Formulation of the Categorical Imperative and Its Derivation]

The first part of our task is to see whether perhaps the mere concept of a categorical imperative might also give us the formula containing the only proposition that can be a categorical imperative. Showing how such an absolute commandment is possible will still require special and difficult effort, even when we know what the commandment asserts. But we postpone this to the last section.

If I think of a *hypothetical* imperative as such, I do not know before-hand what it will contain—not until I am given its condition. But if I think of a *categorical imperative*, I know right away what it contains. For since this imperative contains, besides the law, only the necessity that the maxim* conform to this law, while the law, as we have seen, contains no condition limiting it, there is nothing left over to which the maxim of action should conform except the universality of a law as such; and it is only this conformity that the imperative asserts to be necessary.

There is therefore only one categorical imperative and it is this: 'Act only on that maxim by which you can at the same time will[26] that it should become a universal law.'

> connection only objectively—that is to say, under the Idea of a power of reason that would have complete control over all subjective motives). Hence we have here a practical proposition in which the willing of an action is not derived analytically from some other volition already presupposed (for we do not possess any such perfect will); rather, the willing of the action is connected directly with the concept of the will of a rational being [but] as something that is not contained in this concept.

* A *maxim* is a subjective principle of action and must be distinguished from an *objective principle*—namely, a practical law. The former contains a practical rule determined by reason in accordance with the conditions of the subject (often his ignorance or his inclinations); it is thus a principle on which the subject *acts*. A law, on the other hand, is an objective principle, valid for every rational being; and it is a principle on which he *ought to act*—that is, an imperative.

26. *die du zugleich wollen kannst*

Now if all imperatives of duty can be derived from this one imperative as their principle, then even though we leave it unsettled whether what we call duty is or is not an empty concept, we shall still be able to indicate at least what we understand by it and what the concept means.

26. [A Variation: The Universal Law of Nature Formulation]

Because the universality of law according to which effects occur constitutes what is properly called nature in its most general sense (nature as regards its form)—that is, the existence of things so far as this is determined by universal laws—the universal imperative of duty could also be formulated as follows: 'Act as though the maxim of your action were to become by your will a universal law of nature.'

27. [Four Examples]

We shall now enumerate some duties, dividing them in the usual way into duties towards ourselves and duties towards others and into perfect and imperfect duties.**

I. A man feels sick of life as the result of a mounting series of misfortunes that has reduced him to hopelessness, but he still possesses enough of his reason to ask himself whether it would not be contrary to his duty to himself to take his own life. Now he tests whether the maxim of his action could really become a universal law of nature. His maxim, however, is: 'I make it my principle out of self-love to shorten my life if its continuance threatens more evil than it promises advantage.' The only further question is whether this principle of self-love can become a universal law of nature. But one sees at once that a nature whose law was that the very same feeling meant

** It should be noted that I reserve the division of duties entirely for a future *Metaphysic of Morals* and that my present division is put forward as an arbitrary one (merely for the purpose of arranging my examples). Further, I understand here by a perfect duty one that allows no exception in the interests of inclination, and so I recognize among *perfect duties*, both outer and inner duties. This runs contrary to the standard usage in the schools, but I do not intend to justify it here, since for my purpose it makes no difference whether this point is conceded or not.

to promote life should actually destroy life would contradict itself, and hence would not endure as nature. The maxim therefore could not possibly be a general law of nature and thus it wholly contradicts the supreme principle of all duty.

2. Another finds himself driven by need to borrow money. He knows very well that he will not be able to pay it back, but he sees too that nobody will lend him anything unless he firmly promises to pay it back within a fixed time. He wants to make such a promise, but he still has enough conscience to ask himself, 'Isn't it impermissible and contrary to duty to get out of one's difficulties this way?' Suppose, however, that he did decide to do it. The maxim of his action would run thus: 'When I believe myself short of money, I will borrow money and promise to pay it back, even though I know that this will never be done.' Now this principle of self-love or personal advantage is perhaps quite compatible with my own entire future welfare; only there remains the question 'Is it right?' I therefore transform the unfair demand of self-love into a universal law and frame my question thus: 'How would things stand if my maxim became a universal law?' I then see immediately that this maxim can never qualify as a self-consistent universal law of nature, but must necessarily contradict itself. For the universality of a law that permits anyone who believes himself to be in need to make any promise he pleases with the intention of not keeping it would make promising, and the very purpose one has in promising, itself impossible. For no one would believe he was being promised anything, but would laugh at any such utterance as hollow pretence.

3. A third finds in himself a talent that, with a certain amount of cultivation, could make him a useful man for all sorts of purposes. But he sees himself in comfortable circumstances, and he prefers to give himself up to pleasure rather than to bother about increasing and improving his fortunate natural aptitudes. Yet he asks himself further 'Does my maxim of neglecting my natural gifts, besides agreeing with my taste for amusement, agree also with what is called duty?' He then sees that a nature could indeed endure under such a universal law, even if (like the South Sea Islanders) every man should let his talents rust and should be bent on devoting his life solely to idleness, amusement, procreation—in a word, to

enjoyment. Only he cannot possibly *will*[27] that this should become a universal law of nature or should be implanted in us as such a law by a natural instinct. For as a rational being he necessarily wills that all his powers should be developed, since they are after all useful to him and given to him for all sorts of possible purposes.

4. A fourth man, who is himself flourishing but sees others who have to struggle with great hardships (and whom he could easily help) thinks to himself: 'What do I care? Let every one be as happy as Heaven intends or as he can make himself; I won't deprive him of anything; I won't even envy him; but I don't feel like contributing anything to his well-being or to helping him in his distress!' Now admittedly if such an attitude were a universal law of nature, the human race could survive perfectly well and doubtless even better than when everybody chatters about sympathy and good will, and even makes an effort, now and then, to practise them, but, when one can get away with it, swindles, traffics in human rights, or violates them in other ways. But although it is possible that a universal law of nature in accord with this maxim could exist, it is impossible to *will* that such a principle should hold everywhere as a law of nature. For a will that intended this would be in conflict with itself, since many situations might arise in which the man needs love and sympathy from others, and in which, by such a law of nature generated by his own will, he would rob himself of all hope of the help he wants.

28. [The Two Kinds of Maxims That Fail the Test]

These are some of the many actual duties—or at least of what we take to be actual—whose derivation from the single principle cited above is perspicuous. We must be able to will that a maxim of our action should become a universal law— this is the authoritative model[28] for moral judging of action generally. Some actions are so constituted that we cannot even *conceive* without contradiction that their maxim be a universal law of nature, let alone that we could *will* that it *ought* to become one. In the case of other actions, we do

27. *Er kann unmöglich wollen*
28. *Kanon*

not find this inner impossibility, but it is still impossible to *will* that their maxim should be raised to the universality of a law of nature, because such a will would contradict itself. We see readily that the first kind of action is opposed to strict or narrow duty, the second opposed only to wide (meritorious) duty; Thus all duties—so far as the type of obligation (not the object of its action) is concerned—are fully set out in these examples as dependent on our single principle.

29. [The Typical Problem: Making Exceptions for Ourselves]

If we now look at ourselves whenever we transgress a duty, we find that we in fact do not intend that our maxim should become a universal law. For this is impossible for us. What we really intend is rather that its opposite should remain a law generally; we only take the liberty of making an *exception* to it, for ourselves or (of course just this once) to satisfy our inclination. Consequently if we weighed it all up from one and the same perspective—that of reason—we should find a contradiction in our own will, the contradiction that a certain principle should be objectively necessary as a universal law and yet subjectively should not hold universally but should admit of exceptions. But there is actually no contradiction here, since we are first considering our action from the perspective of a will wholly in accord with reason, and then considering exactly the same action from the point of view of a will affected by inclination. What we have is rather an opposition (antagonism) of inclination to the precept of reason whereby the universality of the principle (*universalitas*) is transformed into a mere generality (*generalitas*) in order that the practical principle of reason can meet the maxim halfway. This procedure, though unjustifiable in our own impartial judgement, proves nevertheless that we in fact recognize the validity of the categorical imperative and (with all respect to it) merely allow ourselves a few exceptions that are, as we pretend, unimportant and apparently forced upon us.

30. [The Proof Still Missing and Why It Must Be A Priori]

We have thus at least shown this much—that if duty is a concept that is to have meaning and actual legislative authority for our actions, it can

be expressed only in categorical imperatives and not at all in hypothetical ones. At the same time—and this is already a great deal—we have set forth clearly, and defined for every use, the content of the categorical imperative, which must contain the principle of all duty (if there is to be such a thing at all). But we are still not so far advanced as to prove a priori that there actually is an imperative of this kind—that there is a practical law which by itself commands absolutely and without any further motivation,[29] and that it is our duty to follow this law.

If we really intend to arrive at this proof it is extremely important to remember that we should not let ourselves think for a moment that the reality of this principle can be derived from *the particular characteristics of human nature*. For duty has to be a practical, unconditional necessity of action; it must therefore hold for all rational beings (to whom alone an imperative can apply at all), and *only for that reason* a law that holds also for all human wills. Whatever, on the other hand, is derived from the special predisposition of humanity, from certain feelings and propensities, and even, if this were possible, from some special bent peculiar to human reason and not holding necessarily for the will of every rational being— all this can indeed supply a personal maxim, but not a law: it can give us a subjective principle— one on which we have a natural disposition and inclination to act—but not an objective principle on which we should be directed to act even though our every propensity, inclination, and natural bent were opposed to it. This is so much the case that the sublimity and inner dignity of the commandment is even more manifest in a duty, the fewer subjective causes there are for obeying it and the more there are against it, but without this weakening in the slightest the constraint exercised by the law or diminishing its validity.

Here we see philosophy placed in what is actually a precarious position, a position that is supposed to be firm though it is neither suspended from heaven nor supported by the earth. Here she must show her purity as the sustainer of her own laws—not as the herald of laws that some implanted sense or who knows what guardian-like nature has whispered to her. Such laws,

29. *Triebfeder*

though perhaps always better than nothing, can never furnish us with fundamental principles dictated by reason, principles whose origin must be completely a priori and, because of this, have commanding authority. Such fundamental principles expect nothing from human inclinations but everything from the supremacy of the law and the respect owed it. Without this they condemn human beings to self-contempt and inner disgust.

Everything empirical is thus not only wholly unfit to contribute to the principle of morality; it is highly damaging to the purity of moral practices themselves. For, in morality, the proper worth of an absolutely good will, a worth exalted above all price, lies precisely in the freedom of its principle of action from any influence by contingent reasons that only experience can provide. We cannot warn too strongly or too often against the slack, or indeed vulgar, attitude which searches among empirical motives[30] and laws for the principle; for human reason in its weariness is glad to rest on this cushion, and in a dream of sweet illusions (which allow it to embrace a cloud instead of Juno) to substitute for morality a bastard patched up from limbs of very diverse parentage, looking like anything one wishes to see in it, only not resembling virtue to anyone who has once beheld her in her true form.*

Our question then is this: 'Is it a necessary law *for all rational beings* to judge their actions always in accordance with those maxims which they can themselves will that they should serve as universal laws?' If it is a necessary law, it must already be connected (entirely a priori) with the concept of the will of a rational being as such. But in order to discover this connection we must, however reluctantly, venture into metaphysics, although into a region of metaphysics different from that of speculative philosophy, namely, the metaphysics of morals. In a practical philosophy we are not concerned with assuming reasons for what happens, but with acknowledging laws for what ought to

happen, even if it may never happen—that is, objective practical laws. And here we have no need to investigate the reasons why anything pleases or displeases, how the pleasure of mere sensation differs from taste, and whether the latter is distinct from general satisfaction of reason. We need not inquire on what the feelings of pleasure and displeasure are based, or how from these feelings there arise desires and inclinations; and how from these, with the co-operation of reason, there arise maxims. For all this belongs to empirical psychology,[31] which would constitute the second part of the study of nature, if we regard the latter as the *philosophy of nature* to the extent to which it rests on *empirical laws*. Here, however, we are discussing objective practical laws, and consequently the relation of a will to itself insofar as it determines itself solely by reason. Everything related to the empirical then falls away of itself; for if *reason all by itself* determines conduct (and the possibility of this is what we now wish to investigate), it must necessarily do so a priori.

31. [Objective and Relative Ends]

We think of the will as a power of determining oneself to act *in conformity with the idea of certain laws*. And such a power can be found only in rational beings. Now, what serves the will as the objective ground of its self-determining is an *end*; and this end, if it is given by reason alone, must be equally valid for all rational beings. On the other hand, something that contains merely the ground of the possibility of an action, where the result of that action is the end, is called a *means*. The subjective ground of desiring is a *driving-spring*,[32] the objective ground of willing[33] is *a motivating reason*.[34] Hence the difference between subjective ends, which depend on driving-springs,[35] and objective ends, which depend on motivating reasons[36] that are valid for every rational being. Practical principles are *formal* if they abstract from all subjective ends; they are *material*, on the other hand, if they are based on[37] subjective ends and

---

30. *Bewegursachen*

* To behold virtue in her true form means nothing other than to show morality stripped of any admixture with what is sensuous and of all the inauthentic adornments of reward or self-love. How much she then casts into the shade all else that appears enticing to the inclinations can be readily perceived by anyone willing to exert his reason in the slightest, if it is not entirely spoiled for all abstract thinking.

31. *empirischen Seelenlehre*
32. *Triebfeder*
33. *des Wollens*
34. *Bewegungsgrund*
35. *Triebfeder*
36. *Beweggründe*
37. *zum Grunde legen*

consequently on certain driving-springs. Those ends that a rational being at his own discretion sets for himself as *what he intends to accomplish* through his action (material ends) are in every case only relative; for what gives them worth is only their relation to some subject's particularly constituted faculty of desire. Such worth can therefore provide no universal principles, no principles valid and necessary for all rational beings and for every act of will[38]—that is, it can provide no practical laws. Consequently all these relative ends are only the ground of hypothetical imperatives.

Suppose, however, there were something *whose existence in itself* had an absolute worth, something that, as an end *in itself*, could be a ground of definite laws. Then in it and in it alone, would the ground of a possible categorical imperative, that is, of a practical law, reside.

32. [The Humanity as an End Formulation]

Now, I say, a human being, and in general every rational being, *does exist* as an end in himself, *not merely as a means* to be used by this or that will as it pleases. In all his actions, whether they are directed to himself or to other rational beings, a human being must always be viewed *at the same time as an end*. All the objects of inclination have only a conditional worth; for if these inclinations and the needs based on them did not exist, their object would be worthless. But inclinations themselves, as sources of needs, are so far from having absolute value to make them desirable for their own sake that it must rather be the universal wish of every rational being to be wholly free of them. Thus the value of any object *that is to be acquired* by our action is always conditional. Beings whose existence depends not on our will but on nature still have only a relative value as means and are therefore called *things*, if they lack reason. Rational beings, on the other hand, are called *persons* because, their nature already marks them out as ends in themselves—that is, as something which ought not to be used *merely* as a means—and consequently imposes restrictions on all choice making[39] (and is an object of respect).

Persons, therefore, are not merely subjective ends whose existence as an effect of our actions has a value *for us*. They are *objective ends*—that is, things whose existence is in itself an end, and indeed an end such that no other end can be substituted for it, no end to which they should serve *merely* as a means. For if this were not so, there would be nothing at all having *absolute value* anywhere. But if all value were conditional, and thus contingent, then no supreme principle could be found for reason at all.

If then there is to be a supreme practical principle and a categorical imperative for the human will, it must be such that it forms an objective principle of the will from the idea of something which is necessarily an end for everyone because *it is an end in itself*, a principle that can therefore serve as a universal practical law. The ground of this principle is: *Rational nature exists as an end in itself.* This is the way in which a human being necessarily conceives his own existence, and it is therefore a *subjective* principle of human actions. But it is also the way in which every other rational being conceives his existence, on the same rational ground which holds also for me;* hence it is at the same time an *objective* principle from which, since it is a supreme practical ground, it must be possible to derive all laws of the will. The practical imperative will therefore be the following: *Act in such a way that you treat humanity, whether in your own person or in any other person, always at the same time as an end, never merely as a means.* We will now see whether this can be carried out in practice.

33. [Examples]

Let us keep to our previous examples.

First, as regards the concept of necessary duty to oneself, the man who contemplates suicide will ask himself whether his action could be compatible with the Idea of humanity as *an end in itself*. If he damages himself in order to escape from a painful situation, he is making use of a person *merely as a means* to maintain a tolerable state of affairs till the end of his life. But a human being is not a thing—not something to be used *merely* as a means: he must always in all his actions be

---

38. *jedes Wollen*
39. *Willkür*

* This proposition I put forward here as a postulate. The grounds for it will be found in the final chapter.

regarded as an end in himself. Hence I cannot dispose of a human being in my own person, by maiming, corrupting, or killing him. (I must here forego a more precise definition of this principle that would forestall any misunderstanding—for example, as to having limbs amputated to save myself or exposing my life to danger in order to preserve it, and so on—this discussion belongs to ethics proper.)

Secondly, as regards necessary or strict duty owed to others, the man who has in mind making a false promise to others will see at once that he is intending to make use of another person *merely as a means* to an end which that person does not share. For the person whom I seek to use for my own purposes by such a promise cannot possibly agree with my way of treating him, and so cannot himself share the end of the action. This incompatibility with the principle of duty to others can be seen more distinctly when we bring in examples of attacks on the freedom and property of others. For then it is manifest that a violator of the rights of human beings[40] intends to use the person of others merely as a means without taking into consideration that, as rational beings, they must always at the same time be valued as ends—that is, treated only as beings who must themselves be able to share in the end of the very same action.[*]

Thirdly, as regards contingent (meritorious) duty to oneself, it is not enough that an action not conflict with humanity in our own person as an end in itself: it must also *harmonize with this end*. Now there are in humanity capacities for greater perfection that form part of nature's purpose for humanity in our own person. To neglect these can

perhaps be compatible with the *survival* of humanity as an end in itself, but not with the *promotion* of that end.

Fourthly, as regards meritorious duties to others, the natural end that all human beings seek is their own perfect happiness. Now the human race might indeed exist if everybody contributed nothing to the happiness of others but at the same time refrained from deliberately impairing it. This harmonizing with humanity *as an end in itself* would, however, be merely negative and not positive, unless everyone also endeavours, as far as he can, to further the ends of others. For the ends of any person who is an end in himself must, if this idea is to have its full effect in me, be also, as far as possible, *my* ends.

34. [The Autonomy Formulation]

This principle of humanity, and in general of every rational agent,[41] *as an end in itself* (a principle which is the supreme limiting condition on every person's freedom of action) is not borrowed from experience: first, because it is universal, applying to all rational beings generally, and no experience is sufficient to determine anything about all such beings; secondly, because in this principle we conceive of humanity not as an end that one happens to have (a subjective end)—that is, as an object which people, as a matter of fact, happen to make their end. We conceive of it rather as an objective end—one that, as a law, should constitute the supreme limiting condition on all subjective ends, whatever those ends may be. This principle must therefore spring from pure reason.

That is to say, the ground of every practical legislating lies *objectively in the rule* and in the form of universality that (according to our first principle) makes the rule fit to be a law (and possibly a law of nature);[42] *subjectively*, however, the ground of practical legislating lies in the *end*. But, according to our second principle, the *subject* of all ends is every rational being as an end in itself. From this there follows our third practical principle of the will: the supreme condition of the will's harmony with universal practical reason is the Idea of

---

40. *Rechte der Menschen*

[*] Let no one think that the trivial '*quod tibi non vis fieri,* etc.' could here serve as a guide or principle. For it is merely a derivation from our principle, and subject to various qualifications: it cannot be a universal law since it contains the ground neither of duties to oneself nor of duties of kindness to others (for many a man would gladly consent that others should not benefit him if only he could be excused from showing benevolence to them. Nor, finally, does this rule contain the ground of strict duties owed to others; for the criminal would be able to argue on this basis against the judge who sentences him, and so on. [Ed. note: This refers to a negative version of the Golden Rule: Do not do to others what you do not want done to you.]

41. *vernünftigen Natur*
42. *allenfalls Naturgesetz*

the will of every rational being as a will that legislates universal law.

By this principle all maxims are rejected which are inconsistent with the will's own universal law-giving. The will is therefore not merely subject to the law, but subject in such a way that it must be considered as also *giving the law to itself*[43] and only for this reason as first of all subject to the law (of which it can regard itself as the author).

Imperatives as formulated above excluded from their legislative authority every admixture of interest as a motivation.[44] They either commanded a conformity of actions to universal law, a conformity analogous to a *natural order*, or they asserted the prerogative of rational beings to be regarded universally as *supreme ends* in themselves. (This followed from the mere fact that these imperatives were conceived as categorical.) But the imperatives were only *assumed* to be categorical because we had to make this assumption if we wished to explain the concept of duty. That there were practical propositions that command categorically could not itself be proved, any more than it can be proved here in this chapter. But one thing might have been done—namely, to show that in willing something just out of duty[45] the renunciation of all interest is the specific mark distinguishing a categorical from a hypothetical imperative. This is what we are doing in the present third formulation of the principle—namely, in the Idea of the will of every rational being as *a will that legislates universal law*.

For once we think of a will of this kind, it becomes clear that while a will *that is subject to laws* may be bound to this law by some interest, a will that is itself a supreme lawgiver cannot possibly depend on any interest; for such a dependent will would itself require yet another law in order to restrict the interest of self-love by the condition that this interest must be valid as a universal law.

Thus the *principle* that every human will is *a will that enacts universal laws in all its maxims* would be well adapted* to be a categorical imperative, provid-

ed only that this principle is correct in other ways. Because of the Idea of giving universal law, it is *based on no interest*, and consequently, of all possible imperatives it alone can be *unconditional*. Or better still, let us take the converse of this proposition: if there is a categorical imperative (a law that applies to the will of every rational being), it can command us only to act always on the maxim of its will as one which could at the same time look upon itself as giving universal laws. For only then is the practical principle, and the imperative that the will obeys, unconditional, because the imperative cannot be based on any interest.

If we look back on all the previous efforts to discover the principle of morality, it is no wonder that they have all had to fail. One saw that human beings are bound to laws by their duty, but it never occurred to anyone that they are subject only to *laws which they themselves have given* but which are nevertheless *universal*, and that people are bound only to act in conformity with a will that is their own but that is, according to nature's purpose, a will that gives universal law.[46] For when one thought of human beings merely as subject to a law (whatever it might be), the law had to carry with it some interest, as stimulus or compulsion to obedience, because it did not spring as law from their *own* will: in order to conform to the law, their will had to be compelled by *something else* to act in a certain way. But this strictly necessary consequence meant that all the labour spent in trying to find a supreme foundation for duty was irrevocably lost. For what one discovered was never duty, but only the necessity of acting from a certain interest. This interest might be one's own or another's. But the resulting imperative was bound to be always a conditional one and could not at all serve as a moral commandment. I therefore want to call my principle the principle of the *Autonomy* of the will in contrast with all others, which I therefore count as *Heteronomy*.

35. [The Kingdom[47] of Ends Formulation]

The concept of every rational being as a being who must regard itself as making universal law by

---

43. *selbstgesetzgebend*

44. *Triebfeder*

45. *im wollen aus Pflicht*

*   I may be excused from citing examples to illustrate this principle, since those that were already used to illustrate the categorical imperative and its formula can all serve the same purpose here.

46. *allgemein gesetzgebenden Willen*

47. *Reich*. The word *Reich* can mean a kingdom, realm, empire, or commonwealth. 'Commonwealth', ('a state

all the maxims of its will, and must seek to judge itself and its actions from this standpoint, leads to a closely connected and very fruitful concept—namely, that of *a kingdom of ends*.

I understand by a 'kingdom' the systematic union of different rational beings under common laws. Now since laws determine ends as regards their universal validity, we can—if we abstract from the personal differences between rational beings, and also from the content of their private ends—conceive a whole of all ends systematically united (a whole composed of rational beings as ends in themselves and also of the personal ends which each may set for himself); that is, we can conceive of a kingdom of ends which is possible in accordance with the aforesaid principles.

For rational beings all stand under the *law* that each of them should treat himself and all others *never merely as a means* but always *at the same time as an end in himself.* But from this there arises a systematic union of rational beings through shared objective laws—that is, a kingdom. Since these laws aim precisely at the relation of such beings to one another as ends and means, this kingdom may be called a kingdom of ends (admittedly only an ideal).

A rational being, however, belongs to the kingdom of ends as a *member*, if, while legislating its universal laws, he is also subject to these laws. He belongs to the kingdom as its *head*,[48] if, as legislating, he is not subject to the will of any other being.

A rational being must always regard himself as lawgiving in a kingdom of ends made possible through freedom of the will—whether as member or as head. But he cannot maintain the position of head merely through the maxim of his will, but only if he is a completely independent being, without needs and with an unlimited power adequate to his will.

founded on law and united by compact or tacit agreement of the people for the common good,' is one dictionary definition), seems closer than 'kingdom' to Kant's meaning, retaining the political metaphor while not suggesting an absolute monarch or emperor as sovereign. However, 'kingdom' and 'kingdom of ends' have become fairly standard in English discussions of Kant and are therefore used here.

48. *Oberhaupt.* Some translators prefer 'sovereign' but that word, like 'kingdom' for *Reich*, may be misleading. Kant's *Oberhaupt* is not an absolute ruler or *Herrscher*.

Thus morality consists in the relation of all action to just that lawgiving through which a kingdom of ends is made possible. But this lawgiving must be found in every rational being itself and must be capable of arising from the will of that being. The principle of its will is therefore this: never to perform any action except one whose maxim could also be a universal law, and thus to act only on a maxim *through which the will could regard itself at the same time as enacting universal law.* If maxims are not already by their very nature in harmony with this objective principle of rational beings as legislating universal law, the necessity of acting on this principle is called a constraint on the choice of actions,[49] i.e., *duty.* Duty does not apply to the head in a kingdom of ends, but it does apply to every member and to all of them in equal measure.

The practical necessity of acting on this principle—that is, duty—is not based at all on feelings, impulses, and inclinations, but only on the relation of rational beings to one another, a relation in which the will of a rational being must always be regarded as *lawgiving*, because otherwise it could not be thought of as *an end in itself.* Reason thus relates every maxim of a universally legislating will to every other will and also to every action towards oneself: it does so, not because of any further motive or future advantage, but from the Idea of the *dignity*[50] of a rational being who obeys no law other than one which he himself also enacts.

36. [Dignity and Price]

In the kingdom of ends everything has either a *price* or a *dignity*. Whatever has a price can be replaced by something else as *equivalent*. Whatever by contrast is exalted above all price and so admits of no equivalent has a dignity.

Whatever is relative to universal human inclinations and needs has a *market price*. Whatever, even without presupposing a need, accords with a certain taste—that is, with satisfaction in the mere random[51] play of our mental powers—has an *attachment price.*[52] But that which constitutes the

49. Literally, 'practical necessitation', *praktische Nötigung*.
50. *Würde*
51. *zwecklos*, without purpose
52. *Affektionspreis*, the value something has because of someone's inclinations or personal valuation. Both

sole condition under which anything can be an end in itself has not mere relative worth, i.e., a price, but an inner worth—i.e., *dignity*.

Now morality is the only condition under which a rational being can be an end in itself; for only through this is it possible to be a lawgiving member in the kingdom of ends. Therefore morality, and humanity so far as it is capable of morality, is the only thing that has dignity. Skill and diligence in work have a market price; wit, lively imagination, and humour have an attachment price but fidelity to promises and benevolence out of basic principles (not out of instinct) have an inner worth. Nature and art alike offer nothing that could replace their lack; for their worth consists not in the effects which result from them, not in the advantage or profit they produce, but in the intentions[53]—that is, in the maxims of the will—which are ready in this way to reveal themselves in action even if they are not favoured by success. Such actions too need no recommendation from any subjective disposition or taste in order to be regarded with immediate favour and approval; they need no direct predilection or feeling for them. They exhibit as an object of immediate respect the will that performs them; since nothing but reason is required in order to *impose* them on the will. Nor is the will to be *coaxed* into them, which would anyhow be a contradiction in the case of duties. This assessment lets us recognize the value of such a mental attitude as dignity and puts it infinitely above all price, with which it cannot be brought into comparison or computation without, as it were, violating its holiness.

And what is it then that justifies a morally good disposition, or virtue, in making such lofty claims? It is nothing less than the *sharing* which it allows to a rational being in *giving universal laws*, which therefore renders him fit to be a member in a possible kingdom of ends. His own nature as an end in himself already marked out this fitness

and therefore his status as lawgiver in a kingdom of ends and as free from all laws of nature, obedient only to those laws which he himself prescribes, laws according to which his maxims can participate in the making of universal law (to which he at the same time subjects himself). For nothing can have worth other than that determined for it by the law. But the lawgiving that determines all worth must therefore have a dignity, i.e., an unconditional and incomparable worth. The word '*respect*' is the only suitable expression for the esteem that a rational being must necessarily feel for such lawgiving. *Autonomy* is thus the basis of the dignity of human nature and of every rational nature.

37. [Summary of the Formulations]

Our three ways of presenting the principle of morality are basically only so many formulations of precisely the same law, each one of them by itself uniting the other two within it. There is nevertheless a difference among them, which, however, is more subjectively than objectively practical: that is to say, the different formulations aim to bring an Idea of reason closer to intuition (by means of a certain analogy) and thus nearer to feeling. All maxims have:

1. A *form*, which consists in universality; and in this respect the formula of the moral imperative is expressed thus: 'Maxims must be chosen as if they were to hold as universal laws of nature.'
2. A *matter*—that is, an end; and in this respect the formula says: 'A rational being, as by its very nature an end and thus an end in itself, must serve every maxim as the limiting condition restricting the pursuit of all merely relative and arbitrary ends.'
3. A *complete determination* of all maxims by means of the following formula: 'All maxims which stem from autonomous lawgiving are to harmonize with a possible kingdom of ends and with a kingdom of nature.'* Progression that

---

market price and attachment price are opposed to 'inner worth' or dignity, which is 'beyond price'.

53. *Gesinnung*, disposition, mental attitude, the agent's settled state of mind or character. Also, in *Religion within the Boundaries of Mere Reason*, Kant refers to '*Gesinnung*' as a sort of basic capacity the will has to bind itself to a fundamental practical principle that privileges either morality or happiness (R 6:25). In Kant's *Anthropology* notes (Ak 7: 292), a similar idea is expressed.

---

* Teleology considers nature as a kingdom of ends, morality considers a possible kingdom of ends as a kingdom of nature. In the former, the kingdom of ends is a theoretical Idea that aims to explain what exists. In the latter, it is a practical Idea, aiming to bring about that

takes place here as elsewhere is through the categories of unity, plurality, and totality: *unity* of the form of the will (its universality); *plurality* of its matter (its objects—that is, its ends); and the totality or *all-comprehensiveness*[54] of its system of ends. It is, however, better if in moral *judgement* one proceeds always in accordance with the strict method and takes as one's basic principle the universal formula of the categorical imperative: '*Act on that maxim that can at the same time make itself into a universal law.*' If, however, we wish also to *gain a hearing* for the moral law, it is very useful to bring one and the same action under the three stated formulae and thereby, as far as possible, bring the moral law closer to intuition.

38. [Comprehensive Review]

We can now end at the point from which we began—namely, with the concept of an unconditionally good will. A *will* is *absolutely good* if it cannot be evil—that is, if its maxim, when made into a universal law, can never be in conflict with itself. This principle is therefore also its supreme law: 'Act always on that maxim whose universality as a law you can at the same time will.' This is the one principle on which a will can never be in conflict with itself, and such an imperative is categorical. Since the validity of the will, as a universal law for possible actions, is analogous to the universal connection of the existence of things under universal laws, which is the formal aspect of nature in general, we can also express the categorical imperative as follows: '*Act on maxims which can at the same time have as their object [making] themselves into universal laws of nature.*'[55] This then gives us the formula for an absolutely good will.

A rational nature distinguishes itself from others by the fact that it sets itself an end. That end would be the matter[56] for every good will. But in the idea of an absolutely good will, good without any limiting condition (the attaining of this or that end), we must abstract completely from every

which does not exist but which could actually become real through our conduct.

54. *Allheit*
55. . . . *Maxime die sich selbst zugleich als allgemeine Naturgesetze zum Gegenstande haben können.*
56. *Materie*

end that has to be *brought about* (for such an end would make any will only relatively good). Hence the proposed end must here be conceived, not as an end to be produced, *but as a self-sufficient*[57] end. It must therefore be conceived only negatively— that is, as an end which we should never act against, and consequently one which in all our willing we must never value merely as a means, but always at the same time as an end. Now this end can be nothing other than the subject of all possible ends itself, because this subject is also the subject of a will that may be absolutely good; for such a will cannot without contradiction be subordinated to any other object. The principle 'So act in relation to every rational being (both yourself and others) that this being may at the same time count in your maxim as an end in itself' is thus basically the same as the principle 'Act on a maxim which at the same time embodies in itself its own universal validity for every rational being.' For to say that, in using means to any end, I ought to restrict my maxim by the condition that it should also be universally valid as a law for every subject, is just the same as to say this: a subject of ends, i.e., a rational being itself, must be made the foundation of all maxims of action, and must thus be treated never merely as a means, but as the supreme condition restricting the use of all means—that is, always at the same time as an end.

Now from this it unquestionably follows that every rational being, as an end in itself, must be able to regard himself as also the maker of universal law in respect of any law whatever to which he may be subject; for it is precisely the fitness of his maxims to make universal law that marks him out as an end in himself. It follows equally that this dignity (or prerogative) he possesses above all merely natural beings carries with it the necessity of always choosing his maxims from the point of view of himself, but also of every other rational being (which is why they are called persons) as lawgiving beings. It is in this way that a world of rational beings (*mundus intelligibilis*) [intelligible world] is possible as a kingdom of ends—possible, that is, through the giving of their own laws by all persons as its members. Accordingly every rational being must act as if he were always by his maxims a lawgiving member in the universal

57. *Selbstständig*

kingdom of ends. The formal principle of such maxims is 'Act as if your maxims had to serve at the same time as a universal law (for all rational beings).' A kingdom of ends is thus possible only by analogy with a kingdom of nature. A kingdom of ends is possible only through maxims—that is, self-imposed rules—while nature is possible only through laws of efficient causes externally necessitated. In spite of this difference, we give to nature as a whole, even though it is regarded as a machine, the name of a 'kingdom of nature' so far as and because rational beings are its ends. Now a kingdom of ends would actually come into existence through maxims whose rule the categorical imperative prescribes for all rational beings, *if these maxims were universally followed*. Yet even if a rational being were himself to follow such a maxim strictly, he cannot count on everybody else therefore being faithful to the same maxim, nor can he count on the kingdom of nature and its purposive order harmonizing with him, as a fitting member, towards a kingdom of ends made possible through himself, i.e., that the kingdom of nature will favour his expectations of perfect happiness. Nevertheless the law 'Act on the maxims of a universally lawgiving member of a merely possible kingdom of ends' remains in full force, because it commands categorically. And precisely here we encounter the paradox that, without any further end or advantage to be attained by it, the mere dignity of humanity as rational nature—and consequently respect for a mere Idea—should serve as an inflexible precept for the will; and that it is just this independence from any motivations based on his expectations of perfect happiness that constitutes the sublimity of a maxim and the worthiness of every rational subject to be a lawgiving member in the kingdom of ends; for otherwise he would have to be regarded as subject only to the natural law of his own needs. Even if both the kingdom of nature and the kingdom of ends were imagined to be united under one head and thus the kingdom of ends ceased to be a mere Idea and achieved genuine reality, the Idea would indeed gain additional motivating power by this, but no increase in its inner worth. For, even if this were so, this unique and absolute lawgiver would have to be conceived as judging the worth of rational beings solely by the disinterested behaviour they prescribed to themselves from this Idea

alone. The essence of things is not changed by their external relations; and, leaving aside such relations, whatever constitutes by itself the absolute worth of human beings is that by which they must be judged—by everyone whatsoever, even by the Supreme Being. *Morality* is thus the relation of actions to the autonomy of the will—that is, to a possible universal lawgiving by means of its maxims. An action that is compatible with the autonomy of the will is *permitted*; one that does not harmonize with it is *forbidden*. A will whose maxims necessarily agree with the laws of autonomy is a *holy*, absolutely good will. The dependence of a will not absolutely good on the principle of autonomy (that is, moral necessitation) is *obligation*.[58] Obligation can thus not apply to a holy being. The objective necessity of an action out of obligation is called *duty*.[59]

From what has just been said we can now easily explain how it happens that, although the concept of duty includes the idea of a person's subjection to the law, we nevertheless attribute a certain sublimity and *dignity* to the person who fulfils all his duties. For although there is nothing sublime about him just in so far as he is *subject* to the law, there is sublimity to him in his being at the same time its *author* and being subordinated only for this reason to this very same law. We have also shown above how neither fear nor inclination, but only respect for the law, is the motivation[60] that can give an action moral worth. Our own will, provided it would act only under the condition of being able to give universal law by means of its maxims—this ideal will, which is possible for us, is the proper object of respect. The dignity of humanity consists precisely in this power of giving universal law, though only on condition of also being subject to this same lawgiving.

Autonomy of the Will: *As the Supreme Principle of Morality*

Autonomy of the will is the property the will has of being a law to itself (independently of any property of the objects of volition). Hence the

58. *Verbindlichkeit*
59. *Pflicht*
60. *Triebfeder*

principle of autonomy is 'Never choose except in such a way that the maxims of your choice are also comprehended as universal law in the same act of will.'[61] That this practical rule is an imperative, that is, that the will of every rational being is necessarily bound to the rule as a condition, cannot be proved by a mere analysis of the concepts contained in it, since it is a synthetic proposition. To prove it we would have to go beyond knowledge of objects and to a critique of the subject—that is, to a critique of pure practical reason—since this synthetic proposition, which commands apodictically, must be capable of being known entirely a priori. This task does not belong to the present chapter. However, by mere analysis of the concepts of morality we can quite well show that the above principle of autonomy is the sole principle of ethics. For analysis discloses that the principle of morality must be a categorical imperative, and that the imperative in turn commands nothing neither more nor less than precisely this autonomy of the will.

Heteronomy of the Will: *As the Source of all Spurious Principles of Morality*

If the will seeks the law that is to determine it *anywhere else* than in the fitness of its maxims for its own giving of universal law, and if therefore it goes outside itself and seeks this law in a property of any of its objects—the result is always *heteronomy*. In that case the will does not give itself the law; rather, the object gives the law to it, in virtue of its relation to the will. This relation, whether based on inclination or on rational ideas, can give rise only to hypothetical imperatives: 'I ought to do something *because I want something else*'. As against this, the moral, and therefore categorical imperative, says, 'I ought to act thus or thus, even though I did not want anything else.' For example, the first says 'I ought not to lie if I want to maintain my reputation' while the second says 'I ought not to lie even if it would not bring me the slightest disgrace.' The second imperative must therefore leave out of consideration all objects to this extent; that they have no *influence* at all on the will, so that practical reason

(the will) may not merely administer some alien interest but may simply manifest its own sovereign authority as the supreme legislation. Thus, for example, the reason why I ought to promote the happiness of others is not because the realization of their happiness concerns me (whether because of direct inclination or on account of some satisfaction gained indirectly through reason,) but simply because a maxim that excludes this cannot be included as a universal law in one and the same act of will.

Classification of all Possible Principles of Morality based on Heteronomy as their Assumed Foundation

Here, as everywhere else in the pure use of reason—so long as a critique of it is lacking—human reason tries every possible wrong way before it succeeds in finding the only true way.

All the principles that can be adopted from this point of view are either *empirical* or *rational*. Principles of the *first* kind, drawn from the principle of *perfect happiness*,[62] are built on either physical or moral, feeling. Principles of the *second* kind, drawn from the principle of *perfection*, are built either on the rational concept of perfection as a possible effect of our will or on the concept of an independently existing perfection (God's will) as a determining cause of our will.

39. [Special Problems with Previous Empiricist Principles]

Empirical principles are never fit to serve as a foundation for moral laws. For the universality with which these laws must hold for all rational beings without exception—the unconditioned practical necessity that they thus impose—is lost if their basis is taken from the *particular constitution of human nature* or from the accidental circumstances in which it is placed. The principle of *one's own perfect happiness* is, however, the most objectionable, not just because it is false and because its claim that well-being always adjusts itself to well-doing is contradicted by experience; nor merely because it contributes nothing whatever towards

---

61. *in demselben Wollen*

62. *Glückseligkeit*

establishing morality, since making people happy is quite different from making them good, and making them prudent or clever in seeking their own advantage is quite different from making them virtuous. It is most objectionable because by basing morality on sensuous motives which undermine it and totally destroy its sublimity, since it puts the motives of virtue in the same class as those of vice and teaches us only to become better at calculation, the specific difference between virtue and vice is completely obliterated. On the other hand, moral feeling, this alleged special sense* (however shallow be the appeal to it, when people who are unable to *think* hope to help themselves out by *feeling*, even when the question is solely one of universal law, and however little feelings, differing as they naturally do from one another by an infinity of degrees, can supply a uniform measure of good and evil—let alone the fact that one person by his feeling can make no valid judgements at all for others)—moral feeling still remains closer to morality and to its dignity in this respect: it does virtue the honour of ascribing to her *directly* the approval and esteem in which she is held, and does not, as it were, tell her to her face that we are attached to her, not for her beauty, but only for our own advantage.

40. [Special Problems with Previous Rationalist Principles]

Among the *rational* or reason-based foundations of morality, the ontological concept of *perfection*[63] is better than the theological concept that derives morality from a divine and supremely perfect will. It is of course empty, indefinite, and consequently useless for discovering in the boundless field of possible reality, the greatest sum

---

* I classify the principle of moral feeling with that of happiness because every empirical principle promises a contribution to our well-being merely from the satisfaction that something leads us to expect—whether this satisfaction occurs directly and without any consideration of advantage or with a view to such advantage. Similarly we must, with *Hutcheson*,** classify the principle of sympathy for the happiness of others with the principle of moral sense which he assumed. [**Ed. note: The Scottish philosopher Francis Hutcheson (1694–1746).]

63. *Volkommenheit*

which is appropriate to us; and, in trying to distinguish specifically between the reality here in question from every other reality, it inevitably tends to move in a circle and cannot avoid tacitly presupposing the morality it is meant to explain. Still, it is better than the theological concept, which derives morality from an all-perfect, divine will, not merely because we cannot directly apprehend[64] God's perfection and can only derive it from our own concepts, among which that of morality is pre-eminent; but because, if we do not do this (and to do it would be to give a grossly circular explanation), the concept of God's will that remains for us is made up of such attributes as lust for glory and dominion, bound up with frightful ideas of power and vengefulness—inevitably the foundation for a moral system that would be directly opposed to morality.

Yet if I had to choose between the concept of moral sense and that of perfection in general (both of which at least do not undermine morality, though they are totally unfit to support it as its foundation), I should decide for the latter. For this, since it at least withdraws the decision of this question from sensibility and brings it before the court of pure reason, even though it there decides nothing, does still preserve undistorted the indeterminate Idea (of a will good in itself) for more precise definition.

41. [The General Problem with All Principles of Heteronomy]

For the rest I believe I may be excused from a lengthy refutation of all these systems. This is so easy and is presumably so well understood even by those whose office requires them to declare themselves for one or other of these theories (since their audience will not lightly put up with a suspension of judgement) that to spend time on it would be merely superfluous labour. But what is of more interest to us here is to know that these principles never lay down anything but heteronomy as the first basis of morality and must in consequence necessarily fail in their objective.

Whenever an object of the will has to be assumed as prescribing the rule that is to determine the will, the rule is nothing but heteronomy.

---

64. *anschauen*

The imperative is then conditional: '*If*, or *because* one wants this object, one ought to act thus or thus'. Consequently this imperative can never command morally, that is, categorically. In whatever way the object determines the will—whether by means of inclination, as in the principle of one's own perfect happiness, or by means of reason directed to objects of our possible volitions generally, as in the principle of perfection—the will in these cases never determines itself *directly* by the thought of an action, but only by the motivation which the anticipated effect of the action exercises on the will: '*I ought to do something because I want something else*'.[65] And the basis for this imperative must be the assumption of yet another law in my person, whereby I necessarily will[66] this 'something else'—and this law in turn requires an imperative to limit this maxim. Because the idea of an object commensurate to our own powers stimulates in the will of the subject an impulse in accordance with our natural constitution, this impulse belongs to the nature of the subject, whether to sensibility, (i.e., inclinations and taste,) or to understanding and reason, whose operation on an object is accompanied by delight due to the particular constitution of their nature. Strictly speaking, therefore, it is nature that would prescribe the law. This law, as a law of nature, not only must be known and proved by experience and therefore is in itself contingent and consequently unfitted to serve as an apodictic rule of action such as a moral rule must be, but it is *always merely heteronomy of the will*: The will would not prescribe the law to itself, but an alien stimulus would do so through the medium of the subject's own nature which is attuned to receive it.

42. [What Remains to Be Established]

An absolutely good will, whose principle must be a categorical imperative, will therefore be undetermined with respect to all objects and will contain only the *form* of *willing* in general and that form is autonomy. In other words, the fitness of the maxim of every good will to make itself a universal law is itself the sole law that the will of every rational being spontaneously imposes on

itself without requiring any incentive[67] or interest for support.

How such a synthetic practical proposition is possible a priori and why it is necessary—that is a problem whose solution does not lie within the boundaries of the metaphysics of morals; nor have we claimed it to be true or, still less, pretended to have a proof of it in our power. We have merely shown by developing the generally accepted concept of morality that autonomy of the will is unavoidably bound up with it or rather is its very foundation. Whoever therefore takes morality to be something real and not merely an illusory idea that lacks truth, must at the same time admit its principle, which we have presented here. This chapter, consequently, like the first, has been merely analytical. To prove that morality is not a mere phantom of the brain—a conclusion that follows if the categorical imperative, and with it the autonomy of the will is true and is absolutely necessary as an a priori principle—requires a *possible synthetic use of pure practical reason*. But we cannot venture on this synthetic use of reason without prefacing it by a *critique* of this faculty of reason itself. In our final chapter we outline, sufficiently for our purpose, the main features of such a critique.

Chapter Three. Final Step from a Metaphysics of Morals to a Critique of Pure Practical Reason

The Concept of Freedom is the Key to Explain Autonomy of the Will

The will is a kind of causality that living beings have so far as they are rational. *Freedom* would then be that property whereby this causality can be active, independently of alien causes *determining* it; just as *natural necessity* is a property characterizing the causality of all non-rational beings—the property of being determined to activity by the influence of alien causes.

The above definition of freedom is *negative* and therefore sterile when it comes to grasping freedom's essence; but a *positive* concept springs from it, which is richer and more fruitful. Since the

65. *weil ich etwas anderes will*
66. or want, *will*

67. *Triebfeder*

concept of causality carries with it that of *laws*, implying that because of something we call a cause, something else—namely, its effect—must be posited,[68] so freedom, although it is not a property the will has by virtue of natural laws, is not for that reason totally lawless. Freedom must rather be a causality that accords with immutable laws, though laws of a special kind; for otherwise a free will would be a fiction. Natural necessity, as we have seen, is a heteronomy of efficient causes; for we saw that every effect was only possible according to the law that something else gets the efficient cause to act as a cause. What else then can freedom of will be but autonomy—that is, the property that a will has of being a law to itself? However, the proposition 'Will is in all its actions a law to itself' expresses only the principle of acting on no other maxim than one that can also have being itself a universal law for its object. But this is precisely the formula of the Categorical Imperative and the principle of morality. Thus a free will and a will under moral laws are one and the same.

Consequently if freedom of the will is presupposed, then morality, together with its principle, follows from this presupposition by mere analysis of its concept. Nevertheless the principle of morality is still a synthetic proposition, namely: An absolutely good will is one whose maxim can always include itself considered as a universal law; for this characteristic of its maxim cannot be discovered by analysis of the concept of an absolutely good will. Such synthetic propositions are however possible only if two cognitions are bound together by their connection with a third in which both of them are to be found. The *positive* concept of freedom supplies this third cognition, which cannot, as is the case with physical causes, be the nature of the sensible world (in the concept of which the concepts of something as a cause in relation to *something else* as effect come together). What this third cognition is, to which freedom directs us and of which we have an Idea a priori, cannot yet be shown here; nor can we as yet make comprehensible the deduction of the concept of freedom from pure practical reason and so the possibility of a categorical imperative. Some further preparation is needed.

1. Freedom Must be Presupposed as a Property of the Will of all Rational Beings

It is not enough to ascribe freedom to our will, on whatever basis unless we have sufficient reason to attribute the same freedom to all rational beings. For since morality serves as a law for us only insofar as we are *rational beings*, it must be equally valid for all rational beings; and since it must be derived solely from the property of freedom, we need to prove that freedom too is a property of the will of all rational beings. And it is not enough to demonstrate freedom by appeal to certain alleged experiences of human nature (though to demonstrate freedom in this way is in any case absolutely impossible—it can be demonstrated only a priori). Rather, we must prove that freedom belongs universally to the activity of rational beings endowed with a will. Now I say that every being who cannot act except *under the Idea of freedom* is just for that reason really free—from the standpoint of practice. That is to say, all laws inseparably bound up with freedom are valid for such a being just as if his will could be proved to be free in itself and by means of proofs taken from theoretical philosophy.* I maintain too that we must necessarily grant the idea of freedom to every rational being who has a will, since only under that idea can such a being act. For we think of such a being as having a power of reason that is practical, i.e., that has causality in regard to its aims.[69] But it is impossible to conceive of a power of reason that consciously regards its own judgements as directed from outside; for in that case the subject would attribute the determination of his power of judgement to some impulse, not to his reason. Reason must regard itself as the author of its own principles independently of alien influences. It follows that reason, as practical reason, or as the will of a rational being, must regard itself as

---

* I use this approach here because I take it as sufficient for our purpose if all rational beings in their actions presuppose freedom merely *as an Idea*. Thus I avoid having to prove freedom also from a theoretical point of view. For even if this latter problem is left unsettled, the laws that would obligate a being who was really free are equally valid for a being who cannot act except under the Idea of his own freedom. In this way we can escape from the burden that weighs upon the theory.

68. *gesetzt*

69. *Objekte*

free. That is to say, the will of a rational being can be a will of its own only under the idea of freedom, and it must therefore—for purposes of action[70]—be attributed to all rational beings.

2. Of the Interest Attached to the Ideas of Morality

43. [The Apparently Circular Reasoning]

We have at last traced the distinct concept of morality back to the Idea of freedom, but we could not demonstrate freedom as something real in human nature nor even in ourselves. We saw only that we must presuppose it if we want to conceive a being as rational and as endowed with consciousness of his causality in regard to actions—that is, as endowed with a will. Thus we find that on precisely the same grounds we must attribute to every being endowed with reason and a will this property of determining himself to action under the Idea of his freedom.

From the presupposition of this Idea there sprang also, as we saw, the consciousness of a law governing action, the law that subjective principles of action—that is, maxims—must always be so chosen that they can also hold as objective principles—that is, universally—and can there fore serve for our own enactment of universal law. But why should I subject myself to this principle simply as a rational being and in so doing also subject to it every other being endowed with reason? I am willing to admit that no interest *drives* me to do so, since that would not produce a categorical imperative. Yet I must necessarily *take* an interest in it and understand how this happens; for this 'I ought to' is actually an 'I intend to'[71] that would hold necessarily for every rational being—if reason in him were practical without hindrance. For beings like us, who are affected also by the senses—that is, by motives of a different kind—and who do not always act as reason by itself would act, this necessity of action is only an 'ought' and the subjective necessity is distinguished from the objective.

It thus looks as though we have in fact merely presupposed the moral law in our Idea of free-

dom—that is, presupposed the principle of the autonomy of the will itself—without being able to give an independent proof of its reality and objective necessity. But in that case we would still have gained something quite considerable, since we would at least have formulated the genuine principle more precisely than has been done before. However, we would have made no progress at all with proving the principle's validity and the practical necessity of subjecting ourselves to it. For if someone asks us: Why must the universal validity of our maxim as a law be the condition that restricts our action, and what is the basis of the worth we ascribe to this way of acting—a worth supposedly so great that there cannot be any interest higher than it—and asks how it happens that human beings believe this alone to be the source of their personal worth, in contrast to which the worth of a pleasant or painful condition counts as nothing? To these questions we could give no sufficient answer.

We do indeed find that we can take an interest in a personal characteristic that involves no interest in any condition, but only if that characteristic makes us fit to share in the latter condition in case reason were to determine its distribution. That is to say, the mere fact of deserving to be happy, even without the motive of sharing in this happiness, can by itself interest us. But such a judgement is in fact merely the result of the importance we have already assumed moral laws to have (when by means of the Idea of freedom we detach ourselves from every empirical interest). But we cannot as yet see why we ought to detach ourselves from such interest—that is, why we ought to regard ourselves as free in our actions and yet bound by certain laws, in order to find solely in our own person a worth that can compensate us for the loss of everything that makes our condition valuable. We do not see how this is possible nor consequently *on what grounds the moral law can be binding.*

We must frankly admit that a kind of circle shows up here, from which there seems to be no escape. We suppose ourselves to be free in the order of efficient causes in order that we may conceive ourselves to be under moral laws in the order of ends; and then we proceed to think of ourselves as subject to moral laws on the ground that we have ascribed freedom of will to ourselves.

70. *in praktischer Absicht*
71. It is difficult to render Kant's phrase naturally in English, retaining his nice rhyme: *dieses Sollen ist eigentlich ein Wollen.*

For freedom and the will's lawgiving of its own laws are both autonomy, and therefore reciprocal concepts. But just for this reason one of them cannot be used to explain the other or to furnish its ground. It can at most be used for the logical purpose of reducing seemingly different ideas of the same object to a single concept (as different fractions of the same value can be reduced to the lowest common terms).

44. [The Solution: Two Perspectives on Human Agency]

One route, however, still remains open to us. We can inquire whether we do not take one standpoint when, through freedom, we think of ourselves as causes acting a priori, and another standpoint when we contemplate ourselves in the light of our actions as effects that we see before our eyes.

A remark that does not require any subtle reflection and that we may assume even the most ordinary intelligence can make—no doubt in its own way, by some obscure distinction in the power of judgement that it calls 'feeling', is this: all ideas that come to us involuntarily (as do those of the senses) allow us to know objects only as they affect us: what those objects may be in themselves remains unknown. Consequently, ideas of this kind, no matter how strenuously the understanding attempts to exert focus and clarity on them, serve only to give us knowledge of *appearances*, never of *things in themselves*. Once this distinction is drawn (it may be merely by noting the difference between ideas given to us from without, where we ourselves are passive, and ideas which we produce entirely from ourselves, ideas that therefore manifest our own activity), it follows directly that behind appearances we must admit and assume something else which is not appearance—namely, things in themselves. Since we can never be acquainted with these, but only with the way in which they affect us, we must however resign ourselves to the fact that we can never get any nearer to them and can never know what they are in themselves. This thought must yield a distinction, however rough, between a *sensible world* and the *intelligible world*, the first of which can vary a great deal because of differences in sensibility among different observers, while the

second, which is its foundation, always remains the same. Even as regards himself—so far as a human being is acquainted with himself by inner sensation—he has no right to claim to know what he is in himself. For since he does not as it were create himself, and since he acquires his concept of himself not a priori but empirically, it is natural that he can get information even about himself only through inner sense and so only through the way his nature appears and the way his consciousness is affected. Beyond this constitution of himself as a subject, compounded of nothing but appearances, he must assume that there is something else that is its foundation—namely, his ego,[72] however it may be constituted in itself. Thus, as far as mere perception and the capacity for receiving sensations are concerned, he must count himself as belonging to the *world of sense*, but as regards whatever pure activity there may be in him (whatever reaches consciousness directly and not by affecting the senses), he must count himself as belonging to the *intellectual world*. Of that world, however, he knows nothing more.

A reflective human being must reach a conclusion of this kind about all things that may present themselves to him. Such a conclusion is presumably to be found even in the most common understanding, which, as is well known, is always inclined to look behind the objects of the senses for something further that is invisible and is spontaneously active. But such an understanding goes on to spoil this invisible something by immediately trying to make it into something sensible—that is to say, it wants to make it an object of intuition, so by this procedure the common understanding does not become the least bit wiser.

Now, a human being actually finds in himself a power by which he distinguishes himself from all other things—and even from himself so far as he is affected by objects. That power is *reason*. As pure spontaneity, reason is elevated even above the *understanding* in the following respect: although the latter too is spontaneous activity and is not, like sense, confined to ideas that arise only when we are affected by things (and therefore are passive), it can produce by its own activity only concepts whose sole purpose is *to bring sensuous representations under rules* and so to unite them in

72. *sein Ich*

one consciousness. Without using sensibility, the understanding would think nothing at all. Reason, on the other hand—in what are called 'Ideas'—shows a spontaneity so pure that it goes far beyond anything sensibility can offer. It manifests its highest function in distinguishing the world of sense from the intelligible world and thereby prescribing limits to the understanding itself.

Because of this a rational being must regard himself, *as an intelligence* (i.e., not from the perspective of his lower powers), as belonging to the world of the understanding rather than the world of sense. Consequently he has two perspectives from which he can consider himself and from which he can acknowledge the laws governing the use of his powers and consequently governing all his actions. He can consider himself *first* so far as he belongs to the world of sense, under laws of nature (heteronomy); and *secondly*—so far as he belongs to the intelligible world—under laws that are not empirical but, being independent of nature, are founded on reason alone.

As a rational being, and consequently as a being who belongs to the intelligible world, a human being can never conceive the causality of his own will except under the Idea of freedom; for independence from the determining causes of the sensible world (and this is what reason must always ascribe to itself) is freedom. To the Idea of freedom there is inseparably attached the concept of *autonomy*, but to the latter in turn the universal principle of morality—a principle which ideally is the ground of all the actions of *rational* beings, just as the law of nature is the ground of all appearances.

We have now removed the suspicion which we raised earlier, namely, that there might be a hidden circle in our reasoning from freedom to autonomy and from autonomy to the moral law, the suspicion that in effect we had perhaps assumed the Idea of freedom only because of the moral law in order later to derive the moral law from freedom; and that we were thus unable to offer any ground at all for the moral law, but had merely begged the question by putting forward a principle which well-meaning souls would gladly concede us, but never as a demonstrable proposition. We see now that when we think of ourselves as free, we transfer ourselves into the world of the understanding as members and we recognize the autonomy of the will together with its consequence, morality; whereas when we think of ourselves as under obligation, we view ourselves as belonging to the world of sense and yet simultaneously to the world of understanding.

3. How Is a Categorical Imperative Possible?

As an intelligence, a rational being counts himself as belonging to the world of the understanding, and simply as an efficient cause belonging to that world, he calls his causality a *will*. On the other hand, however, he is also conscious of himself as a part of the world of sense, where his actions are encountered as mere appearances of that causality. But we can have no insight into how these actions are possible by means of such a causality, since we have no direct acquaintance with it. Instead, these actions, when viewed as belonging to the world of sense, have to be understood as determined by other appearances—namely, by desires and inclinations. Hence, if I were solely a member of the world of understanding, all my actions would conform perfectly to the principle of the autonomy of a pure will; if I were solely a part of the sensible world, they would have to be taken as conforming completely to the natural law of desires and inclinations, consequently to the heteronomy of nature. (In the first case they would rest on the supreme principle of morality; in the second case on that of happiness.) But since *the world of understanding contains the ground of the world of sense and therefore also of its laws*, it thus gives laws directly to my will (which belongs entirely to the world of understanding) and must be conceived as thus lawgiving. Therefore, although I regard myself from one point of view as a being that belongs to the world of sense, I shall have to recognize that, as an intelligence, I am subject to the law of the world of understanding—that is, of reason, which contains this law in the Idea of freedom, and thus in the autonomy of the will. I must therefore regard the laws of the world of the understanding as imperatives for me and see the actions that conform to this principle as duties.

And thus categorical imperatives are possible, because the Idea of freedom makes me a member of an intelligible world. If I were only that, then all my actions *would* thereby invariably be in accord with the autonomy of the will. But since I see myself at the same time as a member of the world of sense, my actions *ought* to be in accord with it. This *categorical* 'ought' presents us with a synthetic a priori proposition, since to my will as affected by sensuous desires there is added the Idea of that same will, viewed, however, as a pure will belonging to the world of understanding and active of its own accord—a will which, according to reason, contains the supreme condition of the former, my sensuously affected will. This is similar to the way in which concepts of the understanding, which by themselves signify nothing but lawful form in general, are added to intuitions of the world of sense and so make possible synthetic a priori propositions on which all knowledge of nature is based.

The use of common human reason in matters of conduct confirms the correctness of this deduction. There is no one, not even the most malicious villain, provided only that he is otherwise accustomed to use reason, who, when presented with examples of honesty of purpose, of faithfulness to good maxims, of sympathy, and of general benevolence even when requiring great sacrifice of advantages and comfort, does not wish that he too might have these qualities. He cannot bring this about in himself, only because of his desires and impulses, but at the same time he wishes he could be free from these burdensome inclinations. By such a wish he proves that with a will free from sensuous impulses he transfers himself in thought into an order of things altogether different from that of his desires in the field of sensibility. For he cannot expect that the fulfillment of this wish would gratify any of his sensuous desires, nor that any of his actual or even conceivable inclinations will be satisfied (since such an expectation would cause the very Idea that elicited the wish to forfeit its excellence). All he can expect is a greater inner worth of his own person. He believes himself to be this better person when he transfers himself to the standpoint of a member of the world of understanding. It is the Idea of freedom that involuntarily constrains him to do this—that is, the Idea of being independent of *determining* causes of the world of sense; and from this standpoint he is conscious of possessing a good will

which, on his own admission, constitutes the law for his evil will as a member of the world of sense—a law of whose authority he is conscious even while transgressing it. The moral 'I ought' is thus his own necessary 'I will' as a member of the intelligible world; and he thinks of it as an 'I ought' only insofar as he regards himself at the same time to be a member of the world of sense.

4. The Extreme Limit of Practical Philosophy

45. [The Apparent Contradiction between Free Will and Natural Necessity]

All human beings think of themselves as having free will. That is the basis of all the judgements of actions that say they *ought to have been done*, although they *were not done*. But this freedom is not an empirical concept, nor can it be, since it still holds although experience shows the contrary of those requirements that are viewed as necessary under the presupposition of freedom. On the other hand, it is equally necessary that everything that takes place should be inexorably determined in accordance with the laws of nature; and this necessity of nature is likewise not an empirical concept, precisely because it carries with it the concept of necessity and thus the concept of an a priori cognition. This concept of a system of nature[73] is, however, confirmed by experience and must unavoidably be presupposed if experience—that is, coherent knowledge of sensible objects in accordance with universal laws—is to be possible. Hence, while freedom is only an Idea of Reason whose objective reality is in itself questionable, nature is a *concept of the understanding*, which proves, and must necessarily prove, its reality in examples from experience.

From this there arises a dialectic of reason, since the freedom ascribed to the will seems to contradict the necessity of nature. Although at this parting of the ways reason, for *cognitive*[74] purposes, finds the path of natural necessity much more beaten and serviceable than that of freedom, yet for *purposes of action*[75] the footpath of

73. *eine Natur*
74. *spekulativer Absicht*
75. *in praktischer Absicht*

freedom is the only one on which we can make use of our reason in our conduct. Hence it is as impossible for the subtlest philosophy as it is for the most common human reason to argue freedom away. Philosophy must therefore presuppose that no genuine contradiction will be found between freedom and natural necessity ascribed to the very same human actions, for it cannot give up the concept of nature any more than that of freedom.

46. [Resolution Sought in the Two Perspectives]

All the same, even if we should never be able to grasp how freedom is possible, this seeming contradiction must at least be eradicated convincingly. For if even the thought of freedom contradicts itself or contradicts nature—a concept which is equally necessary—freedom would have to be given up altogether in favour of natural necessity.

It would be impossible to escape from this contradiction if the subject who believes himself free thought of himself *in the same sense*, or *in precisely the same relationship*, when he calls himself free as when he assumes that in the same action he is subject to the law of nature. Hence speculative philosophy has the unavoidable task of showing at least that its illusion about the contradiction rests on our thinking of the human being in one sense and relation when we call him free and in another when we consider him, as a part of nature, to be subject to nature's laws. And philosophy must show not merely that both characteristics *can* very well coexist, but that they must be thought of as *necessarily united* in one and the same subject. For otherwise we could not explain why we should burden reason with an Idea which—even if it can *without contradiction* be united with another concept that has been adequately justified—entangles us in a perplexity that sorely embarrasses reason in its theoretical use. This duty is imposed on speculative philosophy only in order that it may clear a path for practical philosophy. Thus philosophers have no choice as to whether they will remove the seeming contradiction or leave it untouched; for in the latter case the theory on this topic would be *bonum vacans* [unoccupied property—a good that belongs to no

one], of which the fatalist can justifiably take possession and can chase all of morality out of its supposed property, which it has no title to hold.

Nevertheless we cannot yet say that at this point the boundary of practical philosophy begins. For the settlement of this controversy is not part of practical philosophy, which merely requires speculative reason to bring to an end the dissension in which it is entangled on theoretical questions, so that practical reason may have peace and security from external attacks which could contest its right to the ground on which it seeks to build.

The legitimate title to freedom of the will claimed even by common human reason is grounded on the consciousness and the accepted presupposition that reason is independent of purely subjective determining causes which collectively make up all that belongs to sensation and comes under the general name of sensibility. In thus regarding himself as an intelligence, a human being puts himself into another order of things, and into relation with determining causes of quite another sort, when he thinks of himself as an intelligence endowed with a will and consequently with causality, than he does when he perceives himself as a phenomenon (which he actually is as well) in the world of sense, and sees his causality as the result of external determination in accordance with laws of nature. He then soon realizes that both of these can, and indeed must, take place at the same time. For there is not the slightest contradiction in holding that a thing *as an appearance* (as belonging to the world of sense) is subject to certain laws, laws of which it is independent *as a thing* or a being *in itself*. That he must think and conceive of himself in this twofold way rests, as regards the first way, on the consciousness of himself as an object affected through the senses; as concerns the second way, it rests on the consciousness of himself as an intelligence—that is, as independent of sensible impressions in his use of reason (and so as belonging to the world of understanding).

This is why the human being claims for himself a will that does not allow him to be accountable for anything that belongs merely to his desires and inclinations. Rather, he conceives of actions that can be done only by disregarding all desires and incitements of sense as possible—indeed as necessary—through this will. The causality of such actions lies in him as intelligence and in the laws of effects and actions according to the principles of an intelligible world. Of that world he knows nothing but this—that in that intelligible world, reason alone, and indeed pure reason independent of sensibility, is the source of law; and also that since in that world he is his true self, an intelligence only (while as a human being he is merely an appearance of himself), these laws apply to him directly and categorically. It follows that what desires and impulses (and therefore the whole nature of the sensible world) spur him to do cannot impair the laws of his will as intelligence. Indeed he does not even hold himself responsible for those desires and impulses nor impute them to his true self, that is, to his will, though he does impute to himself the indulgence he would show them if he were to let them influence his maxims to the detriment of the rational laws of his will.

47. [The Limits of What We Can Know and Explain: The Intelligible World, Freedom, and Interest in Morality]

Practical reason does not overstep its limits in the least by *thinking* itself into the world of understanding. It would do so only if it sought to *inspect [hineinschauen]* or *feel* itself into that world. That thinking is a merely negative thought—that the world of sense gives reason no laws for determining the will. It is a positive thought only in one point: that that freedom, as a negative characteristic, is combined with a (positive) power as well—a causality of reason we call a will—the power to act so that the principle of our actions accords with the essential character of a rational cause, that is, with the condition that the maxim of these actions have the universal validity of a law. But if practical reason were also to take from the intelligible world *an object of the will*, that is, a motivating cause of action, it would overstep its limits and pretend to be acquainted with something of which it knows nothing. The concept of a world of understanding is thus only a *standpoint* that reason finds itself constrained to adopt outside of appearances, *in order to think of itself as practical*. If the influences of sensibility were determining for human beings, this would be impossible. It is nev-

ertheless necessary unless the human being is to be denied the consciousness of himself as an intelligence and consequently as a rational and rationally active cause—that is, a cause that is free in its operation. This thought certainly brings on the Idea of another order and another lawgiving than that of the mechanism of nature, which applies to the world of sense. It makes necessary the concept of an intelligible world (that is, the concept of the totality of rational beings as things in themselves) but it makes not the slightest pretence of doing more than to conceive of such a world with respect to its *formal* condition—that is, as conforming to the condition that the maxim of the will should have the universality of a law, and so as conforming to the autonomy of the will, which alone is compatible with its freedom. In contrast with this, all laws determined by reference to an object give us heteronomy, which can be found only in laws of nature and can apply only to the world of sense.

But reason would overstep all its limits if it took it upon itself to *explain how* pure reason can be practical. This would be exactly the same task as explaining *how freedom is possible*.

For we cannot explain anything unless we can bring it under laws whose object can be given in some possible experience. Freedom, however, is a mere Idea: its objective reality can in no way be exhibited according to laws of nature nor, consequently, in any possible experience. And since no example can ever illustrate it even by analogy, we can have no full comprehension or insight into the Idea of freedom. It holds only as a necessary presupposition of reason in a being that believes itself to be conscious of a will—that is, of a power distinct from the mere faculty of desire (a power, namely, of determining itself to act as intelligence and consequently to act in accordance with laws of reason independently of natural instincts). But where determination by laws of nature comes to an end, all *explanation* comes to an end as well. Nothing remains but *defence*—that is, to repulse the objections of those who pretend to have seen more deeply into the essence of things and therefore boldly declare freedom to be impossible. We can only show them that the contradiction they pretend to have discovered in it consists just in this: in order to make the law of nature apply validly to human actions, they must necessarily consider the human being as an appearance; and now that they are asked to think of him as an intelligence and also as a thing in himself, they persist in looking at him as an appearance in this respect also. In that case, admittedly, to exempt the human being's causality (that is, his will) from all the natural laws of the sensible world, in one and the same subject, would yield a contradiction. But that contradiction would fall away if they were willing to reflect and to admit, as is only fair, that behind appearances there must lie things in themselves as their hidden ground, and that we cannot expect the laws by which things in themselves act to be identical with those laws that govern their appearances.

The subjective impossibility of explaining the freedom of the will is one and the same as the impossibility of locating and making comprehensible an *interest** that a human being can take in moral laws; and yet he does really take such an interest. We call the foundation in us of this interest "moral feeling"—a feeling that has been mistakenly taken by some people to be the standard for our moral judgement. It ought to be regarded rather as the *subjective* effect exercised on our will by the law. It is reason alone that supplies the objective grounds for that law.

In order to will actions that reason by itself prescribes to a rational, yet sensuously affected being as what he ought to do, it is certainly necessary that reason should have a power of *infusing a feeling of pleasure* or a feeling of satisfaction in the fulfilment of duty, and consequently that it should possess a kind of causality by which it can deter-

---

* An interest is that by which reason becomes practical—that is, becomes a cause determining the will. Therefore only of a rational being can one say that he takes an interest in something: non-rational creatures feel only sensuous impulses. Reason takes a direct interest in an action only when the universal validity of the maxim of the action is a ground sufficient to determine the will. Only such an interest is pure. If reason can motivate the will only by means of some further object of desire or under the presupposition of some special feeling in the subject, then it takes only an indirect interest in the action; and since reason all by itself, without the help of experience, can discover neither objects of the will nor a special feeling underlying the will, the latter interest would be merely empirical, and not a pure rational interest. The logical interest of reason (interest in furthering its insights) is never direct, but presupposes purposes for its use.

mine sensibility in accordance with rational principles. It is, however, wholly impossible to comprehend—that is, to make intelligible a priori—how a mere thought containing nothing sensible in itself can bring about a sensation of pleasure or displeasure; for there is here a special kind of causality, and—as with all causality—we are totally unable to determine its character a priori. For any knowledge of such a causality, we must consult experience alone. But experience cannot provide us with a relation of cause and effect except between two objects of experience—whereas here pure reason by means of mere Ideas (which furnish absolutely no objects for experience) has to be the cause of an effect admittedly found in experience. Hence for us human beings it is wholly impossible to explain how and why the *universality of a maxim as a law*—and therefore morality—should interest us. This much only is certain: the law is not valid for us *because it interests us* (for this is heteronomy and makes practical reason dependent on sensibility—that is to say, on an underlying feeling—in which case practical reason could never give us moral laws). The law interests us because it is valid for us as human beings in virtue of having sprung from our will as intelligence and so from our true self. *But what belongs to mere appearance is necessarily subordinated by reason to the character of the thing in itself.*

48. [Review]

Thus the question 'How is a categorical imperative possible?' can be answered to this extent: We can supply the sole presupposition under which it is possible—namely, the Idea of freedom—and we can discern the necessity of this presupposition. This is sufficient for the *practical use* of reason—that is, to convince us of the *validity of this imperative*, and so too of the moral law. But human reason will forever lack insight into how this presupposition itself is possible. On the presupposition that the will of an intelligence is free, its *autonomy* follows necessarily as the formal condition under which alone it can be determined. It is not only perfectly *possible* to presuppose such freedom of the will (as speculative philosophy can prove, and without contradicting the principle that natural necessity governs the interconnection of appearances in the world of sense); it is also

198 Chapter VI Kant: Freedom as Autonomy

unconditionally *necessary*, that is, necessary in Idea that a rational being conscious of exercising his causality by means of reason and so of having a will (which is distinct from desires) should take such freedom as the fundamental condition of all his voluntary actions. But *how* pure reason can be practical by itself without any further motives drawn from some other source; that is, how the bare principle of *the universal validity of all its maxims as laws* (which would certainly be the form of a pure practical reason) can by itself—without any material (or object) of the will in which we might take some prior interest—how pure reason can supply a motive and create an interest which could be called purely *moral*; or, in other words, *how pure reason can be practical*—all human reason is totally incapable of explaining this, and all the pains and labour to seek such an explanation are wasted.

It is precisely the same as if I sought to fathom how freedom itself as the causality of a will is possible. For in doing this I would abandon the philosophical basis of explanation, and I have no other. I could, no doubt, proceed to daydream in the intelligible world, which still remains to me— the world of intelligences; but although I have a well-founded *Idea* of it, I have not the slightest *knowledge* of it and cannot hope to arrive at any by all the efforts of my natural power of reason. My Idea of this intelligible world signifies only a 'something' that remains when I have excluded from the grounds determining my will everything that belongs to the world of sense; its sole purpose is to restrict the principle of motivating causes [*Bewegursachen*] from the field of sensibility, by setting bounds to this field and by showing that it does not encompass absolutely everything within itself, but that there is still more beyond it; yet with this 'more' I have no further acquaintance. All that remains for me of the pure reason that formulates this ideal, after I have excluded all material—that is, all knowledge of objects—from it, is its form: the practical law that maxims should be universally valid, plus the corresponding conception of reason, in its relation to a purely intelligible world, as a possible efficient cause, that is, as a cause determining the will. Here the sensuous motive [*Triebfeder*] must be entirely absent; for this Idea of an intelligible world would itself have to be the motive or that in which reason took a

direct interest. But to make this comprehensible is precisely the problem that we cannot solve.

Here then is the supreme limit of all moral inquiry. To define it is of great importance so that reason may not, on the one hand, hunt around in the sensible world, to the detriment of morality, for the supreme motive and for some comprehensible but empirical interest; and so that it will not, on the other hand, impotently flap its wings in the space (for it, an empty space) of transcendent concepts known as 'the intelligible world', flailing without moving from the spot, and thus losing itself among phantoms of the brain. For the rest, the Idea of a pure world of the understanding, as a whole of all intelligences to which we ourselves belong as rational beings (although from another point of view we are also members of the world of sense), remains always as a useful and permitted Idea for the purposes of a reasonable faith[74] though all knowledge ends at its border. It serves to produce in us a lively interest in the moral law by means of the splendid ideal of a universal kingdom of ends in themselves (rational beings), to which we can belong as members only if we are scrupulous to conduct ourselves in accordance with maxims of freedom, as if they were laws of nature.

Concluding Remark

The speculative use of reason *in regard to nature* leads to the absolute necessity of some supreme cause of the *world*; the practical use of reason *with respect to freedom* leads also to absolute necessity, but only to the absolute necessity *of the laws of actions* for a rational being as such. Now it is an essential *principle* for every use of reason to push its knowledge to a consciousness of its *necessity* (for without necessity it would not be rational knowledge). But it is an equally essential *limitation* of this same reason that it cannot have insight into the necessity either of what is or of what happens, or of what ought to happen, unless a *condition* is presupposed under which it is or happens or ought to happen. In this way, however, by continual asking for the condition, reason's satisfaction is merely postponed

---

74. *vernünftigen Glaubens*. This can also mean a rational faith or belief.

again and again. Hence reason restlessly seeks the unconditionally necessary and sees itself compelled to assume it without any means of making it comprehensible, though it is happy enough if only it can find a concept compatible with this presupposition. Thus it is no discredit to our deduction of the supreme principle of morality, but rather a reproach which must be brought against reason as such, that it cannot make comprehensible the absolute necessity of an unconditional practical law (such as the categorical imperative must be). For reason cannot be blamed for its unwillingness to do this by means of a condition—namely, by basing this necessity on some underlying interest—since in that case there would be no moral law, that is, no supreme law of freedom. And thus, while we do not comprehend the practical unconditional necessity of the moral imperative, we do comprehend its *incomprehensibility*. This is all that can fairly be demanded of a philosophy that presses forward in its principles to the very frontier of human reason.

ON A SUPPOSED RIGHT TO LIE BECAUSE OF PHILANTHROPIC CONCERNS[1]

Immanuel Kant

Translated by James W. Ellington

In the periodical *France*[2] for 1797, Part VI, No. 1, page 123, in an article bearing the title "On Political Reactions"[3] by Benjamin Constant[4] there is contained on p. 123 the following passage:

"The moral principle stating that it is a duty to tell the truth would make any society impossible if that principle were taken singly and unconditionally. We have proof of this in the very direct consequences which a German philosopher has drawn from this principle. This philosopher goes as far as to assert that it would be a crime to tell a lie to a murderer who asked whether our friend who is being pursued by the murderer had taken refuge in our house."[5]

The French philosopher [Constant] on p. 124 [of the periodical *France*] refutes this [moral] principle in the following way:

"It is a duty to tell the truth. The concept of duty is inseparable from the concept of right. A duty is what in one man corresponds to the right of another. Where there are no rights, there are no duties. To tell the truth is thus a duty, but is a duty only with regard to one who has a right to the truth. But no one has a right to a truth that harms others."

The πρῶτον ψεῦδος[8], here lies in the statement, "To tell the truth is a duty, but is a duty only with regard to one who has a right to the truth."

1. [This essay appeared in September of 1799 in *Berlinische Blätter (Berlin Press)*, published by Biester. See H. J. Paton, "An Alleged Right to Lie" in *Kant-Studien* 45 (1953–54).]
2. [The periodical *Frankreich im Jahre 1797. Aus den Briefen deutscher Männer in Paris (France in the Year 1797. From Letters of German Men in Paris)*, published in Altona.]
3. [*Des réactions politiques* had appeared in May of 1796, and it was translated into German in this periodical *Frankreich*.]
4. [Henri Benjamin Constant de Rebecque (1767–1830), the renowned French statesman and writer.]
5. "J. D. Michaelis in Göttingen [Johann Daniel Michaelis (1717–91), professor of theology in the University of Göttingen] had propounded this unusual opinion even before Kant. But the author of this article [viz., Constant] has informed me that Kant is the philosopher

referred to[6] in this passage."—K. F. Cramer. [Karl Friedrich Cramer (1752–1807), the editor of the periodical *Frankreich*, was formerly professor of Greek, oriental languages, and homiletics at Kiel until his dismissal in 1794 because of his open sympathy for the French Revolution, after which dismissal he became a book dealer in Paris.]
6. I hereby admit that this was actually said by me somewhere,[7] though I cannot now recollect the place.—I. Kant.
7. [Kant does say something similar in the "Casuistical Questions" appended to the article on "Lying" contained in the *Metaphysical Principles of the Doctrine of Virtue* (Part II of the *Metaphysics of Morals*). See the Royal Prussian Academy edition, Vol. VI, p. 431.]
8. [the first fallacy.]

Firstly it must be noted that the expression "to have a right to truth" is meaningless. One must say, rather, that man has a right to his own truthfulness (*veracitas*), i.e., to subjective truth in his own person. For to have objectively a right to truth would be the same as to say that it is a matter of one's will (as in cases of *mine* and *thine* generally) whether a given statement is to be true or false; this would produce an unusual logic.

Now, the first question is whether a man (in cases where he cannot avoid answering Yea or Nay) has the warrant (right) to be untruthful. The second question is whether he is not actually bound to be untruthful in a certain statement which he is unjustly compelled to make in order to prevent a threatening misdeed against himself or someone else.

Truthfulness in statements that cannot be avoided is the formal duty of man to everyone,[9] however great the disadvantage that may arise therefrom for him or for any other. And even though by telling an untruth I do no wrong to him who unjustly compels me to make a statement, yet by this falsification, which as such can be called a lie (though not in a juridical sense), I do wrong to duty in general in a most essential point. That is, as far as in me lies I bring it about that statements (declarations) in general find no credence, and hence also that all rights based on contracts[13] become void and lose their force, and this is a wrong done to mankind in general.

Hence a lie defined merely as an intentionally untruthful declaration to another man does not require the additional condition that it must do harm to another, as jurists require in their definition (*mendacium est falsiloquium in praeiudicium alterius*).[14]

9. I do not want to sharpen this principle to the point of saying "Untruthfulness is a violation of one's duty to himself." For this principle belongs to ethics,[10] but here the concern is with a duty of right [*Rechtspflicht*].[11] The *Doctrine of Virtue* [*Tugendlehre*] sees in this transgression only worthlessness, the reproach of which the liar draws upon himself.[12]

10. [As contained in the *Metaphysical Principles of the Doctrine of Virtue* [*Tugendlehre*], which is Part II of the *Metaphysics of Morals*.]

11. [Duties of right are treated in the *Metaphysical Principles of the Doctrine of Right* [*Rechtslehre*], which is Part I of the *Metaphysics of Morals*.]

12. [See the *Doctrine of Virtue*, Ak.VI, 429–31.]

13. [See the opus cited above in note 11, Ak.VI, 271–75.]

14. [a lie is a falsehood that harms another.]

For a lie always harms another; if not some other human being, then it nevertheless does harm to humanity in general, inasmuch as it vitiates the very source of right [*Rechtsquelle*].

However, this well-intentioned lie can become punishable in accordance with civil law because of an accident (*casus*); and that which avoids liability to punishment only by accident can also be condemned as wrong even by external laws. For example,[15] if by telling a lie you have in fact hindered someone who was even now planning a murder, then you are legally responsible for all the consequences that might result therefrom. But if you have adhered strictly to the truth, then public justice cannot lay a hand on you, whatever the unforeseen consequence might be. It is indeed possible that after you have honestly answered Yes to the murderer's question as to whether the intended victim is in the house, the latter went out unobserved and thus eluded the murderer, so that the deed would not have come about. However, if you told a lie and said that the intended victim was not in the house, and he has actually (though unbeknownst to you) gone out, with the result that by so doing he has been met by the murderer and thus the deed has been perpetrated, then in this case you may be justly accused as having caused his death. For if you had told the truth as best you knew it, then the murderer might perhaps have been caught by neighbors who came running while he was searching the house for his intended victim, and thus the deed might have been prevented. Therefore, whoever tells a lie, regardless of how good his intentions may be, must answer for the consequences resulting therefrom even before a civil tribunal and must pay the penalty for them, regardless of how unforeseen those consequences may be. This is because truthfulness is a duty that must be regarded as the basis of all duties founded on contract, and the laws of such duties would be rendered uncertain and useless if even the slightest exception to them were admitted.

To be truthful (honest) in all declarations is, therefore, a sacred and unconditionally commanding law of reason that admits of no expediency whatsoever.

15. [This ensuing instance is similar to the one cited in note 7 above.]

Monsieur Constant remarks thoughtfully and correctly with regard to the decrying of such principles that are so strict as to be alleged to lose themselves in impracticable ideas and that are therefore to be rejected. He says on page 123 [of the German translation of Constant's piece that appeared in the periodical *Frankreich*], "In every case where a principle that has been proved to be true appears to be inapplicable, the reason for this inapplicability lies in the fact that we do not know the middle principle that contains the means of its application." He adduces (p. 121) the doctrine of equality as being the first link of the social chain when he says (p. 122): "No man can be bound by any laws other than these to whose formation he has contributed. In a very limited society this principle can be applied directly and requires no middle principle in order to become a common principle. But in a very numerous society there must be added a new principle to the one that has been stated. The middle principle is this: individuals can contribute to the formation of laws either in their own person or through their representatives. Whoever wanted to apply the former principle to a numerous society without also using the middle principle would unfailingly bring about the destruction of such a society. But this circumstance, which would show only the ignorance or the incompetence of the legislator, would prove nothing against the principle." He concludes (p. 125) thus: "A principle acknowledged as true must hence never be abandoned, however obviously there seems to be danger involved in it." (And yet the good man himself abandoned the unconditional principle of truthfulness on account of the danger which that principle posed for society, inasmuch as he could not find any middle principle that could serve to prevent this danger; and indeed there is no such principle to do the mediating here.)

If the names of the persons as they have here been introduced be retained, then the "French philosopher" confuses the action whereby someone does harm (*nocet*) to another by telling the truth when its avowal cannot be avoided with the action whereby someone does wrong to (*laedit*) another. It was merely an accident (*casus*) that the truth of the statement did harm [but not wrong] to the occupant of the house, but it was not a free act (in the juridical sense). For from a right to demand that another should lie for the sake of one's own advantage there would follow a claim that conflicts with all lawfulness. For every man has not only a right but even the strictest duty to be truthful in statements that are unavoidable, whether this truthfulness does harm [but not wrong] to himself or to others. Therefore he does not himself by this [truthfulness] actually harm [*nocet*] the one who suffers because of it; rather, this harm is caused by accident [*casus*]. For he is not at all free to choose in such a case, inasmuch as truthfulness (if he must speak [i.e., must answer Yea or Nay]) is an unconditional duty. The "German philosopher" will, therefore, not take as his principle the proposition (p. 124), "To tell the truth is a duty, but is a duty only with regard to the man who has a right to the truth." He will not do so, first, because of the confused formulation of the proposition, inasmuch as truth is not a possession the right to which can be granted to one person but refused to another. But, secondly, he will not do so mainly because the duty of truthfulness (which is the only thing under consideration here) makes no distinction between persons to whom one has this duty and to whom one can be excused from this duty; it is, rather, an unconditional duty which holds in all circumstances.

Chapter 7

Rawls: Justice as Fairness

One way of thinking about justice is to imagine a social contract in which people come together to choose the basic principles that will govern their society. Would the principles chosen in this way be fair? Not necessarily. Some parties to the social contract might be stronger, or wealthier, or savvier than others. Some might take advantage of a superior bargaining position. Now try to imagine a social contract that would not be subject to these contingencies. This is what John Rawls (1921–2002) invites us to imagine in his book *A Theory of Justice* (1971). According to Rawls, the way to think about justice is to ask what principles would be chosen by people who came together behind a "veil of ignorance" that temporarily deprived them of any knowledge about where they would wind up in society. Only a hypothetical contract such as this, carried out in an original position of equality, would produce principles of justice untainted by differences of bargaining power or knowledge.

Here are some questions to consider as you read Rawls: Is the idea of a hypothetical contract behind a veil of ignorance a compelling way of thinking about justice? What principles does Rawls think would be chosen in the original position? Do you agree that these principles would be chosen? As you think about the veil of ignorance, notice a certain similarity between Rawls and Kant. Both seem to agree that moral reasoning requires us to abstract from the particular circumstances in which we find ourselves. Do you agree?

A Theory of Justice

John Rawls

The Role of Justice

Justice is the first virtue of social institutions, as truth is of systems of thought. A theory however elegant and economical must be rejected or revised if it is untrue; likewise laws and institutions no matter how efficient and well-arranged must be reformed or abolished if they are unjust. Each person possesses an inviolability founded on justice that even the welfare of society as a whole cannot override. For this reason justice denies that the loss of freedom for some is made right by a greater good shared by others. It does not allow that the sacrifices imposed on a few are outweighed by the larger sum of advantages enjoyed by many. Therefore in a just society the liberties of equal citizenship are taken as settled; the rights secured by justice are not subject to political bargaining or to the calculus of social interests. The only thing that permits us to acquiesce in an

203

erroneous theory is the lack of a better one; analogously, an injustice is tolerable only when it is necessary to avoid an even greater injustice. Being first virtues of human activities, truth and justice are uncompromising.

These propositions seem to express our intuitive conviction of the primacy of justice. No doubt they are expressed too strongly. In any event I wish to inquire whether these contentions or others similar to them are sound, and if so how they can be accounted for. To this end it is necessary to work out a theory of justice in the light of which these assertions can be interpreted and assessed. I shall begin by considering the role of the principles of justice. Let us assume, to fix ideas, that a society is a more or less self-sufficient association of persons who in their relations to one another recognize certain rules of conduct as binding and who for the most part act in accordance with them. Suppose further that these rules specify a system of cooperation designed to advance the good of those taking part in it. Then, although a society is a cooperative venture for mutual advantage, it is typically marked by a conflict as well as by an identity of interests. There is an identity of interests since social cooperation makes possible a better life for all than any would have if each were to live solely by his own efforts. There is a conflict of interests since persons are not indifferent as to how the greater benefits produced by their collaboration are distributed, for in order to pursue their ends they each prefer a larger to a lesser share. A set of principles is required for choosing among the various social arrangements which determine this division of advantages and for underwriting an agreement on the proper distributive shares. These principles are the principles of social justice: they provide a way of assigning rights and duties in the basic institutions of society and they define the appropriate distribution of the benefits and burdens of social cooperation. [. . .]

The Main Idea of the Theory of Justice

My aim is to present a conception of justice which generalizes and carries to a higher level of abstraction the familiar theory of the social contract as found, say, in Locke, Rousseau, and Kant.[1] In order to do this we are not to think of the original contract as one to enter a particular society or to set up a particular form of government. Rather, the guiding idea is that the principles of justice for the basic structure of society are the object of the original agreement. They are the principles that free and rational persons concerned to further their own interests would accept in an initial position of equality as defining the fundamental terms of their association. These principles are to regulate all further agreements; they specify the kinds of social cooperation that can be entered into and the forms of government that can be established. This way of regarding the principles of justice I shall call justice as fairness.

Thus we are to imagine that those who engage in social cooperation choose together, in one joint act, the principles which are to assign basic rights and duties and to determine the division of social benefits. Men are to decide in advance how they are to regulate their claims against one another and what is to be the foundation charter of their society. Just as each person must decide by rational reflection what constitutes his good, that is, the system of ends which it is rational for him to pursue, so a group of persons must decide once and for all what is to count among them as just and unjust. The choice which rational men would make in this hypothetical situation of equal liberty, assuming for the present that this choice problem has a solution, determines the principles of justice.

In justice as fairness the original position of equality corresponds to the state of nature in the traditional theory of the social contract. This original position is not, of course, thought of as an

1. As the text suggests, I shall regard Locke's *Second Treatise of Government*, Rousseau's *The Social Contract*, and Kant's ethical works beginning with *The Foundations of the Metaphysics of Morals* as definitive of the contract tradition. For all of its greatness, Hobbes's *Leviathan* raises special problems. A general historical survey is provided by J. W. Gough, *The Social Contract*, 2nd ed. (Oxford, The Clarendon Press, 1957), and Otto Gierke, *Natural Law and the Theory of Society*, trans. with an introduction by Ernest Barker (Cambridge, The University Press, 1934). A presentation of the contract view as primarily an ethical theory is to be found in G. R. Grice, *The Grounds of Moral Judgment* (Cambridge, The University Press, 1967). See also §19, note 30.

actual historical state of affairs, much less as a primitive condition of culture. It is understood as a purely hypothetical situation characterized so as to lead to a certain conception of justice.[2] Among the essential features of this situation is that no one knows his place in society, his class position or social status, nor does any one know his fortune in the distribution of natural assets and abilities, his intelligence, strength, and the like. I shall even assume that the parties do not know their conceptions of the good or their special psychological propensities. The principles of justice are chosen behind a veil of ignorance. This ensures that no one is advantaged or disadvantaged in the choice of principles by the outcome of natural chance or the contingency of social circumstances. Since all are similarly situated and no one is able to design principles to favor his particular condition, the principles of justice are the result of a fair agreement or bargain. For given the circumstances of the original position, the symmetry of everyone's relations to each other, this initial situation is fair between individuals as moral persons, that is, as rational beings with their own ends and capable, I shall assume, of a sense of justice. The original position is, one might say, the appropriate initial status quo, and thus the fundamental agreements reached in it are fair. This explains the propriety of the name "justice as fairness": it conveys the idea that the principles of justice are agreed to in an initial situation that is fair. The name does not mean that the concepts of justice and fairness are the same, any more than the phrase "poetry as metaphor" means that the concepts of poetry and metaphor are the same.

Justice as fairness begins, as I have said, with one of the most general of all choices which persons might make together, namely, with the choice of the first principles of a conception of justice which is to regulate all subsequent criticism and reform of institutions. Then, having chosen a conception of justice, we can suppose that they are to choose a constitution and a legislature to enact laws, and so on, all in accordance with the principles of justice initially agreed upon. Our social situation is just if it is such that by this sequence of hypothetical agreements we would have contracted into the general system of rules which defines it. Moreover, assuming that the original position does determine a set of principles (that is, that a particular conception of justice would be chosen), it will then be true that whenever social institutions satisfy these principles those engaged in them can say to one another that they are cooperating on terms to which they would agree if they were free and equal persons whose relations with respect to one another were fair. They could all view their arrangements as meeting the stipulations which they would acknowledge in an initial situation that embodies widely accepted and reasonable constraints on the choice of principles. The general recognition of this fact would provide the basis for a public acceptance of the corresponding principles of justice. No society can, of course, be a scheme of cooperation which men enter voluntarily in a literal sense; each person finds himself placed at birth in some particular position in some particular society, and the nature of this position materially affects his life prospects. Yet a society satisfying the principles of justice as fairness comes as close as a society can to being a voluntary scheme, for it meets the principles which free and equal persons would assent to under circumstances that are fair. In this sense its members are autonomous and the obligations they recognize self-imposed.

One feature of justice as fairness is to think of the parties in the initial situation as rational and mutually disinterested. This does not mean that the parties are egoists, that is, individuals with only certain kinds of interests, say in wealth, prestige, and domination. But they are conceived as not taking an interest in one another's interests. They are to presume that even their spiritual aims may be opposed, in the way that the aims of those of different religions may be opposed. Moreover, the concept of rationality must be interpreted as far as possible in the narrow sense, standard in

---

2. Kant is clear that the original agreement is hypothetical. See *The Metaphysics of Morals*, pt. I (*Rechislehre*), especially §§ 47, 52; and pt. II of the essay "Concerning the Common Saying: This May Be True in Theory but It Does Not Apply in Practice," in *Kant's Political Writings*, ed. Hans Reiss and trans. by H. B. Nisbet (Cambridge, The University Press, 1970), pp. 73–87. See Georges Vlachos, *La Pensée politique de Kant* (Paris, Presses Universitaires de France, 1962), pp. 326–335; and J. G. Murphy, *Kant: The Philosophy of Right* (London, Macmillan, 1970), pp. 109–112, 133–136, for a further discussion.

economic theory, of taking the most effective means to given ends. I shall modify this concept to some extent, as explained later..., but one must try to avoid introducing into it any controversial ethical elements. The initial situation must be characterized by stipulations that are widely accepted.

In working out the conception of justice as fairness one main task clearly is to determine which principles of justice would be chosen in the original position. To do this we must describe this situation in some detail and formulate with care the problem of choice which it presents. These matters I shall take up in the immediately succeeding chapters. It may be observed, however, that once the principles of justice are thought of as arising from an original agreement in a situation of equality, it is an open question whether the principle of utility would be acknowledged. Offhand it hardly seems likely that persons who view themselves as equals, entitled to press their claims upon one another, would agree to a principle which may require lesser life prospects for some simply for the sake of a greater sum of advantages enjoyed by others. Since each desires to protect his interests, his capacity to advance his conception of the good, no one has a reason to acquiesce in an enduring loss for himself in order to bring about a greater net balance of satisfaction. In the absence of strong and lasting benevolent impulses, a rational man would not accept a basic structure merely because it maximized the algebraic sum of advantages irrespective of its permanent effects on his own basic rights and interests. Thus it seems that the principle of utility is incompatible with the conception of social cooperation among equals for mutual advantage. It appears to be inconsistent with the idea of reciprocity implicit in the notion of a well-ordered society. Or, at any rate, so I shall argue.

I shall maintain instead that the persons in the initial situation would choose two rather different principles: the first requires equality in the assignment of basic rights and duties, while the second holds that social and economic inequalities, for example inequalities of wealth and authority, are just only if they result in compensating benefits for everyone, and in particular for the least advantaged members of society. These principles rule out justifying institutions on the grounds that the

hardships of some are offset by a greater good in the aggregate. It may be expedient but it is not just that some should have less in order that others may prosper. But there is no injustice in the greater benefits earned by a few provided that the situation of persons not so fortunate is thereby improved. The intuitive idea is that since everyone's well-being depends upon a scheme of cooperation without which no one could have a satisfactory life, the division of advantages should be such as to draw forth the willing cooperation of everyone taking part in it, including those less well situated. Yet this can be expected only if reasonable terms are proposed. The two principles mentioned seem to be a fair agreement on the basis of which those better endowed, or more fortunate in their social position, neither of which we can be said to deserve, could expect the willing cooperation of others when some workable scheme is a necessary condition of the welfare of all.[3] Once we decide to look for a conception of justice that nullifies the accidents of natural endowment and the contingencies of social circumstance as counters in quest for political and economic advantage, we are led to these principles. They express the result of leaving aside those aspects of the social world that seem arbitrary from a moral point of view.

The problem of the choice of principles, however, is extremely difficult. I do not expect the answer I shall suggest to be convincing to everyone. It is, therefore, worth noting from the outset that justice as fairness, like other contract views, consists of two parts: (1) an interpretation of the initial situation and of the problem of choice posed there, and (2) a set of principles which, it is argued, would be agreed to. One may accept the first part of the theory (or some variant thereof), but not the other, and conversely. The concept of the initial contractual situation may seem reasonable although the particular principles proposed are rejected. To be sure, I want to maintain that the most appropriate conception of this situation does lead to principles of justice contrary to utilitarianism and perfectionism, and therefore that the contract doctrine provides an alternative to these views. Still, one may dispute this contention even

---

3. For the formulation of this intuitive idea I am indebted to Allan Gibbard.

though one grants that the contractarian method is a useful way of studying ethical theories and of setting forth their underlying assumptions. . . .

The Original Position and Justification

I have said that the original position is the appropriate initial status quo which insures that the fundamental agreements reached in it are fair. This fact yields the name "justice as fairness." It is clear, then, that I want to say that one conception of justice is more reasonable than another, or justifiable with respect to it, if rational persons in the initial situation would choose its principles over those of the other for the role of justice. Conceptions of justice are to be ranked by their acceptability to persons so circumstanced. Understood in this way the question of justification is settled by working out a problem of deliberation: we have to ascertain which principles it would be rational to adopt given the contractual situation. This connects the theory of justice with the theory of rational choice.

If this view of the problem of justification is to succeed, we must, of course, describe in some detail the nature of this choice problem. A problem of rational decision has a definite answer only if we know the beliefs and interests of the parties, their relations with respect to one another, the alternatives between which they are to choose, the procedure whereby they make up their minds, and so on. As the circumstances are presented in different ways, correspondingly different principles are accepted. The concept of the original position, as I shall refer to it, is that of the most philosophically favored interpretation of this initial choice situation for the purposes of a theory of justice.

But how are we to decide what is the most favored interpretation? I assume, for one thing, that there is a broad measure of agreement that principles of justice should be chosen under certain conditions. To justify a particular description of the initial situation one shows that it incorporates these commonly shared presumptions. One argues from widely accepted but weak premises to more specific conclusions. Each of the presumptions should by itself be natural and plausible; some of them may seem innocuous or even trivial. The aim of the contract approach is to establish that taken together they impose significant bounds on acceptable principles of justice. The ideal outcome would be that these conditions determine a unique set of principles; but I shall be satisfied if they suffice to rank the main traditional conceptions of social justice.

One should not be misled, then, by the somewhat unusual conditions which characterize the original position. The idea here is simply to make vivid to ourselves the restrictions that it seems reasonable to impose on arguments for principles of justice, and therefore on these principles themselves. Thus it seems reasonable and generally acceptable that no one should be advantaged or disadvantaged by natural fortune or social circumstances in the choice of principles. It also seems widely agreed that it should be impossible to tailor principles to the circumstances of one's own case. We should insure further that particular inclinations and aspirations, and persons' conceptions of their good do not affect the principles adopted. The aim is to rule out those principles that it would be rational to propose for acceptance, however little the chance of success, only if one knew certain things that are irrelevant from the standpoint of justice. For example, if a man knew that he was wealthy, he might find it rational to advance the principle that various taxes for welfare measures be counted unjust; if he knew that he was poor, he would most likely propose the contrary principle. To represent the desired restrictions one imagines a situation in which everyone is deprived of this sort of information. One excludes the knowledge of those contingencies which sets men at odds and allows them to be guided by their prejudices. In this manner the veil of ignorance is arrived at in a natural way. This concept should cause no difficulty if we keep in mind the constraints on arguments that it is meant to express. At any time we can enter the original position, so to speak, simply by following a certain procedure, namely, by arguing for principles of justice in accordance with these restrictions.

It seems reasonable to suppose that the parties in the original position are equal. That is, all have the same rights in the procedure for choosing principles; each can make proposals, submit reasons for their acceptance, and so on. Obviously the purpose of these conditions is to represent equality between human beings as moral persons, as creatures having a conception of their good and capable of a sense of justice. The basis of equality is taken to be similarity in these two respects. Systems of ends are not ranked in value; and each man is presumed to have the requisite ability to understand and to act upon whatever principles are adopted. Together with the veil of ignorance, these conditions define the principles of justice as those which rational persons concerned to advance their interests would consent to as equals when none are known to be advantaged or disadvantaged by social and natural contingencies.

There is, however, another side to justifying a particular description of the original position. This is to see if the principles which would be chosen match our considered convictions of justice or extend them in an acceptable way. We can note whether applying these principles would lead us to make the same judgments about the basic structure of society which we now make intuitively and in which we have the greatest confidence; or whether, in cases where our present judgments are in doubt and given with hesitation, these principles offer a resolution which we can affirm on reflection. There are questions which we feel sure must be answered in a certain way. For example, we are confident that religious intolerance and racial discrimination are unjust. We think that we have examined these things with care and have reached what we believe is an impartial judgment not likely to be distorted by an excessive attention to our own interests. These convictions are provisional fixed points which we presume any conception of justice must fit. But we have much less assurance as to what is the correct distribution of wealth and authority. Here we may be looking for a way to remove our doubts. We can check an interpretation of the initial situation, then, by the capacity of its principles to accommodate our firmest convictions and to provide guidance where guidance is needed.

In searching for the most favored description of this situation we work from both ends. We begin by describing it so that it represents generally shared and preferably weak conditions. We then see if these conditions are strong enough to yield a significant set of principles. If not, we look for further premises equally reasonable. But if so,

and these principles match our considered convictions of justice, then so far well and good. But presumably there will be discrepancies. In this case we have a choice. We can either modify the account of the initial situation or we can revise our existing judgments, for even the judgments we take provisionally as fixed points are liable to revision. By going back and forth, sometimes altering the conditions of the contractual circumstances, at others withdrawing our judgments and conforming them to principle, I assume that eventually we shall find a description of the initial situation that both expresses reasonable conditions and yields principles which match our considered judgments duly pruned and adjusted. This state of affairs I refer to as reflective equilibrium.[4] It is an equilibrium because at last our principles and judgments coincide; and it is reflective since we know to what principles our judgments conform and the premises of their derivation. At the moment everything is in order. But this equilibrium is not necessarily stable. It is liable to be upset by further examination of the conditions which should be imposed on the contractual situation and by particular cases which may lead us to revise our judgments. Yet for the time being we have done what we can to render coherent and to justify our convictions of social justice. We have reached a conception of the original position.

I shall not, of course, actually work through this process. Still, we may think of the interpretation of the original position that I shall present as the result of such a hypothetical course of reflection. It represents the attempt to accommodate within one scheme both reasonable philosophical conditions on principles as well as our considered judgments of justice. In arriving at the favored interpretation of the initial situation there is no point at which an appeal is made to self-evidence in the traditional sense either of general conceptions or particular convictions. I do not claim for the principles of justice proposed that they are necessary truths or derivable from such truths. A conception of justice cannot be deduced from

4. The process of mutual adjustment of principles and considered judgments is not peculiar to moral philosophy. See Nelson Goodman, *Fact, Fiction, and Forecast* (Cambridge, Mass., Harvard University Press, 1955), pp. 65–68, for parallel remarks concerning the justification of the principles of deductive and inductive inference.

self-evident premises or conditions on principles; instead, its justification is a matter of the mutual support of many considerations, of everything fitting together into one coherent view.

A final comment. We shall want to say that certain principles of justice are justified because they would be agreed to in an initial situation of equality. I have emphasized that this original position is purely hypothetical. It is natural to ask why, if this agreement is never actually entered into, we should take any interest in these principles, moral or otherwise. The answer is that the conditions embodied in the description of the original position are ones that we do in fact accept. Or if we do not, then perhaps we can be persuaded to do so by philosophical reflection. Each aspect of the contractual situation can be given supporting grounds. Thus what we shall do is to collect together into one conception a number of conditions on principles that we are ready upon due consideration to recognize as reasonable. These constraints express what we are prepared to regard as limits on fair terms of social cooperation. One way to look at the idea of the original position, therefore, is to see it as an expository device which sums up the meaning of these conditions and helps us to extract their consequences. On the other hand, this conception is also an intuitive notion that suggests its own elaboration, so that led on by it we are drawn to define more clearly the standpoint from which we can best interpret moral relationships. We need a conception that enables us to envision our objective from afar: the intuitive notion of the original position is to do this for us.[5]

Classical Utilitarianism

We may note first that there is, indeed, a way of thinking of society which makes it easy to suppose that the most rational conception of justice is utilitarian. For consider: each man in realizing his own interests is certainly free to balance his own losses against his own gains. We may impose a sacrifice on ourselves now for the sake of a

greater advantage later. A person quite properly acts, at least when others are not affected, to achieve his own greatest good, to advance his rational ends as far as possible. Now why should not a society act on precisely the same principle applied to the group and therefore regard that which is rational for one man as right for an association of men? Just as the well-being of a person is constructed from the series of satisfactions that are experienced at different moments in the course of his life, so in very much the same way the well-being of society is to be constructed from the fulfillment of the systems of desires of the many individuals who belong to it. Since the principle for an individual is to advance as far as possible his own welfare, his own system of desires, the principle for society is to advance as far as possible the welfare of the group, to realize to the greatest extent the comprehensive system of desire arrived at from the desires of its members. Just as an individual balances present and future gains against present and future losses, so a society may balance satisfactions and dissatisfactions between different individuals. And so by these reflections one reaches the principle of utility in a natural way: a society is properly arranged when its institutions maximize the net balance of satisfaction. The principle of choice for an association of men is interpreted as an extension of the principle of choice for one man. Social justice is the principle of rational prudence applied to an aggregative conception of the welfare of the group.[6]

This idea is made all the more attractive by a further consideration. The two main concepts of

5. Henri Poincaré remarks: "Il nous faut une faculté qui nous fasse voir le but de loin, et, cette faculté, c'est l'intuition." *La Valeur de la science* (Paris, Flammarion, 1909), p. 27.

6. On this point see also D. P. Gauthier, *Practical Reasoning* (Oxford, Clarendon Press, 1963), pp. 126f. The text elaborates the suggestion found in "Constitutional Liberty and the Concept of Justice," *Nomos VI: Justice*, ed. C. J. Friedrich and J. W. Chapman (New York, Atherton Press, 1963), pp. 124f, which in turn is related to the idea of justice as a higher-order administrative decision. See "Justice as Fairness," *Philosophical Review*, 1958, pp. 185–187.... That the principle of social integration is distinct from the principle of personal integration is stated by R. B. Perry *General Theory of Value* (New York, Longmans, Green, and Company, 1926), pp. 674–677. He attributes the error of overlooking this fact to Emile Durkheim and others with similar views. His conception of social integration is that brought about by a shared and dominant benevolent purpose. ["The Veil of Ignorance"]

ethics are those of the right and the good; the concept of a morally worthy person is, I believe, derived from them. The structure of an ethical theory is, then, largely determined by how it defines and connects these two basic notions. Now it seems that the simplest way of relating them is taken by teleological theories: the good is defined independently from the right, and then the right is defined as that which maximizes the good.[7] More precisely, those institutions and acts are right which of the available alternatives produce the most good, or at least as much good as any of the other institutions and acts open as real possibilities (a rider needed when the maximal class is not a singleton). Teleological theories have a deep intuitive appeal since they seem to embody the idea of rationality. It is natural to think that rationality is maximizing something and that in morals it must be maximizing the good. Indeed, it is tempting to suppose that it is self-evident that things should be arranged so as to lead to the most good.

It is essential to keep in mind that in a teleological theory the good is defined independently from the right. This means two things. First, the theory accounts for our considered judgments as to which things are good (our judgments of value) as a separate class of judgments intuitively distinguishable by common sense, and then proposes the hypothesis that the right is maximizing the good as already specified. Second, the theory enables one to judge the goodness of things without referring to what is right. For example, if pleasure is said to be the sole good, then presumably pleasures can be recognized and ranked in value by criteria that do not presuppose any standards of right, or what we would normally think of as such. Whereas if the distribution of goods is also counted as a good, perhaps a higher order one, and the theory directs us to produce the most good (including the good of distribution among others), we no longer have a teleological view in the classical sense. The problem of distribution falls under the concept of right as one intuitively understands it, and so the theory lacks an independent definition of the

good. The clarity and simplicity of classical teleological theories derives largely from the fact that they factor our moral judgments into two classes, the one being characterized separately while the other is then connected with it by a maximizing principle.

Teleological doctrines differ, pretty clearly, according to how the conception of the good is specified. If it is taken as the realization of human excellence in the various forms of culture, we have what may be called perfectionism. This notion is found in Aristotle and Nietzsche, among others. If the good is defined as pleasure, we have hedonism; if as happiness, eudaimonism, and so on. I shall understand the principle of utility in its classical form as defining the good as the satisfaction of desire, or perhaps better, as the satisfaction of rational desire. This accords with the view in all essentials and provides, I believe, a fair interpretation of it. The appropriate terms of social cooperation are settled by whatever in the circumstances will achieve the greatest sum of satisfaction of the rational desires of individuals. It is impossible to deny the initial plausibility and attractiveness of this conception.

The striking feature of the utilitarian view of justice is that it does not matter, except indirectly, how this sum of satisfactions is distributed among individuals any more than it matters, except indirectly, how one man distributes his satisfactions over time. The correct distribution in either case is that which yields the maximum fulfillment. Society must allocate its means of satisfaction whatever these are, rights and duties, opportunities and privileges, and various forms of wealth, so as to achieve this maximum if it can. But in itself no distribution of satisfaction is better than another except that the more equal distribution is to be preferred to break ties.[8] It is true that certain common sense precepts of justice, particularly those which concern the protection of liberties and rights, or which express the claims of desert, seem to contradict this contention. But from a utilitarian standpoint the explanation of these precepts and of their seemingly stringent character is that they are those precepts which experience shows should be strictly respected and departed from only under exceptional circumstances if the sum

---

7. Here I adopt W. K. Frankena's definition of teleological theories in *Ethics* (Englewood Cliffs, N.J., Prentice Hall, Inc., 1963), p. 13

8. On this point see Sidgwick, *The Methods of Ethics*, pp. 416f.

of advantages is to be maximized.[9] Yet, as with all other precepts, those of justice are derivative from the one end of attaining the greatest balance of satisfaction. Thus there is no reason in principle why the greater gains of some should not compensate for the lesser losses of others; or more importantly, why the violation of the liberty of a few might not be made right by the greater good shared by many. It simply happens that under most conditions, at least in a reasonably advanced stage of civilization, the greatest sum of advantages is not attained in this way. No doubt the strictness of common sense precepts of justice has a certain usefulness in limiting men's propensities to injustice and to socially injurious actions, but the utilitarian believes that to affirm this strictness as a first principle of morals is a mistake. For just as it is rational for one man to maximize the fulfillment of his system of desires, it is right for a society to maximize the net balance of satisfaction taken over all of its members.

The most natural way, then, of arriving at utilitarianism (although not, of course, the only way of doing so) is to adopt for society as a whole the principle of rational choice for one man. Once this is recognized, the place of the impartial spectator and the emphasis on sympathy in the history of utilitarian thought is readily understood. For it is by the conception of the impartial spectator and the use of sympathetic identification in guiding our imagination that the principle for one man is applied to society. It is this spectator who is conceived as carrying out the required organization of the desires of all persons into one coherent system of desire; it is by this construction that many persons are fused into one. Endowed with ideal powers of sympathy and imagination, the impartial spectator is the perfectly rational individual who identifies with and experiences the desires of others as if these desires were his own. In this way he ascertains the intensity of these desires and assigns them their appropriate weight in the one system of desire the satisfaction of which the ideal legislator then tries to maximize by adjusting the rules of the social system. On this conception of society separate individuals are thought of as so many different lines along which rights and duties are to be assigned and scarce

means of satisfaction allocated in accordance with rules so as to give the greatest fulfillment of wants. The nature of the decision made by the ideal legislator is not, therefore, materially different from that of an entrepreneur deciding how to maximize his profit by producing this or that commodity, or that of a consumer deciding how to maximize his satisfaction by the purchase of this or that collection of goods. In each case there is a single person whose system of desires determines the best allocation of limited means. The correct decision is essentially a question of efficient administration. This view of social cooperation is the consequence of extending to society the principle of choice for one man, and then, to make this extension work, conflating all persons into one through the imaginative acts of the impartial sympathetic spectator. Utilitarianism does not take seriously the distinction between persons.

Some Related Contrasts

It has seemed to many philosophers, and it appears to be supported by the convictions of common sense, that we distinguish as a matter of principle between the claims of liberty and right on the one hand and the desirability of increasing aggregate social welfare on the other; and that we give a certain priority, if not absolute weight, to the former. Each member of society is thought to have an inviolability founded on justice or, as some say, on natural right, which even the welfare of every one else cannot override. Justice denies that the loss of freedom for some is made right by a greater good shared by others. The reasoning which balances the gains and losses of different persons as if they were one person is excluded. Therefore in a just society the basic liberties are taken for granted and the rights secured by justice are not subject to political bargaining or to the calculus of social interests.

Justice as fairness attempts to account for these common sense convictions concerning the priority of justice by showing that they are the consequence of principles which would be chosen in the original position. These judgments reflect the rational preferences and the initial equality of the contracting parties. Although the utilitarian recognizes that, strictly speaking, his doctrine conflicts with these sentiments of justice, he maintains that common

9. See J. S. Mill, *Utilitarianism*, ch. V, last two pars.

sense precepts of justice and notions of natural right have but a subordinate validity as secondary rules; they arise from the fact that under the conditions of civilized society there is great social utility in following them for the most part and in permitting violations only under exceptional circumstances. Even the excessive zeal with which we are apt to affirm these precepts and to appeal to these rights is itself granted a certain usefulness, since it counterbalances a natural human tendency to violate them in ways not sanctioned by utility. Once we understand this, the apparent disparity between the utilitarian principle and the strength of these persuasions of justice is no longer a philosophical difficulty. Thus while the contract doctrine accepts our convictions about the priority of justice as on the whole sound, utilitarianism seeks to account for them as a socially useful illusion.

A second contrast is that whereas the utilitarian extends to society the principle of choice for one man, justice as fairness, being a contract view, assumes that the principles of social choice, and so the principles of justice, are themselves the object of an original agreement. There is no reason to suppose that the principles which should regulate an association of men is simply an extension of the principle of choice for one man. On the contrary: if we assume that the correct regulative principle for anything depends on the nature of that thing, and that the plurality of distinct persons with separate systems of ends is an essential feature of human societies, we should not expect the principles of social choice to be utilitarian. To be sure, it has not been shown by anything said so far that the parties in the original position would not choose the principle of utility to define the terms of social cooperation. This is a difficult question which I shall examine later on. It is perfectly possible, from all that one knows at this point, that some form of the principle of utility would be adopted, and therefore that contract theory leads eventually to a deeper and more roundabout justification of utilitarianism. In fact a derivation of this kind is sometimes suggested by Bentham and Edgeworth, although it is not developed by them in any systematic way and to my knowledge it is not found in Sidgwick.[10] For the present I shall

simply assume that the persons in the original position would reject the utility principle and that they would adopt instead, for the kinds of reasons previously sketched, the two principles of justice already mentioned. In any case, from the standpoint of contract theory one cannot arrive at a principle of social choice merely by extending the principle of rational prudence to the system of desires constructed by the impartial spectator. To do this is not to take seriously the plurality and distinctness of individuals, nor to recognize as the basis of justice that to which men would consent. Here we may note a curious anomaly. It is customary to think of utilitarianism as individualistic, and certainly there are good reasons for this. The utilitarians were strong defenders of liberty and freedom of thought, and they held that the good of society is constituted by the advantages enjoyed by individuals. Yet utilitarianism is not individualistic, at least when arrived at by the more natural course of reflection, in that, by conflating all systems of desires, it applies to society the principle of choice for one man. And thus we see that the second contrast is related to the first, since it is this conflation, and the principle based upon it, which subjects the rights secured by justice to the calculus of social interests.

The last contrast that I shall mention now is that utilitarianism is a teleological theory whereas justice as fairness is not. By definition, then, the latter is a deontological theory, one that either does not specify the good independently from the right, or does not interpret the right as maximizing the good. (It should be noted that deontological theories are defined as non-teleological ones, not as views that characterize the rightness of institutions and acts independently from their consequences. All ethical doctrines worth our attention take consequences into account in judging rightness. One which did not would simply be irrational, crazy.) Justice as fairness is a deontological theory in the second way. For if it is assumed that the persons in the original position would choose a principle of equal liberty and restrict economic and social inequalities to those

10. For Bentham see *The Principles of International Law*, Essay I, in *The Works of Jeremy Bentham*, ed. John

Bowring (Edinburgh, 1838–1843), vol. II, p. 537; for Edgeworth see *Mathematical Psychics*, pp. 52–56, and also the first pages of "The Pure Theory of Taxation," *Economic Journal*, vol. 7 (1897), where the same argument is presented more briefly.

in everyone's interests, there is no reason to think that just institutions will maximize the good. (Here I suppose with utilitarianism that the good is defined as the satisfaction of rational desire.) Of course, it is not impossible that the most good is produced but it would be a coincidence. The question of attaining the greatest net balance of satisfaction never arises in justice as fairness; this maximum principle is not used at all.

There is a further point in this connection. In utilitarianism the satisfaction of any desire has some value in itself which must be taken into account in deciding what is right. In calculating the greatest balance of satisfaction it does not matter, except indirectly, what the desires are for.[11] We are to arrange institutions so as to obtain the greatest sum of satisfactions; we ask no questions about their source or quality but only how their satisfaction would affect the total of well-being. Social welfare depends directly and solely upon the levels of satisfaction or dissatisfaction of individuals. Thus if men take a certain pleasure in discriminating against one another, in subjecting others to a lesser liberty as a means of enhancing their self-respect, then the satisfaction of these desires must be weighed in our deliberations according to their intensity, or whatever, along with other desires. If society decides to deny them fulfillment, or to suppress them, it is because they tend to be socially destructive and a greater welfare can be achieved in other ways.

In justice as fairness, on the other hand, persons accept in advance a principle of equal liberty and they do this without a knowledge of their more particular ends. They implicitly agree, therefore, to conform their conceptions of their good to what the principles of justice require, or at least not to press claims which directly violate them. An individual who finds that he enjoys seeing others in positions of lesser liberty understands that he has no claim whatever to this enjoyment. The pleasure he takes in other's deprivations is wrong in itself: it is a satisfaction which requires the violation of a principle to which he would agree in the original position. The principles of right, and so of justice, put limits on which satisfactions have value; they impose restrictions on

what are reasonable conceptions of one's good. In drawing up plans and in deciding on aspirations men are to take these constraints into account. Hence in justice as fairness one does not take men's propensities and inclinations as given, whatever they are, and then seek the best way to fulfill them. Rather, their desires and aspirations are restricted from the outset by the principles of justice which specify the boundaries that men's systems of ends must respect. We can express this by saying that in justice as fairness the concept of right is prior to that of the good. A just social system defines the scope within which individuals must develop their aims, and it provides a framework of rights and opportunities and the means of satisfaction within and by the use of which these ends may be equitably pursued. The priority of justice is accounted for, in part, by holding that the interests requiring the violation of justice have no value. Having no merit in the first place, they cannot override its claims.[12]

This priority of the right over the good in justice as fairness turns out to be a central feature of the conception. It imposes certain criteria on the design of the basic structure as a whole; these arrangements must not tend to generate propensities and attitudes contrary to the two principles of justice (that is, to certain principles which are given from the first a definite content) and they must insure that just institutions are stable. Thus certain initial bounds are placed upon what is good and what forms of character are morally worthy, and so upon what kinds of persons men should be. Now any theory of justice will set up some limits of this kind, namely, those that are required if its first principles are to be satisfied given the circumstances. Utilitarianism excludes those desires and propensities which if encouraged or permitted would, in view of the situation, lead to a lesser net balance of satisfaction. But this restriction is largely formal, and in the absence of fairly detailed knowledge of the circumstances it does not give much indication of what these

11. Bentham, *The Principles of Morals and Legislation*, ch. I, sec. IV.

12. The priority of right is a central feature of Kant's ethics. See, for example, *The Critique of Practical Reason*, ch. II, bk. I of *pt. I*, esp. pp. 62–65 of vol. 5 of *Kants Gesammelte Schriften, Preussische Akademie der Wissenschaften* (Berlin, 1913). A clear statement is to be found in "Theory and Practice" (to abbreviate the title), *Political Writings*, pp. 67f.

desires and propensities are. This is not, by itself, an objection to utilitarianism. It is simply a feature of utilitarian doctrine that it relies very heavily upon the natural facts and contingencies of human life in determining what forms of moral character are to be encouraged in a just society. The moral ideal of justice as fairness is more deeply embedded in the first principles of the ethical theory. This is characteristic of natural rights views (the contractarian tradition) in comparison with the theory of utility. [. . .]

Two Principles of Justice

I shall now state in a provisional form the two principles of justice that I believe would be chosen in the original position. In this section I wish to make only the most general comments, and therefore the first formulation of these principles is tentative. As we go on I shall run through several formulations and approximate step by step the final statement to be given much later. I believe that doing this allows the exposition to proceed in a natural way.

The first statement of the two principles reads as follows.

First: each person is to have an equal right to the most extensive basic liberty compatible with a similar liberty for others.

Second: social and economic inequalities are to be arranged so that they are both (a) reasonably expected to be to everyone's advantage, and (b) attached to positions and offices open to all. There are two ambiguous phrases in the second principle, namely "everyone's advantage" and "open to all." Determining their sense more exactly will lead to a second formulation of the principle in ["Democratic Equality and the Difference Principle"] . . .

By way of general comment, these principles primarily apply, as I have said, to the basic structure of society. They are to govern the assignment of rights and duties and to regulate the distribution of social and economic advantages. As their formulation suggests, these principles presuppose that the social structure can be divided into two more or less distinct parts, the first principle applying to the one, the second to the other. They distinguish between those aspects of the social system that define and secure the equal liberties of citizenship and those that specify and establish social and economic inequalities. The basic liberties of citizens are, roughly speaking, political liberty (the right to vote and to be eligible for public office) together with freedom of speech and assembly; liberty of conscience and freedom of thought; freedom of the person along with the right to hold (personal) property; and freedom from arbitrary arrest and seizure as defined by the concept of the rule of law. These liberties are all required to be equal by the first principle, since citizens of a just society are to have the same basic rights.

The second principle applies, in the first approximation, to the distribution of income and wealth and to the design of organizations that make use of differences in authority and responsibility, or chains of command. While the distribution of wealth and income need not be equal, it must be to everyone's advantage, and at the same time, positions of authority and offices of command must be accessible to all. One applies the second principle by holding positions open, and then, subject to this constraint, arranges social and economic inequalities so that everyone benefits.

These principles are to be arranged in a serial order with the first principle prior to the second. This ordering means that a departure from the institutions of equal liberty required by the first principle cannot be justified by, or compensated for, by greater social and economic advantages. The distribution of wealth and income, and the hierarchies of authority, must be consistent with both the liberties of equal citizenship and equality of opportunity.

It is clear that these principles are rather specific in their content, and their acceptance rests on certain assumptions that I must eventually try to explain and justify. A theory of justice depends upon a theory of society in ways that will become evident as we proceed. For the present, it should be observed that the two principles (and this holds for all formulations) are a special case of a more general conception of justice that can be expressed as follows.

All social values—liberty and opportunity, income and wealth, and the bases of self-respect—are to be distributed equally unless an unequal distribution of any, or all, of these values is to everyone's advantage.

Injustice, then, is simply inequalities that are not to the benefit of all. . . .

Interpretations of the Second Principle

I have already mentioned that since the phrases "everyone's advantage" and "equally open to all" are ambiguous, both parts of the second principle have two natural senses. Because these senses are independent of one another, the principle has four possible meanings. Assuming that the first principle of equal liberty has the same sense throughout, we then have four interpretations of the two principles. These are indicated in the table below.

I shall sketch in turn these three interpretations: the system of natural liberty, liberal equality, and democratic equality. In some respects this sequence is the more intuitive one, but the sequence via the interpretation of natural aristocracy is not without interest and I shall comment on it briefly. In working out justice as fairness, we must decide which interpretation is to be preferred. I shall adopt that of democratic equality, explaining in this chapter what this notion means. The argument for its acceptance in the original position does not begin until the next chapter.

The first interpretation (in either sequence) I shall refer to as the system of natural liberty. In this rendering the first part of the second principle is understood as the principle of efficiency adjusted so as to apply to institutions or, in this case, to the basic structure of society; and the second part is understood as an open social system in which, to use the traditional phrase, careers are open to talents. I assume in all interpretations that the first principle of equal liberty is satisfied and that the economy is roughly a free market system, although the means of production may or may not be privately owned. The system of natural liberty asserts, then, that a basic structure satisfying

the principle of efficiency and in which positions are open to those able and willing to strive for them will lead to a just distribution. Assigning rights and duties in this way is thought to give a scheme which allocates wealth and income, authority and responsibility, in a fair way whatever this allocation turns out to be. . . . The system of natural liberty selects an efficient distribution roughly as follows. Let us suppose that we know from economic theory that under the standard assumptions defining a competitive market economy, income and wealth will be distributed in an efficient way, and that the particular efficient distribution which results in any period of time is determined by the initial distribution of assets, that is, by the initial distribution of income and wealth, and of natural talents and abilities. With each initial distribution, a definite efficient outcome is arrived at. Thus it turns out that if we are to accept the outcome as just, and not merely as efficient, we must accept the basis upon which over time the initial distribution of assets is determined.

In the system of natural liberty the initial distribution is regulated by the arrangements implicit in the conception of careers open to talents (as earlier defined). These arrangements presuppose a background of equal liberty (as specified by the first principle) and a free market economy. They require a formal equality of opportunity in that all have at least the same legal rights of access to all advantaged social positions. But since there is no effort to preserve an equality, or similarity, of social conditions, except insofar as this is necessary to preserve the requisite background institutions, the initial distribution of assets for any period of time is strongly influenced by natural and social contingencies. The existing distribution of income and wealth, say, is the cumulative effect of prior distributions of natural assets—that is, natural talents and abilities—as these have been developed or left unrealized, and their use favored or disfavored over time by social circumstances and such chance

"Equally open"	"Everyone's advantage"	
	Principle of efficiency	Difference principle
Equality as careers open to talents	System of Natural Liberty	Natural Aristocracy
Equality as equality of fair opportunity	Liberal Equality	Democratic Equality

Liberal int.

contingencies as accident and good fortune. Intuitively, the most obvious injustice of the system of natural liberty is that it permits distributive shares to be improperly influenced by these factors so arbitrary from a moral point of view.

The liberal interpretation, as I shall refer to it, tries to correct for this by adding to the requirement of careers open to talents the further condition of the principle of fair equality of opportunity. The thought here is that positions are to be not only open in a formal sense, but that all should have a fair chance to attain them. Offhand it is not clear what is meant, but we might say that those with similar abilities and skills should have similar life chances. More specifically, assuming that there is a distribution of natural assets, those who are at the same level of talent and ability, and have the same willingness to use them, should have the same prospects of success regardless of their initial place in the social system, that is, irrespective of the income class into which they are born. In all sectors of society there should be roughly equal prospects of culture and achievement for everyone similarly motivated and endowed. The expectations of those with the same abilities and aspirations should not be affected by their social class.[13]

The liberal interpretation of the two principles seeks, then, to mitigate the influence of social contingencies and natural fortune on distributive shares. To accomplish this end it is necessary to impose further basic structural conditions on the social system. Free market arrangements must be set within a framework of political and legal institutions which regulates the overall trends of economic events and preserves the social conditions necessary for fair equality of opportunity. The elements of this framework are familiar enough, though it may be worthwhile to recall the importance of preventing excessive accumulations of property and wealth and of maintaining equal opportunities of education for all. Chances to acquire cultural knowledge and skills should not depend upon one's class position, and so the school system, whether public or private, should be designed to even out class barriers.

While the liberal conception seems clearly preferable to the system of natural liberty, intuitively it still appears defective. For one thing, even if it works to perfection in eliminating the influence of social contingencies, it still permits the distribution of wealth and income to be determined by the natural distribution of abilities and talents. Within the limits allowed by the background arrangements, distributive shares are decided by the outcome of the natural lottery; and this outcome is arbitrary from a moral perspective. There is no more reason to permit the distribution of income and wealth to be settled by the distribution of natural assets than by historical and social fortune. Furthermore, the principle of fair opportunity can be only imperfectly carried out, at least as long as the institution of the family exists. The extent to which natural capacities develop and reach fruition is affected by all kinds of social conditions and class attitudes. Even the willingness to make an effort, to try, and so to be deserving in the ordinary sense is itself dependent upon happy family and social circumstances. It is impossible in practice to secure equal chances of achievement and culture for those similarly endowed, and therefore we may want to adopt a principle which recognizes this fact and also mitigates the arbitrary effects of the natural lottery itself. That the liberal conception fails to do this encourages one to look for another interpretation of the two principles of justice.

Before turning to the conception of democratic equality, we should note that of natural aristocracy. On this view no attempt is made to regulate social contingencies beyond what is required by formal equality of opportunity, but the advantages of persons with greater natural endowments are to be limited to those that further the good of the poorer sectors of society. The aristocratic ideal is applied to a system that is open, at least from a legal point of view, and the better situation of those favored by it is regarded as just only when less would be had by those below, if less were given to those above.[14] In this

13. This definition follows Sidgwick's suggestion in *The Methods of Ethics*, p. 285n. See also R. H. Tawney, *Equality* (London, George Allen and Unwin, 1931), ch. II, sec. ii; and B. A. O. Williams, "The Idea of Equality," in *Philosophy, Politics, and Society*, ed. Peter Laslett and W. G. Runciman (Oxford, Basil Blackwell, 1962), pp. 125f.

14. This formulation of the aristocratic ideal is derived from Santayana's account of aristocracy in ch. IV of *Reason and Society* (New York, Charles Scribner, 1905), pp. 109f. He says, for example, "an aristocratic regimen

way the idea of *noblesse oblige* is carried over to the conception of natural aristocracy.

Now both the liberal conception and that of natural aristocracy are unstable. For once we are troubled by the influence of either social contingencies or natural chance on the determination of distributive shares, we are bound, on reflection, to be bothered by the influence of the other. From a moral standpoint the two seem equally arbitrary. So however we move away from the system of natural liberty, we cannot be satisfied short of the democratic conception. This conception I have yet to explain. And, moreover, none of the preceding remarks are an argument for this conception, since in a contract theory all arguments, strictly speaking, are to be made in terms of what it would be rational to choose in the original position. But I am concerned here to prepare the way for the favored interpretation of the two principles so that these criteria, especially the second one, will not strike the reader as too eccentric or bizarre. I have tried to show that once we try to find a rendering of them which treats everyone equally as a moral person, and which does not weight men's share in the benefits and burdens of social cooperation according to their social fortune or their luck in the natural lottery, it is clear that the democratic interpretation is the best choice among the four alternatives. With these comments as a preface, I now turn to this conception.

Democratic Equality and the Difference Principle

The democratic interpretation, as the table suggests, is arrived at by combining the principle of fair equality of opportunity with the difference principle. This principle removes the indeterminateness of the principle of efficiency by singling out a particular position from which the social and economic inequalities of the basic structure are to be judged. Assuming the framework of institutions required by equal liberty and fair equality of opportunity, the higher expectations of those better situated are just if and only if they work as part of a scheme which improves the expectations of the least advantaged members of society. The intuitive idea is that the social order

is not to establish and secure the more attractive prospects of those better off unless doing so is to the advantage of those less fortunate. [. . .]

The Tendency to Equality

I wish to conclude this discussion of the two principles by explaining the sense in which they express an egalitarian conception of justice. Also I should like to forestall the objection to the principle of fair opportunity that it leads to a callous meritocratic society. In order to prepare the way for doing this, I note several aspects of the conception of justice that I have set out.

First, we may observe that the difference principle gives some weight to the considerations singled out by the principle of redress. This is the principle that undeserved inequalities call for redress; and since inequalities of birth and natural endowment are undeserved, these inequalities are to be somehow compensated for.[15] Thus the principle holds that in order to treat all persons equally, to provide genuine equality of opportunity, society must give more attention to those with fewer native assets and to those born into the less favorable social positions. The idea is to redress the bias of contingencies in the direction of equality. In pursuit of this principle greater resources might be spent on the education of the less rather than the more intelligent, at least over a certain time of life, say the earlier years of school.

Now the principle of redress has not to my knowledge been proposed as the sole criterion of justice, as the single aim of the social order. It is plausible as most such principles are only as a prima facie principle, one that is to be weighed in the balance with others. For example, we are to weigh it against the principle to improve the

can only be justified by radiating benefit and by proving that were less given to those above, less would be attained by those beneath them." I am indebted to Robert Rodes for pointing out to me that natural aristocracy is a possible interpretation of the two principles of justice and that an ideal feudal system might also try to fulfill the difference principle.

15. See Herbert Spiegelberg, "A Defense of Human Equality," *Philosophical Review*, vol. 53 (1944), pp. 101, 113–123; and D. D. Raphael, "Justice and Liberty," *Proceedings of the Aristotelian Society*, vol. 51 (1950–1951), pp. 187f.

average standard of life, or to advance the common good.[16] But whatever other principles we hold, the claims of redress are to be taken into account. It is thought to represent one of the elements in our conception of justice. Now the difference principle is not of course the principle of redress. It does not require society to try to even out handicaps as if all were expected to compete on a fair basis in the same race. But the difference principle would allocate resources in education, say, so as to improve the long-term expectation of the least favored. If this end is attained by giving more attention to the better endowed, it is permissible; otherwise not. And in making this decision, the value of education should not be assessed only in terms of economic efficiency and social welfare. Equally if not more important is the role of education in enabling a person to enjoy the culture of his society and to take part in its affairs, and in this way to provide for each individual a secure sense of his own worth.

Thus although the difference principle is not the same as that of redress, it does achieve some of the intent of the latter principle. It transforms the aims of the basic structure so that the total scheme of institutions no longer emphasizes social efficiency and technocratic values. We see then that the difference principle represents, in effect, an agreement to regard the distribution of natural talents as a common asset and to share in the benefits of this distribution whatever it turns out to be. Those who have been favored by nature, whoever they are, may gain from their good fortune only on terms that improve the situation of those who have lost out. The naturally advantaged are not to gain merely because they are more gifted, but only to cover the costs of training and education and for using their endowments in ways that help the less fortunate as well. No one deserves his greater natural capacity nor merits a more favorable starting place in society. But it does not follow that one should eliminate these distinctions. There is another way to deal with them. The basic structure can be arranged so that these contingencies work for the good of the least fortunate. Thus we are led to the difference principle if we wish to set up the social system so that no one gains or loses from his arbitrary place in the

16. See, for example, Spiegelberg, pp. 120f.

distribution of natural assets or his initial position in society without giving or receiving compensating advantages in return.

In view of these remarks we may reject the contention that the ordering of institutions is always defective because the distribution of natural talents and the contingencies of social circumstance are unjust, and this injustice must inevitably carry over to human arrangements. Occasionally this reflection is offered as an excuse for ignoring injustice, as if the refusal to acquiesce in injustice is on a par with being unable to accept death. The natural distribution is neither just nor unjust; nor is it unjust that men are born into society at some particular position. These are simply natural facts. What is just and unjust is the way that institutions deal with these facts. Aristocratic and caste societies are unjust because they make these contingencies the ascriptive basis for belonging to more or less enclosed and privileged social classes. The basic structure of these societies incorporates the arbitrariness found in nature. But there is no necessity for men to resign themselves to these contingencies. The social system is not an unchangeable order beyond human control but a pattern of human action. In justice as fairness men agree to share one another's fate. In designing institutions they undertake to avail themselves of the accidents of nature and social circumstance only when doing so is for the common benefit. The two principles are a fair way of meeting the arbitrariness of fortune; and while no doubt imperfect in other ways, the institutions which satisfy these principles are just.

A further point is that the difference principle expresses a conception of reciprocity. It is a principle of mutual benefit. We have seen that, at least when chain connection holds, each representative man can accept the basic structure as designed to advance his interests. The social order can be justified to everyone, and in particular to those who are least favored; and in this sense it is egalitarian. But it seems necessary to consider in an intuitive way how the condition of mutual benefit is satisfied. Consider any two representative men A and B, and let B be the one who is less favored. Actually, since we are most interested in the comparison with the least favored man, let us assume that B is this individual. Now B can accept A's being better off since A's advantages have been gained in ways that improve B's prospects. If A were not allowed his better position, B would be even worse off than he is. The difficulty is to show that A has no grounds for complaint. Perhaps he is required to have less than he might since his having more would result in some loss to B. Now what can be said to the more favored man? To begin with, it is clear that the well-being of each depends on a scheme of social cooperation without which no one could have a satisfactory life. Secondly, we can ask for the willing cooperation of everyone only if the terms of the scheme are reasonable. The difference principle, then, seems to be a fair basis on which those better endowed, or more fortunate in their social circumstances, could expect others to collaborate with them when some workable arrangement is a necessary condition of the good of all.

There is a natural inclination to object that those better situated deserve their greater advantages whether or not they are to the benefit of others. At this point it is necessary to be clear about the notion of desert. It is perfectly true that given a just system of cooperation as a scheme of public rules and the expectations set up by it, those who, with the prospect of improving their condition, have done what the system announces that it will reward are entitled to their advantages. In this sense the more fortunate have a claim to their better situation; their claims are legitimate expectations established by social institutions, and the community is obligated to meet them. But this sense of desert presupposes the existence of the cooperative scheme; it is irrelevant to the question whether in the first place the scheme is to be designed in accordance with the difference principle or some other criterion.

Perhaps some will think that the person with greater natural endowments deserves those assets and the superior character that made their development possible. Because he is more worthy in this sense, he deserves the greater advantages that he could achieve with them. This view, however, is surely incorrect. It seems to be one of the fixed points of our considered judgments that no one deserves his place in the distribution of native endowments, any more than one deserves one's initial starting place in society. The assertion that a man deserves the superior character that enables him to make the effort to cultivate his abilities is

equally problematic; for his character depends in large part upon fortunate family and social circumstances for which he can claim no credit. The notion of desert seems not to apply to these cases. Thus the more advantaged representative man cannot say that he deserves and therefore has a right to a scheme of cooperation in which he is permitted to acquire benefits in ways that do not contribute to the welfare of others. There is no basis for his making this claim. From the standpoint of common sense, then, the difference principle appears to be acceptable both to the more advantaged and to the less advantaged individual. Of course, none of this is strictly speaking an argument for the principle, since in a contract theory arguments are made from the point of view of the original position. But these intuitive considerations help to clarify the nature of the principle and the sense in which it is egalitarian. [. . .]

The Veil of Ignorance

The idea of the original position is to set up a fair procedure so that any principles agreed to will be just. The aim is to use the notion of pure procedural justice as a basis of theory. Somehow we must nullify the effects of specific contingencies which put men at odds and tempt them to exploit social and natural circumstances to their own advantage. Now in order to do this I assume that the parties are situated behind a veil of ignorance. They do not know how the various alternatives will affect their own particular case and they are obliged to evaluate principles solely on the basis of general considerations.[17]

It is assumed, then, that the parties do not know certain kinds of particular facts. First of all, no one knows his place in society, his class position or social status; nor does he know his fortune in the distribution of natural assets and abilities, his intelligence and strength, and the like. Nor, again, does anyone know his conception of the

17. The veil of ignorance is so natural a condition that something like it must have occurred to many. The closest express statement of it known to me is found in J. C. Harsanyi, "Cardinal Utility in Welfare Economics and in the Theory of Risk-Taking," *Journal of Political Economy*, vol. 61 (1953). Harsanyi uses it to develop a utilitarian theory. . . .

good, the particulars of his rational plan of life, or even the special features of his psychology such as his aversion to risk or liability to optimism or pessimism. More than this, I assume that the parties do not know the particular circumstances of their own society. That is, they do not know its economic or political situation, or the level of civilization and culture it has been able to achieve. The persons in the original position have no information as to which generation they belong. These broader restrictions on knowledge are appropriate in part because questions of social justice arise between generations as well as within them, for example, the question of the appropriate rate of capital saving and of the conservation of natural resources and the environment of nature. There is also, theoretically anyway, the question of a reasonable genetic policy. In these cases too, in order to carry through the idea of the original position, the parties must not know the contingencies that set them in opposition. They must choose principles the consequences of which they are prepared to live with whatever generation they turn out to belong to. [. . .]

These remarks show that the original position is not to be thought of as a general assembly which includes at one moment everyone who will live at some time; or, much less, as an assembly of everyone who could live at some time. It is not a gathering of all actual or possible persons. To conceive of the original position in either of these ways is to stretch fantasy too far; the conception would cease to be a natural guide to intuition. In any case, it is important that the original position be interpreted so that one can at any time adopt its perspective. It must make no difference when one takes up this viewpoint, or who does so: the restrictions must be such that the same principles are always chosen. The veil of ignorance is a key condition in meeting this requirement. It insures not only that the information available is relevant, but that it is at all times the same.

It may be protested that the condition of the veil of ignorance is irrational. Surely, some may object, principles should be chosen in the light of all the knowledge available. There are various replies to this contention. Here I shall sketch those which emphasize the simplifications that need to be made if one is to have any theory at all. (Those based on the Kantian interpretation of

the original position are given later.) To begin with, it is clear that since the differences among the parties are unknown to them, and everyone is equally rational and similarly situated, each is convinced by the same arguments. Therefore, we can view the choice in the original position from the standpoint of one person selected at random. If anyone after due reflection prefers a conception of justice to another, then they all do, and a unanimous agreement can be reached. We can, to make the circumstances more vivid, imagine that the parties are required to communicate with each other through a referee as intermediary, and that he is to announce which alternatives have been suggested and the reasons offered in their support. He forbids the attempt to form coalitions, and he informs the parties when they have come to an understanding. But such a referee is actually superfluous, assuming that the deliberations of the parties must be similar.

Thus there follows the very important consequence that the parties have no basis for bargaining in the usual sense. No one knows his situation in society nor his natural assets, and therefore no one is in a position to tailor principles to his advantage. We might imagine that one of the contractees threatens to hold out unless the others agree to principles favorable to him. But how does he know which principles are especially in his interests? The same holds for the formation of coalitions: if a group were to decide to band together to the disadvantage of the others, they would not know how to favor themselves in the choice of principles. Even if they could get everyone to agree to their proposal, they would have no assurance that it was to their advantage, since they cannot identify themselves either by name or description. The one case where this conclusion fails is that of saving. Since the persons in the original position know that they are contemporaries (taking the present time of entry interpretation), they can favor their generation by refusing to make any sacrifices at all for their successors; they simply acknowledge the principle that no one has a duty to save for posterity. Previous generations have saved or they have not; there is nothing the parties can now do to affect that. So in this instance the veil of ignorance fails to secure the desired result. Therefore I resolve the question of justice between generations in a different way by altering the motivation assumption. But with this adjustment no one is able to formulate principles especially designed to advance his own cause. Whatever his temporal position, each is forced to choose for everyone.[18]

The restrictions on particular information in the original position are, then, of fundamental importance. Without them we would not be able to work out any definite theory of justice at all. We would have to be content with a vague formula stating that justice is what would be agreed to without being able to say much, if anything, about the substance of the agreement itself. The formal constraints of the concept of right, those applying to principles directly, are not sufficient for our purpose. The veil of ignorance makes possible a unanimous choice of a particular conception of justice. Without these limitations on knowledge the bargaining problem of the original position would be hopelessly complicated. Even if theoretically a solution were to exist, we would not, at present anyway, be able to determine it.

The notion of the veil of ignorance is implicit, I think, in Kant's ethics. Nevertheless the problem of defining the knowledge of the parties and of characterizing the alternatives open to them has often been passed over, even by contract theories. Sometimes the situation definitive of moral deliberation is presented in such an indeterminate way that one cannot ascertain how it will turn out. Thus Perry's doctrine is essentially contractarian: he holds that social and personal integration must proceed by entirely different principles, the latter by rational prudence the former by the concurrence of persons of good will. He would appear to reject utilitarianism on much the same grounds suggested earlier: namely, that it improperly extends the principle of choice for one person to choices facing society. The right course of action is characterized as that which best advances social aims as these would be formulated by reflective agreement given that the parties have full knowledge of the circumstances and are moved by a benevolent concern for one another's interests. No effort is made, however, to specify in any precise way the possible outcomes of this sort of agreement. Indeed, without a far more elaborate account, no conclusions can be drawn.[19] I do not wish here to criticize others; rather, I want to explain the necessity for what may seem at times like so many irrelevant details.

Now the reasons for the veil of ignorance go beyond mere simplicity. We want to define the original position so that we get the desired solution. If a knowledge of particulars is allowed, then the outcome is biased by arbitrary contingencies. As already observed, to each according to his threat advantage is not a principle of justice. If the original position is to yield agreements that are just, the parties must be fairly situated and treated equally as moral persons. The arbitrariness of the world must be corrected for by adjusting the circumstances of the initial contractual situation. Moreover, if in choosing principles we required unanimity even when there is full information, only a few rather obvious cases could be decided. A conception of justice based on unanimity in these circumstances would indeed be weak and trivial. But once knowledge is excluded, the requirement of unanimity is not out of place and the fact that it can be satisfied is of great importance. It enables us to say of the preferred conception of justice that it represents a genuine reconciliation of interests. [. . .]

18. Rousseau, *The Social Contract*, bk, II, ch. IV, par. 5.

19. See R. B. Perry, *The General Theory of Value* (New York, Longmans, Green and Company, 1926), pp. 674–682.

Chapter 8

DISTRIBUTIVE JUSTICE: EQUALITY, ENTITLEMENT, AND MERIT

John Rawls and Robert Nozick both reject utilitarianism. Both believe that certain individual rights are so fundamental that utilitarian considerations should not override them. But they disagree about what rights are fundamental. For Nozick and other libertarians, people have a right to the money they earn in a free market; it is unjust to tax their earnings to help those who have less. Rawls disagrees. He does not believe that the results of a free market are necessarily fair.

Why not? Recall the second of his two principles of justice. Only those inequalities are just that work to the benefit of the least advantaged members of society. What are the reasons that lead Rawls to this principle? How persuasive do you find them? What sorts of inequalities might be acceptable under this principle? As you consider these questions, think about the distinction Rawls makes between moral desert and legitimate expectations. Why does he claim that distributive justice is not a matter of moral desert? Do you agree? In what sense, if any, do people morally deserve the benefits that result from the exercise of their talents—good grades; college admission; income and wealth; fulfilling work; social prestige?

A THEORY OF JUSTICE

John Rawls

Legitimate Expectations and Moral Desert

There is a tendency for common sense to suppose that income and wealth, and the good things in life generally, should be distributed according to moral desert. Justice is happiness according to virtue. While it is recognized that this ideal can never be fully carried out, it is the appropriate conception of distributive justice, at least as a prime facie principle, and society should try to

realize it as circumstances permit.[1] Now justice as fairness rejects this conception. Such a principle

1. See, for example, W. D. Ross, *The Right and the Good* (Oxford, The Clarendon Press, 1930), pp. 21, 26–28, 35, 57f. Similarly, Leibniz in "On the Ultimate Origin of Things" (1697) speaks of the law of justice which "declares that each one [each individual] participate in the perfection of the universe and in a happiness of his own in proportion to his own virtue and to the good will he entertains toward the common good." *Leibniz,* ed. P. P. Wiener (New York, Charles Scribner's Sons, 1951), p. 353.

would not be chosen in the original position. There seems to be no way of defining the requisite criterion in that situation. Moreover, the notion of distribution according to virtue fails to distinguish between moral desert and legitimate expectations. Thus it is true that as persons and groups take part in just arrangements, they acquire claims on one another defined by the publicly recognized rules. Having done various things encouraged by the existing arrangements, they now have certain rights, and just distributive shares honor these claims. A just scheme, then, answers to what men are entitled to; it satisfies their legitimate expectations as founded upon social institutions. But what they are entitled to is not proportional to nor dependent upon their intrinsic worth. The principles of justice that regulate the basic structure and specify the duties and obligations of individuals do not mention moral desert, and there is no tendency for distributive shares to correspond to it.

This contention is borne out by the preceding account of common sense precepts and their role in pure procedural justice. For example, in determining wages a competitive economy gives weight to the precept of contribution. But as we have seen, the extent of one's contribution (estimated by one's marginal productivity) depends upon supply and demand. Surely a person's moral worth does not vary according to how many offer similar skills, or happen to want what he can produce. No one supposes that when someone's abilities are less in demand or have deteriorated (as in the case of singers) his moral deservingness undergoes a similar shift. All of this is perfectly obvious and has long been agreed to.[2] It simply reflects the fact noted before ["The Tendency to Equality"] that it is one of the fixed points of our moral judgments that no one deserves his place in the distribution of natural assets any more than he deserves his initial starting place in society.

Moreover, none of the precepts of justice aims at rewarding virtue. The premiums earned by scarce natural talents, for example, are to cover the costs of training and to encourage the efforts of learning, as well as to direct ability to where it best furthers the common interest. The distribu-

tive shares that result do not correlate with moral worth, since the initial endowment of natural assets and the contingencies of their growth and nurture in early life are arbitrary from a moral point of view. The precept which seems intuitively to come closest to rewarding moral desert is that of distribution according to effort, or perhaps better, conscientious effort.[3] Once again, however, it seems clear that the effort a person is willing to make is influenced by his natural abilities and skills and the alternatives open to him. The better endowed are more likely, other things equal, to strive conscientiously, and there seems to be no way to discount for their greater good fortune. The idea of rewarding desert is impracticable. And certainly to the extent that the precept of need is emphasized, moral worth is ignored. Nor does the basic structure tend to balance the precepts of justice so as to achieve the requisite correspondence behind the scenes. It is regulated by the two principles of justice which define other aims entirely.

The same conclusion may be reached in another way. In the preceding remarks the notion of moral worth as distinct from a person's claims based upon his legitimate expectations has not been explained. Suppose, then, that we define this notion and show that it has no correlation with distributive shares. We have only to consider a well-ordered society, that is, a society in which institutions are just and this fact is publicly recognized. Its members also have a strong sense of justice, an effective desire to comply with the existing rules and to give one another that to which they are entitled. In this case we may assume that everyone is of equal moral worth. We have now defined this notion in terms of the sense of justice, the desire to act in accordance with the principles that would be chosen in the original position. But it is evident that understood in this way, the equal moral worth of persons does not entail that distributive shares are equal. Each is to receive what the principles of justice say he is entitled to, and these do not require equality.

The essential point is that the concept of moral worth does not provide a first principle of distributive justice. This is because it cannot be introduced until after the principles of justice and

2. See F. H. Knight, *The Ethics of Competition* (New York, Harper and Brothers, 1935), pp. 54–57.

3. See Knight, *ibid.*, p. 56n.

of natural duty and obligation have been acknowledged. Once these principles are on hand, moral worth can be defined as having a sense of justice; and as I shall discuss later, the virtues can be characterized as desires or tendencies to act upon the corresponding principles. Thus the concept of moral worth is secondary to those of right and justice, and it plays no role in the substantive definition of distributive shares. The case is analogous to the relation between the substantive rules of property and the law of robbery and theft. These offenses and the demerits they entail presuppose the institution of property which is established for prior and independent social ends. For a society to organize itself with the aim of rewarding moral desert as a first principle would be like having the institution of property in order to punish thieves. The criterion to each according to his virtue would not, then, be chosen in the original position. Since the parties desire to advance their conceptions of the good, they have no reason for arranging their institutions so that distributive shares are determined by moral desert, even if they could find an antecedent standard for its definition.

In a well-ordered society individuals acquire claims to a share of the social product by doing certain things encouraged by the existing arrangements. The legitimate expectations that arise are the other side, so to speak, of the principle of fairness and the natural duty of justice. For in the way that one has a duty to uphold just arrangements, and an obligation to do one's part when one has accepted a position in them, so a person who has complied with the scheme and done his share has a right to be treated accordingly by others. They are bound to meet his legitimate expectations. Thus when just economic arrangements exist, the claims of individuals are properly settled by reference to the rules and precepts (with their respective weights) which these practices take as relevant. As we have seen, it is incorrect to say that just distributive shares reward individuals according to their moral worth. But what we can say is that, in the traditional phrase, a just scheme gives each person his due: that is, it allots to each what he is entitled to as defined by the scheme itself. The principles of justice for institutions and individuals establish that doing this is fair.

Now it should be noted that even though a person's claims are regulated by the existing rules, we can still make a distinction between being entitled to something and deserving it in a familiar although nonmoral sense.[4] To illustrate, after a game one often says that the losing side deserved to win. Here one does not mean that the victors are not entitled to claim the championship, or whatever spoils go to the winner. One means instead that the losing team displayed to a higher degree the skills and qualities that the game calls forth, and the exercise of which gives the sport its appeal. Therefore the losers truly deserved to win but lost out as a result of bad luck, or from other contingencies that caused the contest to miscarry. Similarly even the best economic arrangements will not always lead to the more preferred outcomes. The claims that individuals actually acquire inevitably deviate more or less widely from those that the scheme is designed to allow for. Some persons in favored positions, for example, may not have to a higher degree than others the desired qualities and abilities. All this is evident enough. Its bearing here is that although we can indeed distinguish between the claims that existing arrangements require us to honor, given what individuals have done and how things have turned out, and the claims that would have resulted under more ideal circumstances, none of this implies that distributive shares should be in accordance with moral worth. Even when things transpire in the best way, there is still no tendency for distribution and virtue to coincide.

No doubt some may still contend that distributive shares should match moral worth at least to the extent that this is feasible. They may believe that unless those who are better off have superior moral character, their having greater advantages is an affront to our sense of justice. Now this opinion may arise from thinking of distributive justice as somehow the opposite of retributive justice. It is true that in a reasonably well-ordered society those who are punished for violating just laws have normally done something wrong. This is because the purpose of the criminal law is to uphold basic natural duties, those which forbid us to injure other persons in their life and limb, or to

4. Here I borrow from Joel Feinberg, *Doing and Deserving* (Princeton, Princeton University Press, 1970), pp. 64f.

deprive them of their liberty and property, and punishments are to serve this end. They are not simply a scheme of taxes and burdens designed to put a price on certain forms of conduct and in this way to guide men's conduct for mutual advantage. It would be far better if the acts proscribed by penal statutes were never done.[5] Thus a propensity to commit such acts is a mark of bad character, and in a just society legal punishments will only fall upon those who display these faults.

It is clear that the distribution of economic and social advantages is entirely different. These arrangements are not the converse, so to speak, of the criminal law so that just as the one punishes certain offenses, the other rewards moral worth.[6] The function of unequal distributive shares is to cover the costs of training and education, to

5. See H. L. A. Hart, *The Concept of Law* (Oxford, The Clarendon Press, 1961), p. 39; and Feinberg, *Doing and Deserving*, ch. V.
6. On this point, see Feinberg, *ibid.*, pp. 62, 69n.

attract individuals to places and associations where they are most needed from a social point of view, and so on. Assuming that everyone accepts the propriety of self- or group-interested motivation duly regulated by a sense of justice, each decides to do those things that best accord with his aims. Variations in wages and income and the perquisites of position are simply to influence these choices so that the end result accords with efficiency and justice. In a well-ordered society there would be no need for the penal law except insofar as the assurance problem made it necessary. The question of criminal justice belongs for the most part to partial compliance theory whereas the account of distributive shares belongs to strict compliance theory and so to the consideration of the ideal scheme. To think of distributive and retributive justice as converses of one another is completely misleading and suggests a different justification for distributive shares than the one they in fact have.

ANARCHY, STATE, AND UTOPIA

Robert Nozick

Natural Assets and Arbitrariness

Rawls comes closest to considering the entitlement system in his discussion of what he terms the system of natural liberty:

The system of natural liberty selects an efficient distribution roughly as follows. Let us suppose that we know from economic theory that under the standard assumptions defining a competitive market economy, income and wealth will be distributed in an efficient way, and that the particular efficient distribution which results in any period of time is determined by the initial distribution of assets, that is, by the initial distribution of income and wealth, and of natural talents and abilities. With each initial distribution, a definite efficient outcome is arrived at. Thus it turns out that if we are to accept the outcome as just, and not merely as efficient, we must accept the basis upon which over time the initial distribution of assets is determined.

In the system of natural liberty the initial distribution is regulated by the arrangements implicit in the conception of careers open to talents. These arrangements presuppose a background of equal liberty (as specified by the first principle) and a free market economy. They require a formal equality of opportunity in that all have at least the same legal rights of access to all advantaged social positions. But since there is no effort to preserve an equality or similarity, of social conditions, except insofar as this is necessary to preserve the requisite background institutions, the initial distribution of assets for any period of time is strongly influenced by natural and social contingencies. The existing distribution of income and wealth, say, is the cumulative effect of prior distributions of natural assets—that is, natural talents and abilities—as these have been developed or left unrealized, and their use favored or disfavored over time by social circumstances and such chance contingencies as accident and good fortune. Intuitively, the most obvious injustice of the system of natural liberty is that it permits distributive shares to be improperly influenced by these factors so arbitrary from a moral point of view.

Here we have *Rawls'* reason for rejecting a system of natural liberty: it "permits" distributive shares to be improperly influenced by factors that are so arbitrary from a moral point of view. These factors are: "prior distribution ... of natural talents and abilities as these have been developed over time by social circumstances and such chance contingencies as accident and good fortune." Notice that there is no mention *at all* of how persons have chosen to develop their own natural assets. Why is that simply left out? Perhaps because such choices also are viewed as being the products of factors outside the person's control, and hence as "arbitrary from a moral point of view." "The assertion that a man deserves the superior character that enables him to make the effort to cultivate his abilities is equally problematic; for his character depends in large part upon fortunate family and social circumstances for which he can claim no credit." (What view is presupposed here of character and its relation to action?) "The initial endowment of natural assets and the contingencies of their growth and nurture in early life are arbitrary from a moral point of view ... the effort a person is willing to make is influenced by his natural abilities and skills and the alternatives open to him. The better endowed are more likely, other things equal, to strive conscientiously...." This line of argument can succeed in blocking the introduction of a person's autonomous choices and actions (and their results) only by attributing *everything* noteworthy about the person completely to certain sorts of "external" factors. So denigrating a person's autonomy and prime responsibility for his actions is a risky line to take for a theory that otherwise wishes to buttress the dignity and self-respect of autonomous beings; especially for a theory that founds so much (including a theory of the good) upon persons' choices. One doubts that the unexalted picture of human beings Rawls' theory presupposes and rests upon can be made to fit together with the view of human dignity it is designed to lead to and embody.

Before we investigate Rawls' reasons for rejecting the system of natural liberty, we should note the situation of those in the original position. The system of natural liberty is *one* interpretation of a principle that (according to Rawls) they *do* accept: social and economic inequalities are to be arranged so that they both are reasonably expected to be to everyone's advantage, and are attached to positions and offices open to all. It is left unclear whether the persons in the original position explicitly consider and choose among *all* the various interpretations of this principle, though this would seem to be the most reasonable construal.... Certainly they explicitly consider one interpretation, the difference principle. Rawls does not state why persons in the original position who considered the system of natural liberty would reject it. Their reason cannot be that it makes the resulting distribution depend upon a *morally* arbitrary distribution of natural assets. What we must suppose, as we have seen before, is that the self-interested calculation of persons in the original position does not (and cannot) lead them to adopt the entitlement principle. We, however, and Rawls, base our evaluations on different considerations.

Rawls has explicitly *designed* the original position and its choice situation so as to embody and realize his negative reflective evaluation of allowing shares in holdings to be affected by natural assets: "Once we decide to look for a conception of justice that nullifies the accidents of natural endowment and the contingencies of social circumstance...." (Rawls makes many scattered references to this theme of nullifying the accidents of natural endowment and the contingencies of social circumstance.) This quest crucially shapes Rawls' theory, and it underlies his delineation of the original position. It is not that persons who *did* deserve their natural endowments would choose differently if placed in Rawls' original position, but rather that, presumably, for such persons, Rawls would not hold that the principles of justice to govern *their* mutual relations were fixed by what they would choose in the original position. It is useful to remember how much of Rawls' construction rests upon this foundation. For example, Rawls argues that certain egalitarian demands are not motivated by envy but rather, because they are in accord with his two principles of justice, by resentment of injustice. This argument can be undercut, as Rawls realizes, if the very considerations which underlie the original position (yielding Rawls' two principles of justice) themselves embody or are based upon envy. So in addition to wanting to understand Rawls' rejection of alternative conceptions and to assess how powerful a criticism he makes of the entitlement conception, reasons internal to his theory provide motivation to explore the basis of the requirement that a conception of justice be geared to nullify differences in social circumstances and in natural assets (and any differences in social circumstances they result in).

Why shouldn't holdings partially depend upon natural endowments? (They will also depend on how these are developed and on the uses to which they are put.) Rawls' reply is that these natural endowments and assets, being undeserved, are "arbitrary from a moral point of view." There are two ways to understand the relevance of this reply: It might be part of an argument to establish that the distributive effects of natural differences ought to be nullified, which I shall call the positive argument; or it might be part of an argument to rebut a possible counterargument holding that the distributive effects of natural differences oughtn't to be nullified, which I shall call the negative argument. Whereas the positive argument attempts to establish that the distributive effects of natural differences ought to be nullified, the negative one, by merely rebutting *one* argument that the differences oughtn't to be nullified, leaves open the possibility that (for other reasons) the differences oughtn't to be nullified. (The negative argument also leaves it possibly a matter of moral *indifference* whether the distributive effects of natural differences are to be nullified; note the difference between saying that something ought to be the case and saying that it's not that it oughtn't to be the case.)

The Positive Argument

We shall begin with the positive argument. How might the point that differences in natural endowments are arbitrary from a moral point of view function in an argument meant to establish that differences in holdings stemming from differ-

ences in natural assets ought to be nullified? We shall consider four possible arguments; the first, the following argument A:

1. Any person should morally deserve the holdings he has; it shouldn't be that persons have holdings they don't deserve.
2. People do not morally deserve their natural assets.
3. If a person's X partially determines his Y, and his X is undeserved then so is his Y.

Therefore,

4. People's holdings shouldn't be partially determined by their natural assets.

This argument will serve as a surrogate for other similar, more complicated ones. But Rawls explicitly and emphatically *rejects* distribution according to moral desert.

> There is a tendency for common sense to suppose that income and wealth, and the good things in life generally, should be distributed according to moral desert. Justice is happiness according to virtue. While it is recognized that this ideal can never be fully carried out, it is the appropriate conception [according to common sense] of distributive justice, at least as a *prima facie* principle, and society should try to realize it as circumstances permit. Now justice as fairness rejects this conception. Such a principle would not be chosen in the original position.

Rawls could not, therefore, accept any premiss like the first premiss in argument A, and so no variant of this argument underlies his rejection of differences in distributive shares stemming from undeserved differences in natural assets. Not only does Rawls reject premiss I, his theory is not coextensive with it. He favors giving incentives to persons if this most improves the lot of the least well off, and it often will be because of their natural assets that these persons will receive incentives and have larger shares. We noted earlier that the entitlement conception of justice in holdings, not being a patterned conception of justice, does not accept distribution in accordance with moral desert either. Any person may give to anyone else any holding he is entitled to, independently of whether the recipient morally deserves to be the recipient. To each according to the legitimate entitlements that legitimately have been transferred to him, is not a patterned principle.

If argument A and its first premiss are rejected, it is not obvious how to construct the positive argument. Consider next argument B:

1. Holdings ought to be distributed according to some pattern that is not arbitrary from a moral point of view.
2. That persons have different natural assets *is* arbitrary from a moral point of view.

Therefore,

3. Holdings ought not to be distributed according to natural assets.

But differences in natural assets might be *correlated* with other differences that are not arbitrary from a moral point of view and that are clearly of some possible moral relevance to distributional questions. For example, Hayek argued that under capitalism distribution generally is in accordance with perceived service to others. Since differences in natural assets will produce differences in ability to serve others, there will be some correlation of differences in distribution with differences in natural assets. The principle of the system is *not* distribution in accordance with natural assets; but differences in natural assets will lead to differences in holdings under a system whose principle is distribution according to perceived service to others. If conclusion 3 above is to be interpreted in extension so as to exclude this, it should be made explicit. But to add the premiss that any pattern that has some roughly coextensive description that is arbitrary from a moral point of view is itself arbitrary from a moral point of view would be far too strong, because it would yield the result that *every* pattern is arbitrary from a moral point of view. Perhaps the crucial thing to be avoided is not mere coextensiveness, but rather some morally arbitrary feature's *giving rise to* differences in distributive shares. Thus consider argument C:

1. Holdings ought to be distributed according to some pattern that is not arbitrary from a moral point of view.
2. That persons have different natural assets is arbitrary from a moral point of view.
3. If part of the explanation of why a pattern contains differences in holdings is that other differences in persons give rise to these differences in holdings, and if these other differences are arbitrary from a moral point of view, then the pattern also is arbitrary from a moral point of view.

Therefore,

4. Differences in natural assets should not give rise to differences in holdings among persons.

Premiss 3 of this argument holds that any moral arbitrariness that underlies a pattern infects the pattern and makes it too morally arbitrary. But any pattern will have some morally arbitrary facts as part of the explanation of how it arises, including the pattern proposed by Rawls. The difference principle operates to give some persons larger distributive shares than others; which persons receive these larger shares will depend, at least partially, on differences between these persons and others, differences that are arbitrary from a moral point of view, for some persons with special natural assets will be offered larger shares as an incentive to use these assets in certain ways. Perhaps some premiss similar to 3 can be formulated so as to exclude what Rawls wishes to exclude while not excluding his *own* view. Still, the resulting argument would *assume* that the set of holdings should realize some pattern.

Why should the set of holdings be patterned? Patterning is *not* intrinsic to a theory of justice, as we have seen in our presentation of the entitlement theory: a theory that focuses upon the underlying principles that generate sets of holdings rather than upon the pattern a set of holdings realizes. If it be denied that the theory of these underlying principles *is* a separate theory of distributive justice, rather than merely a collection of diverse considerations from other areas, then the question becomes one of whether there *is* any separate subject of distributive justice which requires a separate theory.

On the manna-from-heaven model given earlier, there might be a more compelling reason to search for a pattern. But since things come into being already held (or with agreements already made about how they are to be held), there is no need to search for some pattern for unheld holdings to fit; and since the process whereby holdings actually come into being or are shaped, itself needn't realize any particular pattern, there is no reason to expect any pattern to result. The situation is not an appropriate one for wondering, "After all, what is to become of these things; what are we to do with them." In the non-manna-from-heaven world in which things have to be made or produced or transformed by people, there is no separate process of distribution for a theory of distribution to be a theory of. The reader will recall our earlier argument that (roughly) any set of holdings realizing a particular pattern may be transformed by the voluntary exchanges, gifts, and so forth, of the persons having the holdings under the pattern into *another* set of holdings that does not fit the pattern. The view that holdings *must* be patterned perhaps will seem less plausible when it is seen to have the consequence that people may not choose to do acts that upset the patterning, even with things they legitimately hold....

I turn now to our final positive argument which purports to derive the conclusion that distributive shares shouldn't depend upon natural assets from the statement that the distribution of natural assets is morally arbitrary. This argument focuses on the notion of equality. Since a large part of Rawls' argument serves to justify or show acceptable a particular deviation from equal shares (some may have more if this serves to improve the position of those worst off), perhaps a reconstruction of his underlying argument that places equality at its center will be illuminating. Differences between persons (the argument runs) are arbitrary from a moral point of view if there is no moral argument for the conclusion that there ought to be the differences. Not all such differences will be morally objectionable. That there is no such moral argument will seem important only in the case of those differences we believe oughtn't to obtain unless there is a moral reason establishing that they ought to obtain. There is, so to speak, a presumption against certain differences that can be overridden (can it merely be neutralized?) by moral reasons; in the absence of any such moral reasons of sufficient weight, there ought to be equality. Thus we have argument D:

1. Holdings ought to be equal, unless there is a (weighty) moral reason why they ought to be unequal.
2. People do not deserve the ways in which they differ from other persons in natural assets; there

is no moral reason why people ought to differ in natural assets.
3. If there is no moral reason why people differ in certain traits, then their actually differing in these traits does not provide, and cannot give rise to, a moral reason why they should differ in other traits (for example, in holdings).

Therefore,

4. People's differing in natural assets is not a reason why holdings ought to be unequal.
5. People's holdings ought to be equal unless there is some other moral reason (such as, for example, raising the position of those worst off) why their holdings ought to be unequal.

Statements similar to the third premiss will occupy us shortly. Here let us focus on the first premiss, the equality premiss. Why ought people's holdings to be equal, in the absence of special moral reason to deviate from equality? (Why think there *ought* to be *any* particular pattern in holdings?) Why is equality the rest (or rectilinear motion) position of the system, deviation from which may be caused only by moral forces? Many "arguments" for equality merely *assert* that differences between persons are arbitrary and must be justified. Often writers state a presumption in favor of equality in a form such as the following: "Differences in treatment of persons need to be justified." The most favored situation for this sort of assumption is one in which there is one person (or group) treating everyone, a person (or group) having *no* right or entitlement to bestow the particular treatment as they wish or even whim. But if I go to one movie theater rather than to another adjacent to it, need I justify my different treatment of the two theater owners? Isn't it enough that I felt like going to one of them? That differences in treatment need to be justified *does* fit contemporary *governments*. Here there is a centralized process treating all, with no entitlement to bestow treatment according to whim. The major portion of distribution in a free society does not, however, come through the actions of the government, nor does failure to overturn the results of the localized individual exchanges constitute "state action." When there is no *one* doing the treating, and all are entitled to bestow their holdings as they wish, it is not clear why the maxim that differences in treatment must be justified should be thought to have extensive application. Why must differences between persons be justified? Why think that we must change, or remedy, or compensate for any inequality which can be changed, remedied, or compensated for? Perhaps here is where social cooperation enters in: though there is no presumption of equality (in, say, primary goods, or things people care about) among all persons, perhaps there is one among persons cooperating together. But it is difficult to see an argument for this; surely not all persons who cooperate together explicitly agree to this presumption as one of the terms of their mutual cooperation. And its acceptance would provide an unfortunate incentive for well-off persons to refuse to cooperate with, or to allow any of their number to cooperate with, some distant people who are less well off than any among them. For entering into such social cooperation, beneficial to those less well off, would seriously worsen the position of the well-off group by creating relations of presumptive equality between themselves and the worse-off group. In the next chapter I shall consider the major recent argument for equality, one which turns out to be unsuccessful. Here we need only note that the connection argument D forges between not deserving natural assets and some conclusion about distributive shares *assumes* equality as a norm (that can be deviated from with, and only with, moral reason); and hence argument D itself cannot be used to establish any such conclusion about equality.

The Negative Argument

Unsuccessful in our quest for a convincing positive argument to connect the claim that people don't deserve their natural assets with the conclusion that differences in holdings ought not to be based upon differences in natural assets, we now turn to what we called the negative argument: the use of the claim that people don't deserve their natural assets to rebut a possible counterargument to Rawls' view. (If the equality argument D were acceptable, the negative task of rebutting possible counterconsiderations would form part of the positive task of showing that a presumption for equality holds unoverridden in a particular case.) Consider the following possible counterargument E to Rawls:

1. People deserve their natural assets.
2. If people deserve X, they deserve any Y that flows from X.
3. People's holdings flow from their natural assets.

Therefore,

4. People deserve their holdings.
5. If people deserve something, then they ought to have it (and this overrides any presumption of equality there may be about that thing).

Rawls would rebut this counterargument to his position by denying its first premiss. And so we see *some* connection between the claim that the distribution of natural assets is arbitrary and the statement that distributive shares should not depend upon natural assets. However, no great weight can be placed upon *this* connection. For there are other counterarguments, in a similar vein; for example the argument F that begins:

1. If people have X, and their having X (whether or not they deserve to have it) does *not* violate anyone else's (Lockean) right or entitlement to X, and Y flows from (arises out of, and so on) X by a process that does not itself violate anyone's (Lockean) rights or entitlements,[1] then the person is entitled to Y.
2. People's having the natural assets they do does not violate anyone else's (Lockean) entitlements or rights.

and goes on to argue that people are entitled to what they make, to the products of their labor, to what others give them or exchange. It is not true, for example, that a person earns Y (a right to keep a painting he's made, praise for writing *A Theory of Justice*, and so on) only if he's earned (or otherwise *deserves*) whatever he used (in-

---

1. A process, we might strengthen the antecedent by adding, of the sort that would create an entitlement to Y if the person were entitled to X, I use "Lockean" rights and entitlements to refer to those (discussed in Part I) against force, fraud, and so on, which are to be recognized in the minimal state. Since I believe these are the only rights and entitlements people possess (apart from those they specially acquire), I needn't have included the specification to Lockean rights. One who believes some have a right to the fruits of others' labor will deny the truth of the first premiss as stated. If the Lockean specification were not included, he might grant the truth of 1, while denying that of 2 or of later steps.

cluding natural assets) in the process of earning Y. Some of the things he uses he just may *have*, not illegitimately. It needn't be that the foundations underlying desert are themselves deserved, *all the way down*.

At the very least, we can parallel these statements about desert with ones about entitlements. And if, correctly, we describe people as entitled to their natural assets even if it's not the case that they can be said to deserve them, then the argument parallel to E above, with "are entitled to" replacing "deserve" throughout, *will* go through. This gives us the acceptable argument G:

1. People are entitled to their natural assets.
2. If people are entitled to something, they are entitled to whatever flows from it (via specified types of processes).
3. People's holdings flow from their natural assets.

Therefore,

4. People are entitled to their holdings.
5. If people are entitled to something, then they ought to have it (and this overrides any presumption of equality there may be about holdings).

Whether or not people's natural assets are arbitrary from a moral point of view, they are entitled to them, and to what flows from them.[2]

A recognition of people's entitlements to their natural assets (the first premiss of argument G) might be necessary to avoid the stringent application of the difference principle which would lead, we already have seen, to even stronger property rights in other persons than redistributive theories

usually yield. Rawls feels that he avoids this because people in his original position rank the principle of liberty as lexicographically prior to the difference principle, applied not only to economic well-being but to health, length of life, and so on.

We have found no cogent argument to (help) establish that differences in holding arising from differences in natural assets should be eliminated or minimized. Can the theme that people's natural assets are arbitrary from a moral point of view be used differently, for example, to justify a certain *shaping* of the original position? Clearly if the shaping is designed to nullify differences in holdings due to differences in natural assets, we need an argument for this goal, and we are back to our unsuccessful quest for the route to the conclusion that such differences in holdings ought to be nullified. Instead, the shaping might take place by excluding the participants in the original position from knowing of their own natural endowments. In this way the fact that natural endowments are arbitrary from a moral point of view would help to impose and to justify the veil of ignorance. But how does it do this; why should knowledge of natural endowments be excluded from the original position? Presumably the underlying principle would be that if any particular features are arbitrary from a moral point of view, then persons in the original position should not know they possess them. But this would exclude their knowing *anything* about themselves, for each of their features (including rationality, the ability to make choices, having a life span of more than three days, having a memory, being able to communicate with other organisms like themselves) will be based upon the fact that the sperm and ovum which produced them contained particular genetic material. The physical fact that those particular gametes contained particular organized chemicals (the genes for people rather than for muskrats or trees) is arbitrary *from a moral point of view*, it is, from a moral point of view, an accident. Yet the persons in the original position are to know some of their attributes.

Perhaps we are too quick when we suggest excluding knowledge of rationality, and so forth, merely because these features *arise from* morally arbitrary facts. For these features also have moral significance; that is, moral facts depend upon or

---

2. If nothing of moral significance could flow from what was arbitrary, then no particular person's existence could be of moral significance, since which of the many sperm cells succeeds in fertilizing the egg cell is (so far as we know) arbitrary from a moral point of view. This suggests another, more vague, remark directed to the spirit of Rawls' position rather than to its letter. Each existing person is the product of a process wherein the one sperm cell which succeeds is no more deserving than the millions that fail. Should we wish that process had been "fairer" as judged by Rawls' standards, that all "inequities" in it had been rectified? We should be apprehensive about any principle that would condemn morally the very sort of process that brought us to be, a principle that therefore would undercut the legitimacy of our very existing.

arise from them. Here we see an ambiguity in saying that a fact is arbitrary from a moral point of view. It might mean that there is no moral reason why the fact ought to be that way, or it might mean that the fact's being that way is of no moral significance and has no moral consequences. Rationality, the ability to make choices, and so on, are not morally arbitrary in this second sense. But if they escape exclusion on this ground, now the problem is that the natural assets, knowledge of which Rawls wishes to exclude from the original position, are not morally arbitrary in this sense either. At any rate, the entitlement theory's claim that moral entitlements may arise from or be partially based upon such facts is what is now at issue. Thus, in the absence of an argument to the effect that differences in holdings due to differences in natural assets ought to be nullified, it is not clear how anything about the original position can be based upon the (ambiguous) claim that differences in natural assets are arbitrary from a moral point of view.

Collective Assets

Rawls' view seems to be that everyone has some entitlement or claim on the totality of natural assets (viewed as a pool), with no one having differential claims. The distribution of natural abilities is viewed as a "collective asset."

> We see then that the difference principle represents, in effect, an agreement to regard the distribution of natural talents as a common asset and to share in the benefits of this distribution whatever it turns out to be. Those who have been favored by nature, whoever they are, may gain from their good fortune only on terms that improve the situation of those who have lost out. . . . No one deserves his greater natural capacity nor merits a more favorable starting place in society. But it does not follow that one should eliminate these distinctions. There is another way to deal with them. The basic structure can be arranged so that these contingencies work for the good of the least fortunate.

People will differ in how they view regarding natural talents as a common asset. Some will complain, echoing Rawls against utilitarianism, that

this "does not take seriously the distinction between persons"; and they will wonder whether any reconstruction of Kant that treats people's abilities and talents as resources for others can be adequate. "The two principles of justice . . . rule out even the tendency to regard men as means to one another's welfare." Only if one presses *very* hard on the distinction between men and their talents, assets, abilities, and special traits. Whether any coherent conception of a person remains when the distinction is so pressed is an open question. Why we, thick with particular traits, should be cheered that (only) the thus purified men within us are not regarded as means is also unclear.

People's talents and abilities *are* an asset to a free community; others in the community benefit from their presence and are better off because they are there rather than elsewhere or nowhere. (Otherwise they wouldn't choose to deal with them.) Life, over time, is not a constant-sum game, wherein if greater ability or effort leads to some getting more, that means that others must lose. In a free society, people's talents do benefit others, and not only themselves. Is it the extraction of even more benefit to others that is supposed to justify treating people's natural assets as a collective resource? What justifies this extraction?

> No one deserves his greater natural capacity nor merits a more favorable starting place in society. But it does not follow that one should eliminate these distinctions. There is another way to deal with them. The basic structure can be arranged so that these contingencies work for the good of the least fortunate.

And if there weren't "another way to deal with them"? Would it then follow that one should eliminate these distinctions? What exactly would be contemplated in the case of natural assets? If people's assets and talents *couldn't* be harnessed to serve others, would something be done to remove these exceptional assets and talents, or to forbid them from being exercised for the person's own benefit or that of someone else he chose, even though this limitation wouldn't improve the absolute position of those somehow unable to harness the talents and abilities of others for their own benefit? Is it so implausible to claim that envy underlies this conception of justice, forming part of its root notion?[3]

We have used our entitlement conception of justice in holdings to probe Rawls' theory, sharpening our understanding of what the entitlement conception involves by bringing it to bear upon an alternative conception of distributive justice, one that is deep and elegant. Also, I believe, we have probed deep-lying inadequacies in Rawls' theory. I am mindful of Rawls' reiterated point that a theory cannot be evaluated by focusing upon a single feature or part of it; instead the whole theory must be assessed (the reader will not know how whole a theory can be until he has read all of Rawls' book), and a perfect theory is not to be expected. However we have examined an important part of Rawls' theory, and its crucial underlying assumptions. I am as well aware as anyone of how sketchy my discussion of the

entitlement conception of justice in holdings has been. But I no more believe we need to have formulated a complete alternative theory in order to reject Rawls' undeniably great advance over utilitarianism, than Rawls needed a complete alternative theory before he could reject utilitarianism. What more does one need or can one have, in order to begin progressing toward a better theory, than a sketch of a plausible alternative view, which from its very different perspective highlights the inadequacies of the best existing well-worked-out theory? Here, as in so many things, we learn from Rawls.

We began this chapter's investigation of distributive justice in order to consider the claim that a state more extensive than the minimal state could be justified on the grounds that it was necessary, or the most appropriate instrument, to achieve distributive justice. According to the entitlement conception of justice in holdings that we have presented, there is no argument based upon the first two principles of distributive justice, the principles of acquisition and of transfer, for such a more extensive state. If the set of holdings is properly generated, there is no argument for a more extensive state based upon distributive justice. (Nor, we have claimed, will the Lockean proviso actually provide occasion for a more extensive state.) If, however, these principles are violated, the principle of rectification comes into play. Perhaps it is best to view some patterned principles of distributive justice as rough rules of thumb meant to approximate the general results of applying the principle of rectification of injustice. For example, lacking much historical information, and assuming (1) that victims of injustice generally do worse than they otherwise would and (2) that those from the least well-off group in the society have the highest probabilities of being the (descendants of) victims of the most serious injustice who are owed compensation by those who benefited from the injustices (assumed to be those better off, though sometimes the perpetrators will be others in the worst-off group), then a *rough* rule of thumb for rectifying injustices might seem to be the following: organize society so as to maximize the position of whatever group ends up least well-off in the society. This particular example may well be implausible, but an important question for each

---

3. Will the lexicographic priority that Rawls claims for liberty in the original position prevent the difference principle from requiring a head tax on assets and abilities? The legitimacy of a head tax is *suggested* by Rawls' speaking of "collective assets" and "common assets." Those underutilizing their assets and abilities are misusing a public asset. (Squandering public property?) Rawls may intend no such strong inferences from his terminology, but we need to hear more about why those in the original position wouldn't accept the strong interpretation. The notion of liberty needs elaboration which is to exclude a head tax and yet allow the other taxation schemes. Assets and abilities can be harnessed without a head tax; and "harnessing" is an appropriate term—as it would be for a horse harnessed to a wagon which doesn't *have* to move ever, but if it does, it must draw the wagon along

With regard to envy, the difference principle, applied to the choice between either *A* having ten and *B* having five or A having eight and B having five, would favor the latter. Thus, despite Rawls' view (pp. 79–80), the difference principle is inefficient in that it sometimes will favor a status quo against a Pareto-better but more unequal distribution. The inefficiency could be removed by shifting from the simple difference principle to a staggered difference principle, which recommends the maximization of the position of the least well-off group, and *subject to that constraint* the maximization of the position of the next least well-off group, and this point also is made by A. K. Sen (*Collective Choice and Social Welfare.* p. 138, note) and is acknowledged by Rawls (p. 83). But such a staggered principle does not embody a presumption in favor of equality of the sort used by Rawls. How then could Rawls justify an inequality *special* to the staggered principle to someone in the least well-off group? Perhaps these issues underlie the unclarity (see p. 83) as to whether Rawls accepts the staggered principle.

society will be the following: given *its* particular history, what operable rule of thumb best approximates the results of a detailed application in that society of the principle of rectification? These issues are very complex and are best left to a full treatment of the principle of rectification. In the absence of such a treatment applied to a particular society, one *cannot* use the analysis and theory presented here to condemn any particular scheme of transfer payments, unless it is clear that no considerations of rectification of injustice could to justify it. Although to introduce socialism as the punishment for our sins would be to go too far, past injustices might be so great as to make necessary in the short run a more extensive state in order to rectify them.

Chapter 9

AFFIRMATIVE ACTION: REVERSE DISCRIMINATION?

Is it unjust to consider race as a factor in college and university admissions? Some say yes; it is unfair to bestow benefits or impose burdens on people based on characteristics they cannot control. Others point out that many traits that count—including academic, athletic, and musical talent—may not be wholly within the control of the students who possess them (or who do not possess them in sufficient measure to gain admission). This is even more clearly the case with factors such as geographical diversity and "legacy" status (being the child of an alumnus). To what extent is race similar to or different from these traits?

Here are some further questions to bear in mind while considering the arguments for and against affirmative action: If you believe that universities should count race as a factor, on what grounds should they do so? How would you reply to a disappointed applicant like Cheryl Hopwood, who argues that, given her grades and test scores, she would have been admitted had she been an African American or Hispanic applicant? Should universities be free to define their admissions policies to serve any social purpose they deem desirable? Is there a principled distinction between the discrimination practiced by universities in the days of the segregated South, and the use of race in contemporary affirmative action programs?

RACIAL DISCRIMINATION OR RIGHTING PAST WRONGS?

Richard Bernstein

AUSTIN, Tex.—From Cheryl J. Hopwood's point of view, if overcoming past hardship was counted as a plus when applying to the University of Texas Law School, she should have been among the more qualified candidates.

Ms. Hopwood's father died when she was a girl and she was reared under difficult circumstances by her mother. She worked all through high school and put herself through both community college and the California State University at Sacramento, where she graduated with a 3.8 grade point average. Then, having become a Texas resident, she did well enough on the law school admissions test to get into a category of law school applicant that is almost automatically admitted at Texas.

But Cheryl Hopwood was not admitted, and she believes the reason is that she is white. That has put her at the center of a lawsuit against the University of Texas that, if she wins, could make it far more difficult for universities nationwide to follow the affirmative action policies that have guided them for two decades. A decision in the matter is expected in the next few days, certainly weeks.

"The Texas approach to affirmative action is in the mainstream of the approach used by law schools and other schools throughout the country," said Harry Reasoner, a lawyer for the university. "That would be put at risk if this were formally condemned by the court and no alternatives are offered."

Race as a Factor

The suit brought by Ms. Hopwood and three other plaintiffs is being widely compared to a landmark case of 16 years ago, *Bakke v. Regents of the University of California*. The United States Supreme Court, in a 5-to-4 decision, required that Allan P. Bakke be admitted to medical school, ruling that the school violated his rights when it rejected him on the ground that he was white.

The Court endorsed affirmative action in the Bakke case, saying that taking race and ethnicity into account in university admissions is permissible, but only if done in a flexible way and for the purpose of redressing the effects of past racial injustice. Race, in other words, can be a factor in selecting candidates for admission, but not the sole factor, the Court said.

Ms. Hopwood has argued that in setting up admissions targets for black and Mexican-American applicants, the university went far beyond what the Supreme Court permitted in Bakke, using race and ethnicity as the all-important criteria for admission and thus violating the plaintiffs' rights to equal treatment.

"Race should just not be a determining factor in admissions policy at the level of law school," she said in a recent telephone interview from her home in San Antonio. "At that level I'm competing with others who have B.A. degrees and they're not people who necessarily have more disadvantaged backgrounds than I have."

Different Criteria

The case, argued last month before Judge Sam Sparks in Federal District Court in Austin, offered an unusually candid look at the admissions process used by a major law school, a process normally shrouded in secrecy. Called by the plaintiffs as hostile witnesses, university officials said that the institution set aside roughly 15 percent of its law school seats for blacks and Mexican-Americans, who are admitted under different criteria from all other students, including other minority students. Law school deans from Stanford University and the universities of Minnesota, Michigan and North Carolina testified that they used similar preferences for minority applicants.

The Texas system, portrayed as a discriminatory quota by the plaintiffs, was defended by the university on several grounds, among them that race is only one factor among many considered by the admissions panel and that since the Texas affirmative action program is "narrowly tailored" to remedy the effects of past bias, it is permitted by *Bakke*.

Most important, university officials said, in a state that is 40 percent black and Mexican-American, the law school's affirmative action program works. Although minority students are admitted at a lower standard than whites, they said, all can do the required work and almost all graduate and pass the bar exam.

"We see minority graduates of ours as elected officials, working in prominent law firms, as members of the Texas Legislature and the Federal bench," said Michael Charlot, the law school's acting dean. Federico F. Pena, the Secretary of Transportation, is among the school's minority graduates. "To the extent that there are minorities in important offices in Texas, they are often our graduates," Mr. Charlot said.

Almost Full Circle

There is a historic poignancy to the renewed legal conflict over affirmative action occurring at the University of Texas, the scene of one of the early landmark Supreme Court decisions leading to the dismantling of segregation in higher education.

In that case, *Sweatt v. Painter*, the Court decided in 1950 that the university's ban on black students in the law school—and Texas's creation of the Law School for Coloreds—was unconstitutional. Heman Sweatt, who brought the case, became the first black student at the university's law school, but he dropped out, citing its atmosphere of racism.

Judge Sparks must weigh the merits of a nearly inverse accusation: that the university discriminates so avidly in favor of blacks and Mexican-Americans that the rights of whites are being violated.

Witnesses testified during the trial, for example, that virtually every black and Mexican-American student admitted to the law school is given a scholarship, without regard for financial need. As a result, said Terral R. Smith, a lawyer for the plaintiffs: "The university is not helping poor black people with affirmative action. It is denying people like Hopwood and giving special privileges to upper-middle-class black people and Mexican-Americans."

By the Numbers

While there are no data to support this assertion, the anecdotal evidence is compelling, Mr. Smith said in an interview. "When you talk to professors, they admit that the black students who can do the work are usually those whose parents have been successful," he said.

According to the law school, its affirmative action policy works like this: Every one of roughly 4,000 applicants is assigned a Texas Index number, a combination of undergraduate grade point average and law school admissions test score. The numbers range from about 145 to 220. Under examination by plaintiffs' lawyers, law school officials acknowledged that blacks and Mexican-Americans are given something close to automatic admission at index numbers substantially below those of many whites who are rejected, including all four plaintiffs in the case.

The head of the law school's admissions committee, Stanley Johanson, said under questioning that no black or Mexican-American applicants who were state residents and had a Texas Index of 185 or higher were denied admission. Ms. Hopwood's index was 199 and the three other plaintiffs, white men, had 198.

Mr. Johanson also said that had Ms. Hopwood been black or Mexican-American she would "in all probability" have been accepted.

"Hopwood is the epitome of who is harmed by affirmative action," said Mr. Smith, a former state legislator. "If she had been black, she would have been admitted. Every black applicant that

had her credentials got a $7,000 scholarship and free tuition."

"Nature of Racial Preference"

A law school memorandum entered into evidence by plaintiffs' lawyers showed that in 1992, the year Ms. Hopwood applied, the law school rejected 668 white candidates before it rejected a single black candidate. And admissions statistics indicated that among candidates with indexes between 189 and 192, 6 percent of the more than 500 white applicants were admitted while 89 percent of the 23 Mexican-American applicants and all 4 black applicants were admitted.

"Six percent versus 100 percent shows that you're giving quite a bit of weight to race," said Michael Rosman, a lawyer for the Center for Individual Rights in Washington, a public interest firm that represents clients in First Amendment and civil rights cases. The center devised much of the plaintiffs' legal strategy and drafted most of the briefs in the Hopwood case.

The university maintains that the national pool of minority candidates able to compete on an equal basis with whites is so small that, if affirmative action were abandoned, the law school would revert almost to the kind of all-white institution it was in the days of Jim Crow. And in the entering class of 1992, they noted, there were 41 blacks and 55 Mexican-Americans.

"Are there white applicants who were not admitted who would have gotten in if they had been black?" asked Samuel Issacharoff, a law professor at the school and member of the legal team that argued the case. "The answer is clearly yes. That's the nature of a racial preference."

But, he said, while affirmative action is not "cost free," it is an essential tool to enable minorities to overcome a legacy of past discrimination.

Possibilities Elsewhere?

Minority students who testified in the university's behalf agreed that if there were no serious effort to recruit blacks and Mexican-Americans, they would probably have gone to law school elsewhere.

As for Ms. Hopwood, the university's lawyers said that her studies at a university with generally low academic standards counted against her and could have explained her rejection just as much as her race.

But in a trial involving few disputes over facts, Ms. Hopwood's educational credentials may be relatively unimportant. Indeed, the case seems to come down to a value judgment about what price it is fair and legal to ask whites to pay to provide opportunities previously denied nonwhites. "The law school has never denied that there are costs to affirmative action," said Barry D. Burgdorf, a lawyer for the university. "Hopwood is a cost. But the Supreme Court has said several times that you can have innocent victims to get the benefit."

Cheryl J. Hopwood v. State of Texas

United States Court of Appeals for the Fifth Circuit
March 18, 1996

Before SMITH, WIENER, DeMOSS, POLITZ, and STEWART, Circuit Judges.

Opinion: Jerry E. Smith, Circuit Judge

With the best of intentions, in order to increase the enrollment of certain favored classes of minority students, the University of Texas School of Law ("the law school") discriminates in favor of those applicants by giving substantial racial preferences in its admissions program. The beneficiaries of this system are blacks and Mexican Americans, to the detriment of whites and non-preferred minorities. The question we decide today in No. 94-50664 is whether the Fourteenth Amendment permits the school to discriminate in this way.

We hold that it does not. The law school has presented no compelling justification, under the Fourteenth Amendment or Supreme Court precedent, that allows it to continue to elevate some races over others, even for the wholesome purpose of correcting perceived racial imbalance in the student body. "Racial preferences appear to 'even the score' . . . only if one embraces the proposition that our society is appropriately viewed as divided into races, making it right that an injustice rendered in the past to a black man should be compensated for by discriminating against a white." *City of Richmond v. J.A. Croson Co.*, 488 U.S. 469, 528, 102 L. Ed. 2d 854, 109 S. Ct. 706 (1989) (Scalia, J., concurring in the judgment).

As a result of its diligent efforts in this case, the district court concluded that the law school may continue to impose racial preferences. See *Hopwood v. Texas*, 861 F. Supp. 551 (W.D. Tex. 1994). In No. 94-50664, we reverse and remand, concluding that the law school may not use race as a factor in law school admissions. . . .

The University of Texas School of Law is one of the nation's leading law schools, consistently ranking in the top twenty. See, e.g., America's Best Graduate Schools, *U.S. News & World Report* Mar. 20, 1995, at 84 (national survey ranking of seventeenth). Accordingly, admission to the law school is fiercely competitive, with over 4,000 applicants a year competing to be among the approximately 900 offered admission to achieve an entering class of about 500 students. Many of these applicants have some of the highest grades and test scores in the country.

Numbers are therefore paramount for admission. In the early 1990's, the law school largely based its initial admissions decisions upon an applicant's so-called Texas Index ("TI") number, a composite of undergraduate grade point average ("GPA") and Law School Aptitude Test ("LSAT") score. The law school used this number as a matter of administrative convenience in order to rank candidates and to predict, roughly, one's probability of success in law school. Moreover, the law school relied heavily upon such numbers to estimate the number of offers of admission it needed to make in order to fill its first-year class.

Of course, the law school did not rely upon numbers alone. The admissions office necessarily exercised judgment in interpreting the individual scores of applicants, taking into consideration factors such as the strength of a student's undergraduate education, the difficulty of his major, and significant trends in his own grades and the undergraduate grades at his respective college (such as grade inflation). Admissions personnel also considered what qualities each applicant might bring to his law school class. Thus, the law school could consider an applicant's background, life experiences, and outlook. Not surprisingly, these hard-to-quantify factors were especially significant for marginal candidates.

Because of the large number of applicants and potential admissions factors, the TI's administrative usefulness was its ability to sort candidates. For the class entering in 1992 the admissions group at issue in this case the law school placed the typical applicant in one of three categories according to his TI scores: "presumptive admit," "presumptive deny," or a middle "discretionary zone." An applicant's TI category determined how extensive a review his application would receive. . . .

Blacks and Mexican Americans were treated differently from other candidates, however. First, compared to whites and non-preferred minorities, the TI ranges that were used to place them into the three admissions categories were lowered to allow the law school to consider and admit more of them. In March 1992, for example, the presumptive TI admission score for resident whites and non-preferred minorities was 199. Mexican Americans and blacks needed a TI of only 189 to be presumptively admitted. The difference in the presumptive-deny ranges is even more striking. The presumptive denial score for "nonminorities" was 192; the same score for blacks and Mexican Americans was 179.

While these cold numbers may speak little to those unfamiliar with the pool of applicants, the results demonstrate that the difference in the two ranges was dramatic. According to the law school, 1992 resident white applicants had a mean GPA of 3.53 and an LSAT of 164. Mexican Americans scored 3.27 and 158; blacks scored 3.25 and 157.

The category of "other minority" achieved a 3.56 and 160.

These disparate standards greatly affected a candidate's chance of admission. For example, by March 1992, because the presumptive denial score for whites was a TI of 192 or lower, and the presumptive admit TI for minorities was 189 or higher, a minority candidate with a TI of 189 or above almost certainly would be admitted, even though his score was considerably below the level at which a white candidate almost certainly would be rejected. Out of the pool of resident applicants who fell within this range (189-192 inclusive), 100% of blacks and 90% of Mexican Americans, but only 6% of whites, were offered admission.

The stated purpose of this lowering of standards was to meet an "aspiration" of admitting a class consisting of 10% Mexican Americans and 5% blacks, proportions roughly comparable to the percentages of those races graduating from Texas colleges. The law school found meeting these "goals" difficult, however, because of uncertain acceptance rates and the variable quality of the applicant pool. In 1992, for example, the entering class contained 41 blacks and 55 Mexican Americans, respectively 8% and 10.7% of the class.

In addition to maintaining separate presumptive TI levels for minorities and whites, the law school ran a segregated application evaluation process. Upon receiving an application form, the school color-coded it according to race. If a candidate failed to designate his race, he was presumed to be in a nonpreferential category. Thus, race was always an overt part of the review of any applicant's file. . . .

Cheryl Hopwood, Douglas Carvell, Kenneth Elliott, and David Rogers (the "plaintiffs") applied for admission to the 1992 entering law school class. All four were white residents of Texas and were rejected.

The plaintiffs were considered as discretionary zone candidates. Hopwood, with a GPA of 3.8 and an LSAT of 39 (equivalent to a three-digit LSAT of 160), had a TI of 199, a score barely within the presumptive-admit category for resident whites, which was 199 and up. She was dropped into the discretionary zone for resident whites (193 to 198), however, because Johanson decided her educational background overstated the strength of her GPA. . . .

The plaintiffs sued primarily under the Equal Protection Clause of the Fourteenth Amendment. . . . The central purpose of the Equal Protection Clause "is to prevent the States from purposefully discriminating between individuals on the basis of race.". . . In order to preserve [this] principle, the Supreme Court recently has required that any governmental action that expressly distinguishes between persons on the basis of race be held to the most exacting scrutiny. Furthermore, there is now absolutely no doubt that courts are to employ strict scrutiny when evaluating all racial classifications, including those characterized by their proponents as "benign" or "remedial." . . . .

Under the strict scrutiny analysis, we ask two questions: (1) Does the racial classification serve a compelling government interest, and (2) is it narrowly tailored to the achievement of that goal?

With these general principles of equal protection in mind, we turn to the specific issue of whether the law school's consideration of race as a factor in admissions violates the Equal Protection Clause. The district court found both a compelling remedial and a non-remedial justification for the practice.

First, the court approved of the non-remedial goal of having a diverse student body, reasoning that "obtaining the educational benefits that flow from a racially and ethnically diverse student body remains a sufficiently compelling interest to support the use of racial classifications." Second, the court determined that the use of racial classifications could be justified as a remedy for the "present effects at the law school of past discrimination in both the University of Texas system and the Texas educational system as a whole." . . . .

We agree with the plaintiffs that any consideration of race or ethnicity by the law school for the purpose of achieving a diverse student body is not a compelling interest under the Fourteenth Amendment. . . . [T]here has been no indication from the Supreme Court, other than Justice Powell's lonely opinion in Bakke, that the state's interest in diversity constitutes a compelling justification for governmental race-based discrimination. . . .

Within the general principles of the Fourteenth Amendment, the use of race in admissions for diversity in higher education contradicts, rather than furthers, the aims of equal protection. Diversity fosters, rather than minimizes, the use of race. It treats minorities as a group, rather than as individuals. It may further remedial purposes but, just as likely, may promote improper racial stereotypes, thus fueling racial hostility.

The use of race, in and of itself, to choose students simply achieves a student body that looks different. Such a criterion is no more rational on its own terms than would be choices based upon the physical size or blood type of applicants. Thus, the Supreme Court has long held that governmental actors cannot justify their decisions solely because of race. . . .

While the use of race per se is proscribed, state-supported schools may reasonably consider a host of factors—some of which may have some correlation with race—in making admissions decisions. The federal courts have no warrant to intrude on those executive and legislative judgments unless the distinctions intrude on specific provisions of federal law or the Constitution. A university may properly favor one applicant over another because of his ability to play the cello, make a downfield tackle, or understand chaos theory. An admissions process may also consider an applicant's home state or relationship to school alumni. Law schools specifically may look at things such as unusual or substantial extracurricular activities in college, which may be atypical factors affecting undergraduate grades. Schools may even consider factors such as whether an applicant's parents attended college or the applicant's economic and social background.

For this reason, race often is said to be justified in the diversity context, not on its own terms, but as a proxy for other characteristics that institutions of higher education value but that do not raise similar constitutional concerns. Unfortunately, this approach simply replicates the very harm that the Fourteenth Amendment was designed to eliminate.

The assumption is that a certain individual possesses characteristics by virtue of being a member of a certain racial group. This assumption, however, does not withstand scrutiny. "The use of a racial characteristic to establish a presumption that the individual also possesses other, and socially relevant, characteristics, exemplifies, encourages, and legitimizes the mode of thought and behavior that underlies most prejudice and bigotry in modern America." Richard A. Posner, The *DeFunis* Case and the Constitutionality of Preferential Treatment of Racial Minorities, 1974 SUP. CT. REV. 12 (1974).

To believe that a person's race controls his point of view is to stereotype him. The Supreme Court, however, "has remarked a number of times, in slightly different contexts, that it is incorrect and legally inappropriate to impute to women and minorities 'a different attitude about such issues as the federal budget, school prayer, voting, and foreign relations.'" . . . .

Instead, individuals, with their own conceptions of life, further diversity of viewpoint. Plaintiff Hopwood is a fair example of an applicant with a unique background. She is the now-thirty-two-year-old wife of a member of the Armed Forces stationed in San Antonio and, more significantly, is raising a severely handicapped child. Her circumstance would bring a different perspective to the law school. The school might consider this an advantage to her in the application process, or it could decide that her

family situation would be too much of a burden on her academic performance.

We do not opine on which way the law school should weigh Hopwood's qualifications; we only observe that "diversity" can take many forms. To foster such diversity, state universities and law schools and other governmental entities must scrutinize applicants individually, rather than resorting to the dangerous proxy of race. . . .

In summary, we hold that the University of Texas School of Law may not use race as a factor in deciding which applicants to admit in order to achieve a diverse student body, to combat the perceived effects of a hostile environment at the law school, to alleviate the law school's poor reputation in the minority community, or to eliminate any present effects of past discrimination by actors other than the law school. Because the law school has proffered these justifications for its use of race in admissions, the plaintiffs have satisfied their burden of showing that they were scrutinized under an unconstitutional admissions system. The plaintiffs are entitled to reapply under an admissions system that invokes none of these serious constitutional infirmities.

BARBARA GRUTTER, PETITIONER v. LEE BOLLINGER ET AL.

Supreme Court of the United States
June 23, 2003

Justice **O'Connor** delivered the opinion of the Court.

This case requires us to decide whether the use of race as a factor in student admissions by the University of Michigan Law School (Law School) is unlawful.

The Law School ranks among the Nation's top law schools. It receives more than 3,500 applications each year for a class of around 350 students. Seeking to "admit a group of students who individually and collectively are among the most capable," the Law School looks for individuals with "substantial promise for success in law school" and "a strong likelihood of succeeding in the practice of law and contributing in diverse

ways to the well-being of others." More broadly, the Law School seeks "a mix of students with varying backgrounds and experiences who will respect and learn from each other."

The hallmark of that policy is its focus on academic ability coupled with a flexible assessment of applicants' talents, experiences, and potential "to contribute to the learning of those around them." . . . . The policy aspires to "achieve that diversity which has the potential to enrich everyone's education and thus make a law school class stronger than the sum of its parts." The policy does not restrict the types of diversity contributions eligible for "substantial weight" in the admissions process, but instead recognizes "many possible bases for diversity admissions." The policy does, however, reaffirm the Law School's longstanding commitment to "one particular type of diversity," that is, "racial and ethnic diversity with special reference to the inclusion of students from groups which have been historically discriminated against, like African-Americans, Hispanics and Native Americans, who without this commitment might not be represented in our student body in meaningful numbers." By enrolling a "'critical mass' of [underrepresented] minority students," the Law School seeks to "ensure their ability to make unique contributions to the character of the Law School." . . . .

Petitioner Barbara Grutter is a white Michigan resident who applied to the Law School in 1996 with a 3.8 grade point average and 161 LSAT score. The Law School initially placed petitioner on a waiting list, but subsequently rejected her application. In December 1997, petitioner filed suit . . . [alleging] that respondents discriminated against her on the basis of race in violation of the Fourteenth Amendment. . . .

We granted certiorari to resolve the disagreement among the Courts of Appeals on a question of national importance: Whether diversity is a compelling interest that can justify the narrowly tailored use of race in selecting applicants for admission to public universities. Compare *Hopwood v. Texas*, 78 F.3d 932 (CA5 1996) (*Hopwood I*) (holding that diversity is not a compelling state interest). . . .

Before this Court, as they have throughout this litigation, respondents assert only one justification for their use of race in the admissions process: obtaining "the educational benefits that flow from a diverse student body." In other words, the Law School asks us to recognize, in the context of higher education, a compelling state interest in student body diversity. . . . Today, we hold that the Law School has a compelling interest in attaining a diverse student body.

The Law School's educational judgment that such diversity is essential to its educational mission is one to which we defer. The Law School's assessment that diversity will, in fact, yield educational benefits is substantiated by respondents and their *amici*. Our scrutiny of the interest asserted by the Law School is no less strict for taking into account complex educational judgments in an

area that lies primarily within the expertise of the university. Our holding today is in keeping with our tradition of giving a degree of deference to a university's academic decisions, within constitutionally prescribed limits. . . .

As part of its goal of "assembling a class that is both exceptionally academically qualified and broadly diverse," the Law School seeks to "enroll a 'critical mass' of minority students." The Law School's interest is not simply "to assure within its student body some specified percentage of a particular group merely because of its race or ethnic origin." *Bakke*, 438 U.S., at 307, 57 L Ed 2d 750, 98 S Ct 2733 (opinion of Powell, J.). That would amount to outright racial balancing, which is patently unconstitutional. Rather, the Law School's concept of critical mass is defined by reference to the educational benefits that diversity is designed to produce.

These benefits are substantial. As the District Court emphasized, the Law School's admissions policy promotes "cross-racial understanding," helps to break down racial stereotypes, and "enables [students] to better understand persons of different races." These benefits are "important and laudable," because "classroom discussion is livelier, more spirited, and simply more enlightening and interesting" when the students have "the greatest possible variety of backgrounds."

The Law School's claim of a compelling interest is further bolstered by its *amici*, who point to the educational benefits that flow from student body diversity. In addition to the expert studies and reports entered into evidence at trial, numerous studies show that student body diversity promotes learning outcomes, and "better prepares students for an increasingly diverse workforce and society, and better prepares them as professionals."

These benefits are not theoretical but real, as major American businesses have made clear that the skills needed in today's increasingly global marketplace can only be developed through exposure to widely diverse people, cultures, ideas, and viewpoints. What is more, high-ranking retired officers and civilian leaders of the United States military assert that, "based on [their] decades of experience," a "highly qualified, racially diverse officer corps . . . is essential to the military's ability to fulfill its principle mission to provide national security." The primary sources for the Nation's officer corps are the service academies and the Reserve Officers Training Corps (ROTC), the latter comprising students already admitted to participating colleges and universities. At present, "the military cannot achieve an officer corps that is *both* highly qualified *and* racially diverse unless the service academies and the ROTC used limited race-conscious recruiting and admissions policies." To fulfill its mission, the military "must be selective in admissions for training and education for the officer corps, *and* it must train and educate a highly qualified, racially diverse officer corps in a racially diverse setting." We agree that "it requires only a small step from this analysis to conclude that our country's other most selective institutions must remain both diverse and selective." . . . .

Moreover, universities, and in particular, law schools, represent the training ground for a large number of our Nation's leaders. *Sweatt* v. *Painter,* 339 U.S. 629, 634, 94 L. Ed. 1114, 70 S. Ct. 848 (1950) (describing law school as a "proving ground for legal learning and practice"). Individuals with law degrees occupy roughly half the state governorships, more than half the seats in the United States Senate, and more than a third of the seats in the United States House of Representatives. The pattern is even more striking when it comes to highly selective law schools. A handful of these schools accounts for 25 of the 100 United States Senators, 74 United States Courts of Appeals judges, and nearly 200 of the more than 600 United States District Court judges.

In order to cultivate a set of leaders with legitimacy in the eyes of the citizenry, it is necessary that the path to leadership be visibly open to talented and qualified individuals of every race and ethnicity. All members of our heterogeneous society must have confidence in the openness and integrity of the educational institutions that provide this training. As we have recognized, law schools "cannot be effective in isolation from the individuals and institutions with which the law interacts." Access to legal education (and thus the legal profession) must be inclusive of talented and qualified individuals of every race and ethnicity, so that all members of our heterogeneous society may participate in the educational institutions

that provide the training and education necessary to succeed in America.

The Law School does not premise its need for critical mass on "any belief that minority students always (or even consistently) express some characteristic minority viewpoint on any issue." To the contrary, diminishing the force of such stereotypes is both a crucial part of the Law School's mission, and one that it cannot accomplish with only token numbers of minority students. Just as growing up in a particular region or having particular professional experiences is likely to affect an individual's views, so too is one's own, unique experience of being a racial minority in a society, like our own, in which race unfortunately still matters. The Law School has determined, based on its experience and expertise, that a "critical mass" of underrepresented minorities is necessary to further its compelling interest in securing the educational benefits of a diverse student body.

Even in the limited circumstance when drawing racial distinctions is permissible to further a compelling state interest, government is still "constrained in how it may pursue that end: [T]he means chosen to accomplish the [government's] asserted purpose must be specifically and narrowly framed to accomplish that purpose." . . . . We find that the Law School's admissions program bears the hallmarks of a narrowly tailored plan. As Justice Powell made clear in *Bakke*, truly individualized consideration demands that race be used in a flexible, nonmechanical way. It follows from this mandate that universities cannot establish quotas for members of certain racial groups or put members of those groups on separate admissions tracks. Nor can universities insulate applicants who belong to certain racial or ethnic groups from the competition for admission. Universities can, however, consider race or ethnicity more flexibly as a "plus" factor in the context of individualized consideration of each and every applicant.

We are satisfied that the Law School's admissions program, like the Harvard plan described by Justice Powell, does not operate as a quota. . . . Here, the Law School engages in a highly individualized, holistic review of each applicant's file, giving serious consideration to all the ways an applicant might contribute to a diverse educational environment. The Law School affords this individualized consideration to applicants of all races. There is no policy, either *de jure* or *de facto*, of automatic acceptance or rejection based on any single "soft" variable.... We also find that, like the Harvard plan Justice Powell referenced in *Bakke*, the Law School's race-conscious admissions program adequately ensures that all factors that may contribute to student body diversity are meaningfully considered alongside race in admissions decisions. With respect to the use of race itself, all underrepresented minority students admitted by the Law School have been deemed qualified. By virtue of our Nation's struggle with racial inequality, such students are both likely to have experiences of particular importance to the Law School's mission, and less likely to be admitted in meaningful numbers on criteria that ignore those experiences....

We are mindful, however, that "[a] core purpose of the Fourteenth Amendment was to do away with all governmentally imposed discrimination based on race." Accordingly, race-conscious admissions policies must be limited in time. This requirement reflects that racial classifications, however compelling their goals, are potentially so dangerous that they may be employed no more broadly than the interest demands. Enshrining a permanent justification for racial preferences would offend this fundamental equal protection principle. We see no reason to exempt race-conscious admissions programs from the requirement that all governmental use of race must have a logical end point.... We take the Law School at its word that it would "like nothing better than to find a race-neutral admissions formula" and will terminate its race-conscious admissions program as soon as practicable. It has been 25 years since Justice Powell first approved the use of race to further an interest in student body diversity in the context of public higher education. Since that time, the number of minority applicants with high grades and test scores has indeed increased. We expect that 25 years from now, the use of racial preferences will no longer be necessary to further the interest approved today.

In summary, the Equal Protection Clause does not prohibit the Law School's narrowly tailored use of race in admissions decisions to further a compelling interest in obtaining the educational benefits that flow from a diverse student body.

Justice Thomas dissent

Justice Thomas, with whom Justice Scalia joins as to Parts I-VII, concurring in part and dissenting in part:

Frederick Douglass, speaking to a group of abolitionists almost 140 years ago, delivered a message lost on today's majority:

> In regard to the colored people, there is always more that is benevolent, I perceive, than just, manifested towards us. What I ask for the negro is not benevolence, not pity, not sympathy, but simply *justice*. The American people have always been anxious to know what they shall do with us.... I have had but one answer from the beginning. Do nothing with us! Your doing with us has already played the mischief with us. Do nothing with us! If the apples will not remain on the tree of their own strength, if they are worm-eaten at the core, if they are early ripe and disposed to fall, let them fall! ...And if the negro cannot stand on his own legs, let him fall also. All I ask is, give him a chance to stand on his own legs! Let him alone! ...Your interference is doing him positive injury. "What the Black Man Wants: An Address Delivered in Boston, Massachusetts, on 26 January 1865," reprinted in 4 *The Frederick Douglass Papers* 59, 68 (J. Blassingame & J. McKivigan eds. 1991) (emphasis in original).

Like Douglass, I believe blacks can achieve in every avenue of American life without the meddling of university administrators. Because I wish to see all students succeed whatever their color, I share, in some respect, the sympathies of those who sponsor the type of discrimination advanced by the University of Michigan Law School (Law School). The Constitution does not, however, tolerate institutional devotion to the status quo in admissions policies when such devotion ripens into racial discrimination. Nor does the Constitution countenance the unprecedented deference the Court gives to the Law School, an approach inconsistent with the very concept of "strict scrutiny." ....

The Constitution abhors classifications based on race, not only because those classifications can harm favored races or are based on illegitimate motives, but also because every time the government places citizens on racial registers and makes race relevant to the provision of burdens or benefits, it demeans us all. . . .

Unlike the majority, I seek to define with precision the interest being asserted by the Law School before determining whether that interest is so compelling as to justify racial discrimination. The Law School maintains that it wishes to obtain "educational benefits that flow from student body diversity." This statement must be evaluated carefully, because it implies that both "diversity" and "educational benefits" are components of the Law School's compelling state interest. Additionally, the Law School's refusal to entertain certain changes in its admissions process and status indicates that the compelling state interest it seeks to validate is actually broader than might appear at first glance. . . .

One must. . . consider the Law School's refusal to entertain changes to its current admissions system that might produce the same educational benefits. The Law School adamantly disclaims any race-neutral alternative that would reduce "academic selectivity," which would in turn "require the Law School to become a very different institution, and to sacrifice a core part of its educational mission." In other words, the Law School seeks to improve marginally the education it offers without sacrificing too much of its exclusivity and elite status.[1]

The proffered interest that the majority vindicates today, then, is not simply "diversity." Instead the Court upholds the use of racial discrimination as a tool to advance the Law School's interest in offering a marginally superior education while maintaining an elite institution. . . . Under the proper standard, there is no pressing public necessity in maintaining a public law school at all and, it follows, certainly not an elite law school. Likewise, marginal improvements in legal education do not qualify as a compelling state interest.

As the foregoing makes clear, Michigan has no compelling interest in having a law school at all, much less an *elite* one. . . . The interest in remaining elite and exclusive that the majority thinks so obviously critical requires the use of admissions "standards" that, in turn, create the Law School's "need" to discriminate on the basis of race. . . . The Court never explicitly holds that the Law School's desire to retain the status quo in "academic selectivity" is itself a compelling state interest, and, as I have demonstrated, it is not. Therefore, the Law School should be forced to choose between its classroom aesthetic and its exclusionary admissions system—it cannot have it both ways.

With the adoption of different admissions methods, such as accepting all students who meet minimum qualifications, the Law School could achieve its vision of the racially aesthetic student body without the use of racial discrimination. The Law School concedes this, but the Court holds, implicitly and under the guise of narrow tailoring, that the Law School has a compelling state interest in doing what it wants to do. I cannot agree. . . .

Putting aside the absence of any legal support for the majority's reflexive deference, there is much to be said for the view that the use of tests and other measures to "predict" academic performance is a poor substitute for a system that gives every applicant a chance to prove he can succeed in the study of law. The rallying cry that in the absence of racial discrimination in admissions there would be a true meritocracy ignores the fact that the entire process is poisoned by numerous exceptions to "merit." For example, in the national debate on racial discrimination in higher education admissions, much has been made of the fact that elite institutions utilize a so-called "legacy" preference to give the children of alumni an advantage in admissions. This, and other, exceptions to a "true" meritocracy give the lie to protestations that merit admissions are in fact the order of the day at the Nation's universities. The Equal Protection Clause does not, however, prohibit the use of unseemly legacy preferences or many other kinds of arbitrary admissions procedures. What the Equal Protection Clause does prohibit are classifications made on the basis of race. So while legacy preferences can

---

1. The Law School believes both that the educational benefits of a racially engineered student body are large and that adjusting its overall admissions standards to achieve the same racial mix would require it to sacrifice its elite status. If the Law School is correct that the educational benefits of "diversity" are so great, then achieving them by altering admissions standards should not compromise its elite status. The Law School's reluctance to do this suggests that the educational benefits it alleges are not significant or do not exist at all.

stand under the Constitution, racial discrimination cannot.[2] I will not twist the Constitution to invalidate legacy preferences or otherwise impose my vision of higher education admissions on the Nation. The majority should similarly stay its impulse to validate faddish racial discrimination the Constitution clearly forbids.

In any event, there is nothing ancient, honorable, or constitutionally protected about "selective" admissions. The University of Michigan should be well aware that alternative methods have historically been used for the admission of students, for it brought to this country the German certificate system in the late-19th century. Under this system, a secondary school was certified by a university so that any graduate who completed the course offered by the school was offered admission to the university. The certification regime supplemented, and later virtually replaced (at least in the Midwest), the prior regime of rigorous subject-matter entrance examinations. The facially race-neutral "percent plans" now used in Texas, California, and Florida, are in many ways the descendents of the certificate system. . . .

Having decided to use the LSAT, the Law School must accept the constitutional burdens that come with this decision. The Law School may freely continue to employ the LSAT and other allegedly merit-based standards in whatever fashion it likes. What the Equal Protection Clause forbids, but the Court today allows, is the use of these standards hand-in-hand with racial discrimination. An infinite variety of admissions methods are available to the Law School. Considering all of the radical thinking that has historically occurred at this country's universities, the Law School's intractable approach toward admissions is striking.

The Court will not even deign to make the Law School try other methods, however, preferring instead to grant a 25-year license to violate the Constitution. And the same Court that had the courage to order the desegregation of all public schools in the South now fears, on the basis of platitudes rather than principle, to force the

Law School to abandon a decidedly imperfect admissions regime that provides the basis for racial discrimination. . . .

I must [also] contest the notion that the Law School's discrimination benefits those admitted as a result of it. . . . The Law School tantalizes unprepared students with the promise of a University of Michigan degree and all of the opportunities that it offers. These overmatched students take the bait, only to find that they cannot succeed in the cauldron of competition. And this mismatch crisis is not restricted to elite institutions. See T. Sowell, *Race and Culture* 176–177 (1994) ("Even if most minority students are able to meet the normal standards at the 'average' range of colleges and universities, the systematic mismatching of minority students begun at the top can mean that such students are generally overmatched throughout all levels of higher education"). Indeed, to cover the tracks of the aestheticists, this cruel farce of racial discrimination must continue—in selection for the Michigan Law Review, and in hiring at law firms and for judicial clerkships—until the "beneficiaries" are no longer tolerated. While these students may graduate with law degrees, there is no evidence that they have received a qualitatively better legal education (or become better lawyers) than if they had gone to a less "elite" law school for which they were better prepared. . . .

Beyond the harm the Law School's racial discrimination visits upon its test subjects, no social science has disproved the notion that this discrimination "engenders attitudes of superiority or, alternatively, provoke[s] resentment among those who believe that they have been wronged by the government's use of race." "These programs stamp minorities with a badge of inferiority and may cause them to develop dependencies or to adopt an attitude that they are 'entitled' to preferences."

It is uncontested that each year, the Law School admits a handful of blacks who would be admitted in the absence of racial discrimination. Who can differentiate between those who belong and those who do not? The majority of blacks are admitted to the Law School because of discrimination, and because of this policy all are tarred as undeserving. This problem of stigma does not depend on determinacy as to whether those

2. Were this Court to have the courage to forbid the use of racial discrimination in admissions, legacy preferences (and similar practices) might quickly become less popular—a possibility not lost, I am certain, on the elites (both individual and institutional) supporting the Law School in this case.

stigmatized are actually the "beneficiaries" of racial discrimination. When blacks take positions in the highest places of government, industry, or academia, it is an open question today whether their skin color played a part in their advancement. The question itself is the stigma—because either racial discrimination did play a role, in which case the person may be deemed "otherwise unqualified," or it did not, in which case asking the question itself unfairly marks those blacks who would succeed without discrimination. . . .

The Court . . . holds that racial discrimination in admissions should be given another 25 years before it is deemed no longer narrowly tailored to the Law School's fabricated compelling state interest. While I agree that in 25 years the practices of the Law School will be illegal, they are, for the reasons I have given, illegal now. The majority does not and cannot rest its time limitation on any evidence that the gap in credentials between black and white students is shrinking or will be gone in that timeframe. In recent years there has been virtually no change, for example, in the proportion of law school applicants with LSAT scores of 165 and higher who are black. In 1993 blacks constituted

1.1% of law school applicants in that score range, though they represented 11.1% of all applicants. In 2000 the comparable numbers were 1.0% and 11.3%. No one can seriously contend, and the Court does not, that the racial gap in academic credentials will disappear in 25 years. Nor is the Court's holding that racial discrimination will be unconstitutional in 25 years made contingent on the gap closing in that time. . . .

For the immediate future, however, the majority has placed its *imprimatur* on a practice that can only weaken the principle of equality embodied in the Declaration of Independence and the Equal Protection Clause. "Our Constitution is color-blind, and neither knows nor tolerates classes among citizens." *Plessy* v. *Ferguson*, 163 U.S. 537, 559, (1896) (Harlan, J., dissenting). It has been nearly 140 years since Frederick Douglass asked the intellectual ancestors of the Law School to "[d]o nothing with us!" and the Nation adopted the Fourteenth Amendment. Now we must wait another 25 years to see this principle of equality vindicated. I therefore respectfully dissent from the remainder of the Court's opinion and the judgment.

BAKKE'S CASE: ARE QUOTAS UNFAIR?

Ronald Dworkin

On October 12, *1997*, the Supreme Court heard oral argument in the case of *The Regents of the University of California v. Allan Bakke*. No lawsuit has ever been more widely watched or more thoroughly debated in the national and international press before the Court's decision. Still, some of the most pertinent facts set before the Court have not been clearly summarized.

The medical school of the University of California at Davis has an affirmative action program (called the "task force program") designed to admit more black and other minority students. It sets sixteen places aside for which only members of "educationally and economically disadvantaged minorities" compete. Allan Bakke, white, applied for one of the remaining eighty-four places; he was rejected but, since his

test scores were relatively high, the medical school has conceded that it could not prove that he would have been rejected if the sixteen places reserved had been open to him. Bakke sued, arguing that the task force program deprived him of his constitutional rights. The California Supreme Court agreed, and ordered the medical school to admit him. The university appealed to the Supreme Court.

The Davis program for minorities is in certain respects more forthright (some would say cruder) than similar plans now in force in many other American universities and professional schools. Such programs aim to increase the enrollment of black and other minority students by allowing the fact of their race to count affirmatively as part of the case for admitting them. Some schools set a "target" of a particular number of minority places instead of setting aside a flat number of places. But Davis would not fill the number of places set aside unless there were sixteen minority candidates it considered clearly qualified for medical education. The difference is therefore one of administrative strategy and not of principle.

So the constitutional question raised by *Bakke* is of capital importance for higher education in America, and a large number of universities and schools have entered briefs *amicus curiae* urging the Court to reverse the California decision. They believe that if the decision is affirmed then they will no longer be free to use explicit racial criteria in any part of their admissions programs, and that they will therefore be unable to fulfill what they take to be their responsibilities to the nation.

It is often said that affirmative action programs aim to achieve a racially conscious society divided into racial and ethnic groups, each entitled, as a group, to some proportionable share of resources, careers, or opportunities. That is a perverse description. American society is currently a racially conscious society; this is the inevitable and evident consequence of a history of slavery, repression, and prejudice. Black men and women, boys and girls, are not free to choose for themselves in what roles—or as members of which social groups—others will characterize them. They are black, and no other feature of personality or allegiance or ambition will so thoroughly influence how they will be perceived and treated by others, and the range and character of the lives that will be open to them.

The tiny number of black doctors and professionals is both a consequence and a continuing cause of American racial consciousness, one link in a long and self-fueling chain reaction. Affirmative action programs use racially explicit criteria because their immediate goal is to increase the number of members of certain races in these professions. But their long-term goal is to *reduce* the degree to which American society is over-all a racially conscious society.

The programs rest on two judgments. The first is a judgment of social theory: that America will continue to be pervaded by racial divisions as long as the most lucrative, satisfying, and impor-

tant careers remain mainly the prerogative of members of the white race, while others feel themselves systematically excluded from a professional and social elite. The second is a calculation of strategy: that increasing the number of blacks who are at work in the professions will, in the long run, reduce the sense of frustration and injustice and racial self-consciousness in the black community to the point at which blacks may begin to think of themselves as individuals who can succeed like others through talent and initiative. At that future point the consequences of nonracial admissions programs, whatever these consequences might be, could be accepted with no sense of racial barriers or injustice.

It is therefore the worst possible misunderstanding to suppose that affirmative action programs are designed to produce a balkanized America, divided into racial and ethnic subnations. They use strong measures because weaker ones will fail; but their ultimate goal is to lessen not to increase the importance of race in American social and professional life.

According to the 1970 census, only 2.1 percent of US doctors were black. Affirmative action programs aim to provide more black doctors to serve black patients. This is not because it is desirable that blacks treat blacks and whites treat whites, but because blacks, for no fault of their own, are now unlikely to be well served by whites, and because a failure to provide the doctors they trust will exacerbate rather than reduce the resentment that now leads them to trust only their own. Affirmative action tries to provide more blacks as classmates for white doctors, not because it is desirable that a medical school class reflect the racial makeup of the community as a whole, but because professional association between blacks and whites will decrease the degree to which whites think of blacks as a race rather than as people, and thus the degree to which blacks think of themselves that way. It tries to provide "role models" for future black doctors, not because it is desirable for a black boy or girl to find adult models only among blacks, but because our history has made them so conscious of their race that the success of whites, for now, is likely to mean little or nothing for them.

The history of the campaign against racial injustice since 1954, when the Supreme Court decided *Brown* v. *Board of Education*, is a history in large part of failure. We have not succeeded in reforming the racial consciousness of our society by racially neutral means. We are therefore obliged to look upon the arguments for affirmative action with sympathy and an open mind. Of course, if Bakke is right that such programs, no matter how effective they may be, violate his constitutional rights then they cannot be permitted to continue. But we must not forbid them in the name of some mindless maxim, like the maxim that it cannot be right to fight fire with fire, or that the end cannot justify the means. If the strategic claims for affirmative action are cogent, they cannot be dismissed simply on the ground that racially explicit tests are distasteful. If such tests are distasteful it can only be for reasons that make the underlying social realities the programs attack more distasteful still.

The New Republic, in a recent editorial opposing affirmative action, missed that point. "It is critical to the success of a liberal pluralism," it said, "that group membership itself is not among the permissible criteria of inclusion and exclusion." But group membership is in fact, as a matter of social reality rather than formal admission standards, part of what determines inclusion or exclusion for us now. If we must choose between a society that is in fact liberal and an illiberal society that scrupulously avoids formal racial criteria, we can hardly appeal to the ideals of liberal pluralism to prefer the latter.

Professor Archibald Cox of Harvard Law School, speaking for the University of California in oral argument, told the Supreme Court that this is the choice the United States must make. As things stand, he said, affirmative action programs are the only effective means of increasing the absurdly small number of black doctors. The California Supreme Court, in approving Bakke's claim, had urged the university to pursue that goal by methods that do not explicitly take race into account. But that is unrealistic. We must distinguish, as Cox said, between two interpretations of what the California court's recommendation means. It might mean that the university should aim at the same immediate goal, of increasing the propor-

tion of black and other minority students in the medical school, by an admissions procedure that on the surface is not racially conscious.

That is a recommendation of hypocrisy. If those who administer the admissions standards, however these are phrased, understand that their immediate goal is to increase the number of blacks in the school, then they will use race as a criterion in making the various subjective judgments the explicit criteria will require, because that will be, given the goal, the only right way to make those judgments. The recommendation might mean, on the other hand, that the school should adopt some non-racially conscious goal, like increasing the number of disadvantaged students of all races, and then hope that that goal will produce an increase in the number of blacks as a by-product. But even if that strategy is less hypocritical (which is far from plain), it will almost certainly fail because no different goal, scrupulously administered in a non-racially conscious way, will in fact significantly increase the number of black medical students.

Cox offered powerful evidence for that conclusion, and it is supported by the recent and comprehensive report of the Carnegie Council on Policy Studies in Higher Education. Suppose, for example, that the medical school sets aside separate places for applicants "disadvantaged" on some racially neutral test, like poverty, allowing only those disadvantaged in that way to compete for these places. If the school selects those from that group who scored best on standard medical school aptitude tests, then it will take almost no blacks, because blacks score relatively low even among the economically disadvantaged. But if the school chooses among the disadvantaged on some basis other than test scores, just so that more blacks will succeed, then it will not be administering the special procedure in a non-racially conscious way.

So Cox was able to put his case in the form of two simple propositions. A racially conscious test for admission, even one that sets aside certain places for qualified minority applicants exclusively, serves goals that are in themselves unobjectionable and even urgent. Such programs are, moreover, the only means that offer any significant promise of achieving these goals. If these programs are halted, then no more than a trickle of black students will enter medical or other professional schools for another generation at least.

If these propositions are sound, then on what ground can it be thought that such programs are either wrong or unconstitutional? We must notice an important distinction between two different sorts of objections that might be made. These programs are intended, as I said, to decrease the importance of race in the United States in the long run. It may be objected, first, that the programs will in fact harm that goal more than they will advance it. There is no way now to prove that that is not so. Cox conceded, in his argument, that there are costs and risks in these programs.

Affirmative action programs seem to encourage, for example, a popular misunderstanding, which is that they assume that racial or ethnic groups are entitled to proportionate shares of opportunities, so that Italian or Polish ethnic minorities are, in theory, as entitled to their proportionate shares as blacks or Chicanos or American Indians are entitled to the shares the present programs give them. That is a plain mistake: the programs are not based on the idea that those who are aided are entitled to aid, but only on the strategic hypothesis that helping them is now an effective way of attacking a national problem. Some medical schools may well make that judgment, under certain circumstances, about a white ethnic minority. Indeed it seems likely that some medical schools are even now attempting to help white Appalachian applicants, for example, under programs of regional distribution.

So the popular understanding is wrong, but so long as it persists it is a cost of the program because the attitudes it encourages tend to a degree to make people more rather than less conscious of race. There are other possible costs. It is said, for example, that some blacks find affirmative action degrading; they find that it makes them more rather than less conscious of prejudice against their race as such. This attitude is also based on a misperception, I think, but for a small minority of blacks at least it is a genuine cost.

In the view of the many important universities who have such programs, however, the gains will very probably exceed the losses in reducing racial consciousness over-all. This view is hardly so implausible that it is wrong for these universities

to seek to acquire the experience that will allow us to judge whether they are right. It would be particularly silly to forbid these experiments if we know that the failure to try will mean, as the evidence shows, that the status quo will almost certainly continue. In any case, this first objection could provide no argument that would justify a decision by the Supreme Court holding the programs unconstitutional. The Court has no business substituting its speculative judgment about the probable consequences of educational policies for the judgment of professional educators.

So the acknowledged uncertainties about the long-term results of such programs could not justify a Supreme Court decision making them illegal. But there is a second and very different form of objection. It may be argued that even if the programs *are* effective in making our society less a society dominated by race, they are nevertheless unconstitutional because they violate the individual constitutional rights of those, like Allan Bakke, who lose places in consequence. In the oral argument Reynold H. Colvin of San Francisco, who is Bakke's lawyer, made plain that his objection takes this second form. Mr. Justice White asked him whether he accepted that the goals affirmative action programs seek are important goals. Mr. Colvin acknowledged that they were. Suppose, Justice White continued, that affirmative action programs are, as Cox had argued, the only effective means of seeking such goals. Would Mr. Colvin nevertheless maintain that the programs are unconstitutional? Yes, he insisted, they would be, because his client has a constitutional right that the programs be abandoned, no matter what the consequences.

Mr. Colvin was wise to put his objections on this second ground; he was wise to claim that his client has rights that do not depend on any judgment about the likely consequences of affirmative action for society as a whole, because if he makes out that claim then the Court must give him the relief he seeks.

But can he be right? If Allan Bakke has a constitutional right so important that the urgent goals of affirmative action must yield, then this must be because affirmative action violates some fundamental principle of political morality. This is not a case in which what might be called formal or technical law requires a decision one way or the other. There is no language in the Constitution whose plain meaning forbids affirmative action. Only the most naïve theories of statutory construction could argue that such a result is required by the language of any earlier Supreme Court decision or of the Civil Rights Act of 1964 or of any other congressional enactment. If Mr. Colvin is right it must be because Allan Bakke has not simply some technical legal right but an important moral right as well.

What could that right be? The popular argument frequently made on editorial pages is that Bakke has a right to be judged on his merit. Or that he has a right to be judged as an individual rather than as a member of a social group. Or that he has a right, as much as any black man, not to be sacrificed or excluded from any opportunity because of his race alone. But these catch phrases are deceptive here, because, as reflection demonstrates, the only genuine principle they describe is the principle that no one should suffer from the prejudice or contempt of others. And that principle is not at stake in this case at all. In spite of popular opinion, the idea that the *Bakke* case presents a conflict between a desirable social goal and important individual rights is a piece of intellectual confusion.

Consider, for example, the claim that individuals applying for places in medical school should be judged on merit, and merit alone. If that slogan means that admissions committees should take nothing into account but scores on some particular intelligence test, then it is arbitrary and, in any case, contradicted by the long-standing practice of every medical school. If it means, on the other hand, that a medical school should choose candidates that it supposes will make the most useful doctors, then everything turns on the judgment of what factors make different doctors useful. The Davis medical school assigned to each regular applicant, as well as to each minority applicant, what it called a "benchmark score." This reflected not only the results of aptitude tests and college grade averages, but a subjective evaluation of the applicant's chances of functioning as an effective doctor, in view of society's present needs for medical service. Presumably the qualities deemed important were different from the

qualities that a law school or engineering school or business school would seek, just as the intelligence tests a medical school might use would be different from the tests these other schools would find appropriate.

There is no combination of abilities and skills and traits that constitutes "merit" in the abstract; if quick hands count as "merit" in the case of a prospective surgeon, this is because quick hands will enable him to serve the public better and for no other reason. If a black skin will, as a matter of regrettable fact, enable another doctor to do a different medical job better, then that black skin is by the same token "merit" as well. That argument may strike some as dangerous; but only because they confuse its conclusion—that black skin may be a socially useful trait in particular circumstances—with the very different and despicable idea that one race may be inherently more worthy than another.

Consider the second of the catch phrases I have mentioned. It is said that Bakke has a right to be judged as an "individual," in deciding whether he is to be admitted to medical school and thus to the medical profession, and not as a member of some group that is being judged as a whole. What can that mean? Any admissions procedure must rely on generalizations about groups that are justified only statistically. The regular admissions process at Davis, for example, set a cutoff figure for college grade-point averages. Applicants whose averages fell below that figure were not invited to any interview, and therefore rejected out of hand.

An applicant whose average fell one point below the cutoff might well have had personal qualities of dedication or sympathy that would have been revealed at an interview, and that would have made him or her a better doctor than some applicant whose average rose one point above the line. But the former is excluded from the process on the basis of a decision taken for administrative convenience and grounded in the generalization, unlikely to hold true for every individual, that those with grade averages below the cutoff will not have other qualities sufficiently persuasive. Indeed, even the use of standard Medical College Aptitude Tests (MCAT) as part of the admissions procedure requires judging people as part of groups because it assumes that test scores are a guide to medical intelligence which is in turn a guide to medical ability. Though this judgment is no doubt true statistically, it hardly holds true for every individual.

Allan Bakke was himself refused admission to two other medical schools, not because of his race but because of his age: these schools thought that a student entering medical school at the age of thirty-three was likely to make less of a contribution to medical care over his career than someone entering at the standard age of twenty-one. Suppose these schools relied, not on any detailed investigation of whether Bakke himself had abilities that would contradict the generalization in his specific case, but on a rule of thumb that allowed only the most cursory look at applicants over (say) the age of thirty. Did these two medical schools violate his right to be judged as an individual rather than as a member of a group?

The Davis medical school permitted whites to apply for the sixteen places reserved for members of "educationally or economically disadvantaged minorities," a phrase whose meaning might well include white ethnic minorities. In fact several whites have applied, though none has been accepted, and the California Court found that the special committee charged with administering the program had decided, in advance, against admitting any. Suppose that decision had been based on the following administrative theory: it is so unlikely that any white doctor can do as much to counteract racial imbalance in the medical professions as a well-qualified and trained black doctor can do that the committee should for reasons of convenience proceed on the presumption no white doctor could. That presumption is, as a matter of fact, more plausible than the corresponding presumption about medical students over the age of thirty, or even the presumption about applicants whose grade-point averages fall below the cutoff line. If the latter presumptions do not deny the alleged right of individals to be judged as individuals in an admissions procedure, then neither can the former.

Mr. Colvin, in oral argument, argued the third of the catch phrases I mentioned. He said that his client had a right not to be excluded from medical school because of his race alone, and this as a

statement of constitutional right sounds more plausible than claims about the right to be judged on merit or as an individual. It sounds plausible, however, because it suggests the following more complex principle. Every citizen has a constitutional right that he not suffer disadvantage, at least in the competition for any public benefit, because the race or religion or sect or region or other natural or artificial group to which he belongs is the object of prejudice or contempt.

That is a fundamentally important constitutional right, and it is that right that was systematically violated for many years by racist exclusions and anti-Semitic quotas. Color bars and Jewish quotas were not unfair just because they made race or religion relevant or because they fixed on qualities beyond individual control. It is true that blacks or Jews do not choose to be blacks or Jews. But it is also true that those who score low in aptitude or admissions tests do not choose their levels of intelligence. Nor do those denied admission because they are too old, or because they do not come from a part of the country underrepresented in the school, or because they cannot play basketball well, choose not to have the qualities that made the difference.

Race seems different because exclusions based on race have historically been motivated not by some instrumental calculation, as in the case of intelligence or age or regional distribution or athletic ability, but because of contempt for the excluded race or religion as such. Exclusion by race was in itself an insult, because it was generated by and signaled contempt.

Bakke's claim, therefore, must be made more specific than it is. He says he was kept out of medical school because of his race. Does he mean that he was kept out because his race is the object of prejudice or contempt? That suggestion is absurd. A very high proportion of those who were accepted (and, presumably, of those who run the admissions program) were members of the same race. He therefore means simply that if he had been black he would have been accepted, with no suggestion that this would have been so because blacks are thought more worthy or honorable than whites.

That is true: no doubt he would have been accepted if he were black. But it is also true, and in exactly the same sense, that he would have been accepted if he had been more intelligent, or made a better impression in his interview, or, in the case of other schools, if he had been younger when he decided to become a doctor. Race is not, in *his* case, a different matter from these other factors equally beyond his control. It is not a different matter because in his case race is not distinguished by the special character of public insult. On the contrary the program presupposes that his race is still widely if wrongly thought to be superior to others.

In the past, it made sense to say that an excluded black or Jewish student was being sacrificed because of his race or religion; that meant that his or her exclusion was treated as desirable in itself, not because it contributed to any goal in which he as well as the rest of society might take pride. Allan Bakke is being "sacrificed" because of his race only in a very artificial sense of the word. He is being "sacrificed" in the same artificial sense because of his level of intelligence, since he would have been accepted if he were more clever than he is. In both cases he is being excluded not by prejudice but because of a rational calculation about the socially most beneficial use of limited resources for medical education.

It may now be said that this distinction is too subtle, and that if racial classifications have been and may still be used for malign purposes, then everyone has a flat right that racial classifications not be used at all. This is the familiar appeal to the lazy virtue of simplicity. It supposes that if a line is difficult to draw, or might be difficult to administer if drawn, then there is wisdom in not making the attempt to draw it. There may be cases in which that is wise, but those would be cases in which nothing of great value would as a consequence be lost. If racially conscious admissions policies now offer the only substantial hope for bringing more qualified black and other minority doctors into the profession, then a great loss is suffered if medical schools are not allowed voluntarily to pursue such programs. We should then be trading away a chance to attack certain and present injustice in order to gain protection we may not need against speculative abuses we have other means to prevent. And such abuses cannot, in any case, be worse than the injustice to which we would then surrender.

We have now considered three familiar slogans, each widely thought to name a constitutional right that enables Allan Bakke to stop programs of affirmative action no matter how effective or necessary these might be. When we inspect these slogans, we find that they can stand for no genuine principle except one. This is the important principle that no one in our society should suffer because he is a member of a group thought less worthy of respect, as a group, than other groups. We have different aspects of that principle in mind when we say that individuals should be judged on merit, that they should be judged as individuals, and that they should not suffer disadvantages because of their race. The spirit of that fundamental principle is the spirit of the goal that affirmative action is intended to serve. The principle furnishes no support for those who find, as Bakke does, that their own interests conflict with that goal.

It is of course regrettable when any citizen's expectations are defeated by new programs serving some more general concern. It is regrettable, for example, when established small businesses fail because new and superior roads are built; in that case people have invested more than Bakke has. And they have more reason to believe their businesses will continue than Bakke had to suppose he could have entered the Davis medical school at thirty-three even without a task force program.

There is, of course, no suggestion in that program that Bakke shares in any collective or individual guilt for racial injustice in America; or that he is any less entitled to concern or respect than any black student accepted in the program. He has been disappointed, and he must have the sympathy due that disappointment, just as any other disappointed applicant—even one with much worse test scores who would not have been accepted in any event—must have sympathy. Each is disappointed because places in medical schools are scarce resources and must be used to provide what the more general society most needs. It is hardly Bakke's fault that racial justice is now a special need—but he has no right to prevent the most effective measures of securing that justice from being used.

DOUBLE REVERSE DISCRIMINATION

Jefferson Morley

What was fifteen years ago a garbage dump on the eastern edge of Brooklyn is now Starrett City, the country's largest federally subsidized, middle-income housing project. Fifteen thousand people live in its forty-six buildings. Kids play on the grassy plazas amid the tan brick high-rises, and young mothers chat on the benches. A shopping center in the middle of the project has a Waldbaum's, a medical center, a Fayva shoe store; it is busy with shoppers even on a Sunday morning. But one of the most impressive things about Starrett City is also one of the most troubling: it is racially integrated. Impressive because white and black people peacefully live side by side all too infrequently. Troubling because only one thing keeps Starrett City integrated, and that is the management's use of "occupancy controls"— a policy of limiting black and Hispanic tenants to around 40 percent of the total. Starrett City thrives on the paradox of achieving integration by discriminating against blacks.

You could not invent a better test of the affirmative action principle than Starrett City. The only way to be philosophically consistent in judging the rightness of occupancy controls is to be racially disinterested. Should conservatives applaud Starrett City for protecting middle-class city dwellers or condemn it for violating the ideal that society be color blind? Should liberals support Starrett because integration is a worthy goal, or oppose it for discriminating against blacks? Some liberals deny that affirmative action is reverse discrimination against whites. But they can't deny that blacks shut out of Starrett City *are* victims of discrimination—double reverse discrimination. More importantly, though, those who insist that "affirmative discrimination" (Nathan Glazer's phrase) is in the interests of neither blacks nor whites must confront a vivid example of why it is in the interests of both.

On May 2, *1984,* the Federal District Court in Brooklyn decided that society could live with Starrett's paradox. It approved an out-of-court settlement between Starrett City and five black rental applicants, represented by the N.A.A.C.P.

and others, who filed a class action discrimination suit in 1979. Under the settlement, Starrett can maintain its occupancy controls, although it must rent an additional 3 percent of its 5,881 apartments to minority families by 1989. As part of the same settlement, the State of New York has pledged to expand traditional affirmative action. It will increase minority tenancy to 20 percent at eight-six other publicly assisted projects in the city by 1999. In addition, the plaintiffs and all others on Starrett's waiting list will be notified of openings at the other projects.

In one sense the settlement is nothing new. Occupancy controls are a color-conscious policy philosophically identical to many affirmative action programs. With the aim of ending society's racial divisions, occupancy controls make distinctions based on race. But like a photographic negative, the Starrett City case neatly neverses the places of black and white, and forces us to think about the affirmative action debate in a new way.

The Starrett City story begins with the end of liberal illusion. In 1972 Starrett City Associates, a limited investor's partnership, was organized to finance a proposed housing project located on a large tract of unused land between the black poor neighborhood of East New York and the white working-class neighborhood of Canarsie. But the residents of Canarsie fiercely opposed the project, saying it would bring the ghetto closer to their doorsteps. This wasn't an unreasonable fear. East New York had gone from two-thirds white to three-quarters black between 1960 and 1970 and had deteriorated in the process, its property values plummeting and its crime rate rising.

Starrett faced up to the recent unhappy experience of many New York City housing projects. If the minority population at Starrett grew much larger than 30 percent, Starrett would almost certainly "tip"—whites would begin to move out, at first slowly, and then more and more rapidly until all whites, except the elderly on Social Security, were gone. Starrett was sure to attract black tenants. But if it wanted a stable middle-income project, it had to attract—and keep—a larger number of whites. Integration was a practical necessity, an admirable idea, and an unlikely prospect.

Starrett considered—and rejected—three solutions and settled on a fourth.

First, it recognized that a simple policy of nondiscrimination wouldn't work. Choosing tenants on a first-come, first-served basis from an applicant pool with a sizable fraction of blacks would eventually result in segregation.

Second, it knew that even the most sincere intentions to maintain integration would not prevent tipping. The proof was right down the street in Linden Plaza, a middle-income project that opened in 1975. Linden Plaza started out more than half black, well over the generally accepted 30 percent "tipping point." It pledged to stay integrated: nevertheless, within four years it became 95 percent black. Even though Linden Plaza, after tipping, had a higher average household income than Starrett City, it was enculfed in crime, vandalism, and management neglect, while Starrett remained relatively safe and clean. The reasons for this are complex: middle-class blacks show higher crime rates than their white counterparts. Residents and security guards are more reluctant to report crime and criminals in all-black projects than in integrated projects. And middle-class black households are more likely than white households to have both parents working full-time, which means less supervision of adolescents who are responsible for most crime and vandalism. No wonder Starrett City was, in the words of a Department of Housing and Urban Development report in 1974, "singularly driven to achieve an occupancy that is 70 percent white."

Third, Starrett realized from the beginning that it would have to go beyond affirinative action in its original sense—that is, seeking out members of a targeted racial group without extending preferential treatment to them. Starrett did make an extensive effort to attract white applicants. Ads in ethnic neighborhood newspapers emphasized Starrett's stability and safety, terms calculated to ease racial apprehensions. Amenities such as indoor tennis courts and lobbies lined with Italian marble were also highlighted. But there was no illusion that such niceties would prevent tipping.

A deeper realization underlay all of Starrett's assumptions. The uniformity and sickening speed which characterized the tipping phenomena could not be solely explained by white racism. Rather, it was undeniable that the social disorganization afflicting largely black populations—unsupervised youth, discouraged workers, and above all, a higher crime rate—simply became intolerable at some point to their white neighbors. White fears might originate in racism and might be worsened by it, but they were also fed by the reality of muggings. It was Nathan Glazer who most forcefully made the point in the early 1970s that whites' fears of blacks were profound and in many ways justified. Middle-class blacks, of course, have many of these same fears but fewer opportunities to live elsewhere.

Starrett had an answer: it would make sure too many whites didn't leave by making sure too many blacks didn't get in. It delayed opening buildings because there were not enough qualified white applicants to maintain the 70 percent goal. (Starrett carefully monitors the race of outgoing tenants. It has since let the white population drop down to 59 percent without tipping.) By the summer of 1981, minorities constituted three-quarters of Starrett's waiting list but only two-fifths of its tenants. A qualified black family on the list had to wait about twenty months for a two-bedroom apartment. A white family had to wait two months. In defense of integration, Starrett's weapon of last resort was preferential treatment for whites.

What makes the Starrett dilemma especially difficult is that the stakes go beyond the project itself. Without occupancy controls, Starrett would tip—within four years, according to Oscar Newman, a well-known urban planner and consultant to Starrett. Blacks who had hoped to leave the ghetto might well find that it had caught up with them. But because of the pervasiveness of housing discrimination, they would find it far harder than their white neighbors to move on again to better neighborhoods. One pleasant area blacks might be able to move into would be nearby Canarsie, where increasingly apprehensive whites might begin to move out. Canarsie itself might approach the tipping point, and the whole devastating downward spiral of urban decline could begin yet again.

No one got caught between principles more prominently than Starrett's lawyer, Morris B. Abram. Starrett hired Abram in 1979 when the five blacks sued for discrimination. Abram had first become well known in the 1960s when he was a lawyer for Martin Luther King Jr. and numerous civil rights causes. More recently he had made a name for himself with his emphatic opposition to reverse discrimination, which he said amounted to racial quotas. His stand prompted President Reagan to name him to the United States Civil Rights Commission in 1983.

There is simply no way to reconcile Abram's opposition to quotas with his defense of Starrett. In January 1980 Abram wrote a categorical denunciation of preferential treatment in *Commentary*. He chastised the "leading elements of the civil rights community" who "baldly claimed the rightness and legality of imposed goals or quotas for identified members of disadvantaged groups." Race, he said, was an "absurd, unfair, and counterproductive" basis for treating people, and it was a "total reversal of form" for liberals who had supported the color-blind ideals of the civil rights movement to employ it.

In his own total reversal of form, Abram had agreed one month before in December 1979 to defend occupancy controls. As the case approached trial, he filed papers asserting the rightness and legality of Starrett's quota:

> Race remains a significant factor in our society. . . . In the circumstances that actually confront Starrett City today, race-conscious tenant selection methods are the only way in which to preserve an integrated community.

Voicing the convictions of leading elements of the civil rights movement. Justice Thurgood Marshall had made the same argument in his dissent in the *Bakke* case—although not quite as baldly.

> It is because of a legacy of unequal treatment that we now must permit the institutions of this society to give consideration to race. . . . If we are ever to become a fully integrated society, . . . we must be willing.

It's worth examining Abram's apparent about-face in some detail. Are quotas acceptable to Abram at Starrett City because they benefit whites instead of blacks? Of course not. Why then? Abram declined to talk to me for this article, but he did tell Ann Mariano of *The Washington Post* that Starrett's preferential treat-

ment was permissible because it did not "restrict and assign people of lesser qualifications into opportunities denied people of more qualifications on the grounds of race." In other words, where "qualifications" are not a factor, it is permissible to make color-conscious choices.

Abram's explanation only underlines the contradiction he is trying to resolve. In the pages of *Commentary* and in the halls of Congress, Abram has never offered the slightest hint that housing, or decisions not involving qualifications could constitute legitimate areas of race-conscious decision-making. And his unequivocal language leaves no room for any unspecified exceptions. As recently as June 12 Abram wrote an attack on affirmative action in *The Wall Street Journal*, saying that the American people "do not believe that racial distinctions should have any place in our laws or public practice, or that persons should be judged on the basis of the group to which they belong." He did not mention Starrett City in the article.

Despite Abram's implication in the *Post*, qualifications of a sort *are* a part of Starrett's selection process. To qualify for an apartment at Starrett City, applicants must meet a minimum income requirement of about $10,000 per year. Occupancy controls still give preference to a white applicant who makes $15,000 a year over a black applicant who earns $17,000. In this case, the white is less qualified to pay the rent; the more qualified black is denied the opportunity to move into Starrett City on the grounds of race. If Abram followed the logic of his explanation to the *Post*, he would have represented the black plaintiffs, not Starrett.

One might rightly respond that once the two applicants prove they are qualified to pay the rent, it is irrelevant who makes more above the minimum. This would require refining Abram's formulation to something like: in cases in which added qualifications don't make a real difference—where minimum qualifications have been met—color-conscious decisions are O.K. But this wouldn't resolve Abram's inconsistency either. Say that the white and the black applying to live at Starrett both work as security guards, and that they both also apply for jobs as police officers. The white does better on the tests, but both demonstrate the minimum abilities to do the job. Under this logic it would be permissible, not to lower the minimum, but to hire the less qualified black for the sake of some pressing social objective, e.g., an integrated police force.

Of course qualifications figure less importantly in picking a tenant than in, say, picking a brain surgeon. And additional qualifications above and beyond the required minimum are often important. But qualifications can also be easily exaggerated. It is difficult to say with any precision, for example, what additional qualifications will make for a better lawyer. Take a white law school applicant who scores 600 on the law school entrance exam and a black who scores 590. The white's better qualifications are conceivably less valuable to society than the presence of one more black lawyer. There are also cases where additional qualifications are ignored altogether because we choose to reward other values. Veteran's preferences, admissions for alumni children, and college football recruiting are three uncontroversial examples. And there are the many cases where qualifications are so necessary and clear cut that they must take precedence over racial considerations. Abram's basic case on behalf of Starrett City still applies. Racial considerations can be important enough to justify taking race into account. This, of course, is exactly what the supporters of affirmative action contend: it is permissible to be color conscious in the service of an overriding social goal. Abram's defense of Starrett profoundly subverts the neoconservative position on quotas.

But defenders of affirmative action shouldn't throw too many stones at Abram. The N.A.A.C.P.'s role is equally inconsistent. Why did the N.A.A.C.P. go to court to abolish the sort of color-conscious policy it had supported in the *Bakke* case and elsewhere? Was it because this time quotas benefited whites, and not blacks? James Meyerson, a former N.A.A.C.P. attorney who represented the plaintiffs, argues that occupancy controls are inherently different than affirmative action. Starrett's quota, Meyerson says, is "stigmatizing and exclusionary," designed to keep out blacks, while traditional affirmative action employs "inclusionary quotas," designed to bring in the previously excluded.

This is a distinction without a difference. Traditional affirmative action is also "exclusionary," at least for those whites who would not be hired or admitted to law school because of it. And

occupancy controls at Starrett City can be viewed as "inclusionary"—for whites and, notably, for blacks who would otherwise not get to live in an integrated community. Inclusion and exclusion are merely the two faces of any kind of preferential treatment. The whole premise of affirmative action is that the benefits of racial inclusion to society outweigh the damages of exclusion to individuals. Starrett was committed to maximum integration—that is, the maximum amount of inclusion. As occupancy controls were the crucial instrument to that end, they were a model of affirmative action.

Meyerson is right that occupancy controls are "stigmatizing." They are based on the judgment that Starrett would deteriorate if only blacks lived there. There are two possible objections to this unpleasant assumption. One holds that it is wrong and racist, and therefore an illegal basis for public decision-making. The plaintiffs in the Starrett case made this point, though not very convincingly. It is realistic, not racist, to believe that an all-black community in Starrett City would probably suffer more serious social problems than an integrated one. The other objection holds that, whether or not the assumption is correct. Starrett's quota does not treat applicants as individuals but as undifferentiated blacks, thereby violating their rights.

The N.A.A.C.P. and the plaintiffs made this point too, and it only compounded their difficulties. They argued that, whatever the group benefits of integration, individual blacks should not have to suffer to achieve it. As the plaintiffs put it in their concluding argument: "This case is not . . . one of conflict between those supporting integration and those opposing it. . . . The question is whether integration, as the defendants arbitrarily define it, can justify the costs and burdens the black plaintiffs here are being asked to bear." This was not an unfamiliar argument. It was just an uncomfortable one for the N.A.A.C.P. to be offering: substitute "white" for "black," and you have the essence of Abram's usual argument against affirmative action—which the N.A.A.C.P. had long opposed.

To reject the legitimacy of group judgments as the basis of public decisions is to reject the legitimacy of affirmative action. After all, traditional affirmative action doesn't require any individual black to prove discrimination in order to reap the benefits of affirmative action: it doesn't require that any individual white be shown to be guilty of discrimination in order for him or her to be denied benefits he or she might otherwise obtain.

The long and ugly history of exclusion of blacks makes the N.A.A.C.P.'s position more understandable but no less contradictory. The justification for treating individuals as undifferentiated members of a group (in eminent domain decisions, progressive income tax codes, and affirmative action programs) is not simply to distribute benefits to politically preferred groups. If it were, the N.A.A.C.P. would be saying that affirmative action is, and should be, nothing more than aid to blacks. Given the history of racism, society will usually choose not to make group judgments that impose additional "costs and burdens" on individual blacks. But it is perfectly within the spirit of affirmative action to do so for some compelling purpose.

Thus, the implications of the plaintiffs' case undermined affirmative action on an even more fundamental level. Critics of affirmative action often assert that we should conceive of our society, not as a collection of groups with varying claims, but as a collection of individuals with rights. By siding with the plaintiffs, the N.A.A.C.P. recognized the force of this argument. To put group claims ahead of individual rights is unfair, especially when the groups are defined by color alone; no matter how good the intentions are, putting aside the principle of color blindness hurts. If nothing else, the Starrett case ought to give advocates of affirmative action a deeper appreciation of why Allen Bakke, Brian Weber, and other whites have felt unjustly treated by traditional affirmative action, and have gone to court in protest.

But neoconservatives themselves, in their writings on other subjects, have provided two of the best arguments for recognizing the importance of group claims.

The first argument is practicality. Neoconservatism's defense of urban ethnic communities is (at its best) a defense of old-fashioned institutions like neighborhoods. Communities in a city are said to be more than just collections of individuals. They are more akin to organisms whose complex workings ought not be taken for granted. Imposing lofty plans, such as busing for school integration, however well-intentioned, can do irreparable

damage. It seems in this spirit that Abram recognized that rigid adherence to the worthy principle of color blindness at Starrett City made no sense. It might well condemn a model community to segregation and deterioration.

Starrett City, though, is not the only place in the United States where suspending the color-blind principle is justified. Abram—and his colleagues in the Reagan Administration who believe in the color-blind principle—ought to examine the practical limitations of that principle in other situations as well. Color blindness can do real damage to fragile and worthy black communities like East New York by rejecting an obvious method of redressing the legacy of racism—as well as to white communities like Canarsie threatened by the problems of the black community.

The second neoconservative argument that is ironically useful in defending affirmative action is more philosophical. Neoconservatives often lament the expansion of individual rights. Their point is that "rights" have become a sign of confused thinking, or worse, a cover for selfishness and sloth. As Abram put it in another attack on affirmative action on June 11 in *The New York Times Magazine*, "the new [civil rights] movement treated economic claims as civil rights, by embracing an idea of 'rights' that included economic entitlements—a 'right' to shelter, a 'right' to health care, a 'right' to day care for children." The other half of this argument asserts that instead of claiming our rights extend ever further, we ought to be accepting more social responsibilities. It would seem reasonable to temper the right to always be treated in a color-blind manner with the responsiblity of sometimes paying a real price for a more racially just community. Abram demanded that the black plaintiffs in the Starrett case pay a real price. Is it really "absurd, unfair, and counterproductive" to demand that white people sometimes pay a price too?

The final irony of the Starrett case is that nobody will own up to the settlement—even though it is the logical extension of what all sides believe. If you believe in preserving and enhancing urban neighborhoods and housing projects, you have to support Starrett, and if you support Starrett, you logically have to accept the principle of affirmative action. The settlement confirmed that occupancy controls are a form of affirnative action. Abram accepted affirmative action at New York

State's other projects in return for the N.A.A.C.P. tacitly accepting occupancy controls. Nonetheless, the plaintiffs did not acknowledge the lawfulness of occupancy controls, and Abram said nothing about the racial "goals" at the other projects.

This was not just mutual hypocrisy. The fact is that even after resolving all the intellectual twists and turns, the Starrett case is still not resolved. By encapsulating so many of our racial dilemmas, the case continues to make one uneasy. And we should be uneasy about the costs of affirmative action, about the burdens of our racial history, and above all about the state of race relations today: they are bitter, ugly, and sad. Learning from our mistakes, recognizing the limits of our preconceptions, even contradicting ourselves, is the only way to rise above the wreckage of recrimination, mutual suspicion, and fear. If Starrett City proves anything, it proves that we can do worse than to start building on a garbage-dump.

Proxy War

Liberals denounce racial profiling. Conservatives denounce affirmative action. What's the difference?

Michael Brus

In Brent Staples' memoir *Parallel Time*, he recounts a game he used to play while a student at the University of Chicago. Staples, who is black, would pace the streets surrounding the campus after dark. When he spied a white couple strolling toward him arm in arm, he would walk directly at them, at a normal pace. The couple would first tighten their grip on each other. Then, as Staples continued to head toward them, they would panic, release their grip, and scurry apart. Staples would breeze between them, without losing a step, without looking back. He called it "scattering the pigeons."

The "pigeons" feared Staples because of his blackness—they were using his race as a proxy for potential criminality. Using superficial traits to infer deeper characteristics in people is common and need not be racist. Generalizing from what is easily and quickly knowable to something that is hard to know for sure is what economists think of as minimizing information costs. If the clouds turn dark and ominous and it starts to thunder while you're out for a stroll, you can find a phone and call the weather service, or you can ignore them on the grounds that predictions about the weather are often wrong, or you can take cover under the assumption that it's probably going to rain. But using race as a proxy is sensitive, for good and obvious reasons.

If skin color as a proxy for criminal intentions were a precise tool—that is, if every young black man strolling the sidewalks were a mugger—it would be hard to criticize. And if the implied generalization had no validity—if a young black male was no more likely to be a mugger than anyone else approaching on the sidewalk—it would be easy to label as racist. But, like most such generalizations, it is valid but not perfect. A young black man is more likely to be a mugger than a young white man—but the assumption that any particular young black man is a mugger will usually be wrong. So is using race as a proxy racist?

This is what the current "racial profiling" controversy is about. Racial profiling is when police use race as a reason to search someone's car or to frisk a pedestrian. Almost all black men have tales of being stopped by a cop for no reason other than their skin color. It's derisively known as "DWB": the crime of driving while black. Earlier this year the governor of New Jersey, Christine Todd Whitman, fired the state police superintendent for telling a journalist that blacks were more likely to commit crimes than whites. But she has since admitted that state police systematically stop cars simply because the driver is black. And racial profiling has many defenders who say it is sensible, hard-nosed policing of the sort that has led to a dramatic drop in the nation's crime rate.

One generalization that can be made about racial profiling—a valid but not perfect generalization, of course—is that conservatives tend to support it, while liberals tend to regard it as racist. In another controversy, the one over affirmative action, the opposite generalization holds: Liberals tend to support it, while conservatives tend to regard it as reverse racism.

And yet affirmative action and racial profiling are essentially the same. Affirmative action amounts to the use of race as a proxy for other, harder-to-discern qualities: racial victimization, poverty, cultural deprivation. Few critics of affirmative action are against compensating victims of specific and proven acts of racial discrimination. And the critics often positively endorse programs giving a special break to people who've overcome economic or cultural disadvantage. What they object to is generalizing these conditions from a person's race. Defenders of affirmative action say, in essence, that as policy-making generalizations go, this one is overwhelmingly valid—and that more justice will be lost than gained by insisting on scientific precision.

Defenders of affirmative action and defenders of racial profiling even resort to the same dodge in defending their cause against colorblind absolutists. They say they, too, think it's wrong for a person to be promoted and/or arrested just because of his or her race. But, they say, it's OK for race to be one factor among many.

Here is Gov. Whitman, quoted in the *New York Times Magazine* last month, explaining the difference between profiling (good) and racial profiling (bad):

> Profiling means a police officer using cumulative knowledge and training to identify certain indicators of possible criminal activity. Race may be one of those factors, but it cannot stand alone. Racial profiling is when race is the only other factor. There's no other probable cause.

This precisely echoes Justice Lewis Powell's famous explanation of permissible affirmative action in the 1978 Bakke case:

> Ethnic diversity is only one element in a range of factors a university properly may consider in attaining the goal of a heterogeneous student body. . . . In [a constitutional] admissions program, race or ethnic background may be deemed a "plus" in a particular applicant file, yet it does not insulate the individual from comparison with all other candidates for the available seats.

The factor fudge satisfies some critics, but it doesn't solve the racial proxy dilemma. Stopping and frisking a driver or admitting a student to Yale is a yes-or-no decision. As legal scholar Randall Kennedy wrote in his book *Race, Crime, and the Law*, "Even if race is only one of several factors behind a decision, tolerating it at all means tolerating it as potentially the decisive factor." When it's the decisive factor, it might as well have been the only factor. If it's never decisive, it's not really a factor at all.

The main difference between affirmative action and racial profiling is that one singles out blacks for something desirable and the other singles them out for something undesirable. Reasonable people can differ about whether using race as a proxy is OK. Obviously it depends on how valid the generalization is in any given case, and how costly or impractical it would be to get alternative information. When you fear a man approaching you may be a mugger, you may not be able to find out in the next five seconds whether he happens to be a University of Chicago intellectual headed for the *New York Times* editorial board. On the other hand, race is not just any proxy, and probably should be used more sparingly—especially by the government—than the narrow logic of probabilities would justify.

Racial proxies are a tough call. But it's safe to say that anyone who is outraged by racial profiling but tolerates affirmative action, or vice versa, has got it wrong.

Chapter 10

ARISTOTLE: JUSTICE AND VIRTUE

Despite their differences, the rights-oriented theories we have studied so far share some important assumptions. One is the assumption that distributive justice is not a matter of rewarding virtue or moral desert. Both Hayek, a libertarian, and Rawls, an egalitarian liberal, emphasize this point. Another is the idea that the measure of a just society is not whether it produces virtuous citizens, but whether it provides a fair framework of rights within which individuals can pursue their own values. Aristotle (384–322 BC) rejects both of these assumptions. He believes that justice consists in giving people what they deserve, and that a just society is one that enables human beings to realize their highest nature, to attain the good life. For Aristotle, political activity is not simply one way among others to pursue our interests; it is an essential ingredient of the good life.

Turning to Aristotle after having read philosophers such as Bentham, Locke, Kant, Mill, and Rawls enables us to glimpse some of the contrasts between ancient and modern political thought, and to examine some key assumptions of contemporary thinking about justice. Here are some questions to think about when reading Aristotle: Why does he think that politics is essential to the good life? Is he right? What virtues, or qualities of character, are developed by participating in political activity? In contemporary political theory, distributive justice is primarily about the allocation of income, wealth, and opportunity; for Aristotle, distributive justice is primarily about the allocation of offices and honors. What is the significance of this difference? Who does Aristotle consider worthy of the highest offices and honors in the political community?

Finally, what do you make of Aristotle's idea that justice is a matter of fit— between persons and the social roles appropriate to their virtues? Is there a connection between this notion of justice and Aristotle's defense of slavery? Does Aristotle's defense of slavery reveal a defect in his philosophy as a whole, or can it be challenged within the terms that he himself provides?

The Politics

Aristotle

Translated by Ernest Barker

Book I. The Household and the City

The Political Association and Its Relation to Other Associations (Chapters 1–2)

Chapter 1

All associations have ends: the political association has the highest; but the principle of association expresses itself in different forms, and through different modes of government.

1252ª1 Observation shows us, first, that every city [*polis*] is a species of association, and, secondly, that all associations come into being for the sake of some good—for all men do all their acts with a view to achieving something which is, in their view, a good. It is clear therefore that all associations aim at some good, and that the particular association which is the most sovereign of all, and includes all the rest, will pursue this aim most, and will thus be directed to the most sovereign of all goods. This most sovereign and inclusive association is the city [or *polis*], as it is called, or the political association.

1252ª7 It is a mistake to believe that the statesman is the same as the monarch of a kingdom, or the manager of a household, or the master of a number of slaves. Those who hold this view consider that each one of these differs from the others not with a difference of kind, but according to the number, large or small, of those with whom he deals. On this view someone who is concerned with few people is a master, someone who is concerned with more is the manager of a household, and someone who is concerned with still more is a statesman, or a monarch. This view abolishes any real difference between a large household and a small city; and it also reduces the difference between the "statesman" and the monarch to the one fact that the latter has an uncontrolled and sole authority, while the former exercises his authority in conformity with the rules imposed by the art of statesmanship and as one who rules and is ruled in turn. But this is a view which cannot be accepted as correct.

1252ª18 Our point will be made clear if we proceed to consider the matter according to our normal method of analysis. Just as, in all other fields, a compound should be analysed until we reach its simple elements (or, in other words, the smallest parts of the whole which it constitutes), so we must also consider analytically the elements of which a city is composed. We shall then gain a better insight into the way in which these differ from one another; and we shall also be in a position to discover whether there is any kind of expertise to be acquired in connection with the matters under discussion.

Chapter 2

To distinguish the different forms of association we must trace the development successively of the association of the household, that of the village, and that of the city or polis. The polis, or political association, is the crown: it completes and fulfils the nature of man: it is thus natural to him, and he is himself "naturally a polis-animal"; it is also prior to him, in the sense that it is the presupposition of his true and full life.

1252ª24 In this, as in other fields, we shall be able to study our subject best if we begin at the beginning and consider things in the process of their growth. First of all, there must necessarily be a union or pairing of those who cannot exist without one another. Male and female must unite for the reproduction of the species—not from deliberate intention, but from the natural impulse, which exists in animals generally as it also exists in plants, to leave behind them something of the same nature as themselves. Next, there must necessarily be a union of the naturally ruling element with the element which is naturally ruled, for the preservation of both. The element which is able, by virtue of its intelligence, to exercise forethought, is naturally a ruling and master element; the element which is able, by virtue of its bodily power, to do the physical work, is a ruled element, which is naturally in a state of slavery; and master and slave have accordingly a common interest.

1252ᵇ2 The female and the slave are naturally distinguished from one another. Nature makes nothing in a miserly spirit, as smiths do when they make the Delphic knife to serve a number of purposes: she makes each separate thing for a separate end; and she does so because the instrument is most perfectly made when it serves a single purpose and not a variety of purposes. Among barbarians, however, the female and the slave occupy the same position—the reason being that no naturally ruling element exists among them, and conjugal union thus comes to be a union of a female who is a slave with a male who is also a slave. This is why our poets have said,

Meet it is that barbarous peoples should be
governed by the Greeks

the assumption being that barbarian and slave are by nature one and the same.

The first result of these two elementary associations is the household or family. Hesiod spoke truly in the verse,

First house, and wife, and ox to draw the
plough,

for oxen serve the poor in lieu of household slaves. The first form of association naturally instituted for the satisfaction of daily recurrent needs is thus the family; and the members of the family are accordingly termed by Charondas "associates of the breadchest", as they are also termed by Epimenides the Cretan "associates of the manger".

1252ᵇ17 The next form of association—which is also the first to be formed from more households than one, and for the satisfaction of something more than daily recurrent needs—is the village. The most natural form of the village appears to be that of a colony [or offshoot] from a family; and some have thus called the members of the village by the name of "sucklings of the same milk", or, again, of "sons and the sons of sons". This, it may be noted, is the reason why cities were originally ruled, as the peoples of the barbarian world still are, by kings. They were formed of people who were already monarchically governed, for every household is monarchically governed by the eldest of the kin, just as villages,

when they are offshoots from the household, are similarly governed in virtue of the kinship between their members. This is what Homer describes:

Each of them ruleth
Over his children and wives,

a passage which shows that they lived in scattered groups, as indeed men generally did in ancient times. The fact that men generally were governed by kings in ancient times, and that some still continue to be governed in that way, is the reason that leads everyone to say that the gods are also governed by a king. People make the lives of the gods in the likeness of their own—as they also make their shapes.

1252ᵇ27 When we come to the final and perfect association, formed from a number of villages, we have already reached the city [or *polis*]. This may be said to have reached the height of full self-sufficiency; or rather we may say that while it comes into existence for the sake of mere life, it exists for the sake of a good life. For this reason every city exists by nature, just as did the earlier associations [from which it grew]. It is the end or consummation to which those associations move, and the "nature" of things consists in their end or consummation; for what each thing is when its growth is completed we call the nature of that thing, whether it be a man or a horse or a family. Again the end, or final cause, is the best and self-sufficiency is both the end, and the best.

1253ᵃ2 From these considerations it is evident that the city belongs to the class of things that exist by nature, and that man is by nature a political animal. He who is without a city, by reason of his own nature and not of some accident, is either a poor sort of being, or a being higher than man: he is like the man of whom Homer wrote in denunciation:

Clanless and lawless and heartless is he.

The man who is such by nature at once plunges into a passion of war; he is in the position of a solitary advanced piece in a game of draughts.

1253ᵃ7 It is thus clear that man is a political animal, in a higher degree than bees or other gregarious animals. Nature, according to our theory, makes nothing in vain; and man alone of the animals is furnished with the faculty of language. The mere making of sounds serves to indicate pleasure and pain, and is thus a faculty that belongs to animals in general: their nature enables them to attain the point at which they have perceptions of pleasure and pain, and can signify those perceptions to one another. But language serves to declare what is advantageous and what is the reverse, and it is the peculiarity of man, in comparison with other animals, that he alone possesses a perception of good and evil, of the just and the unjust, and other similar qualities; and it is association in these things which makes a family and a city.

1253ª18 We may now proceed to add that the city is prior in the order of nature to the family and the individual. The reason for this is that the whole is necessarily prior to the part. If the whole body is destroyed, there will not be a foot or a hand, except in that ambiguous sense in which one uses the same word to indicate a different thing, as when one speaks of a "hand" made of stone; for a hand, when destroyed [by the destruction of the whole body], will be no better than a stone "hand". All things derive their essential character from their function and their capacity; and it follows that if they are no longer fit to discharge their function, we ought not to say that they are still the same things, but only that, by an ambiguity, they still have the same names.

1253ª25 We thus see that the city exists by nature and that it is prior to the individual. For if the individual is not self-sufficient when he is isolated he will stand in the same relation to the whole as other parts do to their wholes. The man who is isolated, who is unable to share in the benefits of political association, or has no need to share because he is already self-sufficient, is no part of the city, and must therefore be either a beast or a god. There is therefore a natural impulse in all men towards an association of this sort. But the man who first constructed such an association was none the less the greatest of benefactors. Man, when perfected, is the best of animals; but if he be isolated from law and justice he is the worst of all. Injustice is all the graver when it is armed injustice; and man is furnished from birth with weapons which are intended to serve the purposes of wisdom and goodness, but which may be used in preference for opposite ends. That is why, if he be without goodness [of mind and character], he is a most unholy and savage being, and

worse than all others in the indulgence of lust and gluttony. The virtue of justice belongs to the city; for justice is an ordering of the political association, and the virtue of justice consists in the determination of what is just.

The Association of the Household and Its Different Factors (Chapters 3–13)

Chapter 3

1. The constituent elements of the household. The three relations of master and slave, husband and wife, parent and child. The fourth element of "acquisition".

1253ᵇ1 Having ascertained, from the previous analysis, what are the elements of which the city is constituted, we must first consider the management of the household; for every city is composed of households. The parts of household management will correspond to the parts of which the household itself is constituted. A complete household consists of slaves and freemen. But every subject of inquiry should first be examined in its simplest elements; and the primary and simplest elements of the household are the connection of master and slave, that of the husband and wife, and that of parents and children. We must accordingly consider each of these connections, examining the nature of each and the qualities it ought to possess. The factors to be examined are therefore three: first, the relationship of master and slave; next, what may be called the marital relationship (for there is no word in our language which exactly describes the union of husband and wife); and lastly, what may be called the parental relationship, which again has no single word in our language peculiar to itself. But besides the three factors which thus present themselves for examination there is also a fourth, which some regard as identical with the whole of household management, and others as its principal part. This is the element called "the art of acquisition"; and we shall have to consider its nature.

1253ᵇ14 We may first speak of master and slave, partly in order to gather lessons bearing on the necessities of practical life, and partly in order to discover whether we can attain any view, superior to those now generally held, which is likely to promote an understanding of the subject. There are some who hold that the exercise of authority over slaves is a kind of knowledge. They believe (as we said in the beginning) that household management, slave ownership, statesmanship, and kingship are all the same. There are others, however, who regard the control of slaves by a master as contrary to nature. In their view the distinction of master and slave is due to law or convention; there is no natural difference between them: the relation of master and slave is based on force, and so has no warrant in justice.

Chapter 4

*2. **Slavery.** The instruments of the household form its stock of property: they are animate and inanimate: the slave is an animate instrument, intended (like all the instruments of the household) for action, and not for production.*

1253ᵇ23 Property is part of the household and the art of acquiring property is part of household management, for it is impossible to live well, or indeed at all, unless the necessary conditions are present. Thus the same holds true in the sphere of household management as in the specialized arts: each must be furnished with its appropriate instruments if its function is to be fulfilled. Instruments are partly inanimate and partly animate: the steersman of a ship, for instance, has an inanimate instrument in the rudder, and an animate instrument in the look-out man (for in the arts a subordinate is of the nature of an instrument). Each article of property is thus an instrument for the purpose of life, property in general is a quantity of such instruments, the slave is an animate article of property, and subordinates, or servants, in general may be described as instruments which are prior to other instruments. We can imagine a situation in which each instrument could do its own work, at the word of command or by intelligent anticipation, like the statues of Daedalus or the tripods made by Hephaestus, of which the poet relates that

> Of their own motion they entered the
> conclave of Gods on Olympus.

A shuttle would then weave of itself, and a plectrum would do its own harp-playing. In this situation managers would not need subordinates and masters would not need slaves.

1254ᵃ1 The instruments of which we have just been speaking are instruments of production; but property is an instrument of action. From the shuttle there issues something which is different, and exists apart, from the immediate act of its use; but from garments or beds there comes only the one fact of their use. We may add that, since production and action are different in kind, and both of them need instruments, those instruments must also show a corresponding difference. Life is action and not production; and therefore the slave is a servant in the sphere of action.

1254ᵃ8 The term "article of property" is used in the same way in which the term "part" is also used. A part is not only a part of something other than itself: it also belongs entirely to that other thing. It is the same with an article of property. Accordingly, while the master is merely the master of the slave, and does not belong to him, the slave is not only the slave of his master; he also belongs entirely to him.

1254ᵃ13 From these considerations we can see clearly what is the nature of the slave and what is his capacity: anybody who by his nature is not his own man, but another's, is by his nature a slave; anybody who, being a man, is an article of property is another's man; an article of property is an instrument intended for the purpose of action and separable from its possessor.

Chapter 5

There is a principle of rule and subordination in nature at large: it appears especially in the realm of animate creation. By virtue of that principle, the soul rules the body; and by virtue of it the master, who possesses the rational faculty of the soul, rules the slave, who possesses only bodily powers and the faculty of understanding the directions given by another's reason. But nature, though she intends, does not always succeed in achieving a clear distinction between men born to be masters and men born to be slaves.

1254ᵃ17 We have next to consider whether there are, or are not, some people who are by nature such as are here defined; whether, in other words, there are some people for whom slavery is the better and just condition, or whether the reverse is the case and all slavery is contrary to nature. The issue is not difficult, whether we study it philosophically in the light of reason, or consider it empirically on the basis of the actual facts. The relation of ruler and ruled is one of those things which are not only necessary, but also beneficial;

and there are species in which a distinction is already marked, immediately at birth, between those of its members who are intended for being ruled and those who are intended to rule. There are also many kinds both of ruling and ruled elements. (Moreover the rule which is exercised over the better sort of subjects is a better sort of rule— as, for example, rule exercised over a man is better than rule over an animal. The reason is that the value of something which is produced increases with the value of those contributing to it; and where one element rules and the other is ruled, there is something which they jointly produce.) In all cases where there is a compound, constituted of more than one part but forming one common entity, whether the parts be continuous or discrete, a ruling element and a ruled can always be traced. This characteristic is present in animate beings by virtue of the whole constitution of nature; for even in things which are inanimate there is a sort of ruling principle, such as is to be found, for example, in a musical harmony. But such considerations perhaps belong to a more popular method of inquiry; and we may content ourselves here with saying that animate beings are composed, in the first place, of soul and body, with the former naturally ruling and the latter naturally ruled. When investigating the natural state of things, we must fix our attention, not on those which are in a corrupt, but on those which are in a natural condition. It follows that we must consider the man who is in the best state both of body and soul, and in whom the rule of soul over body is accordingly evident; for with vicious people or those in a vicious condition, the reverse would often appear to be true—the body ruling the soul as the result of their evil and unnatural condition.

1254ᵇ2 It is possible, as we have said, to observe first in animate beings the presence of a ruling authority, both of the sort exercised by a master over slaves and of the sort exercised by a statesman over fellow citizens. The soul rules the body with the authority of a master: reason rules the appetite with the authority of a statesman or a monarch. In this sphere it is clearly natural and beneficial to the body that it should be ruled by the soul, and again it is natural and beneficial to the affective part of the soul that it should be ruled by the reason and the rational part; where-

as the equality of the two elements, or their reverse relation, is always detrimental. The same principle is true of the relation of man to other animals. Tame animals have a better nature than wild, and it is better for all such animals that they should be ruled by man because they then get the benefit of preservation. Again, the relation of male to female is naturally that of the superior to the inferior, of the ruling to the ruled. This general principle must similarly hold good of all human beings generally.

1254ᵇ16 We may thus conclude that all men who differ from others as much as the body differs from the soul, or an animal from a man (and this is the case with all whose function is bodily service, and who produce their best when they supply such service)—all such are by nature slaves. In their case, as in the other cases just mentioned, it is better to be ruled by a master. Someone is thus a slave by nature if he is capable of becoming the property of another (and for this reason does actually become another's property) and if he participates in reason to the extent of apprehending it in another, though destitute of it himself. Other animals do not apprehend reason but obey their instincts. Even so there is little divergence in the way they are used; both of them (slaves and tame animals) provide bodily assistance in satisfying essential needs.

1254ᵇ27 It is nature's intention also to erect a physical difference between the bodies of freemen and those of the slaves, giving the latter strength for the menial duties of life, but making the former upright in carriage and (though useless for physical labour) useful for the various purposes of civic life—a life which tends, as it develops, to be divided into military service and the occupations of peace. The contrary of nature's intention, however, often happens: there are some slaves who have the bodies of freemen, as there are others who have a freeman's soul. But, if there were men who were as distinguished in their bodies alone as are the statues of the gods, all would agree that the others should be their slaves. And if this is true when the difference is one of the body, it may be affirmed with still greater justice when the difference is one of the soul; though it is not as easy to see the beauty of the soul as it is to see that of the body.

1254ᵇ39 It is thus clear that, just as some are by nature free, so others are by nature slaves, and for these latter the condition of slavery is both bene-ficial and just.

Chapter 6

Legal or conventional slavery: the divergence of views about its justice, and the reason for this divergence. In spite of the divergence, there is a general consensus—though it is not clearly formulated—that superiority in goodness justifies the owning and controlling of slaves. Granted such superiority in the master, slavery is a ben-eficial and just system.

1255ª3 But it is easy to see that those who hold an opposite view are also in a way correct. "Slavery" and "slave" are terms which are used in two different senses; for there is also a kind of slave, and of slavery, which owes its existence to law. (The law in question is a kind of understand-ing that those vanquished in war are held to belong to the victors.) That slavery can be justi-fied by such a convention is a principle against which a number of jurists bring an "indictment of illegality", as one might against an orator. They regard it as a detestable notion that someone who is subjugated by force should become the slave and subject of one who has the capacity to sub-jugate him, and is his superior in power. Even among men of judgement there are some who accept this and some who do not. The cause of this divergence of view, and the reason why the opposing contentions overlap one another, is to be found in the following consideration. There is a sense in which good qualities, when they are furnished with the right resources, have the great-est power to subjugate; and a victor is always pre-eminent in respect of some sort of good. It thus appears that "power never goes without good qualities"; and the dispute between the two sides thus comes to turn exclusively on the point of justice. (In this matter some think that being just consists in goodwill while others hold that the rule of the stronger is in itself justice.) If these dif-ferent positions are distinguished from one anoth-er, no other argument has any cogency, or even plausibility, against the view that one who is supe-rior in goodness ought to rule over, and be the master of, his inferiors.

1255ª21 There are some who, clinging, as they think, to a sort of justice (for law is a sort of jus-tice), assume that slavery in war is just.

Simultaneously, however, they contradict that assumption; for in the first place it is possible that the original cause of a war may not be just, and in the second place no one would ever say that someone who does not deserve to be in a condi-tion of slavery is really a slave. If such a view were accepted, the result would be that men reputed to be of the highest rank would be turned into slaves or the children of slaves, if they [or their parents] happened to be captured and sold into slavery. This is the reason why they do not like to call such people slaves, but prefer to confine the term to barbarians. But by this use of terms they are, in reality, only seeking to express that same idea of the natural slave which we began by mentioning. They are driven, in effect, to admit that there are some who are everywhere slaves, and others who are everywhere free. The same line of thought is followed in regard to good birth. Greeks regard themselves as well born not only in their own country, but absolutely and in all places; but they regard barbarians as well born only in their own country—thus assuming that there is one sort of good birth and freedom which is absolute, and another which is only relative. We are reminded of what Helen says in the play of Theodectes:

Scion of Gods, by both descent alike,
Who would presume to call me serving-maid?

When they use such terms as these, men are using the one criterion of the presence, or absence, of goodness for the purpose of distinguishing between slave and freeman, or again, between the well-born and the low-born. They are claiming that just as man is born of man, and animal of animal, so a good man is born of good men. It is often the case, however, that nature wishes but fails to achieve this result.

1255ᵇ4 It is thus clear that there is some rea-son for the divergence of view which has been discussed—it is not true that the one group are natural slaves and the other natural freemen. It is also clear that there are cases where such a dis-tinction exists, and that here it is beneficial and just that the former should actually be a slave and the latter a master—the one being ruled, and the other exercising the kind of rule for which he is naturally intended and therefore acting as master. But a wrong exercise of his rule by a master is a thing which is disadvantageous for both master and slave. The part and the whole, like the body and the soul, have an identical interest; and the slave is a part of the master, in the sense of being a living but separate part of his body. There is thus a community of interest, and a relation of friendship, between master and slave, when both of them naturally merit the position in which they stand. But the reverse is true, when matters are otherwise and slavery rests merely on legal sanction and superior power.

Chapter 7

The training of slaves, and the art of using them properly. How they may be justly acquired.

1255ᵇ16 The argument makes it clear that the rule of the master and that of the statesman are different from one another, and that it is not the case that all kinds of rule are, as some thinkers hold, identical. One kind of rule is exercised over those who are naturally free; the other over slaves; and again the rule exercised over a household by its head is that of a monarch (for all households are monarchically governed), while the rule of the statesman is rule over freemen and equals. Now masters are not so termed in virtue of any knowledge which they have acquired, but in virtue of their own endowment; and the same is true of slaves and freemen generally. But there may be a kind of knowledge which belongs to masters, and another which belongs to slaves; and the latter would be of the nature of the knowledge taught by the man of Syracuse, who instructed servants for pay in the discharge of their ordinary duties. Instruction in such subjects might be extended further: it might include, for example, the art of cookery and other similar forms of skilled domestic service. The reason why this might be done is that the duties differ; some are of a higher standing, even if others are needed more. As the proverb says:

> Slave may go before slave, and master may go
> before master.

All such forms of knowledge are necessarily of a servile character. But there is also a form of knowledge belonging to the master, which consists in the use of slaves: a master is such in virtue not of acquiring, but of using slaves. This knowledge belonging to the master is something which

has no great or majestic character: the master must simply know how to command what the slave must know how to do. This is why those who are in a position to escape from being troubled by it delegate the management of slaves to a steward, and spend on politics or philosophy the time they are thus able to save. The art of acquiring slaves for ownership differs both from the art of being a master and from that of being a slave—that is to say, when it is justly practised; for in that case it is a particular form of the art of war, or of the art of hunting.

1255ᵇ39 This should be an adequate account of the distinction between master and slave.

Chapter 8

*3. **Property and the art of acquisition.** The art of household management is distinct from that of acquisition. It has to provide a stock of requisites for the household; and the different methods by which this is done produce different ways of life—the hunting, the pastoral, the agricultural, and so forth. Nature intends and provides the requisites for household use; and the acquisition of such requisites is a natural mode of acquisition. Property in them is limited to the amount required by household needs; and it is the nature of all true wealth to be so limited.*

1256ᵃ1 We may now study generally all forms of property and the art of acquiring it, following our normal method; for we have already seen that the slave is an article of property. The first problem which may be raised is whether the art of acquiring property is identical with that of household management, or is a part of it, or is ancillary to it; and whether, if it is ancillary, it is so in the sense in which the art of making shuttles is ancillary to the art of weaving, or in the sense in which the art of casting bronze is ancillary to the art of sculpture. These are ancillary in a different way; the one provides instruments, and the other the material. (By "material" we mean the substance from which a product is made; as wool, for instance, serves the weaver; and bronze the sculptor.) That the art of household management is not identical with the art of acquiring property is obvious. It is the function of the latter simply to provide, but it is the function of the former to use what has been provided; for what art can there be, other than that of household management, which will use the resources of the household? But the question whether the art of acquisition is a part of it, or a separate art altogether, is one which admits of a divergence of views. If someone who is engaged in acquisition has to consider from what different sources he can get goods and property, and if property and wealth include many different parts, we shall first have to consider whether farming is a part of the art of acquisition, or a separate art: indeed we shall have to ask that question generally, in regard to all modes of occupation and gain which are concerned with the provision of subsistence. There are a number of different modes of subsistence; and the result is a number of different ways of life, among both animals and human beings. It is impossible to live without means of subsistence; and among the animals we may notice that differences in the means of subsistence have produced consequent differences in ways of life. Some wild animals live in herds, and others are scattered in isolation, according as they find it convenient for the purpose of getting subsistence—some of them being carnivorous, some herbivorous, and some, again, omnivorous. Nature has thus distinguished their ways of life, with a view to their greater comfort and their better attainment of these things: indeed, as the same sort of food is not naturally agreeable to all the members of a class, and as different sorts suit different species, there are also different ways of life even within the class of carnivorous animals—and equally in that of the herbivorous. The same is also true of men. Their ways of life also differ considerably. The most indolent are the pastoral nomads. They acquire a subsistence from domestic animals, at their leisure, and without any trouble; and as it is necessary for their flocks to move for the sake of pasturage, they also are forced to follow and to cultivate what may be called a living farm. There are others who live by hunting; and of these, again, there are different kinds, according to their different modes of hunting. Some live by being freebooters; some, who live near lakes and marshes and rivers, or by a sea which is suitable for the purpose, gain a livelihood by fishing; others live by hunting birds or wild animals. Most of mankind, however, derive their livelihood from the soil, and from cultivated plants.

1256ᵃ40 The different ways of life (at any rate if we take into account only those who follow an occupation dependent on their own labours, and do not provide themselves with subsistence by exchange and petty trade) may be roughly classified as pastoral, freebooting, fishing, hunting, and farming. But there are some who live comfortably by means of a combination of different methods, and who supplement the shortcomings of one way of life, when it tends to fall short of being sufficient in itself, by adding some other way. For example, some combine the pastoral way of life with the freebooting; others combine farming with hunting; and similar combinations may be made of other ways of life; as need impels people so they shape their lives.

1256ᵇ7 This kind of capacity for acquisition is evidently given by nature to all living beings, from the moment when they are first born to the days when their growth is finished. There are animals which, when their offspring is born, bring forth along with it food enough to support it until it can provide for itself: this is the case with those which reproduce themselves by grubs, and with animals which do so by eggs. Animals which are viviparous have food for their offspring in themselves, for a certain time, of the nature of what is called milk.

1256ᵇ15 Likewise we must evidently believe that similar provision is made for adults. Plants exist for the benefit of animals, and some animals exist for the benefit of others. Those which are domesticated, serve human beings for use as well as for food; wild animals, too, in most cases if not in all, serve to furnish us not only with food, but also with other kinds of assistance, such as the provision of clothing and similar aids to life. Accordingly, if nature makes nothing purposeless or in vain, all animals must have been made by nature for the sake of men. It also follows that the art of war is in some sense a natural mode of acquisition. Hunting is a part of that art; and hunting ought to be practised, not only against wild animals, but also against human beings who are intended by nature to be ruled by others and refuse to obey that intention, because this sort of war is naturally just.

1256ᵇ26 It follows that one form of acquisition is naturally a part of the art of household management, in the sense that the manager of a household must either have available or ensure the availability of a supply of objects which are capable of being stored and are either necessary for life or useful to the association of the city [*polis*] or the household. These are the objects which may be regarded as constituting true wealth, for the amount of household property which suffices for a good life is not unlimited, nor of the nature described by Solon in the verse,

> There is no bound to wealth stands fixed for men.

There is a bound fixed, as is also the case in the means required by the other arts. All the instruments needed by all the arts are limited, both in number and size, and wealth may be defined as a number of instruments used in a household or city.

1256ᵇ37 It is thus clear that there is a natural art of acquisition which has to be practised by managers of households and statesmen; and the reason for its existence is also clear.

Chapter 9

The "art of acquisition", as a way of acquiring property distinct from the natural way of the household. It originates in exchange, when exchange is conducted through the medium of currency and for profit. The view thus arises that the art of acquisition is specially concerned with accumulating a fund of currency. But there is a contrary view that currency is a mere convention, and not the true object of the art of acquisition. This contrary view has its truth. There is a natural form of the art of acquisition, which is not distinct from, but a part of, the art of household management. This natural form of acquisition aims at the accumulation not of currency, but of true wealth— and therefore not at the infinite, but at the finite.

1256ᵇ40 But there is a second form of the art of getting property, which is particularly called, and which it is just to call, "the art of acquisition". It is this second form which gives rise to the opinion that there is no limit to wealth and property. There are many who hold it to be identical with the other form previously mentioned, because it has affinities with it. In fact it is not identical, and yet it is not far removed. The other form previously mentioned is natural: this second form is not natural, but is rather the product of a certain sort of experience and skill.

1257ᵃ5 We may start our discussion of this [second] form from the following point of view.

All articles of property have two possible uses. Both of these uses belong to the article as such, but they do not belong to it in the same manner, or to the same extent. The one use is proper and peculiar to the article concerned; the other is not. A shoe, for example, can be used both for wearing and for exchange. Both of these uses are uses of the shoe as such. Even the man who exchanges a shoe, in return for money or food, with someone who needs the article, is using the shoe as a shoe; but since the shoe has not been made for the purpose of being exchanged, the use which he is making of it is not its proper and peculiar use. The same is true of all other articles of property. Exchange is possible in regard to them all: it arises from the natural facts of the case, and is due to some men having more, and others less, than suffices for their needs. We can thus see that retail trade is not naturally a part of the art of acquisition. If that were the case, it would only be necessary to practise exchange to the extent that sufficed for the needs of both parties.

1257ᵃ19 In the first form of association, which is the household, it is obvious that there is no purpose to be served by the art of exchange. Such a purpose only emerged when the scope of association had already been extended. The members of the household had shared all things in common: those who lived separately from one another, had at their disposal a number of different things, which they had to exchange as need arose, by way of barter—much as many barbarian tribes still do to this day. On this basis things which are useful are exchanged themselves, and directly, for similar useful things, but the transaction does not go any further; wine, for instance, is given, or taken, in return for wheat, and other similar commodities are similarly bartered for one another. When used in this way, the art of exchange is not contrary to nature, nor in any way a form of the art of acquisition. Exchange simply serves to satisfy the natural requirements of sufficiency. None the less it was from exchange, as thus practised, that the art of acquisition developed, in the sort of way we might reasonably expect. The supply of men's needs came to depend on more foreign sources, as men began to import for themselves what they lacked, and to export what they had in superabundance: and in this way the use of a money currency was inevitably instituted. The reason for this was that all the naturally necessary commodities were not easily portable; and people therefore agreed, for the purpose of their exchanges, to give and receive some commodity which itself belonged to the category of useful things and possessed the advantage of being easily handled for the purpose of getting the necessities of life. Such commodities were iron, silver, and other similar metals. At first their value was simply determined by their size and weight; but finally a stamp was imposed on the metal which, serving as a definite indication of the quantity, would save people the trouble of determining the value on each occasion.

1257ª41 When in this way a currency had once been instituted, there next arose, from the necessary process of exchange, the second form of the art of acquisition, the one which consists in retail trade. At first, we may allow, it was perhaps practised in a simple way: but in process of time, and as the result of experience, it was practised with a more studied technique, which sought to discover the sources from which, and the methods by which, the greatest profit could be made. The result has been the emergence of the view that the art of acquisition is specially concerned with currency, and that its function consists in an ability to discover the sources from which a fund of money can be derived. In support of this view it is urged that the art is one which produces wealth and money; indeed those who hold the view often assume that wealth is simply a fund of currency, on the ground that the arts of acquisition and of retail trade are concerned with currency. In opposition to this view it is sometimes held that currency is a sham, and entirely a convention. Naturally and inherently [the supporters of the view argue] a currency is a nonentity; for if those who use a currency give it up in favour of another, that currency is worthless, and useless for any of the necessary purposes of life. A man rich in currency [they proceed to urge] will often be at a loss to procure the necessities of subsistence; and surely it is absurd that a thing should be counted as wealth which a man may possess in abundance, and yet none the less die of starvation—like Midas in the fable, when everything set before him was turned at once into gold through the granting of his own avaricious prayer.

1257ᵇ17 For this reason some people seek a different conception of wealth and of the art of acquisition. They are right to do so. The natural form of the art of acquisition, like the natural form of wealth, is something different. It is part of the management of the household while retail trade serves to make money, and that only by the exchange of commodities. The latter may be seen as concerned with currency; for currency is both a basic unit and a limiting factor in exchange.

1257ᵇ23 A further point of difference is that the wealth produced by this [second] form of the art of acquisition is unlimited. The art of medicine recognizes no limit in respect of the production of health, and the arts generally admit no limit in respect of the production of their ends (each seeking to produce its end to the greatest possible extent)—though medicine, and the arts generally, recognize and practise a limit to the means they use to attain their ends, since the end itself constitutes a limit. The same is true of the retail form of the art of acquisition. There is no limit to the end it seeks; and the end it seeks is wealth of the sort we have mentioned and the mere acquisition of money. But the art of household management, as distinct from the art of acquisition, has a limit; and the object of that art is not an unlimited amount of wealth. It would thus appear, if we look at the matter in this light, that all wealth must have a limit. In actual experience, however, we see the opposite happening, and all who are engaged in acquisition increase their fund of currency without any limit or pause.

1257ᵇ35 The cause [of this contradiction] lies in the close connection between the two different modes of acquisition. They overlap in the sense that they both use the same object, that is, they use the same property but not in the same way. The object of the one is simply accumulation, and that of the other something quite different. This explains why some men believe that mere accumulation is the object of household management; and why they stick to the idea that they must keep intact their wealth in currency, or increase it indefinitely. But the fundamental cause of this state of mind is concern about living, rather than about living well; and since their desire for that is unlimited, their desire for the things that produce it is equally unlimited. Even those who do aim at well-being seek the means of obtaining physical enjoyments; and, as what they seek appears to depend on the activity of of acquisition, they are thus led to occupy themselves wholly in the making of money. This is why the second form of the art of acquisition has come into vogue. Because enjoyment depends on superfluity, men address themselves to the art which produces the superfluity necessary to enjoyment; and if they cannot get what they want by the art of acquisition, they attempt to do so by other means, using each and every capacity in a way not consonant with its nature. The proper function of courage, for example, is not to produce money but to give confidence. The same is true of military and medical ability: neither has the function of producing money: the one has the function of producing victory, and the other that of producing health. But those of whom we are speaking turn all such capacities into forms of the art of acquisition, as though to make money were the one aim and everything else must contribute to that aim.

1258ᵃ14 We have thus discussed the unnecessary form of the art of acquisition: we have described its nature, and we have explained why men need its services. We have also discussed the necessary form: we have shown that it is different from the other, and is naturally a branch of the art of household management, concerned with the provision of subsistence, and not therefore unlimited in its scope, as the other form is, but subject to definite bounds.

Chapter 10

Household management is concerned with the use, and not (except in the way of general supervision) with the acquisition, of property; generally the householder should be able to count on nature supplying the means he needs. Acquisition for acquisition's sake shows its worst side in usury, which makes barren metal breed.

1258ᵃ19 The argument of the last chapter provides a clear solution to the problem which we originally raised. "Does the art of acquisition belong to the province of the manager of the household and the statesman? Or is it outside that province, and should property be regarded as something which they can simply take as given?" It may be urged, in favour of the second alternative, that just as the art of the statesman does not produce human stock, but counts on its being supplied by nature and proceeds to use her sup-

ply, so nature must also provide the physical means of subsistence—the land, or sea, or whatever it be. Then, and upon that basis, it is the province of the householder to manage properly these means. It is not the business of the art of weaving to produce wool, but to use it, and to distinguish the sorts of wool which are good and suitable from those which are poor and unsuitable. If the art of acquisition were held to be a part of the art of household management, the question might be raised why the art of medicine should not equally be held to be a part; and it might be argued that the members of a household must needs have health, in the same way as they must needs have life or any of the other necessaries. There is a sense in which it is the business of the manager of a household or of a ruler to see to the health of the members of his household or city; but there is another sense in which it is not their business but that of the doctor. Similarly, in the matter of property, there is a sense in which it is the business of the manager of a household to see to its acquisition and another sense in which that is not his business, but part of an ancillary art. But in general, as we have already noticed, a supply of property should be ready to hand.

1258ᵃ35 It is the business of nature to furnish subsistence for each being brought into the world; and this is shown by the fact that the offspring of animals always gets nourishment from the residuum of the matter that gives it its birth. The natural form, therefore, of the art of acquisition is always, and in all cases, acquisition from fruits and animals. That art, as we have said, has two forms: one which is connected with retail trade, and another which is connected with the management of the household. Of these two forms, the latter is necessary and laudable; the former is a method of exchange which is justly censured, because the gain in which it results is not naturally made, but is made at the expense of other men. The trade of the petty usurer is hated with most reason: it makes a profit from currency itself, instead of making it from the process which currency was meant to serve. Currency came into existence merely as a means of exchange; usury tries to make it increase. This is the reason why it got its name; for as the offspring resembles its parent, so the interest bred by money is like the principal which breeds it, and it may be called "currency the son of currency." Hence we can understand why, of all modes of acquisition, usury is the most unnatural.

Chapter 11

A practical consideration of the art of acquisition. The divisions of that art which may be made on practical grounds. Instances of the successful practice of the art, especially by the creation of monopolies.

1258ᵇ9 We have now discussed sufficiently that part of our subject which is related to pure knowledge: it remains to consider the part which is related to actual use. All subjects of this nature may be treated liberally in theory, but have to be handled in practice as circumstances demand. The parts of the art of acquisition which are of actual use are the following. The first is an experience of farm-stock. This involves knowing which are the most profitable breeds, and on what soil, and with what treatment, they will give us the greatest profit—knowing, for example, the right way of stocking horses, or cattle, or sheep, or any other kind of farm-stock. We need experience to tell how different breeds compare with one another in point of profit, or what breeds are most profitable on what sorts of soil: for some breeds thrive on one sort of soil, and some on another sort. Other useful parts of the art of acquisition are experience in cultivation, not only of cornland but also of land planted with vines and olives; experience in bee-keeping; and experience in the rearing of such fish and fowl as may help to provide subsistence. These are the parts and the original elements of the art of acquisition in its most proper form. We now come to exchange. This includes, first and foremost, commerce (which is divided into the three operations of the provision of a ship, the carriage of freight, and offering for sale—operations which differ from one another in the sense that some have a greater margin of safety, and others a greater margin of profit); it includes, in the second place, investment at interest; and it also includes, in the third place, service for hire. This last part of exchange is partly a matter of skilled craftsmen in the mechanical arts, and partly of unskilled workers who can render only the service of bodily labour. A third form of the art of acquisition is a form intermediate between the first and second; for it possesses elements both of the first, or natural, form, and of the form which consists in exchange. It is concerned with things extracted from the earth or with products of the earth which bear no fruit but are still of use; and we may thus cite, as examples, lumbering and all [forms of] mining. Mining, in its turn, has many forms, because there are many species of metals extracted from the earth.

1258ᵇ33 A general account has now been given of the various forms of acquisition: to consider them minutely, and in detail, might be useful for practical purposes; but to dwell long upon them would be in poor taste. Suffice it to say that the occupations which require most skill are those in which there is least room for chance: the meanest are those in which most damage is done to physique: the most servile are those in which most use is made of physical strength: the least noble are those in which there is least need for the exercise of goodness.

1258ᵇ39 There are books on these subjects by several writers: Charetides of Paros and Apollodoros of Lemnos have written on the cultivation of cornland and land planted with vines and olives: others have written on other themes; anyone who is interested should study these subjects with the aid of these writings. A collection ought also to be made of the scattered stories about the ways in which different people have succeeded in making a fortune. They are all useful to those who value the art of acquisition. There is, for example, the story which is told of Thales of Miletus. It is a story about a scheme for making money, which is fathered on Thales owing to his reputation for wisdom; but it involves a principle of general application. He was reproached for his poverty, which was supposed to show the uselessness of philosophy; but observing from his knowledge of meteorology (so the story goes) that there was likely to be a heavy crop of olives, and having a small sum at his command, he paid deposits, early in the year, for the hire of all the olive-presses in Miletus and Chios; and he managed, in the absence of any higher offer, to secure them at a low rate. When the season came, and there was a sudden and simultaneous demand for a number of presses, he let out the stock he had collected at any rate he chose to fix; and making a considerable fortune he succeeded in proving that it is easy for philosophers to become rich if they so desire, though it is not the business which they are really about. The story is told as showing that Thales proved his own wisdom; but as we have said, the plan he adopted, which was, in effect, the creation of a monopoly, involves a principle which can be generally applied in the art of acquisition. Some cities, therefore, as well as individuals, adopt this resource when in need of money: they establish, for instance, a monopoly in provisions. In Sicily a man with whom a sum of money had been deposited bought up all the iron from the ironworks; and afterwards, when retailers came from their shops to get a supply, he was the only seller from whom they could buy. He did not raise the price to any extent; but he gained, none the less, a profit of a 100 talents on an outlay of 50. This speculation came to the notice of Dionysius [the ruler of Syracuse] and he ordered the man to leave the city, though he allowed him to take his gains: the reason was his discovery of a way of making profit which was injurious to the interests of Dionysius himself. Yet his idea was simply the same as that of Thales; and what both of them did was merely to establish a private monopoly. But a knowledge of these methods is useful to statesmen—cities, like households, but to an even greater extent, are often in want of financial resources and in need of more ways of gaining them. This is the reason why some of those who adopt a political career confine their political activity to matters of finance.

children is like that of a monarch over subjects. The male is naturally fitter to command than the female, except where there is some departure from nature; and age and maturity are similarly fitter to command than youth and immaturity. In most cases where rule of the statesman's sort is exercised there is an interchange of ruling and being ruled: the members of a political association aim by their very nature at being equal and differing in nothing. It is none the less true that when one rules and the other is ruled, [the former] desires to establish a difference, in outward forms, in modes of address, and in titles of respect. This may remind us of the saying of Amasis about his foot-pan. The relation of the male to the female is permanently that in which the statesman stands to his fellow citizens. Paternal rule over children, on the other hand, is like that of a king over his subjects. The male parent is in a position of authority both in virtue of the affection to which he is entitled and by right of his seniority; and his position is thus in the nature of royal authority. Homer was right, therefore, to use the invocation.

Father of Gods and of men

to address Zeus, who is king of them all. A king ought to be naturally superior to his subjects, and yet of the same stock as they are; and this is the case with the relation of age to youth, and of parent to child.

Chapter 12

4. Marriage, parenthood, and the general management of the household. The nature of marital authority, which is like that exercised by a statesman over his fellow citizens. The nature of parental authority, which is like that of a king over his subjects.

1259ª37 We said, in a previous passage, that there were three parts of the art of household management—the first, of which we have already spoken, being the art of controlling slaves: the second, the art of exercising paternal authority; and the third, that of exercising marital authority. While the head of the household rules over both wife and children, and rules over both as free members of the household, he exercises a different sort of rule in each case. His rule over his wife is like that of a statesman over fellow citizens; his rule over his

Chapter 13

The art of household management is a moral art, aiming at the moral goodness of the members of the household; and this is true in regard to slaves as well as to other members. The goodness of the head of the household has a quality of its own: the different classes of members have also different qualities of goodness. This is part of a general law that goodness is relative to function, and that it is the function of some to guide, and of others to be guided—and guided, too, in different ways. The master's duty of guiding the slaves of the household. The subjects of marriage and parenthood (only briefly mentioned in the previous chapter) are to be reserved for future treatment, in connection with the city and the proper mode of its government (Book VII, Chapters 17–18).

1259ᵇ18 It is clear from the previous argument that the business of household management is concerned more with human beings than it is with inanimate property; that it is concerned more with the good condition of human beings than with a good condition of property (which is what we call wealth); and, finally, that it is concerned more with the goodness of the free members of the household than with that of slaves. Here a preliminary question may be raised in regard to the slave. Has he any "goodness" beyond that of discharging his function as an instrument and performing his menial service—any goodness of a higher value, such as temperance, fortitude, justice, and the rest of such moral qualities? Or has he no "goodness" outside the area of the bodily services he renders? Either alternative presents difficulties. If slaves have a "goodness" of the higher sort, in what respect will they differ from freemen? If they have not it would be surprising since they are human beings, with a share in reason. Practically the same question may be asked in regard to a woman and a child. Do they have their own forms of goodness? Must a woman be temperate, brave, and just? Is it, or is it not, possible for a child to be licentious or temperate?

1259ᵇ32 In general we must raise the following question about those who are naturally ruled and about those who rule: "Is their goodness the same or does it differ?" If we say that both of them ought to share in the nobility of goodness, why should one of them permanently rule, and the other be permanently ruled? The difference between them cannot be simply a difference of degree: the difference between ruler and ruled is one of kind, and degree has nothing to do with the matter. On the other hand, it would be strange if one of them ought to share and the other ought not. How can the ruler rule properly, or the subject be properly ruled, unless they are both temperate and just? Anyone who is licentious or cowardly will utterly fail to do his duty. The conclusion which clearly emerges is that both classes must share in goodness, but that there must be different kinds of goodness, just as [there are also different kinds of goodness] among those who are naturally ruled.

1260ᵃ4 The view here suggested takes us straight to the nature of the soul. The soul has naturally two elements, a ruling and a ruled; and each has its different goodness, one belonging to the rational and ruling element, and the other to the

irrational and ruled. What is true of the soul is evidently also true of the other cases; and we may thus conclude that it is natural in most cases for there to be both a ruling element and one that is ruled. The rule of the freeman over the slave is one kind of rule; that of the male over the female another; that of the grown man over the child another still. It is true that all these people possess in common the different parts of the soul; but they possess them in different ways. The slave is entirely without the faculty of deliberation; the female indeed possesses it, but in a form which lacks authority; and children also possess it, but only in an immature form. We must assume that the same holds with regard to moral goodness: they must all share in it, but not in the same way—each sharing only to the extent required for the discharge of his or her function. The ruler, accordingly, must possess moral goodness in its full and perfect form, because his function is essentially that of a master-craftsman, and reason is such a master-craftsman; but other people need only to possess moral goodness to the extent required of them. It is thus clear that while moral goodness is a quality of all those mentioned, the fact still remains that temperance—and similarly courage and justice—are not, as Socrates held, the same in a woman as they are in a man. One kind of courage is concerned with ruling, the other with serving; and the same is true of the other forms of goodness.

1260ᵃ24 This conclusion also emerges clearly when we examine the subject in more detail. To speak in general terms, and to maintain that goodness consists in "a good condition of the soul", or in "right action", or in anything of the kind, is to be guilty of self-deception. Far better than such general definitions is the method of simple enumeration of the different forms of goodness, as followed by Gorgias. We must therefore hold that what the poet said of women.

A modest silence is a woman's crown

contains a general truth—but a truth which does not apply to men. And since a child is immature its goodness is obviously not a matter of its relation to itself, but of its relation to its end and to the authority that guides it. Similarly, too, the goodness of the slave is a matter of his relation to his master.

1260ᵃ33 We laid it down, in treating of slaves, that they were useful for the necessary purposes of life. It is clear, on that basis, that they need but little goodness; only so much, in fact, as will prevent them from falling short of their duties through intemperance or cowardice. If this be true, the question may be raised whether artisans too ought not to have goodness, seeing that they often fall short of their duties through intemperance. But does not the case of the artisan differ greatly from that of the slave? The slave is a partner in his master's life: the artisan is less closely attached to a master. The extent of the goodness incumbent on him is proportionate to the extent of the servitude to which he is subject; since the mechanical type of artisan is subject only to what may be called a limited servitude. Again the slave belongs to the class of those who are naturally what they are; but no shoemaker, or any other artisan, belongs to that class. It is therefore clear that the task of producing in the slave the sort of goodness we have been discussing belongs to the master of the household, not to whoever instructs him in his work. This is why those who withhold reason from slaves, and argue that only command should be employed, are making a mistake: admonition ought to be applied to slaves even more than it is to children.

1260ᵇ8 This may be sufficient as a discussion of these topics. There remain for discussion a number of questions: the relation of husband and wife, and that of parent and child; the nature of the goodness proper to each partner in these relations; the character of the mutual association of the partners, with its qualities and defects and the methods of attaining those qualities and escaping those defects. All these are questions which must be treated later in the discourses which deal with constitutions. Every household is a part of a city and the relationships we have mentioned are parts of the house-hold. Moreover, the goodness of every part must be considered with reference to the goodness of the whole. We must therefore consider the constitution before we proceed to deal with the training of children and women—at any rate if we hold that the goodness of children and of women makes any difference to the goodness of the city. And it must make a difference. Women are a half of the free population: children grow up to be partners in the constitution.

1260ᵇ20 As we have already discussed some aspects [of the household], and as we are to discuss the rest at a later stage, we may dismiss our present inquiry as finished, and make a new start. Let us first examine the theories of those who have expressed opinions about the best form of constitution.

Book III. The Theory of Citizenship and Constitutions

Citizenship (Chapters 1–5)

Chapter 1

To understand what a constitution (politeia) is, we must inquire into the nature of the city (polis); and to understand that—since the city is a body of citizens (politai)—we must examine the nature of citizenship. Citizenship is not determined by residence, or by merely having access to the courts of law. Rather "a citizen is one who permanently shares in the administration of justice and the holding of office". This definition is more especially true in a democracy: to make it generally applicable, we must modify it to run, "a citizen is one who shares for any period of time in judicial and deliberative office".

1274ᵇ32 When we are dealing with constitutions, and seeking to discover the essence and the attributes of each form, our first investigation may well be directed to the city [the *polis*] itself; and we may begin by asking, "What is the city?" This is at present a disputed question—while some say, "It was the city that did such and such an act", others say, "It was not the city, but the oligarchy or the tyrant." All the activity of the statesman and the lawgiver is obviously concerned with the city, and a constitution is a way of organizing the inhabitants of a city.

1274ᵇ38 A city belongs to the order of "compounds", just like any other thing which forms a single "whole", while being composed, none the less, of a number of different parts. This being the case, it clearly follows that we must inquire first about the citizen. In other words, a city is a certain number of citizens; and so we must consider who should properly be called a citizen and what a citizen really is. The definition of a citizen is a question which is often disputed: there is no general agreement on who is a citizen. It may be that someone who is a citizen in a democracy is not one in an oligarchy. We may leave out of consideration those who enjoy the title of "citizen" in some special sense, for example, naturalized citizens. A citizen proper is not one by virtue of residence in a given place: for even aliens and slaves may share the common place of residence. Nor [can the title of "citizen" be given to] those who share in legal processes only to the extent of being entitled to sue and be sued in the courts. This is something which belongs also to aliens who share it by virtue of a treaty; though it is to be noted that there are many places where resident aliens are obliged to choose a legal protector, so that they only share to a limited extent in this form of association. They are like children who are still too young to be entered on the roll of citizens, or men who are old enough to have been excused from civic duties. There is a sense in which these may be called citizens, but it is not altogether an unqualified sense: we must add the reservation that the young are undeveloped, and the old superannuated citizens, or we must use some other qualification; the exact term we apply does not matter, for the meaning is clear.

1275ª19 We are seeking to discover the citizen in the strict sense, who has no such defect to be made good. Similar questions may also be raised and answered about those who are exiled or disenfranchised. The citizen in this strict sense is best defined by the one criterion that he shares in the administration of justice and in the holding of office. Offices may be divided into two kinds. Some are discontinuous in point of time: in other words, they are of the sort that either cannot be held at all for more than a single term or can only be held for a second term after some definite interval. Others, however, have no limit of time, for example, the office of jurymen, or the office of a member of the popular assembly. It may possibly be contended that such people are not holders of "office", and do not share in "office" by virtue of their position. But it would be ridiculous to exclude from the category of holders of office those who actually hold the most sovereign position in the city; and, since the argument turns on a word, we should not let it make a difference. The point is that we have no word to denote what is common to the juryman and the member of the assembly, or to describe the position held by both. Let us, in the interest of a clear analysis, call it "indeterminate office". On that basis we may lay it down that citizens are those who share in the holding of office as so defined.

1275ª33 The definition of citizen which will most satisfactorily cover the position of all who bear the name is of this general kind. We must also notice that there are certain kinds of thing which may be based on different kinds of principle, one of them standing first, another second, and so on down the series. Things belonging to this class, when considered purely as such, have no common denominator whatever, or, if they have one, they have it only to a meagre extent. Constitutions obviously differ from one another in kind, with some of them coming later in the order and others earlier; for constitutions which are defective and perverted (we shall explain later in what sense we are using the term "perverted") are necessarily secondary to those which are free from defects. It follows that the citizen under each different kind of constitution must also necessarily be different. We may thus conclude that the citizen of our definition is particularly and especially the citizen of a democracy. Citizens living under other kinds of constitution may possibly, but do not necessarily, correspond to the definition. There are some cities, for example, in which there is no popular element: such cities have no regular meetings of the assembly, but only meetings specially summoned; and they decide different kinds of legal case by different means. In Sparta, for example, the Ephors take cases of contracts (not as a body, but each sitting separately); the Council of Elders take cases of homicide; and some other authority may take other cases. Much the same is also true of Carthage, where a number of official bodies are entitled to decide cases of all kinds.

1275ᵇ13 But our definition of citizenship can be amended. In other kinds of constitution members of the assembly and the courts do not hold that office for an indeterminate period. They hold it for a limited term; and it is to some or all of these that the citizen's function of deliberating and judging (whether on all issues or only a few) is assigned. From these considerations it emerges clearly who a citizen is. We say that one who is entitled to share in deliberative or judicial office is thereby a citizen of that city, and a city, in its simplest terms, is a body of such people adequate in number for achieving a self-sufficient existence.

Chapter 2

A popular and pragmatic view of citizenship makes it depend on birth, i.e. descent from a citizen parent or two citizen parents. This does not carry us far, and in any case it only relates to old established citizens. A more serious question is raised when we consider new citizens, who have been allowed to participate in the constitution as the result of a revolution. Are they actually citizens? On the criterion of sharing in judicial and deliberative office (which is a functional criterion), they are actually citizens when once they possess that function.

1275ᵇ22 For practical purposes, it is usual to define a citizen as "one born of citizen parents on both sides", and not on the father's or mother's side only; but sometimes this requirement is carried still farther back, to the length of two, three, or more stages of ancestry. This popular and facile definition has induced some thinkers to raise the question, "How did the citizen of the third or fourth stage of ancestry himself come to be a citizen?" Gorgias of Leontini—perhaps partly from a sense of this difficulty and partly in irony—said, "As mortars are things which are made by the craftsmen who are mortarmakers, so Larissaeans are made by the craftsmen who are Larissaean-makers". But the matter is really simple. If, in their day, they had a share in the constitution in the sense of our own definition, they were certainly citizens. It is obviously impossible to apply the requirement of descent from a citizen father or a citizen mother to those who were the first inhabitants or original founders of a city.

1275ᵇ34 A more serious difficulty is perhaps raised by the case of those who have acquired a share as the result of a change in the constitution. We may take as an example the action of Cleisthenes at Athens, when after the expulsion of the tyrants he enrolled in the tribes a number of resident aliens both foreigners and slaves. The question raised by such an addition to the civic body is not "Who is actually a citizen?" but, "Are they rightly or wrongly such?" It must be admitted, however, that someone might also raise the further question whether a man who is not justly a citizen is really a citizen, on the grounds that the unjust comes to the same as the false. Obviously there are office-holders who have no just title to their office; but we still say that they hold office, though we do not say it is just for them to do so. The citizen also is defined by the fact of holding a sort of office (for the definition we have given to the citizen involves his sharing in office of the deliberative and judicial kind); and it follows, therefore, that these people must be called citizens.

Chapter 3

The question, "Are they justly citizens?" leads to the further question "When can a given act be considered an act of the city or polis?" This in turn raises the general question of the identity of the city. Is the city identical with the government for the time being? Generally, what are the factors which constitute its identity? The identity of a city does not depend on its being surrounded by one set of walls, or on its consisting of one stock of inhabitants. The city is a compound; and its identity, like that of all compounds, is determined by the scheme of its composition, i.e. by its constitution.

1276ᵃ6 The question whether these people are, in justice, citizens or not is a different matter, which is closely connected with a larger question already mentioned. Some people have wondered when a given act can, and when it cannot, be considered to be the act of the city. We may take as an example the case of an oligarchy or tyranny which changes into a democracy. In such a case some people are reluctant to fulfil public contracts, on the grounds that these were made, not by the city, but by the governing tyrant, and they are unwilling to meet other obligations of a similar nature because they hold that some constitutions exist by virtue of force, and not for the sake of the common good. It would follow that if a democracy exists in this fashion [i.e. by force] we have to admit that acts done under the government of such a democracy are no more acts of the city concerned than were acts done under the oligarchy or tyranny.

1276ᵃ17 Our discussion would seem to be closely connected with the following problem: "On what principles ought we to say that a city has retained its identity, or conversely, that it has lost its identity and become a different city?" The most obvious mode of dealing with this question is to consider simply territory and population. On this basis we may note that the territory and population of a city may be divided into sections, with some of the population residing in one block of territory, and some of it in another. This question need not be regarded as particularly difficult: the issue which it raises can easily be met if we remember that the word "city" is used in different senses.

1276ᵃ24 In the case of a population which inhabits a single territory, we may likewise ask "When should we consider that there is a single city?" For, of course, the identity of a city is not constituted by its walls—it would be possible to surround the whole of the Peloponnese by a single wall. Babylon (which, it is said, had been captured for three whole days before some of its inhabitants knew of the fact) may perhaps be counted a city of this dubious nature: so, too, might any city which had the dimensions of a people [*ethnos*] rather than those of a city [or *polis*]. But it will be better to reserve the consideration of this question for some other occasion. (To determine the size of a city—to settle how large it can properly be, and whether it ought to consist of the members of several races—is a duty incumbent on the statesman.)

1276ᵃ34 Assuming a single population inhabiting a single territory, shall we say that the city retains its identity as long as the stock of its inhabitants continues to be the same (although the old members are always dying and new members are always being born), and shall we thus apply to the city the analogy of rivers and fountains, to which we ascribe a constant identity in spite of the fact that part of their water is always flowing in and part always flowing out? Or must we take a different view, and say that even though the population remains the same, the city, for the reason already mentioned, may none the less change?

1276ᵇ1 If a city is a form of association, and if this form of association is an association of citizens in a constitution, it would seem to follow inevitably that when the constitution undergoes a change in form, and becomes a different constitution, the city will likewise cease to be the same city. We say that a chorus which appears at one time as a comic and at another as a tragic chorus is not the same—and this in spite of the fact that the members often remain the same. What is true

of the chorus is also true of every other kind of association, and of all other compounds generally. If the form of its composition is different, the compound becomes a different compound. A scale composed of the same notes will be a different scale depending on whether it is in the Dorian or the Phrygian mode. If this is the case, it is obvious that in determining the identity of the city we must look to the constitution. Whether the same group of people inhabits a city, or a totally different group, we are free to call it the same city, or a different city. It is a different question whether it is right to pay debts or to repudiate them when a city changes its constitution into another form.

Chapter 4

Aristotle now raises the question, "What is the relation of the excellence of the good citizen to the excellence of the good man?" If we look at constitutions generally, we must note that different constitutions require different types of good citizen, while the good man is always the same. If we look at the best constitution, we may argue that even here there must be different types of good citizen, because there are different sorts of civic function; and thus here too the good citizen cannot be identified with the good man. On the whole, therefore, the good citizen and the good man cannot be identified. But there is one case in which they can be. This is the case of the good ruler who possesses the quality of moral wisdom required for being a good subject. The quality of moral wisdom which he possesses is the essential quality of the good man; and in his case the excellence of the good citizen is identical with that of the good man.

1276ᵇ16 A question connected with those which have just been discussed is the question whether the excellence of a good man and that of a good citizen are identical or different. If this question is to be investigated, we must first describe the excellence of the citizen in some sort of outline. Just as a sailor is a member of an association, so too is a citizen. Sailors differ from one another in virtue of the different capacities in which they act: one is a rower, another a steersman, another a look-out man; and others will have still other such titles. It is, nevertheless, clear that, while the most accurate definition of the excellence of each sailor will be special to the man concerned, a common definition of excellence will apply to all, inasmuch as safety in navigation is the common task of all and the object at which each of the sailors aims. The same is also true of citizens. Though they differ, the end which they all serve is the safety of their association; and this association consists in the constitution. The conclusion to which we are thus led is that the excellence of the citizen must be an excellence relative to the constitution. It follows that if there are several different kinds of constitution there cannot be a single absolute excellence of the good citizen. But the good man is a man so called in virtue of a single absolute excellence.

1276ᵇ34 It is thus clear that it is possible to be a good citizen without possessing the excellence by which one is a good man. But we may reach the same conclusion in another way, by discussing the question with particular reference to the best constitution. Although it is impossible for a city to be composed entirely of good men, each citizen must, none the less, perform well his particular function and this requires [the appropriate kind of] excellence. But, since it is impossible for all the citizens to be alike, the excellence of a citizen cannot be identical with that of a good man. The excellence of a good citizen must belong to all citizens, because that is the condition necessary for the city being the best city; but the excellence of a good man cannot possibly belong to all—unless, indeed, we hold that every citizen of a good city must also be a good man. Furthermore, the city is composed of unlike elements. Just as a living being is composed of soul and body, or the soul of the different elements of reason and appetite, or the household of man and wife, or property of master and slave, so the city too is composed of different and unlike elements, among them not only the various elements already mentioned, but also others in addition. It follows that there cannot be a single excellence common to all the citizens, any more than there can be a single excellence common to the leader of a dramatic chorus and his assistants.

1277ᵃ12 Although it is clear from these considerations why they are not in all cases identical, the question may still be raised whether there are not some cases in which the excellence of the good man and that of the good citizen are the same. We say that a good ruler is a good man and possesses practical wisdom, while the citizen does

not need to have practical wisdom. Indeed there are some who hold that the very training of the ruler should be, from the first, of a different kind; and it is a matter of observation that the sons of kings are specially trained in riding and the art of war. Thus Euripides says

> No subtleties for me,
> But what the city most needs,

which implies a special training for the ruler. We may thus assume that the excellence of the good ruler is identical with that of the good man. But subjects too are citizens. It follows that the excellence of the good citizen cannot be identical with that of the good man in all cases, though it may be so in a particular case. The excellence of the ordinary citizen is different from that of the ruler; and this may well be the reason why Jason [the tyrant of Pherae] said that he was "a hungry man except when he was tyrant", meaning that he did not know how to live as an ordinary person.

1277ᵃ25 On the other hand, people hold in esteem the capacity both to rule and to obey, and they regard the excellence of a good citizen as being a matter of ruling and obeying well. Now if the excellence of the good man is in ruling, while that of the good citizen is in both ruling and obeying, these two excellences cannot be held in the same esteem.

1277ᵃ29 Since it thus seems that ruler and ruled should acquire different kinds of knowledge, rather than the same kind, while the citizen should have both sorts of knowledge, and share in both, we can now see the next step which our argument has to take. There is rule of the sort which is exercised by a master; and by this we mean the sort of rule connected with the necessary functions of life. Here it is not necessary for the ruler to know how to do the task himself, but only to know how to use those who do: indeed the former kind of knowledge (by which we mean an ability to do menial services personally) has a servile character. There are a number of kinds of servant, because there are a number of kinds of menial service which have to be rendered. One of these forms of service is that which is rendered by manual labourers. These, as their very name signifies, are those who live by the work of their hands; and the menial craftsman [or mechanic] belongs to this class. This is the reason why is some cities the manual workers were once upon a time excluded from office, in the days before the institution of the extreme form of democracy. The occupations pursued by those who are subject to rule of the sort just mentioned need never be studied by the good man, or by the statesman, or by the good citizen—except occasionally and in order to satisfy some personal need, in which case there ceases to be any question of the relation of master and slave.

1277ᵇ7 But there is also rule of the sort which is exercised over those who are similar in birth to the ruler, and are similarly free. Rule of this sort is what we call political rule; and this is the sort of rule which the ruler must begin to learn by being ruled—just as one learns to be a commander of cavalry by serving under another commander, or to be a general of infantry by serving under another general and by acting first as colonel and, even before that, as captain. This is why it is a good saying that "you cannot be ruler unless you have first been ruled". Ruler and ruled have indeed different excellences; but the fact remains that the good citizen must possess the knowledge and the capacity requisite for ruling as well as for being ruled, and the excellence of a citizen may be defined as consisting in "a knowledge of rule over free men from both points of view".

1277ᵇ16 A good man, also, will need both, even though the temperance and justice required for ruling have a different character. Equally, the excellence (justice, for example) of a good man who is a subject in a free city will not be of a single kind. It will include different sorts: one sort which fits him to act as a ruler, and one which fits him to act as a subject. The temperance and the courage of a man differ from those of a woman in much the same sort of way. A man would be thought cowardly if his courage were only the same as that of a courageous woman; and conversely a woman would be thought a gossip if she showed no more decorum than that which befits a good man. The function of the man in the household is different from that of the woman: it is the function of the one to acquire, and of the other to keep.

1277ᵇ25 Practical wisdom is the only form of excellence which is peculiar to the ruler. The other forms must, it would seem, belong equally to rulers and subjects. The excellence of subjects cannot be practical wisdom, and may be defined as "right opinion". The ruled may be compared to a flute-maker: the ruler is like a flute-player who uses what the flute-maker makes.

1277ᵇ30 These considerations will show whether the excellence of the good man and that of the good citizen are identical or different—or in what sense they are identical and in what sense they are different.

Chapter 5

There is a further question relating to citizenship, "Can mechanics and labourers be citizens, and if they cannot be citizens, how are they to be described?" They should not be citizens, because they cannot achieve the excellence of the good citizen, though they are necessary to the existence of the city. But the answer varies from one kind of constitution to another: in an aristocratic constitution, mechanics and labourers cannot be citizens; in an oligarchy, a rich mechanic may.

1277ᵇ33 There is still a question which remains to be considered in regard to the citizen. Is the citizen in the true sense one who is entitled to share in office, or must mechanics be also included in the ranks of citizens? If we hold that those, who have no share in public offices, are also to be included, we shall have some citizens who can never achieve the excellence of the good citizen (for this man will also be a citizen). If, on the other hand, someone of this sort is not a citizen, in what class is he to be placed? He is not a resident alien, neither is he a foreigner. Or shall we say that this point does not involve us in any absurdity? For the same is true of slaves and freedmen. The truth is that we cannot include as citizens all who are necessary to the city's existence. Similarly, too, children are not citizens in the same sense as adult males. Adults are citizens absolutely; children are citizens only in a qualified sense—they are citizens but undeveloped ones. There were some places, in ancient times, where the class of mechanics was actually composed of slaves or foreigners only, and this explains why a great number of mechanics are slaves or foreigners even today.

1278ᵃ8 The best form of city will not make the mechanic a citizen. Where mechanics are admitted to citizenship we shall have to say that the citizen excellence of which we have spoken cannot be attained by every citizen, by all who are simply free men, but can only be achieved by those who are free from the necessary tasks of life. Those who do the necessary tasks may be divided into two classes, slaves, who do them for individuals, and mechanics and labourers, who do them for the community.

1278ª13 If we start from this basis, and carry our inquiry a little further, the position of these mechanics and labourers will soon become evident; in fact, enough has already been said to make it clear, once the bearing of the argument is grasped. Constitutions are various: there must thus be various kinds of citizens; more especially, there must be various kinds of citizens who are subjects. In one variety of constitution it will be necessary that mechanics and labourers should be citizens: in other varieties it will be impossible. It will be impossible, for example, where there is a constitution of the type termed "aristocratic", with offices distributed on the basis of worth and excellence; for one who lives the life of a mechanic or labourer cannot pursue the things which belong to excellence. The case is different in oligarchies. Even there, it is true, a labourer cannot be a citizen (participation in office depending on a high property qualification); but a mechanic may, for the simple reason that craftsmen often become rich. Yet in Thebes there was a law that no one could share in office who had not abstained from selling in the market for a period of ten years. On the other hand, there are many constitutions where the law goes to the length of admitting aliens to citizenship. There are, for example, some democracies where someone who has only a citizen mother is admitted; and there are many cities where the same privilege is given to those of illegitimate birth. But the policy of extending citizenship so widely is [generally] due to a dearth of genuine citizens; and it is only shortage of population which produces such legislation. When they have sufficient numbers they gradually disqualify such people: first sons of a slave father or slave mother are disqualified; then those who are born of a citizen mother but an alien father; and finally citizenship is confined to those who are of citizen parentage on both sides.

1278ª34 These considerations prove two things: that there are several different kinds of cit-

izens, and that the name of citizen is particularly applicable to those who share in the offices and honours of the city. Homer accordingly speaks in the *Iliad* of a man being treated

like an alien man, without honour;

and it is true that those who do not share in positions of honour in the city are just like resident aliens. When restrictions are imposed by subterfuge their only object is to hoodwink those inhabitants who are not citizens.

1278ª40 Two conclusions also emerge from our discussion of the question, "Is the excellence of the good man identical with that of the good citizen, or different from it?" The first is that there are some cities in which the good man and the good citizen are identical, and some in which they are different. The second is that, in cities of the former type, it is not all good citizens who are also good men, but only those among them who hold the position of statesmen—in other words, those who direct or are capable of directing, either alone or in conjunction with others, the conduct of public affairs.

Constitutions and Their Classification (Chapters 6–8)

Chapter 6

The definition of a constitution. The classification of constitutions depends on (1) the ends pursued by cities, and (2) the kind of rule exercised by their governments. The true end of a city is a good life, and it is the common interest to achieve this: the right kind of rule is authority exercised in the common interest. We may thus distinguish "right" constitutions, which are directed to the common interest, and "wrong" or "perverted" constitutions directed to the selfish interest of the ruling body.

1278ᵇ6 Having determined these matters we have next to consider whether there is a single type of constitution, or whether there are a number of types. If there are a number of types, what are these types; how many of them are there; and how do they differ? A constitution [or *politeia*] may be defined as "the organization of a city [or *polis*], in respect of its offices generally, but especially in respect of that particular office which is sovereign in all issues". The civic body is everywhere the sovereign of the city; in fact the civic body is the constitution itself. In democratic cities, for example, the people [*dēmos*] is sovereign: in oligarchies, on the other hand, the few [or *oligoí*] have that position; and this difference in the sovereign bodies is the reason why we say that the two types of constitution differ—as we may equally apply the same reasoning to other types besides these.

1278ᵇ15 We must first ascertain two things: the nature of the end for which a city exists, and the various kinds of rule to which mankind and its associations are subject. It has already been stated, in our first book (where we were concerned with the management of the household and the control of slaves), that "man is a political animal". For this reason people desire to live a social life even when they stand in no need of mutual succour; but they are also drawn together by a common interest, in proportion as each attains a share in the good life. The good life is the chief end, both for the community as a whole and for each of us individually. But people also come together, and form and maintain political associations, merely for the sake of life; for perhaps there is some element of the good even in the simple fact of living, so long as the evils of existence do not preponderate too heavily. It is an evident fact that most people cling hard enough to life to be willing to endure a good deal of suffering, which implies that life has in it a sort of healthy happiness and a natural quality of pleasure.

1278ᵇ30 It is easy enough to distinguish the various kinds of rule of which people commonly speak; and indeed we have often had occasion to define them ourselves in works intended for the general public. The rule of a master is one kind; and here, though there is really a common interest which unites the natural master and the natural slave, the fact remains that the rule is primarily exercised with a view to the master's interest, and only incidentally with a view to that of the slave, who must be preserved in existence if the rule is to remain. Rule over wife and children, and over the household generally, is a second kind of rule, which we have called by the name of household management. Here the rule is either exercised in the interest of the ruled or for

the attainment of some advantage common to both ruler and ruled. Essentially it is exercised in the interest of the ruled, as is also plainly the case with other arts besides that of ruling, such as medicine and gymnastics—though an art may incidentally be exercised for the benefit of its practitioner, and there is nothing to prevent (say) a trainer from becoming occasionally a member of the class he instructs, in the same sort of way as a steersman is always one of the crew. Thus a trainer or steersman primarily considers the good of those who are subject to his authority; but when he becomes one of them personally, he incidentally shares in the benefit of that good— the steersman thus being also a member of the crew, and the trainer (though still a trainer) becoming also a member of the class which he instructs.

1279ᵃ8 For this reason, when the constitution of a city is constructed on the principle that its members are equals and peers, the citizens think it proper that they should hold office by turns. At any rate this is the natural system, and the system which used to be followed in the days when people believed that they ought to serve by turns, and each assumed that others would take over the duty of considering his benefit, just as he himself, during his term of office, had considered their interest. Today because of the profits to be derived from office and the handling of public property, people want to hold office continuously. It is as if they were invalids, who got the benefit of being healthy by being permanently in office: at any rate their ardour for office is just what it would be if that were the case. The conclusion which follows is clear: those constitutions which consider the common interest are right constitutions, judged by the standard of absolute justice. Those constitutions which consider only the personal interest of the rulers are all wrong constitutions, or perversions of the right forms. Such perverted forms are despotic; whereas the city is an association of freemen.

Chapter 7

These two types of constitution each fall into three subdivisions on the basis of number, i.e. according as the One, or the Few, or the Many are the ruling authority in each type. We have thus, as the three subdivisions of the "right" type, Kingship, Aristocracy, and "Constitutional Government" or "Polity": as the three subdivisions of the "wrong" type, Tyranny, Oligarchy, and Democracy.

1279ª22 Now that these matters have been determined, the next subject for consideration is the number and nature of the different constitutions. We may first examine those constitutions that are rightly formed, since, when these have been determined, the different perversions will at once be apparent.

1279ª25 The term "constitution" [*politeia*] signifies the same thing as the term "civic body" [*politeuma*]. The civic body in every city [*polis*] is the sovereign [*to kurion*]; and the sovereign must necessarily be either One, or Few, or Many. On this basis we may say that when the One, or the Few, or the Many rule with a view to the common interest, the constitutions under which they do so must necessarily be right constitutions. On the other hand, the constitutions directed to the personal interest of the One, or the Few, or the Masses, must necessarily be perversions. Either we should say that those who do not share in the constitution are not citizens, or they ought to have their share of the benefits. According to customary usage, among monarchical forms of government the type which looks to the common interest is called Kingship; among forms of government by a few people (but more than one) it is called Aristocracy—that name being given to this species either because the best [*aristoi*] are the rulers, or because its object is what is best [*ariston*] for the city and its members. Finally, when the masses govern the city with a view to the common interest, the form of government is called by the generic name common to all constitutions (or polities)—the name of "Constitutional Government". There is a good reason for this usage: it is possible for one man, or a few, to be of outstanding excellence; but when it comes to a large number, we can hardly expect precision in all the varieties of excellence. What we can expect particularly is the military kind of excellence, which is the kind that shows itself in a mass. This is the reason why the defence forces are the most sovereign body under this constitution, and those who possess arms are the ones who participate in it.

1279ᵇ4 The perversions that correspond to the constitutions just mentioned are: Tyranny, [the perversion of] Kingship; Oligarchy [the perversion of] Aristocracy; and Democracy [the perversion of] "Constitutional Government" [or polity]. Tyranny is a government by a single person directed to the interest of that person; Oligarchy is directed to the interest of the well-to-do; Democracy is directed to the interest of the poor. None of these benefits the common interest.

Chapter 8

The basis of number is not, however, adequate. The real basis, at any rate so far as oligarchy and democracy are concerned, is social class: what makes an oligarchy is the rule of the rich (rather than the few), and what makes a democracy is the rule of the poor (rather than the many). Number is an accidental, and not an essential, attribute; but the accidental generally accompanies the essential.

1279ᵇ11 We must consider at somewhat greater length what each of these constitutions is. There are certain difficulties involved; and when one is pursuing a philosophical method of inquiry in any branch of study, and not merely looking to practical considerations, the proper course is to set out the truth about every particular with no neglect or omission.

1279ᵇ16 Tyranny, as has just been said, is single-person government of the political association on the lines of despotism; oligarchy exists where those who have property are the sovereign authority of the constitution; and, conversely, democracy exists where the sovereign authority is composed of the poorer classes, who are without much property.

1279ᵇ20 The first difficulty which arises is a matter of definition. It could be that the majority are well-to-do and that these hold the sovereignty in a city; but when the majority is sovereign there is [said to be] democracy. Similarly it could happen that the poorer classes were fewer in number than the well-to-do, and yet were stronger and had sovereign authority in the constitution; but where a small number has sovereignty there is said to be oligarchy. Thus is may seem that the definitions we have given of these constitutions cannot be correct.

1279ᵇ26 We might attempt to overcome the difficulty by combining both of the factors:

wealth with paucity of numbers, and poverty with mass. On this basis oligarchy might be defined as the constitution under which the rich, being also few in number, hold the public offices; and similarly democracy might be defined as the constitution under which the poor, being also many in number, are in control. But this involves us in another difficulty. If there are no forms of oligarchy and democracy other than those enumerated, what names are we to give to the constitutions just suggested as conceivable—those where the wealthy form a majority and the poor a minority, and where the wealthy majority in the one case, and the poor minority in the other, are the sovereign authority of the constitution? The course of the argument thus appears to show that whether the sovereign body is small or large in number (as it is respectively in oligarchies or in democracies) is an accidental attribute, due to the simple fact that the wealthy are generally few and the poor are generally numerous. Therefore the causes originally mentioned are not in fact the real causes of the difference between oligarchies and democracies. The real ground of the difference between oligarchy and democracy is poverty and riches. It is inevitable that there should be an oligarchy where the rulers, whether they are few or many, owe their position to riches; and it is equally inevitable that there should be democracy where the poor rule.

1280ª2 It happens, however, as we have just remarked, that the former [i.e. the wealthy] are few and the latter [i.e. the poor] are numerous. It is only a few who have riches, but all alike share in free status; and it is on these grounds that the two parties dispute the control of the constitution.

The Principles of Oligarchy and Democracy and the Nature of Distributive Justice (Chapters 9–13)

Chapter 9

The principle of a constitution is its conception of justice; and this is the fundamental ground of difference between oligarchy and democracy. Democrats hold that if men are equal by birth, they should in justice have an equal share in office and honours: oligarchs hold that if

they are unequal in wealth, they should in justice have unequal shares in these things. True justice means that those who have contributed to the end of the city should have privileges in proportion to their contribution to that end. The end of the city is not mere life, nor an alliance for mutual defence; it is the common promotion of a good quality of life. Thus although the citizens of a city must always inhabit a single territory, engage in inter-marriage, and co-operate with each other in economic matters, the operative aim is always the promotion of a good quality of life. Those who contribute most to the realization of that aim should in justice have the largest share of office and honour.

1280ª7 We must next ascertain what are said to be the distinctive principles of oligarchy and democracy, and what are the oligarchical and the democratic conceptions of justice. All parties have a hold on a sort of conception of justice; but they both fail to carry it far enough, and do not express the true conception of justice in the whole of its range. For example, justice is considered to mean equality. It does mean equality—but equality for those who are equal, and not for all. Again, inequality is considered to be just; and indeed it is—but only for those who are unequal, and not for all. These people fail to consider for whom there should be equality or inequality and thus make erroneous judgements. The reason is that they are judging in their own case; and most people, as a rule, are bad judges where their own interests are involved. Justice is concerned with people; and a just distribution is one in which there is proportion between the things distributed and those to whom they are distributed, a point which has already been made in the *Ethics*. There is general agreement about what constitutes equality in the thing, but disagreement about what constitutes it in people. The main reason for this is the reason just stated, they are judging, and judging erroneously, in their own case; but there is also another reason, they are misled by the fact that they are professing a sort of conception of justice, and professing it up to a point, into thinking that they profess one which is absolute and complete. Some think that if they are superior in one point, for example in wealth, they are superior in all: others believe that if they are equal in one respect, for instance in free birth, they are equal all round.

1280ª25 Both sides, however, fail to mention the really cardinal factor. If property is the end for which people come together and form an association, one's share of the city would be proportionate to one's share of the property; and in that case the argument of the oligarchical side would appear to be strong: they say that is not just for someone who has contributed one mina to share in a sum of a hundred minae on equal terms with one who has contributed all the rest and that this applies both to the original sum and to the interest accruing upon it. But the end of the city is not mere life; it is, rather, a good quality of life. Otherwise, there might be a city of slaves, or even a city of animals; but in the world as we know it any such city is impossible, because slaves and animals do not share in happiness nor in living according to their own choice. Similarly, it is not the end of the city to provide an alliance for mutual defence against all injury, nor does it exist for the purpose of exchange or [commercial] dealing. If that had been the end, the Etruscans and the Carthaginians would be in the position of belonging to a single city; and the same would be true to all peoples who have commercial treaties with one another. It is true that such peoples have agreements about imports; treaties to ensure just conduct; and written terms of alliance for mutual defence. On the other hand, they have no common offices to deal with these matters: each, on the contrary, has its own offices, confined to itself. Neither party concerns itself to ensure a proper quality of character among the members of the other; neither of them seeks to ensure that all who are included in the scope of the treaties are just and free from any form of vice; and they do not go beyond the aim of preventing their own members from committing injustice against one another. But it is the goodness or badness in the life of the city which engages the attention of those who are concerned to secure good government.

1280ᵇ6 The conclusion which clearly follows is that any city which is truly so called, and is not merely one in name, must devote itself to the end of encouraging goodness. Otherwise, a political association sinks into a mere alliance, which only differs in space [i.e. in the contiguity of its members] from other forms of alliance where the members live at a distance from one another. Otherwise, too, law becomes a mere covenant—or (in the phrase of the sophist Lycophron) "a guarantor of just claims"—but lacks the capacity to make the citizens good and just.

1280ᵇ12 That this is the case may be readily proved. If two different sites could be united in one, so that the city [i.e. the *polis*] of Megara and that of Corinth were embraced by a single wall, that would not make a single city. If the citizens of two cities intermarried with one another, that would not make a single city, even though intermarriage is one of the forms of social life which are characteristic of a city. Nor would it make a city if a number of people, living at a distance from one another, but not at so great a distance but they could still associate, had a common system of laws to prevent their injuring one another in the course of exchange. We can imagine, for instance, one being a carpenter, another a farmer, a third a shoemaker, and others producing other goods; and we can imagine a total number of as many as 10,000. But if these people were associated in nothing further than matters such as exchange and alliance, they would still have failed to reach the stage of a city. Why should this be the case? It cannot be ascribed to any lack of contiguity in such an association. The members of a group so constituted might come together on a single site; but if that were all—if each still treated his private house as if it were a city, and all of them still confined their mutual assistance to action against aggressors (as if it were only a question of a defensive alliance)—if, in a word, they associated with each other in the same fashion after coming together as they did when they were living apart—their association, even on its new basis, could not be deemed by any accurate thinker to be a city.

1280ᵇ29 It is clear, therefore, that a city is not an association for residence on a common site, or for the sake of preventing mutual injustice and easing exchange. These are indeed conditions which must be present before a city can exist; but the presence of all these conditions is not enough, in itself, to constitute a city. What constitutes a city is an association of households and clans in a good life, for the sake of attaining a perfect and self-sufficing existence. This, however, will not come about unless the members inhabit one and the self-same place and practise intermarriage. It was for this reason that the various institutions of a common social life—marriage-connections, kin-groups, religious gatherings, and social pastimes generally—arose in cities. This sort of thing is the business of friendship, for the pursuit of a common social life is friendship. Thus the purpose of a city is the good life, and these institutions are means to that end. A city is constituted by the association of families and villages in a perfect and self-sufficing existence; and such an existence, on our definition, consists in living a happy and truly valuable life.

1281ª2 It is therefore for the sake of actions valuable in themselves, and not for the sake of social life, that political associations must be considered to exist. Those who contribute most to this association have a greater share in the city than those who are equal to them (or even greater) in free birth and descent, but unequal in civic excellence, or than those who surpass them in wealth but are surpassed by them in excellence. From what has been said it is plain that all sides in the dispute about constitutions profess only a partial conception of justice.

Chapter 10

What person or body of people should be sovereign in a city: the people, the rich, the better sort of citizens, the one best, or the tyrant? All these alternatives present difficulties; and there is a difficulty even in a further alternative, that no person or body of people, but law, should be sovereign.

1281ª11 A difficulty arises when we turn to consider what body should be sovereign in the city. The people at large, the wealthy, the better sort, the one who is best of all, the tyrant. But all these alternatives appear to involve unpleasant results: indeed, how can it be otherwise? What if the poor, on the ground of their being a majority, proceed to divide among themselves the possessions of the wealthy—will not this be unjust? "No, by heaven" (someone may reply); "it has been justly decreed so by the sovereign body." But if this is not the extreme of injustice, what is? Whenever a majority takes everything and divides among its members the possessions of a minority, that majority is obviously ruining the city. But goodness does not ruin whatever pos-

sesses it, nor can justice be such as to ruin a city. It is therefore clear that a law of this kind cannot possibly be just. The tyrant's acts too would necessarily be just; for he too uses coercion by virtue of superior power in just the same sort of way as the people coerce the wealthy. Is it just that a minority composed of the wealthy should rule? Then if they too behave like the others—if they plunder and confiscate the property of the people—their action is just. If it is, then this behaviour would also be just in the former case. It is clear that all these acts of oppression are mean and unjust. But should the better sort have authority and be sovereign in all matters? In that case, the rest of the citizens will necessarily be deprived of honour, since they will not enjoy the honour of holding civic office. We speak of offices as honours; and when the same people hold office all the time, the rest of the community must necessarily be deprived of honour. Is it better that the one best man should rule? This is still more oligarchical because the number of those deprived of honour is even greater. It may perhaps be urged that it is a poor sort of policy to vest sovereignty in a human being, rather than in law; for human beings are subject to the passions that beset their souls. But the law itself may incline either towards oligarchy or towards democracy; and what difference will the sovereignty of law then make in the problems which have just been raised? The consequences already stated will follow just the same.

Chapter 11

It is possible, however, to defend the alternative, that the people should be sovereign. The people, when they are assembled, have a combination of qualities which enables them to deliberate wisely and to judge soundly. This suggests that they have a claim to be the sovereign body; it also suggests the scope of affairs in which they should be sovereign, or the powers which they should exercise. They should exercise deliberative and judicial functions; in particular, they should elect the magistrates and examine their conduct at the end of their tenure. Two objections may be raised. (1) It may be argued that experts are better judges than the non-expert; but this objection may be met by reference to (a) the combination of qualities in the assembled people (which makes them collectively better judges than the expert), and (b) the fact that in some cases laymen are in as good a position to judge as experts (which enables them to pass judgement on the behaviour of magistrates). (2) It may be urged that the people, if they have such powers, have more authority than the better sort of citizens who hold office as magistrates, though they are not of so good a quality; but we may answer to this that the people as a whole may well be of a high quality. We have always, however, to remember that rightly constituted laws should be the final sovereign, and that personal authority of any sort should only act in the particular cases which cannot be covered by a general law.

1281ª39 The other alternatives may be reserved for later inquiry; but the suggestion that the people at large should be sovereign rather than the few best men would [seem to present problems which] need resolution, and while it presents some difficulty it perhaps also contains some truth. There is this to be said for the many: each of them by himself may not be of a good quality; but when they all come together it is possible that they may surpass—collectively and as a body, although not individually—the quality of the few best, in much the same way that feasts to which many contribute may excel those provided at one person's expense. For when there are many, each has his share of goodness and practical wisdom; and, when all meet together, the people may thus become something like a single person, who, as he has many feet, many hands, and many senses, may also have many qualities of character and intelligence. This is the reason why the many are also better judges of music and the writings of poets: some appreciate one part, some another, and all together appreciate all. The thing which makes a good man differ from a unit in the crowd—as it is also the thing which is generally said to make a beautiful person differ from one who is not beautiful, or an artistic representation differ from ordinary reality—is that elements which are elsewhere scattered and separate are here combined in a unity. If the elements are taken separately, one may say of an artistic representation that it is surpassed by the eye of this person and by some other feature of that.

1281ᵇ15 It is not clear, however, that this contrast between the many, on the one hand, and the few good men, on the other, can apply to every people and to every large group. Perhaps, by heav-

en, there are some of which it clearly cannot be true; for otherwise the same argument would apply to the beasts. Yet what difference, one may ask, is there between some men and the beasts? All the same, there is nothing to prevent the view we have stated from being true of a particular group.

1281ᵇ21 It would thus seem possible to solve, by the considerations we have advanced, both the problem raised in the previous chapter ["Which people should be sovereign?"] and the further problem which follows upon it, "What are the matters over which freemen, or the general body of citizens—the sort of people who neither have wealth nor can make any claim on the ground of goodness—should properly exercise sovereignty?" Of course there is a danger in people of this sort sharing in the highest offices, as injustice may lead them into wrongdoing, and thoughtlessness into error. But there is also a serious risk in not letting them have some share of power; for a city with a body of disfranchised citizens who are numerous and poor must necessarily be a city which is full of enemies. The alternative left is to let them share in the deliberative and judicial functions. This is why Solon, and some of the other legislators, allow the people to elect officials and to call them to account at the end of their tenure of office, but not to hold office themselves in their individual capacity. When they all meet together, the people display a good enough gift of perception, and combined with the better class they are of service to the city (just as impure food, when it is mixed with pure, makes the whole concoction more nutritious than a small amount of the pure would be); but each of them is imperfect in the judgements he forms by himself.

1281ᵇ38 But this arrangement of the constitution presents some difficulties. The first difficulty is that it may well be held that the function of judging when medical attendance has been properly given should belong to those whose profession it is to attend patients and cure the complaints from which they suffer—in a word, to members of the medical profession. The same may be held to be true of all other professions and arts; and just as medical men should have their conduct examined before a body of medics, so, too, should those who follow other professions have their examined before a body of members of their own profession. But the term "medic" is applied to the ordinary practitioner, to the specialist who directs the course of treatment, and to someone who has some general knowledge of the art of medicine. (There are people of this last type to be found in connection with nearly all the arts.) We credit those who have a general knowledge with the power of judging as much as we do the experts. When we turn to consider the matter of election, the same principles would appear to apply. To make a proper election is equally the work of experts. It is the work of those who are versed in geometry to choose a geometrician, or again, of those who are acquainted with steering to choose a steersman; and even if, in some occupations and arts, there are some non-experts who also share in the ability to choose, they do not share in a higher degree than the experts. It would thus appear, on this line of argument, that the people should not be made sovereign, either in the matter of election of magistrates or in that of their examination.

1282ª14 It may be, however, that these arguments are not altogether well founded for the reason given above—provided, that is to say, that the people is not too debased in character. Each individual may indeed be a worse judge than the experts; but all, when they meet together, are either better than experts or at any rate no worse. In the second place, there are a number of arts in which the craftsman is not the only, or even the best, judge. These are the arts whose products can be understood even by those who do not possess any skill in the art. A house, for instance, is something which can be understood by others besides the builder: indeed the user of a house, or in other words the householder, will judge it even better than he does. In the same way a steersman will judge a rudder better than a shipwright does; and the diner, not the cook, will be the best judge of a feast.

1282ª23 The first difficulty would appear to be answered sufficiently by these considerations. But there is a second difficulty still to be faced, which is connected with the first. It would seem to be absurd that people of poor character should be sovereign on issues which are more important than those assigned to the better sort of citizens. The election of officials, and their examination at the end of their tenure, are the most important of issues; and yet there are constitutions, as we have

seen, under which these issues are assigned to the people, since the assembly is sovereign in all such matters. To add to the difficulty, membership of the assembly, which carries deliberative and judicial functions, is vested in people of little property and of any age; but a high property qualification is demanded from those who serve as treasurers or generals, or hold any of the highest offices.

1282ª32 This difficulty too may, however, be met in the same way as the first; and the practice followed in these constitutions is perhaps, after all, correct. It is not the individual juryman, councillor, or assemblyman, who is vested with office, but the court, the council, or the popular assembly; and in these bodies each member, whether he be a councillor, an assemblyman, or a juryman, is simply a part of the whole. It is therefore just that the people should be sovereign on the more important issues, since the assembly, the council, and the court consist of many people. Moreover, the property owned by all these people is greater than that of those who either as individuals or as members of small bodies hold the highest offices.

1282ª41 This may serve as a settlement of the difficulties which have been discussed. But the discussion of the first of these difficulties leads to one conclusion above all others. Rightly constituted laws should be [the final] sovereign; but rulers, whether one or many, should be sovereign in those matters on which law is unable, owing to the difficulty of framing general rules for all contingencies, to make an exact pronouncement. But what rightly constituted laws ought to be is a matter that is not yet clear; and here we are still confronted by the difficulty stated at the end of the previous chapter. Laws must be good or bad, just or unjust in the same way as the constitutions to which they belong. The one clear fact is that laws must be laid down in accordance with constitutions; and if this is the case, it follows that laws which are in accordance with right constitutions must necessarily be just, and laws which are in accordance with perverted constitutions must be unjust.

Chapter 12

Justice is the political good. It involves equality, or the distribution of equal amounts to those who are equal. But who are equals, and by what criterion are they to be reckoned as equals? Many criteria can be applied; but the only proper criterion, in a political society, is that of contribution to the function of that society. Those who are equal in that respect should receive equal amounts: those who are superior or inferior should receive superior or inferior amounts, in proportion to the degree of their superiority or inferiority. If all are thus treated proportionately to the contribution they make, all are really receiving equal treatment; for the proportion between contribution and reward is the same in every case. The sort of equality which justice involves is thus proportionate equality; and this is the essence of distributive justice.

1282ᵇ14 In all branches of knowledge and in every kind of craft the end in view is some good. In the most sovereign of these, the capacity for [leadership in] political matters, the end in view is the greatest good and the good which is most to be pursued. The good in the sphere of politics is justice; and justice consists in what tends to promote the common interest. General opinion makes it consist in some sort of equality. Up to a point this agrees with the philosophical inquiries which contain our conclusions on ethics. In other words, it holds that justice involves two factors—things, and those to whom things are assigned—and it considers that those who are equal should have assigned to them equal things. But here there arises a question which must not be overlooked. Equals and unequals—yes; but equals and unequals in what? This is a question which raises difficulties, and involves us in philosophical speculation on politics. It is possible to argue that offices and honours ought to be distributed unequally on the basis of superiority in any kind of goodness whatsoever—even if those concerned are similar, and do not differ, in any other respect. The reason is that where people differ from one another there must be a difference in what is just and proportionate to their merits. If this argument were right, the mere fact of a better complexion, or greater height, or any other such advantage, would establish a claim for a greater share of political rights to be given to its possessor. But is not the argument obviously wrong? To be clear that it is, we have only to consider other kinds of knowledge and ability. In dealing with a number of equally skilled flute-players, you should not assign a better supply of

flutes to those who are better born. Rather those who are better at the job should be given the better supply of tools. If our point is not yet plain, it can be made so if we push it still further. Let us suppose someone who is superior to others in flute-playing, but far inferior in birth and beauty. Even if birth and beauty are greater goods than ability to play the flute, and even if those who possess them may surpass the flute-player proportionately more in these qualities than he surpasses them in his flute-playing, the fact remains that he is the one who ought to get the superior flutes. Superiority, whether in birth or in wealth, ought to contribute something to the performance of that function; and here these qualities contribute nothing to such performance.

1283ᵃ3 There is a further objection. If we accept this argument, every quality will have to be commensurable with every other. You will begin by reckoning a given degree of (say) height as superior to a given degree of some other quality, and you will thus be driven to pit height in general against (say) wealth and birth in general. But on this basis—i.e. that, *in a given case*, A is counted as excelling in height to a greater degree than B does in goodness, and that, *in general*, height is counted as excelling to a greater degree than goodness does—qualities are made commensurable. [We are involved in mere arithmetic]; for if amount X of some quality is "better" than amount Y of some other, some amount which is other than X must clearly be equal to it [i.e. must be *equally* good]. This is impossible. It is therefore clear that in matters political there is no good reason for basing a claim to the exercise of authority on any and every kind of superiority. (Some may be swift and others slow; but this is no reason why the one should have more, and the other less—it is in athletic contests that the superiority of the swift receives its reward.) Claims must be based on the elements which constitute the being of the city. There are thus good grounds for the claims to honour which are made by people of good descent, free birth, or wealth, since those who hold office must necessarily be free men and pay the property assessment. (A city could not be composed entirely of those without means, any more than it could be composed entirely of slaves.) But we must add that if wealth and free birth are necessary elements, the qualities of being just and being a good soldier are also necessary. These too are elements which must be present if people are to live together in a city. The one difference is that the first two elements are necessary for the simple existence of a city, and the last two for its good life.

Chapter 13

This raises the question, What constitutes a contribution to the purpose of a political society? Wealth, birth, goodness, and the aggregate quality of numbers, may all claim to be contributors. How are these rival claims to be reconciled when they all coexist in the same society? A case may be made in favour of the aggregate quality of numbers; but a case may also be made in favour of the single man of exceptional and outstanding goodness. Such a man must either be made a king or sent into exile. The democratic policy of ostracism means a choice of the latter alternative; and the proportion, or balance, needed in a constitution is certainly disturbed if any one element is outstandingly eminent. On the other hand it cannot be just, in a good constitution, to refuse the recognition which is due to a man of outstanding goodness; and such a man should not be banished, but should rather be made a king. We are thus brought to the subject of kingship.

1283ª23 If we are thinking in terms of contribution to the state's existence, all of the elements mentioned, or at any rate several of them, may properly calim to be recognized [in the award of honours and office]; but if we are thinking in terms of contribution to its good life, then culture and goodness, as we have noted already, may be regarded as having the justest claim. On the other hand—since it is not right for those who are equal in one respect, and only in one, to have an equal share of all things, or for those who are unequal in one respect to have unequal shares of everything—all such constitutions must be perversions. We have noted already that there is a certain sense in which all are justified in the claims they advance, though none of them is absolutely justified. (*a*) The rich are justified to the extent that they have a larger share of the land, which is a matter of common concern: they are also, as a rule, more reliable in matters of contract. (*b*) The free and the nobly born may claim recognition together as being closely connected. The better-born are citizens to a greater extent than the low-born; and good birth has always honour in its own country. In addition the descendants of better men are likely to be better; good birth means goodness of stock. (*c*) Similarly we may also allow that goodness [of mind and character] has a just claim; for in our view the virtue of justice is goodness in matters of common concern and is necessarily accompanied by all other forms of goodness. (*d*) Lastly, the many have a justified claim against the few: taken together and compared with the few they are stronger, richer, and better.

1283ª42 Suppose these—I mean the good, the wealthy, and well-born, and some general body of citizens—all living together in a single city. Will there or will there not be a dispute about which of them is to rule? The decision about who should rule is not a matter of dispute in any of the constitutions we have mentioned. These constitutions differ in virtue of different groups being sovereign: one of them is distinguished by sovereignty being vested in the wealthy; another by its being vested in the good; and so with each of the rest. But we should consider how the matter is to be decided when these claims are present at the same time. Suppose, for example, that the good are exceedingly few in number: how are we to settle their claim? Should we consider the fact that they are few in the light of the function they have to discharge and ask therefore whether they will be able to manage a city? Or should we ask whether they are numerous enough to compose one?

1283ᵇ13 Here there arises a difficulty which applies to all the different claimants for political honours. It may be held that those who base their claim to rule on the ground of wealth have no case, and neither do those who base it on birth. The reason for thinking this is that if there is any one man who in turn is richer than all the rest, this one man must rule over all on the very same ground of justice; and similarly any one man who is pre-eminent in point of good birth must carry the day over those who base their claim on the ground of free birth. The same thing could perhaps happen even in aristocracies based on the claim of goodness. If someone is a better man than all the other good men who belong to the civic body, this one man should be sovereign on the very same ground of justice. Similarly if the reason why the Many should be sovereign is their being stronger than the Few, then if one man is stronger than all the rest—or if a group of more than one, but fewer than the Many, is stronger— these should be sovereign instead of the Many.

1283ᵇ27 All these considerations would seem to prove that none of the principles, in virtue of which people claim to rule and to have all others subject to their rule, is right. Take, for example, those who claim to be sovereign over the citizen body on the ground of goodness; or, equally, those who base their claim on the ground of wealth. The claims of both may be justly challenged by the masses; for there is nothing to prevent the Many— collectively if not individually—from being better, or richer, than the Few. This last reflection enables us to meet a difficulty which is sometimes raised and discussed. The difficulty is this. Suppose that the situation just mentioned does occur [i.e. that the Many are actually better, taken as a whole, than the Few]: what, in that case, is the proper policy for a lawgiver who wishes to enact right laws to the best of his power? Should he direct his legisla- tion to the benefit of the better sort or should he direct it to that of the majority? [We may reply that] what is "right" should be understood as what is "equally right"; and what is "equally right" is what is for the benefit of the whole city and for the common good of its citizens. The citizen is, in general, one who shares in the civic life of ruling and being ruled in turn. But this varies from con- stitution to constitution; and under the best con- stitution he must be one who is able and willing to rule and be ruled with a view to attaining a way of life in keeping with goodness.

1284ᵃ3 If there is one person (or several people, but yet not enough to form the full complement of a city) so pre-eminently superior in goodness that there can be no comparison between the goodness and political capacity which he shows (or several show, when there is more than one) and what is shown by the rest, such a person, or such people, can no longer be treated as part of a city. An injustice will be done to them if they are treated as worthy only of an equal share, when they are so greatly superior to others in goodness and political capacity; for someone of this sort may very well be like a god among men. This being the case, it is clear that legislation is necessarily limited to those

who are equal in birth and capacity. There can be no law governing people of this kind. They are a law in themselves. It would be a folly to attempt to legislate for them: they might reply to such an attempt with the words used by the lions, in the fable of Antisthenes, when the hares were making orations and claiming that all the animals should have equal status.

1284ᵃ17 Reasons of this nature will serve to explain why democratic cities institute the rule of ostracism. Such cities are held to aim at equality above anything else; and with that aim in view they used to pass a sentence of ostracism on those whom they regarded as having too much influence owing to their wealth or the number of their connections or any other form of political strength. There is a story that the Argonauts left Heracles behind for this sort of reason; and the Argo itself refused to have him among the crew because he was so great- ly superior to all the others. From this point of view we cannot altogether regard as just the strictures passed by the critics of tyranny on the advice once given by Periander to Thrasybulus. According to the story, Periander said nothing to the messenger who had been sent [by Thrasybulus] for his advice; he simply chopped off the outstanding ears and thus levelled the corn [in the field where he was stand- ing]. The messenger did not understand the mean- ing of his action, and merely reported the incident; but Thrasybulus guessed that he should cut off the outstanding men in the city. It is not only tyrants who may derive some benefit from this policy; nor is it only tyrants who put it into practice. Oligarchies and democracies are both in the same position; and ostracism has, in its way, the same effect of pulling down and banishing men of out- standing influence. Those who have gained an ascendancy apply the same sort of policy to other cities and peoples. The Athenians, for instance, acted in this way to Samos, Chios, and Lesbos: once they had gained a firm grip of their empire, they hum- bled these cities, in violation of their former treaties. The King of the Persians did the same to the Medes, the Babylonians, and any of the others who were made presumptuous by memories of having once had an empire themselves.

1284ᵇ3 The difficulty which we are discussing is one which is common to all forms of govern- ment, the right as well as the wrong; perverted forms adopt this policy of levelling with a view to their own particular interest, but the same is also true even of forms which look to the common good. This rule of proportion may also be observed in the arts and sciences generally. A painter would not permit a figure to have a foot which exceeded the bounds of symmetry, however beautiful it might be. A shipwright would not tolerate a stern, or any other part of a ship, which was out of proportion. A choirmaster would not admit to a choir a singer with a stronger and a finer voice than any of the other members. For this reason nothing prevents monarchs who behave in this way from being in harmony with the cities [over which they rule]—provided that their own rule is beneficial to these cities; and thus the argument in favour of ostracism possesses a kind of political justice in relation to any recognized forms of pre-eminence. It is better if the legislator so frames a constitution initially that it never needs any such remedy; but the next best course, should the need arise, is to correct it by this sort of device. Actually, this is not what has happened in cities; instead of looking to

the interest of their own particular constitution, they have resorted to acts of ostracism in a spirit of faction.

1284ᵇ22 So far as perverted forms are concerned, it is clear that the ostracism is expedient and just from their own point of view—though perhaps it is also clear that it is not absolutely just. But in the best constitution a serious difficulty arises. It does not arise in regard to pre-eminence in other qualities such as political strength, or wealth, or an abundance of connections but where there is someone of outstanding excellence. "What is to be done in that case?" Nobody would say that such a man ought to be banished and sent into exile. But neither would any one say that he ought to be subject to others. That would be like claiming to rule over Zeus, according to some division of offices. The only alternative left—and this would also appear to be the natural course—is for all others to pay a willing obedience to the man of outstanding goodness. Such men will accordingly be the permanent kings in their cities.

Nicomachean Ethics

Aristotle

Translated by W. D. Ross

Book II. Moral Virtue

1. Virtue, then, being of two kinds, intellectual and moral, intellectual virtue in the main owes both its birth and its growth to teaching (for which reason it requires experience and time), while moral virtue comes about as a result of habit, whence also its name (ethike) is one that is formed by a slight variation from the word ethos (habit). From this it is also plain that none of the moral virtues arises in us by nature; for nothing that exists by nature can form a habit contrary to its nature. For instance the stone which by nature moves downwards cannot be habituated to move upwards, not even if one tries to train it by throwing it up ten thousand times; nor can fire be habituated to move downwards, nor can anything else that by nature

behaves in one way be trained to behave in another. Neither by nature, then, nor contrary to nature do the virtues arise in us; rather we are adapted by nature to receive them, and are made perfect by habit.

Again, of all the things that come to us by nature we first acquire the potentiality and later exhibit the activity (this is plain in the case of the senses; for it was not by often seeing or often hearing that we got these senses, but on the contrary we had them before we used them, and did not come to have them by using them); but the virtues we get by first exercising them, as also happens in the case of the arts as well. For the things we have to learn before we can do them, we learn by doing them, e.g. men become builders by building and lyreplayers by playing the lyre; so too we become just by doing just acts, temperate by doing temperate acts, brave by doing brave acts.

This is confirmed by what happens in states; for legislators make the citizens good by forming habits in them, and this is the wish of every legislator, and those who do not effect it miss their mark, and it is in this that a good constitution differs from a bad one.

Again, it is from the same causes and by the same means that every virtue is both produced and destroyed, and similarly every art; for it is from playing the lyre that both good and bad lyre-players are produced. And the corresponding statement is true of builders and of all the rest; men will be good or bad builders as a result of building well or badly. For if this were not so, there would have been no need of a teacher, but all men would have been born good or bad at their craft. This, then, is the case with the virtues also; by doing the acts that we do in our transactions with other men we become just or unjust, and by doing the acts that we do in the presence of danger, and being habituated to feel fear or confidence, we become brave or cowardly. The same is true of appetites and feelings of anger; some men become temperate and good-tempered, others self-indulgent and irascible, by behaving in one way or the other in the appropriate circumstances. Thus, in one word, states of character arise out of like activities. This is why the activities we exhibit must be of a certain kind; it is because the states of character correspond to the differences between these. It makes no small difference, then, whether we form habits of one kind or of another from our very youth; it makes a very great difference, or rather all the difference.

2. Since, then, the present inquiry does not aim at theoretical knowledge like the others (for we are inquiring not in order to know what virtue is, but in order to become good, since otherwise our inquiry would have been of no use), we must examine the nature of actions, namely how we ought to do them; for these determine also the nature of the states of character that are produced, as we have said. Now, that we must act according to the right rule is a common principle and must be assumed—it will be discussed later, i.e. both what the right rule is, and how it is related to the other virtues. But this must be agreed upon beforehand, that the whole account of mat-ters of conduct must be given in outline and not precisely, as we said at the very beginning that the accounts we demand must be in accordance with the subject-matter; matters concerned with conduct and questions of what is good for us have no fixity, any more than matters of health. The general account being of this nature, the account of particular cases is yet more lacking in exactness; for they do not fall under any art or precept but the agents themselves must in each case consider what is appropriate to the occasion, as happens also in the art of medicine or of navigation.

But though our present account is of this nature we must give what help we can. First, then, let us consider this, that it is the nature of such things to be destroyed by defect and excess, as we see in the case of strength and of health (for to gain light on things imperceptible we must use the evidence of sensible things); both excessive and defective exercise destroys the strength, and similarly drink or food which is above or below a certain amount destroys the health, while that which is proportionate both produces and increases and preserves it. So too is it, then, in the case of temperance and courage and the other virtues. For the man who flies from and fears everything and does not stand his ground against anything becomes a coward, and the man who fears nothing at all but goes to meet every danger becomes rash; and similarly the man who indulges in every pleasure and abstains from none becomes self-indulgent, while the man who shuns every pleasure, as boors do, becomes in a way insensible; temperance and courage, then, are destroyed by excess and defect, and preserved by the mean.

But not only are the sources and causes of their origination and growth the same as those of their destruction, but also the sphere of their actualization will be the same; for this is also true of the things which are more evident to sense, e.g. of strength; it is produced by taking much food and undergoing much exertion, and it is the strong man that will be most able to do these things. So too is it with the virtues; by abstaining from pleasures we become temperate, and it is when we have become so that we are most able to abstain from them; and similarly too in the case of courage; for by being habituated to despise things that are terrible and to stand our ground against them we become brave, and it is when we have become so that we shall be most able to stand our ground against them.

3. We must take as a sign of states of character the pleasure or pain that ensues on acts; for the man who abstains from bodily pleasures and delights in this very fact is temperate, while the man who is annoyed at it is self-indulgent, and he who stands his ground against things that are terrible and delights in this or at least is not pained is brave, while the man who is pained is a coward. For moral excellence is concerned with pleasures and pains; it is on account of the pleasure that we do bad things, and on account of the pain that we abstain from noble ones. Hence we ought to have been brought up in a particular way from our very youth, as Plato says, so as both to delight in and to be pained by the things that we ought; for this is the right education. [...]

Book X. Pleasure, Happiness

1. After these matters we ought perhaps next to discuss pleasure. For it is thought to be most intimately connected with our human nature, which is the reason why in educating the young we steer them by the rudders of pleasure and pain; it is thought, too, that to enjoy the things we ought and to hate the things we ought has the greatest bearing on virtue of character. For these things extend right through life, with a weight and power of their own in respect both to virtue and to the happy life, since men choose what is pleasant and avoid what is painful; and such things, it will be thought, we should least of all omit to discuss, especially since they admit of much dispute. For some say pleasure is the good, while others, on the contrary, say it is thoroughly bad—some no doubt being persuaded that the facts are so, and others thinking it has a better effect on our life to exhibit pleasure as a bad thing even if it is not; for most people (they think) incline towards it and are the slaves of their pleasures, for which reason they ought to lead them in the opposite direction, since thus they will reach the middle state. But surely this is not correct. For arguments about matters concerned with feelings and actions are less reliable than facts: and so when they clash with the facts of perception they are despised, and discredit the truth as well; if a man

who runs down pleasure is once seen to be aiming at it, his inclining towards it is thought to imply that it is all worthy of being aimed at; for most people are not good at drawing distinctions. True arguments seem, then, most useful, not only with a view to knowledge, but with a view to life also; for since they harmonize with the facts they are believed, and so they stimulate those who understand them to live according to them. Enough of such questions; let us proceed to review the opinions that have been expressed about pleasure.

2. Eudoxus thought pleasure was the good because he saw all things, both rational and irrational, aiming at it, and because in all things that which is the object of choice is what is excellent, and that which is most the object of choice the greatest good; thus the fact that all things moved towards the same object indicated that this was for all things the chief good (for each thing, he argued, finds its own good, as it finds its own nourishment); and that which is good for all things and at which all aim was the good. His arguments were credited more because of the excellence of his character than for their own sake; he was thought to be remarkably self-controlled, and therefore it was thought that he was not saying what he did say as a friend of pleasure, but that the facts really were so. He believed that the same conclusion followed no less plainly from a study of the contrary of pleasure; pain was in itself an object of aversion to all things, and therefore its contrary must be similarly an object of choice. And again that is most an object of choice which we choose not because or for the sake of something else, and pleasure is admittedly of this nature; for no one asks to what end he is pleased, thus implying that pleasure is in itself an object of choice. Further, he argued that pleasure when added to any good, e.g. to just or temperate action, makes it more worthy of choice, and that it is only by itself that the good can be increased.

This argument seems to show it to be one of the goods, and no more a good than any other; for every good is more worthy of choice along with another good than taken alone. And so it is by an argument of this kind that Plato proves the good not to be pleasure; he argues that the pleasant life is more desirable with wisdom than without, and that if the mixture is better, pleasure is not the good; for the good cannot become more desirable by the addition of anything to it. Now it is clear that nothing else, any more than pleasure, can be the good if it is made more desirable by the addition of any of the things that are good in themselves. What, then, is there that satisfies this criterion, which at the same time we can participate in? It is something of this sort that we are looking for. Those who object that that at which all things aim is not necessarily good are, we may surmise, talking nonsense. For we say that that which every one thinks really is so; and the man who attacks this belief will hardly have anything more credible to maintain instead. If it is senseless creatures that desire the things in question, there might be something in what they say; but if intelligent creatures do so as well, what sense can there be in this view? But perhaps even in inferior creatures there is some natural good stronger than themselves which aims at their proper good.

Nor does the argument about the contrary of pleasure seem to be correct. They say that if pain is an evil it does not follow that pleasure is a good; for evil is opposed to evil and at the same time both are opposed to the neutral state—which is correct enough but does not apply to the things in question. For if both pleasure and pain belonged to the class of evils they ought both to be objects of aversion, while if they belonged to the class of neutrals neither should be an object of aversion or they should both be equally so; but in fact people evidently avoid the one as evil and choose the other as good; that then must be the nature of the opposition between them.

3. Nor again, if pleasure is not a quality, does it follow that it is not a good; for the activities of virtue are not qualities either, nor is happiness. They say, however, that the good is determinate, while pleasure is indeterminate, because it admits of degrees. Now if it is from the feeling of pleasure that they judge thus, the same will be true of justice and the other virtues, in respect of which we plainly say that people of a certain character are so more or less, and act more or less in accordance with these virtues; for people may be more just or brave, and it is possible also to act justly or temperately more or less. But if their judgment is based on the various pleasures, surely they are not stating the real cause, if in fact some pleasures are unmixed and others mixed. Again, just as health

admits of degrees without being indeterminate, why should not pleasure? The same proportion is not found in all things, nor a single proportion always in the same thing, but it may be relaxed and yet persist up to a point, and it may differ in degree. The case of pleasure also may therefore be of this kind.

Again, they assume that the good is perfect while movements and comings into being are imperfect, and try to exhibit pleasure as being a movement and a coming into being. But they do not seem to be right even in saying that it is a movement. For speed and slowness are thought to be proper to every movement, and if a movement, e.g. that of the heavens, has not speed or slowness in itself, it has it in relation to something else; but of pleasure neither of these things is true. For while we may become pleased quickly as we may become angry quickly, we cannot be pleased quickly, not even in relation to some one else, while we can walk, or grow, or the like, quickly. While, then, we can change quickly or slowly into a state of pleasure, we cannot quickly exhibit the activity of pleasure, i.e. be pleased. Again, how can it be a coming into being? It is not thought that any chance thing can come out of any chance thing, but that a thing is dissolved into that out of which it comes into being; and pain would be the destruction of that of which pleasure is the coming into being.

They say, too, that pain is the lack of that which is according to nature, and pleasure is replenishment. But these experiences are bodily. If then pleasure is replenishment with that which is according to nature, that which feels pleasure will be that in which the replenishment takes place, i.e. the body; but that is not thought to be the case; therefore the replenishment is not pleasure, though one would be pleased when replenishment was taking place, just as one would be pained if one was being operated on. This opinion seems to be based on the pains and pleasures connected with nutrition; on the fact that when people have been short of food and have felt pain beforehand they are pleased by the replenishment. But this does not happen with all pleasures; for the pleasures of learning and, among the sensuous pleasures, those of smell, and also many sounds and sights, and memories and hopes, do not presuppose pain. Of what then will these be the coming into being? There has not been lack of anything of which they could be the supplying anew.

In reply to those who bring forward the disgraceful pleasures one may say that these are not pleasant; if things are pleasant to people of vicious constitution, we must not suppose that they are also pleasant to others than these, just as we do not reason so about the things that are wholesome or sweet or bitter to sick people, or ascribe whiteness to the things that seem white to those suffering from a disease of the eye. Or one might answer thus—that the pleasures are desirable, but not from these sources, as wealth is desirable, but not as the reward of betrayal, and health, but not at the cost of eating anything and everything. Or perhaps pleasures differ in kind; for those derived from noble sources are different from those derived from base sources, and one cannot the pleasure of the just man without being just, nor that of the musical man without being musical, and so on.

The fact, too, that a friend is different from a flatterer seems to make it plain that pleasure is not a good or that pleasures are different in kind; for the one is thought to consort with us with a view to the good, the other with a view to our pleasure, and the one is reproached for his conduct while the other is praised on the ground that he consorts with us for different ends. And no one would choose to live with the intellect of a child throughout his life, however much he were to be pleased at the things that children are pleased at, nor to get enjoyment by doing some most disgraceful deed, though he were never to feel any pain in consequence. And there are many things we should be keen about even if they brought no pleasure, e.g. seeing, remembering, knowing, possessing the virtues. If pleasures necessarily do accompany these, that makes no odds; we should choose these even if no pleasure resulted. It seems to be clear, then, that neither is pleasure the good nor is all pleasure desirable, and that some pleasures are desirable in themselves, differing in kind or in their sources from the others. So much for the things that are said about pleasure and pain.

Chapter 11

ABILITY, DISABILITY, AND DISCRIMINATION: CHEERLEADERS AND GOLF CARTS

At least two features of Aristotle's political theory fit uncomfortably with modern sensibilities. One is the idea that thinking about justice and rights requires us to determine the telos, or purpose, or essential nature of the social practice in question. Another is the idea that debates about justice are, at least in part, debates about the allocation of honor. But contemporary controversies over disability and discrimination suggest that Aristotle's approach may not be as foreign as it seems at first glance.

Consider, for example, the debate about whether a golfer with a congenital leg disease had a right to use a golf cart in professional golf tournaments. The case found its way to the U.S. Supreme Court, where the justices disagreed. Notice how the disagreement involved competing views about whether walking the course is essential to the game of golf. Notice too the strong convictions that the case called forth from other professional golfers. To what extent does the debate about the golf cart call into question the athletic nature of golf, and the honor due those who excel at it?

A "SAFETY" BLITZ: TEXAS CHEERLEADER LOSES STATUS AFTER OTHERS' PARENTS COMPLAIN

Sue Anne Pressley

ANDREWS, Tex.—In this West Texas, football-crazy town, many young girls still long to be high school cheerleaders, reigning happily over the star-lit Friday night games, and Callie Smartt was always one of them. It made no difference to her that she was born with cerebral palsy and moved about in a wheelchair. She had plenty of school spirit to go around.

Last year, at Andrews High School, her dream came true: She was a freshman cheerleader. The fans seemed to delight in her. The football players said they loved to see her dazzling smile. And then last spring, at the end of the school sports season,

Smartt was abruptly kicked off the squad. Safety reasons, she was told.

Shocked and hurt, the 15-year-old began crying and couldn't stop. Her mother had to pick her up at school, and it took hours to calm her down.

"I hate people treating me like I'm a baby," Smartt said, making a face. "No one makes fun of me at school or on the field. They always yell, 'Go, Callie!' "

Smartt was relegated this fall to honorary cheerleader on the junior varsity team, and her activities have been sharply curtailed. She is no longer allowed to cheer at away games, no longer allowed to participate in cheerleading fund-raisers, no longer allowed to wheel her chair up and down the sidelines at games.

What's more, she has been told that the honorary cheerleading position is being abolished, and that if she wants to continue, she will have to try out next spring just like anyone else—a rigorous routine involving splits and tumbles that she could never master.

School officials imposed the new strictures at the urging of some of the other cheerleaders and their parents, several of whom appear to resent the extra attention being lavished on Smartt. All this is enough to make Fonda Smartt, Callie's mother, question the critics' motives and the exalted status of cheerleading in this remote oil-field town of 10,000.

After consulting with a state agency, she has vowed to fight for "what is right" for her daughter.

"I think it's just—I don't know what to call it—a big mix-up," said Fonda Smartt, 43, a bookkeeper and divorced mother of four. "I think maybe people have forgotten—especially in a little town maybe, you've got a group that runs things, they forget they're not God—that there are laws supporting people like Callie. She has every right to be there. If she's an inconvenience for somebody, we can fix it. But I don't think that's what it is."

Andrews, about 35 miles north of Midland in a seemingly endless expanse of pasture and oil pumps, pays high tribute to the Andrews High School Mustangs. As many as 4,000 people from the town and the surrounding countryside attend the home games, and the allegiance is obvious in the many town businesses that use the team name (Mustang Lumber, Mustang Printing, Mustang Video). The marquee outside the Sonic Drive-In regularly honors the Mustang Player of the Week.

During the freshman games last year, Callie, dressed in an Andrews High T-shirt and a black cheerleading skirt, wheeled up and down the sidelines in her chair—waving a set of black-and-gold pompoms and shouting the cheers along with the other squad members.

Callie is a familiar and active figure in town, earning the nickname "Hot Rod" for the speed and skill with which she maneuvers her wheelchair. Never one to get discouraged, she belongs to the school choir and the art club and, in 10 busy years in 4-H, has won dozens of awards for activities such as baking and pig-raising. An "A" and "B" student, she has often amazed her mother with her daring—she proudly lists bungee-jumping as one of her accomplishments. And on Friday and Saturday nights, like any teenager, she can be found at the mall in Odessa or cruising the streets of Andrews with a carload of friends.

Peter Francis, a local businessman whose daughter, Jennifer, is the head cheerleader on the JV team, has led the opposition to Callie's participation on the squad. He said last week that his stance has "nothing to do with the young girl. She's smart, she's intelligent, there's always a smile on her face, she's a fine young lady. It's not her at all, period. There's the safety factor... and then the issue of a baby-sitting service—I don't like to call it that.

"In my opinion," said Francis, who emphasized that he was speaking as a parent and not as a school board member, "she was chosen as an honorary cheerleader from a sponsor who took it upon herself to do that. The girls did not have any voice in it, as far as voting to see if they wanted her. I don't think there is a position as honorary cheerleader, but they made one, and that's fine."

On the sidelines, he said, "if a player comes flying off or a ball is overthrown, a cheerleader can be hit as well as a handicapped girl sitting in a wheelchair. The cheerleader girls who aren't handicapped could move out of the way a little faster. I raised the issue, what about the safety of this person?"

But Fonda Smartt wonders why the safety issue suddenly surfaced, because Callie was never hurt or threatened during her freshman year of cheerleading. Smartt noted that an injured football player was recently carried away by ambulance and that other cheerleaders have suffered sprained ankles and wrists simply from performing their routines.

But Francis said his daughter, as head cheerleader, carried much of the responsibility for Callie's welfare. "Callie was a situation where we had to make sure everything was being taken care of," he said. "I did help her in and out of vehicles to go to games, to restaurants."

Fonda Smartt countered that even when she was unable to make a game because of work,

Callie was always accompanied by one of her friends and the friend's mother. Nothing, she said, makes Callie angrier than to be characterized as a burden to others.

Schools Superintendent Ervin Huddleston justified the decision by saying: "All students in the Andrews Independent School District may participate in any activity to the extent that they are capable. As a school district, one of our paramount concerns is always the safety of the student."

As she grew increasingly upset by the situation, Fonda Smartt consulted with Stephon Breedlove, an attorney with Advocacy Inc. in Lubbock, a federally funded state agency that fights for the rights of the disabled. Breedlove is concerned that the school system may be discouraging an enthusiastic and able student.

"At first it seems they were making an extra effort to include Callie, and now it seems they're making an extra effort to exclude her," said Breedlove, who is blind and competed as a wrestler in high school and college. "I think safety reasons may be based more on stereotypes and general fears, instead of someone actually doing a well-thought-out analysis of what would be safe for her as compared to the other girls. People with disabilities are not barred by any law from taking risks.

"I have no idea," he added, "why they would bar her from doing a fund-raiser. You usually want kids to try and be involved."

Perhaps, Breedlove suggested, the cheerleading program is taken a little too seriously at Andrews High. "Maybe only the few, the proud, can do it," he said dryly.

Undaunted for now, Callie joked on a recent afternoon about her upcoming tryout for varsity cheerleader. "I can touch my toes, see?" she said, nimbly placing one foot on top of the other as she sat in her wheelchair.

"That was good, man, that deserves a double," said her best friend Jayne Reid, 17, as Jayne and Callie exchanged high-fives—twice.

Moments later Jayne expertly packed Callie's chair in her car, helped her friend into the seat, buckled her in, and the two took off for an afternoon at the mall. "Chasing boys," Callie said with a grin.

Honor and Resentment

Michael J. Sandel

The politics of the ancients was about virtue and honor, but we moderns are concerned with fairness and rights. There is some truth in this familiar adage, but only to a point. On the surface, our political debates make little mention of honor, a seemingly quaint concern best suited to a status-ridden world of chivalry and duels. Not far beneath the surface, however, some of our fiercest debates about fairness and rights reflect deep disagreement about the proper basis of social esteem.

Consider the fuss over Callie Smartt, a 15 year-old cheerleader at a high school in West Texas. Last year she was a popular freshman cheerleader, despite the fact that she has cerebral palsy and moves about in a wheelchair. As Sue Anne Pressley reported recently in *The Washington Post*, "She had plenty of school spirit to go around. . . .

The fans seemed to delight in her. The football players said they loved to see her dazzling smile." But at the end of the season, Callie was kicked off the squad.

Earlier this fall, she was relegated to the status of honorary cheerleader; now, even that position is being abolished. At the urging of some other cheerleaders and their parents, school officials have told Callie that, to make the squad next year, she will have to try out like anyone else, in a rigorous routine involving splits and tumbles.

The head cheerleader's father opposes Callie's participation. He claims he is only concerned for Callie's safety. If a player comes flying off the field, he worries, "the cheerleader girls who aren't handicapped could move out of the way a little faster." But Callie has never been hurt cheerleading. Her mother suspects the opposition may be motivated by resentment of the acclaim Callie has received.

But what kind of resentment might motivate the head cheerleader's father? It cannot be fear that Callie's inclusion deprives his daughter of a place; she is already on the team. Nor is it the simple envy he might feel toward a girl who outshines his daughter at tumbles and splits, which Callie, of course, does not. The resentment more likely reflects the conviction that Callie is being accorded an honor she does not deserve, in a way that mocks the pride he takes in his daughter's cheerleading prowess. If great cheerleading is something that can be done from a wheelchair, then what becomes of the honor accorded those who excel at tumbles and splits? Indignation at misplaced honor is a moral sentiment that figures prominently in our politics, complicating and sometimes inflaming arguments about fairness and rights.

Should Callie be allowed to continue on the team? Some would answer by invoking the right of nondiscrimination: provided she can perform well in the role, Callie should not be excluded from cheerleading simply because, through no fault of her own, she lacks the physical ability to perform gymnastic routines. But the nondiscrimination argument begs the question at the heart of the controversy: What does it mean to perform well in the role of cheerleader? This question, in turn, is about the virtues and excellences that the practice of cheerleading honors and rewards. The case for Callie is that, by roaring up and down the sidelines in her wheelchair, waving her pom-poms and motivating the team, she does well what cheerleaders are supposed to do: inspire school spirit.

But if Callie should be a cheerleader because she displays, despite her disability, the virtues appropriate to her role, her claim does pose a certain threat to the honor accorded the other cheerleaders. The gymnastic skills they display no longer appear essential to excellence in cheerleading, only one way among others of rousing the crowd. Ungenerous though he was, the father of the head cheerleader correctly grasped what was at stake. A social practice once taken as fixed in its purpose and in the honors it bestowed was now, thanks to Callie, redefined.

Disputes about the allocation of honor underlie other controversies about fairness and rights.

Consider, for example, the debate over affirmative action in university admissions. Here too, some try to resolve the question by invoking a general argument against discrimination. Advocates of affirmative action argue it is necessary to remedy the effects of discrimination, while opponents maintain that taking race into account amounts to reverse discrimination. Again the nondiscrimination argument begs a crucial question. All admissions policies discriminate on some ground or other. The real issue is, what kind of discrimination is appropriate to the purposes universities serve? This question is contested, not only because it decides how educational opportunities are distributed but also because it determines what virtues universities define as worthy of honor.

If the sole purpose of a university were to promote scholarly excellence and intellectual virtues, then it should admit the students most likely to contribute to these ends. But if another mission of a university is to cultivate leadership for a pluralistic society, then it should seek students likely to advance civic purposes as well as intellectual ones. In a recent court case challenging its affirmative action program, the University of Texas Law School invoked its civic purpose, arguing that its minority admissions program had helped equip black and Mexican-American graduates to serve in the Texas legislature, on the federal bench and even in the president's Cabinet.

Some critics of affirmative action resent the idea that universities should honor qualities other than intellectual ones, for to do so implies that standard meritocratic virtues lack a privileged moral place. If race and ethnicity can be relevant to university admissions, then what becomes of the proud parent's conviction that his daughter is worthy of admission by virtue of her grades and test scores alone? Like the father's pride in his cheerleader daughter's tumbles and splits, it would have to be qualified by the recognition that honor is relative to social institutions, whose purposes are open to argument and revision.

Perhaps the most potent instance of the politics of honor plays itself out in debates about work. One reason many working-class voters despise welfare is not that they begrudge the money it costs but that they resent the message it conveys about what is worthy of honor and reward. Liberals who defend welfare in terms of fairness and rights often miss this point. More than an incentive to elicit effort and skills in socially useful ways, income is a measure of the things we prize. For many who "work hard and play by the rules, " rewarding those who stay at home mocks the effort they expend and the pride they take in the work they do. Their resentment against welfare is not a reason to abandon the needy. But it does suggest that liberals need to articulate more convincingly the notions of virtue and honor that underlie their arguments for fairness and rights.

SORRY, FREE RIDES NOT RIGHT

Bob Ryan

I can't believe I find myself on the side of repression and regression. I can't believe I am lining up with people whose schnozzolas so readily and relentlessly point skyward.

I happen to be one of these people who believe there should be all kinds of hootin' and hollerin' involved in golf. (Tennis, too.) Why should Shaquille O'Neal be forced to stride to the free throw line in an enemy arena accompanied by the sound of 20,000-plus shrieking enemy fans while the entire world must come to a stop when Tiger, Gil Morgan, or Annika Sorenstam lines up a putt or addresses a drive? It has never made any sense to me.

I definitely believe golf should loosen up. It needs to set aside its patrician airs and become more like a real sport.

And yet . . . and yet there is no doubt in my mind that golf should dig in and fight on this Casey Martin business. If you can't walk the course, you can't play; it really is no more complicated than that.

I can admire Casey Martin. I can root for him to succeed in life. But that doesn't mean I think he should be riding a cart on a golf tour. If everyone else does, well, there's nothing to talk about. Until then, I say no.

In the event you've just returned from a vacation in Antarctica, Casey Martin is the 25-year-old golfer—a onetime Stanford roommate of Tiger Woods, interestingly enough—who is afflicted with a congenital circulatory condition in his lower right leg known as Klippel-Trenaunay-Weber syndrome. Said condition makes it very painful for him to walk. He can hit the shots, but in order to be in a position to do so, he must get to the ball with the aid of a golf cart.

Martin has done more than petition the PGA for the use of a cart. He has gone to court, using as his weapon of choice the wide-ranging and much-feared Americans with Disabilities Act, a necessary and well-meaning piece of legislation that, in addition to working to the benefit of its intended constituency, has often terrorized institutions with its rigid and uncompromising interpretation. And as so often happens in our notoriously litigious society, the ADA has also very often been hijacked by people who should be ashamed of themselves for comparing their situations to those of truly disabled people.

I'm not about to suggest that Casey Martin should be ashamed of himself for any reason whatsoever. All he wants is the opportunity to make a living from golf. Wishing for that is his prerogative. But just because he wants it does not mean he is automatically entitled to it, and it certainly does not mean that the courts should compel anyone to give it to him.

Let's reverse it a bit. Suppose Martin were a similarly disabled baseball player who was in possession of superb hand-eye contact and could make great contact with a pitched baseball. The only problem: He couldn't run to first, or any other base. And suppose he decided life would be lovely if he were granted a surrogate runner, right out of the batter's box. And suppose he was adamant enough in his stance to invoke this very same ADA in pursuit of his goal. It wouldn't surprise me in the slightest if his attorneys could locate a judge who would rule against organized baseball and mandate a surrogate runner for Martin.

Preposterous? I don't think so. We've all seen crazier legal decisions in the last quarter-century. As sympathetic a figure as Martin is, we've got to draw the line. He knew what golf was all about when he took up the sport. Did he assume from the very beginning that someday he could force the PGA to see things his way, in the event he got proficient enough as a shotmaker to consider becoming a member? I don't know the answer, but if he did, he didn't have that right. He talks about pursuing his dream. That dream was unrealistic to begin with.

The eternal debate about whether golf is a sport—whatever that is—as opposed to a game—whatever that is—will rage well into the next century, I am sure. The fact is that there are times when the physical act of walking the course does become a factor in performance, and a man who could slip into a cart and ride to his next destination on those occasions would have an advantage. Period.

Martin can certainly play—his way. He won a Nike tournament at the outset of the controversy, and that means he has the shots. But the issue here is fairness. In this case, the word applies both ways. Life was certainly not fair to Casey Martin when he was born with this terrible condition. But that is his life, and it's not as if he had been left unequipped to deal with life on a basis that does not include playing on the PGA Tour. This man got into Stanford. The Man Upstairs may not have given him much of a right leg, but He definitely gave him a superior brain. I'm sure he can use it to earn a living.

The bothersome thing here is his sense of entitlement. I want it; therefore, I should have it. And if I can't get it, maybe the courts will get it for me. Aren't we all tired of this?

This is no issue for the courts. The PGA has a rule, and that rule says you walk the course. The PGA has to fight this. There is more at stake here than the fate of one bright and basically charming young man from Stanford. The Rolling Stones spelled it out for us a long time ago: You Can't Always Get What You Want.

Nor should you.

Keep the PGA on Foot

Tom Kite

AUSTIN, Tex.—A Federal court hearing is scheduled for today to decide whether a golfer afflicted with a circulatory disease should be allowed to use a motorized cart to compete in PGA Tour and Nike Tour events. The golfer, Casey Martin, a very talented young player, argues that, under the Americans With Disabilities Act, he should be exempt from the rule that players must walk the course.

From what I understand, Casey Martin is a fine young gentleman. I have not met him personally or played golf with him, and I do not know the finer points of the law. But I do know something about competitive golf, having played the sport for more than 25 years on the PGA Tour.

It seems to me that those who support Casey Martin's right to use a cart are ignoring the fact that we are talking about a competitive sport. We aren't talking about allowing someone to use a cart for a casual game of golf on a weekend; we are talking about an athletic event. And anyone who doesn't think professional golf is an athletic sport simply hasn't been there or done that.

Two weeks ago, Emmitt Smith and Marcus Allen, two of the best football running backs of all time and two excellent athletes, played in my group at the Bob Hope Chrysler Classic. As we neared the end of our fourth consecutive competitive round, Marcus said to me: "Man, I am beat. I've used muscles I don't normally use, and I'm just beat." Emmitt agreed, saying he was also tired. And we were playing one of the easiest walking courses on the Tour in ideal weather conditions.

Play 36 holes in the heat of the Ryder Cup competition, or walk up the 17th hole at Castle Pines Golf Club in Colorado, or play 18 holes at the Tournament Players Club at Southwind in Memphis in July—and then tell me that physical conditioning isn't part of competitive golf.

How much of an advantage is there in having a cart? It would vary from one week to another and one course to another, so there is no way to keep a level playing field without changing the fundamental nature of the competition.

I have to work harder every year to stay competitive, but I would not think about asking for a cart. No one could have benefited more from using a cart than Ben Hogan, who won the United States Open in 1950 after recovering from injuries sustained in a car crash, even though every step he took was a painful ordeal. Hogan is considered perhaps the greatest shotmaker the game has ever seen, but he knew that shotmaking is only part of the game.

The mental, physical and emotional aspects of the sport are closely linked. Fatigue can cause loss of concentration, which can cause poor shot selection, which can cause poor shotmaking, which can cause stress, which can cause more loss of concentration. I have seen a lot of tournaments over the years that were won or lost on the last few holes, when you have to be sharp mentally, physically and emotionally.

No matter how much some may be rooting for Casey Martin and how we sympathize with his disability, we cannot change an integral aspect of our sport for any one person.

PGA TOUR, INC., *v.* CASEY MARTIN

Supreme Court of the United States
May 29, 2001

JUSTICE STEVENS delivered the opinion of the Court.

This case raises two questions concerning the application of the Americans with Disabilities Act of 1990, Stat. 328, 42 U. S. C. §12101 *et seq.*, to a gifted athlete first, whether the Act protects access to professional golf tournaments by a qualified entrant with a disability: and second, whether a disabled contestant may be denied the use of a golf cart because it would "fundamentally alter the nature" of the tournaments, §12182(b) (2)(A) (ii). to allow him to ride when all other contestants must walk.

At trial, petitioner did not contest the conclusion that Martin has a disability covered by the ADA, or the fact "that his disability prevents him from walking the course during a round of golf." 994 F.Supp. 1242, 1244 (Ore. 1998). Rather, petitioner asserted that the condition of walking is a substantive rule of competition, and that waiving it as to any individual for any reason would fundamentally alter the nature of the competition. Petitioner's evidence included the testimony of a number of experts, among them some of the greatest golfers in history. Arnold

Palmer,[1] Jack Nicklaus,[2] and Ken Venturi[3] explained that fatigue can be a critical factor in a tournament, particularly on the last day when psychological pressure is at a maximum. Their testimony makes it clear that, in their view, permis-

1. "And fatigue is one of the factors that can cause a golfer at the PGA Tour level to lose one stroke or more?
"A. Oh, it is. And it has happened.
"Q. And can one stroke be the difference between winning and not winning a tournament at the PGA Tour level?
"A. As I said, I've lost a few national opens by one stroke." App. 177.
2. "Q. Mr. Nicklaus, what is your understanding of the reason why in these competitive events ... that competitors are required to walk the course?
"A. Well, in my opinion, physical fitness and fatigue are part of the game of golf." *Id.*, at 190.
3. "Q. So are you telling the court that this fatigue factor tends to accumulate over the course of the four days of the tournament?
"A. Oh definitely. There's no doubt.
"Q. Does this fatigue factor that you've talked about, Mr. Venturi, affect the manner in which you-you perform as a professional out on the golf course?
"A. Oh, there's no doubt, again, but that, that fatigue does play a big part. It will influence your game. It will influence your shot-making. It will influence your decisions." *Id.*, at 236–237.

sion to use a cart might well give some players a competitive advantage over other players who must walk. They did not, however, express any opinion on whether a cart would give Martin such an advantage.[4]

Rejecting petitioner's argument that an individualized inquiry into the necessity of the walking rule in Martin's case would be inappropriate, the District Court stated that it had "the independent duty to inquire into the purpose of the rule at issue, and to ascertain whether there can be a reasonable modification made to accommodate plaintiff without frustrating the purpose of the rule" and thereby fundamentally altering the nature of petitioner's tournaments. *Id.*, at 1246. The judge found that the purpose of the rule was to inject fatigue into the skill of shot-making, but that the fatigue injected "by walking the course cannot be deemed significant under normal circumstances." *Id.*, at 1250. Furthermore, Martin presented evidence, and the judge found, that even with the use of a cart, Martin must walk over a mile during an 18-hole round, and that the fatigue he suffers from coping with his disability is "undeniably greater" than the fatigue his able-bodied competitors endure from walking the course. *Id.*, at 1251. As the judge observed:

> [P]laintiff is in significant pain when he walks, and even when he is getting in and out of the cart. With each step, he is at risk of fracturing his tibia and hemorrhaging. The other golfers have to endure the psychological stress of competition as part of their fatigue; Martin has the same stress plus the added stress of pain and risk of serious injury. As he put it, he would gladly trade the cart for a good leg. To perceive that the cart puts him—with

his condition—at a competitive advantage is a gross distortion of reality. *Id.*, at 1251–1252.

As a result, the judge concluded that it would "not fundamentally alter the nature of the PGA Tour's game to accommodate him with a cart." *Id.*, at 1252. The judge accordingly entered a permanent injunction requiring petitioner to permit Martin to use a cart in tour and qualifying events.

As we have noted, 42 U. S. C. §12182(a) sets forth Title III's general rule prohibiting public accommodations from discriminating against individuals because of their disabilities. The question whether petitioner has violated that rule depends on a proper construction of the term "discrimination," which is defined by Title III to include:

> a failure to make reasonable modifications in policies, practices, or procedures, when such modifications are necessary to afford such goods, services, facilities, privileges, advantages, or accommodations to individuals with disabilities, *unless the entity can demonstrate that making such modifications would fundamentally alter the nature* of such goods, services, facilities, privileges, advantages, or accommodations. §12182(b)(2)(A)(ii) (emphasis added).

Petitioner does not contest that a golf cart is a reasonable modification that is necessary if Martin is to play in its tournaments. Martin's claim thus differs from one that might be asserted by players with less serious afflictions that make walking the course uncomfortable or difficult, but not beyond their capacity. In such cases, an accommodation might be reasonable but not necessary. In this case, however, the narrow dispute is whether allowing Martin to use a golf cart, despite the walking requirement that applies to the PGA TOUR, the NIKE TOUR, and the third stage of the Q-School, is a modification that would "fundamentally alter the nature" of those events.

In theory, a modification of petitioner's golf tournaments might constitute a fundamental alteration in two different ways. It might alter such an essential aspect of the game of golf that it would be unacceptable even if it affected all competitors equally; changing the diameter of the hole from three to six inches might be such a modification.[5]

---

4. "Q. Based on your experience, do you believe that it would fundamentally alter the nature of the competition on the PGA Tour and the Nike Tour if competitors in those events were permitted to use golf carts?
"A. Yes, absolutely.
"Q. Why do you say so, sir?
"A. It would—it would take away the fatigue factor in many ways. It would—it would change the game.
"Q. Now, when you say that the use of carts takes away the fatigue factor, it would be an aid, et cetera, again, as I understand it, you are not testifying now about the plaintiff. You are just talking in general terms?
"A. Yes, sir." *Id.*, at 238. See also *id.*, at 177–178 (Palmer); *id.*, at 191 (Nicklaus).

5. Cf. *post*, at 11 (Scalia, J., dissenting) ("I suppose there is some point at which the rules of a well-known game are changed to such a degree that no reasonable person would call it the same game").

Alternatively, a less significant change that has only a peripheral impact on the game itself might nevertheless give a disabled player, in addition to access to the competition as required by Title III, an advantage over others and, for that reason, fundamentally alter the character of the competition.[6] We are not persuaded that a waiver of the walking rule for Martin would work a fundamental alteration in either sense.[7]

As an initial matter, we observe that the use of carts is not itself inconsistent with the fundamental character of the game of golf. From early on, the essence of the game has been shot-making–using clubs to cause a ball to progress from the teeing ground to a hole some distance away with as few strokes as possible.[8] That essential aspect of the game is still reflected in the very first of the Rules of Golf, which declares: "The

Game of Golf consists in playing a ball from the *teeing ground* into the hole by a *stroke* or successive strokes in accordance with the rules." Rule 1–1, Rules of Golf, App. 104 (italics in original). Over the years, there have been many changes in the players' equipment, in golf course design, in the Rules of Golf, and in the method of transporting clubs from hole to hole.[9] Originally, so few clubs were used that each player could carry them without a bag. Then came golf bags, caddies, carts that were pulled by hand, and eventually motorized carts that carried players as well as clubs. "Golf carts started appearing with increasing regularity on American golf courses in the 1950's. Today they are everywhere. And they are encouraged. For one thing, they often speed up play, and

---

6. Accord, *post*, at 13 (SCALIA, J., dissenting) ("The statute seeks to assure that a disabled person's disability will not deny him *equal access* to (among other things) competitive sporting events—not that his disability will not deny him an *equal chance to win* competitive sporting events").

7. As we have noted, the statute contemplates three inquiries: whether the requested modification is "reasonable," whether it is "necessary" for the disabled individual, and whether it would "fundamentally alter the nature of" the competition. 42 U. S. C. §12182(b)(2)(A)(ii). Whether one question should be decided before the others likely will vary from case to case, for in logic there seems to be no necessary priority among the three. In routine cases, the fundamental alteration inquiry may end with the question whether a rule is essential. Alternatively, the specifics of the claimed disability might be examined within the context of what is a reasonable or necessary modification. Given the concession by petitioner that the modification sought is reasonable and necessary, and given petitioner's reliance on the fundamental alteration provision, we have no occasion to consider the alternatives in this case.

8. Golf is an ancient game, tracing its ancestry to Scotland, and played by such notables as Mary Queen of Scots and her son James. That shot-making has been the essence of golf since early in its history is reflected in the first recorded rules of golf, published in 1744 for a tournament on the Leith Links in Edinburgh:
   "*Articles & Laws in Playing at Golf*

   "1. You must Tee your Ball, within a Club's length of the [previous] Hole.
   "2. Your Tee must be upon the Ground.
   "3. You are not to change the Ball which you Strike off the Tee.
   "4. You are not to remove, Stones, Bones or any Break Club for the sake of playing your Ball, Except upon

the fair Green/& that only/within a Club's length of your Ball.
   "5. If your Ball comes among Water, or any Watery Filth, you are at liberty to take out your Ball & bringing it behind the hazard and Teeing it, you may play it with any Club and allow your Adversary a Stroke for so getting out your Ball.
   "6. If your Balls be found anywhere touching one another, You are to lift the first Ball, till you play the last.
   "7. At Holling, you are to play your Ball honestly for the Hole, and, not to play upon your Adversary's Ball, not lying in your way to the Hole.
   "8. If you should lose your Ball, by its being taken up, or any other way, you are to go back to the Spot, where you struck last & drop another Ball, And allow your Adversary a Stroke for the misfortune.
   "9. No man at Holling his Ball, is to be allowed, to mark his way to the Hole with his Club or, any thing else.
   "10. If a Ball be stopp'd by any person, Horse, Dog, or any thing else, The Ball so stop'd must be play'd where it lyes.
   "11. If you draw your Club, in order to Strike & proceed so far in the Stroke, as to be bringing down your Club; If then, your Club shall break, in, any way, it is to be Accounted a Stroke.
   "12. He, whose Ball lyes farthest from the Hole is obliged to play first.
   "13. Neither Trench, Ditch, or Dyke, made for the preservation of the Links, nor the Scholar's Holes or the Soldier's Lines, Shall be accounted a Hazard; But the Ball is to be taken out/Teed/and play'd with any Iron Club." K. Chapman, Rules of the Green 14–15 (1997).

9. See generally M. Campbell, *The Random House International Encyclopedia of Golf* 9–57 (1991): *Golf Magazine's Encyclopedia of Golf* 1–17 (2d ed. 1993).

for another, they are great revenue producers."[10] There is nothing in the Rules of Golf that either forbids the use of carts, or penalizes a player for using a cart. That set of rules, as we have observed, is widely accepted in both the amateur and professional golf world as the rules of the game.[11] The walking rule that is contained in petitioner's hard cards, based on an optional condition buried in an appendix to the Rules of Golf,[12] is not an essential attribute of the game itself.

Indeed, the walking rule is not an indispensable feature of tournament golf either. As already mentioned, petitioner permits golf carts to be used in the SENIOR PGA TOUR, the open qualifying events for petitioner's tournaments, the first two stages of the Q-School, and, until 1997, the third stage of the Q-School as well. See *supra*, at 2–4. Moreover, petitioner allows the use of carts during certain tournament rounds in both the PGA TOUR and the NIKE TOUR. See *supra*, at 4, and n. 6. In addition, although the USGA enforces a walking rule in most of the tournaments that it sponsors, it permits carts in the Senior Amateur and the Senior Women's Amateur championships.[13]

Petitioner, however, distinguishes the game of golf as it is generally played from the game that it sponsors in the PGA TOUR, NIKE TOUR, and (at least recently) the last stage of the Q-School—golf at the "highest level." According to petitioner, "[t]he goal of the highest-level competitive athletics is to assess and compare the performance of different competitors, a task that is meaningful only if the competitors are subject to identical substantive rules."[14] The waiver of any possibly "outcome-affecting" rule for a contestant would violate this principle and therefore, in petitioner's view, fundamentally alter the nature of the highest level athletic event.[15] The walking rule is one such rule, petitioner submits, because its purpose is "to inject the element of fatigue into the skill of shot-making,[16] and thus its effect may be the critical loss of a stroke. As a consequence, the reasonable modification Martin seeks would fundamentally alter the nature of petitioner's highest level tournaments even if he were the only person in the world who has both the talent to compete in those elite events and a disability sufficiently serious that he cannot do so without using a cart.

The force of petitioner's argument is, first of all, mitigated by the fact that golf is a game in which it is impossible to guarantee that all competitors will play under exactly the same conditions or that an individual's ability will be the sole determinant of the outcome. For example, changes in the weather may produce harder greens and more head winds for the tournament leader than for his closest pursuers. A lucky bounce may save a shot or two.[17] Whether such happenstance events are more or less probable than the likelihood that a golfer afflicted with Klippel-Trenaunay-Weber Syndrome would one day qualify for the NIKE TOUR and PGA TOUR, they at least demonstrate that pure chance may have a greater impact on the outcome of elite golf tournaments

10. *Olinger v. United States Golf Assn.*, 205 F. 3d 1001, 1003 (CA7 2000).
11. On this point, the testimony of the immediate past president of the USGA (and one of petitioner's witnesses at trial) is illuminating:
"Tell the court, if you would, Ms. Bell, who it is that plays under these Rules of Golf . . .?
"A. Well, these are the rules of the game, so all golfers. These are for all people who play the game.
"Q. So the two amateurs that go out on the weekend to play golf together would—would play by the Rules of Golf?
"A. We certainly hope so.
"Q. Or a tournament that is conducted at a private country club for its members, is it your understanding that that would typically be conducted under the Rules of Golf?
"A. Well, that's—that's right. If you want to play golf, you need to play by these rules." App. 239.
12. See n. 3, *supra*.
13. Furthermore, the USGA's handicap system, used by over 4 million amateur golfers playing on courses rated by the USGA, does not consider whether a player walks or rides in a cart, or whether she uses a caddy or carries her own clubs. Rather, a player's handicap is determined by a formula that takes into account the average score in the 10 best of her 20 most recent rounds, the difficulty of the different courses played, and whether or not a round was a "tournament" event.

14. Brief for Petitioner 13.
15. *Id.*, at 37.
16. 994 F. Supp., at 1250.
17. A drive by Andrew Magee earlier this year produced a result that he neither intended nor expected. While the foursome ahead of him was still on the green, he teed off on a 322-yard par four. To his surprise, the ball not only reached the green, but also bounced off Tom Byrum's putter and into the hole. Davis, Magee Gets Ace on Par-4, Ariz. Republic, Jan. 26 2001, p. C16, 2001 WL 8510792.

than the fatigue resulting from the enforcement of the walking rule.

Further, the factual basis of petitioner's argument is undermined by the District Court's finding that the fatigue from walking during one of petitioner's 4-day tournaments cannot be deemed significant. The District Court credited the testimony of a professor in physiology and expert on fatigue, who calculated the calories expended in walking a golf course (about five miles) to be approximately 500 calories—"nutritionally . . . less than a Big Mac." 994 F. Supp., at 1250. What is more, that energy is expended over a 5-hour period, during which golfers have numerous intervals for rest and refreshment. In fact, the expert concluded, because golf is a low intensity activity, fatigue from the game is primarily a psychological phenomenon in which stress and motivation are the key ingredients. And even under conditions of severe heat and humidity, the critical factor in fatigue is fluid loss rather than exercise from walking.

To be sure, the waiver of an essential rule of competition for anyone would fundamentally alter the nature of petitioner's tournaments. As we have demonstrated, however, the walking rule is at best peripheral to the nature of petitioner's athletic events, and thus it might be waived in individual cases without working a fundamental alteration.

Under the ADA's basic requirement that the need of a disabled person be evaluated on an individual basis, we have no doubt that allowing Martin to use a golf cart would not fundamentally alter the nature of petitioner's tournaments. As we have discussed, the purpose of the walking rule is to subject players to fatigue, which in turn may influence the outcome of tournaments. Even if the rule does serve that purpose, it is an uncontested finding of the District Court that Martin "easily endures greater fatigue even with a cart than his able-bodied competitors do by walking." 994 F. Supp., at 1252. The purpose of the walking rule is therefore not compromised in the slightest by allowing Martin to use a cart. A modification that provides an exception to a peripheral tournament rule without impairing its purpose cannot be said to "fundamentally alter" the tournament. What it can be said to do, on the other hand, is to allow Martin the chance to qualify for and compete in the athletic events petitioner offers to those members of the public who

have the skill and desire to enter. That is exactly what the ADA requires. As a result, Martin's request for a waiver of the walking rule should have been granted.

JUSTICE SCALIA, with whom JUSTICE THOMAS joins, dissenting

In my view today's opinion exercises a benevolent compassion that the law does not place it within our power to impose. The judgment distorts the text of Title III, the structure of the ADA, and common sense. I respectfully dissent.

The Court attacks this "fundamental alteration" analysis by asking two questions: first, whether the "essence" or an "essential aspect" of the sport of golf has been altered; and second, whether the change, even if not essential to the game, would give the disabled player an advantage over others and thereby "fundamentally alter the character of the competition." *Ante*, at 20-21. It answers no to both.

Before considering the Court's answer to the first question, it is worth pointing out that the assumption which underlies that question is false. Nowhere is it writ that PGA TOUR golf must be classic "essential" golf. Why cannot the PGA TOUR, if it wishes, promote a new game, with distinctive rules (much as the American League promotes a game of baseball in which the pitcher's turn at the plate can be taken by a "designated hitter")? If members of the public do not like the new rules—if they feel that these rules do not truly test the individual's skill at "real golf" (or the team's skill at "real baseball") they can withdraw their patronage. But the rules are the rules. They are (as in all games) entirely arbitrary, and there is no basis on which anyone—not even the Supreme Court of the United States—can pronounce one or another of them to be "nonessential" if the rulemaker (here the PGA TOUR) deems it to be essential.

If one assumes, however, that the PGA TOUR has some legal obligation to play classic, Platonic golf—and if one assumes the correctness of all the other wrong turns the Court has made to get to this point—then we Justices must confront what is indeed an awesome responsibility. It has been rendered the solemn duty of the Supreme Court of the United States, laid upon it by Congress in pursuance of the Federal Government's power "[t]o regulate Commerce with foreign Nations, and among the several States," U. S. Const., Art. I. §8, cl. 3, to decide What Is Golf. I am sure that the Framers of the Constitution, aware of the 1457 edict of King James II of Scotland prohibiting golf because it interfered with the practice of archery, fully expected that sooner or later the paths of golf and government, the law and the links, would once again cross, and that the judges of this august Court would some day have to wrestle with that age-old juris-prudential question, for which their years of study in the law have so well prepared them: Is someone riding around a golf course from shot to shot *really* a golfer? The answer, we learn, is yes. The Court ultimately concludes, and it will henceforth be the Law of the Land, that walking is not a "fundamental" aspect of golf.

Either out of humility or out of self-respect (one or the other) the Court should decline to answer this incredibly difficult and incredibly silly question. To say that something is "essential" is ordinarily to say that it is necessary to the achievement of a certain object. But since it is the very nature of a game to have no object except amusement (that is what distinguishes games from productive activity), it is quite impossible to say that any of a game's arbitrary rules is "essential." Eighteen-hole golf courses, 10-foot-high basketball hoops, 90-foot baselines, 100-yard football fields—all are arbitrary and none is essential. The only support for any of them is tradition and (in more modern times) insistence by what has come to be regarded as the ruling body of the sport—both of which factors support the PGA TOUR's position in the present case. (Many, indeed, consider walking to be *the central feature* of the game of golf—hence Mark Twain's classic criticism of the sport: "a good walk spoiled.") I suppose there is some point at which the rules of a well-known game are changed to such a degree that no reasonable person would call it the same game. If the PGA TOUR competitors were required to dribble a large, inflated ball and put it through a round hoop, the game could no longer reasonably be called golf. But this criterion—destroying recognizability as the same generic game—is surely not the test of "essentialness" or "fundamentalness" that the Court applies, since it apparently thinks that merely changing the diam-

eter of the *cup* might "fundamentally alter" the game of golf, *ante*, at 20.

Having concluded that dispensing with the walking rule would not violate federal-Platonic "golf" (and, implicitly, that it is federal-Platonic golf, and no other, that the PGA TOUR can insist upon) the Court moves on to the second part of its test: the competitive effects of waiving this non-essential rule. In this part of its analysis, the Court first finds that the effects of the change are "mitigated" by the fact that in the game of golf weather, a "lucky bounce," and "pure chance" provide different conditions for each competitor and individual ability may not "be the sole determinant of the outcome." *Ante*, at 25. I guess that is why those who follow professional golfing consider Jack Nicklaus the *luckiest* golfer of all time, only to be challenged of late by the phenomenal *luck* of Tiger Woods. The Court's empiricism is unpersuasive. "Pure chance" is randomly distributed among the players, but allowing respondent to use a cart gives him a "lucky" break every time he plays. Pure chance also only matters at the margin—a stroke here or there: the cart substantially improves this respondent's competitive prospects beyond a couple of strokes. But even granting that there are significant nonhuman variables affecting competition, that fact does not justify adding another variable that always favors one player.

In an apparent effort to make its opinion as narrow as possible, the Court relies upon the District Court's finding that even with a cart, respondent will be at least as fatigued as everyone else. *Ante*, at 28. This, the Court says, *proves* that competition will not be affected. Far from thinking that reliance on this finding cabins the effect of today's opinion, I think it will prove to be its most expansive and destructive feature. Because step one of the Court's two-part inquiry into whether a requested change in a sport will "fundamentally alter [its] nature," § 12182(b)(2)(A)(ii), consists of an utterly unprincipled ontology of sports (pursuant to which the Court is not even sure whether golf's "essence" requires a 3-inch hole), there is every reason to think that in future cases involving requests for special treatment by would-be athletes the second step of the analysis will be determinative. In resolving that second step—determining whether waiver of the "nonessential" rule will have an impermissible "competitive effect"—by measuring the athletic capacity of the requesting individual, and asking whether the special dispensation would do no more than place him on a par (so to speak) with other competitors, the Court guarantees that future cases of this sort will have to be decided on the basis of individualized factual findings. Which means that future cases of this sort will be numerous, and a rich source of lucrative litigation. One can envision the parents of a Little League player with attention deficit disorder trying to convince a judge that their son's disability makes it at least 25% more difficult to hit a pitched ball. (If they are successful, the only thing that could prevent a court order giving the kid four strikes would be a judicial determination that, in baseball, three strikes are metaphysically necessary, which is quite absurd.)

The statute, of course, provides no basis for this individualized analysis that is the Court's last step on a long and misguided journey. The statute seeks to assure that a disabled person's disability will not deny him *equal access* to (among other things) competitive sporting events—not that his disability will not deny him an *equal chance to win* competitive sporting events. The latter is quite impossible, since the very *nature* of competitive sport is the measurement, by uniform rules, of

unevenly distributed excellence. This unequal distribution is precisely what determines the winners and losers—and artificially to "even out" that distribution, by giving one or another player exemption from a rule that emphasizes his particular weakness, is to destroy the game. That is why the "handicaps" that are customary in social games of golf—which, by adding strokes to the scores of the good players and subtracting them from scores of the bad ones, "even out" the varying abilities—are *not* used in professional golf. In the Court's world, there is one set of rules that is "fair with respect to the able-bodied" but "individualized" rules, mandated by the ADA, for "talented but disabled athletes." *Ante,* at 29. The ADA mandates no such ridiculous thing. Agility, strength, speed, balance, quickness of mind, steadiness of nerves, intensity of concentration—these talents are not evenly distributed. No wildeyed dreamer has ever suggested that the managing bodies of the competitive sports that test precisely these qualities should try to take account of the uneven distribution of God-given gifts when writing and enforcing the rules of competition. And I have no doubt Congress did not authorize misty-eyed judicial supervision of such a revolution.

Chapter 12

JUSTICE, COMMUNITY, AND MEMBERSHIP

Contemporary critics of Kant and Rawls challenge their political theory on two grounds. First, they argue that the liberalism of Kant and Rawls rests on a notion of persons as freely choosing, individual selves that does not leave room for loyalties and obligations antecedent to choice. Because these critics emphasize the moral claims that may arise from our membership in particular communities and traditions, they are sometimes called communitarians. They also challenge the idea, shared by Kant and Rawls, that principles of justice can be defined and defended without affirming a particular conception of the good. Arguments about justice and rights, say the critics, cannot be neutral with respect to competing conceptions of the good life.

Here are some questions to consider while reading the contemporary critics of Kant and Rawls: If justice and rights unavoidably depend on conceptions of the good life, does this mean that justice depends on the values that happen to prevail in any given community at any given time? If so, doesn't this make justice the hostage of convention, and deprive it of its critical character? And if communitarians claim that we are bound by ties of solidarity or membership we have not chosen, then what becomes of freedom? Shouldn't we think of ourselves instead as capable of reflecting on the communities and traditions we inherit, deciding for ourselves which ones to affirm and which to reject?

AFTER VIRTUE

Alasdair MacIntyre

The Virtues, the Unity of a Human Life and the Concept of a Tradition

Any contemporary attempt to envisage each human life as a whole, as a unity, whose character provides the virtues with an adequate *telos* encounters two different kinds of obstacle, one social and one philosophical. The social obstacles derive from the way in which modernity partitions each human life into a variety of segments, each with its own norms and modes of behav-

iour. So work is divided from leisure, private life from public, the corporate from the personal. So both childhood and old age have been wrenched away from the rest of human life and made over into distinct realms. And all these separations have been achieved so that it is the distinctiveness of each and not the unity of the life of the individual who passes through those parts in terms of which we are taught to think and to feel.

The philosophical obstacles derive from two distinct tendencies, one chiefly, though not only,

315

domesticated in analytical philosophy and one at home in both sociological theory and in existentialism. The former is the tendency to think atomistically about human action and to analyse complex actions and transactions in terms of simple components. Hence the recurrence in more than one context of the notion of "a basic action". That particular actions derive their character as parts of larger wholes is a point of view alien to our dominant ways of thinking and yet one which it is necessary at least to consider if we are to begin to understand how a life may be more than a sequence of individual actions and episodes.

Equally the unity of a human life becomes invisible to us when a sharp separation is made either between the individual and the roles that he or she plays—a separation characteristic not only of Sartre's existentialism, but also of the sociological theory of Ralf Dahrendorf—or between the different role—and quasi-role—enactments of an individual life so that life comes to appear as nothing but a series of unconnected episodes—a liquidation of the self characteristic, as I noticed earlier, of Goffman's sociological theory. I already also suggested in Chapter 3 that both the Sartrian and the Goffmanesque conceptions of selfhood are highly characteristic of the modes of thought and practice of modernity. It is perhaps therefore unsurprising to realise that the self as thus conceived cannot be envisaged as a bearer of the Aristotelian virtues.

For a self separated from its roles in the Sartrian mode loses that arena of social relationships in which the Aristotelian virtues function if they function at all. The patterns of a virtuous life would fall under those condemnations of conventionality which Sartre put into the mouth of Antoine Roquentin in *La Nausée* and which he uttered in his own person in *L'Etre et le niant*. Indeed the self's refusal of the inauthenticity of conventionalised social relationships becomes what integrity is diminished into in Sartre's account.

At the same time the liquidation of the self into a set of demarcated areas of role-playing allows no scope for the exercise of dispositions which could genuinely be accounted virtues in any sense remotely Aristotelian. For a virtue is not a disposition that makes for success only in some one particular type of situation. What are spoken of as the virtues of a good committee man or of a good administrator or of a gambler or a pool hustler are

professional skills professionally deployed in those situations where they can be effective, not virtues. Someone who genuinely possesses a virtue can be expected to manifest it in very different types of situation, many of them situations where the practice of a virtue cannot be expected to be effective in the way that we expect a professional skill to be. Hector exhibited one and the same courage in his parting from Andromache and on the battlefield with Achilles: Eleanor Marx exhibited one and the same compassion in her relationship with her father, in her work with trade unionists and in her entanglement with Aveling. And the unity of a virtue in someone's life is intelligible only as a characteristic of a unitary life, a life that can be conceived and evaluated as a whole. Hence just as in the discussion of the changes in and fragmentation of morality which accompanied the rise of modernity in the earlier parts of this book, each stage in the emergence of the characteristically modern views of the moral judgment was accompanied by a corresponding stage in the emergence of the characteristically modern conceptions of selfhood; so now, in defining the particular premodern concept of the virtues with which I have been preoccupied, it has become necessary to say something of the concomitant concept of selfhood, a concept of a self whose unity resides in the unity of a narrative which links birth to life to death as narrative beginning to middle to end.

Such a conception of the self is perhaps less unfamiliar than it may appear at first sight. Just because it has played a key part in the cultures which are historically the predecessors of our own, it would not be surprising if it turned out to be still an unacknowledged presence in many of our ways of thinking and acting. Hence it is not inappropriate to begin by scrutinising some of our most taken-for-granted, but clearly correct conceptual insights about human actions and selfhood in order to show how natural it is to think of the self in a narrative mode.

It is a conceptual commonplace, both for philosophers and for ordinary agents, that one and the same segment of human behaviour may be correctly characterised in a number of different ways. To the question "What is he doing?" the answers may with equal truth and appropriateness be "Digging", "Gardening", "Taking exercise", "Preparing for winter" or "Pleasing his wife".

Some of these answers will characterise the agent's intentions, others unintended consequences of his actions, and of these unintended consequences some may be such that the agent is aware of them and others not. What is important to notice immediately is that any answer to the questions of how we are to understand or to explain a given segment of behaviour will presuppose some prior answer to the question of how these different correct answers to the question "What is he doing?" are related to each other. For if someone's primary intention is to put the garden in order before the winter and it is only incidentally the case that in so doing he is taking exercise and pleasing his wife, we have one type of behaviour to be explained; but if the agent's primary intention is to please his wife by taking exercise, we have quite another type of behaviour to be explained and we will have to look in a different direction for understanding and explanation.

In the first place the episode has been situated in an annual cycle of domestic activity, and the behaviour embodies an intention which presupposes a particular type of household-cum-garden setting with the peculiar narrative history of that setting in which this segment of behaviour now becomes an episode. In the second instance the episode has been situated in the narrative history of a marriage, a very different, even if related, social setting. We cannot, that is to say, characterise behaviour independently of intentions, and we cannot characterise intentions independently of the settings which make those intentions intelligible both to agents themselves and to others.

I use the word "setting" here as a relatively inclusive term. A social setting may be an institution, it may be what I have called a practice, or it may be a milieu of some other human kind. But it is central to the notion of a setting as I am going to understand it that a setting has a history, a history within which the histories of individual agents not only are, but have to be, situated, just because without the setting and its changes through time the history of the individual agent and his changes through time will be unintelligible. Of course one and the same piece of behaviour may belong to more than one setting. There are at least two different ways in which this may be so.

In my earlier example the agent's activity may be part of the history both of the cycle of household activity and of his marriage, two histories which have happened to intersect. The household may have its own history stretching back through hundreds of years, as do the histories of some European farms, where the farm has had a life of its own, even though different families have in different periods inhabited it; and the marriage will certainly have its own history, a history which itself presupposes that a particular point has been reached in the history of the institution of marriage. If we are to relate some particular segment of behaviour in any precise way to an agent's intentions and thus to the settings which that agent inhabits, we shall have to understand in a precise way how the variety of correct characterisations of the agent's behaviour relate to each other first by identifying which characteristics refer us to an intention and which do not and then by classifying further the items in both categories.

Where intentions are concerned, we need to know which intention or intentions were primary, that is to say, of which it is the case that, had the agent intended otherwise, he would not have performed that action. Thus if we know that a man is gardening with the self-avowed purposes of healthful exercise and of pleasing his wife, we do not yet know how to understand what he is doing until we know the answer to such questions as whether he would continue gardening if he continued to believe that gardening was healthful exercise, but discovered that his gardening no longer pleased his wife, *and* whether he would continue gardening, if he ceased to believe that gardening was healthful exercise, but continued to believe that it pleased his wife, *and* whether he would continue gardening if he changed his beliefs on both points. That is to say, we need to know both what certain of his beliefs are and which of them are causally effective; and, that is to say, we need to know whether certain contrary-to-fact hypothetical statements are true or false. And until we know this, we shall not know how to characterise correctly what the agent is doing.

Consider another equally trivial example of a set of compatibly correct answers to the question "What is he doing?" "Writing a sentence"; "Finishing his book"; "Contributing to the debate on the theory of action"; "Trying to get tenure". Here the intentions can be ordered in terms of the stretch of time to which reference is made. Each of the shorter-term intentions is, and can only be made, intelligible by reference to some longer-term intentions; and the characterisation of the behaviour in terms of the longer-term intentions can only be correct if some of the characterisations in terms of shorter-term intentions are also correct. Hence the behaviour is only characterised adequately when we know what the longer and longest-term intentions invoked are and how the shorter-term intentions are related to the longer. Once again we are involved in writing a narrative history.

Intentions thus need to be ordered both causally and temporally and both orderings will make references to settings, references already made obliquely by such elementary terms as "gardening", "wife", "book" and "tenure". Moreover the correct identification of the agent's beliefs will be an essential constituent of this task; failure at this point would mean failure in the whole enterprise. (The conclusion may seem obvious; but it already entails one important consequence. There is no such thing as "behaviour", to be identified prior to and independently of intentions, beliefs and settings. Hence the project of a science of behaviour takes on a mysterious and somewhat outré character. It is not that such a science is impossible; but there is nothing for it to be but a science of uninterpreted physical movement such as B.F. Skinner aspires to. It is no part of my task here to examine Skinner's problems; but it is worth noticing that it is not at all clear what a scientific experiment could be, if one were a Skinnerian; since the conception of an experiment is certainly one of intention- and belief-informed behaviour. And what would be utterly doomed to failure would be the project of a science of, say, *political* behaviour, detached from a study of intentions, beliefs and settings. It is perhaps worth noting that when the expression "the behavioural sciences" was given its first influential use in a Ford Foundation Report of 1953, the term "behaviour" was defined so as to include what were called "such subjective behaviour as attitudes, beliefs, expectations, motivations and aspirations" as well as "overt acts". But what the Report's wording seems to imply is that it is cataloguing two distinct sets of items, available for

independent study. If the argument so far is correct, then there is only one set of items.)

Consider what the argument so far implies about the interrelationships of the intentional, the social and the historical. We identify a particular action only by invoking two kinds of context, implicitly if not explicitly. We place the agent's intentions, I have suggested, in causal and temporal order with reference to their role in his or her history; and we also place them with reference to their role in the history of the setting or settings to which they belong. In doing this, in determining what causal efficacy the agent's intentions had in one or more directions, and how his short-term intentions succeeded or failed to be constitutive of long-term intentions, we ourselves write a further part of these histories. Narrative history of a certain kind turns out to be the basic and essential genre for the characterisation of human actions.

It is important to be clear how different the standpoint presupposed by the argument so far is from that of those analytical philosophers who have constructed accounts of human actions which make central the notion of "a" human action. A course of human events is then seen as a complex sequence of individual actions, and a natural question is: How do we individuate human actions? Now there are contexts in which such notions are at home. In the recipes of a cookery book for instance actions are individuated in just the way that some analytical philosophers have supposed to be possible of all actions. "Take six eggs. Then break them into a bowl. Add flour, salt, sugar, etc." But the point about such sequences is that each element in them is intelligible as an action only as a-possible-element-in-a-sequence. Moreover even such a sequence requires a context to be intelligible. If in the middle of my lecture on Kant's ethics I suddenly broke six eggs into a bowl and added flour and sugar, proceeding all the while with my Kantian exegesis, I have *not*, simply in virtue of the fact that I was following a sequence prescribed by Fanny Farmer, performed an intelligible action.

To this it might be related that I certainly performed an action or a set of actions, if not an intelligible action. But to this I want to reply that the concept of an intelligible action is a more fundamental concept than that of an action as such. Unintelligible actions are failed candidates for the status of intelligible action; and to lump unintelligible actions and intelligible actions together in a single class of actions and then to characterise action in terms of what items of both sets have in common is to make the mistake of ignoring this. It is also to neglect the central importance of the concept of intelligibility.

The importance of the concept of intelligibility is closely related to the fact that the most basic distinction of all embedded in our discourse and our practice in this area is that between human beings and other beings. Human beings can be held to account for that of which they are the authors; other beings cannot. To identify an occurrence as an action is in the paradigmatic instances to identify it under a type of description which enables us to see that occurrence as flowing intelligibly from a human agent's intentions, motives, passions and purposes. It is therefore to understand an action as something for which someone is accountable, about which it is always appropriate to ask the agent for an intelligible account. When an occurrence is apparently the intended action of a human agent, but none the less we cannot so identify it, we are both intellectually and practically baffled. We do not know how to respond; we do not know how to explain; we do not even know how to characterise minimally as an intelligible action; our distinction between the humanly accountable and the merely natural seems to have broken down. And this kind of bafflement does indeed occur in a number of different kinds of situation; when we enter alien cultures or even alien social structures within our own culture, in our encounters with certain types of neurotic or psychotic patient (it is indeed the unintelligibility of such patient's actions that leads to their being treated as patients; actions unintelligible to the agent as well as to everyone else are understood—rightly—as a kind of suffering), but also in everyday situations. Consider an example.

I am standing waiting for a bus and the young man standing next to me suddenly says: "The name of the common wild duck is *Histrionicus histrionicus histrionicus*." There is no problem as to the meaning of the sentence he uttered: the problem is, how to answer the question, what was he doing in uttering it? Suppose he just uttered such sentences at random intervals; this would be one possible form of

madness. We would render his act of utterance intelligible if one of the following turned out to be true. He has mistaken me for someone who yesterday had approached him in the library and asked: "Do you by any chance know the Latin name of the common wild duck?" *Or* he has just come from a session with his psychotherapist who has urged him to break down his shyness by talking to strangers. "But what shall I say?" "Oh, anything at all." *Or* he is a Soviet spy waiting at a pre-arranged rendez-vous and uttering the ill-chosen code sentence which will identify him to his contact. In each case the act of utterance becomes intelligible by finding its place in a narrative.

To this it may be replied that the supplying of a narrative is not necessary to make such an act intelligible. All that is required is that we can identify the relevant type of speech act (e.g. "He was answering a question") or some purpose served by his utterance (e.g. "He was trying to attract your attention"). But speech acts and purposes too can be intelligible or unintelligible. Suppose that the man at the bus stop explains his act of utterance by saying "I was answering a question." I reply: "But I never asked you any question to which that could have been the answer." He says, "Oh, I know *that*." Once again his action becomes unintelligible. And a parallel example could easily be constructed to show that the mere fact that an action serves some purpose of a recognised type is not sufficient to render an action intelligible. Both purposes and speech-acts require contexts.

The most familiar type of context in and by reference to which speech-acts and purposes are rendered intelligible is the conversation. Conversation is so all-pervasive a feature of the human world that it tends to escape philosophical attention. Yet remove conversation from human life and what would be left? Consider then what is involved in following a conversation and finding it intelligible or unintelligible. (To find a conversation intelligible is not the same as to understand it; for a conversation which I overhear may be intelligible, but I may fail to understand it.) If I listen to a conversation between two other people my ability to grasp the thread of the conversation will involve an ability to bring it under some one out of a set of descriptions in which the degree and kind of coherence in the conversation is brought out: "a drunken, rambling quarrel", "a serious intellectual disagreement", "a tragic misunderstanding of each other", "a comic, even farcical misconstrual of each other's motives", "a penetrating interchange of views", "a struggle to dominate each other", "a trivial exchange of gossip."

The use of words such as "tragic", "comic", and "farcical" is not marginal to such evaluations. We allocate conversations to genres, just as we do literary narratives. Indeed a conversation is a dramatic work, even if a very short one, in which the participants are not only the actors, but also the joint authors, working out in agreement or disagreement the mode of their production. For it is not just that conversations belong to genres in just the way that plays and novels do; but they have beginnings, middles and endings just as do literary works. They embody reversals and recognitions; they move towards and away from climaxes. There may within a longer conversation be digressions and subplots, indeed digressions within digressions and subplots within subplots.

But if this is true of conversations, it is true also *mutatis mutandis* of battles, chess games, courtships, philosophy seminars, families at the dinner table, businessmen negotiating contracts—that is, of human transactions in general. For conversation, understood widely enough, is the form of human transactions in general. Conversational behaviour is not a special sort or aspect of human behaviour, even though the forms of language-using and of human life are such that the deeds of others speak for them as much as do their words. For that is possible only because they are the deeds of those who have words.

I am presenting both conversations in particular then and human actions in general as enacted narratives. Narrative is not the work of poets, dramatists and novelists reflecting upon events which had no narrative order before one was imposed by the singer or the writer; narrative form is neither disguise nor decoration. Barbara Hardy has written that "we dream in narrative, day-dream in narrative, remember, anticipate, hope, despair, believe, doubt, plan, revise, criticise, construct, gossip, learn, hate and love by narrative" in arguing the same point.

At the beginning of this chapter I argued that in successfully identifying and understanding what someone else is doing we always move towards placing a particular episode in the context of a set of narrative histories, histories both of the individuals concerned and of the settings in which they act and suffer. It is now becoming clear that we render the actions of others intelligible in this way because action itself has a basically historical character. It is because we all live out narratives in our lives and because we understand our own lives in terms of the narratives that we live out that the form of narrative is appropriate for understanding the actions of others. Stories are lived before they are told-except in the case of fiction.

This has of course been denied in recent debates. Louis O. Mink, quarrelling with Barbara Hardy's view, has asserted: "Stories are not lived but told, Life has no beginnings, middles, or ends; there are meetings, but the start of an affair belongs to the story we tell ourselves later, and there are partings, but final partings only in the story. There are hopes, plans, battles and ideas, but only in retrospective stories are hopes unfulfilled, plans miscarried, battles decisive, and ideas seminal. Only in the story is it America which Columbus discovers and only in the story is the kingdom lost for want of a nail."

What are we to say to this? Certainly we must agree that it is only retrospectively that hopes can be characterised as unfulfilled or battles as decisive and so on. But we so characterise them in life as much as in art. And to someone who says that in life there are no endings, or that final partings take place only in stories, one is tempted to reply, "But have you never heard of death?" Homer did not have to tell the tale of Hector before Andromache could lament unfulfilled hope and final parting. There are countless Hectors and countless Andromaches whose lives embodied the form of their Homeric namesakes, but who never came to the attention of any poet. What is true is that in taking an event as a beginning or an ending we bestow a significance upon it which may be debatable. Did the Roman republic end with the death of Julius Caesar, or at Philippi, or with the founding of the principate? The answer is surely that, like Charles II, it was a long time a-dying; but this answer implies the reality of its ending as much as do any of the former. There is a crucial sense in which the principate of Augustus, or the taking of the oath in the tennis court, or the decision to construct an atomic bomb at Los Alamos constitute beginnings; the peace of 404 B.C., the abolition of the Scottish Parliament and the battle of Waterloo equally constitute endings; while there are many events which are both endings and beginnings.

As with beginnings, middles and endings, so also with genres and with the phenomenon of embedding. Consider the question of to what genre the life of Thomas Becket belongs, a question which has to be asked and answered before we can decide how it is to be written. (On Mink's paradoxical view this question could not be asked until *after* the life had been written.) In some of the medieval versions, Thomas's career is presented in terms of the canons of medieval hagiography. In the Icelandic *Thomas Saga* he is presented as a saga hero. In Dom David Knowles's modern biography the story is a tragedy, the tragic relationship of Thomas and Henry II, each of whom satisfies Aristotle's demand that the hero be a great man with a fatal flaw. Now it clearly makes sense to ask who is right, if anyone: the monk William of Canterbury, the author of the saga, or the Cambridge Regius Professor Emeritus? The answer appears to be clearly the last. The true genre of the life is neither hagiography nor saga, but tragedy. So of such modern narrative subjects as the life of Trotsky or that of Lenin, of the history of the Soviet Communist Party or the American presidency, we may also ask: To what genre does their history belong? And this is the same question as: What type of account of their history will be both true and intelligible?

Or consider again how one narrative may be embedded in another. In both plays and novels there are well-known examples: the play within the play in *Hamlet*, Wandering Willie's Tale in *Redgauntlet*, Aeneas' narrative to Dido in book 2 of the *Aeneid*, and so on. But there are equally well-known examples in real life. Consider again the way in which the career of Becket as archbishop and chancellor is embedded within the reign of Henry II, or the way in which the tragic life of Mary Stuart is embedded in that of Elizabeth I, or the history of the Confederacy within the history of the United States. Someone may discover (or not discover) that he or she is a character in a number of narratives at the same time, some of them embedded in others. Or again, what seemed to be an intelligible narrative in which one was playing a part may be transformed wholly or partly into a story of unintelligible episodes. This last is what happened to Kafka's character K. in both *The Trial* and *The Castle*. (It is no accident that Kafka could not end his novels, for the notion of an ending like that of a beginning has its sense only in terms of intelligible narrative.)

I spoke earlier of the agent as not only an actor, but an author. Now I must emphasise that what the agent is able to do and say intelligibly as an actor is deeply affected by the fact that we are never more (and sometimes less) than the co-authors of our own narratives. Only in fantasy do we live what story we please. In life, as both Aristotle and Engels noted, we are always under certain constraints. We enter upon a stage which we did not design and we find ourselves part of an action that was not of our making. Each of us being a main character in his own drama plays subordinate parts in the dramas of others, and each drama constrains the others. In my drama, perhaps, I am Hamlet or Iago or at least the swineherd who may yet become a prince, but to you I am only A Gentleman or at best Second Murderer, while you are my Polonius or my Gravedigger, but your own hero. Each of our dramas exerts constraints on each other's, making the whole different from the parts, but still dramatic.

It is considerations as complex as these which are involved in making the notion of intelligibility the conceptual connecting link between the notion of action and that of narrative. Once we have understood its importance the claim that the concept of an action is secondary to that of an intelligible action will perhaps appear less bizarre and so too will the claim that the notion of "an" action, while of the highest practical importance, is always a potentially misleading abstraction. An action is a moment in a possible or actual history or in a number of such histories. The notion of a history is as fundamental a notion as the notion of an action. Each requires the other. But I cannot say this without noticing that it is precisely this that Sartre denies—as indeed his whole theory of the self, which captures so well the spirit of modernity, requires that he should. In *La Nausée*, Sartre makes Antoine Roquentin argue not just what Mink argues, that narrative is very different from life, but that to present human life in the form of a narrative is always to falsify it. There are not and there cannot be any true stories. Human life is composed of discrete actions which lead nowhere, which have no order; the story-teller imposes on human events retrospectively an order which they did not have while they were lived. Clearly if Sartre/Roquentin is right—I speak of Sartre/Roquentin to distinguish him from such other well-known characters as Sartre/Heidegger and Sartre/Marx—my central contention must be mistaken. There is none the less an important point of agreement between my thesis and that of Sartre/Roquentin. We agree in identifying the intelligibility of an action with its place in a narrative sequence. Only Sartre/Roquentin takes it that human actions are as such unintelligible occurrences: it is to a realisation of the metaphysical implications of this that Roquentin is brought in the course of the novel and the practical effect upon him is to bring to an end his own project of writing an historical biography. This project no longer makes sense. Either he will write what is true or he will write an intelligible history, but the one possibility excludes the other. Is Sartre/Roquentin right?

We can discover what is wrong with Sartre's thesis in either of two ways. One is to ask: what would human actions deprived of any falsifying narrative order be like? Sartre himself never answers this question; it is striking that in order to show that there are no true narratives, he himself writes a narrative, albeit a fictional one. But the only picture that I find myself able to form of human nature *an-sich*, prior to the alleged misinterpretation by narrative is the kind of dislocated sequence which Dr Johnson offers us in his notes of his travels in France: "There we waited on the ladies—Morville's.—Spain. Country towns all beggars. At Dijon he could not find the way to Orleans.—Cross roads of France very bad.— Five soldiers.—Women.—Soldiers escaped.— The Colonel would not lose five men for the sake of one woman.—The magistrate cannot seize a soldier but by the Colonel's permission, etc., etc." What this suggests is what I take to be true, namely that the characterisation of actions allegedly prior to any narrative form being imposed upon them will always turn out to be the presentation of what are plainly the disjointed parts of some possible narrative.

We can also approach the question in another way. What I have called a history is an enacted dramatic narrative in which the characters are also the authors. The characters of course never start literally *ab initio*; they plunge *in medias res*, the beginnings of their story already made for them by what and who has gone before. But when Julian Grenfell or Edward Thomas went off to France in the 1914–18 war they no less enacted a narrative than did Menelaus or Odysseus when *they* went off. The difference between imaginary characters and real ones is not in the narrative form of what they do; it is in the degree of their authorship of that form and of their own deeds. Of course just as they do not begin where they please, they cannot go on exactly as they please either; each character is constrained by the actions of others and by the social settings presupposed in his and their actions, a point forcibly made by Marx in the classical, if not entirely satisfactory account of human life as enacted dramatic narrative, *The Eighteenth Brumaire of Louis Bonaparte*.

I call Marx's account less than satisfactory partly because he wishes to present the narrative of human social life in a way that will be compatible with a view of that life as law-governed and predictable in a particular way. But it is crucial that at any given point in an enacted dramatic narrative we do not know what will happen next. The kind of unpredictability for which I argued [earlier] is required by the narrative structure of human life, and the empirical generalisations and explorations which social scientists discover provide a kind of understanding of human life which is perfectly compatible with that structure.

This unpredictability coexists with a second crucial characteristic of all lived narratives, a certain teleological character. We live out our lives, both individually and in our relationships with each other, in the light of certain conceptions of a possible shared future, a future in which certain possibilities beckon us forward and others repel us, some seem already foreclosed and others perhaps inevitable. There is no present which is not informed by some image of some future and an image of the future which always presents itself in the form of a *telos*—or of a variety of ends or goals—towards which we are either moving or failing to move in the present. Unpredictability and teleology therefore coexist as part of our lives; like characters in a fictional narrative we do not know what will happen next, but none the less our lives have a certain form which projects itself towards our future. Thus the narratives which we live out have both an unpredictable and a partially teleological character. If the narrative of our individual and social lives is to continue intelligibly—and either type of narrative may lapse into unintelligibility—it is always both the case that there are constraints on how the story can continue *and* that within those constraints there are indefinitely many ways that it can continue.

A central thesis then begins to emerge: man is in his actions and practice, as well as in his fictions, essentially a story-telling animal. He is not essentially but becomes through his history, a teller of stories that aspire to truth. But the key question for men is not about their own authorship; I can only answer the question "What am I to do?" if I can answer the prior question "Of what story or stories do I find myself a part?" We enter human society, that is, with one or more imputed characters—roles into which we have been drafted—and we have to learn what they are in order to be able to understand how others respond to us and how our responses to them are apt to be construed. It is through hearing stories about wicked stepmothers, lost children, good but misguided kings, wolves that suckle twin boys, youngest sons who receive no inheritance but must make their own way in the world and eldest sons who waste their inheritance on riotous living and go into exile to live with the swine that children learn or mislearn both what a child and what a parent is, what the cast of characters may be in the drama into which they have been born and what the ways of the world are. Deprive children of stories and you leave then, unscripted, anxious stutterers in their actions as in their words. Hence there is no way to give us an understanding of any society, including our own, except through the stock of stories which constitute its initial dramatic resources Mythology, in its original sense, is at the heart of things. Vico was right and so was Joyce. And so too of course is that moral tradition from heroic society to its medieval heirs according to which the telling of stories has a key part it educating us into the virtues.

I suggested earlier that "an" action is always an episode in a possible history I would now like to make a related suggestion about another concept, that of personal identity. Derek Parfit and others have recently drawn our attention to the contrast between the criteria of strict identity, which is an all-or-nothing matter (*either* the Tichborne claimant *is* the last Tichborne heir; *either* all the properties of the last heir belong to the claimant *or* the claimant is not the heir–Leibniz's Law applies) and the psychological continuities of personality which are a matter of more or less. (Am I the same man at fifty as I was at forty in respect of memory, intellectual powers, critical responses? More or less.) But what is crucial to human beings as characters in enacted narratives is that, possessing only the resources of psychological continuity, we have to be able to respond to the imputation of strict identity. I am forever whatever I have been at any time for others—and I may at any time be called upon to answer for it—no matter how changed I may be now. There is no way of *founding* my identity—or lack of it—on the psychological continuity or discontinuity of the self. The self inhabits a character whose unity is given as the unity of a character. Once again there is a crucial disagreement with empiricist or analytical philosophers on the one hand and with existentialists on the other.

Empiricists, such as Locke or Hume, tried to give an account of personal identity solely in terms of psychological states or events. Analytical philosophers, in so many ways their heirs as well as their critics, have wrestled with the connection between those states and events and strict identity understood in terms of Leibniz's Law. Both have failed to see that a background has been omitted, the lack of which makes the problems insoluble. That background is provided by the concept of a story and of that kind of unity of character which a story requires. Just as a history is not a sequence of actions, but the concept of an action is that of a moment in an actual or possible history abstracted for some purpose from that history, so the characters in a history are not a collection of persons, but the concept of a person is that of a character abstracted from a history.

What the narrative concept of selfhood requires is thus twofold. On the one hand, I am what I may justifiably be taken by others to be in the course of living out a story that runs from my birth to my death; I am the *subject* of a history that is my own and no one else's, that has its own peculiar meaning. When someone complains—as do some of those who attempt or commit suicide—that his or her life is meaningless, he or she is often and perhaps characteristically complaining that the narrative of their life has become unintelligible to them, that it lacks any point, any movement towards a climax or a *telos*. Hence the point of doing any one thing rather than another at crucial junctures in their lives seems to such a person to have been lost.

To be the subject of a narrative that runs from one's birth to one's death is, I remarked earlier, to be accountable for the actions and experiences which compose a narratable life. It is, that is, to be open to being asked to give a certain kind of account of what one did or what happened to one or what one witnessed at any earlier point in one's life the time at which the question is posed. Of course someone may have forgotten or suffered brain damage or simply not attended sufficiently at the relevant times to be able to give the relevant account. But to say of someone under some one description ("The prisoner of the Chateau d'Il") that he is the same person as someone characterised quite differently ("The Count of Monte Cristo") is precisely to say that it makes sense to ask him to give an intelligible narrative account enabling us to understand how he could at different times and different places be one and the same person and yet be so differently characterised. Thus personal identity is just that identify presupposed by the unity of the character which the unity of a narrative requires. Without such unity there would not be subjects of whom stories could be told.

The other aspect of narrative selfhood is correlative: I am not only accountable, I am one who can always ask others for an account, who can put others to the question. I am part of their story, as they are part of mine. The narrative of any one life is part of an interlocking set of narratives. Moreover this asking for and giving of accounts itself plays an important part in constituting narratives. Asking you what you did and why, saying what I did and why, pondering the differences between your account of what I did and my account of what I did, and *vice versa*, these are essential constituents of all but the very simplest and barest of narratives. Thus without the accountability of the self those trains of events that constitute all but the simplest and barest of narratives could not occur; and without that same accountability narratives would lack that continu-

ity required to make both them and the actions that constitute them intelligible.

It is important to notice that I am not arguing that the concepts of narrative or of intelligibility or of accountability are *more* fundamental than that of personal identity. The concepts of narrative, intelligibility and accountability presuppose the applicability of the concept of personal identity, just as it presupposes their applicability and just as indeed each of these three presupposes the applicability of the two others. The relationship is one of mutual presupposition. It does follow of course that all attempts to elucidate the notion of personal identity independently of and in isolation from the notions of narrative, intelligibility and accountability are bound to fail. As all such attempts have.

It is now possible to return to the question from which this enquiry into the nature of human action and identity started: In what does the unity of an individual life consist? The answer is that its unity is the unity of a narrative embodied in a single life. To ask "What is the good for me?" is to ask how best I might live out that unity and bring it to completion. To ask "What is the good for man?" is to ask what all answers to the former question must have in common. But now it is important to emphasise that it is the systematic asking of these two questions and the attempt to answer them in deed as well as in word which provide the moral life with its unity. The unity of a human life is the unity of a narrative quest. Quests sometimes fail, are frustrated, abandoned or dissipated into distractions; and human lives may in all these ways also fail. But the only criteria for success or failure in a human life as a whole are the criteria of success or failure in a narrated or to-be-narrated quest. A quest for what?

Two key features of the medieval conception of a quest need to be recalled. The first is that without some at least partly determinate conception of the final *telos* there could not be any beginning to a quest. Some conception of the good for man is required. Whence is such a conception to be drawn? Precisely from those questions which led us to attempt to transcend that limited conception of the virtues which is available in and through practices. It is in looking for a conception of *the* good which will enable us to order other goods, for a conception of *the* good which will enable us to extend our understanding of the purpose and content of the virtues, for a conception of *the* good which will enable us to understand the place of integrity and constancy in life, that we initially define the kind of life which is a quest for the good. But secondly it is clear the medieval conception of a quest is not at all that of a search for something already adequately characterised, as miners search for gold or geologists for oil. It is in the course of the quest and only through encountering and coping with the various particular harms, dangers, temptations and distractions which provide any quest with its episodes and incidents that the goal of the quest is finally to be understood. A quest is always an education both as to the character of that which is sought and in self-knowledge.

The virtues therefore are to be understood as those dispositions which will not only sustain practices and enable us to achieve the goods internal to practices, but which will also sustain us in the relevant kind of quest for the good, by enabling us to overcome the harms, dangers, temptations and distractions which we encounter, and which will furnish us with increasing self-knowledge and increasing knowledge of the good. The catalogue of the virtues will therefore include the virtues required to sustain the kind of households and the kind of political communities in which men and women can seek for the good together and the virtues necessary for philosophical enquiry about the character of the good. We have then arrived at a provisional conclusion about the good life for man: the good life for man is the life spent in seeking for the good life for man, and the virtues necessary for the seeking are those which will enable us to understand what more and what else the good life for man is. We have also completed the second stage in our account of the virtues, by situating them in relation to the good life for man and not only in relation to practices. But our enquiry requires a third stage.

For I am never able to seek for the good or exercise the virtues only *qua* individual. This is partly because what it is to live the good life concretely varies from circumstance to circumstance even when it is one and the same conception of the good life and one and the same set of virtues which are being embodied in a human life. What the good life is for a fifth-century Athenian general will not be the same as what it was for a medieval nun or a seventeenth-century farmer. But it is not just that different individuals live in different social circumstances; it is also that we all approach our own circumstances as bearers of a particular social identity. I am someone's son or daughter, someone else's cousin or uncle; I am a citizen of this or that city, a member of this or that guild or profession; I belong to this clan, that tribe, this nation. Hence what is good for me has to be the good for one who inhabits these roles. As such, I inherit from the past of my family, my city, my tribe, my nation, a variety of debts, inheritances, rightful expectations and obligations. These constitute the given of my life, my moral starting point. This is in part what gives my life its own moral particularity.

This thought is likely to appear alien and even surprising from the stand-point of modern individualism. From the standpoint of individualism I am what I myself choose to be. I can always, if I wish to, put in question what are taken to be the merely contingent social features of my existence. I may biologically be my father's son; but I cannot be held responsible for what he did unless I choose implicitly or explicitly to assume such responsibility. I may legally be a citizen of a certain country; but I cannot be held responsible for what my country does or has done unless I choose implicitly or explicitly to assume such responsibility. Such individualism is expressed by those modern Americans who deny any responsibility for the effects of slavery upon black Americans, saying "I never owned any slaves". It is more subtly the standpoint of those other modern Americans who accept a nicely calculated responsibility for such effects measured precisely by the benefits they themselves as individuals have indirectly received from slavery. In both cases "being an American" is not in itself taken to be part of the moral identity of the individual. And of course there is nothing peculiar to modern Americans in this attitude; the Englishman who says, "*I* never did any wrong to Ireland; why bring up that old history as though it had something to do with *me*?" or the young German who believes that being born after 1945 means that what Nazis did to Jews has no moral relevance to his relationship to his Jewish contemporaries, exhibit the same attitude, that according to which the self is detachable from its social and historical roles and statuses. And the self so detached is of course a self very much at home in either Sartre's or Goffman's perspective, a self that can have no history. The contrast with the narrative view of the self is clear. For the story of my life is always embedded in the story of those communities from which I derive my identity. I am born with a past; and to try to cut myself off from that past, in the individualist mode, is to deform my present relationships. The possession of an historical identity and the possession of a social identity coincide. Notice that rebellion against my identity is always one possible mode of expressing it.

Notice also that the fact that the self has to find its moral identity in and through its membership in communities such as those of the family, the neighbourhood, the city and the tribe does not entail that the self has to accept the moral *limitations* of the particularity of those forms of community. Without those moral particularities to begin from there would never be anywhere to begin; but it is in moving forward from such particularity that the search for the good, for the universal, consists. Yet particularity can never be simply left behind or obliterated. The notion of escaping from it into a realm of entirely universal maxims which belong to man as such, whether in its eighteenth-century Kantian form or in the presentation of some modern analytical moral philosophies, is an illusion and an illusion with painful consequences. When men and women identify what are in fact their partial and particular causes too easily and too completely with the cause of some universal principle, they usually behave worse than they would otherwise do.

What I am, therefore, is in key part what I inherit, a specific past that is present to some degree in my present. I find myself part of a history and that is generally to say, whether I like it or not, whether I recognise it or not, one of the bearers of a tradition. It was important when I characterised the concept of a practice to notice that practices always have histories and that at any given moment what a practice is depends on a mode of understanding it which has been transmitted often through many generations. And thus, insofar as the virtues sustain the relationships required for practices, they have to sustain relationships to the past—and to the future—as well as in the present. But the traditions through which particular practices are transmitted and reshaped never exist in isolation for larger social traditions. What constitutes such traditions?

We are apt to be misled here by the ideological uses to which the concept of a tradition has been put by conservative political theorists. Characteristically such theorists have followed Burke in contrasting tradition with reason and the stability of tradition with conflict. Both contrasts obfuscate. For all reasoning takes place within the context of some traditional mode of thought, transcending through criticism and invention the limitations of what had hitherto been reasoned in that tradition; this is as true of modern physics as of medieval logic. Moreover when a tradition is in good order it is always partially constituted by an argument about the goods the pursuit of which gives to that tradition its particular point and purpose.

So when an institution—a university, say, or a farm, or a hospital—is the bearer of a tradition of practice or practices, its common life will be partly, but in a centrally important way, constituted by a continuous argument as to what a university is and ought to be or what good farming is or what good medicine is. Traditions, when vital, embody continuities of conflict. Indeed when a tradition becomes Burkean, it is always dying or dead.

The individualism of modernity could of course find no use for the notion of tradition within its own conceptual scheme except as an adversary notion; it therefore all too willingly abandoned it to the Burkeans, who, faithful to Burke's own allegiance, tried to combine adherence in politics to a conception of tradition which would vindicate the oligarchical revolution of property of 1688 and adherence in economics to the doctrine and institutions of the free market. The theoretical incoherence of this mismatch did not deprive it of ideological usefulness. But the outcome has been that modern conservatives are for the most part engaged in conserving only older rather than later versions of liberal individualism. Their own core doctrine is as liberal and as individualist as that of self-avowed liberals.

A living tradition then is an historically extended, socially embodied argument, and an argument precisely in part about the goods which constitute that tradition. Within a tradition the pursuit of goods extends through generations, sometimes through many generations. Hence the individual's search for his or her good is generally and characteristically conducted within a context defined by those traditions of which the individual's life is a part, and this is true both of those goods which are internal to practices and of the goods of a single life. Once again the narrative phenomenon of embedding is crucial: the history of a practice in our time is generally and characteristically embedded in and made intelligible in terms of the larger and longer history of the tradition through which the practice in its present form was conveyed to us; the history of each of our own lives is generally and characteristically embedded in and made intelligible in terms of the larger and longer histories of a number of traditions. I have to say "generally and characteristically" rather than "always", for traditions decay, disintegrate and disappear. What then sustains and strengthens traditions? What weakens and destroys them?

The answer in key part is: the exercise or the lack of exercise of the relevant virtues. The virtues find their point and purpose not only in sustaining those relationships necessary if the variety of goods internal to practices are to be achieved and not only in sustaining the form of an individual life in which that individual may seek out his or her good as the good of his or her whole life, but also in sustaining those traditions which provide both practices and individual lives with their necessary historical context. Lack of justice, lack of truthfulness, lack of courage, lack of the relevant intellectual virtues—these corrupt traditions, just as they do those institutions and practices which derive their life from the traditions of which they are the contemporary embodiments. To recognise this is of course also to recognise the existence of an additional virtue, one whose importance is perhaps most obvious when it is least present, the virtue of having an adequate sense of the traditions to which one belongs or which confront one. This virtue is not to be confused with any form of conservative antiquarianism; I am not praising those who choose the conventional conservative role of *laudator temporss acli*. It is rather the case that an adequate sense of tradition manifests itself in a grasp of those future possibilities which the past has made available to the present. Living traditions, just because they continue a not-yet-completed narrative, confront a future

whose determinate and determinable character, so far as it possesses any, derives from the past.

In practical reasoning the possession of this virtue is not manifested so much in the knowledge of a set of generalisations or maxims which may provide our practical inferences with major premises; its presence or absence rather appears on the kind of capacity for judgment which the agent possesses in knowing how to select among the relevant stack of maxims and how to apply them in particular situations. Cardinal Pole possessed it, Mary Tudor did not; Montrose possessed it, Charles I did not. What Cardinal Pole and the Marquis of Montrose possessed were in fact those virtues which enable their possessors to pursue both their own good and the good of the tradition of which they are the bearers even in situations defined by the necessity of tragic, dilemmatic choice. Such choices, understood in the context of the tradition of the virtues, are very different from those which face the modern adherents of rival and incommensurable moral premises in the debates about which I wrote in Chapter 2. Wherein does the difference lie?

It has often been suggested—by J.L. Austin, for example—that *either* we can admit the existence of rival and contingently incompatible goods which make incompatible claims to our practical allegiance *or* we can believe in some determinate conception of *the* good life for man, but that these are mutually exclusive alternatives. No one can consistently hold both these views. What this contention is blind to is that there may be better or worse ways for individuals to live through the tragic confrontation of good with good. And that to know what the good life for man is may require knowing what are the better and what are the worse ways of living in and through such situations. Nothing *a priori* rules out this possibility; and this suggests that within a view such as Austin's there is concealed an unacknowledged empirical premise about the character of tragic situations.

One way in which the choice between rival goods in a tragic situation differs from the modern choice between incommensurable moral premises is that *both* of the alternative courses of action which confront the individual have to be recognised as leading to some authentic and substantial good. By choosing one I do nothing to diminish or derogate from the claims upon me of the other; and therefore, whatever I do, I shall have left undone what I ought to have done. The tragic protagonist, unlike the moral agent as depicted by Sartre or Hare, is not choosing between allegiance to one moral principle rather than another, nor is he or she deciding upon some principle of priority between moral principles. Hence the "ought" involved has a different meaning and force from that of the "ought" in moral principles understood in a modern way. For the tragic protagonist cannot do everything that he or she ought to do. This "ought", unlike Kant's, does not imply "can". Moreover any attempt to map the logic of such "ought" assertions on to some modal calculus so as to produce a version of deontic logic has to fail.

Yet it is clear that the moral task of the tragic protagonist may be performed better or worse, independently of the choice between alternatives that he or she makes – *ex hypothesi* he or she has no *right* choice to make. The tragic protagonist may behave heroically or unheroically, generously or ungenerously, gracefully or gracelessly, prudently or imprudently. To perform his or her task better rather than worse will be to do both what is better for him or her *qua* individual or *qua* parent or child or *qua* citizen or member of a profession, or perhaps *qua* some or all of these. The existence of tragic dilemmas casts no doubt upon and provides no counter-examples to the thesis that assertions of the form "To do this in this way would be better for X and/or for his or her family, city or profession" are susceptible of objective truth and falsity, any more than the existence of alternative and contingently incompatible forms of medical treatment casts

doubt on the thesis that assertions of the form "To undergo this medical treatment in this way would be better for X and/or his or her family" are susceptible of objective truth and falsity.

The presupposition of this objectivity is of course that we can understand the notion of "good for X" and cognate notions in terms of some conception of the unity of X's life. What is better or worse for X depends upon the character of that intelligible narrative which provides X's life with its unity. Unsurprisingly it is the lack of any such unifying conception of a human life which underlies modern denials of the factual character of moral judgments and more especially of those judgments which ascribe virtues or vices to individuals.

I argued earlier that every moral philosophy has some particular sociology as its counterpart. What I have tried to spell out in this chapter is the kind of understanding of social life which the tradition of the virtues requires, a kind of understanding very different from those dominant in the culture of bureaucratic individualism. Within that culture conceptions of the virtues become marginal and the tradition of the virtues remains central only in the lives of social groups whose existence is on the margins of the central culture. Within the central culture of liberal or bureaucratic individualism new conceptions of the virtues emerge and the concept of a virtue is itself transformed. To the history of that transformation I therefore now turn; for we shall only understand the tradition of the virtues fully if we understand to what kinds of degeneration it has proved liable.

DEMOCRACY'S DISCONTENT

Michael J. Sandel

The Aspiration to Neutrality

The idea that government should be neutral on the question of the good life is distinctive to modern political thought. Ancient political theory held that the purpose of politics was to cultivate the virtue, or moral excellence, of citizens. All associations aim at some good, Aristotle wrote,

and the polis, or political association, aims at the highest, most comprehensive good: "any polis which is truly so called, and is not merely one in name, must devote itself to the end of encouraging goodness. Otherwise, a political association sinks into a mere alliance, which only differs in space from other forms of alliance where the members live at a distance from one another.

Otherwise, too, law becomes a mere covenant—or (in the phrase of the Sophist Lycophron) 'a guarantor of men's rights against one another'—instead of being, as it should be, a rule of life such as will make the members of a polis good and just." [1]

According to Aristotle, political community is more than "an association for residence on a common site, or for the sake of preventing mutual injustice and easing exchange." Although these are necessary conditions for political community, they are not its purpose or ultimate justification. "The end and purpose of a polis is the good life, and the institutions of social life are means to that end." It is only as participants in political association that we can realize our nature and fulfill our highest ends. [2]

Unlike the ancient conception, liberal political theory does not see political life as concerned with the highest human ends or with the moral excellence of its citizens. Rather than promote a particular conception of the good life, liberal political theory insists on toleration, fair procedures, and respect for individual rights—values that respect people's freedom to choose their own values. But this raises a difficult question. If liberal ideals cannot be defended in the name of the highest human good, then in what does their moral basis consist?

It is sometimes thought that liberal principles can be justified by a simple version of moral relativism. Government should not "legislate morality," because all morality is merely subjective, a matter of personal preference not open to argument or rational debate. "Who is to say what is literature and what is filth? That is a value judgment, and whose values should decide?" Relativism usually appears less as a claim than as a question: "Who is to judge?" But the same question can be asked of the values that liberals defend. Toleration and freedom and fairness are values too, and they can hardly be defended by the claim that no values can be defended. So it is a mistake to affirm liberal values by arguing that all values are merely subjective. The relativist defense of liberalism is no defense at all.

Utilitarianism versus Kantian Liberalism

What, then, is the case for the neutrality the liberal invokes? Recent political philosophy has offered two main alternatives—one utilitarian, the other Kantian. The utilitarian view, following John Stuart Mill, defends liberal principles in the name of maximizing the general welfare. The state should not impose on its citizens a preferred way of life, even for their own good, because doing so will reduce the sum of human happiness, at least in the long run. It is better that people choose for themselves, even if, on occasion, they get it wrong.

"The only freedom which deserves the name," writes Mill in *On Liberty*, "is that of pursuing our own good in our own way, so long as we do not attempt to deprive others of theirs, or impede their efforts to obtain it." He adds that his argument does not depend on any notion of abstract right, only on the principle of the greatest good for the greatest number. "I regard utility as the ultimate appeal on all ethical questions; but it must be utility in the largest sense, grounded on the permanent interests of man as a progressive being." [3]

Many objections have been raised against utilitarianism as a general doctrine of moral philosophy. Some have questioned the concept of utility and the assumption that all human goods are in principle commensurable. Others have objected that by reducing all values to preferences and desires, utilitarians are unable to admit qualitative distinctions of worth, unable to distinguish noble desires from base ones. But most recent debate has focused on whether utilitarianism offers a convincing basis for liberal principles, including respect for individual rights.

At first glance, utilitarianism seems well suited to liberal purposes. Seeking to maximize overall happiness does not require judging people's values, only aggregating them. And the willingness to aggregate preferences without judging them suggests a tolerant spirit, even a democratic one. When people go to the polls we count their votes, whatever they are.

But the utilitarian calculus is not always as liberal as it first appears. If enough cheering Romans pack the Coliseum to watch the lion devour the

---

1. Aristotle, *The Politics*, trans. Ernest Barker, book 3, chap. 9 (London: Oxford University Press, 1946), p. 119.
2. Ibid., pp. 119–120

3. John Stuart Mill, *On Liberty* (1859), chap. 1.

Christian, the collective pleasure of the Romans will surely outweigh the pain of the Christian, intense though it be. Or if a big majority abhors a small religion and wants it banned, the balance of preferences will favor suppression, not toleration. Utilitarians sometimes defend individual rights on the grounds that respecting them now will serve utility in the long run. But this calculation is precarious and contingent. It hardly secures the liberal promise not to impose on some the values of others.

The case against utilitarianism was made most powerfully by Immanuel Kant. He argued that empirical principles such as utility were unfit to serve as a basis for morality. A wholly instrumental defense of freedom and rights not only leaves rights vulnerable but fails to respect the inherent dignity of persons. The utilitarian calculus treats people as means to the happiness of others, not as ends in themselves, worthy of respect.[4]

Contemporary liberals extend Kant's argument with the claim that utilitarianism fails to take seriously the distinction between persons. In seeking above all to maximize the general welfare, the utilitarian treats society as a whole as if it were a single person; it conflates our many, diverse desires into a single system of desires. It is indifferent to the distribution of satisfactions among persons, except insofar as this may affect the overall sum. But this fails to respect our plurality and distinctness. It uses some as means to the happiness of all, and so fails to respect each as an end in himself or herself.

In the view of modern-day Kantians, certain rights are so fundamental that even the general welfare cannot override them. As John Rawls writes in *A Theory of Justice*, "Each person possesses an inviolability founded on justice that even the welfare of society as a whole cannot override. . . . The rights secured by justice are not subject to political bargaining or to the calculus of social interests."[5]

4. See Immanuel Kant, *Groundwork of the Metaphysics of Morals* (1785), trans. H.J. Paton (New York: Harper and Row, 1956); idem, *Critique of Practical Reason* (1788), trans. L.W. Beck (Indianapolis: Bobbs-Merrill, 1956); idem, "On the Common Saying: 'This May Be True in Theory, But It Does Not Apply in Practice,'" in *Kant's Political Writings*, ed. Hans Reiss (Cambridge: Cambridge University Press, 1970), pp. 61–92.
5. John Rawls, *A Theory of Justice*, (Cambridge, MA: Harvard University Press, 1971), pp. 3–4.

So Kantian liberals need an account of rights that does not depend on utilitarian considerations. More than this, they need an account that does not depend on any particular conception of the good, that does not presuppose the superiority of one way of life over others. Only a justification neutral among ends could preserve the liberal resolve not to favor any particular ends or to impose on its citizens a preferred way of life. But what sort of justification could this be? How is it possible to affirm certain liberties and rights as fundamental without embracing some vision of the good life, without endorsing some ends over others?

The solution proposed by Kantian liberals is to draw a distinction between the "right" and the "good"—between a framework of basic rights and liberties, and the conceptions of the good that people may choose to pursue within the framework. It is one thing for the state to support a fair framework, they argue, something else to affirm some particular ends. For example, it is one thing to defend the right to free speech so that people may be free to form their own opinions and choose their own ends, but something else to support it on grounds that a life of political discussion is inherently worthier than a life unconcerned with public affairs, or on the grounds that free speech will increase the general welfare. Only the first defense is available on the Kantian view, resting as it does on the ideal of a neutral framework.

Now the commitment to a framework neutral with respect to ends can be seen as a kind of value—in this sense the Kantian liberal is no relativist—but its value consists precisely in its refusal to affirm a preferred way of life or conception of the good. For Kantian liberals, then, the right is prior to the good, and in two senses. First, individual rights cannot be sacrificed for the sake of the general good; and second, the principles of justice that specify these rights cannot be premised on any particular vision of the good life. What justifies the rights is not that they maximize the general welfare or otherwise promote the good, but rather that they constitute a fair framework within which individuals and groups can choose their own values and ends, consistent with a similar liberty for others.

The claim for the priority of the right over the good connects the ideal of neutrality with the primacy of individual rights. For Kantian liberals, rights "function as trump cards held by individuals." They protect individuals from policies, even democratically enacted ones, that would impose a preferred conception of the good and so fail to respect people's freedom to choose their own conceptions.[6]

Of course, proponents of the liberal ethic notoriously disagree about what rights are fundamental and what political arrangements the ideal of the neutral framework requires. Egalitarian liberals support the welfare state and favor a scheme of civil liberties together with certain social and economic rights—rights to welfare, education, health care, and so on. They argue that respecting the capacity of persons to pursue their own ends requires government to assure the minimal prerequisites of a dignified life. Libertarian liberals (usually called conservatives in contemporary politics) defend the market economy and claim that redistributive policies violate people's rights. They argue that respect for persons requires assuring to each the fruits of his or her own labor, and so favor a scheme of civil liberties combined with a strict regime of private property rights. Whether egalitarian or libertarian, Kantian liberalism begins with the claim that we are separate, individual persons, each with our own aims, interests, and conceptions of the good life. It seeks a framework of rights that will enable us to realize our capacity as free moral agents, consistent with a similar liberty for others.

The Liberal Self

The Kantian case against utilitarianism derives much of its force from its contrasting conception of the person, its view of what it means to be a moral agent. Where utilitarians conflate our many desires into a single system of desire, Kantian liberals insist on the separateness of persons. Where the utilitarian self is simply defined as the sum of its desires, the Kantian self is a choosing self, independent of the desires and ends it may have at any moment. Kant expressed this idea by attributing to human beings the capacity to act with an autonomous will. Contemporary liberals rely on the similar notion of a self given prior to and independent of its purposes and ends.

The claim for the priority of the right over the good, and the conception of the person that attends it, oppose Kantian liberalism not only to utilitarianism but also to any view that regards us as obligated to fulfill ends we have not chosen—ends given by nature or God, for example, or by our identities as members of families, peoples, cultures, or traditions. Encumbered identities such as these are at odds with the liberal conception of the person as free and independent selves, unbound by prior moralties, capable of choosing our ends for ourselves. This is the conception that finds expression in the ideal of the state as a neutral framework. For Kantian liberals, it is precisely because we are freely choosing, independent selves that we need a neutral framework, a framework of rights that refuses to choose among competing values and ends. For the liberal self, what matters above all, what is most essential to our personhood, is not the ends we choose but our capacity to choose them. "It is not our aims that primarily reveal our nature," but rather the framework of rights we would agree to if we could abstract from our aims. "For the self is prior to the ends which are affirmed by it; even a dominant end must be chosen from among numerous possibilities."[7]

The liberal ethic derives much of its moral force from the appeal of the self-image that animates it. This appeal has at least two sources. First, the image of the self as free and independent, unencumbered by aims and attachments it does not choose for itself, offers a powerful liberating vision. Freed from the sanctions of custom and tradition and inherited status, unbound by moral ties antecedent to choice, the liberal self is installed as sovereign, cast as the author of the only obligations that constrain. More than the simple sum of circumstance, we become capable of the dignity that consists in being persons of our "own creating, making, choosing."[8] We are agents and not just instruments of the purposes we pursue. We are "self-originating sources of valid claims."[9]

A second appeal of the liberal self-image consists in the case it implies for equal respect. The idea that there is more to a person than the roles

6. Ronald Dworkin, "Liberalism," in Stuart Hampshire, ed., *Public and Private Morality* (Cambridge: Cambridge University Press, 1978). p. 136.

7. Rawls, *A Theory of Justice*, p. 560.
8. George Kateb, "Democratic Individuality and the Claims of Politics," *Political Theory*, 12 (August 1984), 343.
9. John Rawls, "Kantian Constructivism in Moral Theory," *Journal of Philosophy*, 77 (Summer 1980), 543.

he plays or the customs she keeps or the faith he affirms suggests a basis for respect independent of life's contingencies. Liberal justice is blind to such differences between persons as race, religion, ethnicity, and gender, for in the liberal self-image, these features do not really define our identity in the first place. They are not constituents but merely attributes of the self, the sort of things the state should look beyond. "Our social position and class, our sex and race should not influence deliberations made from a moral point of view."[10] Once these contingencies are seen as products of our situation rather than as aspects of our person, they cease to supply the familiar grounds for prejudice and discrimination.

Nor does it matter, from the standpoint of liberal justice, what virtues we display or what values we espouse. "That we have one conception of the good rather than another is not relevant from a moral standpoint. In acquiring it we are influenced by the same sort of contingencies that lead us to rule out a knowledge of our sex and class."[11] Despite their many differences, libertarian and egalitarian liberals agree that people's entitlements should not be based on their merit or virtue or moral desert, for the qualities that make people virtuous or morally deserving depend on factors "arbitrary from a moral point of view."[12] The liberal state therefore does not discriminate; none of its policies or laws may presuppose that any person or way of life is intrinsically more virtuous than any other. It respects persons as persons, and secures their equal right to live the lives they choose.

Critique of Kantian Liberalism

Kantian liberals thus avoid affirming a conception of the good by affirming instead the priority of the right, which depends in turn on a picture of the self given prior to its ends. But how plausible

is this self-conception? Despite its powerful appeal, the image of the unencumbered self is flawed. It cannot make sense of our moral experience, because it cannot account for certain moral and political obligations that we commonly recognize, even prize. These include obligations of solidarity, religious duties, and other moral ties that may claim us for reasons unrelated to a choice. Such obligations are difficult to account for if we understand ourselves as free and independent selves, unbound by moral ties we have not chosen. Unless we think of ourselves as encumbered selves, already claimed by certain projects and commitments, we cannot make sense of these indispensable aspects of our moral and political experience.

Consider the limited scope of obligation on the liberal view. According to Rawls, obligations can arise in only one of two ways, as "natural duties" we owe to human beings as such or as voluntary obligations we incur by consent. The natural duties are those we owe persons *qua* persons—to do justice, to avoid cruelty, and so on. All other obligations, the ones we owe to particular others, are founded in consent and arise only in virtue of agreements we make, be they tacit or explicit.[13]

Conceived as unencumbered selves, we must respect the dignity of all persons, but beyond this, we owe only what we agree to owe. Liberal justice requires that we respect people's rights (as defined by the neutral framework), not that we advance their good. Whether we must concern ourselves with other people's good depends on whether, and with whom, and on what terms, we have agreed to do so.

One striking consequence of this view is that "there is no political obligation, strictly speaking, for citizens generally." Although those who run for office voluntarily incur a political obligation (that is, to serve their country if elected), the ordinary citizen does not. "It is not clear what is the requisite binding action or who has performed it."[14] The average citizen is therefore without any special obligations to his or her fellow citizens, apart from the universal, natural duty not to commit injustice.

10. John Rawls, "Fairness to Goodness," *Philosophical Review*, 84 (October 1985), 537.
11. Ibid.
12. Rawls, *A Theory of Justice*, p. 312, and, generally, pp. 310–315. See also Friedrich A. Hayek, *The Constitution of Liberty* (Chicago: University of Chicago Press, 1960), chap. 7; and Nozick, *Anarchy, State, and Utopia*, pp. 155–160.

13. Rawls, *A Theory of Justice*, pp. 108–117.
14. Ibid., p. 114.

The liberal attempt to construe all obligation in terms of duties universally owed or obligations voluntarily incurred makes it difficult to account for civic obligations and other moral and political ties that we commonly recognize. It fails to capture those loyalties and responsibilities whose moral force consists partly in the fact that living by them is inseparable from understanding ourselves as the particular persons we are—as members of this family or city or nation or people, as bearers of that history, as citizens of this republic. Loyalties such as these can be more than values I happen to have, and to hold, at a certain distance. The moral responsibilities they entail may go beyond the obligations I voluntarily incur and the "natural duties" I owe to human beings as such.[15]

Some of the special responsibilities that flow from the particular communities I inhabit I may owe to fellow members, such as obligations of solidarity. Others I may owe to members of those communities with which my own community has some morally relevant history, such as the morally burdened relations of Germans to Jews, of American whites to American blacks, or of England and France to their former colonies.[16] Whether they look inward or outward, obligations of membership presuppose that we are capable of moral ties antecedent to choice. To the extent that we are, the meaning of our membership resists redescription in contractarian terms.

It is sometimes argued, in defense of the liberal view, that loyalties and allegiances not grounded in consent, however psychologically compelling, are matters of sentiment, not of morality, and so do not suggest an obligation unavailable to unencumbered selves. But it is difficult to make sense of certain familiar moral and political dilemmas without acknowledging obligations of solidarity and the thickly constituted, encumbered selves that they imply.

Consider the case of Robert E. Lee on the eve of the Civil War. Lee, then an officer in the Union army, opposed secession, in fact regarded it as treason. And yet when war loomed, Lee concluded that his obligation to Virginia outweighed his obligation to the Union and also his reported opposition to slavery. "With all my devotion to the Union," he wrote, "I have not been able to make up my mind to raise my hand against my relatives, my children, my home. . . . If the Union is dissolved, and the Government disrupted, I shall return to my native State and share the miseries of my people. Save in her defense, I will draw my sword no more."[17]

One can appreciate the poignance of Lee's predicament without necessarily approving of the choice he made. But one cannot make sense of his dilemma as a *moral* dilemma without acknowledging that the call to stand with his people, even to lead them in a cause he opposed, was a claim of moral and not merely sentimental import, capable at least of weighing in the balance against other duties and obligations. Otherwise, Lee's predicament was not really a moral dilemma at all, but simply a conflict between morality on the one hand and mere sentiment or prejudice on the other.

A merely psychological reading of Lee's predicament misses the fact that we not only sympathize with people such as Lee but often admire them, not necessarily for the choices they make but for the quality of character their deliberation reflects. The quality at stake is the disposition to see and bear one's life circumstance as a reflectively situated being—claimed by the history that implicates me in a particular life, but self-conscious of its particularity, and so alive to other ways, wider horizons. But this is precisely the quality that is lacking in those who would think of themselves as unencumbered selves, bound only by the obligations they choose to incur.

As the Lee example illustrates, the liberal conception of the person is too thin to account for the full range of moral and political obligations we commonly recognize, such as obligations of solidarity. This counts against its plausibility generally. But it may even be too weak to support the less strenuous communal obligations expected of citizens in the modern welfare state. Some

15. See Michael J. Sandel, *Liberalism and the Limits of Justice* (Cambridge: Cambridge University Press, 1982), pp. 179–183.
16. Alasdair MacIntyre, *After Virtue* (Notre Dame: University of Notre Dame Press, 1981), pp. 204–206.
17. Lee quoted in Douglas Southall Freeman, *R. E. Lee* (New York: Charles Scribner's Sons, 1934), pp. 443, 421. See also the discussions of Lee in Morton Grodzins, *The Loyal and the Disloyal* (Chicago: University of Chicago Press, 1965), pp. 142–143; and Judith Shklar, *Ordinary Vices* (Cambridge, Mass.: Harvard University Press, 1984), p. 160.

stronger conception of community may be required, not only to make sense of tragic-heroic dilemmas such as Lee's, but even to sustain the rights that many liberals defend.

While libertarian liberals ask little of citizens, more generous expressions of the liberal ethic support various policies of public provision and redistribution. Egalitarian liberals defend social and economic rights as well as civil and political rights, and so demand of their fellow citizens a high measure of mutual engagement. They insist on the "plurality and distinctness" of individuals but also require that we "share one another's fate" and regard the distribution of natural talents as "a common asset."[18]

Liberalism as an ethic of sharing emphasizes the arbitrariness of fortune and the importance of certain material prerequisites for the meaningful exercise of equal liberties. Since "necessitous men are not free men," and since in any case the distribution of assets and endowments that make for success is "arbitrary from a moral point of view," egalitarian liberals would tax the rich to help the poor secure the prerequisites of a dignified life. Thus the liberal case for the welfare state depends not on a theory of the common good or on some strong notion of communal obligation, but instead on the rights we would agree to respect if we could abstract from our interests and ends.

The liberal case for public provision seems well suited to conditions in which strong communal ties cannot be relied on, and this is one source of its appeal. But it lies vulnerable nonetheless to the libertarian objection that redistributive policies use some people as means to others' ends, and so offend the "plurality and distinctness" of individuals that liberalism seeks above all to secure.[19] In the contractual vision of community alone, it is unclear how the libertarian objection can be met. If those whose fate I am required to share really are, morally speaking, *others*, rather than fellow participants in a way of life with which my identity is bound, then liberalism as an ethic of sharing seems open to the same objections as utilitarianism. Its claim on me is not the claim of a community with which I identify, but rather the claim of an arbitrarily defined collectivity whose aims I may or may not share.

If the egalitarian replies that social and economic rights are required as a matter of equal respect for persons, the question remains why *these* persons, the ones who happen to live in my country, have a claim on my concern that others do not. Tying the mutual responsibilities of citizenship to the idea of respect for persons *qua* persons puts the moral case for welfare on a par with the case for foreign aid—a duty we owe strangers with whom we share a common humanity but possibly little else. Given its conception of the person, it is unclear how liberalism can defend the particular boundaries of concern its own ethic of sharing must presuppose.

What egalitarian liberalism requires, but cannot within its own terms provide, is some way of defining the relevant community of sharing, some way of seeing the participants as mutually indebted and morally engaged to begin with. It needs a way of answering Emerson's challenge to the man who solicited his contribution to the poor—"Are they *my* poor?" Since liberal social and economic rights cannot be justified as expressing or advancing a common life of shared pursuits, the basis and bounds of communal concern become difficult to defend. For as we have seen, the strong notion of community or membership that would save and situate the sharing is precisely the one denied to the liberal self. The moral encumbrances and antecedent obligations it implies would undercut the priority of right.

18. Rawls, *A Theory of Justice*, pp. 101–102.
19. See Nozick, *Anarchy, State, and Utopia*, p. 228.

Spheres of Justice

Michael Walzer

A Theory of Goods

Theories of distributive justice focus on a social process commonly described as if it had this form:

People distribute goods to (other) people.

Here, "distribute" means give, allocate, exchange, and so on, and the focus is on the individuals who stand at either end of these actions: not on producers and consumers, but on distributive agents and recipients of goods. We are as always interested in ourselves, but, in this case, in a special and limited version of ourselves, as people who give and take. What is our nature? What are our rights? What do we need, want, deserve? What are we entitled to? What would we accept under ideal conditions? Answers to these questions are turned into distributive principles, which are supposed to control the movement of goods. The goods, defined by abstraction, are taken to be movable in any direction.

But this is too simple an understanding of what actually happens, and it forces us too quickly to make large assertions about human nature and moral agency—assertions unlikely, ever, to command general agreement. I want to propose a more precise and complex description of the central process:

People conceive and create goods, which they then distribute among themselves.

Here, the conception and creation precede and control the distribution. Goods don't just appear in the hands of distributive agents who do with them as they like or give them out in accordance with some general principle. Rather, goods with their meanings—because of their meanings—are the crucial medium of social relations; they come into people's minds before they come into their hands; distributions are patterned in accordance with shared conceptions of what the goods are and what they are for. Distributive agents are constrained by the goods they hold; one might almost say that goods distribute themselves among people.

Things are in the saddle
And ride mankind.

But these are always particular things and particular groups of men and women. And, of course, we make the things—even the saddle. I don't want to deny the importance of human agency, only to shift our attention from distribution itself to conception and creation: the naming of the goods, and the giving of meaning, and the collective making. What we need to explain and limit the pluralism of distributive possibilities is a theory of goods. For our immediate purposes, that theory can be summed up in six propositions.

1. All the goods with which distributive justice is concerned are social goods. They are not and they cannot be idiosyncratically valued. I am not sure that there are any other kinds of goods; I mean to leave the question open. Some domestic objects are cherished for private and sentimental reasons, but only in cultures where sentiment regularly attaches to such objects. A beautiful sunset, the smell of new-mown hay, the excitement of an urban vista: these perhaps are privately valued goods, though they are also, and more obviously, the objects of cultural assessment. Even new inventions are not valued in accordance with the ideas of their inventors; they are subject to a wider process of conception and creation. God's goods, to be sure, are exempt from this rule—as in the first chapter of Genesis: "and God saw every thing that He had made, and, behold, it was very good" (1:31). That evaluation doesn't require the agreement of manking (who might be doubtful), or of a majority of men and women, or of any group of men and women meeting under ideal conditions (though Adam and Eve in Eden would probably endorse it). But I can't think of any other exemptions. Goods in the world have shared meanings because conception and creation are social processes. For the same reason, goods have different meanings in different societies. The same "thing" is valued for different reasons, or it is valued here and disvalued there. John Stuart Mill once complained that "people like in crowds," but

I know of no other way to like or to dislike social goods. A solitary person could hardly understand the meaning of the goods or figure out the reasons for taking them as likable or dislikable. Once people like in crowds, it becomes possible for individuals to break away, pointing to latent or subversive meanings, aiming at alternative values—including the values, for example, of notoriety and eccentricity. An easy eccentricity has sometimes been one of the privileges of the aristocracy: it is a social good like any other.

2.   Men and women take on concrete identities because of the way they conceive and create, and then possess and employ social goods. "The line between what is me and mine," wrote William James, "is very hard to draw." Distributions can not be understood as the acts of men and women who do not yet have particular goods in their minds or in their hands. In fact, people already stand in a relation to a set of goods; they have a history of transactions, not only with one another but also with the moral and material world in which they live. Without such a history, which begins at birth, they wouldn't be men and women in any recognizable sense, and they wouldn't have the first notion of how to go about the business of giving, allocating, and exchanging goods.

3.   There is no single set of primary or basic goods conceivable across all moral and material worlds—or, any such set would have to be conceived in terms so abstract that they would be of little use in thinking about particular distributions. Even the range of necessities, if we take into account moral as well as physical necessities, is very wide, and the rank orderings are very different. A single necessary good, and one that is always necessary—food, for example—carries different meanings in different places. Bread is the staff of life, the body of Christ, the symbol of the Sabbath, the means of hospitality, and so on. Conceivably, there is a limited sense in which the first of these is primary, so that if there were twenty people in the world and just enough bread to feed the twenty, the primacy of bread-as-staff-of-life would yield a sufficient distributive principle. But that is the only circumstance in which it would do so; and even there, we can't be sure. If the religious uses of bread were to conflict with its nutritional uses—if the gods demanded that bread be baked and burned rather than eaten—it

is by no means clear which use would be primary. How, then, is bread to be incorporated into the universal list? The question is even harder to answer, the conventional answers less plausible, as we pass from necessities to opportunities, powers, reputations, and so on. These can be incorporated only if they are abstracted from every particular meaning—hence, for all practical purposes, rendered meaningless.

4.   But it is the meaning of goods that determines their movement. Distributive criteria and arrangements are intrinsic not to the good-in-itself but to the social good. If we understand what it is, what it means to those for whom it is a good, we understand how, by whom, and for what reasons it ought to be distributed. All distributions are just or unjust relative to the social meanings of the goods at stake. This is in obvious ways a principle of legitimation, but it is also a critical principle.[1] When medieval Christians, for example, condemned the sin of simony, they were claiming that the meaning of a particular social good, ecclesiastical office, excluded its sale and purchase. Given the Christian understanding of office, it followed—I am inclined to say, it necessarily followed—that office holders should be chosen for their knowledge and piety and not for their wealth. There are presumably things that money can buy, but not this thing. Similarly, the words *prostitution* and *bribery*, like *simony*, describe the sale and purchase of goods that, given certain understandings of their meaning, ought never to be sold or purchased.

5.   Social meanings are historical in character; and so distributions, and just and unjust distribu-

---

1. Aren't social meanings, as Marx said, nothing other than "the ideas of the ruling class," "the dominant material relationships grasped as ideas"? I don't think that they are ever only that or simply that, though the members of the ruling class and the intellectuals they patronize may well be in a position to exploit and distort social meanings in their own interests. When they do that, however, they are likely to encounter resistance, rooted (intellectually) in those same meanings. A people's culture is always a joint, even if it isn't an entirely cooperative, production, and it is always a complex production. The common understanding of particular goods incorporates principles, procedures, conceptions of agency, that the rulers would not choose if they were choosing *right now*—and so provides the terms of social criticism. The appeal to what I shall call "internal" principles against the usurpations of powerful men and women is the ordinary form of critical discourse.

tions, change over time. To be sure, certain key goods have what we might think of as characteristic normative structures, reiterated across the lines (but not all the lines) of time and space. It is because of this reiteration that the British philosopher Bernard Williams is able to argue that goods should always be distributed for "relevant reasons"—where relevance seems to connect to essential rather than to social meanings. The idea that offices, for example, should go to qualified candidates—though not the only idea that has been held about offices—is plainly visible in very different societies where simony and nepotism, under different names, have similarly been thought sinful or unjust. (But there has been a wide divergence of views about what sorts of position and place are properly called "offices.") Again, punishment has been widely understood as a negative good that ought to go to people who are judged to deserve it on the basis of a verdict, not of a political decision. (But what constitutes a verdict? Who is to deliver it? How, in short, is justice to be done to accused men and women? About these questions there has been significant disagreement.) These examples invite empirical investigation. There is no merely intuitive or speculative procedure for seizing upon relevant reason.

6. When meanings are distinct, distributions must be autonomous. Every social good or set of goods constitutes, as it were, a distributive sphere within which only certain criteria and arrangements are appropriate. Money is inappropriate in the sphere of ecclesiastical office; it is an intrusion from another sphere. And piety should make for no advantage in the marketplace, as the marketplace has commonly been understood. Whatever can rightly be sold ought to be sold to pious men and women and also to profane, heretical, and sinful men and women (else no one would do much business). The market is open to all comers; the church is not. In no society, of course, are social meanings entirely distinct. What happens in one distributive sphere affects what happens in the others; we can look, at most, for relative autonomy. But relative autonomy, like social meaning, is a critical principle—indeed, as I shall be arguing throughout this book, a radical principle. It is radical even though it doesn't point to a single standard against which all distributions are to be measured. There is no single standard. But there are standards (roughly knowable even when they are also controversial)

for every social good and every distributive sphere in every particular society; and these standards are often violated, the goods usurped, the spheres invaded, by powerful men and women....

The Case of Medical Care

Until recent times, the practice of medicine was mostly a matter of free enterprise. Doctors made their diagnosis, gave their advice, healed or didn't heal their patients, for a fee. Perhaps the private character of the economic relationship was connected to the intimate character of the professional relationship. More likely, I think, it had to do with the relative marginality of medicine itself. Doctors could, in fact, do very little for their patients; and the common attitude in the face of disease (as in the face of poverty) was a stoical fatalism. Or, popular remedies were developed that were not much less effective, sometimes more effective, than those prescribed by established physicians. Folk medicine sometimes produced a kind of communal provision at the local level, but it was equally likely to generate new practitioners, charging fees in their turn. Faith healing followed a similar pattern.

Leaving these two aside, we can say that the distribution of medical care has historically rested in the hands of the medical profession, a guild of physicians that dates at least from the time of Hippocrates in the fifth century B.C. The guild has functioned to exclude unconventional practitioners and to regulate the number of physicians in any given community. A genuinely free market has never been in the interest of its members. But it is in the interest of the members to sell their services to individual patients; and thus, by and large, the well-to-do have been well cared for (in accordance with the current understanding of good care) and the poor hardly cared for at all. In a few urban communities—in the medieval Jewish communities, for example—medical services were more widely available. But they were virtually unknown for most people most of the time. Doctors were the servants of the rich, often attached to noble houses and royal courts. With regard to this practical outcome, however, the profession has always had a collective bad conscience. For the distributive logic of the practice of medicine seems to be this: that care should be proportionate to illness and not to wealth. Hence, there have always been doctors, like those honored in ancient Greece, who served the poor on the side, as it were, even while they earned their living from paying patients. Most doctors, present in an emergency, still feel bound to help the victim without regard to his material status. It is a matter of professional Good Samaritanism that the call "Is there a doctor in the house?" should not go unanswered if there is a doctor to answer it. In ordinary times, however, there was little call for medical help, largely because there was little faith in its actual helpfulness. And so the bad conscience of the profession was not echoed by any political demand for the replacement of free enterprise by communal provision.

In Europe during the Middle Ages, the cure of souls was public, the cure of bodies private. Today, in most European countries, the situation is reversed. The reversal is best explained in terms of a major shift in the common understanding of souls and bodies: we have lost confidence in the cure of souls, and we have come increasingly to believe, even to be obsessed with, the cure of bodies. Descartes's famous declaration that the "preservation of health" was the "chief of all goods" may be taken to symbolize the shift—or to herald it, for in the history of popular attitudes, Descartes's *Discourse on Method* came very early. Then, as eternity receded in the popular consciousness, longevity moved to the fore. Among medieval Christians, eternity was a socially recognized need; and every effort was made to see that it was widely and equally distributed, that every Christian had an equal chance at salvation and eternal life: hence, a church in every parish, regular services, catechism for the young, compulsory communion, and so on. Among modern citizens, longevity is a socially recognized need; and increasingly every effort is made to see that it is widely and equally distributed, that every citizen has an equal chance at a long and healthy life; hence doctors and hospitals in every district, regular check-ups, health education for the young, compulsory vaccination, and so on.

Parallel to the shift in attitudes, and following naturally from it, was a shift in institutions: from the church to the clinic and the hospital. But the shift has been gradual: a slow development of communal interest in medical care, a slow erosion of interest in religious care. The first major form of medical provision came in the area of prevention, not of treatment, probably because the former involved no interference with the prerogatives of the guild of physicians. But the beginnings of provision in the area of treatment were roughly simultaneous with the great public health campaigns of the late nineteenth century, and the two undoubtedly reflect the same sensitivity to questions of physical survival. The licensing of physicians, the establishment of state medical schools and urban clinics, the filtering of tax money into the great voluntary hospitals: these measures involved, perhaps, only marginal interference with the profession—some of them, in fact, reinforced its guildlike character; but they already represent an important public commitment. Indeed, they represent a commitment that ultimately can be fulfilled only by turning physicians, or some substantial number of them, into public physicians (as a smaller number once turned themselves into court physicians) and by abolishing or constraining the market in medical care. But before I defend that transformation, I want to stress the unavoidability of the commitment from which it follows.

What has happened in the modern world is simply that disease itself, even when it is endemic rather than epidemic, has come to be seen as a plague. And since the plague can be dealt with, it *must* be dealt with. People will not endure what they no longer believe they have to endure. Dealing with tuberculosis, cancer, or heart failure, however, requires a common effort. Medical research is expensive, and the treatment of many particular diseases lies far beyond the resources of ordinary citizens. So the community must step in, and any democratic community will in fact step in, more or less vigorously, more or less effectively, depending on the outcome of particular political battles. Thus, the role of the American government (or governments, for much of the activity is at the state and local levels): subsidizing research, training doctors, providing hospitals and equipment, regulating voluntary insurance schemes, underwriting the treatment of the very old. All this represents "the contrivance of human wisdom to provide for human wants." And all that is required to make it morally necessary is the development of a "want" so widely and deeply felt that it can plausibly be said that it is the want not of this or that person alone but of the community generally—a "human want" even though culturally shaped and stressed.[2]

But once communal provision begins, it is subject to further moral constraints: it must provide what is "wanted" equally to all the members of the community; and it must do so in ways that respect their membership. Now, even the pattern of medical provision in the United States, though it stops far short of a national health service, is intended to provide minimally decent care to all who need it. Once public funds are committed, public officials can hardly intend anything less. At the same time, however, no political decision has yet been made to challenge directly the system of free enterprise in medical care. And so long as that system exists, wealth will be dominant in (this part of) the sphere of security and welfare; individuals will be cared for in proportion to their ability to pay and not to their need for care. In fact, the situation is more complex than that formula suggests, for communal provision already encroaches upon the free market, and the very sick and the very old sometimes receive exactly the treatment they should receive. But it is clear that poverty remains a significant bar to adequate and consistent treatment. Perhaps the most telling statistic about contemporary American medicine is the correlation of visits to doctors and hospitals with social class rather than with degree or incidence of illness. Middle- and upper-class Americans are considerably more likely to have a private physician and to see him often, and con-

2. Arguing against Bernard Williams's claim that the only proper criterion for the distribution of medical care is medical need, Robert Nozick asks why it doesn't then follow "that the only proper criterion for the distribution of barbering services is barbering need"? Perhaps it does follow if one attends only to the "internal goal" of the activity, conceived in universal terms. But it doesn't follow if one attends to the social meaning of the activity, the place of the good it distributes in the life of a particular group of people. One can conceive of a society in which haircuts took on such central cultural significance that communal provision would be morally required, but it is something more than an interesting fact that no such society has ever existed. I have been helped in thinking about these issues by an article of Thomas Scanlon's; I adopt here his "conventionalist" alternative.

siderably less likely to be seriously ill, than are their poorer fellow citizens. Were medical care a luxury, these discrepancies would not matter much; but as soon as medical care becomes a socially recognized need, and as soon as the community invests in its provision, they matter a great deal. For then deprivation is a double loss—to one's health and to one's social standing. Doctors and hospitals have become such massively important features of contemporary life that to be cut off from the help they provide is not only dangerous but also degrading.

But any fully developed system of medical provision will require the constraint of the guild of physicians. Indeed, this is more generally true: the provision of security and welfare requires the constraint of those men and women who had previously controlled the goods in question and sold them on the market (assuming, what is by no means always true, that the market predates communal provision). For what we do when we declare this or that good to be a needed good is to block or constrain its free exchange. We also block any other distributive procedure that doesn't attend to need—popular election, meritocratic competition, personal or familial preference, and so on. But the market is, at least in the United States today, the chief rival of the sphere of security and welfare; and it is most importantly the market that is pre-empted by the welfare state. Needed goods cannot be left to the whim, or distributed in the interest, of some powerful group of owners or practitioners.

Most often, ownership is abolished, and practitioners are effectively conscripted or, at least, "signed up" in the public service. They serve for the sake of the social need and not, or not simply, for their own sakes: thus, priests for the sake of eternal life, soldiers for the sake of national defense, public school teachers for the sake of their pupils' education. Priests act wrongly if they sell salvation; soldiers, if they set up as mercenaries; teachers, if they cater to the children of the wealthy. Sometimes the conscription is only partial, as when lawyers are required to be officers of the court, serving the cause of justice even while they also serve their clients and themselves. Sometimes the conscription is occasional and temporary, as when lawyers are required to act as "assigned counsels" for defendants unable to pay.

In these cases, a special effort is made to respect the personal character of the lawyer-client relationship. I would look for a similar effort in any fully developed national health service. But I see no reason to respect the doctor's market freedom. Needed goods are not commodities. Or, more precisely, they can be bought and sold only insofar as they are available above and beyond whatever level of provision is fixed by democratic decision making (and only insofar as the buying and selling doesn't distort distributions below that level).

It might be argued, however, that the refusal thus far to finance a national health service constitutes a political decision by the American people about the level of communal care (and about the relative importance of other goods): a minimal standard for everyone—namely, the standard of the urban clinics; and free enterprise beyond that. That would seem to me an inadequate standard, but it would not necessarily be an unjust decision. It is not, however, the decision the American people have made. The common appreciation of the importance of medical care has carried them well beyond that. In fact, federal, state, and local governments now subsidize different levels of care for different classes of citizens. This might be all right, too, if the classification were connected to the purposes of the care—if, for example, soldiers and defense workers were given special treatment in time of war. But the poor, the middle class, and the rich make an indefensible triage. So long as communal funds are spent, as they currently are, to finance research, build hospitals, and pay the fees of doctors in private practice, the services that these expenditures underwrite must be equally available to all citizens.

This, then, is the argument for an expanded American welfare state. It follows from the three principles with which I began, and it suggests that the tendency of those principles is to free security and welfare from the prevailing patterns of dominance. Though a variety of institutional arrangements is possible, the three principles would seem to favor provision in kind; they suggest an important argument against current proposals to distribute money instead of education, legal aid, or medical care. The negative income tax, for example, is a plan to increase the purchasing power of the poor—a modified version of simple equality. This plan would not, however, abolish the dominance of wealth in the sphere of need. Short of a radical equalization, men and women with greater purchasing power could still, and surely would, bid up the price of needed services. So the community would be investing, though now only indirectly, in individual welfare but without fitting provision to the shape of need. Even with equal incomes, health care delivered through the market would not be responsive to need; nor would the market provide adequately for medical research. This is not an argument against the negative income tax, however, for it may be the case that money itself, in a market economy, is one of the things that people need. And then it too, perhaps, should be provided in kind.

I want to stress again that no *a priori* stipulation of what needs ought to be recognized is possible; nor is there any *a priori* way of determining appropriate levels of provision. Our attitudes toward medical care have a history; they have been different; they will be different again. The forms of communal provision have changed in the past and will continue to change. But they don't change automatically as attitudes change. The old order has its clients; there is a lethargy in institutions as in individuals. Moreover, popular attitudes are rarely so clear as they are in the case of medical care. So change is always a matter of political argument, organization, and struggle. All that the philosopher can do is to describe the basic structure of the arguments and the constraints they entail. Hence the three principles, which can be summed up in a revised version of Marx's famous maxim: From each according to his ability (or his resources); to each according to his socially recognized needs. This, I think, is the deepest meaning of the social contract. It only remains to work out the details—but in everyday life, the details are everything. . . .

Tyrannies and Just Societies

The Relativity and the Non-Relativity of Justice

The best account of distributive justice is an account of its parts: social goods and spheres of distribution. But I want now to say something about the whole: first, with regard to its relative character; second, with regard to the form it takes in our own society; and third, with regard to the stability of that form. These three points will conclude my argument. I shall not attempt here to consider the question whether societies where goods are justly distributed are also good societies. Certainly, justice is better than tyranny; but whether one just society is better than another, I have no way of saying. Is there a particular understanding (and then a particular distribution) of social goods that is *good* simply? That is not a question that I have addressed in this book. As a singular conception, the idea of the good does not control our arguments about justice.

Justice is relative to social meanings. Indeed, the relativity of justice follows from the classic non-relative definition, giving each person his due, as much as it does from my own proposal, distributing goods for "internal" reasons. These are formal definitions that require, as I have tried to show, historical completion. We cannot say what is due to this person or that one until we know how these people relate to one another through the things they make and distribute. There cannot be a just society until there is a society; and the adjective *just* doesn't determine, it only modifies, the substantive life of the societies it describes. There are an infinite number of possible lives, shaped by an infinite number of possible cultures, religions, political arrangements, geographical conditions, and so on. A given society is just if its substantive life is lived in a certain way—that is, in a way faithful to the shared understandings of the members. (When people disagree about the meaning of social goods, when understandings are controversial, then justice requires that the society be faithful to the disagreements, providing institutional channels for their expression, adjudicative mechanisms, and alternative distributions.)

In a society where social meanings are integrated and hierarchical, justice will come to the aid of inequality. Consider again the caste system, which has served me before as a test of theoretical coherence. Here is the summary of a detailed account of the distribution of grain in an Indian village:

Each villager participated in the division of the grain heap. There was no bargaining, and no pay-

ment for specific services rendered. There was no accounting, yet each contributor to the life of the village had a claim on its produce, and the whole produce was easily and successfully divided among the villagers.

This is the village as commune, an idealized though not an absurd picture. But if everyone had a claim on the communal grain heap, some people had greater claims than others. The villagers' portions were unequal, significantly so; and the inequalities were tied to a long series of other inequalities, all of them justified by customary rules and an overarching religious doctrine. Distributions were public and "easily" made, so it can't have been difficult to recognize unjust seizures and acquisitions, not only of grain. A landowner, for example, who brought in hired labor to replace the lower caste members of the village community would violate their rights. The adjective *just*, applied to this community, rules out all such violations. But it does not rule out the inequality of the portions; it cannot require a radical redesign of the village against the shared understandings of the members. If it did, justice itself would be tyrannical.

But perhaps we should doubt that the understandings governing village life were really shared. Perhaps the lower caste members were angry and indignant (though they repressed these feelings) even with landowners who took only their "rightful" portions. If that were so, then it would be important to seek out the principles that shaped their anger and indignation. These principles, too, must have their part in village justice; and if they were known among the lower castes, they were not unknown (though perhaps repressed) among the higher. Social meanings need not be harmonious; sometimes they provide only the intellectual structure within which distributions are debated. But that is a necessary structure. There are no external or universal principles that can replace it. Every substantive account of distributive justice is a local account.[3]

3. At the same time, it may be the case, as I suggested in chapter 1, that certain internal principles, certain conceptions of social goods, are reiterated in many, perhaps in all, human societies. That is an empirical matter. It cannot be determined by philosophical argument among ourselves—nor even by philosophical argument among some ideal version of ourselves.

It will be useful at this point to return to one of the questions that I set aside in my preface: By virtue of what characteristics are we one another's equals? One characteristic above all is central to my argument. We are (all of us) culture-producing creatures; we make and inhabit meaningful worlds. Since there is no way to rank and order these worlds with regard to their understanding of social goods, we do justice to actual men and women by respecting their particular creations. And they claim justice, and resist tyranny, by insisting on the meaning of social goods among themselves. Justice is rooted in the distinct understandings of places, honors, jobs, things of all sorts, that constitute a shared way of life. To override those understandings is (always) to act unjustly.

Chapter 13

Moral Argument and Liberal Toleration

In *Political Liberalism* (1993), Rawls argues that the case for detaching justice from substantive moral and religious controversies does not depend on accepting Kantian moral philosophy or a conception of persons as freely choosing, unencumbered selves. Instead, the need to find principles of justice that are neutral among competing conceptions of the good life arises from the fact that people disagree about moral and religious questions. Moreover, these disagreements are reasonable; we should not expect them to give way in the face of arguments that everyone can accept. Political liberalism, Rawls argues, is a response to the fact of reasonable pluralism about the good that prevails in modern democratic societies.

Here are some questions to consider: Does the reasonable pluralism we find in modern democratic societies apply only to questions of morality and religion, or also to questions of justice and rights? If it applies to both, what are the consequences for Rawls's account of liberalism? When we encounter moral and religious views different from our own, do we respect our fellow citizens by setting aside our disagreements for political purposes, or by taking up these disagreements in the political arena?

Political Liberalism

John Rawls

Fundamental Ideas

Political liberalism, the title of these lectures, has a familiar ring. Yet I mean by it something quite different, I think, from what the reader is likely to suppose. Perhaps I should, then, begin with a definition of political liberalism and explain why I call it "political." But no definition would be useful at the outset. Instead I begin with a first fundamental question about political justice in a democratic society, namely what is the most appropriate conception of justice for specifying the fair terms of social cooperation between citizens regarded as free and equal, and as fully cooperating members of society over a complete life, from one generation to the next?

We join this first fundamental question with a second, that of toleration understood in a general way. The political culture of a democratic society is always marked by a diversity of opposing and irreconcilable religious, philosophical, and moral doctrines. Some of these are perfectly reasonable, and this diversity among reasonable doctrines political liberalism sees as the inevitable long-run result of the powers of human reason at work within the background of enduring free institutions. Thus, the second question is what are the grounds of toleration so understood and given the fact of reasonable pluralism as the inevitable outcome of free institutions? Combining both questions we have: how is it possible for there to exist over time a just and stable society of free and equal citizens, who remain profoundly divided by reasonable religious, philosophical, and moral doctrines?

The most intractable struggles, political liberalism assumes, are confessedly for the sake of the highest things: for religion, for philosophical views of the world, and for different moral conceptions of the good. We should find it remarkable that, so deeply opposed in these ways, just cooperation among free and equal citizens is possible at all. In fact, historical experience suggests that it rarely is. If the problem addressed is all too familiar, political liberalism proposes, I believe, a somewhat unfamiliar resolution of it. To state this resolution we need a certain family of ideas. In this lecture I set out the more central of these and offer a definition at the end. . . .

Addressing Two Fundamental Questions

1. Focusing on the first fundamental question, the course of democratic thought over the past two centuries or so makes plain that there is at present no agreement on the way the basic institutions of a constitutional democracy should be arranged if they are to satisfy the fair terms of cooperation between citizens regarded as free and equal. This is shown in the deeply contested ideas about how the values of liberty and equality are best expressed in the basic rights and liberties of citizens so as to answer to the claims of both liberty and equality. We may think of this disagreement as a conflict within the tradition of democratic thought itself, between the tradition associated with Locke, which gives greater weight to what Constant called "the liberties of the moderns," freedom of thought and conscience, certain basic rights of the person and of property, and the rule of law, and the tradition associated with Rousseau, which gives greater weight to what Constant called "the liberties of the ancients," the equal political liberties and the values of public life.[1]

This familiar and stylized contrast may serve to fix ideas.

As a way to answer our first question, justice as fairness[2] tries to adjudicate between these contending traditions, first, by proposing two principles of justice to serve as guidelines for how basic institutions are to realize the values of liberty and equality; and second, by specifying a point of view from which these principles can be seen as more appropriate than other familiar principles of justice to the idea of democratic citizens viewed as free and equal persons. What must be shown is that a certain arrangement of basic political and social institutions is more appropriate to realizing the values of liberty and equality when citizens are so conceived. The two principles of justice (noted above) are as follows:[3]

a. Each person has an equal claim to a fully adequate scheme of equal basic rights and liberties, which scheme is compatible with the same scheme for all; and in this scheme the equal political liberties, and only those liberties, are to be guaranteed their fair value.

b. Social and economic inequalities are to satisfy two conditions: first, they are to be attached to positions and offices open to all under conditions of fair equality of opportunity; and second, they are to be to the greatest benefit of the least advantaged members of society.

Each of these principles regulates institutions in a particular domain not only in regard to basic rights, liberties, and opportunities but also in regard to the claims of equality; while the second part of the second principle underwrites the worth of these institutional guarantees.[4] The two

1. See "Liberty of the Ancients Compared with that of the Moderns," (1819), in Benjamin Constant, *Political Writings*, translated and edited by Biancamaria Fontana (Cambridge: Cambridge University Press, 1988). The discussion in the introduction of the difference between the problem of political philosophy in the ancient and

modern worlds illustrates the significance of Constant's distinction.
2. The conception of justice presented in *Theory*.
3. The statement of these principles differs from that given in *Theory* and follows the statement in "The Basic Liberties and Their Priority," *Tanner Lectures on Human Values*, vol. III (Salt Lake City: University of Utah Press, 1982), p. 5. The reasons for these changes are discussed on pp. 46–55 of that lecture. They are important for the revisions in the account of the basic liberties found in *Theory* and were made to try to answer the forceful objections raised by H. L. A. Hart in his critical review in the *University of Chicago Law Review* 40 (Spring 1973):535–55. . . .
4. The worth of these guarantees is specified by reference to an index of primary goods. . . .

principles together, with the first given priority over the second, regulate the basic institutions that realize these values.

2. Much exposition would be needed to clarify the meaning and application of these principles. Since in these lectures such matters are not our concern, I make only a few comments. First, I view these principles as exemplifying the content of a liberal political conception of justice. The content of such a conception is given by three main features: first, a specification of certain basic rights, liberties and opportunities (of a kind familiar from constitutional democratic regimes); second, an assignment of special priority to those rights, liberties, and opportunities, especially with respect to claims of the general good and of perfectionist values; and third, measures assuring to all citizens adequate all-purpose means to make effective use of their liberties and opportunities. These elements can be understood in different ways, so that there are many variant liberalisms.

Further, the two principles express an egalitarian form of liberalism in virtue of three elements. These are a) the guarantee of the fair value of the political liberties, so that these are not purely formal; b) fair (and again not purely formal) equality of opportunity; and finally c) the so-called difference principle, which says that the social and economic inequalities attached to offices and positions are to be adjusted so that, whatever the level of those inequalities, whether great or small, they are to the greatest benefit of the least advantaged members of society.[5] All these elements are still in place, as they were in *Theory*; and so is the basis of the argument

for them. Hence I pose throughout these lectures the same egan conception of justice as before; and thou mention revisions from time to time, none of affect this feature of it.[6] Our topic, however, litical liberalism and its component ideas, so much of our discussion concerns liberal concos more generally, allowing for all variants, as example when we consider the idea of publion. . . .

Finally, as one migpect, important aspects of the principles are let in the brief statement as given. In particular, first principle covering the equal basic rights liberties may easily be preceded by a lexicallor principle requiring that citizens' basic need met, at least insofar as their being met is nece for citizens to understand and to be able fully to exercise those rights and liberties. Cnly any such principle must be assumed in apng the first principle.[7] But I do not pursue thend other matters here.

3. I return instead bur first question and ask: How might politicailosophy find a shared basis for settling such a ndamental question as that of the most appropr family of institutions to secure democratic libe and equality? Perhaps the most that can be dors to narrow the range of disagreement. Yet evenrmly held convictions gradually change: religis toleration is now accepted, and arguments r persecution are no longer openly professed; nilarly, slavery, which caused our Civil War, is jected as inherently unjust, and however much e aftermath of slavery may persist in social pcies and unavowed

---

5. There are a number of questions that arise concerning the intended interpretation of the difference principle. For example, the least advantaged members of society are given by description and not by a rigid designator (to use Saul Kripke's term in *Naming and Necessity* [Cambridge, Mass.: Harvard University Press, 1972]). Further, the principle does not require continual economic growth over generations to maximize upward indefinitely the expectations of the least advantaged. It is compatible with Mill's idea of a society in a just stationary state where (real) capital accumulation is zero. What the principle does require is that however great inequalities are, and however willing people are to work so as to earn their greater return, existing inequalities are to be adjusted to contribute in the most effective way to the benefit of the least advantaged. These brief remarks are hardly clear; they simply indicate the complexities that are not our concern in these lectures.

6. I make this comment since sde have thought that my working out the ideas of polital liberalism meant giving up the egalitarian concepon of *Theory*. I am not aware of any revisions that imply such a change and think the surmise has no basis.

7. For the statement of such a rinciple, as well as an instructive fuller statement in for parts of the two principles, with important revision see Rodney Peffer's *Marxism, Morality, and Social Justi* (Princeton: Princeton University Press, 1989), p. 14. I sould agree with most of Peffer's statement, but not with is 3(b), which appears to require a socialist form of economic organization. The difficulty here is not with socialism as such: but I should not include its being required in he first principles of political justice. These principles I se (as I did in *Theory*) as setting out fundamental values in terms of which, depending on the tradition and drcumstances of the society in question, one can consider whether socialism in some form is justified.

attitudes, no one is v to defend it. We collect such settled convicts the belief in religious toleration and the ion of slavery and try to organize the basic iand principles implicit in these convictions inoherent political conception of justice. Thesnvictions are provisional fixed points that it s any reasonable conception must account fo start, then, by looking to the public culture as the shared fund of implicitly recognizesic ideas and principles. We hope to formulhese ideas and principles clearly enough to combined into a political conception of justicegenial to our most firmly held convictions. Woress this by saying that a political conceptionjustice, to be acceptable, must accord with ounsidered convictions, at all levels of generality, due reflection, or in what I have called elsewh reflective equilibrium."[8]

The public polit culture may be of two minds at a very deepel. Indeed, this must be so with such an endur controversy as that concerning the most ropriate understanding of liberty and equalityhis suggests that if we are to succeed in findin basis for public agreement, we must find a way of organizing familiar ideas and principles into conception of political justice that expresses tse ideas and principles in a somewhat differenway than before. Justice as fairness tries to dois by using a fundamental organizing idea witn which all ideas and principles can be systenically connected and related. This organizing ideis that of society as a fair system of social coopeion between free and equal persons viewed as lly cooperating members of society over a complete life. It lays a basis for answering the firstfundamental question and is taken up below. . .

8. See *Theory*, pp. 20, 48–51, and 120f. One feature of reflective equilibriım is that it includes our considered convictions at all lvels of generality; no one level, say that of abstract priıciple or that of particular judgments in particular cases is viewed as foundational. They all may have an initial credibility. There is also an important distinction betweın narrow and wide reflective equilibrium, which is implicit in the distinction between the first and second kind of reflective equilibrium on pp. 49–50 (though the terms are not used). The terms *narrow* and *wide* were used first in § 1 of "Independence of Moral Theory," *Proceedings of the American Philosophical Association* 49 (1974).

4. Now suppose justice as fairness were to achieve its aims and a publicly acceptable political conception were found. Then this conception provides a publicly recognized point of view from which all citizens can examine before one another whether their political and social institutions are just. It enables them to do this by citing what are publicly recognized among them as valid and sufficient reasons singled out by that conception itself. Society's main institutions and how they fit together into one system of social cooperation can be assessed in the same way by each citizen, whatever that citizen's social position or more particular interests.

The aim of justice as fairness, then, is practical: it presents itself as a conception of justice that may be shared by citizens as a basis of a reasoned, informed, and willing political agreement. It expresses their shared and public political reason. But to attain such a shared reason, the conception of justice should be, as far as possible, independent of the opposing and conflicting philosophical and religious doctrines that citizens affirm. In formulating such a conception, political liberalism applies the principle of toleration to philosophy itself. The religious doctrines that in previous centuries were the professed basis of society have gradually given way to principles of constitutional government that all citizens, whatever their religious view, can endorse. Comprehensive philosophical and moral doctrines likewise cannot be endorsed by citizens generally, and they also no longer can, if they ever could, serve as the professed basis of society.

Thus, political liberalism looks for a political conception of justice that we hope can gain the support of an overlapping consensus of reasonable religious, philosophical, and moral doctrines in a society regulated by it.[9] Gaining this support of reasonable doctrines lays the basis for answering our second fundamental question as to how citizens, who remain deeply divided on religious, philosophical, and moral doctrines, can still maintain a just and stable democratic society. To this end, it is normally desirable that the comprehensive philosophical and moral views we are wont to use in debating fundamental political issues

9. The idea of an overlapping consensus is defined . . . and discussed further [later].

should give way in public life. Public reason—citizens' reasoning in the public forum about constitutional essentials and basic questions of justice—is now best guided by a political conception the principles and values of which all citizens can endorse. . . . That political conception is to be, so to speak, political and not metaphysical.[10]

Political liberalism, then, aims for a political conception of justice as a freestanding view. It offers no specific metaphysical or epistemological doctrine beyond what is implied by the political conception itself. As an account of political values, a free-standing political conception does not deny there being other values that apply, say, to the personal, the familial, and the associational; nor does it say that political values are separate from, or discontinuous with, other values. One aim, as I have said, is to specify the political domain and its conception of justice in such a way that its institutions can gain the support of an overlapping consensus. In this case, citizens themselves, within the exercise of their liberty of thought and conscience, and looking to their comprehensive doctrines, view the political conception as derived from, or congruent with, or at least not in conflict with, their other values.

The Idea of a Political Conception of Justice

1. To this point I have used the idea of a political conception of justice without explaining its meaning. From what I have said, one can perhaps gather what I mean by it and why political liberalism uses that idea. Yet we need an explicit statement thus: a political conception of justice has three characteristic features, each of which is exemplified by justice as fairness. I assume some but not much acquaintance with that view.

The first concerns the subject of a political conception. While such a conception is, of course, a moral conception,[11] it is a moral conception worked out for a specific kind of subject, namely, for political, social, and economic institutions. In particular, it applies to what I shall call the "basic structure" of society, which for our present purposes I take to be a modern constitutional democracy. (I use "constitutional democracy" and "democratic regime," and similar phrases interchangeably unless otherwise stated.) By the basic structure I mean a society's main political, social, and economic institutions, and how they fit together into one unified system of social cooperation from one generation to the next.[12] The initial focus, then, of a political conception of justice is the framework of basic institutions and the principles, standards, and precepts that apply to it, as well as how those norms are to be expressed in the character and attitudes of the members of society who realize its ideals.

Moreover, I assume that the basic structure is that of a closed society: that is, we are to regard it as self-contained and as having no relations with other societies. Its members enter it only by birth and leave it only by death. This allows us to speak of them as born into a society where they will lead a complete life. That a society is closed is a considerable abstraction, justified only because it enables us to focus on certain main questions free from distracting details. At some point a political conception of justice must address the just relations between peoples, or the law of peoples, as I shall say. In these lectures I do not discuss how a law of peoples might be worked out, starting from justice as fairness as applied first to closed societies.[13]

2. The second feature concerns the mode of presentation: a political conception of justice is presented as a freestanding view. While we want a political conception to have a justification by reference to one or more comprehensive doctrines, it is neither presented as, nor as derived from, such a doctrine applied to the basic structure of society, as if this structure were simply another subject to which that doctrine applied. It is important to stress this point: it means that we must distinguish between how a political conception is presented and its being part of, or as derivable within, a comprehensive doctrine. I assume all citizens to affirm a comprehensive doctrine to which the

---

10. The context here serves to define the phrase: "political not metaphysical."

11. In saying that a conception is moral, I mean, among other things, that its content is given by certain ideals, principles and standards; and that these norms articulate certain values, in this case political values.

12. See *Theory*, §2 and the index, and also "The Basic Structure as Subject," in [*Political Liberalism*], pp. 257–88.

13. See my "Law of Peoples" (an Oxford Amnesty Lecture), . . . published with the other Amnesty Lectures by Basic Books, 1993.

political conception they accept is in some way related. But a distinguishing feature of a political conception is that it is presented as free-standing and expounded apart from, or without reference to, any such wider background. To use a current phrase, the political conception is a module, an essential constituent part, that fits into and can be supported by various reasonable comprehensive doctrines that endure in the society regulated by it. This means that it can be presented without saying, or knowing, or hazarding a conjecture about, what such doctrines it may belong to, or be supported by.

In this respect a political conception of justice differs from many moral doctrines, for these are widely regarded as general and comprehensive views. Utilitarianism is a familiar example: the principle of utility, however understood, is usually said to hold for all kinds of subjects ranging from the conduct of individuals and personal relations to the organization of society as a whole as well as to the law of peoples.[14] By contrast, a political conception tries to elaborate a reasonable conception for the basic structure alone and involves, so far as possible, no wider commitment to any other doctrine.

This contrast will be clearer if we observe that the distinction between a political conception of justice and other moral conceptions is a matter of scope: that is, the range of subjects to which a conception applies and the content a wider range requires. A moral conception is general if it applies to a wide range of subjects, and in the limit to all subjects universally. It is comprehensive when it includes conceptions of what is of value in human life, and ideals of personal character, as well as ideals of friendship and of familial and associational relationships, and much else that is to inform our conduct, and in the limit to our life as a whole. A conception is fully comprehensive if it covers all recognized values and virtues within one rather precisely articulated system; whereas a conception is only partially comprehensive when it comprises a number of, but by no means all, nonpolitical values and virtues and is rather loosely articulated. Many religious and philosophical doctrines aspire to be both general and comprehensive.

3. The third feature of a political conception of justice is that its content is expressed in terms of

certain fundamental ideas seen as implicit in the public political culture of a democratic society. This public culture comprises the political institutions of a constitutional regime and the public traditions of their interpretation (including those of the judiciary), as well as historic texts and documents that are common knowledge. Comprehensive doctrines of all kinds—religious, philosophical, and moral—belong to what we may call the "background culture" of civil society. This is the culture of the social, not of the political. It is the culture of daily life, of its many associations: churches and universities, learned and scientific societies, and clubs and teams, to mention a few. In a democratic society there is a tradition of democratic thought, the content of which is at least familiar and intelligible to the educated common sense of citizens generally. Society's main institutions, and their accepted forms of interpretation, are seen as a fund of implicitly shared ideas and principles.

Thus, justice as fairness starts from within a certain political tradition and takes as its fundamental idea[15] that of society as a fair system of cooperation over time, from one generation to the next. This central organizing idea is developed together with two companion fundamental ideas: one is the idea of citizens (those engaged in cooperation) as free and equal persons; the other

14. See "Basic Structure as Subject," p. 260f.

15. I comment that I use "ideas" as the more general term and as covering both concepts and conceptions. This pair is distinguished as they were in *Theory*, pp. 3f. Roughly, the concept is the meaning of a term, while a particular conception includes as well the principles required to apply it. To illustrate: the concept of justice, applied to an institution, means, say, that the institution makes no arbitrary distinctions between persons in assigning basic rights and duties, and that its rules establish a proper balance between competing claims. Whereas a conception includes, besides this, principles and criteria for deciding which distinctions are arbitrary and when a balance between competing claims is proper. People can agree on the meaning of the concept of justice and still be at odds, since they affirm different principles and standards for deciding those matters. To develop a concept of justice into a conception of it is to elaborate these requisite principles and standards. Thus, to give another example, [elsewhere] I consider the concept of the person in law and in political philsophy, [and] set out the further necessary elements of a conception of the person as a democratic citizen. This distinction between concept and conception I took from H. L. A. Hart's, *The Concept of Law* (Oxford: Clarendon Press, 1961), pp. 155–59.

is the idea of a well-ordered society as a society effectively regulated by a political conception of justice.[16] We suppose also that these ideas can be elaborated into a political conception of justice that can gain the support of an overlapping consensus. Such a consensus consists of all the reasonable opposing religious, philosophical, and moral doctrines likely to persist over generations and to gain a sizable body of adherents in a more or less just constitutional regime, a regime in which the criterion of justice is that political conception itself.[17] Whether justice as fairness (or some similar view) can gain the support of an overlapping consensus so defined is a speculative question. One can reach an educated conjecture only by working it out and exhibiting the way it might be supported. . . .

The Political Conception of the Person

1. I remarked earlier that the idea of the original position and the description of the parties may tempt us to think that a metaphysical doctrine of the person is presupposed. While I said that this interpretation is mistaken, it is not enough simply to disavow reliance on metaphysical doctrines, for despite one's intent they may still be involved. To rebut claims of this nature requires discussing them in detail and showing that they have no foothold. I cannot do that here.[18]

16. Two other fundamental ideas are those of the basic structure . . . ; and of the original position. . . . These are not seen as ideas familiar to educated common sense but rather as ideas introduced for the purpose of presenting justice as fairness in a unified and prespicuous way.

17. The idea of an overlapping consensus, or perhaps better the term, was introduced in *Theory*, pp. 387f., as a way to weaken the conditions for the reasonableness of civil disobedience in a nearly just democratic society. Here and later in these lectures I use it in a different sense and in a far wider context.

18. Part of the difficulty is that there is no accepted understanding of what a metaphysical doctrine is. One might say, as Paul Hoffman has suggested to me, that to develop a political conception of justice without presupposing, or explicitly using, a particular metaphysical doctrine, for example, some particular metaphysical conception of the person, is already to presuppose a metaphysical thesis: namely, that no metaphysical doctrine is required for this purpose. One might also say that our ordinary conception of persons as the basic units of deliberation and responsibility presupposes, or

I can, however, sketch an account of a political conception of the person drawn on in setting up the original position. To understand what is meant by describing a conception of the person as political, consider how citizens are represented in that position as free persons. The representation of their freedom seems to be one source of the idea that a metaphysical doctrine is presupposed. Now citizens are conceived as thinking of themselves as free in three respects, so I survey each of these and indicate the way in which the conception of the person is political.

2. First, citizens are free in that they conceive of themselves and of one another as having the moral power to have a conception of the good. This is not to say that, as part of their political conception, they view themselves as inevitably tied to the pursuit of the particular conception of the good that they affirm at any given time. Rather, as citizens, they are seen as capable of revising and changing this conception on reasonable and rational grounds, and they may do this if they so desire. As free persons, citizens claim the right to view their persons as independent from and not identified with any particular such conception with its scheme of final ends. Given their moral power to form, revise, and rationally pursue a conception of the good, their public identity as free persons is not affected by changes over time in their determinate conception of it.

For example, when citizens convert from one religion to another, or no longer affirm an established religious faith, they do not cease to be, for

in some way involves, certain metaphysical theses about the nature of persons as moral or political agents. Following the precept of avoidance, I should not want to deny these claims. What should be said is the following. If we look at the presentation of justice as fairness and note how it is set up, and note the ideas and conceptions it uses, no particular metaphysical doctrine about the nature of persons, distinctive and opposed to other metaphysical doctrines, appears among its premises, or seems required by its argument. If metaphysical presuppositions are involved, perhaps they are so general that they would not distinguish between the metaphysical views—Cartesian, Leibnizian, or Kantian: realist, idealist, or materialist—with which philosophy has traditionally been concerned. In this case they would not appear to be relevant for the structure and content of a political conception of justice one way or the other. I am grateful to Daniel Brudney and Paul Hoffman for discussion of these matters.

questions of political justice, the same persons they were before. There is no loss of what we may call their public, or institutional, identity, or their identity as a matter of basic law. In general, they still have the same basic rights and duties, they own the same property and can make the same claims as before, except insofar as these claims were connected with their previous religious affiliation. We can imagine a society (history offers many examples) in which basic rights and recognized claims depend on religious affiliation and social class. Such a society has a different political conception of the person. It lacks a conception of equal citizenship, for this conception goes with that of a democratic society of free and equal citizens.

There is a second sense of identity specified by reference to citizens' deeper aims and commitments. Let's call it their noninstitutional or moral identity.[19] Citizens usually have both political and nonpolitical aims and commitments. They affirm the values of political justice and want to see them embodied in political institutions and social policies. They also work for the other values in nonpublic life and for the ends of the associations to which they belong. These two aspects of their moral identity citizens must adjust and reconcile. It can happen that in their personal affairs, or in the internal life of associations, citizens may regard their final ends and attachments very differently from the way the political conception supposes. They may have, and often do have at any given time, affections, devotions, and loyalties that they believe they would not, indeed could and should not, stand apart from and evaluate objectively. They may regard it as simply unthinkable to view themselves apart from certain religious, philosophical, and moral convictions, or from certain enduring attachments and loyalties.

These two kinds of commitments and attachments—political and nonpolitical—specify moral identity and give shape to a person's way of life, what one sees oneself as doing and trying to accomplish in the social world. If we suddenly lost them, we would be disoriented and unable to carry on. In fact, there would be, we might think,

19. I am indebted to Erin Kelly for the distinction between the two kinds of aims that characterize peoples' moral identity as described in this and the next paragraph.

no point in carrying on.[20] But our conceptions of the good may and often do change over time, usually slowly but sometimes rather suddenly. When these changes are sudden, we are likely to say that we are no longer the same person. We know what this means; we refer to a profound and pervasive shift, or reversal, in our final ends and commitments; we refer to our different moral (which includes our religious) identity. On the road to Damascus Saul of Tarsus becomes Paul the Apostle. Yet such a conversion implies no change in our public or institutional identity, not in our personal identity as this concept is understood by some writers in the philosophy of mind.[21]

20. This role of commitments is often emphasized by Bernard Williams, for example, in "Persons, Character and Morality," in *Moral Luck* (Cambridge: Cambridge University Press, 1981), pp. 10–14.

21. Though I have used the term *identity* in the text, it would, I think, cause less misunderstanding to use the phrase "our conception of ourselves," or "the kind of person we want to be." Doing so would distinguish the question with important moral elements from the question of the sameness, or identity, of a substance, continuant, or thing, through different changes in time and space. In saying this I assume that an answer to the problem of personal identity tries to specify the various criteria (for example, psychological criteria of memories and physical continuity of body, or some part thereof) in accordance with which two different psychological states or actions, say, which occur at two different times may be said to be states or actions of the same person who endures over time; and it also tries to specify how this enduring person is to be conceived, whether as a Cartesian or a Leibnizian substance, or a Kantian transcendental ego, or as a continuant of some kind, for example, bodily or physical. See the collection of essays edited by John Perry, *Personal Identity* (Berkeley: University of California Press, 1975), especially Perry's introduction, pp. 1–30; and Sydney Shoemaker's essay in *Personal Identity* (Oxford: Basil Blackwell, 1984), both of which consider a number of views. Sometimes in discussions of this problem, continuity of fundamental aims is largely ignored, for example in views like H. P. Grice's (in Perry's collection), which emphasizes continuity of memory. However, once the continuity of these aims is counted as also basic, as in Derek Parfit's *Reasons and Persons* (Oxford: Clarendon Press, 1984), pt. III, there is no sharp distinction between the problem of a person's nonpublic or moral identity and the problem of their personal identity. The latter problem raises profound questions on which past and current philosophical views widely differ and surely will continue to differ. For this reason it is important to try to develop a political conception of justice that avoids this problem as far

Moreover, in a well-ordered society supported by an overlapping consensus, citizens' (more general) political values and commitments, as part of their noninstitutional or moral identity, are roughly the same.

3. A second respect in which citizens view themselves as free is that they regard themselves as self-authenticating sources of valid claims. That is, they regard themselves as being entitled to make claims on their institutions so as to advance their conceptions of the good (provided these conceptions fall within the range permitted by the public conception of justice). These claims citizens regard as having weight of their own apart from being derived from duties and obligations specified by a political conception of justice, for example, from duties and obligations owed to society. Claims that citizens regard as founded on duties and obligations based on their conception of the good and the moral doctrine they affirm in their own life are also, for our purposes here, to be counted as self-authenticating. Doing this is reasonable in a political conception of justice for a constitutional democracy, for provided the conceptions of the good and the moral doctrines citizens affirm are compatible with the public conception of justice, these duties and obligations are self-authenticating from a political point of view.

When we describe the way in which citizens regard themselves as free, we describe how citizens think of themselves in a democratic society when questions of political justice arise. That this aspect belongs to a particular political conception is clear from the contrast with a different political conception in which people are not viewed as self-authenticating sources of valid claims. Rather, their claims have no weight except insofar as they can be derived from the duties and obligations owed to society, or from their ascribed roles in a social hierarchy justified by religious or aristocratic values.

To take an extreme case, slaves are human beings who are not counted as sources of claims, not even claims based on social duties or obligations, for slaves are not counted as capable of having duties or obligations. Laws that prohibit

the maltreatment of slaves are not based on claims made by slaves, but on claims originating from slaveholders, or from the general interests of society (which do not include the interests of slaves). Slaves are, so to speak, socially dead: they are not recognized as persons at all.[22] This contrast with slavery makes clear why conceiving of citizens as free persons in virtue of their moral powers and their having a conception of the good goes with a particular political conception of justice.

4. The third respect in which citizens are viewed as free is that they are viewed as capable of taking responsibility for their ends and this affects how their various claims are assessed. Very roughly, given just background institutions and given for each person a fair index of primary goods (as required by the principles of justice), citizens are thought to be capable of adjusting their aims and aspirations in the light of what they can reasonably expect to provide for. Moreover, they are viewed as capable of restricting their claims in matters of justice to the kinds of things the principles of justice allow.

Citizens are to recognize, then, that the weight of their claims is not given by the strength and psychological intensity of their wants and desires (as opposed to their needs as citizens), even when their wants and desires are rational from their point of view. The procedure is as before: we start with the basic idea of society as a fair system of cooperation. When this idea is developed into a conception of political justice, it implies that, viewing citizens as persons who can engage in social cooperation over a complete life, they can also take responsibility for their ends: that is, they can adjust their ends so that those ends can be pursued by the means they can reasonably expect to acquire in return for what they can reasonably expect to contribute. The idea of responsibility for ends is implicit in the public political culture and discernible in its practices. A political conception of the person articulates this idea and fits it into the idea of society as a fair system of cooperation.

5. To sum up, I recapitulate three main points of this and the preceding two sections:

as possible. Even so, to refer to the example in the text, all agree, I assume, that for the purposes of public life, Saul of Tarsus and St. Paul the Apostle are the same person. Conversion is irrelevant to our public, or institutional, identity.

22. For the idea of social death, see Orlando Patterson's *Slavery and Social Death* (Cambridge, Mass.: Harvard University Press, 1982), esp. pp. 5–9, 38–45, 337.

First, persons were regarded as free and equal persons in virtue of their possessing to the requisite degree the two powers of moral personality, namely, the capacity for a sense of justice and the capacity for a conception of the good. These powers we associated with the two main elements of the idea of cooperation, the idea of the fair terms of cooperation, and the idea of each participant's rational advantage, or good.

Second, in this section, we surveyed three respects in which persons are regarded as free, and have noted that in the public political culture of a constitutional democratic regime citizens conceive of themselves as free in these ways.

Third, since the question of which conception of political justice is most appropriate for realizing in basic institutions the values of liberty and equality has long been deeply controversial within the very tradition in which citizens are regarded as free and equal, the aim of justice as fairness is to resolve this question by starting from the idea of society as a fair system of cooperation in which the fair terms of cooperation are agreed upon by citizens so conceived. . . . [W]e saw why this approach, once the basic structure of society is taken as the primary subject of justice, leads to the idea of the original position as a device of representation. . . .

The Idea of an Overlapping Consensus

Three Features of an Overlapping Consensus

1. Before beginning, I recall two main points about the idea of an overlapping consensus. The first is that we look for a consensus of reasonable (as opposed to unreasonable or irrational) comprehensive doctrines. The crucial fact is not the fact of pluralism as such, but of reasonable pluralism. This diversity political liberalism sees, as I have said, as the long-run result of the powers of human reason within an enduring background of free institutions. The fact of reasonable pluralism is not an unfortunate condition of human life, as we might say of pluralism as such, allowing for doctrines that are not only irrational but mad and aggressive. In framing a political conception of justice so it can gain an overlapping consensus, we are not bending it to existing unreason, but to the

fact of reasonable pluralism, itself the outcome of the free exercise of free human reason under conditions of liberty.

For the second point about an overlapping consensus, recall that . . . I said that in a constitutional democracy the public conception of justice should be, so far as possible, presented as independent of comprehensive religious, philosophical, and moral doctrines. This meant that justice as fairness is to be understood at the first stage of its exposition as a free-standing view that expresses a political conception of justice. It does not provide a specific religious, metaphysical, or epistemological doctrine beyond what is implied by the political conception itself. As remarked [earlier], the political conception is a module, an essential constituent part, that in different ways fits into and can be supported by various reasonable comprehensive doctrines that endure in the society regulated by it.

2. There are at least four objections likely to be raised against the idea of social unity founded on an overlapping consensus on a political conception of justice. I begin with perhaps the most obvious of these, namely, that an overlapping consensus is a mere modus vivendi.

To fix ideas I shall use a model case of an overlapping consensus to indicate what is meant; and I shall return to this example from time to time. It contains three views: one affirms the political conception because its religious doctrine and account of free faith[23] lead to a principle of toleration and underwrite the fundamental liberties of a constitutional regime; while the second view affirms the political conception on the basis of a

23. This idea is illustrated by various of Locke's statements in *A Letter Concerning Toleration* (1690). He says such things as: 1) God has given no man authority over another (p. 129); 2) no man can abandon the care of his own salvation to the care of another (pp. 129, 139, 154); 3) the understanding cannot be compelled by force to belief (p. 129); 4) the care of men's souls is not given to the magistrate as that would determine faith by where we were born (p. 130); 5) a church is a voluntary society, and no man is bound to any particular church and he may leave it as freely as he entered (p. 131); 6) excommunication does not affect civil relationships (p. 134); 7) only faith and inward sincerity gain our salvation and acceptance with God (p. 143). (Page references are to the edition of J.W. Gough, *Two Treatises of Government with A Letter on Toleration* (Oxford: Basil Blackwell, 1956). Other writers on toleration would have served as well.)

comprehensive liberal moral doctrine such as those of Kant or Mill. The third, however, is not systematically unified: besides the political values formulated by a freestanding political conception of justice, it includes a large family of nonpolitical values. It is a pluralist view, let us say, since each subpart of this family has its own account based on ideas drawn from within it, leaving all values to be balanced against one another, either in groups or singly, in particular kinds of cases.

In this model case the religious doctrine and the liberalisms of Kant and Mill are taken to be general and comprehensive. The third view is only partially comprehensive but holds, with political liberalism, that under reasonably favorable conditions that make democracy possible, political values normally outweigh whatever nonpolitical values conflict with them. The previous views agree with the last in this respect and so all views lead to roughly the same political judgments and thus overlap on the political conception.

3. To begin with the objection: some will think that even if an overlapping consensus were sufficiently stable, the idea of political unity founded on an overlapping consensus must still be rejected, since it abandons the hope of political community and settles instead for a public understanding that is at bottom a mere modus vivendi. To this objection, we say that the hope of political community must indeed be abandoned, if by such a community we mean a political society united in affirming the same comprehensive doctrine. This possibility is excluded by the fact of reasonable pluralism together with the rejection of the oppressive use of the state power to overcome it.[24] The substantive question concerns the

significant features of such a consensus and how these features affect social concord and the moral quality of public life. I turn to why an overlapping consensus is not a mere modus vivendi.

A typical use of the phrase "modus vivendi" is to characterize a treaty between two states whose national aims and interests put them at odds. In negotiating a treaty each state would be wise and prudent to make sure that the agreement proposed represents an equilibrium point: that is, that the terms and conditions of the treaty are drawn up in such a way that it is public knowledge that it is not advantageous for either state to violate it. The treaty will then be adhered to because doing so is regarded by each as in its national interest, including its interest in its reputation as a state that honors treaties. But in general both states are ready to pursue their goals at the expense of the other, and should conditions change they may do so. This background highlights the way in which such a treaty is a mere modus vivendi. A similar background is present when we think of social consensus founded on self- or group interests, or on the outcome of political bargaining: social unity is only apparent, as its stability is contingent on circumstances remaining such as not to upset the fortunate convergence of interests.

4. That an overlapping consensus is quite different from a modus vivendi is clear from our model case. In that example, note two aspects: first, the object of consensus, the political conception of justice, is itself a moral conception. And second, it is affirmed on moral grounds, that is, it includes conceptions of society and of citizens as persons, as well as principles of justice, and an account of the political virtues through which

24. Note that what is impracticable is not all values of community (recall that a community is understood as an association or society whose unity rests on a comprehensive conception of the good) but only political community and its values. Justice as fairness assumes, as other liberal political views do also, that the values of community are not only essential but realizable, first in the various association that carry on their life within the framework of the basic structure, and second in those associations that extend across the boundaries of political societies, such as churches and scientific societies. Liberalism rejects political society as a community because, among other things, it leads to the systematic denial of basic liberties and may allow the oppressive use of the government's monopoly of (legal)

force. Of course, in the well-ordered society of justice as fairness citizens share a common aim, and one that has high priority: namely, the aim of insuring that political and social institutions are just, and of giving justice to persons generally, as what citizens need for themselves and want for one another. It is not true, then, that in a liberal view citizens have no fundamental common aims. Nor is it true that the aim of political justice is not an important part of their noninstitutional, or moral, identity. . . . But this common aim of political justice must not be mistaken for (what I have called) "a conception of the good." For a discussion of this last point, see Amy Gutmann, "Communitarian Critics of Liberalism," *Philosophy and Public Affairs* 14 (Summer 1985): 311, footnote.

those principles are embodied in human character and expressed in public life. An overlapping consensus, therefore, is not merely a consensus on accepting certain authorities, or on complying with certain institutional arrangements, founded on a convergence of self- or group interests. All those who affirm the political conception start from within their own comprehensive view and draw on the religious, philosophical, and moral grounds it provides. The fact that people affirm the same political conception on those grounds does not make their affirming it any less religious, philosophical, or moral, as the case may be, since the grounds sincerely held determine the nature of their affirmation.

The preceding two aspects of an overlapping consensus—moral object and moral grounds—connect with a third aspect, that of stability. This means that those who affirm the various views supporting the political conception will not withdraw their support of it should the relative strength of their view in society increase and eventually become dominant. So long as the three views are affirmed and not revised, the political conception will still be supported regardless of shifts in the distribution of political power. Each view supports the political conception for its own sake, or on its own merits. The test for this is whether the consensus is stable with respect to changes in the distribution of power among views. This feature of stability highlights a basic contrast between an overlapping consensus and a modus vivendi, the stability of which does depend on happenstance and a balance of relative forces.

This becomes clear once we change our example and include the views of Catholics and Protestants in the sixteenth century. At that time there was not an overlapping consensus on the principle of toleration. Both faiths held that it was the duty of the ruler to uphold the true religion and to repress the spread of heresy and false doctrine.[25] In such a case the acceptance of the principle of toleration would indeed be a mere modus vivendi, because if either faith becomes dominant, the principle of toleration would no longer be followed. Stability with respect to the distribution of power is lacking. So long as such views as those of Catholic and Protestant in the sixteenth century are very much in the minority, and are likely to remain so, they do not significantly affect the moral quality of public life and the basis of social concord. For the vast majority in society are confident that the distribution of power will range over and be widely shared by views in the consensus that affirm the political conception of justice for its own sake. But should this situation change, the moral quality of political life will also change in ways that are obvious and require no comment.

5. In conclusion I comment briefly on what we may call "the depth and breadth of an overlapping consensus" and the specificity of its focus; that is, how deep does the consensus go into citizens' comprehensive doctrines? How broad are the institutions to which it applies? And how specific is the conception agreed to?

The preceding account says that the consensus goes down to the fundamental ideas within which justice as fairness is worked out. It supposes agreement deep enough to reach such ideas as those of society as a fair system of cooperation and of citizens as reasonable and rational, and free and equal. As for its breadth, it covers the principles and values of a political conception (in this case those of justice as fairness) and it applies to the basic structure as a whole. This degree of depth and breadth and specificity helps to fix ideas and keeps before us the main question: consistent with plausibly realistic assumptions, what is the deepest and widest feasible conception of political justice?

There are, of course, other possibilities. I have not supposed that an overlapping consensus on a political conception is necessary for certain kinds of social unity and stability. Rather I have said that, with two other conditions, it is sufficient for the most reasonable basis of social unity available to us. Yet as Baier has suggested, a less deep consensus on the principles and rules of a workable political constitution may be sufficient for less demanding purposes and far easier to obtain. He thinks that in fact in the United States we have actually achieved something like that. So rather than supposing that the consensus reaches down

25. See J. W. Allen, *A History of Political Thought in the Sixteenth Century* (London: Methuen, 1941), pt. I, chap. 5, pt. II, chap. 9, pt. III, Chaps. 4, 6, 8; and Quentin Skinner, *The Foundations of Modern Political Thought* (Cambridge: Cambridge University Press, 1978), vol. II, esp. pt. III.

to a political conception covering principles for the whole of the basic structure, a consensus may cover only certain fundamental procedural political principles for the constitution.[26] I return to these matters [later] when we discuss the steps from "constitutional consensus," as I shall call it, to overlapping consensus.

An Overlapping Consensus not Indifferent or Skeptical

1. I turn to a second objection to the idea of an overlapping consensus on a political conception of justice: namely, that the avoidance of general and comprehensive doctrines implies indifference or skepticism as to whether a political conception of justice can be true, as opposed to reasonable in the constructivist sense. This avoidance may appear to suggest that such a conception might be the most reasonable one for us even when it is known not to be true, as if truth were simply beside the point. In reply, it would be fatal to the idea of a political conception to see it as skeptical about, or indifferent to, truth, much less as in conflict with it. Such skepticism or indifference would put political philosophy in opposition to numerous comprehensive doctrines, and thus defeat from the outset its aim of achieving an overlapping consensus.

We try, so far as we can, neither to assert nor to deny any particular comprehensive religious, philosophical, or moral view, or its associated theory of truth and the status of values. Since we assume each citizen to affirm some such view, we hope to make it possible for all to accept the political conception as true or reasonable from the standpoint of their own comprehensive view, whatever it may be. Properly understood, then, a political conception of justice need be no more indifferent, say, to truth in philosophy and morals than the principle of toleration, suitably understood, need be indifferent to truth in religion. Since we seek an agreed basis of public justification in matters of justice, and since no political agreement on those disputed questions can reasonably be expected, we turn instead to the fundamental ideas we seem to share through the public political culture. From these ideas we try to work out a political conception of justice congruent with our considered convictions on due reflection. Once this is done, citizens may within their comprehensive doctrines regard the political conception of justice as true, or as reasonable, whatever their view allows.

2. Some may not be satisfied with this; they may reply that, despite these protests, a political conception of justice must express indifference or skepticism. Otherwise it could not lay aside fundamental religious, philosophical, and moral questions because they are politically difficult to settle, or may prove intractable. Certain truths, it may be said, concern things so important that differences about them have to be fought out, even should this mean civil war. To this we say first that questions are not removed from the political agenda, so to speak, solely because they are a source of conflict. We appeal instead to a political conception of justice to distinguish between those questions that can be reasonably removed from the political agenda and those that cannot. Some questions still on the agenda will be controversial, at least to some degree; this is normal with political issues.

To illustrate: from within a political conception of justice let us suppose we can account both for equal liberty of conscience, which takes the truths of religion off the political agenda, and the equal political and civil liberties, which by ruling out serfdom and slavery take the possibility of those institutions off the agenda.[27] But controversial

---

26. These points are made by Kurt Baier in a valuable discussion. "Justice and the Aims of Political Philosophy," *Ethics* 99 (July 1989): 771–90. His idea of a consensus on constitutional principles (which he thinks we largely have), rather than on a conception of justice, is found at pp. 775f.

27. To explain: when certain matters are taken off the political agenda, they are no longer regarded as appropriate subjects for political decision by majority or other plurality voting. For example, in regard to equal liberty of conscience and the rejection of slavery and serfdom, this means that the equal basic liberties in the constitution that cover these matters are reasonably taken as fixed, as correctly settled once and for all. They are part of the public charter of a constitutional regime and not a suitable topic for ongoing public debate and legislation, as if they can be changed, one way or the other by the requisite majorities. Moreover, the more established political parties likewise acknowledge these matters as settled. See Stephen Holmes, "Gag Rules or the Politics of Omission," in *Constitutional Democracy*, edited by J. Elster and R. Slagstad (Cambridge: Cambridge University Press, 1987).

issues inevitably remain: for example, how more exactly to draw the boundaries of the basic liberties when they conflict (where to set "the wall between church and state"); how to interpret the requirements of distributive justice even when there is considerable agreement on general principles for the basic structure; and finally, questions of policy such as the use of nuclear weapons. These cannot be removed from politics. But by avoiding comprehensive doctrines we try to bypass religion and philosophy's profoundest controversies so as to have some hope of uncovering a basis of a stable overlapping consensus.

3. Nevertheless, in affirming a political conception of justice we may eventually have to assert at least certain aspects of our own comprehensive religious or philosophical doctrine (by no means necessarily fully comprehensive).[28] This will happen whenever someone insists, for example, that certain questions are so fundamental that to insure their being rightly settled justifies civil strife. The religious salvation of those holding a particular religion, or indeed the salvation of a whole people, may be said to depend on it. At this

point we may have no alternative but to deny this, or to imply its denial and hence to maintain the kind of thing we had hoped to avoid.

To consider this, imagine rationalist believers who contend that these beliefs are open to and can be fully established by reason (uncommon though this view may be).[29] In this case the believers simply deny what we have called "the fact of reasonable pluralism." So we say of the rationalist believers that they are mistaken in denying that fact; but we need not say that their religious beliefs are not true, since to deny that religious beliefs can be publicly and fully established by reason is not to say that they are not true. Of course, we do not believe the doctrine believers here assert, and this is shown in what we do. Even if we do not, say, hold some form of the doctrine of free religious faith that supports equal liberty of conscience, our actions nevertheless imply that we believe the concern for salvation does not require anything incompatible with that liberty. Still, we do not put forward more of our comprehensive view than we think needed or useful for the political aim of consensus.

4. The reason for this restraint is to respect, as best we can, the limits of public reason. Let us suppose that by respecting these limits we succeed in reaching an overlapping consensus on a conception of political justice. It will then be, for the moment at least, reasonable. Some might insist that reaching this reflective agreement is itself sufficient grounds for regarding that conception as true, or at any rate highly probable. But we refrain from this further step: it is unnecessary and may interfere with the practical aim of finding an agreed public basis of justification. For many the true, or the religiously and the metaphysically well-grounded, goes beyond the reasonable. The idea of an overlapping consensus leaves this step to be taken by citizens individually in line with their own comprehensive views.[30]

Of course, that certain matters are reasonably taken off the political agenda does not mean that a political conception of justice should not provide the grounds and reasons why this should be done. Indeed, as I note above, a political conception should do precisely this. But normally the fuller discussions of these questions between various political doctrines and their roots in comprehensive doctrines is part of the background culture.

Finally, in saying that certain matters are taken off the political agenda once and for all, some may object that we can be mistaken, as we have been in the past about toleration and slavery. Certainly we have been mistaken, but does anyone doubt for that reason that the principle of toleration may be mistaken or that it is wrong to have abolished slavery? Who seriously thinks so? Is there any real chance of a mistake? And surely we don't want to say: we take certain matters off the agenda for the time being. Or until the next election. Or the next generation. Why isn't "once and for all" the best way to put it? By using that phrase citizens express to one another a firm commitment about their common status. They express a certain ideal of democratic citizenship.

28. As I said [earlier], a doctrine is fully comprehensive if it covers all recognized values and virtues within one rather precisely articulated system; whereas a doctrine is only partially comprehensive when it comprises a number of nonpolitical values and virtues and is rather loosely articulated. This limited scope and looseness turns out to be important with regard to stability.

29. The idea of rationalist believers is adapted from Joshua Cohen's discussion, "Moral Pluralism and Political Consensus." My reply is similar to his, as I understand it. Cohen also discusses the case of nonrationalist believers who do not claim that reason supports their faith but who do claim that since their beliefs are true, state power is properly used to enforce it. . . .

30. Recall here the further important fact: namely, that if any of the reasonable comprehensive doctrines in the

Were justice as fairness to make an overlapping consensus possible it would complete and extend the movement of thought that began three centuries ago with the gradual acceptance of the principle of toleration and led to the nonconfessional state and equal liberty of conscience. This extension is required for an agreement on a political conception of justice given the historical and social circumstances of a democratic society. To apply the principles of toleration to philosophy itself is to leave to citizens themselves to settle the questions of religion, philosophy, and morals in accordance with views they freely affirm.

A Political Conception Need not be Comprehensive

1. A third objection is the following: even if we grant that an overlapping consensus is not a modus vivendi, as I have defined it, some may say that a workable political conception must be general and comprehensive. Without such a doctrine on hand, there is no way to order the many conflicts of justice that arise in public life. The deeper the conceptual and philosophical bases of those conflicts, the objection continues, the more general and comprehensive the level of philosophical reflection must be if their roots are to be laid bare and an appropriate ordering found. It is useless, the objection concludes, to try to work out a political conception of justice expressly for the basic structure apart from any comprehensive doctrine. As we have just seen, we may be forced to refer, at least in some way, to such a view.[31]

existing overlapping consensus is true, then the political conception itself is true, or close thereto in the sense of being endorsed by a true doctrine. The truth of any one doctrine guarantees that all doctrines yield the right conception of political justice, even though all are not right for the right reasons as given by the one true doctrine. So, as we have said, when citizens differ, not all can be fully correct; yet if one of their doctrines should be true, all citizens are correct, politically speaking.

31. There is a distinction between general and comprehensive views and views that are abstract. When justice as fairness begins from the fundamental idea of society as a fair system of cooperation and proceeds to elaborate that idea, the resulting conception of political justice may be said to be abstract. It is abstract in the same way that the conception of a perfectly competitive market, or of general economic equilibrium, is abstract: that is, it singles out certain aspects of society

This objection is perfectly natural, as we are tempted to ask: how else could these conflicting claims be adjudicated? Yet part of the answer is found in the third view of our model case. This view is pluralist, we said, and not systematically unified: besides the political values formulated by a freestanding political conception of justice, it includes a large family of nonpolitical values. Each subpart of this family has its own account based on ideas drawn from within it, leaving all values to be balanced against one another. Thus the political conception can be seen as part of a comprehensive doctrine but it is not a consequence of that doctrine's nonpolitical values. Nevertheless, its political values normally outweigh whatever other values oppose them, at least under the reasonably favorable conditions that make a constitutional democracy possible.

Those who hold this conception recognize values and virtues belonging to other parts of life. They differ from citizens holding the first two views in our model case in having no fully (as opposed to partially) comprehensive doctrine within which they see all values and virtues as being more or less systematically ordered. They do not say such a doctrine is impossible, but rather, practically speaking, unnecessary. Their conviction is that, within the scope allowed by the basic liberties and the other provisions of a just constitutional regime, all citizens can pursue their way of life on fair terms and properly respect its (nonpolitical) values. With those constitutional guarantees secure, they think no conflict of values is likely to arise that justifies their opposing the political conception as a whole, or on such fundamental matters as liberty of conscience, or equal political liberties, or basic civil rights.

2. This partially comprehensive view might be explained as follows. We do best not to assume that there exist generally acceptable answers for all or even for many questions of political justice.

as especially significant from the standpoint of political justice and leaves others aside. But whether the conception that results itself is general and comprehensive, as I have used those terms, is a separate question. I believe the conflicts implicit in the fact of reasonable pluralism force political philosophy to present conceptions of justice that are abstract, if it is to achieve its aims (I:8.2); but the same conflicts prevent those conceptions from being general and comprehensive.

Rather, we must be prepared to accept the fact that only a few questions we are moved to ask can be satisfactorily resolved. Political wisdom consists in identifying those few, and among them the most urgent.

That done, we must frame the institutions of the basic structure so that intractable conflicts are unlikely to arise; we must also accept the need for clear and simple principles, the general form and content of which we hope can be publicly understood. A political conception is at best but a guiding framework of deliberation and reflection which helps us reach political agreement on at least the constitutional essentials and the basic questions of justice. If it seems to have cleared our view and made our considered convictions more coherent; if it has narrowed the gap between the conscientious convictions of those who accept the basic ideas of a constitutional regime, then it has served its practical political purpose.[32]

This remains true even if we cannot fully explain our agreement: we know only that citizens who affirm the political conception, and who have been raised in and are familiar with the fundamental ideas of the public political culture, find that, when they adopt its framework of deliberation, their judgments converge sufficiently so that political cooperation on the basis of mutual respect can be maintained. They view the political conception as itself normally sufficient and may not expect, or think they need, greater political understanding than that.

3. Here we are bound to ask: how can a political conception of justice express values that, under the reasonably favorable conditions that make democracy possible, normally outweigh whatever other values are likely to conflict with them? One reason is this. As I have said, the most reasonable political conception of justice for a democratic regime will be, broadly speaking, liberal. This means that it protects the familiar basic rights and assigns them a special priority; it also includes measures to insure that all citizens have sufficient material means to make effective use of those basic rights. Faced with the fact of reasonable pluralism, a liberal view removes from the political agenda the most divisive issues, serious

contention about which must undermine the bases of social cooperation.

The virtues of political cooperation that make a constitutional regime possible are, then, very great virtues. I mean, for example, the virtues of tolerance and being ready to meet others halfway, and the virtue of reasonableness and the sense of fairness. When these virtues are widespread in society and sustain its political conception of justice, they constitute a very great public good, part of society's political capital.[33] Thus, the values that conflict with the political conception of justice and its sustaining virtues may be normally outweighed because they come into conflict with the very conditions that make fair social cooperation possible on a footing of mutual respect.

4. The other reason political values normally win out is that severe conflicts with other values are much reduced. This is because when an overlapping consensus supports the political conception, this conception is not viewed as incompatible with basic religious, philosophical, and moral values. We need not consider the claims of political justice against the claims of this or that comprehensive view; nor need we say that political values are intrinsically more important than other values and that is why the latter are overridden. Having to say that is just what we hope to avoid, and achieving an overlapping consensus enables us to do so.

To conclude: given the fact of reasonable pluralism, what the work of reconciliation by public reason does, thus enabling us to avoid reliance on general and comprehensive doctrines, is two things: first, it identifies the fundamental role of political values in expressing the terms of fair social cooperation consistent with mutual respect between citizens regarded as free and equal; and second, it uncovers a sufficiently inclusive concordant fit among political and other values seen in a reasonable overlapping consensus. . . .

---

32. See *Theory*, pp. 44f., 89f., 303, 364.

33. The term *capital* is appropriate in this connection because these virtues are built up slowly over time and depend not only on existing political and social institutions (themselves slowly built up), but also on citizens' experience as a whole and their knowledge of the past. Again, like capital, these virtues depreciate, as it were, and must be constantly renewed by being reaffirmed and acted from in the present.

POLITICAL LIBERALISM

Michael J. Sandel

Rare is the work of political philosophy that provokes sustained debate. It is a measure of its greatness that John Rawls's *A Theory of Justice*[1] inspired not one debate, but three.

The first, by now a starting point for students of moral and political philosophy, is the argument between utilitarians and rights-oriented liberals. Should justice be founded on utility, as Jeremy Bentham and John Stuart Mill argue, or does respect for individual rights require a basis for justice independent of utilitarian considerations, as Kant and Rawls maintain? Before Rawls wrote, utilitarianism was the dominant view within Anglo-American moral and political philosophy. Since *A Theory of Justice,* rights-oriented liberalism has come to predominate.[2]

The second debate inspired by Rawls's work is an argument within rights-oriented liberalism. If certain individual rights are so important that even considerations of the general welfare cannot override them, it remains to ask which rights these are. Libertarian liberals, like Robert Nozick and Friedrich Hayek, argue that government should respect basic civil and political liberties, and also the right to the fruits of our labor as conferred by the market economy; redistributive policies that tax the rich to help the poor thus violate our rights.[3] Egalitarian liberals like Rawls disagree. They argue that we cannot meaningfully exercise our civil and political liberties without the provision of basic social and economic needs; government should therefore assure each person, as a matter of right, a decent level of such goods as education, income, housing, health care, and the like. The debate between the libertarian and egalitarian versions of rights-oriented liberalism, which flourished in the academy in the 1970s, corresponds roughly to the debate in American politics, familiar since the New Deal, between

defenders of the market economy and advocates of the welfare state.

The third debate prompted by Rawls's work centers on an assumption shared by libertarian and egalitarian liberals alike. This is the idea that government should be neutral among competing conceptions of the good life. Despite their various accounts of what rights we have, rights-oriented liberals agree that the principles of justice that specify our rights should not depend for their justification on any particular conception of the good life.[4] This idea, central to the liberalism of Kant, Rawls, and many contemporary liberals, is summed up in the claim that the right is prior to the good.[5]

Contesting the Priority of the Right over the Good

For Rawls, as for Kant, the right is prior to the good in two respects, and it is important to distinguish them. First, the right is prior to the good in the sense that certain individual rights "trump," or outweigh, considerations of the common good. Second, the right is prior to the good

---

1. JOHN RAWLS, A THEORY OF JUSTICE (1971).
2. *See, e.g.*, H.L.A. Hart, *Between Utility and Rights, in* THE IDEA OF FREEDOM 77, 77 (Alan Ryan ed., 1979).
3. *See* FRIEDRICH A. HAYEK, THE CONSTITUTION OF LIBERTY (1960); ROBERT NOZICK, ANARCHY, STATE, AND UTOPIA (1974).
4. *See* BRUCE A. ACKERMAN, SOCIAL JUSTICE IN THE LIBERAL STATE 349–78 (1980); RONALD DWORKIN, TAKING RIGHTS SERIOUSLY 90–100, 168–77 (1977); CHARLES FRIED, RIGHT AND WRONG 114–19 (1978); CHARLES E. LARMORE, PATTERNS OF MORAL COMPLEXITY 42–68 (1987); NOZICK, *supra* note 5, at 33; RAWLS, *supra* note 3, at 30–32, 446–51, 560; Ronald Dworkin, *Liberalism, in* PUBLIC AND PRIVATE MORALITY 113, 127–36 (Stuart Hampshire ed., 1978); Thomas Nagel, *Moral Conflict and Political Legitimacy,* 16 PHIL. & PUB. AFF. 215, 227–37 (1987).
5. *See* IMMANUEL KANT, CRITIQUE OF PURE REASON (Norman K. Smith trans., St. Martin's Press 1965) (1788); IMMANUEL KANT, GROUNDWORK OF THE METAPHYSIC OF MORALS (H. J. Paton trans., Harper & Row 3d ed. 1964) (1785); IMMANUEL KANT, *On the Common Saying: "This May Be True in Theory, but It Does Not Apply in Practice," in* KANT'S POLITICAL WRITINGS 61, 73–74 (Hans Reiss ed. & H. B. Nisbet trans., 1970); RAWLS, *supra* note 3, at 30–32, 446–51, 560.

in that the principles of justice that specify our rights do not depend for their justification on any particular conception of the good life. It is this second claim for the priority of the right that prompted the most recent wave of debate about Rawlsian liberalism, an argument that has flourished in the last decade under the somewhat misleading label of the "liberal-communitarian debate."

A number of political philosophers writing in the 1980s took issue with the notion that justice can be detached from considerations of the good. Challenges to contemporary rights-oriented liberalism found in the writings of Alasdair MacIntyre,[6] Charles Taylor,[7] Michael Walzer,[8] and also in my own work,[9] are sometimes described as the "communitarian" critique of liberalism. The term "communitarian" is misleading, however, insofar as it implies that rights should rest on the values or preferences that prevail in any given community at any given time. Few, if any, of those who have challenged the priority of the right are communitarians in this sense.[10] The question is not whether rights should be respected, but whether rights can be identified and justified in a way that does not presuppose any particular conception of the good. At issue in the third wave of debate about Rawls's liberalism is not the relative weight of individual and communal claims, but the terms of relation between the right and the good.[11] Those who dispute the priority of the

6. See ALASDAIR MACINTYRE, AFTER VIRTUE (2d ed. 1984) [hereinafter MACINTYRE, AFTER VIRTUE]; ALASDAIR MACINTYRE, IS PATRIO-TISM A VIRTUE?: THE LINDLEY LECTURE (1984) [hereinafter MACINTYRE, IS PATRIOTISM A VIRTUE?]; ALASDAIR MACINTYRE, WHOSE JUSTICE? WHICH RATIONALITY? (1988).

7. See CHARLES TAYLOR, The Nature and Scope of Distributive Justice, in PHILOSOPHY AND THE HUMAN SCIENCES, 2 PHILOSOPHICAL PAPERS 289 (1985); CHARLES TAYLOR, SOURCES OF THE SELF: THE MAKING OF THE MODERN IDENTITY (1989) [hereinafter TAYLOR, SOURCES OF THE SELF].

8. See MICHAEL WALZER, SPHERES OF JUSTICE: A DEFENSE OF PLURALISM AND EQUALITY (1983).

9. See MICHAEL J. SANDEL, LIBERALISM AND THE LIMITS OF JUSTICE (1982); Michael J. Sandel, The Procedural Republic and the Unencumbered Self, 12 POL. THEORY 81 (1984).

10. Michael Walzer comes close to this view when he writes: "Justice is relative to social meanings. . . . A given society is just if its substantive life is lived . . . in a way faithful to the shared understandings of the members." WALZER, supra note 10, at 312–13. Walzer allows, however, that prevailing practices of rights can be criticized from the standpoint of alternative interpretations of a society's shared understandings. See id. at 84–91.

11. Much of the debate about liberal political philosophy in the last decade has focused on the "communitarian" critique of liberalism, or, more broadly, on the challenge to the priority of the right over the good. The best overall account of this debate is STEPHEN MULHALL & ADAM SWIFT, LIBERALS AND COMMUNITARIANS (1992). Edited volumes on the subject include COMMUNITARIANS AND INDIVIDUALISM (Shlomo Avineri & Avner de-Shalit eds., 1992); LIBERALISM AND ITS CRITICS (Michael J. Sandel ed., 1984); LIBERALISM AND THE GOOD (R. Bruce Douglass, Gerald M. Mara & Henry S. Richardson eds., 1990); LIBERALISM AND THE MORAL LIFE (Nancy L. Rosenblum ed., 1989); and UNIVERSALISM VS. COMMUNI-TARIANISM (David Rasmussen ed., 1990). Notable book-length works include DANIEL BELL, COM-MUNITARIANISM AND ITS CRITICS (1993); WILL KYMLICKA, LIBERALISM, COMMUNITY AND CULTURE (1989); CHARLES E. LAR-MORE, PATTERNS OF MORAL COMPLEXITY (1987); and STEPHEN MACEDO, LIBERAL VIRTUES: CITIZENSHIP, VIRTUE, AND COM-MUNITY IN LIBERAL CONSTITUTIONALISM (1990). The vast literature on the subject includes, among others: JEREMY WALDRON, Particular Values and Critical Morality, in LIBERAL RIGHTS 168 (1993); C. Edwin Baker, Sandel on Rawls, 133 U. PA. L. REV. 895 (1985); Sheyla Benhabib, Autonomy, Modernity and Community: Communitarianism and Critical Social Theory in Dialogue, in ZWISCHENBE-TRACHTUNGEN IM PROZESS DER AUFK-LAERUNG 373 (Axel Honneth, Thomas McCarthy, Claus Offe & Albrecht Welmer eds., 1989); Allen E. Buchanan, Assessing the Communitarian Critique of Liberalism, 99 ETHICS 852 (1989); Gerald Doppelt, Is Rawls's Kantian Liberalism Coherent and Defensible?, 99 ETHICS 815 (1989); Stephen A. Gardbaum, Law, Politics, and the Claims of Community, 90 MICH. L. REV. 685 (1992); Emily R. Gill, Goods, Virtues, and the Constitution of the Self, in LIBERALS ON LIBER-ALISM III (Alfonso J. Damico ed., 1986); Amy Gutmann, Communitarian Critics of Liberalism, 14 PHIL. & PUB. AFF. 308 (1985); H. N. Hirsch, The Threnody of Liberalism, 14 POL. THEORY 423 (1986); Will Kymlicka, Liberalism and Communitarianism, 18 CAN. J. PHIL. 181 (1988); Will Kymlicka, Rawls on Teleology and Deontology, 17 PHIL. & PUB. AFF. 173 (1988); Christopher Lasch, The Communitarian Critique of Liberalism, 69 SOUNDINGS 60 (1986); David Miller, In What Sense Must Socialism Be Communitarian?, 6 SOC. PHIL. & POL. 57 (1989); Chantal Mouffe,

right argue that justice is relative to the good, not independent of it. As a philosophical matter, our reflections about justice cannot reasonably be detached from our reflections about the nature of the good life and the highest human ends. As a political matter, our deliberations about justice and rights cannot proceed without reference to the conceptions of the good that find expression in the many cultures and traditions within which those deliberations take place.

Much of the debate about the priority of the right has focused on competing conceptions of the person and of how we should understand our relation to our ends. Are we, as moral agents, bound only by the ends and roles we choose for ourselves, or can we sometimes be obligated to fulfill certain ends we have not chosen—ends given by nature or

American Liberalism and Its Critics: Rawls, Taylor, Sandel and Walzer, 8 PRAXIS INT'L 193 (1988); Patrick Neal, *A Liberal Theory of the Good?*, 17 CAN. J. PHIL. 567 (1987); Jeffrey Paul & Fred D. Miller Jr., *Communitarian and Liberal Theories of the Good*, 43 REV. META-PHYSICS 803 (1990); Milton C. Regan, Jr., *Community and Justice in Constitutional Theory*, 1985 WIS. L. REV. 1073; Richard Rorty, *The Priority of Democracy to Philosophy*, in THE VIRGINIA STATUTE OF RELI-GIOUS FREEDOM 257, 257–82 (Merrill D. Peterson & Robert C. Vaughan eds., 1988); George Sher, *Three Grades of Social Involvement*, 18 PHIL. & PUB. AFF. 133 (1989); Tom Sorell, *Self, Society, and Kantian Impersonality*, 74 MONIST 30 (1991); Symposium, *Law, Community, and Moral Reasoning*, 77 CAL. L. REV. 475 (1989); Charles Taylor, *Cross-Purposes: The Liberal-Communitarian Debate*, in LIBERALISM AND THE MORAL LIFE, *supra*; Robert B. Thigpen & Lyle A. Downing, *Liberalism and the Communitarian Critique*, 31 AM. J. POL. SCI. 637 (1987); John Tomasi, *Individual Rights and Community Virtues*, 101 ETHICS 521 (1991); John R. Wallach, *Liberals, Communitarians, and the Tasks of Political Theory*, 15 POL. THEORY 581 (1987); Michael Walzer, *The Communitarian Critique of Liberalism*, 18 POL. THEORY 6 (1990); Iris M. Young, *The Ideal of Community and the Politics of Difference*, 12 SOC. THEORY & PRAC. 1 (1986); and Joel Feinberg, *Liberalism, Community and Tradition*, TIKKUN, May–June 1988, at 38. Prior to *Political Liberalism*, Rawls addressed these issues in a number of essays, including *The Idea of an Overlapping Consensus*, 7 OXFORD J. LEGAL STUD. 1 (1987); *Justice as Fairness: Political Not Metaphysical*, 14 PHIL. & PUB. AFF. 223 (1985); and *The Priority of Right and Ideas of the Good*, 17 PHIL. & PUB. AFF. 251 (1987). In *Political Liberalism*, however, he states: "The changes in the later essays are sometimes said to be replies to criti-cisms raised by communitarians and others. I don't believe there is a basis for saying this" (p. xvii).

God, for example, or by our identities as members of families, peoples, cultures, or traditions? In vari-ous ways, those who have criticized the priority of right have resisted the notion that we can make sense of our moral and political obligations in wholly voluntarist or contractual terms.

In *A Theory of Justice*, Rawls linked the priori-ty of the right to a voluntarist, or broadly Kantian, conception of the person. According to this conception, we are not simply defined as the sum of our desires, as utilitarians assume, nor are we beings whose perfection consists in realizing certain purposes or ends given by nature, as Aristotle held. Rather, we are free and independ-ent selves, unbound by antecedent moral ties, capable of choosing our ends for ourselves. This is the conception of the person that finds expression in the ideal of the state as a neutral framework. It is precisely because we are free and independent selves, capable of choosing our own ends, that we need a framework of rights that is neutral among ends. To base rights on some conception of the good would impose on some the values of others and so fail to respect each person's capacity to choose his or her own ends.

This conception of the person, and its link to the case for the priority of the right, are expressed throughout *A Theory of Justice*. Its most explicit statement comes toward the end of the book, in Rawls's account of "the good of justice." There Rawls argues, following Kant, that teleological doctrines are "radically misconceived" because they relate the right and the good in the wrong way:

> We should not attempt to give form to our life by first looking to the good independently defined. It is not our aims that primarily reveal our nature but rather the principles that we would acknowledge to govern the background conditions under which these aims are to be formed and the manner in which they are to be pursued. For the self is prior to the ends which are affirmed by it; even a dominant end must be chosen from among numerous possibilities. . . . We should therefore reverse the relation between the right and the good proposed by teleological doctrines and view the right as prior.[12]

12. RAWLS, *supra* note 3, at 560.

In *A Theory of Justice,* the priority of the self to its ends supports the priority of the right to the good. "[A] moral person is a subject with ends he has chosen, and his fundamental preference is for conditions that enable him to frame a mode of life that expresses his nature as a free and equal rational being as fully as circumstances permit."[13] The notion that we are free and independent selves, unclaimed by prior moral ties, assures that considerations of justice will always outweigh other, more particular aims. In an eloquent expression of Kantian liberalism, Rawls explains the moral importance of the priority of the right in the following terms:

> [T]he desire to express our nature as a free and equal rational being can be fulfilled only by acting on the principles of right and justice as having first priority. . . . It is acting from this precedence that expresses our freedom from contingency and happenstance. Therefore in order to realize our nature we have no alternative but to plan to preserve our sense of justice as governing our other aims. This sentiment cannot be fulfilled if it is compromised and balanced against other ends as but one desire among the rest. . . . [H]ow far we succeed in expressing our nature depends upon how consistently we act from our sense of justice as finally regulative. What we cannot do is express our nature by following a plan that views the sense of justice as but one desire to be weighed against others. For this sentiment reveals what the person is, and to compromise it is not to achieve for the self free reign but to give way to the contingencies and accidents of the world.[14]

In different ways, those who disputed the priority of the right took issue with Rawls's conception of the person as a free and independent self, unencumbered by prior moral ties.[15] They argued that a conception of the self given prior to its aims and attachments could not make sense of certain important aspects of our moral and political experience. Certain moral and political obligations that we commonly recognize—such as obligations of solidarity, for example, or religious duties—may claim us for reasons unrelated to a choice. Such obligations are difficult to dismiss as merely confused, and yet difficult to account for if we understand ourselves as free and independent selves, unbound by moral ties we have not chosen.[16]

Defending the Priority of the Right over the Good

In *Political Liberalism,* Rawls defends the priority of the right over the good. He sets aside, for the most part, issues raised in the first two waves of debate, about utility versus rights and libertarian versus egalitarian notions of distributive justice. *Political Liberalism* focuses instead on issues posed by the third wave of debate, about the priority of the right.

Given the controversy over the Kantian conception of the person that supports the priority of the right, at least two lines of reply are possible. One is to defend liberalism by defending the Kantian conception of the person; the other is to defend liberalism by detaching it from the Kantian conception. In *Political Liberalism,* Rawls adopts the second course. Rather than defend the Kantian conception of the person as a moral ideal, he argues that liberalism as he conceives it does not depend on that conception of the person after all. The priority of the right over the good does not presuppose any particular conception of the person, not even the one advanced in Part III of *A Theory of Justice.*

Political versus Comprehensive Liberalism

The case for liberalism, Rawls now argues, is political, not philosophical or metaphysical, and so does not depend on controversial claims about

13. *Id.* at 561.
14. *Id.* at 574–75.
15. The objection to the conception of the person presented in *A Theory of Justice* does not depend on failing to see the original position as a device of representation. It can be stated wholly in terms of the conception of the person presented in Part III of *A Theory of Justice,* which Rawls now recasts as a political conception. Not only critics, but also defenders of Rawls's liberalism interpreted *A Theory of Justice* as affirming a Kantian conception of the person. *See, e.g.,* LARMORE, *supra* note 6, at 118–30.

16. *See* MACINTYRE, AFTER VIRTUE, *supra* note 8, at 190–209; MACINTYRE, IS PATRIOTISM A VIRTUE?, *supra* note 8, *passim;* SANDEL, *supra* note 11, at 175–83; TAYLOR, SOURCES OF THE SELF, *supra* note 9, at 508.

the nature of the self (pp. 29–35). The priority of the right over the good is not the application to politics of Kantian moral philosophy, but a practical response to the familiar fact that people in modern democratic societies typically disagree about the good. Because people's moral and religious convictions are unlikely to converge, it is more reasonable to seek agreement on principles of justice that are neutral with respect to those controversies (pp. xvi–xvii).

Central to Rawls's revised view is the distinction between political liberalism and liberalism as part of a comprehensive moral doctrine (pp. 154–58). Comprehensive liberalism affirms liberal political arrangements in the name of certain moral ideals, such as autonomy or individuality or self-reliance. Examples of liberalism as a comprehensive moral doctrine include the liberal visions of Kant and John Stuart Mill.[17] As Rawls acknowledges, the version of liberalism presented in *A Theory of Justice* is also an instance of comprehensive liberalism. "An essential feature of a well-ordered society associated with justice as fairness is that all its citizens endorse this conception on the basis of what I now call a comprehensive philosophical doctrine" (p. xvi). It is this feature that Rawls now revises, by recasting his theory as a "political conception of justice" (p. xvi).

Unlike comprehensive liberalism, political liberalism refuses to take sides in the moral and religious controversies that arise from comprehensive doctrines, including controversies about conceptions of the self. "Which moral judgments are true, all things considered, is not a matter for political liberalism" (p. xx). "To maintain impartiality between comprehensive doctrines, it does not specifically address the moral topics on which those doctrines divide" (p. xxviii). Given the difficulty of securing agreement on any comprehensive conception, it is unreasonable to expect that, even in a well-ordered society, all people will

support liberal institutions for the same reason—as expressing the priority of the self to its ends, for example. Political liberalism abandons this hope as unrealistic and contrary to the aim of basing justice on principles that adherents of various moral and religious conceptions can accept. Rather than seek a philosophical foundation for principles of justice, political liberalism seeks the support of an "overlapping consensus" (p. 134). This means that different people can be persuaded to endorse liberal political arrangements, such as equal basic liberties, for different reasons, reflecting the various comprehensive moral and religious conceptions they espouse. Because political liberalism does not depend for its justification on any one of those moral or religious conceptions, it is presented as a "freestanding" view; it "applies the principle of toleration to philosophy itself" (p. 10).

Although political liberalism renounces reliance on the Kantian conception of the person, it does not do without a conception of the person altogether. As Rawls acknowledges, some such conception is necessary to the idea of the original position, the hypothetical social contract that gives rise to the principles of justice. The way to think about justice, Rawls argued in *A Theory of Justice,* is to ask which principles would be agreed to by persons who found themselves gathered in an initial situation of equality, each in temporary ignorance of his or her race and class, religion and gender, aims and attachments.[18] But in order for this way of thinking about justice to carry weight, the design of the original position must reflect something about the sort of persons we actually are, or would be in a just society.

One way of justifying the design of the original position would be to appeal to the Kantian conception of the person that Rawls advanced in Part III of *A Theory of Justice.* If our capacity to choose our ends is more fundamental to our nature as moral persons than are the particular ends we choose, if "[i]t is not our aims that primarily reveal our nature but rather the principles that we would acknowledge to govern the background conditions under which these aims are to be formed,"[19] if "the self is prior to the ends which are affirmed by it,"[20] then it makes sense to think

17. For contemporary examples of comprehensive liberalism, see GEORGE KATEB, THE INNER OCEAN: INDIVIDUALISM AND DEMOCRATIC CULTURE (1992); and JOSEPH RAZ, THE MORALITY OF FREEDOM (1986). Ronald Dworkin describes his view as a version of comprehensive liberalism in *Foundations of Liberal Equality, in* II THE TANNER LECTURES ON HUMAN VALUES 1 (Grethe B. Peterson ed., 1990).

18. *See* RAWLS, *supra* note 3, at 11–12.
19. *Id.* at 560.
20. *Id.*

about justice from the standpoint of persons deliberating prior to any knowledge of the ends they will pursue. If "a moral person is a subject with ends he has chosen, and his fundamental preference is for conditions that enable him to frame a mode of life that expresses his nature as a free and equal rational being as fully as circumstances permit,"[21] then the original position can be justified as an expression of our moral personality and the "fundamental preference" that flows from it.

Once Rawls disavows reliance on the Kantian conception of the person, however, this way of justifying the original position is no longer available. But this raises a difficult question: what reason remains for insisting that our reflections about justice should proceed without reference to our purposes and ends? Why must we "bracket," or set aside, our moral and religious convictions, our conceptions of the good life? Why should we not base the principles of justice that govern the basic structure of society on our best understanding of the highest human ends?

The Political Conception of the Person

Political liberalism replies as follows: the reason we should think about justice from the standpoint of persons who abstract from their ends is not that this procedure expresses our nature as free and independent selves given prior to our ends. Rather, this way of thinking about justice is warranted by the fact that, for *political* purposes, though not necessarily for all moral purposes, we should think of ourselves as free and independent citizens, unclaimed by prior duties or obligations (pp. 29–35). For political liberalism, what justifies the design of the original position is a "political conception of the person" (p. 29). The political conception of the person embodied in the original position closely parallels the Kantian conception of the person, with the important difference that its scope is limited to our public identity, our identity as citizens. Thus, for example, our freedom as citizens means that our public identity is not claimed or defined by the ends we espouse at any given time. As free persons, citizens view themselves "as independent from and not identified with any particular such conception with its

scheme of final ends" (p. 30). Our public identity is not affected by changes over time in our conceptions of the good.

In our personal or nonpublic identity, Rawls allows, we may regard our "ends and attachments very differently from the way the political conception supposes" (p. 31). There, persons may find themselves claimed by loyalties and commitments "they believe they would not, indeed could and should not, stand apart from and evaluate objectively. They may regard it as simply unthinkable to view themselves apart from certain religious, philosophical, and moral convictions, or from certain enduring attachments and loyalties" (p. 31). But however encumbered we may be in our personal identities, however claimed by moral or religious convictions, we must bracket our encumbrances in public, and regard ourselves, *qua* public selves, as independent of any particular loyalties or attachments or conceptions of the good (p. 31).

A related feature of the political conception of the person is that we are "self-authenticating sources of valid claims" (p. 32). The claims we make as citizens carry weight, whatever they are, simply by virtue of our making them (provided they are not unjust). That some claims may reflect high moral or religious ideals, or notions of patriotism and the common good, while others express mere interests or preferences, is not relevant from the standpoint of political liberalism. From a political point of view, claims founded on duties and obligations of citizenship or solidarity or religious faith are just things people want—nothing more, nothing less. Their validity as political claims has nothing to do with the moral importance of the goods they affirm, but consists solely in the fact that someone asserts them. Even divine commandments and imperatives of conscience count as "self-authenticating" claims, politically speaking.[22] This ensures that even those

---

21. *Id.* at 561.

22. The notion that we should regard our moral and religious duties as "self-authenticating from a political point of view" (p. 33) accords with Rawls's statement, in *A Theory of Justice,* that "from the standpoint of justice as fairness, these [moral and religious] obligations are self-imposed." RAWLS, *supra* note 3, at 206. But it is not clear what the justification can be on such a view for according religious beliefs or claims of conscience a special respect not accorded other preferences that people may hold with equal or greater intensity. *See id.* at 205–11.

who regard themselves as claimed by moral or religious or communal obligations are nonetheless, for political purposes, unencumbered selves.

This political conception of the person explains why, according to political liberalism, we should reflect about justice as the original position invites us to do, in abstraction from our ends. But this raises a further question: why should we adopt the standpoint of the political conception of the person in the first place? Why should our political identities not express the moral and religious and communal convictions we affirm in our personal lives? Why insist on the separation between our identity as citizens and our identity as moral persons more broadly conceived? Why, in deliberating about justice, should we set aside the moral judgments that inform the rest of our lives?

Rawls's answer is that this separation or "dualism" between our identity as citizens and our identity as persons "originates in the special nature of democratic political culture" (p. xxi). In traditional societies, people sought to shape political life in the image of their comprehensive moral and religious ideals. But in a modern democratic society like our own, marked as it is by a plurality of moral and religious views, we typically distinguish between our public and personal identities. Confident though I may be of the truth of the moral and religious ideals I espouse, I do not insist that these ideals be reflected in the basic structure of society. Like other aspects of political liberalism, the political conception of the person as a free and independent self is "implicit in the public political culture of a democratic society" (p. 13).

But suppose Rawls is right, and the liberal self-image he attributes to us is implicit in our political culture. Would this provide sufficient grounds for affirming it, and for adopting the conception of justice it supports? Some have read Rawls's recent writings as suggesting that justice as fairness, being a political conception of justice, requires no moral or philosophical justification apart from an appeal to the shared understandings implicit in our political culture. Rawls seemed to invite this interpretation when he wrote, in an article published after *A Theory of Justice* but before *Political Liberalism,* as follows:

What justifies a conception of justice is not its being true to an order antecedent to and given to

us, but its congruence with our deeper understanding of ourselves and our aspirations, and our realization that, given our history and the traditions embedded in our public life, it is the most reasonable doctrine for us.[23]

Richard Rorty, in an insightful article, interprets (and welcomes) Rawls's revised view as "thoroughly historicist and antiuniversalist."[24] Although *A Theory of Justice* seemed to base justice on a Kantian conception of the person, Rorty writes, Rawls's liberalism "no longer seems committed to a philosophical account of the human self, but only to a historico-sociological description of the way we live now."[25] On this view, Rawls is not "supplying philosophical foundations for democratic institutions, but simply trying to systematize the principles and intuitions typical of American liberals."[26] Rorty endorses what he takes to be Rawls's pragmatic turn, a turn away from the notion that liberal political arrangements require a philosophical justification, or "extrapolitical grounding" in a theory of the human subject. "[I]nsofar as justice becomes the first virtue of a society," Rorty writes, "the need for such legitimation may gradually cease to be felt. Such a society will become accustomed to the thought that social policy needs no more authority than successful accommodation among individuals, individuals who find themselves heir to the same historical traditions and faced with the same problems."[27]

In *Political Liberalism,* Rawls pulls back from this purely pragmatic account. Although justice as fairness begins "by looking to the public culture itself as the shared fund of implicitly recognized basic ideas and principles" (p. 8), it does not affirm these principles simply on the grounds that they are widely shared. Though Rawls argues that his principles of justice could gain the support of an overlapping consensus, the overlapping consensus he seeks "is not a mere modus vivendi" (p. 147), or compromise among conflicting views. Adherents of different moral and religious conceptions begin by endorsing the principles of justice for reasons

23. John Rawls, *Kantian Constructivism in Moral Theory: Rational and Full Autonomy,* 77 J. PHIL. 515, 519 (1980).
24. Rorty, *supra* note 13, at 257, 262.
25. *Id.* at 265.
26. *Id.* at 268.
27. *Id.* at 264.

drawn from within their own conceptions. But, if all goes well, they come to support those principles as expressing important political values. As people learn to live in a pluralist society governed by liberal institutions, they acquire virtues that strengthen their commitment to liberal principles.

> The virtues of political cooperation that make a constitutional regime possible are . . . very great virtues. I mean, for example, the virtues of tolerance and being ready to meet others halfway, and the virtue of reasonableness and the sense of fairness. When these virtues are widespread in society and sustain its political conception of justice, they constitute a very great public good . . . (p. 157).

Rawls emphasizes that affirming liberal virtues as a great public good and encouraging their cultivation is not the same as endorsing a perfectionist state based on a comprehensive moral conception. It does not contradict the priority of the right over the good. The reason is that political liberalism affirms liberal virtues for political purposes only—for their role in supporting a constitutional regime that protects people's rights. Whether and to what extent these virtues should figure in people's moral lives generally is a question that political liberalism does not claim to answer (pp. 194–95).

Assessing Political Liberalism

If *Political Liberalism* defends the priority of right by detaching it from the Kantian conception of the person, how convincing is its defense? As I shall try to argue, *Political Liberalism* rescues the priority of the right from controversies about the nature of the self only at the cost of rendering it vulnerable on other grounds. Specifically, I shall try to show that liberalism conceived as a political conception of justice is open to three objections.

First, notwithstanding the importance of the "political values" to which Rawls appeals, it is not always reasonable to bracket, or set aside for political purposes, claims arising from within comprehensive moral and religious doctrines. Where grave moral questions are concerned, whether it is reasonable to bracket moral and religious controversies for the sake of political agreement

partly depends on which of the contending moral or religious doctrines is true.

Second, for political liberalism, the case for the priority of the right over the good depends on the claim that modern democratic societies are characterized by a "fact of reasonable pluralism" about the good (p. xvii). Though it is certainly true that people in modern democratic societies hold a variety of conflicting moral and religious views, it cannot be said that there is a "fact of reasonable pluralism" about morality and religion that does not also apply to questions of justice.

Third, according to the ideal of public reason advanced by political liberalism, citizens may not legitimately discuss fundamental political and constitutional questions with reference to their moral and religious ideals. But this is an unduly severe restriction that would impoverish political discourse and rule out important dimensions of public deliberation.

Bracketing Grave Moral Questions

Political liberalism insists on bracketing our comprehensive moral and religious ideals for political purposes, and on separating our political from our personal identities. The reason is this: in modern democratic societies like ours, where people typically disagree about the good life, bracketing our moral and religious convictions is necessary if we are to secure social cooperation on the basis of mutual respect. But this raises a question that political liberalism cannot answer within its own terms. Even granting the importance of securing social cooperation on the basis of mutual respect, what is to guarantee that this interest is always so important as to outweigh any competing interest that could arise from within a comprehensive moral or religious view?

One way of assuring the priority of the political conception of justice (and hence the priority of the right) is to deny that any of the moral or religious conceptions it brackets could be true.[28]

28. Thomas Hobbes, who can be interpreted as advancing a political conception of justice, ensured the priority of his political conception with respect to claims arising from contending moral and religious conceptions by denying the truth of those conceptions. *See* THOMAS HOBBES, LEVIATHAN 168–83 (C.B. Macpherson ed., Penguin Books 1985) (1651).

But this would implicate political liberalism in precisely the sort of philosophical claim it seeks to avoid. Time and again Rawls emphasizes that political liberalism does not depend on skepticism about the claims of comprehensive moral and religious doctrines. If political liberalism therefore allows that some such doctrines might be true, then what is to assure that none can generate values sufficiently compelling to burst the brackets, so to speak, and morally outweigh the political values of toleration, fairness, and social cooperation based on mutual respect?

One might reply that political values and values arising from within comprehensive moral and religious doctrines address different subjects. Political values, one might say, apply to the basic structure of society and to constitutional essentials, whereas moral and religious values apply to the conduct of personal life and voluntary associations. But if it were simply a difference of subject matter, no conflict between political values and moral and religious values could ever arise, and there would be no need to assert, as Rawls repeatedly does, that in a constitutional democracy governed by political liberalism, "political values normally outweigh whatever nonpolitical values conflict with them" (p. 146).

The difficulty of asserting the priority of "political values" without reference to the claims of morality and religion can be seen by considering two political controversies that bear on grave moral and religious questions. One is the contemporary debate about abortion rights. The other is the famous debate between Abraham Lincoln and Stephen Douglas over popular sovereignty and slavery.

Given the intense disagreement over the moral permissibility of abortion, the case for seeking a political solution that brackets the contending moral and religious issues—that is neutral with respect to them—would seem especially strong. But whether it is reasonable to bracket, for political purposes, the comprehensive moral and religious doctrines at stake largely depends on which of those doctrines is true. If the doctrine of the Catholic Church is true, if human life in the relevant moral sense does begin at conception, then bracketing the moral-theological question when human life begins is far less reasonable than it would be on rival moral and religious assumptions.

The more confident we are that fetuses are, in the relevant moral sense, different from babies, the more confident we can be in affirming a political conception of justice that sets aside the controversy about the moral status of fetuses.

The political liberal might reply that the political values of toleration and equal citizenship for women are sufficient grounds for concluding that women should be free to choose for themselves whether to have an abortion; government should not take sides on the moral and religious controversy over when human life begins.[29] But if the Catholic Church is right about the moral status of the fetus, if abortion is morally tantamount to murder, then it is not clear why the political values of toleration and women's equality, important though they are, should prevail. If the Catholic doctrine is true, the political liberal's case for the priority of political values must become an instance of just-war theory; he or she would have to show why these values should prevail even at the cost of some 1.5 million civilian deaths each year.

Of course, to suggest the impossibility of bracketing the moral-theological question of when human life begins is not to argue against a right to abortion. It is simply to show that the case for abortion rights cannot be neutral with respect to that moral and religious controversy. It must engage rather than avoid the comprehensive moral and religious doctrines at stake. Liberals often resist this engagement because it violates the priority of the right over the good. But the abortion debate shows that this priority cannot be sustained. The case for respecting a woman's right to decide for herself whether to have an abortion depends on showing—as I believe can be shown—that there is a relevant moral difference between aborting a fetus at a relatively early stage of development and killing a child.

A second illustration of the difficulty with a political conception of justice that tries to bracket controversial moral questions is offered by the 1858 debates between Abraham Lincoln and Stephen Douglas. Douglas's argument for the doctrine of popular sovereignty is perhaps the

29. Rawls seems to take this view in a footnote on abortion. But he does not explain why political values should prevail even if the Catholic doctrine were true (p. 243 n.32).

most famous case in American history for bracketing a controversial moral question for the sake of political agreement. Because people were bound to disagree about the morality of slavery, Douglas argued, national policy should be neutral on that question. The doctrine of popular sovereignty he defended did not judge slavery right or wrong, but left the people of each territory free to make their own judgments. "[T]o throw the weight of federal power into the scale, either in favor of the free or the slave states," would violate the fundamental principles of the Constitution and run the risk of civil war. The only hope of holding the country together, he argued, was to agree to disagree, to bracket the moral controversy over slavery and respect "the right of each state and each territory to decide these questions for themselves."[30]

Lincoln argued against Douglas's case for a political conception of justice. Policy should express rather than avoid a substantive moral judgment about slavery. Though Lincoln was not an abolitionist, he believed government should treat slavery as the moral wrong that it was, and prohibit its extension to the territories. "The real issue in this controversy—the one pressing upon every mind—is the sentiment on the part of one class that looks upon the institution of slavery *as a wrong,* and of another class that *does not* look upon it as a wrong."[31] Lincoln and the Republican party viewed slavery as a wrong and insisted that it "*be treated* as a wrong, and one of the methods of treating it as a wrong is to *make provision that it shall grow no larger.*"[32]

Whatever his personal moral views, Douglas claimed that, for political purposes at least, he was agnostic on the question of slavery; he did not care whether slavery was "voted up or voted down."[33] Lincoln replied that it was reasonable to bracket the question of the morality of slavery only on the assumption that it was not the moral evil he regarded it to be. Any man can advocate political neutrality

who does not see anything wrong in slavery, but no man can logically say it who does see a wrong in it; because no man can logically say he don't care whether a wrong is voted up or voted down. He may say he don't care whether an indifferent thing is voted up or down, but he must logically have a choice between a right thing and a wrong thing. He contends that whatever community wants slaves has a right to have them. So they have if it is not a wrong. But if it is a wrong, he cannot say people have a right to do wrong.[34]

The debate between Lincoln and Douglas was not primarily about the morality of slavery, but about whether to bracket a moral controversy for the sake of political agreement. In this respect, their debate over popular sovereignty is analogous to the contemporary debate over abortion rights. As some contemporary liberals argue that government should not take a stand one way or the other on the morality of abortion, but let each woman decide the question for herself, so Douglas argued that national policy should not take a stand one way or the other on the morality of slavery, but let each territory decide the question for itself. There is of course the difference that in the case of abortion rights, those who would bracket the substantive moral question typically leave the choice to the individual, while in the case of slavery, Douglas's way of bracketing was to leave the choice to the territories.

But Lincoln's argument against Douglas was an argument against bracketing as such, at least where grave moral questions are at stake. Lincoln's point was that the political conception of justice defended by Douglas depended for its plausibility on a particular answer to the substantive moral question it claimed to bracket. This point applies with equal force to those arguments for abortion rights that claim to take no side in the controversy over the moral status of the fetus. Even in the face of so dire a threat to social cooperation as the prospect of civil war, Lincoln argued that it made neither moral nor political sense to bracket the most divisive moral controversy of the day.

I say, where is the philosophy or the statesmanship based on the assumption that we are to quit talking about it . . . and that the public mind is all

---

30. CREATED EQUAL?: THE COMPLETE LINCOLN-DOUGLAS DEBATES OF 1858, at 369, 374 (Paul M. Angle ed., 1958) [hereinafter CREATED EQUAL?].
31. *Id.* at 390.
32. *Id.*
33. *Id.* at 392.

34. *Id.*

at once to cease being agitated by it? Yet this is the policy . . . that Douglas is advocating—that we are to care nothing about it! I ask you if it is not a false philosophy? Is it not a false statesmanship that undertakes to build up a system of policy upon the basis of caring nothing about *the very thing that every body does care the most about?*[35]

Present-day liberals will surely resist the company of Douglas and want national policy to oppose slavery, presumably on the grounds that slavery violates people's rights. The question is whether liberalism conceived as a political conception of justice can make this claim consistent with its own strictures against appeals to comprehensive moral ideals. For example, a Kantian liberal can oppose slavery as a failure to treat persons as ends in themselves, worthy of respect. But this argument, resting as it does on a Kantian conception of the person, is unavailable to political liberalism. Other historically important arguments against slavery are unavailable to political liberalism for similar reasons. American abolitionists of the 1830s and 1840s, for example, typically cast their arguments in religious terms, arguments that political liberalism cannot invoke.

How, then, can political liberalism escape the company of Douglas and oppose slavery without presupposing some comprehensive moral view? It might be replied that Douglas was wrong to seek social peace at any price; not just any political agreement will do. Even conceived as a political conception, justice as fairness is not merely a modus vivendi. Given the principles and self-understandings implicit in our political culture, only an agreement on terms that treat persons fairly, as free and equal citizens, can provide a reasonable basis for social cooperation. For us twentieth-century Americans, at least, the rejection of slavery is a settled matter. The historical demise of Douglas's position is by now a fact of our political tradition that any political agreement must take as given.

This appeal to the conception of citizenship implicit in our political culture might explain how political liberalism can oppose slavery today; our present political culture was importantly shaped, after all, by the Civil War, Reconstruction, the adoption of the Thirteenth, Fourteenth, and Fifteenth Amendments, *Brown v. Board of*

35. *Id.* at 388–89.

Education,[36] the civil rights movement, the Voting Rights Act,[37] and so on. These experiences, and the shared understanding of racial equality and equal citizenship they formed, provide ample grounds for holding that slavery is at odds with American political and constitutional practice as it has developed over the past century.

But this does not explain how political liberalism could oppose slavery in 1858. The notions of equal citizenship implicit in American political culture of the mid-nineteenth century were arguably hospitable to the institution of slavery. The Declaration of Independence proclaimed that all men are created equal, endowed by their Creator with certain unalienable rights, but Douglas argued, not implausibly, that the signers of the Declaration were asserting the right of the colonists to be free of British rule, not the right of their Negro slaves to equal citizenship.[38] The Constitution itself did not prohibit slavery, but to the contrary accommodated it by allowing states to count three-fifths of their slave population for apportionment purposes,[39] providing that Congress could not prohibit the slave trade until 1808,[40] and requiring the return of fugitive slaves.[41] And in the notorious *Dred Scott* case,[42] the Supreme Court upheld the property rights of slaveholders in their slaves and ruled that African-Americans were not citizens of the United States.[43] To the extent that political liberalism refuses to invoke comprehensive moral ideals and relies instead on notions of citizenship implicit in the political culture, it would have a hard time explaining, in 1858, why Lincoln was right and Douglas was wrong.

The Fact of Reasonable Pluralism

The abortion debate today and the Lincoln-Douglas debate of 1858 illustrate the way a political conception of justice must presuppose some answer to the moral questions it purports to

36. 347 U.S. 483 (1954).
37. Voting Rights Act of 1965, 42 U.S.C. §§ 1971, 1973 (1988).
38. *See* CREATED EQUAL?, *supra* note 32, at 374.
39. *See* U.S. CONST. art. I, § 2, cl. 3.
40. *See id.* art. I, § 9, cl. 1.
41. *See id.* art. IV, § 2, cl. 3.
42. Scott v. Sandford, 60 U.S. (19 How.) 393 (1857).
43. *See id.* at 404–05.

bracket, at least where grave moral questions are concerned. In cases such as these, the priority of the right over the good cannot be sustained. A further difficulty with political liberalism concerns the reason it gives for asserting the priority of the right over the good in the first place. For Kantian liberalism, the asymmetry between the right and the good arises from a certain conception of the person. Because we must think of ourselves as moral subjects given prior to our aims and attachments, we must regard the right as regulative with respect to the particular ends we affirm; the right is prior to the good because the self is prior to its ends.

For political liberalism, the asymmetry between the right and the good is not based on a Kantian conception of the person but instead on a certain feature of modern democratic societies. Rawls describes this feature as "the fact of reasonable pluralism" (p. xvii). "A modern democratic society is characterized not simply by a pluralism of comprehensive religious, philosophical, and moral doctrines but by a pluralism of incompatible yet reasonable comprehensive doctrines. No one of these doctrines is affirmed by citizens generally" (p. xvi). Nor is it likely that sometime in the foreseeable future this pluralism will cease to hold. Disagreement about moral and religious questions is not a temporary condition but "the normal result of the exercise of human reason" under free institutions (p. xvi).

Given the "fact of reasonable pluralism," the problem is to find principles of justice that free and equal citizens can affirm despite their moral, philosophical, and religious differences. "This is a problem of political justice, not a problem about the highest good" (p. xxv). Whatever principles it generates, the solution to this problem must be one that upholds the priority of the right over the good. Otherwise, it will fail to provide a basis for social cooperation among adherents of incompatible but reasonable moral and religious convictions.

But here there arises a difficulty. For even if the fact of reasonable pluralism is true, the asymmetry between the right and the good depends on a further assumption. This is the assumption that, despite our disagreements about morality and religion, we do not have, or on due reflection would not have, similar disagreements about justice. Political liberalism must assume not only that the exercise of human reason under conditions of freedom will produce disagreements about the good life, but also that the exercise of human reason under conditions of freedom will *not* produce disagreements about justice. The "fact of reasonable pluralism" about morality and religion only creates an asymmetry between the right and the good when coupled with the further assumption that there is no comparable "fact of reasonable pluralism" about justice.

It is not clear, however, that this further assumption is justified. We need only look around us to see that modern democratic societies are teeming with disagreements about justice. Consider, for example, contemporary debates about affirmative action, income distribution and tax fairness, health care, immigration, gay rights, free speech versus hate speech, and capital punishment, to name just a few. Or consider the divided votes and conflicting opinions of Supreme Court Justices in cases involving religious liberty, freedom of speech, privacy rights, voting rights, the rights of the accused, and so on. Do not these debates display a "fact of reasonable pluralism" about justice? If so, how does the pluralism about justice that prevails in modern democratic societies differ from the pluralism about morality and religion? Is there reason to think that, sometime in the foreseeable future, our disagreements about justice will dissolve even as our disagreements about morality and religion persist?

The political liberal might reply by distinguishing two different kinds of disagreement about justice. There are disagreements about what the principles of justice should be and disagreements about how these principles should be applied. Many of our disagreements about justice, it might be argued, are of the second kind. Although we generally agree, for example, that freedom of speech is among the basic rights and liberties, we disagree about whether the right to free speech should protect racial epithets, or violent pornographic depictions, or commercial advertising, or unlimited contributions to political campaigns. These disagreements, vigorous and even intractable though they may be, are consistent with our agreeing at the level of principle that a just society includes a basic right to free speech.

Our disagreements about morality and religion, by contrast, might be seen as more fundamental. They reflect incompatible conceptions of the good life, it might be argued, not disagreements about how to put into practice a conception of the good life that commands, or on reflection would command, widespread agreement. If our controversies about justice concern the application of principles we share or would share on due reflection, while our controversies about morality and religion run deeper, then the asymmetry between the right and the good advanced by political liberalism would be vindicated.

But with what confidence can this contrast be asserted? Do all of our disagreements about justice concern the application of principles we share or would share on due reflection, rather than the principles themselves? What of our debates about distributive justice? Here it would seem that our disagreements are at the level of principle, not application. Some maintain, consistent with Rawls's difference principle, that only those social and economic inequalities that improve the condition of the least-advantaged members of society are just. They argue, for example, that government must ensure the provision of certain basic needs, such as income, education, health care, housing, and the like, so that all citizens will be able meaningfully to exercise their basic liberties. Others reject the difference principle. Libertarians argue, for example, that it may be a good thing for people to help those less fortunate than themselves, but that this should be a matter of charity, not entitlement. Government should not use its coercive power to redistribute income and wealth, but should respect people's rights to exercise their talents as they choose, and to reap their rewards as defined by the market economy.[44]

The debate between liberal egalitarians like Rawls and libertarians like Robert Nozick and Milton Friedman is a prominent feature of political argument in modern democratic societies. This debate reflects disagreement about what the correct principle of distributive justice is, not

disagreement about how to apply the difference principle. But this would suggest that there exists in democratic societies a "fact of reasonable pluralism" about justice as well as about morality and religion. And if this is the case, the asymmetry between the right and the good does not hold.

Political liberalism is not without a reply to this objection, but the reply it must make departs from the spirit of toleration it otherwise evokes. Rawls's reply must be that, although there is a fact of pluralism about distributive justice, there is no fact of *reasonable* pluralism. Unlike disagreements about morality and religion, disagreements about the validity of the difference principle are not reasonable; libertarian theories of distributive justice would not be sustained on due reflection. Our differences about distributive justice, unlike our differences of morality and religion, are not the natural outcome of the exercise of human reason under conditions of freedom.[45]

At first glance, the claim that disagreements about distributive justice are not reasonable may seem arbitrary, even harsh, at odds with political liberalism's promise to apply "the principle of toleration to philosophy itself" (p. 10). It contrasts sharply with Rawls's apparent generosity toward differences of morality and religion. These differences, Rawls repeatedly writes, are a normal, indeed desirable feature of modern life, an expression of human diversity that only the oppressive use of state power can overcome (pp. 303–04). Where comprehensive moralities are concerned, "it is not to be expected that conscientious persons with full powers of reason, even after free discussion, will all arrive at the same conclusion" (p. 58). Since the exercise of human reason produces a plurality of reasonable moral and religious doctrines, "it is unreasonable or worse to want to use the sanctions of state power to correct, or to punish, those who disagree with us" (p. 138). But this spirit of toleration does not extend to our disagreements about justice. Because disagreements

44. *See* MILTON FRIEDMAN, CAPITALISM AND FREEDOM 200 (1962); MILTON FRIEDMAN & ROSE FRIEDMAN, FREE TO CHOOSE 134–36 (1980); HAYEK, *supra* note 5, at 85–86, 99–100; NOZICK, *supra* note 5, at 149, 167–74.

45. Although Rawls does not state this view explicitly, it is necessary in order to make sense of the "fact of reasonable pluralism" and the role it plays in supporting the priority of the right. He notes that reasonable disagreements may arise over what policies fulfill the difference principle, but adds, "[t]his is not a difference about what are the correct principles but simply a difference in the difficulty of seeing whether the principles are achieved" (p. 230).

between, say, libertarians and advocates of the difference principle do not reflect a reasonable pluralism, there is no objection to using state power to implement the difference principle.

Intolerant though it may seem at first glance, the notion that theories of distributive justice at odds with the difference principle are not reasonable, or that libertarian theories of justice would not survive due reflection, is no arbitrary claim. To the contrary, in *A Theory of Justice* Rawls offers a rich array of compelling arguments on behalf of the difference principle and against libertarian conceptions: the distribution of talents and assets that enables some to earn more and others less in the market economy is arbitrary from a moral point of view; so is the fact that the market happens to prize and reward, at any given moment, the talents you or I may have in abundance; libertarians would agree that distributive shares should not be based on social status or accident of birth (as in aristocratic or caste societies), but the distribution of talents given by nature is no less arbitrary; the notion of freedom that libertarians invoke can be meaningfully exercised only if persons' basic social and economic needs are met; if people deliberated about distributive justice without reference to their own interests, or without prior knowledge of their talents and the value of those talents in the market economy, they would agree that the natural distribution of talents should not be the basis of distributive shares; and so on.[46]

My point is not to rehearse Rawls's argument for the difference principle, but only to recall the kind of reasons he offers. Viewing justification as a process of mutual adjustment between principles and considered judgments that aims at a "reflective equilibrium,"[47] Rawls tries to show that the difference principle is more reasonable than the alternative offered by libertarians. To the extent that his arguments are convincing—as I believe they are—and to the extent they can be convincing to citizens of a democratic society, the principles they support are properly embodied in public policy and law. Disagreement will doubtless remain. Libertarians will not fall silent or dis-

appear. But their disagreement need not be regarded as a "fact of reasonable pluralism" in the face of which government must be neutral.

But this leads to a question that goes to the heart of political liberalism's claim for the priority of the right over the good: if moral argument or reflection of the kind Rawls deploys enables us to conclude, despite the persistence of conflicting views, that some principles of justice are more reasonable than others, what guarantees that reflection of a similar kind is not possible in the case of moral and religious controversy? If we can reason about controversial principles of distributive justice by seeking a reflective equilibrium, why can we not reason in the same way about conceptions of the good? If it can be shown that some conceptions of the good are more reasonable than others, then the persistence of disagreement would not necessarily amount to a "fact of reasonable pluralism" that requires government to be neutral.

Consider, for example, the controversy in our public culture about the moral status of homosexuality, a controversy based in comprehensive moral and religious doctrines. Some maintain that homosexuality is sinful, or at least morally impermissible; others argue that homosexuality is morally permissible, and in some cases gives expression to important human goods. Political liberalism insists that neither of these views about the morality of homosexuality should play a role in public debates about justice or rights. Government must be neutral with respect to them. This means that those who abhor homosexuality may not seek to embody their view in law; it also means that proponents of gay rights may not base their arguments on the notion that homosexuality is morally defensible. From the standpoint of political liberalism, each of these approaches would wrongly base the right on some conception of the good; each would fail to respect the "fact of reasonable pluralism" about comprehensive moralities.

But does the disagreement in our society about the moral status of homosexuality constitute a "fact of reasonable pluralism" any more than does the disagreement about distributive justice? According to political liberalism, the libertarian's objection to the difference principle does not constitute a "fact of reasonable pluralism" that requires government neutrality, because there are

46. *See* RAWLS, *supra* note 3, at 72–75, 100–07, 136–42, 310–15.
47. *See id.* at 20–21, 48–51, 120, 577–87.

good reasons to conclude, on due reflection, that the arguments for the difference principle are more convincing than the ones that support libertarianism. But isn't it possible to conclude, with equal or greater confidence, that on due reflection, the arguments for the moral permissibility of homosexuality are more convincing than the arguments against it? Consistent with the search for a reflective equilibrium among principles and considered judgments, such reflection might proceed by assessing the reasons advanced by those who assert the moral inferiority of homosexual to heterosexual relations.

Those who consider homosexuality immoral often argue, for example, that homosexuality cannot fulfill the highest end of human sexuality, the good of procreation.[48] To this it might be replied that many heterosexual relations also do not fulfill this end, such as contracepted sex, or sex among sterile couples, or sex among partners beyond the age of reproduction. This might suggest that the good of procreation, important though it is, is not necessary to the moral worth of human sexual relations; the moral worth of sexuality might also consist in the love and responsibility it expresses, and these goods are possible in homosexual as well as heterosexual relations. Opponents might reply that homosexuals are often promiscuous, and hence less likely to realize the goods of love and responsibility. The reply to this claim might consist in an empirical showing to the contrary, or in the observation that the existence of promiscuity does not argue against the moral worth of homosexuality as such, only against certain instances of it.[49]

48. In this paragraph, I draw on some of the arguments for and against the morality of homosexuality that appear in John Finnis & Martha Nussbaum, *Is Homosexual Conduct Wrong?: A Philosophical Exchange,* NEW REPUBLIC, Nov. 15, 1993, at 12–13; Stephen Macedo, *The New Natural Lawyers,* HARV. CRIMSON, Oct. 29, 1993, at 2; and Harvey C. Mansfield, *Saving Liberalism From Liberals,* HARV. CRIMSON, Nov. 8, 1993, at 2.

49. An alternative line of reply might undertake to defend promiscuity and to deny that the goods of love and responsibility are necessary to the moral worth of sexuality. From this point of view, the line of argument I suggest mistakenly seeks to defend the moral legitimacy of homosexuality by way of an analogy with heterosexuality. *See* BONNIE HONIG, POLITICAL THEORY AND THE DISPLACEMENT OF POLITICS 186–95 (1993).

Heterosexuals also engage in promiscuity and other practices at odds with the goods that confer on sexuality its moral worth, but this fact does not lead us to abhor heterosexuality as such. And so on.

My point is not to offer a full argument for the moral permissibility of homosexuality, only to suggest the way such an argument might proceed. Like Rawls's argument for the difference principle, it would proceed by seeking a reflective equilibrium between our principles and considered judgments, adjusting each in the light of the other. That the argument for the morality of homosexuality, unlike the argument for the difference principle, explicitly addresses claims about human ends and conceptions of the good does not mean that the same method of moral reasoning cannot proceed. It is unlikely, of course, that such moral reasoning would produce conclusive or irrefutable answers to moral and religious controversies. But as Rawls acknowledges, such reasoning does not produce irrefutable answers to questions of justice either; a more modest notion of justification is appropriate. "[I]n philosophy questions at the most fundamental level are not usually settled by conclusive argument," writes Rawls, referring to arguments about justice. "What is obvious to some persons and accepted as a basic idea is unintelligible to others. The way to resolve the matter is to consider after due reflection which view, when fully worked out, offers the most coherent and convincing account" (p. 53). The same could be said of arguments about comprehensive moralities.

If it is possible to reason about the good as well as the right, then political liberalism's claim for the asymmetry between the right and good is undermined. For political liberalism, this asymmetry rests on the assumption that our moral and religious disagreements reflect a "fact of reasonable pluralism" that our disagreements about justice do not. What enables Rawls to maintain that our disagreements about distributive justice do not amount to a "fact of reasonable pluralism" is the strength of the arguments he advances on behalf of the difference principle and against libertarianism. But the same could be said of other controversies, including, conceivably, some moral and religious controversies. The public culture of democratic societies includes controversies about justice and comprehensive moralities alike.

If government can affirm the justice of redistributive policies even in the face of disagreement by libertarians, why cannot government affirm in law, say, the moral legitimacy of homosexuality, even in the face of disagreement by those who regard homosexuality as sin?[50] Is Milton Friedman's objection to redistributive policies a less "reasonable pluralism" than Pat Robertson's objection to gay rights?

With morality as with justice, the mere fact of disagreement is no evidence of the "reasonable pluralism" that gives rise to the demand that government must be neutral. There is no reason in principle why in any given case, we might not conclude that, on due reflection, some moral or religious doctrines are more plausible than others. In such cases, we would not expect all disagreement to disappear, nor would we rule out the possibility that further deliberation might one day lead us to reverse our view. But neither would we have grounds to insist that our deliberations about justice and rights may make no reference to moral or religious ideals.

The Limits of Liberal Public Reason

Whether it is possible to reason our way to agreement on any given moral or political controversy is not something we can know until we try. This is why it cannot be said in advance that controversies about comprehensive moralities reflect a "fact of reasonable pluralism" that controversies about justice do not. Whether a moral or political controversy reflects reasonable but incompatible conceptions of the good, or whether it can be resolved by due reflection and deliberation, can only be determined by reflecting and deliberating. But this raises a further difficulty with political liberalism. For the political life it describes leaves little room for the kind of public deliberation necessary to test the plausibility of contending comprehensive moralities—to persuade others of the merits of our moral ideals, to be persuaded by others of the merits of theirs.

Although political liberalism upholds the right to freedom of speech, it severely limits the kinds of arguments that are legitimate contributions to political debate, especially debate about constitutional essentials and basic justice.[51] This limitation reflects the priority of the right over the good. Not only may government not endorse one or another conception of the good, but citizens may not even introduce into political discourse their comprehensive moral or religious convictions, at least when debating matters of justice and rights (pp. 15–16).[52] Rawls maintains that this limitation is required by the "ideal of public reason" (p. 218). According to this ideal, political discourse should be conducted solely in terms of "political values" that all citizens can reasonably be expected to accept. Because citizens of democratic societies do not share comprehensive moral and religious conceptions, public reason should not refer to such conceptions (pp. 216–20).

The limits of public reason do not apply, Rawls allows, to our personal deliberations about political questions, or to the discussions we may have as members of associations such as churches and universities, where "religious, philosophical, and moral considerations" (p. 215) may properly play a role.

> But the ideal of public reason does hold for citizens when they engage in political advocacy in the public forum, and thus for members of political parties and for candidates in their campaigns and for other groups who support them. It holds equally for how citizens are to vote in elections when constitutional essentials and matters of basic justice are at stake. Thus, the ideal of public reason not only governs the public disclosure of elections insofar as the issues involve those fundamental questions, but also how citizens are to cast their vote on these questions (p. 215).

How can we know whether our political arguments meet the requirements of public reason,

---

50. It is possible to argue for certain gay rights on grounds that neither affirm nor deny the morality of homosexuality. The question here is whether government is justified in supporting laws or policies (such as gay marriage, for example) on grounds that affirm the moral legitimacy of homosexuality.

51. Rawls states that the limits of public reason apply to all discussions involving constitutional essentials and basic justice. As for other political questions, he writes that "it is usually highly desirable to settle political questions by invoking the values of public reason. Yet this may not always be so" (pp. 214–15).

52. This idea is repeated at several other points (pp. 215, 224, 254).

suitably shorn of any reliance on moral or religious convictions? Rawls offers a novel test. "To check whether we are following public reason we might ask: how would our argument strike us presented in the form of a supreme court opinion?" (p. 254). For citizens of a democracy to allow their political discourse about fundamental questions to be informed by moral and religious ideals is no more legitimate, Rawls suggests, than for a judge to read his or her moral and religious beliefs into the Constitution.

The restrictive character of this notion of public reason can be seen by considering the sorts of political arguments it would rule out. In the debate about abortion rights, those who believe that the fetus is a person from the moment of conception and that abortion is therefore murder could not seek to persuade their fellow citizens of this view in open political debate. Nor could they vote for a law that would restrict abortion on the basis of this moral or religious conviction. Although adherents of the Catholic teaching on abortion could discuss the issue of abortion rights in religious terms within their church, they could not do so in a political campaign, or on the floor of the state legislature, or in the halls of Congress. Nor for that matter could opponents of the Catholic teaching on abortion argue their case in the political arena. Relevant though it clearly is to the question of abortion rights, Catholic moral doctrine cannot be debated in the political arena that political liberalism defines.

The restrictive character of liberal public reason can also be seen in the debate about gay rights. At first glance, these restrictions might seem a service to toleration. Those who consider homosexuality immoral and therefore unworthy of the privacy rights accorded heterosexual intimacy could not legitimately voice their views in public debate. Nor could they act on their belief by voting against laws that would protect gay men and lesbians from discrimination. These beliefs reflect comprehensive moral and religious convictions and so may not play a part in political discourse about matters of justice.

But the demands of public reason also limit the arguments that can be advanced in support of gay rights, and so restrict the range of reasons that can be invoked on behalf of toleration. Those who oppose anti-sodomy laws of the kind at issue in *Bowers v. Hardwick*[53] cannot argue that the moral judgments embodied in those laws are wrong, only that the law is wrong to embody any moral judgments at all.[54] Advocates of gay rights cannot contest the substantive moral judgment lying behind anti-sodomy laws or seek, through open political debate, to persuade their fellow citizens that homosexuality is morally permissible, for any such argument would violate the canons of liberal public reason.

The restrictive character of liberal public reason is also illustrated by the arguments offered by American abolitionists of the 1830s and 1840s. Rooted in evangelical Protestantism, the abolitionist movement argued for the immediate emancipation of the slaves on the grounds that slavery is a heinous sin.[55] Like the argument of some present-day Catholics against abortion rights, the abolitionist case against slavery was explicitly based on a comprehensive moral and religious doctrine.

In a puzzling passage, Rawls tries to argue that the abolitionist case against slavery, religious though it was, did not violate the ideal of liberal public reason. If a society is not well-ordered, he explains, it may be necessary to resort to comprehensive moralities in order to bring about a society in which public discussion is conducted solely in terms of "political values" (p. 251 n.41). The religious arguments of the abolitionists can be justified as hastening the day when religious arguments would no longer play a legitimate role in public discourse. The abolitionists "did not go against the ideal of public reason," Rawls concludes, "provided they thought, or on reflection would have thought (as they certainly could have thought), that the comprehensive reasons they appealed to were required to give sufficient strength to the political conception to be subsequently realized" (p. 251).

---

53. 478 U.S. 186 (1986).
54. *See* Michael J. Sandel, *Moral Argument and Liberal Toleration: Abortion and Homosexuality*, 77 CAL. L. REV. 521, 534–38 (1989).
55. *See* ERIC FONER, POLITICS AND IDEOLOGY IN THE AGE OF THE CIVIL WAR 72 (1980); AILEEN S. KRADITOR, MEANS AND ENDS IN AMERICAN ABOLITIONISM 78, 91–92 (1967); JAMES M. MCPHERSON, BATTLE CRY OF FREEDOM: THE CIVIL WAR ERA 7–8 (1988).

376 Chapter XIII Moral Argument and Liberal Toleration

It is difficult to know what to make of this argument. There is little reason to suppose, and I do not think Rawls means to suggest, that the abolitionists opposed slavery on secular political grounds and simply used religious arguments to win popular support. Nor is there reason to think that the abolitionists sought by their agitation to make a world safe for secular political discourse. Nor can it be assumed that, even in retrospect, the abolitionists would take pride in having contributed, by their religious arguments against slavery, to the emergence of a society inhospitable to religious argument in political debate. If anything the opposite is more likely the case, that by advancing religious arguments against so conspicuous an injustice as slavery, the evangelicals who inspired the abolitionist movement were hoping to encourage Americans to view other political questions in moral and religious terms as well. In any case, it is reasonable to suppose that the abolitionists meant what they said, that slavery is wrong because it is contrary to God's law, a heinous sin, and that this is the reason it should be ended. Absent some extraordinary assumptions, it is difficult to interpret their argument as consistent with the priority of the right over the good, or with the ideal of public reason advanced by political liberalism.

The cases of abortion, gay rights, and abolitionism illustrate the severe restrictions liberal public reason would impose on political debate. Rawls argues that these restrictions are justified as essential to the maintenance of a just society, in which citizens are governed by principles they may reasonably be expected to endorse, even in the light of their conflicting comprehensive moralities. Although public reason requires that citizens decide fundamental political questions without reference "to the whole truth as they see it" (p. 216), this restriction is justified by the political values, such as civility and mutual respect, that it makes possible. "[T]he political values realized by a well-ordered constitutional regime are very great values and not easily overridden and the ideals they express are not to be lightly abandoned" (p. 218). Rawls compares his case for restrictive public reason with the case for restrictive rules of evidence in criminal trials. There too we agree to decide without reference to the whole truth as we know it—through illegally obtained evidence, for example—in order to advance other goods (pp. 218–19).

The analogy between liberal public reason and restrictive rules of evidence is instructive. Setting aside the whole truth as we know it carries moral and political costs, for criminal trials and for public reason alike. Whether those costs are worth incurring depends on how significant they are compared to the goods they make possible, and whether those goods can be secured in some other way. To assess restrictive rules of evidence, for example, we need to know how many criminals go free as a result and whether less restrictive rules would unduly burden innocent persons suspected of a crime, lead to undesirable law enforcement practices, violate important ideals such as respect for privacy (exclusionary rule) and spousal intimacy (spousal privilege), and so on. We arrive at rules of evidence by weighing the importance of deciding in the light of the whole truth against the importance of the ideals that would be sacrificed if all evidence were admissible.

Similarly, to assess restrictive rules of public reason, we need to weigh their moral and political costs against the political values they are said to make possible; we must also ask whether these political values—of toleration, civility, and mutual respect—could be achieved under less-restrictive rules of public reason. Although political liberalism refuses to weigh the political values it affirms against competing values that may arise from within comprehensive moralities, the case for restrictive rules of public reason must presuppose some such comparison.

The costs of liberal public reason are of two kinds. The strictly moral costs depend on the validity and importance of the moral and religious doctrines liberal public reason requires us to set aside when deciding questions of justice. These costs will necessarily vary from case to case. They will be at their highest when a political conception of justice sanctions toleration of a grave moral wrong, such as slavery in the case of Douglas's argument for popular sovereignty. In the case of abortion, the moral cost of bracketing is high if the Catholic doctrine is correct, otherwise much lower. This suggests that, even given the moral and political importance of toleration, the argument for tolerating a given practice must take some account of the moral status of the practice, as well as the good of avoiding social conflict, letting people decide for themselves, and so on.

This way of thinking about the moral cost of liberal public reason is admittedly at odds with political liberalism itself. Although Rawls repeatedly states that a political conception of justice expresses values that normally outweigh whatever other values conflict with them (pp. 138, 146, 156, 218), he also insists that this involves no substantive comparison of the political values to the moral and religious values they override.

> We need not consider the claims of political justice against the claims of this or that comprehensive view; nor need we say that political values are intrinsically more important than other values and that is why the latter are overridden. Having to say that is just what we hope to avoid . . . (p. 157).

But because political liberalism allows that comprehensive moral and religious doctrines can be true, such comparisons cannot reasonably be avoided.

Beyond the moral costs of liberal public reason are certain political costs. These costs are becoming increasingly apparent in the politics of those countries, notably the United States, whose public discourse most closely approximates the ideal of public reason advanced by political liberalism. With a few notable exceptions, such as the civil rights movement, American political discourse in recent decades has come to reflect the liberal resolve that government be neutral on moral and religious questions, that fundamental questions of public policy be debated and decided without reference to any particular conception of the good.[56] But democratic politics cannot long abide a public life as abstract and decorous, as detached from moral purposes, as Supreme Court opinions are supposed to be. A politics that brackets morality and religion too completely soon generates its own disenchantment. Where political discourse lacks moral resonance, the yearning for a public life of larger meanings finds undesirable expressions. Groups like the Moral Majority seek to clothe the naked public square with narrow, intolerant moralisms. Fundamentalists rush in where liberals fear to tread. The disenchantment also assumes more secular forms. Absent a political agenda that addresses the moral dimension of public questions, public attention becomes riveted on the private vices of public officials. Public discourse becomes increasingly preoccupied with the scandalous, the sensational, and the confessional as purveyed by tabloids, talk shows, and eventually the mainstream media as well.

It cannot be said that the public philosophy of political liberalism is wholly responsible for these tendencies. But its vision of public reason is too spare to contain the moral energies of a vital democratic life. It thus creates a moral void that opens the way for the intolerant and the trivial and other misguided moralisms.

If liberal public reason is too restrictive, it remains to ask whether a more spacious public reason would sacrifice the ideals that political liberalism seeks to promote, notably mutual respect among citizens who hold conflicting moral and religious views. Here it is necessary to distinguish two conceptions of mutual respect. On the liberal conception, we respect our fellow citizens' moral and religious convictions by ignoring them (for political purposes), by leaving them undisturbed, or by carrying on political debate without reference to them. To admit moral and religious ideals into political debate about justice would undermine mutual respect in this sense.

But this is not the only, or perhaps even the most plausible way of understanding the mutual respect on which democratic citizenship depends. On a different conception of respect—call it the deliberative conception—we respect our fellow citizen's moral and religious convictions by engaging, or attending to them—sometimes by challenging and contesting them, sometimes by listening and learning from them—especially if those convictions bear on important political questions. There is no guarantee that a deliberative mode of respect will lead in any given case to agreement or even to appreciation for the moral and religious convictions of others. It is always possible that learning more about a moral or religious doctrine will lead us to like it less. But the respect of deliberation and engagement affords a more spacious public reason than liberalism allows. It is also a more suitable ideal for a pluralist society. To the extent that our moral and religious disagreements reflect the ultimate plurality of human goods, a deliberative mode of respect will better enable us to appreciate the distinctive goods our different lives express.

---

56. I elaborate this claim in my book *Democracy's Discontent: America in Search of a Public Philosophy*.

Chapter 14

MORALITY AND LAW: SAME-SEX MARRIAGE, FOR AND AGAINST

The debate over same-sex marriage illustrates competing views, not only about the meaning of marriage but also about the relation of law and morality. What do you consider the best arguments for and against same-sex marriage? Is it possible to decide whether the state should recognize same-sex marriage without taking sides in the moral and religious controversy over the purpose of marriage and the moral status of homosexuality? If it is not possible to find a solution that is neutral on these moral and religious questions, what are the implications for the relation of law and morality?

HILLARY GOODRIDGE & OTHERS VS. DEPARTMENT OF PUBLIC HEALTH

Supreme Judicial Court of Massachusetts, November 18, 2003

Marshall, C.J.

Marriage is a vital social institution. The exclusive commitment of two individuals to each other nurtures love and mutual support; it brings stability to our society. For those who choose to marry, and for their children, marriage provides an abundance of legal, financial, and social benefits. In return it imposes weighty legal, financial, and social obligations. The question before us is whether, consistent with the Massachusetts Constitution, the Commonwealth may deny the protections, benefits, and obligations conferred by civil marriage to two individuals of the same sex who wish to marry. We conclude that it may not. The Massachusetts Constitution affirms the dignity and equality of all individuals. It forbids the creation of second-class citizens. In reaching our conclusion we have given full deference to the arguments made by the Commonwealth. But it has failed to identify any constitutionally adequate reason for denying civil marriage to same-sex couples.

We are mindful that our decision marks a change in the history of our marriage law. Many people hold deep-seated religious, moral, and ethical convictions that marriage should be limited to the union of one man and one woman, and that homosexual conduct is immoral. Many hold equally strong religious, moral, and ethical convictions that same-sex couples are entitled to be married, and that homosexual persons should be treated no differently than their heterosexual neighbors. Neither view answers the question before us. Our concern is with the Massachusetts Constitution as a charter of governance for every person properly within its reach. "Our obligation is to define the liberty of all, not to mandate our own moral code." *Lawrence v. Texas,* 123 S.Ct. 2472, 2480 (2003) (*Lawrence*), quoting *Planned Parenthood of Southeastern Pa.* v. *Casey,* 505 U.S. 833, 850 (1992). . . .

Barred access to the protections, benefits, and obligations of civil marriage, a person who enters into an intimate, exclusive union with another of the same sex is arbitrarily deprived of membership in one of our community's most rewarding and cherished institutions. That exclusion is incompatible with the constitutional principles of respect for individual autonomy and equality under law. . . .

The plaintiffs' claim that the marriage restriction violates the Massachusetts Constitution can be analyzed in two ways. Does it offend the Constitution's guarantees of equality before the law? Or do the liberty and due process provisions of the Massachusetts Constitution secure the plaintiffs' right to marry their chosen partner? . . . .

We begin by considering the nature of civil marriage itself. Simply put, the government creates civil marriage. . . . In a real sense, there are three partners to every civil marriage: two willing spouses and an approving State. While only the parties can mutually assent to marriage, the terms of the marriage—who may marry and what obligations, benefits, and liabilities attach to civil marriage—are set by the Commonwealth. Conversely, while only the parties can agree to end the marriage. . . , the Commonwealth defines the exit terms.

Civil marriage is created and regulated through exercise of the police power. "Police power" (now more commonly termed the State's regulatory authority) is an old-fashioned term for the Commonwealth's lawmaking authority, as bounded by the liberty and equality guarantees of the Massachusetts Constitution and its express delegation of power from the people to their government. In broad terms, it is the Legislature's power to enact rules to regulate conduct, to the extent that such laws are "necessary to secure the health, safety, good order, comfort, or general welfare of the community."

Without question, civil marriage enhances the "welfare of the community." It is a "social institution of the highest importance." Civil marriage anchors an ordered society by encouraging stable relationships over transient ones. It is central to the way the Commonwealth identifies individuals, provides for the orderly distribution of property, ensures that children and adults are cared for and supported whenever possible from private rather than public funds, and tracks important epidemiological and demographic data.

Marriage also bestows enormous private and social advantages on those who choose to marry. Civil marriage is at once a deeply personal commitment to another human being and a highly public celebration of the ideals of mutuality, companionship, intimacy, fidelity, and family. . . . Because it fulfils yearnings for security, safe haven, and connection that express our common humanity, civil marriage is an esteemed institution, and the decision whether and whom to marry is among life's momentous acts of self-definition. . . .

For decades, indeed centuries, in much of this country (including Massachusetts) no lawful marriage was possible between white and black Americans. That long history availed not when the Supreme Court of California held in 1948 that a legislative prohibition against interracial marriage violated the due process and equality guarantees of the Fourteenth Amendment, *Perez v. Sharp,* 32 Cal.2d 711, 728 (1948), or when, nineteen years later, the United States Supreme Court also held that a statutory bar to interracial marriage violated the Fourteenth Amendment, *Loving v. Virginia,* 388 U.S. 1 (1967). As both *Perez* and *Loving* make clear, the right to marry means little if it does not include the right to marry the person of one's choice, subject to appropriate government restrictions in the interests of public health, safety, and welfare. See *Perez v. Sharp, supra* at 717 ("the essence of the right to marry is freedom to join in marriage with the person of one's choice"). See also *Loving v. Virginia, supra* at 12. In this case, as in *Perez* and *Loving,* a statute deprives individuals of access to an institution of fundamental legal, personal, and social significance—the institution of marriage—because of a single trait: skin color in *Perez* and *Loving,* sexual orientation here. As it did in *Perez* and *Loving,* history must yield to a more fully developed understanding of the invidious quality of the discrimination.

The individual liberty and equality safeguards of the Massachusetts Constitution protect both "freedom from" unwarranted government intrusion into protected spheres of life and "freedom to" partake in benefits created by the State for the common good. Both freedoms are involved here. Whether and whom to marry, how to express sexual intimacy, and whether and how to establish a family—these are among the most basic of every individual's liberty and due process rights. And central to personal freedom and security is the assurance that the laws will apply equally to persons in similar situations. "Absolute equality before the law is a fundamental principle of our own Constitution." *Opinion of the Justices,* 211 Mass. 618, 619 (1912). The liberty interest in choosing whether and whom to marry would be hollow if the Commonwealth could, without sufficient justification, foreclose an individual from freely choosing the person with whom to share an exclusive commitment in the unique institution of civil marriage. . . .

The department posits three legislative rationales for prohibiting same-sex couples from marrying: (1) providing a "favorable setting for procreation"; (2) ensuring the optimal setting for child rearing, which the department defines as "a two-parent family with one parent of each sex"; and (3) preserving scarce State and private financial resources. We consider each in turn.

The judge in the Superior Court endorsed the first rationale, holding that "the state's interest in regulating marriage is based on the traditional concept that marriage's primary purpose is procreation." This is incorrect. Our laws of civil marriage do not privilege procreative heterosexual intercourse between married people above every other form of adult intimacy and every other means of creating a family. General Laws c. 207 contains no requirement that the applicants for a marriage license attest to their ability or intention to conceive children by coitus. Fertility is not a condition of marriage, nor is it grounds for divorce. People who have never consummated their marriage, and never plan to, may be and stay married. People who cannot stir from their deathbed may marry. While it is certainly true that many, perhaps most, married couples have

children together (assisted or unassisted), it is the exclusive and permanent commitment of the marriage partners to one another, not the begetting of children, that is the sine qua non of civil marriage.

Moreover, the Commonwealth affirmatively facilitates bringing children into a family regardless of whether the intended parent is married or unmarried, whether the child is adopted or born into a family, whether assistive technology was used to conceive the child, and whether the parent or her partner is heterosexual, homosexual, or bisexual. If procreation were a necessary component of civil marriage, our statutes would draw a tighter circle around the permissible bounds of nonmarital child bearing and the creation of families by noncoital means. The attempt to isolate procreation as "the source of a fundamental right to marry," overlooks the integrated way in which courts have examined the complex and overlapping realms of personal autonomy, marriage, family life, and child rearing. Our jurisprudence recognizes that, in these nuanced and fundamentally private areas of life, such a narrow focus is inappropriate.

The "marriage is procreation" argument singles out the one unbridgeable difference between same-sex and opposite-sex couples, and transforms that difference into the essence of legal marriage. Like "Amendment 2" to the Constitution of Colorado, which effectively denied homosexual persons equality under the law and full access to the political process, the marriage restriction impermissibly "identifies persons by a single trait and then denies them protection across the board." In so doing, the State's action confers an official stamp of approval on the destructive stereotype that same-sex relationships are inherently unstable and inferior to opposite-sex relationships and are not worthy of respect.

The department's first stated rationale, equating marriage with unassisted heterosexual procreation, shades imperceptibly into its second: that confining marriage to opposite-sex couples ensures that children are raised in the "optimal" setting. Protecting the welfare of children is a paramount State policy. Restricting marriage to opposite-sex couples, however, cannot plausibly further this policy. . . . Moreover, the department readily concedes that people in same-sex couples may be "excellent" parents. These couples (including four of the plaintiff couples) have children for the reasons others do—to love them, to care for them, to nurture them. But the task of child rearing for same-sex couples is made infinitely harder by their status as outliers to the marriage laws. . . .

No one disputes that the plaintiff couples are families, that many are parents, and that the children they are raising, like all children, need and should have the fullest opportunity to grow up in a secure, protected family unit. Similarly, no one disputes that, under the rubric of marriage, the State provides a cornucopia of substantial benefits to married parents and their children. The preferential treatment of civil marriage reflects the Legislature's conclusion that marriage "is the foremost setting for the education and socialization of children" precisely because it "encourages parents to remain committed to each other and to their children as they grow."

In this case, we are confronted with an entire, sizeable class of parents raising children who have absolutely no access to civil marriage and its protections because they are forbidden from procuring a marriage license. It cannot be rational under our laws, and indeed it is not permitted, to penalize children by depriving them of State benefits because the State disapproves of their parents' sexual orientation. . . .

The department suggests additional rationales for prohibiting same-sex couples from marrying, which are developed by some amici. It argues that broadening civil marriage to include same-sex couples will trivialize or destroy the institution of marriage as it has historically been fashioned. Certainly our decision today marks a significant change in the definition of marriage as it has been inherited from the common law, and understood by many societies for centuries. But it does not disturb the fundamental value of marriage in our society.

Here, the plaintiffs seek only to be married, not to undermine the institution of civil marriage. They do not want marriage abolished. They do not attack the binary nature of marriage, the consanguinity provisions, or any of the other gate-keeping provisions of the marriage licensing law. Recognizing the right of an individual to marry a person of the same sex will not diminish the validity or dignity of opposite-sex marriage, any more than recognizing the right of an individual to marry a person of a different race devalues the marriage of a person who marries someone of her own race. If anything, extending civil marriage to same-sex couples reinforces the importance of marriage to individuals and communities. That same-sex couples are willing to embrace marriage's solemn obligations of exclusivity, mutual support, and commitment to one another is a testament to the enduring place of marriage in our laws and in the human spirit. . . .

The department has had more than ample opportunity to articulate a constitutionally adequate justification for limiting civil marriage to opposite-sex unions. It has failed to do so. The department has offered purported justifications for the civil marriage restriction that are starkly at odds with the comprehensive network of vigorous, gender-neutral laws promoting stable families and the best interests of children. It has failed to identify any relevant characteristic that would justify shutting the door to civil marriage to a person who wishes to marry someone of the same sex.

The marriage ban works a deep and scarring hardship on a very real segment of the community for no rational reason. The absence of any reasonable relationship between, on the one hand, an absolute disqualification of same-sex couples who wish to enter into civil marriage and, on the other, protection of public health, safety, or general welfare, suggests that the marriage restriction is rooted in persistent prejudices against persons who are (or who are believed to be) homosexual. "The Constitution cannot control such prejudices but neither can it tolerate them. Private biases may be outside the reach of the law, but the law cannot, directly or indirectly, give them effect." *Palmore v. Sidoti,* 466 U.S. 429, 433 (1984) (construing Fourteenth Amendment). Limiting the protections, benefits, and obligations of civil marriage to opposite-sex couples violates the basic premises of individual liberty and equality under law protected by the Massachusetts Constitution.

ABOLISH MARRIAGE

Let's Really Get the Government Out of Our Bedrooms

Michael Kinsley

Critics and enthusiasts of *Lawrence v. Texas*, last week's Supreme Court decision invalidating state anti-sodomy laws, agree on one thing: The next argument is going to be about gay marriage. As Justice Antonin Scalia noted in his tart dissent, it follows from the logic of *Lawrence*. Mutually consenting sex with the person of your choice in the privacy of your own home is now a basic right of American citizenship under the Constitution. This does not mean that the government must supply it or guarantee it. But the government cannot forbid it, and the government also should not discriminate against you for choosing to exercise a basic right of citizenship. Offering an institution as important as marriage to male-female couples only is exactly this kind of discrimination. Or so the gay rights movement will now argue. Persuasively, I think.

Opponents of gay rights will resist mightily, although they have been in retreat for a couple of decades. General anti-gay sentiments are now considered a serious breach of civic etiquette, even in anti-gay circles. The current line of defense, which probably won't hold either, is between social toleration of homosexuals and social approval of homosexuality. Or between accepting the reality that people are gay, even accepting that gays are people, and endorsing something called "the gay agenda." Gay marriage, the opponents will argue, would cross this line. It would make homosexuality respectable and, worse, normal. Gays are welcome to exist all they want, and to do their inexplicable thing if they must, but they shouldn't expect a government stamp of approval.

It's going to get ugly. And then it's going to get boring. So we have two options here. We can add gay marriage to the short list of controversies—abortion, affirmative action, the death penalty—that are so frozen and ritualistic that debates about them are more like kabuki performances than intellectual exercises. Or we can think outside the box. There is a solution that ought to satisfy both camps, and may not be a bad idea even apart from the gay marriage controversy.

That solution is to end the institution of marriage. Or rather (he hastens to clarify, dear) the solution is to end the institution of government-sanctioned marriage. Or, framed to appeal to conservatives: End the government monopoly on marriage. Wait, I've got it: Privatize marriage. These slogans all mean the same thing. Let churches and other religious institutions continue to offer marriage ceremonies. Let department stores and casinos get into the act if they want. Let each organization decide for itself what kinds of couples it wants to offer marriage to. Let couples celebrate their union in any way they choose and consider themselves married whenever they want. Let others be free to consider them not married, under rules these others may prefer. And, yes, if three people want to get married, or one person wants to marry herself, and someone else wants to conduct a ceremony and declare them married, let 'em. If you and your government aren't implicated, what do you care?

In fact, there is nothing to stop any of this from happening now. And a lot of it does happen. But only certain marriages get certified by the government. So, in the United States we are about to find ourselves in a strange situation where the principal demand of a liberation movement is to be included in the red tape of a government bureaucracy. Having just gotten state governments out of their bedrooms, gays now want these governments back in. Meanwhile, social-conservative anti-gays, many of them southerners, are calling on the government in Washington to trample states' rights and nationalize the rules of marriage, if necessary, to prevent gays from getting what they want. The Senate majority leader, Bill Frist of Tennessee, responded to the Supreme Court's *Lawrence* decision by endorsing a constitutional amendment, no less, against gay marriage.

If marriage were an entirely private affair, all the disputes over gay marriage would become irrelevant. Gay marriage would not have the official sanction of government, but neither would straight marriage. There would be official equality between the two, which is the essence of what gays want and are entitled to. And if the other side is sincere in saying that its concern is not what people do in private but government endorsement of a gay "lifestyle" or "agenda," that problem goes away too.

Yes, yes, marriage is about more than sleeping arrangements. There are children, there are finances, there are spousal job benefits such as health insurance and pensions. In all of these areas, marriage is used as a substitute for other factors that are harder to measure, such as financial dependence or devotion to offspring. It

would be possible to write rules that measure the real factors at stake and leave marriage out of the matter. Regarding children and finances, people can set their own rules, as many already do. None of this would be easy. Marriage functions as what lawyers call a "bright line," which saves the trouble of trying to measure a lot of amorphous factors. You're either married or you're not. Once marriage itself becomes amorphous, who-gets-the-kids and who-gets-health-care become trickier questions.

So, sure, there are some legitimate objections to the idea of privatizing marriage. But they don't add up to a fatal objection. Especially when you consider that the alternative is arguing about gay marriage until death do us part.

LAW, MORALITY, AND "SEXUAL ORIENTATION"

John M. Finnis

. . . .

At the heart of the Platonic-Aristotelian and later ancient philosophical rejections of all homosexual conduct, and thus of the modern "gay" ideology, are three fundamental theses: (1) The commitment of a man and woman to each other in the sexual union of marriage is intrinsically good and reasonable, and is incompatible with sexual relations outside marriage. (2) Homosexual acts are radically and peculiarly non-marital, and for that reason intrinsically unreasonable and unnatural. (3) Furthermore, according to Plato, if not Aristotle, homosexual acts have a special similarity to solitary masturbation, and both types of radically non-marital act are manifestly unworthy of the human being and immoral.

1

I want now to offer an interpretation of these three theses which articulates them more clearly than was ever attempted by Plato or, so far as we can tell, by Aristotle. It is, I think, an interpretation faithful to what they do say, but takes up suggestions in Plutarch and in the eighteenth

century Enlightenment philosophy of Immanuel Kant (who likewise rejected all homosexual conduct), though even these writers' indications, too, remain relatively terse. My account also articulates thoughts which have historically been implicit in the judgments of many non-philosophical people, and which have been held to justify the laws adopted in many nations and states both before and after the period when Christian beliefs as such were politically and socially dominant. And it is an application of the theory of morality and natural law developed over the past thirty years by Germain Grisez and others. A fuller exposition can be found in the chapter on marriage, sexual acts, and family life, in the new second volume of Grisez's great work on moral theology.[1]

Plato's mature concern, in the Laws, for familiarity, affection and love between spouses in a chastely exclusive marriage, Aristotle's representation of marriage as an intrinsically desirable friendship between quasi-equals, and as a state of life even more natural to human beings than political

---

1. 2 GERMAIN GRISEZ. THE WAY OF THE LORD JESUS, *Living a Christian Life* 555–574, 633–680 (1993).

life,[2] and Musonius Rufus's conception of the inseparable double goods of marriage, all find expression in Plutarch's celebration of marriage— as a union not of mere instinct but of reasonable love, and not merely for procreation but for mutual help, goodwill and cooperation for their own sake.[3] Plutarch's severe critiques of homosexual conduct (and of the disparagement of women implicit in homosexual ideology),[4] develop Plato's critique of homosexual and all other extra-marital sexual conduct. Like Musonius Rufus, Plutarch does so by bringing much closer to explicit articulation the following thought. Genital intercourse between spouses enables them to actualize and experience (and in that sense express) their marriage itself, as a single reality with two blessings (children and mutual affection).[5] Non-marital intercourse, especially but not only homosexual, has no such point and therefore is unacceptable.

The core of this argument can be clarified by comparing it with Saint Augustine's treatment of marriage in his *De Bono Coniugali*. The good of marital communion is here an instrumental good, in the service of the procreation and education of children so that the intrinsic, non-instrumental good of friendship will be promoted and realized by the propagation of the human race, and the intrinsic good of inner integration be promoted and realized by the "remedying" of the disordered desires of concupiscence.[6] Now, when considering sterile marriages, Augustine had identified a further good of marriage, the natural *societas* (companionship) of the two sexes.[7] Had he truly integrated this into his synthesis, he would have recognized that in sterile and fertile marriages alike, the communion, companionship, *societas* and *amicitia* of the spouses—their being married—*is* the very good of marriage, and is an intrinsic, basic human good, not merely instrumental to any other good. And this communion of married life, this integral amalgamation of the lives of the two persons (as Plutarch[8] put it before John Paul II),[9] has as its intrinsic elements, as essential *parts* of one and the same good, the goods and ends to which the theological tradition, following Augustine, for a long time subordinated that communion. It took a long and gradual process of development of doctrine, through the Catechism of the Council of Trent, the teachings of Pius XI and Pius XII, and eventually those of Vatican II— a process brilliantly illuminated by Germain Grisez[10]—to bring the tradition to the position that procreation and children are neither the *end* (whether primary or secondary) to which marriage is instrumental (as Augustine taught), nor instrumental to the good of the spouses (as much secular and "liberal Christian" thought supposes), but rather: Parenthood and children and family are the intrinsic fulfillment of a communion which, because it is not merely instrumental, can exist and fulfill the spouses even if procreation happens to be impossible for them.

2. ARISTOTLE, NICOMACHEAN ETHICS, VIII.12: 1162a16-30: *see also* the probably pseudo-Aristotle, *Orconomica* I, 3-4: 1343b12-1344a22; III.

3. Plutarch reads this conception back to the dawn of Athenian civilization and, doubtless anachronistically, ascribes it to the great original Athenian law-giver, Solon: Marriage should be "a union of life between man and woman for the delights of love and the getting of children." PLUTARCH, LIFE OF SOLON 20, 4. *See also* PLUTARCH. EROTIKOS 769:

> In the case of lawful wives, physical union is the beginning of friendship, a sharing, as it were, in great mysteries. [The] pleasure is short [or unimportant: *mikron*], but the respect and kindness and mutual affection and loyalty that daily spring from it [conjugal sex] convicts neither the Delphians of raving when they call Aphrodite 'Harmony' nor Homer when he designates such a union 'friendship'. It also proves that Solon was a very experienced legislator of marriage laws. He prescribed that a man should consort with his wife not less than three times a month— not for the pleasure surely, but as cities renew their mutual agreements from time to time, just so he must have wished this to be a renewal of marriage and with such an act of tenderness to wipe out the complaints that accumulate from everyday living.

4. *See* PLUTARCH, EROTIKOS 768D-770A; IX MORALIA 427 (Loeb ed., 1961): *see also* the fine translation in D.A. RUSSELL, PLUTARCH 92 (1973).

5. Plutarch speaks of the union of husband and wife as an "integral amalgamation" [*di' holon krasis*]. PLUTARCH, EROTIKOS 769F; CONIUGALIA PRAECEPTA 142F.

6. ST. AUGUSTINE, DE BONO CONIUGALI, 9.9.

7. *Id*. at 3.3.

8. PLUTARCH, EROTIKOS 769f; CONIUGALIA PRAECEPTA 142f.

9. John Paul II, Address to Young Married Couples at Taranto (October 1989), *quoted in* GRISEZ, *supra* note 35, at 571 n.46 ("a great project: *fusing* your persons to the point of becoming 'one flesh'").

10. GRISEZ, *supra* note 1, at 556-569.

Now if, as the recent encyclical on the foundations of morality, *Veritatis Splendor*, teaches, "the communion of persons in marriage" which is violated by every act of adultery is itself a "fundamental human good,"[11] there fall into place not only the elements of the classic philosophical judgments on non-marital sexual conduct but also the similar judgments reached about such conduct by decent people who cannot articulate explanatory premises for those judgments, which they reach rather by an insight into what is and is not *consistent with* realities whose goodness they experience and understand at least sufficiently to will and choose. In particular, there fall into place the elements of an answer to the question: Why cannot non-marital friendship be promoted and expressed by sexual acts? Why is the attempt to express affection by orgasmic non-marital sex the pursuit of an illusion? Why did Plato and Socrates, Xenophon, Aristotle, Musonius Rufus, and Plutarch, right at the heart of their reflections on the homoerotic culture around them, make the very deliberate and careful judgment that homosexual *conduct* (and indeed all extra-marital sexual gratification) is radically incapable of participating in, actualizing, the common good of friendship?

Implicit in the philosophical and common-sense rejection of extra-marital sex is the answer: The union of the reproductive organs of husband and wife really unites them biologically (and their biological reality is part of, not merely an instrument of, their *personal* reality); reproduction is one function and so, in respect of that function, the spouses are indeed one reality, and their sexual union therefore can *actualize* and allow them to *experience* their *real common good—their marriage* with the two goods, parenthood and friendship, which (leaving aside the order of grace) are the parts of its wholeness as an intelligible common good even if, independently of what the spouses will, their capacity for biological parenthood will not be fulfilled by that act of genital union. But the common good of friends who are not and cannot be married (for example, man and man, man and boy, woman and woman) has nothing to do with their having children by each other, and their reproductive organs cannot make them a biological (and

therefore personal) unit.[12] So their sexual acts together cannot do what they may hope and imagine. Because their activation of one' or even each of their reproductive organs cannot be an actualizing and experiencing of the *marital* good—as marital intercourse (intercourse between spouses in a marital way) can, even between spouses who *happen* to be sterile—it can do no more than provide each partner with an individual gratification. For want of a *common good* that could be actualized and experienced *by and in this bodily union*, that conduct involves the partners in treating their bodies as instruments to be used in the service of their consciously experiencing selves; their choice to engage in such conduct thus dis-integrates each of them precisely as acting persons.[13]

Reality is known in judgment, not in emotion, and *in reality*, whatever the generous hopes and dreams and thoughts of *giving* with which some same-sex partners may surround their sexual acts, those acts cannot express or do more than is expressed or done if two strangers engage in such activity to give each other pleasure, or a prostitute pleasures a client to give him pleasure in return for money, or (say) a man masturbates to give himself pleasure and a fantasy of more human relationships after a gruelling day on the assembly line. This is, I believe, the substance of Plato's judgment—at that moment in the *Gorgias* which is also decisive for the moral and political philosophical critique of

---

11. JOHN PAUL II, VERITATIS SPLENDOR ¶¶ 13, 48 (1984); see also id, at ¶¶ 50, 67, 78. 79.

12. Steven Macedo, *The New Natural Lawyers*, THE HARV. CRIMSON, Oct. 28, 1993, writes:

> In effect, gays can have sex in a way that is open to procreation, and to new life. They can be, and many are, prepared to engage in the kind of loving relations that would result in procreation—were conditions different. Like sterile married couples, many would like nothing better.

Here, fantasy has taken leave of reality. Anal or oral intercourse, whether between spouses or between males, is no more a biological union "open to procreation" than is intercourse with a goat by a shepherd who fantasizes about breeding a faun; each "would" yield the desired mutant "were conditions different". Biological union between humans is the inseminatory union of male genital organ with female genital organ; in most circumstances it does not result in generation, but it is the behavior that unites biologically because it is the behavior which, as behavior, is suitable for generation.

13. For the whole argument, see GRISEZ, *supra* note 1, at 634–39, 648–54, 662–4.

hedonism[14]—that there is no important distinction in essential moral worthlessness between solitary masturbation, being sodomized as a prostitute, and being sodomized for the pleasure of it. Sexual acts cannot *in reality* be self-giving unless they are acts by which a man and a woman actualize and experience sexually the real giving of themselves to each other—in biological, affective and volitional union in mutual commitment, both open-ended and exclusive—which like Plato and Aristotle and most peoples we call marriage.

In short, sexual acts are not unitive in their significance unless they are marital (actualizing the all-level unity of marriage) and (since the common good of marriage has two aspects) they are not marital unless they have not only the generosity of acts of friendship but also the procreative significance, not necessarily of being intended to generate or capable in the circumstances of generating but at least of being, as human conduct, acts of the reproductive kind—actualizations, so far as the spouses then and there can, of the reproductive function in which they are biologically and thus personally one.

The ancient philosophers do not much discuss the case of sterile marriages, or the fact (well known to them) that for long periods of time (e.g. throughout pregnancy) the sexual acts of a married couple are naturally incapable of resulting in reproduction. They appear to take for granted what the subsequent Christian tradition certainly did, that such sterility does not render the conjugal sexual acts of the spouses non-marital. (Plutarch indicates that intercourse with a sterile spouse is a desirable mark of marital esteem and affection.)[15] For: A husband and wife who unite their reproductive organs in an act of sexual intercourse which, so far as they then can make it, is of a kind suitable for generation, do function as a biological (and thus personal) unit and thus can be actualizing and experiencing the two-in-

one-flesh common good and reality of marriage, even when some biological condition happens to prevent that unity resulting in generation of a child. Their conduct thus differs radically from the acts of a husband and wife whose intercourse is masturbatory, for example sodomitic or by fellatio or coitus interruptus.[16] In law such acts do not consummate a marriage, because in reality (whatever the couple's illusions of intimacy and self-giving in such acts) they do not actualize the one-flesh, two-part marital good.

Does this account seek to "make moral judgments based on natural facts"?[17] Yes and no. No, in the sense that it does not seek to infer normative conclusions or theses from non-normative (natural-fact) premises. Nor does it appeal to any norm of the form "Respect natural facts or natural functions." But yes, it does apply the relevant practical reasons (especially that marriage and inner integrity are basic human goods) and moral principles (especially that one may never *intend* to destroy, damage,

---

14. PLATO, GORGIAS 494–5, especially 494cl-5, 495b3.

15. PLUTARCH, LIFE OF SOLON, 20.3. The post-Christian moral philosophy of Kant identified the wrongfulness of masturbation and homosexual (and bestial) conduct as consisting in the instrumentalisation of one's body, and thus ("since a person is an absolute unity") the "wrong to humanity in our own person." But Kant, though he emphasizes the equality of husband and wife (impossible in concubinage or more casual prostitution), did not integrate this insight with an understanding of marriage as a single two-part good

involving, inseparably, friendship as well as procreation. Hence he was puzzled by the question why marital intercourse is right when the woman is pregnant or beyond the menopause. *See* IMMANUEL KANT, THE METAPHYSICS OF MORALS 277–79. 424–26 (Mary Gregor trans., Cambridge Univ. Press 1991, 96–97, 220–22) (1797). The deep source of his puzzlement is his refusal to allow intelligible goods any structural role in his ethics, a refusal which sets him against a classical moral philosophy such as Aristotle's, and indeed against any adequate theory of natural law, and in turn is connected with his dualistic separation of body from mind and body, a separation which conflicts with his own insight, just quoted, that the person is a real unity.

16. Or deliberately contracepted, which I omit from the list in the text only because it would no doubt not now be accepted by secular civil law as preventing consummation—a failure of understanding. *See* discussion, *supra* note 46.

17. Macedo, *supra* note 12, at 2:

All we can say is that conditions would have to be more radically different in the case of gay and lesbian couples than sterile married couples for new life to result from sex . . . but what is the moral force of that? The new natural law theory does not make moral judgments based on natural facts.

Macedo's phrase "based on" equivocates between the first premises of normative arguments (which must be normative) and the other premise(s) (which can and normally should be factual and, where appropriate, can refer to natural facts such as that the human mouth is not a reproductive organ).

impede, or violate any basic human good, or prefer an illusory instantiation of a basic human good to a real instantiation of that or some other human good) to facts about the human personal organism.

2

Societies such as classical Athens and contemporary England (and virtually every other) draw a distinction between behavior found merely (perhaps extremely) offensive (such as eating excrement), and behavior to be repudiated as destructive of human character and relationships. Copulation of humans with animals is repudiated because it treats human sexual activity and satisfaction as something appropriately sought in a manner as divorced from the actualizing of an intelligible common good as is the instinctive coupling of beasts—and so treats human bodily life, in one of its most intense activities, as appropriately lived as merely animal. The deliberate genital coupling of persons of the same sex is repudiated for a very similar reason. It is not simply that it is sterile and disposes the participants to an abdication of responsibility for the future of humankind. Nor is it simply that it cannot *really* actualize the mutual devotion which some homosexual persons hope to manifest and experience by it, and that it harms the personalities of its participants by its dis-integrative manipulation of different parts of their one personal reality. It is also that it treats human sexual capacities in a way which is deeply hostile to the self-understanding of those members of the community who are willing to commit themselves to real marriage in the understanding that its sexual joys are not mere instruments or accompaniments to, or mere compensations for, the accomplishment of marriage's responsibilities, but rather enable the spouses to *actualize and experience* their intelligent commitment to share in those responsibilities, in that genuine self-giving.

Now, as I have said before, "homosexual orientation," in one of the two main senses of that highly equivocal term, is precisely the deliberate willingness to promote and engage in homosexual acts—the state of mind, will, and character whose self-interpretation came to be expressed in the deplorable but helpfully revealing name "gay."

So this willingness, and the whole "gay" ideology, treats human sexual capacities in a way which is deeply hostile to the self-understanding of those members of the community who are willing to commit themselves to real marriage.

Homosexual orientation in this sense is, in fact, a standing denial of the intrinsic aptness of sexual intercourse to actualize and in that sense give expression to the exclusiveness and open-ended commitment of marriage as something good in itself. All who accept that homosexual acts can be a humanly appropriate use of sexual capacities must, if consistent, regard sexual capacities, organs and acts as instruments for gratifying the individual "selves" who have them. Such an acceptance is commonly (and in my opinion rightly) judged to be an active threat to the stability of existing and future marriages; it makes nonsense, for example, of the view that adultery is per se (and not merely because it may involve deception), and in an important way, inconsistent with conjugal love. A political community which judges that the stability and protective and educative generosity of family life is of fundamental importance to that community's present and future can rightly judge that it has a compelling interest in denying that homosexual conduct—a "gay lifestyle"—is a valid, humanly acceptable choice and form of life, and in doing whatever it *properly* can, as a community with uniquely wide but still subsidiary functions, to discourage such conduct.

3

I promised to defend the judgment that the government of political communities is subsidiary, and rationally limited not only by constitutional law and by the moral norms which limit every decent person's deliberation and choice, but also by the inherent limits of its general justifying aim, purpose or rationale. That rationale is, of course, the common good of the political community. And that common good, I shall argue, is not basic, intrinsic or constitutive, but rather is instrumental.

Every community is constituted by the communication and cooperation between its members. To say that a community has a common good is simply to say that communication and cooperation have a point which the members more or less concur in understanding, valuing and pursuing. There are three types of common good which each provide the constitutive point of a distinctive type of open-ended community and directly instantiate a basic human good: (1) the affectionate mutual help and shared enjoyment of the friendship and *communio* of "real friends"; (2) the sharing of husband and wife in married life, united as complementary, bodily persons whose activities make them apt for parenthood—the *communio* of spouses and, if their marriage is fruitful, their children; (3) the *communio* of religious believers cooperating in the devotion and service called for by what they believe to be the accessible truths about the ultimate source of meaning, value and other realities, and about the ways in which human beings can be in harmony with that ultimate source. Other human communities *either* are dedicated to accomplishing a specific goal or set of goals (like a university or hospital) and so are not in the open-ended service of their members, *or* have a common good which is instrumental rather than basic. One should notice here that association and cooperation, even when oriented towards goals which are both specific and instrumentally rather than basically and intrinsically good (as, e.g., in a business enterprise), have a more than merely instrumental character inasmuch as they instantiate the basic good of friendship in one or other of its central or non-central forms.

The political community—properly understood as one of the forms of collaboration needed for the sake of the basic goods, identified in the first principles of natural law—is a community cooperating in the service of a common good which is instrumental, not itself basic. True, it is a good which is "great and god-like"[18] in its ambitious range: "to secure the whole ensemble of material and other conditions, including forms of collaboration, that tend to favor, facilitate, and foster the realization by each individual [in that community] of his or her personal development"[19] (which will in each case include, constitutively, the flourishing of the family, friendship

18. ARISTOTLE, NICOMACHEAN ETHICS, I,1: 1094b9.
19. JOHN FINNIS, NATURAL LAW AND NATURAL RIGHTS 147 (1980). As I indicate, this account of the common good of the political community is close to that

and other communities to which that person belongs). True too, its proper range includes the regulation of friendships, marriage, families, and religious associations, as well as of all the many organizations and associations which are dedicated to specific goals or which, like the state itself, have only an instrumental (e.g. an economic) common good. But such regulation of these associations should never (in the case of the associations with a non-instrumental common good) or only exceptionally (in the case of instrumental associations) be intended to take over the formation, direction or management of these personal initiatives and interpersonal associations. Rather, its purpose must be to carry out the *subsidiary* (i.e. helping, from the Latin *subsidium*, help) function[20] of assisting individuals and groups to coordinate their activities for the objectives and commitments they have chosen, and to do so in ways consistent with the other aspects of the common good of this community, uniquely complex, far-reaching and demanding in its rationale, its requirements of cooperation, and its monopolization of force: the political community.[21]

worked out by French commentators on Aquinas in the early mid-twentieth century. *Id.* at 160. A similar account was adopted by the Second Vatican Council: "the sum of those conditions of social life which allow social groups and their individual members relatively thorough and ready access to their own fulfillment." GAUDIUM ET SPES ¶ 26 (1965); *see also* DIGNITATIS HUMANAE ¶ 6 (1965).
20. *See* FINNIS, *supra* note 19, at 146-47, 159.
21. Of course, the common good of the political community has important elements which are scarcely shared with any other community within the polity: for example, the restoration of justice by punishment of those who have offended against just laws; the coercive repelling and restraint of those whose conduct (including negligent omissions) unfairly threatens the interests of others, particularly those interests identified as moral ("human") or legal rights, and corresponding compulsory measures to secure restitution, compensation or reparation for violations of rights; and the specifying and upholding of a system of holding or property rights which respects the various interests, immediate and vested or remote and contingent, which everyone has in each holding. But the fact that these and various other elements of the political common good are peculiar to the political community and the proper responsibility of its leaders, the government, in no way entails that these elements are basic human goods or

The fundamentally instrumental character of the political common good is indicated by both parts of the Second Vatican Council's teaching about religious liberty, a teaching considered by the Council to be a matter of natural law (i.e. of "reason itself").[22] The *first* part of the teaching is that everyone has the right not to be coerced in matters of religious belief and practice. For, to know the truth about the ultimate matters compendiously called by the Council "religious," and to adhere to and put into practice the truth one has come to know, is so significant a good and so basic a responsibility, and the attainment of that "good of the human spirit"[23] is so inherently and non-substitutably a matter of *personal* assent and *conscientious* decision, that if a government intervenes coercively in people's search for true religious beliefs, or in people's expression of the beliefs they suppose true, it will harm those people and violate their dignity even when its intervention is based on the correct premise that their search has been negligently conducted and/or has led them into false beliefs. Religious acts, according to the Council, "transcend" the sphere which is proper to government; government is to care for the temporal common good, and this includes [the subsidiary function of] acknowledging and fostering the religious life of its citizens; but governments have no responsibility or right to direct religious acts, and "exceed their proper *limits*" if they presume to do so.[24]

The *second* part of the Council's teaching concerns the proper restrictions on religious freedom, namely those restrictions which are

required for [i] the effective *protection of the rights* of all citizens and of their peaceful coexistence, [ii] a sufficient care for the authentic *public peace* of an ordered common life in true justice, and [iii] a proper upholding of *public morality*. All

that the political common good is other than in itself instrumental.
22. DIGNITATIS HUMANAE ¶ 2. In the succeeding part, the Declaration treats the matter as one of divine revelation. *Id.* at ¶¶ 9–14.
23. It is one of the *animi humani bona* mentioned in *id.*, ¶ 1.
24. "Potestas igitur civilis, cuius finis proprius est bonum commune temporale curare, religiosam quidem civium vitam agnoscere eique favere debet, sed *limites suos excedere* dicenda est, si actus religiosos dirigere vel impedire praesumat." *Id.* at ¶ 3.

these factors constitute the fundamental part of the common good, and come under the notion of *ordre public.*[25]

Here, too, the political common good is presented as instrumental, serving the protection of human and legal rights, *public* peace and *public* morality—in other words, the preservation of a social environment conducive to virtue. Government is precisely not presented here as dedicated to the commanding of virtue and the repressing of vice, as such, even though virtue (and vice) are of supreme and constitutive importance for the well-being (or otherwise) of individual persons and the worth (or otherwise) of their associations.

Is the Council's natural law teaching right? Or should we rather adhere to the uncomplicated theory of Aquinas's treatise *On Princely Government*, that government should command whatever leads people towards their ultimate (heavenly) end, forbid whatever deflects them from it, and coercively deter people from evil-doing and induce them to morally decent conduct?[26] Perhaps the most suasive short statement of that teaching is still Aristotle's famous attack on theories which, like the sophist Lycophron's, treat the state as a mere mutual insurance arrangement?[27] But in two

25. *Id.* at ¶ 7.
26. DE REGIMINE PRINCIPUM c.14 (. . . ab iniquitate coerceat et ad opera virtuosa inducat). This thesis is qualified, though not abandoned, in other works of Aquinas. Thus *Summa Theologiae* II-II q.104 a.5c teaches that human government has no authroity over people's minds and the interior motions of their wills. *Id.* I-II q.96 a.2 teaches that governmental pursuit of virtue should be gradual and should not ask too much of the average citizen (who is not virtuous).
27. It states:

[T]he *polis* was formed not for the sake of life only but rather for the good life . . . and . . . its purpose is not [merely] military alliance for defence . . . and it does not exist [merely] for the sake of trade and business relations . . . any *polis* which is truly so called, and is not one merely in name, must have virtue/excellence as an object of its care [*peri aretes epimeles einat*: be solicitous about virtue]. Otherwise a polis sinks into a mere alliance, differing only in space from other forms of alliance where the members live at a distance from each other. Otherwise, too, the law becomes a mere social contract [*syntheke*, covenant]—or (in the phrase of the sophist Lycophron) 'a guarantor of justice as between one man and another'—instead of being, as it

crucial respects, at least, Aristotle (and with him the tradition) has taken things too easily.

First: If the object, point or common good of the political community were indeed a self-sufficient life, and if self-sufficiency (*autarcheia*) were indeed what Aristotle defines it to be—a life lacking in nothing, of complete fulfillment[28]—then we would have to say that the political community has a point it cannot hope to achieve, a common good utterly beyond its reach. For subsequent philosophical reflection has confirmed what one might suspect from Aristotle's own manifest oscillation between different conceptions of *eudaimonia* (and thus of *autarcheia*): Integral human fulfillment is nothing less than the fulfillment of (in principle) all human persons in all communities and cannot be achieved in any community short of the heavenly kingdom, a community envisaged not by unaided reason (natural law theory) but only by virtue of divine revelation and attainable only by a divine gift which transcends the capacities of nature. To be sure, integral human fulfillment can and should be a conception central to a natural law theory of morality and thus of politics, and should be envisaged as a kind of ideal community (to which will answer the reality of the Kingdom which Christian faith's first moral norm directs us to seek).[29] But that ideal community is not, as early

natural law theories such as Aristotle's prematurely proposed, the political community.

Second: When Aristotle speaks of "making" people good, he constantly[30] uses the word *poiesis* which he has so often contrasted with *praxis* and reserved for techniques ("arts") of manipulating matter.[31] But helping citizens to choose and act in line with integral human fulfillment must involve something which goes beyond any art or technique. For only individual acting persons can by their own choices make themselves good or evil. Not that their life should or can be individualistic; their deliberating and choosing will be shaped, and helped or hindered, by the language of their culture, by their family, their friends, their associates and enemies, the customs of their communities, the laws of their polity, and by the impress of human influences of many kinds from beyond their homeland. Their choices will involve them in relationships just or unjust, generous or illiberal, vengeful or charitable, with other persons in all these communities. And as members of all these communities they have some responsibility to encourage their fellow-members in morally good and discourage them from morally bad conduct.

To be sure, the political community is a cooperation which undertakes the unique tasks of giving coercive protection to all individuals and lawful associations within its domain, and of securing an economic and cultural environment in which all these persons and groups can pursue their own proper good. To be sure, this common good of the political community makes it far more than a mere arrangement for "preventing mutual injury and exchanging goods." But it is one thing to maintain, as reason requires, that the political community's

should be, such as will make [*poiein*] the citizens good and just . . . . The polis is not merely a sharing of a common locality for the purpose of preventing mutual injury and exchanging goods. These are necessary preconditions of the existence of a polis . . but a polis is a *communio* [*koinonia*] of clans [and neighborhoods] in living well, with the object of a full and self-sufficient [*autarkous*] life . . . it must therefore be for the sake of truly good (*kalon*) actions, not of merely living together."

ARISTOTLE, POLITICS, III.5: 1280a32, a35, 1280b7–13, b30–31, b34, 1281a1–4.
28. ARISTOTLE, NICOMACHEAN ETHICS, I. 7:1097b8. This, incidentally, differs widely from what STEPHEN MACEDO, LIBERAL VIRTUES 215–17 (1990), means by "an autarchic person."
29. For nothing less than integral human fulfillment, the fulfillment of all persons in all the basic human goods, answers to reason's full knowledge of, and the will's full interest in, the human good in which one can participate by action. And so the first principle of a sound morality must be: In voluntarily acting for human goods and avoiding what is opposed to them, one

ought to choose and will those and only those possibilities whose willing is compatible with integral human fulfillment. To say that immorality is constituted by cutting back on, fettering, reason by passions is equivalent to saying that the sway of feelings over reason constitutes immorality by deflecting one to objectives not in line with integral human fulfillment. This ideal community is thus the good will's most fundamental orientating ideal.
30. Apart from the passage just cited, see ARISTOTLE, NICOMACHEAN ETHICS, I, 10; 1099b32; II, I: 110364; X, 9: 1180b24.
31. *E.g.* ARISTOTLE, NICOMACHEAN ETHICS, VI, 5: 1140a2; ARISTOTLE, POLITICS, I, 2: 1254a5.

rationale requires that its public managing structure, the state, should deliberately and publicly identify, encourage, facilitate and support the truly worthwhile (including moral virtue), should deliberately and publicly identify, discourage and hinder the harmful and evil, and should, by its criminal prohibitions and sanctions (as well as its other laws and policies), assist people with parental responsibilities to educate children and young people in virtue and to discourage their vices. It is another thing to maintain that that rationale requires or authorizes the state to direct people to virtue and deter them from vice by making even secret and truly consensual adult acts of vice a punishable offence against the state's laws.[32]

So there was a sound and important distinction of principle which the Supreme Court of the United States overlooked in moving from

Griswold v. Connecticut[33] (private use of contraceptives by *spouses*) to Eisenstadt v. Baird (*public distribution* of contraceptives to *unmarried* people).[34] The truth and relevance of that distinction, and its high importance for the common good, would be overlooked again if laws criminalizing private acts of sodomy between adults were to be struck down by the Court on any ground which would also constitutionally require the law to tolerate the advertising or marketing of homosexual services, the maintenance of places of resort for homosexual activity, or the promotion of homosexualist "lifestyles" via education and public media of communication, or to recognize homosexual "marriages" or permit the adoption of children by homosexually active people, and so forth.

32. So a third way in which Aristotle takes things too easily is his slide from upholding government's responsibility to assist or substitute for the direct parental discipline of youth, to claiming that this responsibility continues, and in the same direct coercive form, "to cover the whole of a lifetime, since most people obey necessity rather than argument, and punishments rather than the sense of what is truly worthwhile." ARISTOTLE, NICOMACHEAN ETHICS, X.9:1180a1-3.

33. 381 U.S. 479 (1965).
34. 405 U.S. 438 (1972). The law struck down in *Griswold* was the law forbidding use of contraceptives even by married persons; Griswold's conviction as an accessory to such use fell with the fall of the substantive law against the principals in such use. Very different, in principle, would have been a law directly forbidding Griswold's activities as a public promoter of contraceptive information and supplies. If American constitutional law fails to recognize such distinctions, it shows, I suggest, its want of sound principle.

Homosexuality and the Conservative Mind

Stephen Macedo*

[R]espondent asserts that there must be a rational basis for the [antisodomy] law and that there is none in this case other than the presumed belief of a majority of the electorate in Georgia that homosexual sodomy is immoral and unaccept-

able. . . . [R]espondent . . . insists that majority sentiments about the morality of homosexuality should be declared inadequate. We do not agree, and are unpersuaded that the sodomy laws of some 25 States should be invalidated on this basis.

* Michael O. Sawyer Professor of Constitutional Law and Politics, Maxwell School of Citizenship and Public Affairs, Syracuse University. My thanks to Mary E. Becker, Peter Berkowitz, Gayle Binion, David Boaz, Sam Fleischacker, Mary Ann Glendon, Josh Green, Kent Greenawalt, Mark Henrie, Rick Hills, Andrew Koppelman, Harvey C. Mansfield, and Andrew Sabl for helpful comments on previous drafts. I am also deeply grateful to Princeton University's Center for Human Values, and its Director Amy Gutmann, for providing the perfect setting in which to work.

Associate Justice White, *Bowers v. Hardwick*,
Supreme Court of the United States, 1986.[1]

Some of the most divisive political conflicts of our time hang at least partly on the answer to the question of whether legal discrimination against gays and lesbians has a reasoned basis. Is there a reasoned ground for the sharply different evaluations

1. *Bowers v. Hardwick*, 478 U.S. 186, 196 (1986).

of heterosexual and homosexual intimacy embodied in the Supreme Court's privacy jurisprudence?[2] Is the government acting on mere prejudice by excluding active and open homosexuals from military service?[3] Are there any good reasons for not allowing gay marriage?[4] For many ordinary Americans—and perhaps one day for the Supreme Court as well—these questions remain open.

Lawyers and litigants are not the only ones trying to answer these questions. A number of leading conservative academics and intellectuals have also argued for the reasonableness of discrimination against gays and lesbians.[5] They have done this, in part, because they concede that discriminatory laws and public policies are often motivated by popular prejudice and unthinking hostility, which are, on their own, inadequate bases for exercising political power.[6] Moral philosopher and legal scholar John Finnis, for example, argues that "public policies must be based on reasons, not mere emotions, prejudices, and biases."[7] He also concedes, however, that "embarrassment" makes

"most people more than usually inarticulate" with respect to homosexuality.[8] The twenty-four academics and intellectuals composing the Ramsey Colloquium allow that most Americans regard homosexuality with a "largely intuitive and pre-articulate anxiety."[9] These conservative scholars aim to supply the "public" arguments and widely accessible "reasons" that are often missing from popular attacks on the morality of homosexuality, and in this they support what the Court itself has sometimes maintained: that even when fundamental rights are not at stake, and even when the victims of discrimination have no special call on the protection of courts, "private biases" and "mere negative attitudes, or fear" are not proper grounds for lawmaking.[10]

This article critically assesses the state of conservative thinking on homosexuality: Are today's conservatives succeeding in advancing a reasoned, public, secular case for legal discrimination against homosexuals?[11] It proceeds by conceding a good deal to the conservatives. I allow, for example, that

2. *See id.* I should perhaps note that some will regard the "gay-straight" dichotomy that I deploy here as an oversimplifying distortion of reality, and as "essentializing" categories that are historically fluid. My purpose is to use these categories in order to make coherent arguments against others who use them.

3. Under current federal court decisions, homosexuals and bisexuals do not constitute a suspect class. *See, e.g.*, High Tech Gays v. Defense Indus. Sec. Clearance Office, 895 F. 2d 563 (9th Cir. 1990); Steffan v. Cheney, 780 F. Supp. I (D.D.C. 1991).

4. The Hawaii Supreme Court recently held that a law restricting marriage to opposite-sex couples came within the scope of Hawaii's equal rights amendment's prohibition of sex discrimination. Baehr v. Lewin, 852 P.2d 44 (Haw. 1993). See also Andrew Koppelman's provocative discussion of related issues in Andrew Koppelman, *Why Discrimination Against Lesbians and Gay Men is Sex Discrimination*, 69 N.Y.U.L. REV. 197 (1994).

5. "Conservative" and "conservative moralist" refer here to those who argue that homosexual conduct is immoral; it should not be taken to imply that those so designated take conservative positions on other matters.

6. This assertion is explicitly stated by Finnis, the Ramseyites, and several of the other conservatives examined below. It is implicitly stated by other conservative commentators. E.L. Pattullo seeks to provide a "secular reason" for those who resist "the gay rights movement." *See* E.L. Pattullo, *Straight Talk About Gays*, COMMENTARY, Dec. 1992, at 21.

7. John Finnis, *Natural Law and Limited Government, in* LIBERALISM, MODERNITY, AND NATURAL LAW (Robert George & Christopher Wolfe eds., forthcoming 1996) (on file with author).

8. *Id.* Finnis's argument about homosexuality reappears in *Law, Morality, and "Sexual Orientation,"* 69 NOTRE DAME L. REV. 1049 (1994) [hereinafter Finnis, *Sexual Orientation*].

9. *See The Homosexual Movement: A Response by the Ramsey Colloquium.* FIRST THINGS. Mar. 1994, at 16 [hereinafter *The Homosexual Movement*]. An abridged edition appeared as *Morality and Homosexuality,* WALL ST. J., Feb. 24, 1994, at A18 [hereinafter Rumsey Colloquium, *Morality and Homosexuality*]. The members of the Colloquium (sponsored by the Institute on Religion and Public Life) and signatories of both pieces are Hadley Arkes, Matthew Berke. Gerard Bradley, Rabbi David Dalin, Ernest Fortin, Jorge Garcia, Rabbi Marc Gellman, Robert George, The Rev. Hugh Haffenreffer, John Hittinger, Russell Hittinger, Robert Jenson, Gilbert Meilaender, Jerry Muller, Fr. Richard John Neuhaus, Rabbi David Novak, James Neuchterlein, Max Stackhouse, Philip Turner, George Weigel, and Robert Wilken. It should be noted that this list of signatories includes tenured professors of philosophy, law, and political science at such prestigious institutions as Amherst College, Boston College, Princeton University, and Notre Dame.

10. *See The Homosexual Movement, supra* note 9. at 15. 16; Ramsey Colloquium, *Morality and Homosexuality, supra* note 9, at A18; City of Cleburne v. Cleburne Living Ctr., 473 U.S. 432, 448 (1985) (holding that public policies based on "private biases" and "mere negative attitudes, or fear" should not pass even the lowest level of judicial scrutiny).

11. My sources are somewhat disparate because intellectual arguments by conservatives on the subject of homosexuality are not as abundant as one might expect.

they may be correct to regard promiscuity as morally bad, and right to believe that we have good reason for encouraging people to settle down in long-term monogamous relationships. I believe, with the conservatives, that public moral judgment has a legitimate role to play in even the most personal aspects of our lives.[12] Conservatives seem right, as well, to worry about teenage pregnancy, the excesses of sexual permissiveness and promiscuity, and liberationist ideals that condemn all traditional restraints indiscriminately. I admit a degree of sympathy with Germain Grisez's challenge to the libertarianism that certainly characterizes an extreme form of liberalism that came to the fore in the 1960s:

> The promoters of sexual liberation thought it would eliminate the pain of sexual frustration and make society as a whole more joyful. What has happened instead shows how wrong they were. The pain of sexual frustration is slight in comparison with the misery of abandoned women and unwanted children, of people lonely for lack of true marital intimacy, of those dying wretchedly from sexually transmitted disease. Moreover, unchastity's destructive effects on so many families impact on the wider society, whose stability depends on families. . . . Boys and girls coming to maturity without solid formation in a stable family are ill prepared to assume adult social responsibilities.[13]

I feel sure that this is not the whole truth, but it may represent an important part of the truth. Such charges at least need to be taken seriously.

In spite of these and other concessions, a wide range of conservative moral and political thinkers fail to provide a reasoned defense for discrimination against gays and lesbians.[14] The frequency

with which conservatives translate their opposition to promiscuity and liberationism into blanket condemnations of homosexual conduct is as puzzling as it is illegitimate. Such arguments are a form of moral scapegoating that is both unreasonable and unjust. Condemning all gays and lesbians on the basis of opposition to the promiscuous behavior of some gays (and, in truth, many heterosexuals also) is no better than condemning all men because some men rape women. To deny basic public rights and opportunities to a whole class of people on the basis of opposition to the behavior of some within the class is fundamentally arbitrary and unjust.

My analysis is not purely negative. By making various concessions to conservatives—by allowing that promiscuity, teen pregnancy, and other matters are reasonable causes for public concern—I hope to show that acceptance of equal rights for gays and lesbians does not require that we scrap the whole of traditional morality. Indeed, by jettisoning the unreasonable and arbitrary parts of traditional morality, we may well strengthen the elements that remain.

The argument here has another positive element. By examining a range of conservative arguments in some detail, I go beyond showing that conservative moral argument is poor, and try to explain *why*. Conservative moral arguments about homosexuality achieve greater coherence when reformulated as efforts to support fragile social norms that embody imperfect moral generalizations. This way of achieving coherence carries a high moral price, however, for the reformulated argument is open to the charge of complacency in the face of injustice.

Moral arguments against homosexual conduct evince a range of tone and emphasis, and they proceed from a variety of philosophical assumptions. In some cases (especially the case of the "new natural lawyers" considered . . . below), I cannot lay out and analyze the philosophical

---

12. *See generally* Robert P. George, Making Men Moral: Civil Liberties and Public Morality (1993).

13. Germain Grisez, 2 The Way of the Lord Jesus: Living a Christian Life 662 (1993).

14. I realize that some readers (including many who agree with my conclusions) will be unhappy with the concessions I make to conservatives. Some will prefer an argument that endorses more radical revisions of sexual morality and gives far less ground to conservative moralists. I hope that these readers will nevertheless allow that there might be value in showing that equal rights for gays and lesbians need not depend upon the

acceptance of more radical goals, which many Americans regard as controversial or deeply objectionable for reasons that have nothing to do with prejudice against gay, lesbian, and bisexual people. My aim is to show that even those who share some conservative concerns should endorse fundamental equality of treatment for homosexuals, and I hope that even those who do not share those concerns might see some value in the argument.

assumptions in great detail, but must largely confine myself to considering the reasonableness of these arguments as contributions to our *public* deliberations about important and basic matters of political morality.[15] In spite of the differences of philosophical assumptions, we shall see that similar themes and errors recur repeatedly. . . .

Finnis, Grisez, and the New Natural Law[16]

The Broad Sweep of Natural Law Sexual Prohibitions

At least some of the new natural lawyers—secular philosophers such as John Finnis, Germain Grisez, and Robert George, working in one part of the Catholic natural law tradition—allow that some people are homosexual by nature.[17] At least some of these thinkers would *not*, moreover, deploy the criminal law against private homosexual acts.[18]

The law should, however, supervise "the *public realm or environment*," within which young and old are morally educated toward good or bad lives. Finnis argues that *openly* active homosexuals are "deeply hostile to the self-understanding of those members of the community who are willing to commit themselves to real marriage."[19] The law should, therefore, deny "that homosexual conduct—a 'gay lifestyle'—is a valid, humanly acceptable choice and form of life," and it should do "whatever it *properly* can . . . to discourage such conduct."[20]

The new natural lawyers go out of their way to distinguish their position from the narrow prejudice and mere disgust that characterize much popular opposition to equal rights for gays and lesbians. They do not claim that homosexual acts are unique in being distractions from real human goods, or in justly being subject to legal discouragement. The new natural lawyers strikingly treat gay and lesbian sexual activity like most forms of heterosexual activity: like all sex outside of marriage and all contracepted sex, *including* all contracepted sex between married couples.

The new natural law's broad prohibitions against extramarital and "recreational" sexual activity (contracepted or homosexual) are based on the contention that many forms of sexual activity are like masturbation, through which individuals forgo opportunities to participate in real human goods and wrongly use the body as a mere instrument of pleasure.[21] Masturbation involves only fantasy,

---

15. There may be something appropriate about the limited depth in which we can consider the new natural law arguments. As Rawls has recently argued, the reasons offered for justifying and shaping our basic rights and liberties ought to be ones whose force can be appreciated by people lacking specialized intellectual sophistication and by people proceeding from a variety of abstract, not unreasonable, philosophical assumptions. *See generally* JOHN RAWLS, POLITICAL LIBERALISM 47–88, 212–44 (1993).

16. My discussion in this Part is a revised version of part III of *Against the Old Sexual Morality of the New Natural Law, in* LIBERALISM, MODERNITY, AND NATURAL LAW, *supra* note 7. Finnis, George, and Mansfield all testified in *Evans v. Romer*, the successful challenge to the constitutionality of Colorado's Amendment 2. Evans v. Romer, 854 P.2d 1270 (Colo.), *cert. denied*, 114 S. Ct. 419 (1993). This *Evans v. Romer* cite is to the litigation over the preliminary injunction only. *See also* Evans v. Romer, 882 P.2d 1335 (Colo. 1994) (making the injunction permanent), *cert. granted*, 115 S. Ct. 1092 (1995) [hereinafter *Evans II*]. The Supreme Court heard oral arguments in *Evans II* in October 1995.

17. Grisez is fairly explicit in conceding the naturalness of homosexual orientation, though it hardly leads him to endorse homosexual activity: "[A] homosexual orientation is natural only in the sense that any handicap for which an individual is not personally responsible is natural." GRISEZ, *supra* note 13, at 654 n.194.

18. Finnis allows that the Supreme Court might properly have overturned the criminal prosecution of private homosexual acts in *Bowers v. Hardwick*, 478 U.S. 186 (1986), but only while distinguishing such private conduct from "the advertising or marketing of homosexu-

al services, the maintenance of places of resort for homosexual activity, or the promotion of homosexualist 'lifestyles,'" as well as homosexual marriages and the "adoption of children by homosexually active people." Finnis, *Sexual Orientation, supra* note 8, at 1076. Other conservatives press the same line, arguing that "no one cares about someone's private sexual practices," as Schiatly puts it, and urging that "homosexuality should be a private affair," as Kristol puts it, *Sex and God in American Politics, supra* note 18, at 23–24.

19. Finnis, *Sexual Orientation, supra* note 8, at 1069.

20. *Id.* at 1070.

21. Finnis's account of masturbation—and the broader question of whether pleasure is a good—relies upon Robert Nozick's thought experiment of deciding whether to plug oneself into an "experience machine." *See* ROBERT NOZICK, ANARCHY, STATE, AND UTOPIA 42–45 (1974). Nozick asks us to imagine a machine that, by stimulating the brain, can be preprogrammed to provide one with any and every experience that

Finnis insists, rather than real friendship, play, knowledge, and other goods embodied in genuine intimate relations with others.[22] Germain Grisez similarly maintains that "[t]he pleasurable sensations of sexual activity culminating in orgasm are in themselves a private and incommunicable experience."[23] Finnis and Grisez also believe that masturbation violates the good of personal integrity, for it is the use of one's body by the conscious self for the mere production of pleasure, with no connection to any real projects, goods, or other persons.[24]

The sexual act should be subordinate to the real goods that are relevant to the kind of act that it is; and those real goods are the complex of goods united in a permanent heterosexual marriage.[25] Our understanding of proper sexuality should take its bearings from the "specific, intrinsic perfection" of relations between man and woman, which perfection is found in marriage: "[f]or marriage realizes the potentiality of man and woman for unqualified, mutual self-giving," oriented toward not simply the "begetting and raising of children," but also the spouses' own "open-ended community" of mutual love, companionship, willing and loving cooperation, help, and comfort, all of which fulfill the spouses' marital good, even if procreation does not occur on account of infertility, sterility, or some other unchosen condition.[26] Sexual pleasure must be subordinate to these marital goods if it is to be "the experience of loving cooperation in one-flesh communion." Pleasure experienced as an intrinsic part of marriage is good, however intense it may be.[27] As Finnis argues:

---

might be desired over an entire lifetime. Few people would choose a lifetime of being plugged into such a machine, Finnis rightly insists, because such a life would accomplish nothing and would involve no real relations with others. The thought experiment reveals that we care deeply about having real relations with others and doing real things in the world. Realizing basic goods in one's activities in the world will of course often bring with it various feelings of pleasure, and that is entirely appropriate. But the production of pleasure divorced from any real accomplishments and activities is of no value and is a distraction from valuable activity. *See* John M. Finnis, Natural Law and Natural Rights 95–97 (1980) [hereinafter Finnis, Natural Law and Natural Rights]; John M. Finnis, *Personal Integrity, Sexual Morality, and Responsible Personhood, Anthropos,* I Anthropos: Rivistadi Di Studi Sulla Persona E La Famiglia 43, 45–46 (1985) [hereinafter Finnis, *Personal Integrity*]. One problem with this argument is that it only shows the great loss that would come from plugging into an experience machine *for life.* It does not show why plugging in for half an hour several times a week would be such a great disaster (I'd do it!). To make the experience machine analogy helpful with respect to masturbation or pleasure more broadly, one might have to add that plugging in is addictive and so is bound to lead to excess for the majority of people.

22. Among the basic goods are life, knowledge, play, aesthetic experience, sociability or friendship, and practical reasonableness. Finnis, Natural Law and Natural Rights, *supra* note 53, at 81–99. Basic goods are foundational reasons for action: they are self-evident, intrinsic, and incommensurable goods, known to people of ordinary experience, which can be embodied in any number of "commitments, projects and actions," *Id.* at 63–64. Our choice of projects and pursuits becomes explicable and intelligible by reference to the ways in which those choices realize basic goods. *Id.*

23. Grisez, *supra* note 13, at 637.

24. Finnis, *Personal Integrity, supra* note 53, at 47. Grisez elaborates on the argument:

> [I]n choosing to masturbate, one does not choose to act for a goal which fulfills oneself as a unified, bodily person. The only immediate goal is satisfaction for the

conscious self; and so the body, not being part of the whole for whose sake the act is done, serves only as an extrinsic instrument . . . . [T]he choice of self-disintegrity damages the basic good of self-integration . . . . The self-integration damaged by masturbation is the unity of the acting person as conscious subject and sexually functioning body. This specific aspect of self-integration, however, is precisely the aspect necessary so that the bodily union of sexual intercourse will be a communion of persons, as marital intercourse is. Therefore, masturbation damages the body's capacity for the marital act as an act of self-giving which constitutes a communion of bodily persons.

Grisez, *supra* note 13, at 650.

25. As Grisez puts it:

> [T]he sexual acts of a married couple express and foster their communion primarily because they contribute to the common good of marriage, which realizes their specific potentiality as husband and wife. . . . [T]he organic complementarity of man and woman in respect to reproduction is the necessary condition for the very possibility of marriage, and the requirements of human parenting specify the characteristics of marriage as an open-ended community. Therefore, marital acts must realize both the spouses' open-ended community and their organic complementarity.

Grisez, *supra* note 13, at 634.

26. *Id.* at 569–70, 634–35.

27. *Id.* at 636–37.

The union of the reproductive organs of husband and wife really unites them biologically (and their biological reality is part of, not merely an instrument of, their *personal* reality); reproduction is one function and so, in respect of that function, the spouses are indeed one reality, and their sexual union therefore can *actualize* and allow them to *experience* their *real common good—their marriage* with two goods, parenthood and friendship. . . .[28]

Valuable sexual activity, therefore, must take place within a permanent heterosexual marriage, it must involve total mutual self-giving, and it must be open to all of the goods of marital communion, including the transmission of new life (meaning that it must not be contracepted).[29]

All nonprocreative, recreational sexual acts merely instrumentalize bodies for mutual use and pleasure. All are equivalent to mutual masturbation: simultaneous individual gratifications incapable of realizing any shared goods such as friendship or love (which could be better realized in other activities), or any "real communion of persons."[30] This is certainly true of homosexuality, "inasmuch as the coupling of two bodies of the same sex cannot form one complete organism."[31] But Grisez is quite explicit that much heterosexual activity is of the same moral character: "such heterosexual activities—including contracepted intercourse, within or outside marriage—are morally similar to sodomy."[32]

It may be, indeed, that the case against recreational heterosexual sex is even stronger than that against gay sex, for the former risks the great evil of bringing unwanted children into the world. Even when effectively contracepted, recreational heterosexual acts are (in natural law terms) choices to forgo the great good of new life. Gay sex is not, on the new natural law account, a choice against the great integrating goods of heterosexual marriage: the goods of heterosexual intimacy may not be available to those who are gay by nature.[33]

The wrongfulness of gay sex is merely its "self-disintegrity": the failure to act in a way that is consistent with a desire for the real goods that homosexual friends may share in common. When sex is chosen by homosexuals, it is as a source of "subjective satisfactions" through the use and instrumentalization of each other's bodies.[34] The wrongfulness of homosexual acts and of heterosexual fornication is that, in both instances, the coupling of the bodies can form no single organism,

28. Finnis, *Sexual Orientation, supra* note 8, at 1066 (emphasis added).

29. It is perhaps worth noting that the good of practical reason has a special architectonic role: one participates in the good of practical reason "precisely by shaping one's participation in the other basic goods, by guiding one's commitments, one's selection of projects, and what one does in carrying them out." FINNIS, NATURAL LAW AND NATURAL RIGHTS, *supra* note 53, at 100. The good of practical reason is realized by those who reflectively construct a rational plan of life that realizes a rich array of basic goods in projects and activities that harmonize and give meaning, structure, and discipline to one's life as a whole. *Id.* at 103–05. Among the failures of practical reason are arbitrary preferences among basic goods or an unreasonable discounting of any basic good. *Id.* at 104–06. Most important for our purposes, practical reason, as the new natural lawyers conceive it, bars any action or project that represents a direct choice against any of the basic goods. As Finnis asserts:

> To choose an act which in itself simply (or primarily) damages a basic good is thereby to engage oneself willy-nilly (but directly) in an act of opposition to an incommensurable value (an aspect of human personality) which one treats as if it were an object of measurable worth that could be outweighed by commensurable objects of greater (or cumulatively greater) worth. To do this will often accord with our feelings, our generosity, our sympathy. . . . But it can never be justified in reason.

> *Id.* at 120. One of the basic goods that must never be chosen against is "human life in its transmission," "personal integrity," and this is the basis of the new natural law's condemnation of contraception, abortion, and much else.

30. *See* GRISEZ, *supra* note 13, at 654.

31. *Id.*

32. *Id.: see also id.* at 648–56 (claiming that nonmarital sexual acts are wrong); Finnis, *Sexual Orientation, supra* note 8, at 18–20.

33. Grisez seems to allow all this, and says that

> while sodomites may not choose, as fornicators do, an illusory good *instead* of a real one, they do choose to use their own and each other's bodies to provide subjective satisfactions, and thus they choose self-disintegrity as masturbators do. Of course, while masturbators can be interested exclusively in the experience of sexual arousal and orgasm, sodomites also are interested in the illusion of intimacy.

> GRISEZ, *supra* note 13, at 654: *see also id.* at 653 (discussing sodomites' need for intimacy).

34. *Id.* at 653–54.

and so the sexual act can have no real point, or realize any real good in common.[35] That homosexual lovers—or heterosexuals using contraception—think that their sexuality expresses friendship, care, affection, and intimacy is merely illusory: those goods could be better expressed by nonsexual acts of friendship, such as mutual helping at home.

This natural law teaching—the surface of which I have barely scratched—is by far the most elaborate intellectual case for distinguishing between heterosexual and homosexual activity. Unlike the almost offhanded pronouncements of some of the conservatives examined here, the judgments issued by Finnis and Grisez are tied closely to a complex intellectual system. Notice, however, where this system of ideas has taken us: to the extent that the state has an interest in discouraging homosexuality on these natural law grounds, it has an equal interest in acting against all extramarital and contracepted sex. To the extent that the state exhibits no interest in discouraging the use of contraceptives, it has evidently rejected new natural law reasoning and must find some other grounds to justify discouraging homosexuality.[36]

Let us also recall that the very foundation of modern privacy jurisprudence—*Griswold v. Connecticut*—was laid when the Court insisted that married couples should be free to decide for themselves whether to use contraceptives.[37] The Court subsequently extended the right of privacy to the decision of unmarried couples to use contraceptives.[38] The new natural law offers no ground for drawing fundamental distinctions between the privacy rights the Court *has protected* and the privacy rights of homosexuals.

In these ways, the new natural law performs the vital service of revealing the gross and unreflective arbitrariness of public policies and proposals that—in the name of family values—fix their scornful attention on gays and lesbians. Nothing could be easier in the face of heterosexual promiscuity, premarital sex, teenage pregnancy, and skyrocketing divorce rates than to fasten our attention on a long-despised class of people who bear few children. The new natural law shows that, on reflection, such attitudes embody a double standard of permissiveness toward straights and censoriousness toward gays who engage in acts that are essentially the same.

The new natural law has the apparent virtue of consistency. If it rejects equality for homosexuals, it poses an even greater challenge to the *conventional wisdom*—including that of the conservative moralists examined above—that would single out homosexuality as singularly perverse and "unnatural."

This fair-mindedness and broad sweep may also make the new natural law politically irrelevant. It supports only very broad public actions against sexual immorality in general: against divorce, contraception, all sex outside of marriage, and homosexuality. To reject natural law teachings on contraception, for example, is to jettison natural law grounds for acting against homosexuality. This natural law philosophy cannot be of help to any but those few Americans who accept its extremely broad strictures. It provides no aid and comfort to the vast majority of those who would condemn homosexual activity while accepting the availability of divorce, contraception, and premarital sex.

Those sympathetic to natural law's broadly conservative sexual teaching might reply that simply because some justifiable moral strictures have

---

35. As Finnis puts it:

> For want of a *common good* that could be actualized and experienced *by and in this bodily union*, that conduct involves the partners in treating their bodies as instruments to be used in the service of their consciously experiencing selves; their choice to engage in such conduct thus dis-integrates each of them precisely as acting persons.

> Finnis, *Sexual Orientation, supra* note 8, at 1066–67; *see also* Grisez, *supra* note 13, at 649–53 (explaining that although fornicators' and homosexuals' primary motivation may be intimate communion, that experience is only illusory).

36. One might reply that promiscuity is greatest in the gay male population. But if this is true, it is hard to see how it furnishes grounds for discrimination. Why punish all for the wrongs of some? Not all homosexuals are promiscuous and not all promiscuous people are homosexual. Are there not more honorable and just means for discouraging promiscuity? So long as we refuse, moreover, to extend to gay men the inducements to stability and self-control (such as marriage) available to heterosexuals, we should regard promiscuous gay men as (at least in part) victims of fate, circumstance, and public policy rather than of a special moral depravity. In any case, conservatives often greatly exaggerate the levels of promiscuity among homosexuals. *See infra* note 95.

37. 381 U.S. 479 (1965).
38. *See Eisenstadt v. Baird*, 405 U.S. 438 (1972).

been relaxed, that is no reason to relax them all. But it is a reason (both a *moral* reason and a constitutional one) when a long-despised minority is arbitrarily saddled with restrictions that the majority is unwilling to impose on itself.[39] Even if one accepts natural law judgments, therefore, considerations of fairness suggest that they should not be applied against the homosexual minority until we also apply them against the heterosexual majority.

Insuperable obstacles lie in the path of any state that would rely on natural law grounds for selective prohibitions on homosexual conduct. There are, moreover, other problems with the natural law position still to be considered. I have commended the new natural law's sexual teaching for its fair-mindedness and broad sweep, but this may have been premature, for the position is plagued by a major inconsistency, to which we now turn.

The New Natural Law's Double Standard

The new natural lawyers argue that sex within a marriage of sterile heterosexuals is not only permissible but good: "marital union itself fulfills the spouses."[40] But how can we justify this favored treatment of sterile heterosexuals given that their bodies, like those of homosexuals, can form no "single reproductive principle," no "real unity?"[41] If there is no possibility of procreation, then sterile couples are, like homosexuals, incapable of sex acts "open to procreation."[42]

What is the point of sex in an infertile marriage? Not procreation; the partners (let us assume) know that they are infertile. If they have sex, it is for pleasure and to express their love, or friendship, or some other shared good. It will be for precisely the same reasons that committed,

loving gay couples have sex. Why are these good reasons for sterile or elderly married couples but not for gay and lesbian couples? If, on the other hand, sex detracts from the real goods shared by homosexual couples, and indeed undermines their friendship, this should also be the case for infertile heterosexual couples. Sterile couples' experience of sexual intimacy should be as "private and incommunicable" as that of gays.

Of course, sterility is an unchosen condition beyond the control of sterile heterosexual couples. But the new natural lawyers allow that the same is true of homosexuality. Then again, gays and lesbians do not have the physical equipment (the "biological complementarity") such that anyone could have children by doing what they can do in bed. They can, Finnis and Grisez repeatedly tell us, only imitate or fantasize *real* procreative acts. Is not exactly the same thing true of sterile couples?

The new natural lawyers want to widen the circle of valuable sexuality beyond the narrowly procreative to bring in sterile and elderly couples. Sexual activity is itself part of the good of marriage, so long as sexual acts are *open to new life*, and subordinate to "marital love";[43] we must not choose against the good of new life, and we must ensure that what predominates in our sexual relations is "loving cooperation in one-flesh communion."[44] The "one-flesh communion" of sterile couples would appear, however, to be more a matter of appearance than reality. So why should these couples be included while we exclude committed, stable, monogamous gay couples—who, no more than the sterile, choose against the good of new life and who, as much as sterile heterosexual couples, can subordinate sexual passion to love, friendship, and other "marital" goods?

This double standard gives rise to several puzzles. It is hard to know in what sense sterile heterosexual couples (who know themselves to be so) can engage in sexual acts that are "open to procreation," given that procreation is and is known to be just as impossible for gay and lesbian couples. One would think that the crucial distinction between valuable and valueless sex in a sterile marriage is the partners' openness to goods that they *can share*, not to goods that they *cannot share*. From within the natural law framework itself, it

39. As John Hart Ely observes, the doctrine of "suspect classifications" means that special scrutiny should apply to those laws "that disadvantage groups we know to be the object of widespread vilification, groups we know others (specifically those who control the legislative process) might wish to injure." JOHN HART ELY, DEMOCRACY AND DISTRUST: A THEORY OF JUDICIAL REVIEW 153 (1980); *see also* Yick Wo v. Hopkins, 118 U.S. 356 (1886).
40. GRISEZ, *supra* note 13, at 573.
41. I have benefitted greatly in this section from conversations with Andrew Koppelman, and from access to early versions of Koppelman, *supra* note 44.
42. This question might be posed to Mansfield as well.
43. GRISEZ, *supra* note 13, at 636.
44. *Id.* at 637–38.

would seem sensible to focus on the importance for sterile partners of subordinating their passionate impulses to love, affection, mutual devotion, a self-giving desire to please the other, and so on.

Once we focus on the importance of integrating sexual activity into a larger pattern of *attainable* goods, sterile married couples and devoted, loving, committed homosexual partners seem to fall into the same camp. This is one way in which the apparent double standard might be dissolved. Procreation is equally unattainable by sterile and same-sex couples; other goods (mutuality, love, and the like) are attainable by both. Looked at in this way, the natural lawyers' own framework argues for equal treatment for sterile heterosexuals and homosexuals.

We could interpret Finnis's criterion of "openness to procreation" more figuratively, but this also argues for the moral similarity of homosexual and sterile heterosexual couples. We might say that gays and lesbians can have sex in a way that *is* "open to procreation" (albeit *figuratively*) and to new life. They can be, and many are, prepared to engage in the kinds of loving relations that would result in procreation—were conditions different. Like sterile married couples, many would like nothing better. All we can say is that conditions would have to be more radically different in the case of gay and lesbian couples than sterile married couples for new life to result from sex, but what is the moral force of that argument?

Finnis ridicules this argument (which I have made previously elsewhere[45]). "Here," he says, "fantasy has taken leave of reality. Anal or oral intercourse, whether between spouses or males, is no more a biological union 'open to procreation' than is intercourse with a goat by a shepherd who fantasizes about breeding a faun."[46] Finnis insists once again on the importance of "biological union" and "openness to procreation." But the sterile heterosexual couple's "openness to procreation" is as much a fantasy as that of Finnis's kinky shepherd. Sterile heterosexuals have as great a chance of breeding a child as the shepherd and his goat do a faun. The shepherd and goat analogy is poor in any case, for they cannot share the goods

of intelligent friendship, commitment and affection, mutual help and comfort—*among moral equals*—all of which can be shared by sterile heterosexual *and* homosexual couples (once again making these cases appear similar to each other, and radically different from bestiality). The focus on procreation appears opportunistic: selected so as to allow sterile heterosexuals into the tent while keeping all homosexuals out.

Still, Finnis and Grisez seek to avoid this conclusion. Finnis insists that the sexual acts of sterile heterosexuals can actualize their "two-in-one-flesh common good" because they can, unlike homosexuals, be united biologically: fertile or sterile, heterosexual couples have the equipment that allows them to engage in the behavior which, as behavior, is "suitable for generation."[47]

Is sterile heterosexual intercourse "as behavior" suitable for generation? As Koppelman suggests, pointing a gun at someone and pulling the trigger is in general behavior suitable for murder, but not when the gun is unloaded.[48] Nor when the gun shoots water or is made of licorice.

The National Rifle Association might have said, "Guns don't kill people, bullets kill people." Likewise, penises and vaginas do not unite biologically, sperm and eggs do (at least under the right conditions). For Finnis, however, the crucial thing is penises and vaginas, functional or not.

This gives rise to other puzzles. If the presence of nonworking equipment of the "right" sort is a crucial distinguishing feature of permissible sexual relationships, artifice might supply what nature has not. One gay male might have a partial sex-change operation, having his penis removed and a vagina installed. Does this allow a gay couple to re-create the appearance of biological complementarity closely enough to have valuable sex? Or suppose a gay male couple simply eschews oral sex, anal sex, and mutual masturbation in favor of intercrural sex (inserting the penis between the thighs of the partner). Would this *resemble* heterosexual intercourse closely enough to have "procreative significance?"[49]

45. Stephen Macedo, *The New Natural Lawyers*, HARV. CRIMSON, Oct. 28, 1993, at 2.

46. Finnis, *Sexual Orientation, supra* note 8, at 18–19.

47. *Id.*

48. This analogy is from Koppelman, *supra* note 44.

49. Finnis insists that valuable sex must have not only the "generosity of acts of friendship" but also "the procreative significance." Finnis, *Sexual Orientation, supra* note 8, at 20.

In the end, it is hard to see why sex between sterile couples has any more "procreative significance" than gay or lesbian sex. These cases are distinguished by appearances only, and matters of great moral significance should not hang on mere appearances.

The new natural law's double standard could be resolved in more ways than one. The proscriptions against homosexuality could be saved by arguing that involuntarily sterile heterosexual couples, including all women past menopause and their spouses, may not have sex. Elderly and otherwise sterile heterosexuals can enjoy mutual helping and friendship, but sex will distract from these goods, as with homosexuals. Public policy should do "whatever it *properly* can" to deter fornication by the elderly and sterile, including denying them the right to marry and prohibiting the promotion or facilitation of sex among the elderly (though not criminalizing sexual acts, so long as they are committed in private).[50]

There is an alternative, *inclusive* path to consistency that we should prefer: broadening the scope of legitimate sexuality to include committed gay couples. The new natural lawyers furnish no grounds for supposing that the goods shared by infertile and elderly couples cannot be shared by gays in committed relationships. The inclusive path would acknowledge all of this, while preserving the reasonable natural law claim that sexual activity should be channelled into committed and loving relationships, whether heterosexual or homosexual.

The New Natural Law's Cramped View of Valuable Sexual Relations

I have already said enough to suggest that the new natural law fails to supply a reasoned public ground for discrimination against homosexuals. And I have not yet touched on an even more basic problem, namely, the new natural law's extremely narrow view of valuable sexual activity as only that which is open to procreation and within a permanent heterosexual marriage. According to the new natural lawyers, homosexual acts, all contracepted heterosexual acts, and all sex outside of marriage "can *do* no more than provide each partner with an individual gratification."[51] Homosexual sex, like heterosexual "fornication," forgoes opportunities to participate in real goods and undermines the goods that homosexual friends can share. Goodwill and affection can be expressed far more effectively by conversation, mutually beneficial help in work, and shared domestic tasks.

The new natural law seems to exaggerate greatly the subjective, self-centered character of all nonprocreative sexuality. The reductionism here is striking: "whatever the generous hopes and dreams" of "some same-sex partners" (and many heterosexuals), their sexual acts

> cannot express or do more than is expressed or done if two strangers engage in such activity to give each other pleasure, or a prostitute pleasures a client to give him pleasure in return for money, or (say) a man masturbates to give himself a fantasy of more human relationships after a gruelling day on the assembly line.[52]

Homosexual sex, *or* contracepted sex in marriage, *at best* embody no more than anonymous bathhouse sex, a quick trip to a prostitute, or masturbation.

Is it plausible that there are *no* distinctions to be drawn here? My guess is that most committed, loving couples—whether gay or straight—are sensitive to the difference between loving sexual acts expressing a shared intimacy and mere mutual masturbation. Finnis and Grisez may not be all wrong: promiscuous, "anonymous," casual sex very likely tends toward the valueless character he describes. Even sexual acts within marriage may tend to become "masturbatory" if the aim is merely to heighten and intensify one's own erotic pleasure, with no thought given to mutuality, romantic self-giving, or the proper subordination of lust to love. Having said all this, and having agreed with Finnis and Grisez that a healthy sexual life requires a measure of self-control that may

---

50. This path to consistency is not without precedent. Fustel de Coulanges notes that in some ancient cities it may have been obligatory for a man to divorce a wife who proved to be sterile. *See* FUSTEL DE COULANGES. THE ANCIENT CITY 65 (1980). Philo of Alexandria condemned sex with an infertile partner, likening it to copulation with a pig. JOHN BOSWELL, CHRISTIANITY, SOCIAL TOLERANCE, AND HOMOSEXUALITY 148 (1980). Once again, I am here indebted to Andrew Sabl and Andrew Koppelman.

51. Finnis, *Sexual Orientation, supra* note 8, at 1066.
52. *Id.* at 1067.

be hard to achieve for many people—especially in a culture such as ours that is heavily charged with sexuality—it seems, nevertheless, strikingly simplistic and implausible to portray the essential nature of *every form* of nonprocreative sexuality as no better than the *least valuable* form.

Many will find deeply unreasonable, as well, the judgment that pleasure is not in and of itself a good. Consider the analogy between sex and eating. We eat and have sex not only to sustain and reproduce human life, but also for their intrinsic pleasure. Eating is especially pleasurable when shared with others (most think that the same is true of sex): social dining cements friendships, expresses affection, and so on. But suppose eating and nourishment are severed? Is eating for the sake of mere pleasure unnatural or irrational? Is it permissible to chew sugarless gum, which gives pleasure but has no nutritional value, as Andrew Koppelman asks, or is doing so the gastronomic equivalent of masturbation (assuming that we are not doing it to exercise the jaw or clean the teeth)? Is it immoral?[53] Is either sexual or gastronomic pleasure sought and achieved for its own sake immoral, or does the immorality lie in excessive or compulsive pursuit of these pleasures (as seems far more reasonable)?

It also has to be said that certain parts of the natural law's analytic structure are far from clear. The basic good of "self-integration" is obviously crucial, but exactly what this means, and how it is violated, are not clear. It is hardly obvious, for example, that contracepted sexual acts are a direct and significant assault on "the basic good of self-integration," or that masturbation is wrong because it violates "the body's capacity for self-giving."[54]

For the new natural lawyers, the essential nature of sexual acts is known by analytical inquiry, not by consequentialist calculations, or by historical or cultural investigation of actual lives. Sexual activity unconnected with the realization of real goods (as defined by natural law) is objectively valueless. The sexual act is essentially a conjugal act that realizes a tightly knit array of marital goods. Chaste marital communion—open to the transmission of new life—is not only the *highest* expression of our sexuality, as many might be prepared to concede, it is for Finnis and Grisez the *only* legitimate way of expressing our sexuality. All else—from masturbation, to contracepted heterosexual sex, to extramarital sex, to homosexuality—is a set of variations on the same themes: acts of self-disintegrity, using the body as an instrument of pleasure, simulating or fantasizing the conjugal act, and so on. All else is valueless, and not only valueless, but a choice to materially damage the social environment: "masturbation tends to make everyone's body into a sex object and predisposes masturbators to treat their sexual partners as masturbatory tools. . . . [M]asturbation is essentially a social sin against interpersonal communion."[55] And what is true of masturbation is true of contracepted sexual acts and all homosexual acts.

To many, this philosophical approach will seem an odd way to proceed. Many will wonder whether the level of philosophical abstraction and generality employed here is really adequate for drawing all of the distinctions that should be drawn. Sometimes even Finnis does not seem entirely sure. He says, for example, that the "essential features" of "solitary masturbation" are to be found in "casual promiscuous sexual relations, such as heterosexual fornication or adultery *often is* and homosexual activity *usually is*."[56] "Often" and "usually" are very different from "always." "Often" and "usually" suggest a bad tendency that is not inevitable. This is far more plausi-

---

53. Koppelman, *supra* note 44. Or as Sabl suggested to me, suppose a person lost his capacity to digest but not the capacity to eat, so that nutrition had to be delivered intravenously. Would it then be immoral to eat for the sake of mere pleasure, or perhaps for the sake of pleasure as well as the comraderie of dining companions? Would it be incumbent on one in such a state to eat only a healthy, balanced diet, or would it be permissible to binge on chocolate to one's heart's content? Would it be necessary (in Sabl's words) "to go on eating beets and tofu because this would be the kind of eating which, 'as eating,' is suitable for a human being" though useless to the digestively impaired individual? Sabl rightly suggests that this "would not make rational sense (though it might provide psychological solace)." Private communication from Andrew Sabl, June 13, 1994 (on file with author).

The new natural law's teleological ethics assert the universal validity of ends that are *in general* good for the species, even when those ends make no sense as applied to particular individuals. Why should we be required to generalize—or overgeneralize—our ethical judgments in this way? I suggest an explanation for this apparent mistake in Part V of this article.

54. GRISEZ, *supra* note 13, at 650–51.

55. *Id.* at 664.

56. Finnis, *Personal Integrity, supra* note 53, at 47 (emphasis added).

ble than the main line of argument, which suggests that the bad forms are found "always" and inevitably.

The valueless quality of homosexual acts is established analytically for the new natural law, but Finnis also invokes the sorts of unsupported empirical generalizations about homosexual relationships found in Jaffa's work. He refers off-handedly to "the modern 'gay' ideology," which treats "sexual capacities, organs, and acts as instruments to be put to whatever suits the purposes of the individual 'selves' who have them."[57] Millions of homosexual lives are thus presumptively epitomized by a promiscuous, liberationist "gay lifestyle," which rejects all sexual restraints and value judgments.[58] These sweeping generalizations are, however, overgeneralizations. Not all gay people are promiscuous. If gay people are somewhat more likely to be promiscuous than heterosexuals,

many things are likely to contribute to this. Mistakes in judgment about what makes for a good life, the pressures of life in the "closet," mistaken ideology, and other socially contingent factors must be at least partly responsible for the tendency (to the extent that it exists) for homosexual relations to be "often," "usually," or "sometimes" rather casual.[59] But the new natural lawyers know what they know on the basis of abstract philosophical analysis, so none of this matters.

In the end, Finnis relies, in part at least, on the sorts of sweeping stereotypes about actual behavior that are also deployed by other conservatives. He may need these stereotypes to support the new natural law's equally sweeping moral condemnations, which have so little room for complexity or ambiguity.

57. Finnis, *Sexual Orientation, supra* note 8, at 1070. Similarly, the Ramsey Colloquium describes the gay and lesbian movement as of a piece with other "component parts of the sexual revolution," namely, "[p]ermissive abortion, widespread adultery, easy divorce, [and] radical feminism." All of these share "a declared desire for liberation from constraint" as well as "the presupposition that the body is little more than an instrument for the fulfillment of desire." All components of the sexual revolution rest on the view that any "discipline or denial or restraint" with respect to sex is "unhealthy and dehumanizing." *See* Ramsey Colloquium, *Morality and Homosexuality, supra* note 9, at 16, 17.

58. *See generally* Finnis, *Sexual Orientation, supra* note 8.

59. Reliable figures for levels of promiscuity—about which many conservatives pronounce so confidently—are hard to come by. The recent University of Chicago survey of sexual practices—the most extensive ever undertaken in the United States—found that the differences in the mean number of sexual partners between those with exclusively heterosexual relationships and those with at least some same-gender activity "do not appear very large." They also point out that to the extent that differences do exist, they may be misleading, because those who report some same-gender sexual relations also tend to be "younger, more educated, more likely to live in large cities, and generally less religious," and "all these factors are also associated with having more sex partners." EDWARD O. LAUMANN ET AL., THE SOCIAL ORGANIZATION OF SEXUALITY 316 (1994).

UNIVERSALISM, LIBERAL THEORY, AND THE PROBLEM OF GAY MARRIAGE

*Robin West**

Introduction

Liberalism, both contemporary and classical, rests at heart on a theory of human nature, and at the center of that theory lies one core commitment: all human beings, *qua* human beings, are essentially

* Professor of Law, Georgetown University Law Center. This essay is the published version of the 1997 Mason Ladd Lecture delivered at the Florida State University College of Law.

rational. There are two equally important implications. The first we might call the "universalist" assumption: *all* human beings, not just some, are rational—not just white people, men, freemen, property owners, aristocrats, or citizens, but all of us. In this central, defining respect, then, we are all the same: we all share in this universal, natural, human trait. The second implication, we might call the "individualist" assumption: because each one of us is rational, each one of us is not only competent to, but best-equipped to formulate and act on his or her own individually held conception of the good life. We are each capable of deciding for ourselves what to think, believe, and do within the sphere of self-regarding behavior. We all share in this capacity equally. Whatever may be our otherwise terribly and radically unequal endowments, we share equally the capacity to decide for ourselves what is our own best conception of our individual self, future, and interests.[1]

Over the last fifty years of American constitutional law, this liberal conception of our nature has provided the foundation for a distinctly liberal legalist understanding of two of our most central constitutional rights—equal protection and due process. First, at least since *Brown v. Board of Education*[2] the universalist interpretation of human nature has grounded a particular conception of the equality guaranteed by the Fourteenth Amendment. Liberalism holds that we are all in some essential way the same. Accordingly, equality law in the post-*Brown* era holds that we must be treated the same, unless a case can be made for the rationality of various distinctions between us. In this sense, equality law and the rights it entails are all about what follows from our universality. Second, the rationalist conception of human nature, over roughly the same time period, has been at the heart of a particular interpretation of the liberty guaranteed by the Fourteenth Amendment: we are all rational and equally capable of ascertaining what for us would be a good life. At least since *Griswold v. Connecticut*,[3] the liberty we are promised gives us the right to do precisely that, unimpeded by the state. Liberty law in a post-*Griswold* liberal legal conception is, in this sense, the bundle of rights that are entailed by our universally shared but radically differentiating rationality.[4] In the last forty years or so, the constitutional law govern-

ing our liberty has been about the scope of our negative liberty to be and do what we want. More bluntly, it is about what has come to be called "the right to be left alone."

There can be no doubt that this liberal understanding of our nature, and the wide range and bewildering variety of interpretations of constitutional rights and norms that it undergirds, have prompted moments of very real moral progress over the course of the second half of this century. Surely it is fair to say that the acknowledgment of our universality lying at the heart of so much of Fourteenth Amendment jurisprudence over the last forty years has not only prompted the creation of a more equal and free society, but has also enabled us to at least glimpse the expansive and inclusive community that is equality's natural complement. The Court's overruling of *Plessey v. Ferguson*[5] in *Brown*, the various sex equality cases from the 1970s,[6] and the current Court's recent decision in *Romer v. Euans*[7] all rest at the heart of the profoundly liberal and universalist claim that what we share is what makes us human. It is by virtue of our commonality that the state must accord all of us, without regard to race, sex, or sexuality, equal protection of the law and the dignity and respect that it entails. The common message of these great liberal cases is that it is, at root, our commonality—our shared, universal nature—that implies that laws segregating some of us from others, or denying some but not others civic duties and responsibilities, or denying some but not others access to the levers of political change, are unconstitutional. These decisions have given us not only a more just legal order, but a larger and more moral community as well.

Likewise, in decisions over roughly the same time period, the thoroughly liberal acknowledgment of our individual capacity for rationality has inspired dramatic expansions of our liberty. First, the Court's early insistence on the parent's right to educate his child as he sees fit,[8] and then its insistence in *Griswold, Eisenstadt v. Baird*,[9] *Roe v.*

---

1. *See* RONALD DWORKIN, *Liberalism and Justice, in* A MATTER OF PRINCIPLE 179, 188–204 (1985); ISAIAH BERLIN, *Two Concepts of Liberty, in* FOUR ESSAYS ON LIBERTY 118, 131–34 (1970). These may be the best modern statements of the universalist and individualist assumptions at the heart of contemporary liberalism.
2. 347 U.S. 483 (1954).
3. 381 U.S. 479 (1965).
4. *See* RONALD DWORKIN, *The Moral Reading and the Majoritarian Premise, in* FREEDOM'S LAW: THE MORAL READING OF THE AMERICAN CONSTITUTION 1, 21–26 (1996).

5. 163 U.S. 537 (1896).
6. *See* Craig v. Boren, 429 U.S. 190 (1976); Frontiero v. Richardson, 411 U.S. 677 (1973); Reed v. Reed, 404 U.S. 71 (1971).
7. 517 U.S. 620 (1996).
8. *See* Meyer v. Nebraska, 262 U.S. 390 (1923).
9. 405 U.S. 438 (1972).

Wade,[10] and *Planned Parenthood v. Casey*[11] on the individual's right to decide for oneself how, whether, and when to parent all rest at heart on the quintessential liberal and rationalist claim that we are each capable of and must be free to formulate our own fallible responses to life's deepest mysteries, and must therefore be free of the state's meddling desire to do it for us. Because of these constitutional developments over the last fifty years, we, as a culture, are more aware than our ancestors were of our shared universal nature and of the demands that universality places upon the state, the community, and the law. Because of these developments, we, as a culture, are more free than they were to decide individually how to live our intimate and private lives, and on which predicated set of beliefs. We are also more free than our ancestors were to make these decisions rationally and by our own lights and chosen goals rather than acquiesce in the presumed imperatives of state, community, tradition, nature, or fate.

There can also be no doubt, however, that these revolutionary, expansive, and liberal changes in our self-understanding have left serious difficulties in their wake, as scores of critics of liberalism and of legal liberalism, in particular, have made clear over the last thirty years or so. I will focus on what strikes me as the two most intractable problems. First, pointed challenges to the liberal legalists' commitment to universalism have come from a range of identity theorists, activists, and indeed, entire peoples. The question, or challenge, posed to liberalism by this eclectic collection of critics is essentially this: is it really true, as the liberal seems to believe as an article of faith, that the flame of inclusion in a hegemonic community, defined by universally shared human traits, is worth the lost candle of identity or distinctiveness a particular subcommunity or culture may be asked to sacrifice?[12] Does the African American community

sacrifice too much when in the name of liberalism it integrates its strongest members out of the black community and into the enclaves of privilege, all so as to honor a shared universal nature that transcends race? Does liberal feminism hold, as its many detractors claim, to a false and patriarchal ideal, betraying women, if it aims to do nothing more than increase the number of "women in suits."What will happen to gay and lesbian culture, to say nothing of queer theory, when it is no longer queer to be queer? Should we, or when should we, forego the securities, strengths, and challenges of our distinctive identities for the allure of the community's universalistic embrace? If what distinguishes us is oftentimes as dear and precious as what we share, then the justice of liberalism's admonition to forego particularity for the sake of our universality is not so clear. If there are costs involved in accepting the liberal's promise of universality—costs to our sacrificed distinguishing identities—we need to assess what those costs are. We cannot assume them away by blindly holding onto the preemptive moral importance of our shared human traits as an article of faith.

Equally poignant challenges to the individualist side of liberalism, and hence the libertarian thrust of our constitutional law of liberty and substantive due process, have come from communitarians, relational feminists, and various Marxist scholars. The common question posed, in many different ways, by this group of critics who otherwise have little or nothing in common is something like the following: is the flame of individual freedom (to stick with my original metaphor) worth the candle of community, of connection, of relation, of the ethic of care, and of the responsibilities and duties to others it implies, that may

10. 410 U.S. 113 (1973).
11. 505 U.S. 833 (1992).
12. *See generally* DERRICK BELL, AND WE ARE NOT SAVED: THE ELUSIVE QUEST FOR RACIAL JUSTICE (1987) (exploring through allegory why racial inequality has yet to be achieved in the United States); Angela P. Harris, *Race and Essentialism in Feminist Legal Theory*, 42 STAN. L. REV. 581 (1990) (critiquing feminist legal theorists who posit a universal women's experience because it works to subvert and erase the experience of women of different races, classes, and sexual orienta-

tion); Mari J. Matsuda, *Voices of America: Accent, Antidiscrimination Law and Jurisprudence for the Last Reconstruction*, 100 YALE L.J. 1329 (1991) (arguing that linguistic tolerance should be a goal of the law and offering a reinterpretation of Title VII to address the subordination of linguistic difference); Mari J. Matsuda, *Looking to the Bottom: Critical Legal Studies and Reparations*, 22 HARV. C.R.-C.L. L. REV. 323 (1987) (stating that Critical Legal Studies should look to the experience of non-whites in reconstructing legal concepts and strategies); Robin West, *Jurisprudence and Gender*, 55 U. CHI. L. REV. 1 (1988) (arguing that conceptions of "human nature" in modern jurisprudence are untrue of women's lives).

have to be sacrificed to insure it?[13] To put it in selfish terms, does my "right to be left alone" come at too high of a cost to my need not to be? We have a right to be left alone, but needs that can only be met interdependently. For example, we have rights to birth control and early trimester abortions, but grossly unmet needs for quality, publicly funded childcare. Has the right to the former, perhaps, made it more rather than less difficult to meet the need for the latter? Similarly, we have a right, perhaps, to die—or at least prominent liberal legal theorists are now arguing as much—but what we desperately need is quality, publicly funded health care. Might the gain of the right to die make more, rather than less, difficult the campaign to meet the need for the latter? No doubt, we have a right to educate our children in our own home, in private schools, in any language we please, with our own money, and by our own lights away from the prying eye of the state, but what our children need is a decent and civic education. When put more altruistically, the communitarian's complaint is, if anything, even more pressing: does my right to be left alone come at too high of a cost to my civic responsibilities to others? Does my right to ignore the panhandler on the street—to avert my eyes, keep my wallet in my pocket, and preserve my private space—come at too high of a sacrifice to my responsibility and my civic duties to help others in need? We have a right to be left alone, but both a need for and an obligation to engage in civic, public, deliberative life. If our rights of self-deliberation, self-creation, and self-control, all justified and grounded in our presumed rationality, come to threaten our needs for others and our responsibilities and duties toward them, then we need to assess whether the gain is worth the cost. We cannot assume that the question answers itself, or that the context within which any particular trade-off arises might not make a difference.

The alternatives to liberalism, however, are not particularly palatable. Identity theorists and their legions of followers need to critically rethink the politics, policies, ethics, and societies that follow

13. See Michael J. Sandel, Democracy's Discontent: America in Search of a Public Philosophy (1996); Pluralism, Justice, and Equality (David Miller & Michael Walzer eds., 1995); Milton C. Regan, Jr., Family Law and the Pursuit of Intimacy (1993).

from a denial of universalism. To reverse the questions posed above: do we really want, in the name of the integrity of identity, a confederation of separatist communities with ethnic houses for every ethnicity, not only on college campuses but in the larger society as well, with the culture balkanized and the state bosnianized, with our differences both emphasized and infinitely subdivided?

Communitarians also need to tread carefully. What politics will, in practice, follow from a denial of the radical rationalist individualism so squarely at the heart of not only modern liberal theory but of contemporary American life? Do we want a return to the constrained choices of the past in our intimate lives, where young girls face mandatory heterosexuality, back-alley abortions, shotgun weddings, and loveless marriages, where divorce is hard to come by, and child raising—an ennobling profession for some, but a life of drudgery for others—is mandated by fate for all? Likewise, as much as we may legitimately worry about the tethering of our bonds of civic engagement, do we really want to embrace a world in which such engagement displaces independent thought? As much as we may legitimately worry, for example, that the independent schools movement siphons the best students and parents from public schools, and weakens considerably the bonds of democracy and community, do we really want them abolished? Can we even envision, much less endorse, the monotonous, hegemonic conformity that might very well follow on the heels of a serious attack on liberal individualism?

For me, these questions are rhetorical. The answer to all is no. The motivating impulses of both the identity theorists' and the communitarians' critiques of liberalism are understandable, but the political implications of a full-scale rejection of fundamental liberal norms are unacceptable in the end. This Essay will explore the possibility of a mid-way correction, rather than rejection, of liberalism, so as to meet at least some of the objections posed by identity theorists and communitarians respectively. We need to reconstruct liberalism in order to take into account the meaning and weight of these objections without losing the thread of its motivating impulse.

Generally, I propose that liberalism fails to take seriously the differences between groups of people, as identity theorists claim, and the interconnections and interdependencies of all of us, as communitarians insist, and that the failure to do so has had a profound and negative effect on our constitutional law and rhetoric. I suggest it has significantly undermined the classic liberal arguments for many of our most vulnerable and controversial contemporary liberal rights and entitlements. Nevertheless, it would be wrong to jettison either the universalist or individualist aspirations of liberalism, or the liberal legal defenses of the vital and embattled rights that tenuously follow from those assumptions. Rather, in theory, a friendly amendment to liberalism's core convictions is needed. While we share a universal nature, some traits differentiate some of us from the rest of us. While we are in some aspects of our lives individuals first and foremost, we are also interconnected in comparably profound ways to and with others. In liberal constitutional practice and doctrine, we need to recognize that the animating core commitments of liberalism provide, at most, a necessary but insufficient condition for many of the rights that have proven to be most vulnerable today. Where a group seeking a right is different in some way—for example, differently vulnerable to the harms that flow from sexual assault, or differently committed to child-raising, or differently vulnerable to hate speech—what is needed is a showing that the harms occasioned by sexual assault and hate speech are real and demand a response, or that child-raising is a vital human activity and demands greater communal support. Similarly, where an individual right of self-governance impacts social, intimate, or structural connections between persons, as they almost invariably do, we need to show that the interaction is for the good: that abortion rights strengthen the community and the family despite the severance of the connection between mother and fetus; or that birth control, abortion rights, or same-sex marriages would constitute an improvement in, not a threat to, the bonds of tradition tying our modern institution of family to our history and our larger society. I am certain a commitment to liberalism, universalism, and individualism is necessary to provide a floor for these arguments; without such a commitment, there is just no reason for these arguments to be heard, much less honored or heeded. However, a liberal commitment to universality or individualism provides only the floor because it is not sufficient to make the case for virtually any of our modern rights. In addition, an insistence on these commitments, if it blinds us to the differences and interconnections that also define us, will ultimately frustrate rather than further our attempts to articulate such a case.

In the last section of this Essay, I will attempt to apply my friendly amendment to liberal legalism to the current debates swirling around the problem and promise of same-sex marriage. I will argue, in brief, that the more or less standard liberal arguments for gay marriage are flawed in the ways described above. They relentlessly deny morally salient differences between gay and straight sexuality and same-sex and opposite-sex marriage, and they relentlessly deny the essentially communitarian, rather than individualistic, nature of the institution of marriage itself. In so doing, they not only threaten to win the battle but lose the war by securing an entitlement to gay marriage with an argument that carries a potential for very real backfiring, but they also incur a substantial opportunity cost. The best case for same-sex marriage is one that underscores not only the universality of gay and straight culture, but also the salient differences between them and the interdependencies, rather than the independency, of human individuals. By insisting upon those differences and their moral significance we may not only better secure the human rights of this substantial subcommunity among us, but we may immeasurably strengthen the institution of marriage, which despite its many and heralded flaws, continues to enrich the lives of many of us. . . .

Same-Sex Marriage: Problems and Promise

Let me quickly apply these observations to the promise and potential pitfalls of liberal defenses of same-sex marriage, or liberal legal attacks on laws prohibiting the same. I do not mean to suggest a uniformity within either the gay and lesbian community or their advocates where there is none. There is tremendous internal division over the merits of marriage as an institution, the desirability of entering into it, the efficacy of asserting a right to do so at this point in our history, and the meaning of it all—to say nothing of the strengths and weaknesses of particular constitutional or legal arguments asserting the right itself. Nevertheless, at least a liberal legal consensus of sorts is emerging, and it is one that, I suspect, will carry all of the problems of liberal legalism I have tried to identify here, and then some.

The argument is straightforward. Same-sex and opposite sex marriages are in all legally relevant ways identical. They would serve comparable needs for intimacy and stability, and they would entail comparable rights, duties, and liabilities in the various areas of law that impact family life. The only difference between them lies in the sex of the spouse, but this difference is simply immaterial—in all important or essential respects that matter, the union is of the same sort. Gay men and lesbians, in Andrew Sullivan's liberal formulation of the point, are "virtually normal" in all ways relevant to law.[14]

From this claim of sameness follows a straightforward equal protection claim. The state's denial of a marriage license to two women seeking to marry is impermissible discrimination. There is simply no difference, on this account, as the Hawaii Supreme Court has held, between a woman's decision to marry a man—fully protected as a fundamental right—and a woman's decision to marry a woman.[15] The only difference, again, is in the sex of the intended spouse, and that is a difference of no consequence. To differentiate between them—protecting the former and disallowing the latter—is therefore impermissible because it is based on irrational discrimination.[16]

The liberty argument, although not yet elaborated in case law, is not hard to imagine. The right of the individual to marry within his sex is covered by the same right of privacy that protects the

individual's right to marry outside his race, to take birth control, or to procure an abortion. It goes to the heart of our right to make fundamental decisions regarding our individual lives. It is quintessentially self-regarding behavior, a clear-cut example of conduct that is simply no one's business but one's own. Expanding the freedom to marry implicates essentially no negative externalities and would constitute a dramatic expansion of individual liberty. Accordingly, it is a paradigmatic freedom that ought to be, and hence is, protected by the Fourteenth Amendment.

Let me first address the assumption of sameness and the denial of difference at the heart of the equal protection argument. I will skip over, or leave to your imagination, the ways in which the assertion of bland sameness may backfire, and focus instead on the opportunity costs inherent in the denial of differences between opposite and same-sex marriage. My claim, briefly, is that there are at least two such differences that, if recognized, could ground an argument for gay marriage that could transform the cultur, in a badly needed and profoundly liberal direction!

The first difference is that same-sex marriage, unlike traditional marriage, has never been predicated on the presumed desirability of subordinating the female sex. There is no record in the history of same-sex marriage of a "marital rape exemption" according to which one of the partners is entitled to sex on demand, regardless of the consent or desire of the other. There is no expectation on the part of those contemplating same-sex marriage, as there still is with vast numbers of individuals contemplating traditional marriage, that one partner is privileged to demand sex and the other obligated to provide it. There is no cultural construct, in other words, of marital roles, obligations, and identities constituted by an axis of subordination, in turn constituted by legally privileged sexual violence. This is a difference that matters, and it matters a lot.

The difference is important because it carries the promised potential to transform the very institution of marriage itself into a truly liberal and even egalitarian institution. Should same-sex marriage ever become a reality in this culture, it would "normalize" the ideal of a for-life union between sexual equals. It would allow us an opportunity to glimpse the possibility of marital

14. See Andrew Sullivan, Virtually Normal: An Argument About Homosexuality 178–85 (1995).

15. See Baehr v. Lewin, 852 P.2d 44, 67 (Haw. 1993) (holding a Hawaii statute that restricted marriage to male and female partners to be subject to strict scrutiny analysis and unconstitutional on its face); Baehr v. Miike, No. CIV.91-1394, 1996 WL 694235, at *18 (Haw. Cir. Ct. Dec. 3, 1996) (finding no compelling state interest supports the Hawaii ban on same-sex marriage), aff'd, 950 P.2d 1234 (Haw. 1997).

16. See Lewin, 852 P.2d at 67; William N. Eskridge, Jr., A History of Same-Sex Marriage, 79 Va. L. Rev. 1419, 1425 (1993).

life freed of the illiberal, nonegalitarian, and unfree heritage of the institution's deeply patriarchal past. For liberalism to deny that opportunity in the name of formal equality is more than just perverse, although it is surely that. It is also self-defeating. In this instance, denial of difference is a denial, not an affirmation, of liberalism's deepest egalitarian and libertarian impulses.

The second difference between traditional and same-sex marriage is the difference emphasized by conservatives, and particularly by the natural lawyer, John Finnis: same-sex marriage, unlike traditional marriage, would legitimate and sanctify non-reproductive sex acts instead of reproductive sex acts. For Finnis, this difference is fatal because such non-reproductive sex acts are paradigmatically immoral.[17]

Liberals, and most persuasively, Stephen Macedo, have responded true to form by denying the difference. Macedo argues that the differences between the non-reproductive sex acts of a same-sex couple and the non-reproductive sex acts of a sterile, post-menopausal, or heterosexual couple using birth control are surely insignificant.[18] Macedo's point is obviously well-taken. However, here again, we should at least hesitate before insisting so strenuously on sameness in the face of this apparent difference. There may be a relevant difference between a marriage that sanctifies paradigmatically non-reproductive sexual acts and paradigmatically reproductive ones. Further, it may even be a difference that matters morally, but cuts the opposite way of that suggested by Finnis. Reproductive sex acts model a form of physically caring for the other in a marriage that either carries the potential for, or at least symbolizes in the conservative imagination, biological reproduction—an event that, when it occurs, demands considerable altruism, at least on the part of the mother. But it is also an event that, at least as sociobiologists never tire of reminding us, is through and through selfish on a genetic and evolutionary scale.

The care we bestow on family members genetically linked to us carries the same paradox-

ical quality. We might want to consider the possibility that the non-reproductive sex act sanctified by a legal, religious, and socially recognized same-sex marriage between two individuals committed to the care of each other and no less committed than their heterosexual counterparts to the possibility of raising children, presents a model of caring that, precisely because it does not embed the giving of physical care in a genetic replication, is less constrained by egoism. It is often observed—and quite rightly—that our capacity for care ebbs and flows depending on the strength or weakness of the genetic link between the subject and object of caregiving. The creation of a social institution defined by love-making not aimed toward genetic replication, but nevertheless aimed toward care, might at least expand our imaginative understanding of the limits and promise of the affective source of this communal, connective ethic.

I will be much more brief regarding liberty. There is just no good reason, and much to be lost, by denying the communitarian and communal nature of marriage, and hence of gay marriage. It is also unnecessary. There is nothing in the liberal regard for individual autonomy that commits liberalism to the false claim that marriage is an individualistic institution designed to enhance the autonomy of consenting adults by permitting them to contract with each other for sex, affection, and mutual support. Marriage just is, through and through, anti-individualistic. That is precisely its moral strength, and to no small measure the source of its immense appeal.

Advocates of gay marriage in particular, outside of a dubious loyalty to liberalism, have no reason to deny this. First, gay unions have the potential to be significantly better as communities than their heterosexual counterparts. They may be just as violent, oppressive, suffocating, boring, tedious, or dreary, but they simply are not as vulnerable to the disabling and destructive possibilities of rape, legal and otherwise.[19] Second, they share with heterosexual unions the redemptive potential to transform the individual into a person whose self-regarding preferences and desires are defined communally, and that is a morally desirable, not undesirable, transformation of self-regard and identity. Third, the impact of these

17. *See* John Finnis, *Is Natural Law Theory Compatible With Limited Government, in* NATURAL LAW, LIBERALISM, AND MORALITY: CONTEMPORARY ESSAYS 1, 15 (Robert P. George ed., 1996).

18. *See* Stephen Macedo, *Homosexuality and the Conservative Mind,* 84 GEO. L.J. 261, 287–88 (1995).

19. *See* SUSAN ESTRICH, REAL RAPE (1987).

marriages on the larger culture would surely be for the good. Aside from the obvious benefits to gay and lesbian citizens themselves, the availability and legality of gay marriage would strengthen heterosexual marriages as well, leaving them more voluntary, less compulsory, more egalitarian, and for all of these reasons considerably more liberal.

Conclusion

Let me conclude by noting that the liberal denial of difference and connection, in the area of gay marriage, and in the name of equality and liberty respectively, leaves in its wake one additional opportunity cost of a somewhat peculiar theoretical nature. In this culture and at this time, we desperately need a reinvigorated and open dialogue regarding the point of marriage, of married life, and of marital sex. If feminism continues to influence culture in the next century—as it has in the one now ending—then the point of that institution will no longer be, as it was for so much of the last millennium, to order social relations and life through subordinating the female sex. If liberalism holds its ground, nor will its point be the conception and rearing of children—so long as there are individuals who badly want to marry but have no desire or ability to parent. But nor can the point of marriage be what large numbers of liberals and libertarians are now arguing: that marriage is a contract, no different in essence from any other, designed to efficiently coordinate

complementary preferences and to maximize wealth and efficiency for all. Marriage cannot be merely a contract for the straightforward reason that if it becomes that it will wither away.

This leaves a void. What is the point of marriage? One possible answer, I think, is raised by the possibility and promise of gay marriage. It is also an old argument, dating at least from Kierkegaard. The point of marriage, in theory as well as in our private lives, may be to provide a structure within which we learn to define and continually redefine ourselves as caring rather than egoistic beings—as connected to rather than alienated from the concerns and well-being of others.[20] If so, then the central point of marriage would indeed be shared by gay and straight marriage alike. It is a shared trait, however, and a common essence that only comes into focus, and can only come into focus, when the transformative difference gay marriage might make in the institution itself is highlighted, not obscured. It is by highlighting difference, in other words, that we might discard the institution's ignoble but ultimately inessential heterosexual and misogynist past. By blurring or denying those differences, the liberal advocate, perversely, obscures the very universality among us that, entirely to his credit, he relentlessly seeks to foster.

20. See Peter Singer, How Are We to Live: Ethics in an Age of Self Interest 143 (1995); Peter Singer, The Expanding Circle: Ethics and Sociobiology 33 (1981).

CREDITS

Anderson, Elizabeth S., "Is Women's Labor a Commodity?" *Philosophy and Public Affairs*, (19): 71-92. Copyright © Winter 1990. Reproduced with the permission of the author and Blackwell Publishing.

Bernstein, Richard, "Racial Discrimination or Righting Past Wrongs," *The New York Times*: B8. Copyright © July 13, 1994. Reproduced with the permission of The New York Times.

Brus, Michael, "Proxy War: Liberals denounce racial profiling; Conservatives denounce affirmative action: What's the difference?" *MSN Slate Magazine*, Copyright © July 9, 1999, published by Microsoft Network. Reproduced with the permission of Michael Brus.

Calabresi, Guido, and Bobbit, Philip, "The Tragic Dilemma," from *Tragic Choices*, pp. 158-165. Copyright © 1978 by the Fels Center of Government. Used by permission of W.W. Norton & Co., Inc.

Dworkin, Ronald, "Bakke's Case: Are Quotas Unfair?," reprinted by permission of the publisher from *A Matter of Principle* by Ronald Dworkin, pp. 293-303, Cambridge, Mass.: Harvard University Press, Copyright © 1985 by Ronald Dworkin. Originally published in *The New York Review of Books*, November 10, 1977.

Finnis, John M., "Law, Morality, and 'Sexual Orientation,'" *Notre Dame Law Review*, 69 (5): 1049, 1062-1076. Copyright © 1994. Reproduced with the permission of *Notre Dame Law Review*.

Friedman, Milton and Rose, "Created Equal," *Free to Choose, A Personal Statement*, pp. 128-149. Copyright © 1980. Reproduced with the permission of Harcourt Brace & Company and the Random House Group, Ltd.

Hayek, Friedrich A., "Equality, Value, and Merit," *The Constitution of Liberty*, pp. 85-102. Copyright © 1960. Reproduced with the permission of the University of Chicago Press and Taylor & Francis, LLC.

Kant, Immanuel, *The Groundwork for the Metaphysic of Morals*, 189-262. Edited by Thomas E. Hill, Jr. and Arthur Zweig. Copyright © 2002. Reprinted with the permission of Oxford University Press.

——, "On a Supposed Right to Lie Because of Philanthropic Concerns," from *Grounding for the Metaphysics of Morals*, translated by James W. Ellington, pp. 63-66, (Indianapolis: Hackett Publishing Company, Inc., 1993). Third edition with new material copyright © 1993 by Hackett Publishing Company, Inc. Reprinted by permission of Hackett Publishing Company, Inc. All rights reserved.

Kite, Tom, "Keep the PGA on Foot," *The New York Times*, (Sec. A, col.1 Editorial Desk): 23. Copyright © Februrary 2, 1998. Reproduced with permission of *The New York Times*.

Kinsley, Michael, "Abolish Marriage: Let's Really Get the Government Out of Our Bedrooms," *Washington Post*, pp. A23. Copyright © July 3, 2003. Reprinted with permission of Michael Kinsley.

Macedo, Stephen, "Homosexuality and the Conservative Mind," *The Georgetown Law Journal*, (84, No. 2, December 1995): 261-265; 272-284. Copyright © 1995 published by Georgetown Law Journal Association. Reproduced with the permission of Stephen Macedo.

MacIntyre, Alasdair, "The Virtues, the Unity of a Human Life and the Concept of a Tradition," *After Virtue*, pp. 190-209. Copyright © 1981. Reproduced with the permission of the University of Notre Dame Press.

McPherson, James M., "Fire in the Rear," from *Battle Cry of Freedom: The Civil War Era*, pp. 600-611. Copyright © 1988. Reproduced with the permission of Oxford University Press.

Morley, Jefferson, "Double Reverse Discrimination," *New Republic*: 14-18. Copyright © July 9, 1984. Reproduced with the permission of Jefferson Morley.

Nozick, Robert, "Distributive Justice," *Anarchy, State, and Utopia*, pp. 149-164; 167-178; 213-231. Copyright © 1974. Reproduced with the permission of Basic Books, Inc.

Pressley, Sue Anne, "A 'Safety Blitz; Texas Cheerleader Loses Status After Others' Parents Complain," *Washington Post*, pp. A01. Copyright © November 12, 1996. Reproduced with the permission of The Washington Post Company.

Rawls, John. *Political Liberalism*, pp. 3-15; 29-35; 144-158. Copyright © 1993. Reproduced with the permission of Columbia University Press.

——— , excerpts from *A Theory of Justice* reprinted by permission of the publisher, pp. 3-4, 11-16, 17-22, 23-32, 60-62, 65-66, 72-75, 100-104, 136-137, 139-142, Cambridge, Mass.: The Belknap Press of Harvard University Press, Copyright © 1971, 1999 by President and Fellows of Harvard College.

Ryan, Bob, "Sorry, free rides not right," *Boston Globe*, (Sports): E1. January 31, 1998. Reproduced with the permission of the *Boston Globe*.

Sandel, Michael J., "Political Liberalism," Harvard Law Review: 1765-1794. Copyright © May 1994 published by *Harvard Law Review*. Reproduced with the permission of Michael J. Sandel.

——— , "Honor and Resentment," *The New Republic*. Copyright © December 23, 1996. Reproduced with the permission of Michael J. Sandel.

——— , excerpt from *Democracy's Discontent*, pp. 7-17, Cambridge, Mass.: The Belknap Press of Harvard University Press. Belknap Press, 1996. Reproduced with the permission of the publisher and Michael J. Sandel.

Traub, James, "All Go Down Together," *The New York Times*, March 2, 2003, Section 6, Column 3, Magazine Desk, page 21. Reproduced with the permission of *The New York Times*.

Walzer, Michael, "Complex Equality," "Security and Welfare," "Tyrannies and Just Societies," *Spheres of Justice*, pp. 6-10, 86-91, 312-314. Copyright © 1983. Reproduced with the permission of Basic Books, Inc.

West, Robinson, "Universalism, Liberal Theory, and the Problem of Gay Marriage," *Florida State University Law Review*, (Vol. 25, No. 4): 705-711, 726-730. Copyright © Summer 1998. Reproduced with the permission of Florida State University.